HISTORY OF BROADCASTING: RADIO TO TELEVISION

HISTORY OF BROADCASTING: Radio to Television

Big Business and Radio

GLEASON L. ARCHER

ARNO PRESS and THE NEW YORK TIMES

New York • 1971

Reprint Edition 1971 by Arno Press Inc.

Reprinted from a copy in The State Historical Society of Wisconsin Library

LC# 76-161133
ISBN 0-405-03558-6

HISTORY OF BROADCASTING: RADIO TO TELEVISION
ISBN for complete set: 0-405-03555-1
See last pages of this volume for titles.

Manufactured in the United States of America

BIG BUSINESS AND RADIO

BIG BUSINESS

and

RADIO

By GLEASON L. ARCHER, LL.D.

President of Suffolk University

The American Historical Company, Inc.

NEW YORK

PRINTED IN THE UNITED STATES OF AMERICA
AMERICAN BOOK—STRATFORD PRESS, INC., NEW YORK

ILLUSTRATIONS FROM THE AQUATONE PRESSES OF
EDWARD STERN & CO., INC.

PREFACE

THE AUTHOR HAS BEEN especially fortunate in the splendid cooperation that he has enjoyed during the preparation of the text of this volume. He has been aided not only by those who assisted him with data for the first volume in this series, *History of Radio to 1926,*—but also by many other individuals now or formerly connected with the great industry that forms the subject matter of this text.

To David Sarnoff, president of the Radio Corporation of America, is no doubt due chief credit for the widespread assistance previously mentioned. The natural reluctance of leaders of great industrial enterprises to open their files to any historian, however well intentioned, is a fact to be reckoned with. Busy officials, moreover, have little time for conferences concerning past events, yet the author bears grateful testimony to the fact that all down the line, radio officials, high and low, have rendered most courteous and prompt assistance.

Lewis MacConnach, secretary both to the Radio Corporation of America and the National Broadcasting Company, has naturally encountered somewhat more than the traditional lion's share of requests for information. To his credit be it recorded that, however engrossed by the duties of his busy office he may have been at the time, he has nevertheless invariably responded promptly and fully to all such requests. Elmer E. Bucher has rendered invaluable assistance in locating source material. George H. Clark, of RCA, has also been most helpful. Mark J. Woods, treasurer of the National Broadcasting Company, and O. B. Hanson, vice-president of the same organization, have each aided the author greatly.

At the General Electric Company, Miss Lillian V. Morrison and Miss Gertrude Chandler in the office of Owen D. Young have supplied extremely helpful data. Miss Frances Sprague, librarian of the general library of the National Broadcasting Company, and Miss Doris Crooker, librarian of another department of the same corporation, have each rendered highly appreciated aid in locating source material.

At the Columbia Broadcasting System all officials from President Paley down have responded generously and graciously. At the offices of the Mutual Network the same spirit of helpfulness has been displayed. Of those outside the official families of the great corporations but formerly connected with their activities are Frank A. Arnold and Dr. Alfred N. Goldsmith. The author has been very fortunate in having so eminent a scientist as Dr. Goldsmith to whom he could turn for enlightenment on many technical details. In fact, Dr. Goldsmith has generously given of his time to check certain chapters, especially the one dealing with television and facsimile. The author would have been handicapped greatly in dealing with highly technical matters had it not been possible to try out his written text upon those who are familiar with the very type of research that he has been attempting to describe.

The Federal Communications Commission, the National Association of Broadcasters, and the Zenith Radio Corporation, have each cooperated with valuable information. To each of the above and to others too numerous to mention the author is deeply grateful for aid in the preparation of the text of *Big Business and Radio*.

G.L.A.

June 1, 1939.
Boston, Massachusetts.

CONTENTS BY CHAPTER

ILLUSTRATIONS

BIG BUSINESS AND RADIO

CHAPTER
ONE

Behind the Scenes with RCA in 1922

Section 1. Introductory.

ATTENTION, GENTLE READER!

This explanation should properly be in the preface, but some people never read a preface—and this explanation is important! Disabuse your mind at once of any idea that the present volume is a mere continuation of the *History of Radio to 1926*. On the contrary, much of the struggle from which the volume takes its name was fought and won prior to July, 1926. The bulk of this volume consists of a story based upon records opened for the first time to any historian. That so great a conflict within the ranks of "American Big Business" could have been fought without the knowledge of American journalists, or that the story could have slumbered for more than a decade without discovery, is little short of amazing, except for the fact that, generally speaking, great corporations are reticent and, moreover, do not make their records available to historians.

The manner in which the author discovered the story may be of interest. At various times, while interviewing industrial leaders during the preparation of the first volume of this series, vague hints were dropped that aroused speculation. References were made to "legal opinions," "arbitrations," "conferences," "negotiations," and the like. These apparently contradicted the generally accepted theory that the National Broadcasting Company originated simply because the American Telephone Company had grown tired of running Station WEAF and had sold it for a million dollars. The author became convinced that a story of conflict lay sleeping in the files of great corporations.

David Sarnoff, president of the Radio Corporation of America, promised the author in June, 1938, that when he should be ready to write the second volume data in RCA files would be opened for inspection. In October, 1938—the university year having begun and the author having again some leisure for research—the new volume was attempted. Mr. Sarnoff is a man of his word—and his organization has rendered every possible assistance. Files concerning the "Arbitration of 1924"—with correspondence, an accumulation fastened together in chronological order were made available. But examination proved that this accumulation was incomplete. A six months' section, for instance, was missing. The exhibits in the case, moreover, were supposed to be in the files of Boston lawyers who had died since the litigation had ended.

For several weeks the author made himself a nuisance to busy executives and their staffs requesting documents that could not be located until, as a last expedient, he turned to the office of Owen D. Young, of the General Electric Company. Here he was given the privilege of examining correspondence of the period. He then found, in duplicate or original, the missing material. The documents in Boston were located. Thus it became possible to assemble the complete story of the arbitration.

The "Sarnoff-Bloom negotiations" presented even more difficulty. The papers were in RCA files, to be sure, but with a changing personnel none of the present staff knew where to look for them. Mr. Sarnoff finally cut the Gordian knot by calling back from retirement a former official of RCA—a close associate during the hectic years—and assigned him the task of aiding in locating necessary data. Fortunately, Elmer E. Bucher, by diligent search, discovered the time-yellowed folders in which had reposed for fifteen years complete correspondence and memoranda of the Sarnoff-Bloom negotiations—successive drafts of contracts as details were altered in seemingly endless negotiations.

Thus from several distinct sources was assembled the story of one of the greatest epochs in the industrial history of the world. To the author it has been a thrilling adventure into the unknown—discovering for the first time the day-by-day developments in a contest for supremacy in a great industry. The author has realized very keenly the great opportunity that has been accorded him of being the first historian to look upon these records. He has realized, moreover, his responsibility to future generations that no important detail be overlooked—that no incident be colored by partisanship or bias of any sort.

With the foregoing explanation let us proceed with *Big Business and Radio:*

Sec. 2. Origin of the Cross-Licensing Pact.

Many of the chief actors in the great industrial drama that will presently unfold before the reader have already appeared in the pages of the preceding volume. We meet them again—Owen D. Young, David Sarnoff, General James G. Harbord, Harry P. Davis, Albert G. Davis, Charles B. Popenoe, William E. Harkness, and a score of other well-known characters whose deeds enlivened the *History of Radio to 1926.* New and important personages will appear in the present volume.

It is not mere individuals, however, but mighty corporations and corporate groups that concern us in our present recital. We will discover that these corporations eventually divided into two camps—the Telephone Group and the Radio Group—to battle for mastery of a mighty industry that did not exist when the first cross-licensing agreements were signed in the period from 1919 to 1921. Let us consider for a moment how these corporations came into alliance in the beginning.

It has been noted in the *History of Radio to 1926* that the Radio Corporation of America originated in 1919 at the suggestion of certain officials of the United States Government during the hectic days of international reconstruction following the World War. At that time there existed grave danger that Great Britain, already possessing a virtual monopoly of transportation on the seas, and an actual monopoly of the cable systems of the world, would also speedily acquire a monopoly of wireless communications of the world.

The British Marconi Company, prior to the War, had built up the nucleus of a world-girdling system. In the United States, moreover, before the World War, an affiliate of the parent company, the Marconi Wireless Telegraph Company of America, had developed an almost complete domination of wireless communications in the United States. One of the few fortunate results flowing from our entrance into the World War in 1917 was that the national government, under its war powers, took over all wireless stations, thereby suspending for the time being the Marconi dominance of American wireless communications.

It was, no doubt, the unlovely scramble at the Peace Conference at Paris, in which greedy European intrigues revealed themselves to our idealistic President, that set him and other responsible officials of the national government to thinking upon how the United States might safeguard itself against loss to Great Britain of the wireless communications of the nation. The Navy Department, having administered wireless communications during the War, was keenly aware of the strategic value of wireless as a first line of national defense. There was need of haste, moreover, if anything really effective were to be accomplished, since the government would shortly be obliged to return wireless stations to their rightful owners. In such event no American company would exist that could hope to challenge the Marconi Company in its own field. But an American owned and American controlled communications company was needed—imperatively, immediately.

It has been set forth in the preceding volume how, in 1919, Owen D. Young was asked to mobilize the wireless resources of the nation—or rather to mobilize corporate interests engaged in the manufacture of wireless equipment. The fact that Mr. Young's own organization—the General Electric Company—was the manufacturer and owner of patent rights in the Alexanderson Alternator, then recognized as the most efficient long-distance wireless apparatus in the world, no doubt influenced the selection of Mr. Young for this great task. The masterly manner in which Owen D. Young overcame the tremendous obstacles that confronted him in establishing an all-American communications company has already been set forth in considerable detail in *History of Radio to 1926*.

It is probable that in no other way could rival corporations have been induced to meet on a common ground in the manufacture of wireless equipment than by utilizing RCA as the sales outlet of participating corporations. It is likewise obvious that the exchange of patent rights, with each corporation cross-licensing other corporations in the group, was the only feasible plan for breaking the deadlock of conflicting patent rights that had virtually paralyzed the industry. In the author's previous volume it has been pointed out that during the World War the United States Government had accomplished the feat under its wartime powers. Manufacturers were authorized to use one another's patents, the aggrieved parties to seek redress against the government in the Court of Claims. Now that peace had come, the old "log jam" had reasserted itself. The task of breaking the jam could be accomplished only through negotiation and mutual concessions.

A cross-licensing agreement had been set up between the General Electric Company and the Radio Corporation of America on November 20, 1919, when the latter corporation was formed. This was merely a beginning of the process. Since the two corporations controlled only a portion of the patents needful in the development of a truly national communications system, it was found necessary to obtain rights from other corporations owning important patent rights in the wireless field. The American Telephone & Telegraph Company, a continent-girdling public utility owning many wireless patents was the next important corporation to join the group. It made a cross-licensing agreement with the General Electric Company on July 1, 1920. On the same day, an extension agreement was executed that entitled RCA to the same privileges accorded to the General Electric Company, and also included in its provisions the Western Electric Company, a Telephone Company subsidiary which handled the manufacturing end of the latter's vast telephone industry. Thus four great corporations became entitled to reciprocal rights in one another's patents, each in the field of its principal business activity.

By the irony of fate, however, so many corporations held basic patents in the multitude of devices that went to make up the sum total of scientific advance in this field, that even the combined patent rights of the four could not provide a completely efficient wireless communications system. The Westinghouse Electric & Manufacturing Company, the General Electric Company's chief rival, was already setting up a radio position of its own. It controlled patents without which the Radio Corporation of America would be unable to establish a completely efficient system. The United Fruit Company was developing a wireless communications system for its ships and properties in the Caribbean. It obtained its equipment from the Wireless Specialty Apparatus Company, which it owned. (The manner in which negotia-

DAVID SARNOFF
Who played the leading role in the great industrial drama herein portrayed.
Office boy in the office of the American Marconi Company in 1906. President
of Radio Corporation of America since 1930.

tions were conducted by Owen D. Young "in fitting together the jig-saw puzzle of conflicting patent rights" has been set forth in full in the author's previous volume.) Agreements were signed with the United Fruit Company in February and March, 1921, and Westinghouse on July 1, 1921 signed an agreement with the others. At the close of the campaign the following corporations were linked together by cross-licensing covenants:

The Radio Group, so-called:
Radio Corporation of America
General Electric Company
Westinghouse Electric & Manufacturing Company
United Fruit Company
Tropical Radio Telegraph Company
Wireless Specialty Apparatus Company

The Telephone Group, so-called:
American Telephone & Telegraph Company
Western Electric Company

Had conditions remained as they were when the above corporations agreed to exchange patent licenses this story would never have been written. It was a beautiful theory—a League of Nations' idea by which the Titans of Big Business sought to compose their conflicting interests and to live happily ever after—or at least for thirteen years, which was the minimum term of the Telephone Company agreement. Unfortunately, it did not last even that long. Since it is easier to detect lines of cleavage after the catastrophe than before the event, let us give due credit to the idealism that animated the authors of the original cross-licensing plan and then proceed to examine the observable lines of cleavage.

To begin with, the Radio Corporation of America, conceived for a semi-patriotic purpose, was a company in which the chief corporations of the Radio Group held stock for money advanced, for patent rights surrendered to RCA, or for other considerations. In addition to the above, the General Electric Company and the Westinghouse Company, by making RCA the exclusive sales outlet for their wireless apparatus, contributed materially to the welfare of the youthful corporation. Not only that, but they spared it the necessity of spending many millions of dollars for manufacturing facilities needful to produce the equipment necessary in international communications. The worth of these additional contributions of the two manufacturing concerns could not very well be assigned definite value. They were too intangible for that, but on the other hand common stock of RCA given in exchange was likewise of intangible worth. At any rate, the score stood thus in the spring of 1921:

Outstanding or Authorized Stock of RCA

3,955,974 shares of 7% preferred stock, par value $5, of which

General Electric Company held	620,800
Westinghouse and The International Radio Telegraph Company held	1,000,000 (to be issued)
American Telephone Company held	500,000
United Fruit Company held	200,000
Others	1,635,174

Total 3,955,974

5,732,000 shares of common stock, no par value, of which

General Electric Company held	2,364,826	shares
Westinghouse and The International Radio Telegraph Company held	1,000,000	"
The American Telephone Company held	500,000	"
United Fruit Company held	200,000	"
Others	1,667,174	"

Total 5,732,000   "

It should be noted that, unlike most corporations of mammoth proportions, the Radio Corporation of America did not sell bonds or stock to the general public. The hazard of investment was borne largely by great corporate interests that participated in the development of the communications corporation. The author has been assured by high officials of RCA that never in its history has it sold stock to the public—the present individual stockholders, in general, having acquired stock originally issued to one or another of the above corporations.

Even though great industrial rivals had temporarily made peace, new and unexpected developments might easily cause friction in their mutual relations. That the great radio boom was to change the whole industrial picture is now well known; but before discussing this phase of our story it is necessary to pay close attention to the original status of RCA in relation to other corporations in the group, especially the electrical manufacturers—the General Electric Company and the Westinghouse Company.

Sec. 3. RCA Godfathers Miscalculate the Future.

The main purpose for which the Radio Corporation was created was obviously to establish a national wireless communications system. If this purpose had been confined wholly to the nationalistic

phase no great corporate group would have been justified in invest-
ing large sums to set it on its feet. But the fact is that in developing
RCA the great electrical manufacturers were consciously providing
a market for expensive electrical apparatus needful in a communications system. To RCA they might legitimately sell alternators, receiving apparatus vacuum tubes and the like, just as they might have
sold these things to the American Marconi Company.

Prior to the signing of the cross-licensing agreements, the General
Electric Company and the Westinghouse Manufacturing Company
had maintained rival sales organizations. It was a part of Mr. Young's
plan to unify the wireless manufacturing interests of these corporations by making the Radio Corporation the sales outlet for their
combined wireless products. Since the General Electric Company had
a larger volume of wireless business than its rival, the parties agreed
that RCA would purchase for resale 60% of its needs from the General
Electric Company and 40% from the Westinghouse Company. At
the time this arrangement was made—June, 1921—the KDKA experiment was in progress, yet few industrial leaders save David Sarnoff,[1] of the Radio Corporation, had as yet glimpsed the full possibilities of a radio broadcasting boom. Papers were signed without
realization of the possibilities inherent in the commercial angles of
the contract. Going back to the Telephone Company cross-licensing
compact of July 1, 1920, we find an even more contention-breeding
provision concerning which we will learn more hereafter.

Had the activities of the Radio Corporation of America been confined purely and simply to wireless communications the corporation
would have found itself limited in scope and its survival, under the
circumstances which developed later, might have been doubtful. Circumstances unforseen and unpredictable were speedily to arise that
would cause nightmares for those officials charged with the duty of
administering its affairs. Fortunately, in the organization was one man
to whom the corporation was later, in large measure, to owe its continued success. That man was the dynamic general manager of the
corporation—young David Sarnoff.

As before indicated the Radio Corporation of America represented
a mobilization of the financial and business interests of several great
corporations hitherto rivals in the electrical as distinguished from
radio manufacturing field. This is apparent from the following statement of the antecedents of the board of directors of RCA as contained

[1] As early as 1916 Mr. Sarnoff had foreseen radio broadcasting and the "Radio
Music Box," as he designated the future radio receiving set. Again, in January,
1920, he had propounded the same scheme to the officials of RCA. See Archer, *History of Radio to 1926*, pp. 110-113, 189.

in the following tabulation of membership as it stood in December, 1921:

Board of Directors of RCA

Edward J. Nally
James R. Sheffield
Edward W. Harden
John W. Griggs
} American Marconi Company

Owen D. Young
Gordon Abbott
Albert G. Davis
Edwin W. Rice, Jr.
} General Electric Company

Walter S. Gifford
Frederick A. Stevenson
} American Telephone &
Telegraph Company

George S. Davis — United Fruit Company

Guy E. Tripp
Edwin M. Herr
} Westinghouse Electric &
Manufacturing Company

Arthur E. Braun
} International Radio
Telegraph Company

Sec. 4. Why the Telephone Company Joined the Group.

It is obvious that at the time the American Telephone & Telegraph Company signed the cross-licensing agreements in July, 1920, radio broadcasting in the modern sense was not even remotely contemplated. To be sure there is a mention in the contract of broadcasting "news, music and entertainment" by wireless telephony and receiving sets for same, but that obviously did not contemplate mass broadcasting as we now know it. Station KDKA was still four months unborn. Any contract provision, therefore, relating to the wireless telephone or to receiving sets for the same had reference to conditions then existing rather than to future developments. The contract, however, was so drawn as to regulate mutual rights and liabilities for a period of years —thus committing the high contracting parties to whatever fate might have in store for them. Let us consider for a moment why the Telephone Company signed cross-licensing agreements.

It is well known that the vacuum tube was vitally important to long-distance wire telephony—and that no one corporation could manufacture the tube without infringing rights claimed by others. "Interference" decisions might be far reaching. Whoever won might be in a position to hold up all others. The Radio Corporation of America had acquired basic patents in the Fleming invention—of which the Telephone-owned deForest Audion was an infringement. As early as 1912 the Telephone Company had investigated the possibilities of the deForest Audion and, in the summer of 1913, had purchased from the inventor telephonic rights therein.[2] Dr. H. P. Arnold, of the research department of the Telephone Company, had thereafter made important discoveries and improvements in the vacuum tube, and an attempt had been made by the company to patent the improved device. It so happened, however, that Dr. Irving Langmuir, of the technical staff of the General Electric Company, working independently, had perfected a vacuum tube very similar to that of Dr. Arnold. The inventions were so nearly identical that litigation might prevent exploitation of the vacuum tube either for its telephonic or wireless possibilities. A cross-licensing agreement, however, would solve the problem. This was but one phase of the "log jam" that brought the Telephone Company into the agreements for the exchange of patent rights.

Without realizing the fact, however, the cross-licensing agreement between the American Telephone Company and the General Electric Company contained many provisions that would arise thereafter to perplex and baffle the legal departments of the corporations concerned. General language that would have been adequate to meet the problems of communications by wire and by wireless proved inadequate indeed in face of newly arising conditions. When the original cross-licensing contracts between the parties were entered into, it was recognized that there were two major interests to be safeguarded, and each group undertook to obtain rights in its primary field of endeavor. The Telephone Company received rights in the field of wire telephony and wire telegraphy, with some rights in the field of public service wireless telephony. The Radio Group received rights in the fields in which it was then engaged: wireless telegraphy and wireless telephony. That the parties did not fully contemplate the importance that wireless telephony might later have is apparent from the fact that the provisions of the contract relating to "wireless telephony" became thereafter the chief bone of contention.

No one had then contemplated that wireless transmission of the human voice would soon challenge transmission of the voice by wire. The spectacular performance of Station KDKA, however, created a sudden demand for radio broadcasting transmitting apparatus. This demand did not assume impressive proportions until the Westinghouse Company had established other stations—WJZ in the New York area; WBZ in Springfield, Mass.—and independent companies had demonstrated that radio broadcasting had great possibilities.

2 Archer, *History of Radio to 1926*, pp. 107, 109.

Both Westinghouse and General Electric, as well as the American Telephone Company, were thereupon deluged with orders for radio broadcasting transmitters. Neither Westinghouse nor General Electric would fill the orders—all because of the cross-licensing agreement of July, 1920.

The Telephone Company quite naturally regarded transmission of the human voice as a form of telephony which should be within its own domain. While both Westinghouse and General Electric had long manufactured certain devices that were indispensable to wireless telegraphy as well as other devices, such as the vacuum tube, that could be used in wire telephony yet the Telephone Company had inserted in the agreement of July 1, 1920, the following express provision:

"For the protection of the Telephone Company under the licenses hereinbelow granted to it, it is agreed that the General Company has no license to equip wireless telephone receiving apparatus sold under this paragraph with transmitting apparatus, or to sell, lease or otherwise dispose of transmitting apparatus for use in connection with receiving apparatus sold under this paragraph." [3]

Thus the Telephone Company, unless some other legal construction could be discovered, had an apparently ironclad control of that portion of the radio industry that related to the manufacture and sale of broadcasting transmitters. It will later appear that the attorneys for the Radio Group eventually attacked this provision and stoutly maintained that the clause referred only to such types of transmitters as might be manufactured under the Telephone Company patents and did not deprive the Radio Group of the right to manufacture and sell transmitters covered by their own patents. In support of this contention they pointed to subdivision (e) of paragraph 4, Article V of the contract in which the General Electric Company licensed the Telephone Company to manufacture under its patents wireless telephone apparatus to be used "as a part of a public service telephone communication system."

The situation was complicated, however, since it was impossible to manufacture a broadcast transmitter without infringing some basic patent belonging to the Telephone Company. The officials of RCA, General Electric and Westinghouse, moreover, had apparently assumed from the outset that the Telephone Company had a complete monopoly in this field, just as the Radio Group had similar exclusive

[3] License Agreement—General Electric Company and American Telephone Company, Article V, par. 4, clause 2.

rights to manufacture radio receiving apparatus. For more than two years after the contract was signed they turned over all orders or inquiries for radio telephone transmitters to the Telephone Company. It was only when bitterness and controversy had caused their legal departments to scrutinize with great care the provisions of the cross-licensing agreement of July, 1920, that they became alive to the possibility that they also had rights to manufacture and to sell radio telephone transmitters.

Sec. 5. RCA Unprepared for Radio Boom.

From 'the day it took over the wireless stations of the American Marconi Company, on March 1, 1920, the Radio Corporation of America had vigorously pressed on in an effort to develop the field of wireless telegraphy. There was a natural limit, however, to the flow of business over such channels. Commercial messages, over the sea, ship-to-shore communications, and ship-to-ship messages in code, were not great enough in volume to yield substantial profits to the corporation. In the very field, as it later developed, in which it might have hoped to win its greatest financial rewards—the sale of radio apparatus—RCA, for the reasons already stated, found itself endowed with powers as a selling organization but with no manufacturing rights.

The "radio boom," however, that by the spring of 1922 was to spread from the Atlantic seaboard to the Pacific coast, was to create a new type of manufacturing not in existence when the agreements were signed. It was soon to overshadow all other sales. Vacuum tubes for the radio trade, radio parts for home-made sets were suddenly of tremendous importance. Complete radio sets, scientifically constructed in the factory, were soon to be demanded from all over the nation —an unforeseen development that found the Radio Corporation quite unprepared.

To be sure, David Sarnoff had envisioned the "Radio Music Box" prior to 1916. It is a matter of record that in November, 1916, he made a written recommendation concerning it to Edward J. Nally, then general manager of the American Marconi Company. He had renewed the suggestion to officials of RCA in January, 1920, months before radio broadcasting began. Correspondence in the files of RCA show, for instance, that on February 14, 1920, Mr. Sarnoff wrote to Dr. Alfred N. Goldsmith relative to the "Radio Music Box." Dr. Goldsmith's reply, dated February 26, contains his comments on the idea; but most important of all, in this very letter Dr. Goldsmith christens the device "Radiola," a name by which it was afterward to be known.

Significant, indeed, is the fact that the idea continued to be agitated. On May 28, 1920, E. P. Edwards, of the lighting department of the General Electric Company, wrote to David Sarnoff concerning the cost of building a model of the Radiola, setting the figure at $2000, and making the following significant statement:

"Mr. Baker feels that further experimentation along this line should be carried on with the Radiola. Work on the Radiola can be carried on in conjunction with other models we have already started for you and we are preparing to start work as soon as you give us the word to go ahead."

The records of RCA disclose that the technical committee of the board of directors promptly appropriated the requested $2000—a modest sum indeed in the light of the millions later to be spent in radio set development! Presumably, the General Electric Company carried on the suggested experimentation, but it must be remembered that not until November, 1920, did radio broadcasting begin, then only in Pittsburgh to a very limited number of listeners. It is evident, despite the experimentation under the auspices of RCA, as above indicated, that the first complete radio sets sold to the public were produced by the Westinghouse Company [4] some time in 1921, apparently in response to the demand created by the broadcasts at Station KDKA. These sets, moreover, were similar to wireless telephone receivers that various firms had manufactured for the government during the World War.

Because the development of radio sets is of great importance in this story, let us examine such data as may now exist. A Westinghouse catalogue, undated, refers to Conrad's Station 8XK which was, of course, prior to November, 1920. It refers to an RC receiver and to its component separate parts, RA (the tuning device) and DA (crystal detector and amplifier). On August 21, 1921, a Westinghouse price sheet refers to the RC set above described, and also to an "RE" set called "Aeriola, Jr." with crystal detector. In December of the same year Westinghouse added to its list "Aeriola, Sr."

We may conclude from the foregoing that the first genuine radio set offered in assembled form by any company was a "crystal set," RA, which, however, had a tickler and could be used with a tube as a detector. The second type of radio set manufactured by the same company was the RC, consisting of a tuner, vacuum tube detector,

[4] The author has been informed that further development of radio sets was held up by the fact that the Armstrong patents interfered, and that it was only after Westinghouse joined the group in 1921 and cross-licensing privileges were acquired, was the General Electric Company free to proceed with the manufacture of radio sets.

and amplifier. The third type was the Aeriola, Jr., while the fourth was the Aeriola, Sr. All of these developments were prior to December, 1921, and came from the Westinghouse technicians. Whether a speech by David Sarnoff at Schenectady, in the winter of 1920, explaining the "Radio Music Box" idea fired the imagination of wide-awake rivals (Westinghouse and General Electric then being in keen competition in electrical manufacturing) or whether the idea was developed independently is perhaps beyond possibility of proof.

It will be remembered that Westinghouse came into the cross-licensing engagements in July, 1921. From that date onward the Radio Corporation sold the products of General Electric and Westinghouse. In a typewritten list of radio receiving apparatus, dated March 1, 1922, the sales department of RCA lists the following:

A R 1300	GE receiver
A A 1400	GE detector and two step amplifier
E R 753	GE
Aeriola, Jr.	Westinghouse
Aeriola, Sr.	"
Aeriola Grand	"
RC	"
RA and DA	"

In an RCA printed price list of August 21, 1922, we find the General Electric set ER 753 had been renamed "Radiola I," as will appear in the following:

A R 1300	GE receiver
A R 1400	GE detector and amplifier
Radiola I	GE receiver, previously called ER 753
Aeriola Grand	Westinghouse
Aeriola, Sr.	"
Aeriola, Jr.	"
RC (with RA and DA)	"
AR 1375	Wireless Specialty
AA 1520	GE three stage r.f. amplifier
A C	Westinghouse two step amplifier, for Aeriola, Sr.
AA 485	Wireless Specialty detector, radio-audio amplifier.

Because of patent complications, not for two and a half years after Dr. Goldsmith had named David Sarnoff's brain child a "Radiola," and the General Electric Company had started working upon it under that name,[5] did a radio set appear with the "Radiola" label upon it. The Radiola I was a crystal set manufactured by the General Electric Company.

In May, 1923, the term Radiola had become popular, as will be evident in the following:

RCA price list for May 1, 1923

Radiola I	GE
Radiola II	GE
Radiola IV	GE
Radiola V	GE (1400 plus 1300)
Radiola VI	GE (1520 plus 1300)
Radiola Senior	Westinghouse
Two stage amplifier, A C	"
RS Receiver with detector and 1 stage amplifier	"
RG Radiola Grand	"
RT Antenna coupler	"
RA Tuner	"
AR three stage radio amplifier	"
DA Detector-amplifier	"
A A 1520 three stage radio amplifier	GE
A A 485	Wireless Specialty

[5] For evidence of this fact see the following letter:

Schenectady, May 28, 1920

Mr. David Sarnoff,
  Commercial Manager,
    Radio Corporation of America,
      233 Broadway,
        New York City.

Dear Mr. Sarnoff:

SUBJECT: RADIOLA:

With reference to your letter of May 25th, wish to advise that based on Mr. Baker's specifications, a copy of which was handed to you on May 27th, we estimate that $2000 will be necessary to build up the model.

We further estimate that a model built in accordance with these specifications could be produced in from four to six weeks after receipt of authority to proceed.

As pointed out in Mr. Baker's specifications, we are now bringing through our factory some 3½ KW telephone sets which would give us an ideal set to test the radiola with.

Our Mr. Baker has been doing some experimental work in connection with loud speaking apparatus, and to date he has been able to get much better articulation than we have heretofore been able to get with any of the loud speaking devices on the market. Mr. Baker feels that further experimentation along this line should be carried on with the Radiola. Work on the Radiola can be carried on in conjunction with the other models we have already started for you and we are preparing to start work as soon as you give us the word to go ahead.

Yours very truly,
E. P. EDWARDS,
Asst. Mgr., Lighting Dept.,
BY: F. R. DEAKINS

The omission of Radiola III from the foregoing was probably due to some delay in perfecting the set. Not until October, 1924, did Radiola III join the family of Radiola sets. In surveying the slow development of the radio set, so far as RCA and its allies are concerned, we are brought face to face with the fact that had it been possible to heed the words of the youthful prophet in their midst it would have meant much to the Radio Corporation. RCA and its allies would have been in position to supply the radio set market when the great radio boom burst upon the nation in 1922. It will be remembered by those who have read the previous volume in this series that in the winter of 1921–1922 radio broadcasting stations sprang up all over the nation, so that by May 1, 1922, there were 218 licensed radio broadcasting stations in the United States. Since RCA was unprepared to meet the demand for radio sets the way was open for anybody and everybody to enter the manufacturing field. This they did in bewildering numbers all over the United States. It mattered not to these newcomers that RCA and others in the cross-licensing group owned the patents that they were so openly infringing. The American public needed radio sets, and fly-by-night manufacturers were keen to reap a golden harvest, immune by very numbers from restraint by law. Not all of these manufacturers of radio sets were of pirate blood. Some of them bargained for licenses to use RCA patents. Some of them developed large enterprises in the manufacturing of radio parts and radio sets before RCA could get fairly into action.[6]

[6] Public demand and uncertainty as to patent rights no doubt had bearing upon the early history of radio manufacturing. For a considerable period there was chaos in the matter of licensing rival corporations to manufacture radio sets under RCA patents. To the Zenith Radio Corporation goes the distinction of having asked for the first license from RCA, after it established its licensing policy in 1927. While negotiations were pending, however, the All American Radio Corporation secured a license which was terminated a few years later. Zenith's license, issued on March 10, 1927, was the first to be issued to a major company. Zenith was founded by Lieut. Commander Eugene F. McDonald, U.S.N., retired, July 5, 1923, at which time it was incorporated to carry on the radio business of the Chicago Radio Laboratory that had been in existence since 1919. Zenith is one of the leading radio manufacturers of the nation. The second important radio manufacturer to take out an RCA license was the Crosley Radio Corporation, its license being dated May 16, 1927. Powel Crosley, Jr., had organized this company in 1921. It has enjoyed a vigorous corporate life and is still an important figure in the radio field. The Freed-Eisemann Company was licensed by RCA on June 2, 1927, but this license expired December 13, 1929, at which time the company was in receivership. Atwater Kent Manufacturing Company took out an RCA license on August 1, 1927. This company was phenomenally successful until 1934, when the depression closed in on the radio industry. A. Atwater Kent, its founder, is said to have accumulated one of the greatest fortunes to have been won by a radio manufacturer. The Philadelphia Storage Battery Company (Philco), one of the outstanding radio manufacturers of the present day, was first licensed under RCA patents on February 10, 1928.

Sec. 6. The Prophet in Their Midst.

We may well speculate whether there were reasons, aside from patent complications, for failure to heed David Sarnoff's warnings of the coming radio boom. The first observable reason is that the board of directors of RCA were conservative men to whom this prophecy had no doubt seemed like the exuberance of a youthful enthusiast. The second reason is one that takes us into the "backstage" secrets of RCA's beginnings. It is important and should be introduced at this time.

The fact is that David Sarnoff was not at first accepted by some as more than a temporary official left over from the absorbed Marconi Company. His very youth and aggressiveness did not find favor with the conservatives. Then, too, as the infant corporation gave evidence of developing into a powerful organization some subordinate officials in the older electrical corporations began to look with kindling interest upon RCA. It was natural that private intrigues should have been formed looking to future possibilities within the Radio Corporation. It was inevitable that young Sarnoff should have been the target for sharpshooters from without. The fact that Owen D. Young entertained a favorable opinion of him rendered it essential that the latter be "taken down" before Mr. Young could be expected to consent to a change in general managers. There is considerable evidence, unofficial of course, that a hazing process was already going on.

A former official of RCA, closely associated with the young man at the time, has stated to the author that, in the early years of Mr. Sarnoff's service at RCA, if there were any particularly disagreeable job to be done by or for the management it was almost invariably turned over to David Sarnoff. Tasks regarded as impossible were likewise shouldered upon him. Bores were routed to his office. Even before RCA went into the manufacturing of radio equipment unwelcome would-be vendors of lumber or other commodities who applied to Westinghouse or General Electric were likely to be sent to Mr. Sarnoff as the one man who could deal with them, notwithstanding the fact that it was well known to those in authority that Mr. Sarnoff had nothing to do with such matters.

Unfortunately for those who sought to discredit Mr. Sarnoff in early days, but fortunately for the radio industry, the young man not only kept his head but actually made good on the difficult or impossible assignments. He won the approval of the directors of RCA. More than that, he made friends with those who were sent on wild-goose errands to his office. In short, the very efforts to unseat the general manager enabled him to demonstrate how necessary he was to the organization, and left him more firmly seated in the saddle. This by no means indicates that Sarnoff, during his first dozen years at RCA, was ever free from attack. He was in fact the stormy petrel of the organization.

That we may judge how accurately Mr. Sarnoff had envisioned the possibilities of the coming radio boom, let us examine the prophecy and its fulfillment. Mr. Sarnoff estimated in his January 31, 1920, communication to Owen D. Young the following:

1st year—100,000 Radio Music Boxes $ 7,500,000.00
(RCA's actual radio sales in 1922—$11,000,000
out of $60,000,000 total for the entire industry,) [7]
2nd year—300,000 Radio Music Boxes   22,500,000.00
(RCA's actual radio sales in 1923—$22,500,000
out of $136,000,000 for the nation) [7]
3rd year—600,000 Radio Music Boxes   45,000,000.00
(RCA's actual radio sales in 1924—$50,000,000
out of $358,000,000 for the nation) [7]

When we consider that, even though unprepared, RCA under David Sarnoff's administration as general manager contrived to reap even this share of a fabulous harvest, we may wonder what would have happened had the Sarnoff Radiola been ready for the national market at the beginning of the radio boom. At any rate, RCA was in no position to monopolize the market in radio sets and equipment.

Sec. 7. Friction Develops over Wire Lines.

It is well known that the Westinghouse Manufacturing Company, by establishing Station KDKA in Pittsburgh, paved the way for the great radio boom. By broadcasting radio programs of general interest they stimulated the demand for radio sets. KDKA was the only genuine broadcasting station up to the time of the drafting of a cross-licensing agreement between RCA and the Westinghouse Company. This agreement, by the way, was dated June 30, 1921, but was not formally executed until August 8th following.[8] This RCA-Westinghouse agreement by its terms effected an exchange of licenses with the group of corporations that had already made cross-licensing agreements with RCA, among them the American Telephone & Telegraph Company.

An incident was soon to occur that was to bring into the foreground a clash of interests between the new ally and the Telephone Company. Since Station KDKA was the first of all radio stations, pioneering in a new field, it was inevitable that at an early date it should

[7] Statistics of sales for the industry by O. H. Caldwell, editor of *Radio Today*, in *Broadcasting Year Book for 1939*, p. 11.
[8] Archer, *History of Radio to 1926*, p. 210.

have encountered problems that would confront all radio stations. In solving those problems it naturally established precedents of great importance to the future industry.

. As early as January 1, 1921, Station KDKA succeeded in broadcasting the religious services of the Calvary Episcopal Church of Pittsburgh, Pa. This was an engineering feat that required what were later known as pick-up wires, extending from the church auditorium to the broadcasting studio. Fortunately, we have the testimony of Dr. Frank Conrad in the arbitration hearings of May, 1924, to explain how this historic "pick-up" was achieved. Station KDKA did not attempt to string special wires of its own, but tried the experiment, successfully as it proved, of utilizing a local telephone line. Dr. Conrad states that they used the wires of the Pittsburgh & Allegheny Telephone Company. This practice was continued from week to week in connection with the broadcasting of these church services.

On January 15, 1921, a banquet at the Duquesne Club in Pittsburgh—Herbert Hoover the stellar attraction—was broadcast. Pick-up wires were again used. A veritable procession of events broadcast by KDKA and other stations was to follow during the year 1921 before the American Telephone Company was to take official notice of the custom. Obviously the use of pick-up wire involved a phase of wire telephony. The American Telephone & Telegraph Company must look into the situation in order to safeguard its commercial rights. It is quite probable, in the light of subsequent events, that the Telephone Company had already experienced a degree of alarm over radio broadcasting. To be sure wire telephony involved two-way communication, yet radio broadcasting had possibilities of menace to the supremacy of the telephone even though it was still a one-way system of communication. Broadcasting so closely resembled wire telephony that the Telephone Company was apparently up in arms about it, resenting the invasion of the communications field by manufacturing corporations.

On December 21, 1921, Vice-President Walter S. Gifford of the American Telephone Company wrote a letter to Guy E. Tripp, chairman of the board of directors of Westinghouse, which is of considerable historic importance even though it does not throw down the gauntlet to the Westinghouse Company on the subject matter of the letter.

"It has come to our attention," he writes, "that the Westinghouse Company is using wires of both the Bell Telephone Company of Pennsylvania and the Independent Company of Pittsburgh [9] in connection with your radio broadcasting stations. I trust that you have

[9] Doubtless the Pittsburgh & Allegheny Telephone Company.

not forgotten that the license agreement does not permit you to connect radio telephone equipment to the lines of any public service communication system. As you know, we have this matter under consideration at the present time. In the meantime, I am sure you will not wish to do anything in violation of our General Agreement." [10]

So much for the Westinghouse Company's initial venture into the to-be-disputed field of pick-up wires. Now comes a significant event in which the General Electric Company was concerned. It is well known that on February 20, 1922, the General Electric Company entered radio broadcasting by establishing its famous Station WGY in Schenectady, N. Y. Whether pick-up wires were used on opening night is not apparent, but that the plan was in contemplation even before the station was launched is a matter of record. At some time prior to opening day, Albert G. Davis, vice-president of the General Electric Company, requested the American Telephone Company to grant permission for such use in connection with a dinner of the local Rotary Club, at which Governor Miller was to be the speaker. The response of Mr. Gifford is of historic importance.

February 20, 1922

Mr. A. G. Davis, Vice President,
    General Electric Company,
        120 Broadway, New York, N. Y.

Dear Mr. Davis:

The A. T. & T. Company will be pleased to extend to the General Electric Company permission to request the New York Telephone Company to provide them with a special line between the Rotary Club and the General Electric radio broadcasting station in connection with a particular event at the Rotary Club at which Governor Miller is to make an address. This permission is given for this special case only and does not establish a precedent with reference to future requests.

Very truly yours,

(Signed) W. S. Gifford,

Vice-President

Thus we have the opening skirmishes in warfare between great corporations that was destined to continue behind the scenes for several years and to result in eventual elimination of the chief contending parties from the broadcasting arena. Other protests and other letters were to follow, notwithstanding which the radio stations of the allies,

[10] Transcript of Record of Arbitration between Telephone Group and Radio Corporation Group, May-June, 1934, pp. 1162-1163.

if we may call them such, continued to utilize pick-up wires as an adjunct to broadcasting activities. In the nature of things such use was essential. All radio stations—and they were soon to be found in all populous centers—were using pick-up wires. Had the Telephone Company been able to enforce its supposed rights in this matter radio broadcasting might have been tremendously handicapped.

ELMER E. BUCHER
Sales Manager of RCA during its years of expansion.

LEWIS MacCONNACH
Secretary of RCA since 1923. Secretary of NBC since its formation in 1926

DR. ALFRED N. GOLDSMITH
Eminent electrical engineer, aided industrial development of RCA.

HARRY P. DAVIS
Who fathered Station KDKA. First Chairman of Board of NBC.

CHAPTER
TWO

A Prophecy Pigeon-Holed

Section 8. Radio Corporation's Early Sales Difficulties.

REFERENCE WAS MADE in the preceding chapter to the manner in which the godfathers of RCA had attempted to provide for its future. Wise plans had been made for it in its capacity as a communications corporation. Devices which were to be manufactured for RCA were principally required for the transmission and reception of communications —such as the Alexanderson alternators—huge machines which cost in the neighborhood of $125,000 each.

Under RCA's original cross-licensing agreement with the General Electric Company, the youthful corporation obtained the right to purchase such radio devices from General Electric for its own needs or for resale at cost plus 20%, or at fixed prices to be agreed upon between the parties. After Westinghouse joined the Radio Group in the summer of 1921, RCA agreed to purchase such devices from that company also on the same terms. Purchase orders were to be divided as between General Electric and Westinghouse upon a 60-40 basis. In this manner, RCA avoided the expense of a manufacturing plant of its own. It obtained, moreover, the benefit of the world-renowned research and manufacturing facilities of General Electric and Westinghouse.

It should be remembered that at the time of the formation of RCA, broadcasting, public reception thereof, sound pictures, electrical phonographs, improved recording and reproduction of sound generally and television were not yet commercially developed.

With increased demand for radio sets and tubes, RCA entered upon a comparatively new career as a seller of radio apparatus on a large scale. RCA, which purchased its product from two manufacturers, found itself under the necessity of harmonizing the views of three research and engineering departments for design and construction and, at the same time, of harmonizing those views with the public demand as determined by the Sales Department. Orders had to be apportioned between the two manufacturers and some difficulty was encountered in obtaining standardized apparatus. Thus, although apparatus might bear the RCA label and the same name, yet the Westinghouse product was frequently somewhat different from a set supplied by the General Electric Company. Competitors who in one organization controlled the design, manufacture and sale of the radio devices marketed by them, could quickly adjust their production and take care of improved design and technique—a freedom of action that soon excited a desire for similar freedom on the part of RCA.

Sincere efforts were made at coordination of the pertinent engineers and departments of the General Electric Company and Westinghouse and the sales division of RCA, but from the very nature of the tripartite arrangement, delay resulted. Furthermore, even after design and construction had been determined upon, RCA was under the handicap of the necessity of forwarding orders in writing months before the articles ordered could be expected for delivery and moreover of dividing these orders between the General Electric Company and Westinghouse on a 60-40 basis. Such sets and tubes were manufactured by the different companies in their respective plants.

The burden rested largely upon the shoulders of David Sarnoff. He must foresee the public demand for the manufactured goods. He must not over-order. He must not under-order. In other words, he must combine the functions of a clairvoyant and a hard-headed business man. Under a less skillful management, the Radio Corporation would have suffered serious reverses in the rough and tumble competition of those early days.

David Sarnoff had been made General Manager of the Radio Corporation on April 29, 1921. From the vantage point of direct supervision over its activities, he appreciated clearly somewhat earlier than others, perhaps, the desirability from the RCA point of view of manufacturing rights in the radio field. As the time passed, he chafed at the inability of the corporation to manufacture its own radio sets, and thus to be able to take advantage of up-to-the-minute developments in the art. If it could alter designs at will, it might offer to the public only the latest and best in radio equipment.

Despite its difficulties, the Radio Corporation was able to meet competition and to show substantial profits. The General Electric and Westinghouse operating departments expressed the opinion that even though RCA were to obtain manufacturing rights, it could not manufacture as efficiently or as cheaply as the older electric companies. It should also be remembered that the acquisition of manufacturing rights by RCA would entail the turning over to it by the General Electric Company and Westinghouse the results of research and development over a long period of years and would eliminate those companies from certain distinct phases of their existing business. There was no reason why RCA should secure such rights without fair compensation and the value of the manufacturing rights was very great. It is difficult to see how RCA could have paid for such rights at any time during the first ten years of its existence. Moreover, the scope of the rights of the Radio Group in the radio field was not actually to be determined until the agreement with the American Telephone Company was eventually concluded in 1926, as will be seen hereafter.

The original agreements, however, prevented Sarnoff from carrying out his cherished desire of attaining flexibility in the manufacturing process. RCA technicians could not improve or alter this part or that during the process of manufacture. There was no evading the issue

—hence the great opportunity for Atwater Kent, Crosley, Grebe, Grigsby-Grunow, Freed-Eisemann, Fada, Philco, Zenith, and other manufacturers to spring up in the field of radio competition.

Sec. 9. General Electric Company and Telephone Company in Controversy.

It has previously been noted that because of the language of the cross-licensing compacts the American Telephone Company believed that the other corporations joining the group except its own subsidiary, the Western Electric Company, had no right to manufacture and sell broadcast transmitters. Inasmuch as both Westinghouse and General Electric Company had developed types of transmitters prior to the cross-licensing agreements, they clung to the belief that they had not surrendered their rights therein, although they apparently conceded that the equipping of radio broadcasting stations in general should be within the province of the American Telephone Company. The latter company, however, viewed with disfavor exercise by either corporation of the contested privilege even within the "family circle." It is a known fact that the General Electric Company continued to labor upon the development and perfecting of its own transmitting system. The Westinghouse Company had equipped its own pioneer Station KDKA and had continued to manufacture equipment for its other stations that were being established.

The Telephone Company officials were too wise to rely upon mere written agreements to safeguard its rights in the manufacture of broadcast transmitters. Its technical staff had already decided to demonstrate by impressive example that the broadcasting facilities at the command of the Telephone Company were superior to anything possessed by General Electric or Westinghouse. Thus, in their plans for Stations WBAY and WEAF to be opened in the summer of 1922, they were devoting utmost care to render them superior to any broadcasting stations in existence. In fact, they hoped to set a standard of perfection that would virtually eliminate competition in this field.

So many points of controversy had developed between the Telephone Company and the Radio Group that in the spring of 1922 the cross-licensing contract became the object of painstaking legal scrutiny. This action was apparently jointly agreed upon by the General Electric Company and the American Telephone & Telegraph Company— doubtless a fresh demonstration of Owen D. Young's skillful diplomacy. One of the reasons for believing that Mr. Young was the prime mover in this effort at conciliation was that a lawyer who enjoyed Mr. Young's confidence and respect was selected to make the all-important analysis of the respective rights of the parties. This lawyer was Charles Neave, of the influential law firm of Fish, Richardson and Neave, with offices in Boston and New York City. Mr. Neave, moreover, had long been patent counsel for both the General Electric and the Telephone Company. He had assisted in drafting the original agreement.

It was hoped that out of this joint endeavor might come an impartial interpretation of the cross-licensing agreement that would satisfy each party and thus eliminate the friction that was rapidly becoming more acute. It is noteworthy that during the period in which Mr. Neave was studying the document Mr. Gifford and Mr. Stevenson resigned from the board of directors of RCA as previously indicated. More was involved in these resignations, perhaps, than the conflict of views that we have discussed. The Telephone Company was then under attack as a monopoly and membership on the board of directors of RCA might prove awkward. This was true of ownership of stock in the Radio Corporation. It was during the period of Mr. Neave's study of the General Electric-Telephone Company agreement that the Telephone Company began to sell its RCA stock.

Mr. Neave was apparently instructed to consider what rights were actually conferred by the contract with respect to a number of controverted points: so-called "carrier-current" problems had arisen involving the mutual rights of the contending parties. The question of what was meant by the expression, "for amateur purposes," and whether it could be said to include an ordinary listener to a radio broadcast as well as the wireless tinkerer who had originally been intended. Combined wireless telephone and telegraph sets had been manufactured, and a conflict of jurisdiction had arisen over the custom. Radio sets for aircraft and automobiles were also being manufactured, and the rights of the parties were here entangled. The vexed topic of broadcast transmitters was very much in the foreground of Mr. Neave's inquiry. Related to it was the question of whether a loud speaker was properly within the domain of wire or wireless. Public service communication also came in for a share of attention. What could properly be considered a part of wireless receiving apparatus was another of the problems which Mr. Neave was to attempt to solve.

Sec. 10. National Broadcasting Company Foreshadowed.

Reference has been made to the extraordinary ability of David Sarnoff to anticipate future developments in the radio industry. A singular demonstration of this ability occurred on June 17, 1922—more than four years before the National Broadcasting Company was formed. In a letter written on the above date, Mr. Sarnoff made an amazing suggestion which in the light of future events reads like a prophecy. This letter was addressed to E. W. Rice, Jr., one of the directors of RCA and a member of the newly appointed broadcasting committee of the board.

It must be remembered that in June, 1922, very little could have been known by Mr. Sarnoff of broadcasting problems from actual experience. RCA had made a brief trial of broadcasting, but after three months had discontinued its Station WDY and, at the time Mr. Sarnoff's letter was written, the Radio Corporation was a silent partner in the operation of Westinghouse Station WJZ. Thus it will be seen that Mr. Sarnoff's insight into the problems of radio was due more to natural insight than to sage experience. He lays down his major premises in the following language:

"First, it seems to me that in seeking a solution to the broadcasting problem, we must recognize that the answer must be along national rather than local lines, for the problem is distinctly a national one.

"Secondly, I think that the principal elements of broadcasting service are entertainment, information and education, with emphasis on the first feature—entertainment; although not under-estimating the importance of the other two elements. Expressed in other words, and considered from its broadest aspect, this means that broadcasting represents a job of entertaining, informing and educating the nation and should, therefore, be distinctly regarded as a public service."

With admirable directness Mr. Sarnoff went on to point out certain disturbing truths that were destined not to be solved by the great radio manufacturing companies for years to come. In so doing he poses two major problems, as will be seen in the following quotation from his letter of June 17, 1922:

"That this kind of a job calls for specialists in the respective fields and that it requires expert knowledge of the public's taste and the manner in which to cater the public's taste is apparent on the surface. That manufacturing companies or communication companies are not at present organized and equipped to do this kind of a job in a consistent and successful way is to my mind also clear.

"If the foregoing premises be correct, it would seem that the two fundamental problems calling for a solution are—

"1. Who is to pay for broadcasting?

"2. Who is to do the broadcasting job?"

Sec. 11. Radio Costs to Be Borne by Manufacturers and Dealers.

After discussing suggestions by those who were then arguing that the cost of radio broadcasting should be borne by radio listeners Mr. Sarnoff reasoned that all such ideas were impractical and unworkable, arguing that even if the public were to make voluntary contributions for a time there was no certainty of continuance.

"The temptation to discontinue payments on the ground of poor service, etc.," he writes, "is too great to make any system of voluntary public subscription sufficiently secure to justify large financial commitments and the creation of an administrative and collection organization necessary to deal with the general public. Therefore, if I am correct in assuming that such a foundation is insecure over a period of time, the superstructure built on such a foundation is perforce equally weak.[1]

"For these reasons I am led to the conclusion that the cost of broadcasting must be borne by those who derive profits directly or indirectly from the business resulting from radio broadcasting. This means the manufacturer, the national distributor (the Radio Corporation of America), the wholesale distributor, the retail dealer, the licensee and others associated in one way or another with the business.

"When the novelty of radio will have worn off and the public no longer interested in the means by which it is able to receive but rather, in the substance and quality of the material received, I think that the task of reasonably meeting the public's expectations and desires will be greater than any so far tackled by any newspaper, theater, opera or other public information or entertainment agency. The newspaper, after all, caters to a limited list of subscribers. The theater presents its production to a literal handful of people, but the broadcasting station will ultimately be required to entertain a nation. No such audience has ever before graced the effort of even the most celebrated artist or the greatest orator produced by the Ages."

Sec. 12. A Broadcasting Corporation Advocated.

Having laid the foundation for his argument that a new agency for handling the radio situation would soon be imperatively needed, Mr. Sarnoff goes on to declare:

"Because of these reasons, I am of the opinion that neither the General Electric Company, the Westinghouse Company nor the Radio Corporation would in the long run do justice to themselves or render satisfaction to the public if they undertook this tremendous job.

"The service to be rendered distinctly calls for a specialized organization with a competent staff capable of meeting the necessities of the situation."

A structure capable of expansion in accordance with the development of the art seemed to Mr. Sarnoff to be the only possible solution of so vast a problem. How that corporate structure could be erected is set forth in some detail in the following quotation from the letter of June 17, 1922:

[1] Several months later the disappointing experiment of public donations for radio expenses proved the soundness of Mr. Sarnoff's theory.

"The plan I have in mind and one which I respectfully suggest for your consideration and discussion at the first meeting of the Broadcasting Committee is as follows:

"Let us organize a separate and distinct company, to be known as the Public Service Broadcasting Company, or National Radio Broadcasting Company, or American Radio Broadcasting Company, or some similar name.

"This company to be controlled by the Radio Corporation of America, but its board of directors and officers to include members of the General Electric Company, Westinghouse Electric Company and possibly also a few from the outside prominent in national or civic affairs. The administrative and operating staff of this company to be composed of those considered best qualified to do the broadcasting job.

"Such company to acquire the existing broadcasting stations of the Westinghouse Company, General Electric Company, as well as the three stations to be erected by the Radio Corporation; to operate such stations and build such additional broadcasting stations as may be determined upon in the future."

The omission of the third godfather of RCA—the American Telephone & Telegraph Company is easily explained. The latter company was even then at odds with the others and had not at that time established a broadcasting station—Station WEAF being still a future possibility.

Sec. 13. The Corporation to Be on a Non-profit Basis.

A significant feature of Mr. Sarnoff's plan was that the proposed broadcasting corporation should be organized not only as a non-profit organization but also as a corporation devoid of earning power. How then was it to be financed? Let us quote Mr. Sarnoff's own words:

"Since the proposed company is to pay the cost of broadcasting as well as the cost of its own administrative operations, it is, of course, necessary to provide it with a source of income sufficient to defray all its expenses.

"As a means for providing such income, I tentatively suggest that the Radio Corporation pay over to the Broadcasting Company, two per cent of its gross radio sales, that the General Electric and Westinghouse Companies do likewise and that our proposed licensees be required to do the same.

"Assuming, for example, that gross radio sales effected by the Radio Corporation for the year 1923, amount to $20,000,000, which would represent, roughly, $14,000,000 in billing prices for such devices made by the General Electric and Westinghouse Companies and, assuming further, that the gross volume of our proposed licensees' business for the year will be $5,000,000 the contributions to the broadcasting company for the year would be as follows:

"By the Radio Corporation of America—
2% on $20,000,000 would equal $400,000.00
By the General Electric Company—
2% on 60% of $14,000,000 would equal . . 168,000.00
By the Westinghouse Company—
2% on 40% of $14,000,000 would equal . . 112,000.00
By Licensees*—
2% on $5,000,000 . . . . 100,000.00
                                         _____
       Total $780,000.00

"While the total of $780,000.00 may be regarded as inadequate to defray the whole of the expense of the broadcasting company, yet, I think it should be sufficient to provide for a modest beginning. Once the structure is created opportunities for providing additional sources of income to increase the 'pot' will present themselves. For example, if the business expands, the income grows proportionately. Also, we may find it practicable to require our wholesale distributors to pay over to the broadcasting company a reasonable percentage of their gross radio sales for it will be to their interest to support broadcasting. It is conceivable that the same principle may even be extended in time to the dealers."

Sec. 14. Public Service in Radio Programs Advocated.

At the time this letter was written no one had glimpsed the possibilities of revenue from radio advertising—two months were to elapse before Station WEAF was to inaugurate sponsored programs. David Sarnoff was, in fact, to become one of the most persistent critics of radio for revenue, choosing to regard broadcasting as a public service endeavor that should be kept free from the taint of "money-making." The Sarnoff creed as enunciated in this remarkable letter was to continue as his slogan for years to come and, in fact, until radio advertising over the networks became a recognized and reputable practice. Then and then only did Sarnoff bow to the inevitable—because advertising was the only source of revenue upon which radio broadcasting could rely and still preserve its freedom. Mr. Sarnoff feared the systems of some European countries by which radio became the closely fettered propaganda agencies of the government.

"Since the broadcasting company," he wrote, "is to be organized on the basis of rendering a public service commensurate with its financial ability to do so and is not set up for the purpose of earning revenue, or in other words, to be a 'money-making' proposition, it is conceivable that plans may be devised by it whereby it will receive public

* At the time this letter was written there were only a few small companies holding licenses.

support and, in fact, there may even appear on the horizon a public benefactor, who will be willing to contribute a large sum in the form of an endowment. It will be noted that these additional possibilities of income are merely regarded as 'possibilities' and do not in themselves form the foundation upon which the broadcasting company is to operate.

"Once the broadcasting company is established as a Public Service and the General Public educated to the idea that the sole function of the company is to provide the public with a service as good and extensive as its total income permits, I feel that with suitable publicity activities, such a company will ultimately be regarded as a public institution of great value in the same sense that a library, for example, is regarded today. Also, it would remove from the public mind, the thought that those who are doing broadcasting today are doing so because of profit to themselves. In other words, it removes the broadcasting company itself from the atmosphere of being a commercial institution."

It has been pointed out in the author's first volume that on various occasions Mr. Sarnoff advocated endowment of radio stations; the most notable of these a symposium conducted by *Radio Broadcast* in August, 1924.[2] His philosophy, however, was well formulated even as early as June, 1922, as will be seen from the following:

"Mention of a library institution brings to mind the thought that great as is the public benefactor who endows a library for the purpose of educating the general public, the person who in the future may endow a broadcasting station or a broadcasting service will be a still greater public benefactor because of the many advantages which a broadcasting service offers to all classes of people, not only in the matter of education, but also in entertainment and health services, etc. Important as the library is, it can only provide the written word and at that, it is necessary for people to go to the library in order to avail themselves of its services, whereas in the matter of broadcasting the spoken word is projected into the home where all classes of people may remain and listen."

Sec. 15. Sarnoff's Plan Pigeon-Holed by RCA.

It does not appear that Mr. Sarnoff's suggestion of a national broadcasting corporation made a very profound impression upon the Radio Committee of RCA. This is understandable in view of the chaos that reigned in the radio industry at the time. It seemed the world was mad about radio, and the Radio Corporation was more or less swamped by it all. As sales outlet for the great manufacturers of radio equipment the company was literally rushed off its feet. Despite the

[2] Archer, *History of Radio to 1926*, pp. 342, 343.

fact that David Sarnoff had prophesied this very development, and that in this particular his star had risen to such a point that the board of directors were shortly to elect him vice-president and general manager of RCA, yet here was a new prophecy. In this matter young Mr. Sarnoff might be wrong—after all he was only thirty-one years of age.

History was repeating itself. Few people there are who can forecast the future and few there are who can understand and appreciate a genuine prophecy of future events. The prophet must needs educate those whom he would lead to the promised land, whether it be in the realm of earthly territory, business expansion or public service. Mr. Sarnoff had voiced the prophecy. He must now educate his associates. The history of RCA demonstrates that the astute business manager lost no opportunity to preach his doctrine either to Owen D. Young, the all-powerful chairman of the board, or to other members of the governing body.

CHAPTER
THREE

A Vain Attempt at Mediation

Section 16. A Lawyer to Mediate General Electric-Telephone Row.
THREE DAYS AFTER the Sarnoff letter, quoted in the previous chapter, was written, a letter of a totally different nature came to Owen D. Young of the General Electric Company and Walter S. Gifford of the American Telephone & Telegraph Company. This letter was written by Charles Neave, the lawyer who had been engaged to make an impartial interpretation of the controversial cross-licensing agreement. It was dated June 20, 1922, and began as follows:

"In accordance with your request, I have reviewed the License Agreement, dated July 1, 1920, between your companies, for the purpose of making recommendations (binding upon neither of your companies, but for your consideration), based broadly upon the spirit and intent of the parties, and thus to attempt to set at rest various possible uncertainties in the interpretation of that Agreement as written, and to suggest, in some respects, modifications which might tend to minimize the chances of misunderstandings and criticism in the future."

In order to clarify the situation, or at least to lay the groundwork for his discussion, Mr. Neave sets forth six causes for controversy inherent in the license agreement. Five controversial points are thus stated by the lawyer:

"1. In the field of *transoceanic wire telegraphy,* neither party grants any licenses to the other and each may utilize its own inventions, provided that they do not embody inventions of the other, and may dispose of its rights, under its own inventions, in this field. Here is an incentive to each party to attempt to improve its own patent position, with resultant interferences and uncertainties.
"2. In the field of wireless telephone communication by, to and between *automotive devices,* except railway vehicles, the General Company receives non-exclusive licenses to establish, but not to lease or sell, transmitting and receiving stations for communication with such devices, and the Telephone Company receives no licenses for this purpose, except when the communication is through its telephone system. Here is a similar incentive to each company to improve its patent position and weaken that of the other.
"3. In the field of *broadcasting* the General Company receives non-exclusive rights to establish broadcasting stations and to make, use, sell and lease wireless telephone receiving apparatus for broadcasted matter, but no license to equip receiving sets with transmitting apparatus; and the Telephone Company receives no licenses with reference to receiving apparatus except as a part of or for direct use in connection with transmitting apparatus. Obviously, the stronger the patent position of either company becomes with reference to the other, the wider is the field which it may occupy in broadcasting.

"4. The Agreement, is, throughout, one which defines the fields only to the extent that is involved in the granting of licenses in certain fields and withholding them in others. This, in itself, creates an incentive for one party to strengthen its patent position as compared with the other in all instances in which *exclusive* rights are not granted, for then the party owning the patent has a non-exclusive right, and thus has access to that field and may grant licenses to others under its own patents.

* * * *

"6. There is always the incentive for each party to strengthen its patent position at the expense of the other in order to be in a dominant position upon the termination of the Agreement."

Having stated the more obvious features of the agreement, Mr. Neave makes the following analysis of reasons inherent in the nature of the Telephone Company, the General Electric and RCA, that militate against harmonious interrelations:

"The parties were dealing with a situation which was complicated by reason of the fact that the Telephone Company was dealing on behalf of itself, a public service wire telephone and telegraph communications company operating in the United States and adjoining points and developing wireless communication, and on behalf of the Western Electric Company, a manufacturer and distributor of varied kinds of electrical supplies; and the General Company was dealing on behalf of itself, a manufacturer and distributor of electrical apparatus and supplies and engaged in developing wireless apparatus, and on behalf of the Radio Corporation whose primary business was that of a public service wireless telegraph communications company then operating principally in transoceanic communication."

Sec. 17. Mr. Neave Advises Further Exchange of Licenses.

After discussing the difficulties that had arisen under the agreement in the field of transoceanic wire telegraphy and wire telephony, Mr. Neave points out that while "it was certainly the expressed intention that no licenses should be granted by either party to the other, this was certainly inconsistent with the expressed plan that the interests of the parties should be so merged that conflicts would not arise on patent matters and that there might be a free and rapid advance in development and production."

He then speaks of the competition existing between transoceanic cables and transoceanic wireless and points out that the withholding patents from RCA by either of the other two companies cannot fail to hinder its development.

"So far as I know," he continues, "the question here involved relates only to the use of the inventions in the reception of cable telegraph messages, and I understand that those inventions are not at all essential to or controlling in such reception, but may advantageously be used. In view of (a) the impossibility of being able to *control* cable communication by these inventions, (b) the position of the Radio Corporation and its prominence in the transoceanic communication field which opens it to attack, and (c) principally in view of the great importance attributed by the Government to any improvements in our international communications, it is my own impression that it is now a mistake to be apparently in the position of standing in the way of such improvements by creating such a situation that no one, not even either of the parties to the Agreement, may be in a position to furnish apparatus embodying the inventions and developments of both parties and, therefore, presumably, the most efficient apparatus for this purpose. I recommend that you seriously consider the advisability of an exchange of licenses, exclusive except with respect to each granting party. This, under the provisions of the Agreement as it stands, would carry with it no right to grant sub-licenses except such as may be involved in the sale of apparatus and systems. (This would mean a modification of Article V, 3 (a))."

Sec. 18. Recommendations as to Carrier-Current Dispute.

In order to understand the controversy that had arisen over the use of so-called carrier current it is needful to consider what was meant by the parties by the expression itself. Unfortunately for the average reader, the term is highly technical, since it involves phenomena in the high heavens of the science of electricity. One of the first to experiment with the idea was Alexander Graham Bell with his proposed harmonic telegraph scheme. Bell had hoped to transmit several messages simultaneously over the same wire. Not until 1914, however, did engineers succeed in solving the problem of multiple transmission over the same wire.

The vacuum tube and the electric filter device made possible the effective use of carrier currents in wire telephony. Although the vacuum tube had at first been used to amplify ordinary voice frequencies it was soon discovered that it could be used to generate carrier frequencies ranging from the low frequencies of the human voice to the high frequencies employed in radio. Thus, by means of the vacuum tube, currents of any desired frequency might be produced and controlled. In order to operate the system it was necessary to feed to the same set of wires as many types of frequency as were desired up to certain limits. In the period of which we write engineers were accustomed to send as many as four carrier telephone circuits and ten carrier telegraph circuits over a single pair of wires. Obviously, if several messages were being transmitted simultaneously, it was essential that the frequencies used differ sufficiently to permit unscrambling them at their destination.

Thus, if one frequency were 10,000 cycles per second, another 15,000, another 20,000, and a fourth frequency 25,000, then selecting circuits of appropriate frequency will do the unscrambling—that is to say, the 10,000-cycle message will be captured by the 10,000-cycle selective circuit, and so on. After thus being filtered out, as it were, the greatly weakened current passed into a device known as a demodulator. Here again the vacuum tube plays an all important part. Thus by the exercise of a magic that would have been inconceivable to an earlier generation the unscrambled messages might be received through ordinary telephone receivers.

The art of telephony by carrier wave had reached such a degree of perfection by 1922 that engineers were able to use power lines as well as telephone wires. Thus it will be seen that the advent of radio broadcasting and especially the use of pick-up wires might very profoundly affect the carrier-current system that the telephone engineers had developed through years of effort and at great expense to the Telephone Company.

Mr. Neave thus comments on the mutual rights of the parties:

"Some question has been raised as to whether, under Article V, 5, the Telephone Company has licenses under the General Electric patents for 'carrier current' telephone communication over wires, and partly over wires and partly over wireless gaps. It seems clear to me that it has exclusive licenses, in this respect, subject only to the right of both the General Company and Telephone Company, under the patents of both, to make and sell (the Telephone Company but not the General Company having a right to lease) apparatus of this character to electric light, electric power and electric traction companies for the use of such companies and not for the use of the public, nor for toll, nor for operation of a selective train signaling system (V, 5 (a)) and subject to the provision that the Telephone Company's rights with respect to selling or leasing such apparatus for use on electric railroads are limited to sales or leases to the railroads, all sales for installation as a part of the original equipment of cars or locomotives being through the General Company only (IV, 5)."

Sec. 19. "For Amateur Purposes" Defined.

In the contract of July 1, 1920, the Telephone Company had granted to the General Electric Company an "exclusive license to make, use, lease, and sell all wireless telephone apparatus for amateur purposes." This term was undoubtedly understood at the time the contract was made to apply to the army of wireless enthusiasts who were tinkering with home sets. Now that radio broadcasting had created a totally new industry in which the listener was one seeking music or entertainment, it became important to decide whether the term amateur could be applied to the ordinary radio listener. It was obviously to the financial advantage of the General Electric and RCA that the term be construed to include all radio listeners.

On the other hand, if the term could be interpreted to include only those enthusiasts who were experimenting with wireless telephony as a scientific pursuit, it would exclude the multitude who were using radio as they would the phonograph—for entertainment alone. Thus the Telephone Company might gain entrance to the very important field of manufacture of radio sets. Vast financial implications were involved in the word "amateur."

With this explanation we may now proceed to Mr. Neave's pronouncement on the subject.

"6. The General Company has exclusive license to make, use, lease and sell all wireless telephone apparatus '*for amateur purposes.*' I, recommend that 'for amateur purposes' be defined as meaning for purposes of transmission and/or reception (including what would be called broadcasting, if wave lengths assigned to broadcasting were used) on such wave lengths as may, from time to time, be allotted to amateurs by competent authority, but does not include apparatus for the use of professional investigators for experimental purpose only, as to which each party has a non-exclusive license from the other. (This adds to Article V, 4 (d), 3)."

Sec. 20. Controversy over Combined Telephone-Telegraph Sets.

Before the advent of radio broadcasting many thousands of wireless enthusiasts had mastered the Morse Code, which operated on the spark system rather than on continuous waves. These listeners naturally desired to have the advantage of the wireless telephone, or radio set. The Telephone Company and the Radio Group were already in controversy over the custom that had grown up of combining both phases in the same set. In commenting on this angle of the dispute Mr. Neave writes as follows:

"I understand that the receiving set ordinarily used for wireless telephone reception, receives spark telegraphy also, but will not, without some change or readjustment, receive continuous wave heterodyne telegraph messages. Also, combined sets may be desired for both sending and receiving both telephone and telegraph messages, as in the case of brokers' offices, business houses, etc., for such a service as might be given by leased wires, which so far as concerns wireless telephony, is now in the exclusive field of the Telephone Company. It is obviously desirable that someone have the right to meet those demands by furnishing the most efficient sets for the purpose, embodying the improvements of both parties, though not desirable that the General Company should grant such licenses that the Telephone Company might be free to encroach on the Radio Corporation's basic field as an operating telephone communication company.

"There would, however, seem to be such encroachment if the Telephone Company could sell wireless telegraph apparatus, even though combined with wireless telephone apparatus, for uses of such character as might be served by leased wires, for such service, when given by wireless, is a kind that naturally falls in the Radio Corporation's field. Similarly, the Radio Corporation would encroach on the Telephone Company's basic field, if it were free to sell telephone apparatus for a service analogous to that of leased wire service, which service is of great importance to the Telephone Company. A royalty to be paid by one party to the other, would not compensate. I, however, do not like any arrangement which would tend to prevent the public from getting what it wants and the most efficient apparatus. If the demand is sufficiently insistent, other manufacturers will furnish it and take their chances on infringement, which introduces complications, expense, and the injecting of others into a business which might better be done by the parties."

Mr. Neave recommended:

"That for uses other than in connection with a wireless telegraph or telephone public service communication system (as to which each retains its present exclusive rights), and other than fields in which the General Company receives exclusive wireless telephone rights, and the fields in which each now has non-exclusive licenses permitting them to sell combined sets, the Telephone Company grant to the General Company exclusive rights to make, use, sell and lease combined telephone and telegraph receiving sets, and combined telegraph and telephone sending and receiving sets not operated for business purposes or profit (it now has no such right with reference to communication between fixed points and automotive devices, for instance) and that the General Company grant to the Telephone Company exclusive licenses to make, use, lease or sell such sets for all business, public service and commercial uses of such character as might be served by leased wires, as to which its rights are already exclusive with reference to wireless telephony only."

Sec. 21. Broadcasting Devices and Loud Speakers.

An involved controversy had arisen between the Telephone Company and the General Electric not only over the right to make and sell broadcast transmitters but also over the manufacture of loud speaking devices. The language of the contract had been decidedly ambiguous. If construed literally it might mean that the Telephone Company had no right to manufacture transmitters to be used in any way except as a part of a public service telephone communication system. The Radio Group would gladly have limited the Telephone Company to the literal interpretation, except that to construe the clause in this manner would have necessitated a similar literal construction of one of their most cherished rights. Thus, in the grant giving the General Electric Company "non-exclusive licenses" to establish and maintain broadcasting stations, and to make, use, sell and lease wireless telephone receiving apparatus for the reception of matter "so broadcasted," this language might have been interpreted to limit the Radio Group to the manufacture and sale of receiving apparatus to be used only to listen to their own stations. When, therefore, Mr. Neave construed both clauses broadly it had the effect of assuring each of the validity of the position assumed by each manufacturer in producing their own specialty, but it failed to satisfy either in the cross-claims against the other.

In discussing the loud-speaker situation Mr. Neave's letter reads as follows:

"A disagreement has arisen as to the right of the Telephone Company (or the Western Electric Company, to which it has extended rights) to sell or lease loud speaking sets (consisting of an amplifying set and a telephone receiver with horn) for use with wireless telephone receiving apparatus. The General Company asserts that such sets are a part of 'wireless telephone receiving apparatus for the reception of' broadcasted matter. The Telephone and Western Companies assert that these devices are their regular loud speaking sets widely used on wire systems, and that, in connection with wireless receiving sets, they are still being used on a wire system; that it makes no difference that the wire from the receiving set to the loud speaking set may be short, the principle being the same whether it is a foot or two long, or whether it is longer than the distance over which the radio messages come, that is, the principle is the same as when the wireless transmission is an insignificant portion of the whole transmission. As against this broad position, it might be urged that the Telephone Company has never contended that the General and Radio Companies had no license from it to install telephone receivers or amplifiers in and as a part of their wireless telephone receiving sets, though the message has ceased to be wireless, or of radio frequency, and has thus lost all of the attributes of radio and has been conveyed by wires, before it reaches the telephone receivers or the amplifiers. If a telephone receiver is a necessary part of a receiving apparatus, it should make no difference whether that receiver does or does not 'speak loud,' that is, whether it is a receiver of a kind that one holds to the ear or whether it may be placed further away; in each case, it is acted upon by, and is reproducing, waves or impulses which have ceased to be wireless and have been guided to it by wires.

"The Telephone Company suggests, also, that the loud speaker set is a wire, not wireless, set when it is sold to a baseball park, for instance, irrespective of whether it is there joined to a telephone wire or to a broadcasting receiving set—its character does not change when the plug connector is switched from one jack to the other, and the purchaser cannot be controlled in his use of it, and would resent any attempted control. The same line of argument could, however, be made with reference to the sale of tubes which do not change their character whether used for wireless telegraphy within the General Company's field, or for wire telephony within the Telephone Company's field."

Sec. 22. Broadcasting Stations Dispute.

One portion of Mr. Neave's opinion must have been extremely distasteful to the Radio Group. A major controversy had arisen over the relative rights of the parties in broadcasting stations. Members of the Radio Group already owned and operated several powerful stations. The Telephone Company had not yet established a station of its own, although it was well known that the towers of two stations in New York City were already under construction—one for the American Telephone Company and the other for its subsidiary, the Western Electric Company. Hundreds of radio broadcasting stations were in operation throughout the country. Whichever group could establish its right under the complicated patent situation to over-lordship of the great industry would have an immense advantage.

According to Mr. Neave's interpretation of the contract the American Telephone Company not only had the right to manufacture and sell transmitters for radio stations but also to use the same. This meant the right to license others to use them. The only crumb of comfort for the General Electric Company and its allies was Mr. Neave's opinion that General Electric had a non-exclusive right to establish and maintain broadcasting stations of a private character, "and for which no charge is made." This latter clause must have been particularly objectionable to the Radio Group because it was a virtual denial of the means of rendering a radio station self-supporting. It was in exact accord with the contention of the Telephone Company. The language used by Mr. Neave in handing down this highly controversial verdict is as follows:

"(a) Subject to the non-exclusive right of the General Company to establish and maintain wireless telephone broadcasting transmitting stations of a private character, namely, for the use of which no charge is made, and subject to the General Company's exclusive rights with reference to amateur apparatus, the Telephone Company should have the exclusive license to make, sell, lease and use, wireless telephone broadcasting transmitting stations, except that each party is licensed under the patents of the other to sell to the United States Government and to State governments and political subdivisions thereof."

Sec. 23. Multiple Reception.

The final controversy treated by Mr. Neave concerned the vexed question of which group was entitled to jurisdiction over multiple reception of broadcast material. The devices used in halls, public places and apartment houses to render audible the matter so received involved the use of loud speakers and wires from the receiving set. The Telephone Company claimed jurisdiction on two grounds—one that it involved wire telephony, and the other that it was a public use that brought it within the definition of "public service." Since the Telephone Company admittedly had exclusive rights in radio telephony for public service this interpretation would have given it the right to manufacture and sell all such devices.

Mr. Neave denied the validity of the latter reasoning and, in deciding for the General Electric Company, used the following language:

"Reception of telephonic matter necessarily involves and includes rendering the transmitted matter audible and I believe that a reasonable view of the intention of the parties is that 'wireless telephone receiving apparatus' means everything found necessary or desirable in that reception, including amplifiers and telephone receivers, whether or not loud speakers; but that distribution or transmission of the matter received is not to be included in reception. . . .

"Wireless telephone receiving apparatus should be understood to include amplifiers and should also include telephone receivers, whether or not loud speakers, when furnished as an integral part of the receiving set, or for direct use with the receiving set as distinguished from being used to render audible matter received by the receiving set and conducted over wires to a point or points more than say, thirty feet, from the receiving set. . . . Even if their amplifiers did not or may not require any co-ordinating adjustment, I would consider the telephone receivers, whether or not loud speakers, as a part of the receiving apparatus when used at substantially the same point as the wireless receiving set; no idea of transmission or distribution of the received matter enters, under those conditions. If, however, there *is* a substantial transmission to one telephone receiver, whether or not a loud speaker, or to an outlying number or group of them, I would not consider them as forming a part of the receiving apparatus but, rather, as a part of a wire distribution system, as, for instance, head telephone receivers, or loud speakers installed in the rooms of a house, club or hotel, or in nickel-in-the-slot machines, loud speakers distributed around a baseball park, or other public place, etc.

"The General Electric Company should have an exclusive license with reference to wireless telephone broadcasting receiving apparatus, as above defined."

It will be observed that this was a mixed decision. In construing multiple reception as a wire distribution system Mr. Neave would give the Telephone Company the right of control over the terminus of what had begun as an RCA-General Electric undertaking.

By inference, this language would give the Telephone Company jurisdiction over any system of reception that could be termed a wire distribution system—another vexation for the Radio Group.

Sec. 24. *Failure of Neave Mediation.*

The effort of Owen D. Young and Walter S. Gifford to settle their mutual controversies by mediation thus ended in failure. Mr. Neave's valiant efforts had the effect of failing to satisfy either side. The Telephone Company denounced that portion of the decision that ran counter to their own interpretation. The Radio Group likewise refused to be bound by Mr. Neave's opinion in so far as its own contentions were denied.

As early as July, 1922, President Thayer, of the American Telephone Company, wrote to Vice-President Gifford of his company the following dissent from the legal opinion of Mr. Neave:

"As the contract now stands, I have understood it as neither expressing nor implying any obligation on one party to keep out of the field of another, provided getting into that field did not involve the infringement of patent rights of the other."

This ominous contention, coupled with the fact that, weeks before, at a meeting of the board of directors of RCA, Walter S. Gifford, vice-president of the Telephone Company, had made an even more significant remark which had convinced David Sarnoff, Owen D. Young, and others in authority, that future relations between the industrial giants were to be militant indeed. Mr. Gifford's statement was that upon the expiration of certain RCA-controlled patents the American Telephone Company would feel itself at liberty to manufacture and to sell vacuum tubes.

It is obvious that neither group desired to precipitate a major engagement, yet each was resolved to go to extremes if necessary to enforce what it believed to be its rights. Now it was that David Sarnoff was entrusted with the task of negotiating with the opposition —a task in which he was later to demonstrate extraordinary talent. The first important series of conferences were held between Mr.

Sarnoff and Mr. Griswold of the Telephone Company in an effort to arrive at an agreement on certain disputed points; an effort to obtain "definition" of a complex situation. These efforts proved fruitless because neither Sarnoff nor Griswold was willing to make vital concessions to the other.

The net result of the attempt to clarify the cross-licensing agreement by an impartial interpretation of its language had been to widen the breach between the contending groups, rather than to cause them to see eye to eye on any important point of difference. Indeed, it might be said that the very process of analysis of the language used in the cross-licensing agreement had served to convince the RCA Group that, broadly construed, there was ample authority for all its major contentions. By the same process of thought the Telephone Company had arrived at conclusions diametrically opposite. That this phenomenon is not without parallel in human relations we have ample evidence. The classic example is that of various religious sects studying the same text in the Bible and arriving at widely divergent conclusions. Each has found justification for its own point of view. The same is true in construing statutes and legal precedents —each side finds comfort for its own contentions.

It is apparent also that the very process of studying the terms of the agreement of July 1, 1920, had caused each side to discover new "rights" on which to take a decided stand. Each had at first tacitly conceded to the other certain valuable manufacturing prerogatives that might, after all, belong as much to one as to the other. Before signing the agreements each had possessed patent rights of wide range, not enough it is true to make a complete system of wireless telegraphy or to meet the new development of radio broadcasting.

Thus we may explain the Telephone Company's threat to resume manufacture of vacuum tubes. Before July, 1920, it had done much to develop the potentialities of the vacuum tube. It held basic patents therein. The Langmuir and other patents owned by competitors had prevented the Telephone Company from manufacturing the latest type of vacuum tube. The Arnold-Langmuir interference was one of the greatest controversies in radio annals. It will be remembered that Arnold was a Telephone Company technician, whereas Langmuir was in the employ of General Electric Company. As matters stood, however, according to the wording of the license agreement if interpreted as the General Electric Company lawyers and Mr. Neave had construed it, all rights in vacuum tubes for radio purposes were now lodged in the Radio Group. It is small wonder that the Telephone Company repented of the agreement. Believing that it did not express the intention of the parties, it now resolved to maintain acknowledged rights as well as to regain rights inadvertently lost. Thus we may explain the hostile marches and countermarches of the embattled groups that were already in progress behind the scenes.

Mediation had failed to satisfy either party. Efforts were now being made by each to occupy disputed territory and to hold it against all hostile attack. To David Sarnoff, man of action as well as negotiator of unusual talent, this new situation was highly interesting. He entered into the contest with a twofold purpose: first, of winning victory for the Radio Group and, second, of achieving for RCA the manufacturing rights that it had not then obtained.

CHAPTER
FOUR

Hostilities Begin

Section 25. Sarnoff Advocates High-Power Short-Wave Broadcasting.
THE EVENTS OF THE YEAR 1922 in the sales department of the Radio
Corporation had marked David Sarnoff as the man of destiny in the
organization. As early as midsummer it had been noised abroad that
under Mr. Sarnoff's management the volume of sales of RCA had
mounted to incredible figures. It was rumored that the income from
sales for the year had increased about seven hundred per cent over
that of the previous year. Increased income is the most convincing
proof of any man's worth that can be offered to any board of directors. Thus it came to pass that any suggestions for future business
from the pen of RCA's young general manager were now given respectful consideration even by the most conservative of the directors
of RCA.

On August 2, 1922, Mr. Sarnoff addressed a letter to President
Edward J. Nally that is of sufficient historic importance to deserve
attention in any recital that purports to depict the behind-the-scenes
developments in one of the greatest industrial dramas of American
life. It demonstrates how the leaders of the industry were even then
exploring every possibility in their efforts to overcome technical
problems of radio broadcasting. At the time this letter was written
Station WJZ was still being operated by Westinghouse, although RCA
was paying one-half of the expenses of operation. Mr. Sarnoff knew,
nevertheless, the problems that confronted the station—especially
with reference to wave lengths. The Department of Commerce was
still licensing all radio stations to operate on the 360-meter channel
which caused great inconvenience to stations in the same locality.
WJZ was then sharing broadcast hours with a number of stations,
and now the Telephone Company was breaking into the field with
a very powerful station. Mr. Sarnoff's letter reflects the condition existing at the time, as will be seen in the following:

"The recent difficulties experienced in connection with broadcasting schedules and the division of time, coupled with the possibilities
which come into view by the use of short waves, have led me to think
in terms of high-power broadcasting as a possible solution to a number
of problems which face us at present.

"*First* of all, the economic question of 'who is to pay for broadcasting,' is a large one or a small one in proportion to the number
of broadcasting stations which need be erected and operated in order
to give a national broadcasting service. Thus, if it were possible to
cover the country with one, two or three broadcasting stations, the
question of expense of operation and the matter of procuring and
paying suitable artists become very much simplified; indeed simplified

almost to the point where the Radio Corporation alone might be in a position to do the whole job and pay for it out of returns from sales.

"Secondly, the problems of wave-lengths and interference are directly related to the number of stations in operation. Hence, if it were possible satisfactorily to cover the country with one, two or three broadcasting stations and in the case of the latter number, perhaps operated simultaneously by being connected with wires, only one wave length, say 100 meters, or preferably, one band covering the range, say from 75 to 100 meters, would be necessary to do the job.

"Thirdly, if the above were demonstrated as being technically practical, I would suppose that we could with logic and propriety, approach the Department of Commerce or Congress and ask for an exclusive wave length or band to protect such national broadcasting service. . . .

"In exploring the possibilities of high-power operation on a wave length as short as 100 meters, we must recognize that we are entering a totally new and unknown field in radio. No one, I think, can speak with definite knowledge today as to how far or how well telegraph or radio telephone signals on 100 meters will travel if sent off on their journey by 100 kw.

"As you know, I have been a believer in the possibilities of short waves for a number of years and I have had my faith more or less strengthened by what Senatore Marconi told us during his last visit in America, about his experiments and success with short waves. . . .

"Although it is purely a speculative statement and necessarily based on incomplete knowledge and information, yet it would not surprise me if in the next few years we find that a radio signal sent out on 100 meters with 100 or 200 kw. of power will travel around the world and be received through the highly sensitive and delicate receiving instruments which are rapidly projecting themselves into the radio art, for example, the super-regenerative.

"It may well be that some day in the future we will signal and talk across the Atlantic and Pacific with short instead of long waves and if this should come true, the problems of static elimination and high-speed operation would take on a new appearance for it is well known one can signal on short waves at a rate of speed many times that possible on the longer waves and static at the shorter wave lengths is not comparable to that on the long waves. . . .

"If the picture I have painted above should become a real one, it would practically mean a new broadcasting art both on the transmission and reception ends. It may well be that with sufficient power we may ultimately find two stations sufficient to cover the country, in which case one transmitter could be located at radio central and controlled from the New York studio and the second station located at Bolinas, California, and controlled by a wire from San Francisco at our studio. . . ."

Sec. 26. Why the Telephone Company Established Station WEAF.

The radio broadcasting situation in June, 1922, so far as the warring factions were concerned, was that the Westinghouse Company had in operation the following radio stations: KDKA in Pittsburgh, Pa.; WBZ in Springfield, Mass.; KYW in Chicago, Ill., and WJZ in Newark, N. J., the latter station being operated jointly by Westinghouse and RCA. The General Electric Company had opened one station, WGY, in Schenectady, N. Y. Thus the Radio Group were actively operating five radio broadcasting stations before the American Telephone Company entered the broadcasting field. To be sure the General Electric Company and its allies contended that the Telephone Company had no right to broadcast at all, but this contention was disregarded by the latter. In the light of events we may conclude that the opening of radio stations by the Telephone Company had definite significance.

It will be remembered that Station WBAY was first listed as a licensed station in the Department of Commerce Radio Bulletin, May 1, 1922, but was not ready to go on the air until July 25th following. This station was listed in the name of the American Telephone & Telegraph Company, whereas a second radio station, WEAF, was listed on June 1, 1922, in the name of the Western Electric Company, a subsidiary of the American Telephone Company. Thus the parent company had two strings to its bow, so to speak. Station WBAY was to be located at 24 Walker Street, and Station WEAF at 463 West Street, in New York City. The story of the opening of these stations and how they came to be consolidated into one station has been set forth at length by the author in the *History of Radio to 1926*,[1] it may be summarized as follows:

Station WBAY was to have its broadcasting studios in the steel-framed building at 24 Walker Street. Its broadcasting towers were to be on the roof of the building. Station WEAF was doubtless intended to share studio and office accommodations with WBAY at 24 Walker Street. Its broadcasting towers, however, were constructed on the top of the building at 463 West Street. WBAY was to open on July 25th and WEAF on August 15th. By a strange turn of fate the expensive towers of WBAY would not work satisfactorily owing to the steel structure on which they stood. Even before WEAF was scheduled to go on the air the Telephone Company engineers were obliged to try the towers at 463 West Street as a means of broadcasting the WBAY program.

Fortunately, the antenna of WEAF worked admirably. Its signals

[1] Pages 264-269.

were marvelously clear. No radio station then existing could compare with it, and so, by force of circumstances, and the Federal law that required a station to be known by license of its broadcasting towers, Station WBAY faded out of the picture and WEAF succeeded to its offices and studios at 24 Walker Street. Here WEAF remained during the exciting months while it was blazing the trail for commercially sponsored broadcasts. It is obvious, however, that the Telephone Company at first intended to operate their radio stations much as they were accustomed to operate their long-distance wire telephone toll stations. The preliminary announcement was couched in part in the following language:

"Anyone desiring to use these facilities for radio broadcasting should make arrangements with Mr. A. W. Drake, general commercial manager, long lines department, Am. Tel. & Tel. Company, 195 Broadway, New York City. Mr. Drake can advise fully with reference to all particulars concerning the use of the station, including information as to the periods of operation and the charges thereof. He is also in a position to give helpful suggestions with reference to the arrangement of programs and the kind of subject matter which it is thought will be most acceptable to the radio audience.

* * * *

"Recognizing these conditions and bearing in mind that broadcasting facilities should be provided for the general use of the public rather than for the few who might desire to own and operate stations, this Station WBAY has been established as an experiment in toll broadcasting. Its success or failure will depend upon the use of it made by those who employ its facilities. Those who broadcast will not receive general favor from the radio audience unless they broadcast programs of merit and of general interest."

Sec. 27. Rivalry Between WJZ and WEAF.

To the surprise, no doubt, of the Telephone Company, no one "desiring to use these facilities for radio broadcasting" put in an appearance at 24 Walker Street. The company was virtually driven to the expedient of drumming up trade. H. Clinton Smith, an enterprising employee of the commercial department of the American Telephone Company, is conceded to have been the salesman who won the first contract for a sponsored program ever arranged in radio annals. The Queensborough Corporation,[2] a real estate enterprise, was the first customer of WEAF. A ten-minute program on August 28, 1922, proved the inauguration of a most controversial type of radio program.

[2] For a complete story of this event see Archer, *History of Radio to 1926*, pp. 276-277, 397-399 for text of broadcast.

GENERAL JAMES G. HARBORD
Distinguished World War commander. Second President of RCA. Since 1930
Chairman of Board of RCA.

The broadcast became controversial for various reasons. First, it introduced commercial advertising into radio programs; and many people resented the innovation. Second, it produced revenue for the station; and the Telephone Company, claimant for overlordship of radio broadcasting, had forbidden other stations to broadcast for hire. This was considered by the Radio Group to be highly unfair. To be excluded from obtaining means of support for its stations threatened the position of the Radio Group in the broadcasting field. How much this attitude was influenced by the growing rivalry between the two groups is hard to say. Certain it is that crimination and recrimination were soon to characterize the relations between the groups, especially in the radio sector. Between WJZ, the RCA Westinghouse station, and WEAF, the Telephone Company station, there soon grew up a spirit of antagonism and rivalry that was to increase in bitterness for years to come.

Station WJZ was nine months old when WEAF first went on the air, yet the new station, equipped with the Telephone Company's latest and best broadcasting transmitters, immediately overshadowed WJZ in the excellence and clarity of its signals. This could not have failed to arouse chagrin and resentment. Not only that, but WEAF, with a shrewd sense of showmanship, at once added to its staff an announcer who was a talented pianist and capable of staging a live show unaided if need be. Albert V. Llufrio, paragon of his kind, joined the WEAF staff in October, 1922.

Not to be outdone, Station WJZ at once countered by hiring Milton J. Cross, a tenor soloist with a remarkable speaking voice—destined to become one of the most famous of all radio announcers.[3] Thus the rivalry between the two stations at once resulted in improved radio programs. The technical superiority of WEAF also put RCA engineers on their mettle to improve their own broadcasting equipment. However bitter the rivalry between the two stations may have become, it is noteworthy that the listening public profited mightily by the radio war. No doubt the rivalry of the Telephone Company and the Radio Group was vastly intensified in the sector represented by the operating staffs of the broadcasting studios. The rivalry, however, was by this time deep seated.

Prior to the opening of WBAY and WEAF, Station WJZ had enjoyed a pre-eminence on the air. It had perhaps been a bit "cocky"— which was natural, in view of the importance of its sponsors, Westinghouse and RCA. Whenever new stations had been authorized—on the same wave length as WJZ—it had become necessary to divide time on the air with the newcomers. This had led to heartburnings on the

[3] For a detailed story of these events see Archer, *History of Radio to 1926*, pp. 277-279.

part of the latter. They complained that WJZ was using the 360-meter channel a disproportionately large share of the time. Local stations had banded together for the purpose of obliging WJZ to surrender a part of its broadcasting hours. Now, in the midst of these difficulties, came WEAF with its clear and powerful transmitter—on the same wave length!

In the light of present-day knowledge it seems strange that the government should so long have continued its policy of licensing all radio stations on the same wave length. When Station WBAY came on the air on July 25, 1922, it appears from the program sheets of Station WJZ that it was operating from 7:00 P.M. to 9:00 o'clock—the best broadcasting hours, no doubt, but not the lion's share of broadcasting time.

This condition of time-sharing, and frequent trespass, was soon to yield to a more sensible arrangement. On October 2, 1922, Station WEAF was permitted to operate on a 400-meter channel, sharing time with WOR and possibly others. Station WJZ continued on 360 meters, but was given a second wave length of 485 meters. It is interesting to note that WEAF continued to use the 400-meter channel until it opened its new station at 195 Broadway, when its assignment was changed to 492 meters, or 610 kilocycles, as the new frequency was presently labeled. On November 11, 1928, WEAF went on its present frequency of 660 kilocycles.

Another cause for dissatisfaction on the part of the WJZ staff in the beginning of WEAF's competition on the air concerned location of the stations. The WJZ studios were in Newark, N. J. A special pick-up studio had already been established in the Waldorf-Astoria Hotel in New York City,[4] yet even this studio, more accessible to the stars of stage and concert halls than the Newark headquarters, suffered in comparison with WEAF's studios at 24 Walker Street in New York City because the hotel studio was a mere make-shift. This competitive advantage soon led to a decision of RCA chieftains to build real studios in the heart of the metropolis.

Sec. 28. The Telephone Company Clamps Down on Leased Wires.

Coincident with the opening of a radio station it appears that the officials of the American Telephone Company decided to refuse further use of leased wires to the broadcasting stations of the Radio Group. That this was not done in a spirit of meanness or in an effort to exalt their new station is evident from the correspondence that passed between the parties at the time. The Telephone Company apparently believed that valuable rights under the cross-licensing

[4] Archer, *History of Radio to 1926*, p. 219.

covenant would be jeopardized by a continuation of the practice. The matter really came to a head when Charles B. Popenoe, the energetic manager of WJZ, decided to win acclaim for his station by broadcasting the 1922 World Series baseball games—a feat that had never before been attempted.

When Mr. Popenoe applied to the Telephone Company for a leased wire to bring the announcer's description of the games to the WJZ studio the matter was referred to Augustus H. Griswold, then assistant vice-president of the company, who was said by Mr. Popenoe to have "bluntly turned down our request." [5] The matter was to be the subject of further correspondence, as will presently appear. In the meantime, however, the resourceful Popenoe contrived a means of accomplishing his purpose. This can best be told in his own words:

"Needless to say we were disappointed, but recently L. R. Krumm, superintendent of Radio Operators, had been succeeded by C. W. Horn in the same capacity and as Mr. Horn was well connected with the Western Union Company we decided to investigate their wire services. To our great satisfaction we found Mr. J. C. Willever, vice-president of Western Union, willing to help us. . . . We heaved a sigh of relief after ascertaining that Western Union wires could be used. Through the assistance of the New York *Tribune* and their famous sports writer, Mr. Grantland Rice, we did a one hundred per cent job of this broadcasting feature, besides securing a great deal of front-page publicity from the *Tribune*."

The denial of the use of wires of the American Telephone Company was a serious matter to the Radio Group. They evidently saw in it the first genuine skirmish in hostilities of far-reaching nature. On October 9, 1922, Owen D. Young wrote a letter on the subject to Henry B. Thayer, president of the American Telephone Company, complaining of the ungenerous conduct of the Telephone Company. This letter elicited the following reply:

October 13, 1922

Owen D. Young, Chairman,
    Radio Corporation of America,
    233 Broadway, New York City.

Dear Mr. Young:

I am in receipt of yours of the 9th instant.

As you know, under the license agreement between us, broadcasting stations of the Radio Corporation, General Electric, Westinghouse or United Fruit may not be connected with the public service telephone communication system.

[5] Archer, *History of Radio to 1926*, p. 279.

It is not true, however, that the board of directors of this company either have or have not decided that requests for the use of wires for broadcasting stations could not be granted and in fact we have granted several requests for such service with the understanding that they were granted without prejudice to any rights under the contract.

It is our intention to connect to our own broadcasting station or stations for the purpose of giving service to the public in this way, and where we have no broadcasting station but one of the other parties to the license agreement has such a station, we have been ready to consider every case where a connection with toll lines or with subscriber stations has been asked and to give all possible consideration to meeting the needs of the situation, so that the public might obtain this service pending the period in which this whole broadcasting matter is being considered and brought to a definite policy.

Yours very truly,

(Signed) H. B. THAYER,

President

While the concluding paragraph of the above letter is couched in polite language, so astute a man as Owen D. Young could not fail to perceive in it a solemn warning that, in the New York area, where the Telephone Company had a broadcasting station of its own no other radio station could expect to be served by pick-up wires. This letter, moreover, was written on a Friday. It probably did not come to the notice of Mr. Young until Monday, October 16th. It is obvious that Mr. Young at once communicated with the Westinghouse Company, which at this time was operating Station WJZ in conjunction with the Radio Corporation.

No doubt as the result of a conference with Mr. Young, Charles A. Terry, vice-president of Westinghouse, a lawyer by profession, at once telephoned to G. E. Folk, the general patent attorney of the American Telephone Company. It is evident that the conversation was characterized by earnestness, if not by a degree of acrimony. Mr. Terry had been studying the general aspects of the cross-licensing agreement and had developed opinions of his own as to the extent of the Telephone Company's supposed monopoly. In fact, he had concluded that the language, sweeping as it appeared at first glance, could not and did not give the Telephone Company a monopoly of the use of telephone wires except when they were being used as a part of public service communications system. This opinion he voiced to Mr. Folk, who retorted with surprised indignation.

On the following day, October 17, 1922, he wrote a three-page letter to Mr. Terry, the first portion of which was as follows:

Dear Mr. Terry:

I have been giving careful consideration to the question you raised in your telephone conversation yesterday regarding the use of telephone wires in connection with your company's broadcasting stations. That you should raise any doubt regarding the exclusive right of the American Telephone and Telegraph Company under its patents to such use of telephone wires came to me as a complete surprise.

By the contract between the American Telephone and Telegraph Company and the Westinghouse Electric & Manufacturing Company, the respective rights of the two companies with regard to broadcasting are the same as the rights of the American Telephone & Telegraph Company and the General Electric Company respectively, as fixed by the contract of July 1, 1920. By the above-mentioned contracts the Westinghouse Company received

"non-exclusive licenses to establish and maintain transmitting stations for transmitting or broadcasting news, music and entertainment from a transmitting station to outlying points."

The A. T. & T. Company, without any reservation with respect to broadcasting, received

"exclusive licenses in the field of wireless telephony to make, use, lease and sell, all wireless telephone apparatus connected to or operated as a part of a public service telephone communication system, whether wire or wireless."

And also

"exclusive licenses in the field of wire telephony on land. . . ."

It seems clear to me, therefore, that the rights of your company with respect to wireless broadcast transmission relates solely to transmitting *from* wireless transmitting stations and does not include transmission by wires connected to such stations.

Thus, in the proverbial nutshell, Mr. Folk expressed an opinion over which the lawyers for the contesting parties were to wrangle for several years.

Sec. 29. The Telephone Company Aims at Supremacy of WEAF.

It was now apparent that the American Telephone Company had resolved at all costs to establish and maintain a supremacy in radio broadcasting—to begin in the New York area with WEAF as its great weapon of competition. Mr. Thayer had intimated in his letter of October 13th that Station WEAF was to be equipped with pick-up wires "for the purpose of giving service to the public in this way." Mr. Folk's letter, already partially quoted, states very bluntly in the following paragraph this phase of Telephone Company policy:

"With specific reference to the New York metropolitan area, this company, as you know, has a broadcasting station in New York and is prepared to give connection to it over its telephone lines, thus giving to the public the service which it was contemplated in the license agreement should be given by the A. T. & T. Company. Such service is open to your company through this company's station."

The irony of the suggestion that the Radio Group avail itself of the facilities of WEAF must have incensed the vice-president of Westinghouse having jurisdiction over four radio stations. But now Mr. Folk reveals in plain English a thought that had long rankled in the breasts of the Telephone chieftains—that the Radio allies were trespassing against vested rights of the Telephone Company by maintaining public radio broadcasting stations. His letter continues in the following tone of recrimination:

"Since it was contemplated that the maintenance of stations for the use of others than the contracting parties was to be the field of the Telephone Company, we have felt that your company, by offering its stations for the use of others, is further invading this company's field. It was contemplated that your company would use its stations merely for its own publicity and to create a demand for its products, and not for furnishing a service to others. As a matter of fact, your stations are now giving such service to others. For example, as is perfectly obvious, the concerts given by the *Evening Mail* are intended to advertise that newspaper. As an additional example, a lecture recently given through your broadcasting station advertising a brand of candy was another misuse of your station. These are but a few of the many cases in which your station is giving a service for which, under the contract, it is not licensed.

"As you stated in your conversation, the immense popularity of wireless broadcasting has given rise to several situations which were not clearly foreseen at the time the contract was drawn. I think that all parties of the contract have been as lenient as possible in order that the public might obtain all possible service during the period in which this whole broadcasting matter is being brought to a definite policy. We trust that our leniency has not been misconstrued by you as acquiescence in a continuance of such disregard of our rights when the emergency has passed."

It is apparent from another letter written at this time that Mr. Folk was engaged in debate not only with Mr. Terry of the Westinghouse Company but also with Mr. Davis of the General Electric Company —presumably Albert G. Davis, the chief patent attorney of the company. This would be logical in view of the fact that the battle must be fought largely along the lines of patent rights. It is apparent, however, that the commanders-in-chief of the embattled powers were not leaving the contest to their subordinates. On the contrary, it appears that Owen D. Young on October 17, 1922, shortly after receiving Mr. Thayer's letter of October 13th already quoted, fired a broadside of verbal artillery. To this letter, on October 20, 1922, Mr. Thayer replied in part as follows:

"The routines of our business have been laid out on the basis of the contract as we have understood it. Such matters as the connection with Schenectady and others of a similar character would naturally come up as exceptions, because they meant extending rights or permitting infringement of rights which we believe belong to us under the contract. We have been good natured about this, but, as I look at it, it is not possible in any business to provide a routine for exceptions to the operation of a contract. Such matters must be considered by the officers of the company, however unimportant in themselves. . . .

"My contention with our people has been that we should not attempt to consider any variations or modifications in the licenses until there had been a definite conclusion as to the rights under the contract as it stands, so that we could have a basis to start from. I think that Mr. Folk and Mr. Davis have discussed these things pretty fully and have been attempting to arrive at such a conclusion but, as I get it, a conclusion in which we make some sacrifices is the only conclusion which Mr. Davis is inclined to accept. We have even considered whether, for the sake of peace and quietness, we should not make some concessions.

"I am saying this to you just to let you know that I am in sympathy with your troubles and anxious to go just as far as we possibly can towards relieving them."

Sec. 30. The Carrier-Current Controversy.

The net result of conferences, negotiations and letter writing thus far had been to crystallize the contentions of each corporate group. Neither side was apparently willing to give an inch of advantage to the other. In the light of circumstances, it is apparent that each was acting on principle. The language of their compact was very ambiguous. The parties, through much study and many arguments had arrived at their conclusions as to vested rights—conclusions no doubt colored by self interest, as are nearly all human controversies. This was no vulgar struggle of one greedy corporate group to oust another group equally great from a rich, new field of endeavor. It was rather an earnest and dignified struggle of each to protect the rights of its stockholders, each apparently willing to grant to the other all legal rights stipulated in the cross-licensing compact yet unable to agree upon interpretation of language.

There is indeed some evidence of a spirit of conciliation among the high officials of the contending corporations. For instance, on December 14, 1922, President Thayer, of the Telephone Company, wrote to Owen D. Young, evidently after a conference on the vexed topic of carrier currents, suggesting a possible way of marketing apparatus suitable for use in this type of broadcasting. His words are as follows:

"With reference to carrier-current broadcasting on electric light, power and traction lines which we touched on slightly at our last meeting, I wondered whether, without committing ourselves either to develop the apparatus or to manufacture it or to put it on the market, it would be of any material help to your interests if we should agree that that particular line of apparatus, if put on the market, should be put out through the Radio Corporation? I doubt very much whether it is likely to prove a considerable business."

It will be observed that this suggestion does not touch the real issue of carrier-current broadcasting. It affected merely the manufacture and sale of apparatus needful for this type of transmission. The Telephone Company, as Mr. Young knew only too well, was still adamant in its attitude on this score. David Sarnoff approached the matter cautiously. He was strong in the belief that the language of Section 5, Article V of the contract gave the Radio Group the right to broadcast over power lines. To be sure there was no definite grant of such in the contract, yet there was a clause giving the General Electric Company (and its affiliated companies) a right to manufacture and sell devices for "carrier-current" telephone communication over wires, or partly over wires and partly across wireless gaps. This, to Mr. Sarnoff, was evidence that the Telephone Company by inference conceded that it did not reserve the exclusive rights that it now claimed.

The astute general manager of RCA saw in the controversy over carrier-current devices a danger that if the Telephone Company were permitted to sell apparatus for carrier-current purposes the same might be used by the purchasers for ordinary radio broadcasting. There would really be no way of preventing such purchasers from buying ostensibly for one purpose and using the apparatus for another— thus striking a blow at RCA's chief source of revenue: sales of radio tubes and sets.

Mr. Sarnoff feared, moreover, that carrier-current broadcasting might turn out to be more important than radio broadcasting itself. Evidence had already come to Mr. Sarnoff's office that the North American Company, a great power utility combine, had purchased some rights under the Squier patents and was even then carrying on extensive investigations and experimentation. There was also an unconfirmed report that the American Telephone Company itself was already experimenting in carrier-current broadcasting. Thus the contest grew more and more critical as the keen minds of the technicians and tacticians of each group jockeyed for advantage in the great struggle in which they were now fully embarked.

Sec. 31. Open Warfare in Broadcasting Sector.

Thus far, in conferences, joint debates and in letter writing, the chieftains had struggled to convince each other of the justice of their respective claims. Down the line, however, in the ranks of the warring corporations there was no armistice, no diminution of effort. On the contrary, with the zest of battle, each side strove to entrench itself more firmly in the disputed territory. In no phase of the conflict was this more pronounced than in the radio broadcasting sector.

To the casual observer it might seem that the officials of the rival radio stations WEAF and WJZ must have lain awake nights in order to concoct new schemes for triumphing over each other. An experiment of great historic importance was staged by WEAF during the football season of 1922 that took the staff at WJZ by surprise and demonstrated anew the great importance of wire lines as an adjunct of broadcasting. The incident has been described by the author in the previous volume in this series.

"In the light of history a very significant event occurred in the fall of 1922. The Telephone Company engineers decided to test the possibility of long-distance telephone connection in radio transmission. A football game was to be played in Chicago on a certain day. By means of special transmitters and amplifiers located on the football field an oral description of the game, together with the cheering of the spectators, was delivered to a telephone cable circuit connected with the toll office of the Telephone Company in Chicago. This circuit was connected with the toll line to New York City. In Park Row, in New York, a truck in which a radio receiving set was installed had been equipped with a public address system. By this means it became possible for a street throng in New York City to hear a broadcast of a game actually being played in Chicago. This experiment demonstrated the soundness of the principle later successfully employed in chain or network broadcasting." [6]

Then came WJZ's opportunity to steal a march on its rival. In December, 1922, it inaugurated the first grand opera broadcast ever to be heard by radio listeners in the metropolis. To be sure Station KYW had broadcast concerts of the Chicago Opera Company during the previous winter [7] but WJZ's feat was worthy of mention as a pioneer effort owing to the deadlock that existed locally over leased wires. Wires were necessary to pick up the concerts directly from the Opera House but the American Telephone Company not only refused to furnish the wires but also forbade the hiring of lines from other companies. This did not prevent Mr. Popenoe from carrying out the

[6] Archer, *History of Radio to 1926*, pp. 284-285.
[7] *Ibid.*, p. 271.

project. We have no proof of what company assisted him but it was undoubtedly the Western Union that had come to his rescue at the time of the World Series games. At any rate this achievement was a triumph for WJZ.[8]

A development that must have brought keen satisfaction to the RCA-Westinghouse camp was the public reaction to commercial advertising over Station WEAF. Radio listeners had accepted radio broadcasting as manna from heaven. It came to them "without money and without price"—entertainment that was free as air. Station WEAF with its clear tones and high quality programs seems to have been preferred to all other stations—but now an ominous note crept into its broadcasts. Commercial advertising—some of it crude and direct in its appeal—began to creep into the brilliant offerings of this popular station. Criticism and mutterings against the custom were not slow in manifesting themselves.

The most formidable critic of all was no doubt the powerful periodical, *Radio Broadcast*. This magazine had welcomed the advent of Station WEAF both in its news columns and editorial pages. In the November, 1922 issue appeared a feature article entitled "Should Radio Be Used for Advertising?" While the author of the article did not mention the offending station by name, he nevertheless made it perfectly clear what station was being castigated as the leader in a movement that had already spread to other stations. A portion of the article was as follows:

"Anyone who doubts the reality, the imminence of the problem has only to listen about him for plenty of evidence. Driblets of advertising, most of it indirect so far, to be sure, but still unmistakable, are floating through the ether every day. Concerts are seasoned here and there with a dash of advertising paprika. You can't miss it; every little classic number has a slogan all its own, if it is only the mere mention of the name—and the street address, and the phone number—of the music house which arranged the program. More of this sort of thing may be expected. And once the avalanche gets a good start, nothing short of an Act of Congress or a repetition of Noah's excitement will suffice to stop it."

There was much in this article—all demonstrating that the listening public expected to be entertained without rendering any return to the entertainers—without suffering even a wee bit for the cause. As yet, the public in general did not realize that radio broadcasting must find some means of self-support or perish. Manufacturers of radio sets might have an incentive to broadcast until the radio boom should have passed its crest, but so soon as profits might be endangered by

[8] Archer, *History of Radio to 1926*, p. 282.

the expenses of broadcasting they too must close their radio stations. A tax upon radio sets, or radio advertising, were the only choices. Great Britain was to choose the former, the United States of America the latter alternative.

Thus, while the industrial giants carried on their warfare in the background—apart from public gaze and from public knowledge—there were phases of the conflict in which the public was an active participant. In the meantime, the chieftains of the American Telephone Company, realizing the ability and resourcefulness of their antagonists, were busily strengthening the lineup at WEAF. W. E. Harkness, of the long lines department, was transferred to the broadcasting sector on November 1, 1922. The purpose was obviously to have him apply his engineering skill to the problems of the station, with the idea of taking over its official management at an early date. As events were to prove, he was to become station manager April 21, 1923. Functions of the studio were now divided. Samuel L. Ross was musical director; Vischer A. Randall, studio director; R. S. Fenimore, operating supervisor; Edmund R. Taylor, assistant plant supervisor. George F. McClelland came to the station as commercial representative on November 15, 1922. The rapid development of sponsored programs during the next twelve months was due in large measure to the energy and enthusiasm of George F. McClelland, who was later to rise to the position of manager of the station. O. B. Hanson, a long lines engineer, is one of the few officials who has served continuously in radio since the winter of 1923. He is now vice-president and chief engineer of the National Broadcasting Company. Another veteran from WEAF is Mark Woods, who is now vice-president and treasurer of NBC.

Sec. 32. RCA and Radio in December, 1922.

While these changes were occurring at Station WEAF very significant developments were manifest at the head offices of RCA. For some months it had been known within the organization that President Nally, who had devoted his life to communications problems, found current developments overshadowing the original picture. RCA had started as a communications corporation, yet the radio boom had literally overwhelmed it with a new line of endeavor. Not that it had lost ground as a communications corporation—quite the reverse being true—but now the energetic Sarnoff was building up a sales organization of nationwide dimensions.

The Annual Report of the Board of Directors for the year ending December 31, 1922, contains this vivid portrayal of the growth of radio sales:

"While in previous years your corporation had enjoyed in the domestic field a substantial business in the sale of radio apparatus to shipowners, commercial companies, amateurs, experimenters and to governments, it had never been faced with the problem of setting up an organization for merchandising apparatus that would eventually go into every American home. In order to meet this unprecedented demand, your sales organization grew from a personnel of fourteen to approximately two hundred, and district offices were opened in Chicago and San Francisco. The products of your corporation are being distributed today through one hundred and forty-six wholesale distributors throughout the United States who operate one hundred and ninety-six warehouses, and the list of dealers who are handling RCA products now numbers approximately 15,000."

The most significant feature of the report was that while the income from transoceanic communications had increased from $2,138,625.86 to $2,914,283.41 the sales of apparatus had jumped from $1,468,919.95 to $11,286,489.41—a revenue nearly eight times as great as that of 1921. This, no doubt, explains why David Sarnoff was advanced to the position of vice-president and general manager on September 8, 1922.

The foregoing recital of the changes that took place in the fortunes of RCA during the year should sufficiently explain why Edward J. Nally had asked to be relieved of his responsibilities as president of the Radio Corporation. He had made this request of Owen D. Young as early as February, 1922, when the radio flood was beginning to engulf the organization. Mr. Young had given a great deal of care to the task of selecting a successor to Mr. Nally. The story has been told by the author in another connection.[9]

It is significant, at this time when skillful generalship was needed in the camp of the Radio Group, that an actual military man of that exalted rank came to the presidency of RCA. General James G. Harbord, with World War and postwar laurels as an organizer of operations, might well have fancied that he was stepping into a new type of warfare when he became chief executive of the Radio Corporation. It was no small task to take the place just vacated by so able a man as Edward J. Nally. General Harbord was new to his duties, but it must be remembered that Owen D. Young continued as chairman of the board of directors of RCA. The father of the corporation and the architect of its policies, Mr. Young was well qualified to guide the new president in the complicated situation in which he found himself.

The vacancies on the board of directors of RCA, caused by the resignation in June, 1922, of Walter S. Gifford and Frederick A. Stevenson, had now been filled by the election of General Harbord and Harry P. Davis. Mr. Davis will be remembered as the Westing-

9 Archer, *History of Radio to 1926*, pp. 246, 295.

house vice-president who had been responsible for the founding of Station KDKA. Thus, at a critical time, there was added to the board one of the great veterans of radio—although veteran is scarcely the word to use when we reflect that at this time radio broadcasting was only two years old.

In the report of the board of directors for the year 1922 is the following significant entry concerning the development of radio broadcasting:

"In the last year the number of broadcasting stations has grown from less than twenty to almost six hundred. The art itself is advancing very fast, and the ultimate effect of broadcasting upon the economic, social, religious, political, and educational life of the country and the world, is comparable only with that of the discovery of printing 500 years ago. Today, broadcasting stations are sending out news, music, lectures, concerts, crop reports, weather reports, time signals, religious services, as well as fire and police warnings. Systematic broadcasting of educational matter is also being experimented with in many places. Broadcasting has appealed to the imagination as no other scientific development of the time. . . . In many places in the past year, because of the limited number of wave lengths available for broadcasting and the large number of stations trying to operate on these wave lengths, there has been a great deal of interference. Generally, one of two things has happened: either good programs have suffered from this interference, or stations capable of serving many thousands of listeners have been asked to give up time on specific wave lengths to stations less well equipped, which can at best serve only small communities and a limited number of listeners with local programs."

The paragraph last quoted obviously refers to WJZ's tribulations in the New York area. It was indeed equipped to serve a great multitude but, alas! was obliged to surrender a goodly share of its time to other stations. This recalls the controversy raging even before WEAF came, in which local stations had banded together to fight WJZ in the courts. This had been commented upon by *Radio Broadcast* for October, 1922, in the following language:

"It was a foreordained fact that there would eventually be conflicts between various broadcasting stations, especially in the neighborhood of New York, where a large number of them have been installed. This recently came to pass. We have had the experience of listening to a jumble of signals of just the kind anticipated—dance music competing with a lecturer for the ear of the radio audience.

"From the press notices it appears that WJZ, the Radio Corporation-Westinghouse Station at Newark, has been using the 360-meter ether channel during what seems to certain other stations a disproportionately large share of the time, and has refused to agree with these other stations on what they think a reasonable division of hours. It is probably because of this attitude on the part of the Radio Corporation Station that the Radio Broadcasting Society has been organized recently, banding together broadcasting stations for the purpose of allotting them hours in what they regard as a reasonable division, with the idea of averting the kind of interference to which we have recently been treated. It seems that WJZ felt the ether should be unchallenged by later comers, and it was not until the counsel for the Broadcasting Society had started action to have the license of WJZ revoked by the federal authorities that a temporary peace and agreement were made possible."

The editor discusses the crisis in radio affairs that was involved in the controversy, and makes the following pertinent observation:

"It would be sheer nonsense to stop the operation of WJZ for one minute so that some dry goods store might send out a scratchy foxtrot phonograph record which is mixed up with a loud commutator hum and 'blocking' of overmodulated tubes. The time has gone by when the public should have to listen to such stuff, because there are stations which have been properly designed and to which it is a pleasure to listen. . . . The only criterion which must serve to guide in the allocation of hours is excellence of program excellently produced."

CHAPTER
FIVE

Compromise, Arbitrate, or Litigate

CHARLES NEAVE
Eminent lawyer who interpreted G.E.-A. T. & T. contract.

FREDERICK P. FISH
Chief counsel for Radio Group in arbitration of 1924.

ROLAND W. BOYDEN
Boston lawyer who acted as Referee in the famous arbitration of 1924.

ANDREW W. ROBERTSON
Chairman of the Board, Westinghouse Company.

Section 33. Important Developments in Radio Industry.

ATTENTION HAS ALREADY BEEN CALLED to the significant experiment by Station WEAF in picking up a football game being played in Chicago and relaying it by public address system to a street throng in New York City. This was apparently a prelude to an even more important experiment soon to be attempted between WEAF and WNAC, a station then recently established in Boston. On January 4, 1923, the two stations, connected by long-distance telephone wires, successfully staged the first network broadcast in history. The story has been re-cited at length by the author in another connection.[1] It needs merely a passing mention as one of a series of events that marked the progress of the contest for supremacy in the radio field. The experiment did not satisfy the Telephone Company engineers, and they at once re-newed their efforts to perfect a type of land wire suitable for network broadcasting.

In December, 1922, and January, 1923, Station WEAF, disregarding criticism of its sponsored programs, persisted in the practice. No less than sixteen commercial clients had been added to the books of WEAF before the end of January.[2] These sponsors included depart-ment stores, real estate companies, oil dealers, automobile companies, and the Bedford YMCA with the famous Dr. Parkes Cadman at the microphone. The significance of this development was twofold. It demonstrated that advertisers were willing to pay liberally for time on the air, and it brought actual income into the coffers of WEAF. This does not mean that the station was self-supporting—far from it, but it did point the way to financial salvation for radio stations in general.

While these events were transpiring in the radio sector the chief-tains of the contending groups were busily at work on various phases of the controversy. It is apparent that each side had now given up hope of persuading the other to acquiesce in its views. The agreement itself provided for arbitration of differences in case of a deadlock. There was a natural reluctance, however, to take so irrevocable a step since, if the controversy should be submitted to arbitration, each side would be bound by the decision, however distasteful it might be. The fact that they had already tried a sort of informal arbitration in seek-ing the opinion of Mr. Neave, and had found his views unacceptable to either, no doubt contributed to this reluctance to enter into an official arbitration.

There is ample evidence that legal "bigwigs" and technical advisers of each group spent much thought and conference time in an en-

[1] Archer, *History of Radio to 1926*, pp. 286-287.
[2] For a complete list of dates of early "commercials" and the sponsors of them, see Archer, *History of Radio to 1926*, pp. 288-291.

deavor to formulate in the most effective manner the salient points of their contentions. These were apparently submitted to the opposing group. We know, for example, that as early as November 2, 1922, the Telephone Company had presented to the Radio Group a list of five formal complaints. They were couched in the following language:

"1. The Radio Corporation's tubes are being used by outsiders in broadcasting transmitting stations, and are being used by the Magnavox people, and perhaps others, in loud speaker amplifiers.

"2. The Radio Corporation and its associate companies are using their broadcasting stations in a manner not contemplated or intended.

"3. The General Electric Company is announcing inventions as being made by it which were really made by the Telephone Company.

"4. The Telephone Company desires to modify the present contract with reference to exchange of information, limited to information on things which are practically developed.

"5. The Radio Corporation has sold combined telegraph and telephone radio sets for export without specifying that this telephone use was to be confined to the Radio Corporation field, or where it knew that the use was not to be so confined."

This was but the beginning of exchanges of written contentions—all of which served no purpose of conciliation but did have the effect of disclosing the lines along which future legal battles were to be fought. Such was the condition of affairs when General James G. Harbord took office in January, 1923. The controversy with the Telephone Company was only one of several major problems to which the General was introduced during his first few weeks in office.

The question of wave lengths and assignments of channels to broadcasting stations had been under discussion for months. Radio technicians had at last conceived the idea that if stations in a given locality could be assigned differing wave lengths bedlam on the air might be reduced. The experiment had been tried by operating Station WGY on the 400-meter wave length, while Station WHAZ continued on the standard 360-meter plan. These stations had formerly interfered with one another's broadcasts, but now interference was eliminated and the way was opened for a new era in radio broadcasting.

Coincident with this discovery was the announcement of two important technical advances—the condenser type of microphone and RCA's latest offering, vacuum tubes with thoriated tungsten filaments. The new tubes were the famous "UV 199" and "UV 201 A." It must not be supposed, however, that even so great a boon to radio broadcasting as the new vacuum tubes could be any assurance that RCA was to enjoy undisputed pre-eminence in the industry. Quite the reverse was true. If we survey the behind-the-scenes developments in radio during the "gold rush" years when radio was a new Eldorado in American life we find an amazing situation. Not only were rival manufacturers—many of them unscrupulous infringers of patent rights—competing with RCA for trade in every section of the nation, but they had already raised hue and cry against the Radio Corporation, accusing it of being a monopoly that should be proceeded against by the United States Government. It mattered not that RCA owned or controlled the patents under which it had virtually created the industry, and by law was under no obligation to share its patents with others except voluntarily upon a license or royalty basis. Others desired to use the patents in competition with the owner and, because RCA would not license them to use the same, certain manufacturers boldly infringed the patents and cried "monopoly" when RCA proceeded against them.

These developments have been explained by the author in the first volume to which the reader may refer for a more complete recital. They form an essential part in the "battle of the giants" that was now in progress. Verily, General Harbord came to the Radio Corporation at a most bewildering moment in its history. The board of directors had now resolved to take a firm stand against infringement of its patents. It authorized appeal to the courts, little dreaming of the public furor that would shortly be aroused by such action. Infringers all over the country were to make common cause against the Radio Corporation, as will be seen hereafter.

Sec. 34. President Harbord Seeks Advice.

It was only natural that General James G. Harbord should decide at an early date to acquaint himself with the details of the RCA-Telephone Company dispute. This he did by a careful study of all the correspondence, as well as the Neave mediation attempt. The situation was too complicated, however, for him immediately to gain any clear comprehension of the vital issues and so, on January 29, 1923, we find him writing the following terse letter to David Sarnoff:

Mr. Sarnoff:

I have been over these papers which pertain to the telephone situation carefully by myself, and have also had some discussion of the situation with Mr. A. G. Davis.

Among these papers are some from you. I take it that you are probably more familiar with the situation than anyone else in our immediate organization. If not too much trouble I should like to have you give me:

1. A succinct statement of the matters at issue with the A. T. & T. Company, rated in their importance to the RCA, showing concisely their contention and our contention in each case.
2. The points on which the Radio Corporation of America can afford to trade or yield.
3. The concessions most desirable to obtain from the A. T. & T. through trading or yielding under the preceding paragraph.
4. The principal damage now being done to our interest by failure to agree or by non-observance of the contract by the A. T. & T.
5. Your suggested action.

(Signed) JAMES G. HARBORD

It is apparent from the foregoing that General Harbord was not content with watchful waiting. He was willing to trade, if need be, in composing differences, but only when convinced that RCA would gain the full equivalent of whatever concessions it might make to the adversary. Mr. Sarnoff's previous comments in writing, from the layman's viewpoint but direct and penetrating, had apparently convinced the new president of RCA that the vice-president and general manager was able to guide him in a difficult situation. At any rate, in response to this challenge, Mr. Sarnoff wrote a letter on February 6, 1923, from which the following excerpts are taken:

"Replying to request contained in your letter to me dated January 29th, 1923, referring to our present relations and contemplated negotiations with the Telephone Company, I submit the following:

"A. Intent of Existing Contract

"To my mind, this is the base from which discussions of the present situation must start. Where a controversy or ambiguity exists as to the meaning or language of a contract, decision must be arrived at on the basis of the intent of the parties during negotiations preceding the signing of the contract.

"1. Issue

"The position of the Telephone Company is best summarized by President Thayer in his letter to Vice-President Gifford, dated July 10th, 1922, in which Mr. Thayer dissents from the opinion expressed by Mr. Neave in his report of June 20th, 1922.

"Mr. Thayer states:—

" 'As the contract now stands, I have understood it as neither expressing nor implying any obligation on one party to keep out of the field of another, provided getting into that field did not involve the infringement of patent rights of the other.'

"If the above statement does represent the intention of the parties to the contract, I do not see the purpose or force in each party having ceded to the other, exclusive rights in certain fields under its own patents.

"For example, under the present contract, we find the Radio Corporation Group saying, in effect, to the Telephone Company, that in the field of radio telephony, for tolls, as a public service, 'we not only recognize your patents and agree not to infringe them, but we also grant you an exclusive license to use our own patents in this field, from which, we exclude ourselves under your patents and ours.'

"In the field of wireless telegraphy as a public service, we find the Telephone Company saying, in effect, the same thing to the Radio Corporation.

"What was the intent and purpose of placing each group in this position?

"(a) Was it to enter the other party's field by destroying or circumventing its patents or commercial position? By failing to produce new inventions and patents, thereby avoiding the necessity of turning over to the other party exclusive licenses in such fields, under one's own patents?

or

"(b) Was it to remove such uncertainties, stimulate new inventions and patents, thereby protecting each other's reserved fields toward the end that each group would be unhampered to best develop such fields in the interest of public service and its stock holders?

"My understanding is that (a) was not and that (b) was the intent and purpose of the contract.

"Recommendation

"Fortunately, Messrs. Thayer and Young, the principals of both parties to the negotiations which resulted in the contracts, are alive and able to give expression as to what was in their minds at the time and thus clarify the issue in this respect."

Evidently Mr. Sarnoff believed that if the two leaders could get together for a frank discussion they must inevitably agree upon proposition (b) as stated above. On this score we may well entertain some doubts, since Owen D. Young had already held various conferences with Mr. Thayer and they were still far apart in their interpretation of the contract.

Sec. 35. Sarnoff on Broadcasting for Hire.

It is well known that the Telephone Company was insisting upon its own right to maintain radio broadcasting stations and to sell broadcasting time to commercial advertisers. Not only that, but it was disputing the right of the Radio Group to maintain radio broadcasting stations and declaring that to charge for broadcasting time, or even to accept contributions for such service, would be an infringement of its own exclusive rights therein.

In answering General Harbord's questions Mr. Sarnoff discussed these problems frankly and succinctly. He injected into his discussion the basis of a trade with the Telephone Company, as will be seen from the following excerpt from the letter of February 6th:

"B. Broadcast Transmission
"2. Issue

"The contract is ambiguous as to whether or not the Telephone Company has acquired for its fields, full rights under all patents owned or controlled by the Radio Corporation Group, necessary to enable the Telephone Company to operate or control broadcasting transmission without infringement.

"Recommendation

"My view is that regardless of the language of the contract, it was the intention that the Telephone Company should be given full rights referred to above. Therefore, in the negotiations, this ambiguity should be cleared up by granting to the Telephone Company the full rights referred to.

"3. Issue

"The contract is ambiguous as to whether or not the RCA Group is free to accept financial support from the public or outsiders (as, for example, a tax on sales of competitors, jobbers, dealers, etc.) for the purpose of helping to defray the expense of operating broadcasting stations.

"Recommendation

"As to the above, my view is that the present contract does not cover this point but regardless of this, the Telephone Company should offer no objection to our accepting such support or contribution so long as these are used for the purpose of helping to defray the expense of operating broadcasting stations which, under the contract, we are permitted to erect and operate. I offer this view because such stations are operating only in order to develop to the utmost, a field already exclusively reserved to us under the contract, i.e., the sale of broadcast receivers."

Sec. 36. Sale of Loud Speakers, Tubes and Accessories.

Mr. Sarnoff next discusses a topic very close to his heart. The sale of vacuum tubes had at first been regarded by both parties as the exclusive function of RCA. Since the radio boom had caused the vacuum tube to be in tremendous demand, the Telephone Company had awakened to its commercial possibilities. It had decided, moreover, to manufacture and sell tubes in competition with RCA—and to justify its conduct as a right inherent in the contract even though unexpressed in words. In addition to vacuum tubes the Telephone Company was now manufacturing and selling in quantity loud speakers, amplifiers and accessories—ostensibly for its ordinary customers, but admirably suited for use in radio sets. The Telephone Company could not have failed to note that the vast quantities of such goods being sold must be finding their way directly into radio receiving sets in direct competition with RCA. In fact, the sales department of the latter company was making loud protests concerning the serious competition of the Telephone Company. Let us see how Mr. Sarnoff handles this phase of the situation.

"C. Broadcast Reception

"4. Issue

"Sale of Loud Speakers, Vacuum Tubes
and Accessories by the Telephone Group

"The position of the Radio Corporation Group is that it has reserved unto itself, not only an exclusive license to manufacture and sell broadcast receiving devices under its own patents, but that it has also acquired exclusive rights under the patents of the Telephone Group to cover this field.

"In this position, the Radio Corporation is supported—first, by a definite recollection that such was the intent of the parties to the contract and—secondly, by a line of unanimous and concurring legal opinions rendered by Messrs. A. G. Davis, I. J. Adams, Charles Neave, L. F. H. Betts and Governor Griggs.

"The Telephone Company, while not directly disputing the exclusive rights of the Radio Group in this field, is following a line of action which is regarded by our legal advisors as a violation of the agreement and which in effect, is now seriously damaging our business in this reserved field and threatens to damage it still further in the future.

"For example, Mr. Thayer's reference, quoted on page 1 of this letter, would indicate the Telephone Company's view that it can manufacture and sell radio broadcast receiving devices for broadcasting purposes so long as it does not employ patents other than its own.

"Mr. Gifford, vice-president of the A. T. & T., on a previous occasion announced at a meeting of the board of directors of the Radio Corporation, that upon expiration of certain of our patents, the Telephone Company will feel itself at liberty to manufacture and sell vacuum tubes.

"Aside from these opinions, to which we do not subscribe, the Telephone Group (Western Electric Company) is actually manufacturing and selling loud speakers, amplifiers, vacuum tubes, head telephones and other accessories, with full knowledge that such items are being used for the purpose of radio broadcast reception (our exclusive field). The Telephone Group contends that the items enumerated constitute a loud speaker device which it has been selling in the past for wire telephone purposes and therefore feels at liberty to continue to sell even though such devices are attached to and become part of radio broadcast receivers.

"The practical meaning of this activity on the part of the Telephone Company is that its subsidiary, the Western Electric Company, is selling radio devices or parts which constitute about 80 to 90% of a complete broadcast receiver. For example, if one purchased from the Western Electric Company the items above enumerated, the only remaining items necessary to make a complete broadcast receiver are a tuner and a detector tube. As to the latter, tubes sold by the Western Electric Company with their loud speakers, can also be used as detectors, thus making the Western Electric a full-fledged tube competitor in our reserved field of broadcast sales.

"Recommendation

"Since the broadcast reception field has been reserved to the Radio Corporation Group, and the Telephone Group is now violating the contract by its actions above enumerated, the Telephone Company should cease such operations and conform to the intent and letter of the contract in this respect."

Sec. 37. Restaurant and Moving Picture Radios.

Another phase of the RCA-Telephone Company controversy involved the right to sell radios with loud speakers in restaurants and theaters. Because of the public nature of these places the Telephone Company insisted that the Telephone Company alone had the right to sell apparatus to be used therein. Another kindred controversy involved the installation of radio systems in apartment houses, with wire connections to the various apartments. This field also was claimed by the Telephone Company. Mr. Sarnoff's discussion of these questions is illuminating:

"5. Issue

"Sale of Broadcast Receivers
for Public Places or Multiple Uses

"Two typical cases under this heading are cited below:

"(a) A radio receiver, with suitable loud speaker, is installed in a restaurant or moving picture theater. The purpose of such installation is to increase the patronage of the restaurant or theater, thereby increasing the profits of the owner. The Telephone Company maintains that since it has the exclusive rights in radio telephony for public service, that the above constitutes a public service and, therefore, not in the field of the Radio Group. The language of the contract on this subject is not clear and the intent, in my judgment, was not to grant the Telephone Company exclusive rights to such business.

"(b) Another case is one where a broadcast receiver is installed, say in the basement of an apartment house, and the received material distributed to the tenants of the apartment house over wires connecting the main receiver with the apartments.

"Recommendation

"As to (a), since there is no practical way by which to stop a proprietor from purchasing a complete radio receiving device from any dealer and installing it in his restaurant or theater in the same manner as he would do with a phonograph and since such use of a device is for indirect profit only and falls within the broadcast reception field intended to be exclusively reserved to the Radio Corporation Group, my view is that the rights to such business not only under our patents, but those of the Telephone Group as well, should be exclusively vested in the Radio Corporation.

"With respect to (b), the apartment house case, my view is that such business should also be within the exclusive field of the Radio Corporation since the use described merely means that instead of—say twenty tenants living in one apartment house purchasing twenty separate broadcast receiving sets (in which case there would be no issue), the landlord of the apartment house purchases a single receiving set and distributes the output to his tenants over his own electric light wires within the apartment."

Sec. 38. Pick-up Wires and Carrier-Currents.

The distinction between wire line connections or "pick-up" wires and carrier current was made very clear in Mr. Sarnoff's letter, even though in previous writings on the subject the distinction had been left somewhat vague. As we have seen, wire lines for connecting studios with events at a distance were already so necessary to radio stations that station owners were literally ready to fight for them. Had the American Telephone Company agreed to lease them even at a stiff price there would no doubt have been grumbling, but its refusal to lease the wires at all caused stations to hire lines from the Western Union and Postal Telegraph systems. In the immediate future stations were to discover a new and greater use for leased wires in network or chain broadcasting. Carrier current is aptly described by Mr. Sarnoff as "wired wireless." To continue with the Sarnoff letter of February 6, 1923:

"D. Wire-Line Connections

"6. Issue

"The Telephone Company refuses to connect with its wires, broadcasting stations of the Radio Group, though such stations are operated only for the purposes authorized by the contract. The Telephone Company also maintains that we have not the right to use other wire line facilities, as, for example, wires of the Western Union or Postal.

"Recommendation

"My opinion is that in view of the public interest in and importance of broadcasting, the above position of the Telephone Company is untenable. It should agree to connect with its wires broadcast stations of our group upon reasonable payment for such facilities and where the Telephone Company cannot furnish wire lines, it should offer no objection to the use by the Radio Corporation of such lines as can be obtained from others.

"E. Carrier Current (Wired Wireless)

"7. Issue

"Aside from certain reserved and undisputed rights in fields of electric light and power line companies (for purposes of their own communications), the present contract is not clear as to whether or not the Telephone Company has exclusive rights for carrier-current broadcasting over wires under its own patents and those of the Radio Group, whether such wires be those of the Telephone Company or those owned or controlled by electric light, power or other companies. In view of the possibility of developing in the future a practical system of broadcasting over wires, this question is vital both to the Telephone Company and the Radio Group.

"While the language of the contract in this respect is capable of many interpretations, my opinion is that it was the intention of the parties to the contract to place wired wireless exclusively in the field of the Telephone Company so far as its own wires are concerned. The use of carrier current for broadcasting purposes, over lines other than those owned or controlled by the Telephone Company, raises a question which to my mind is either not definitely covered or not covered at all by the present contract. Also, I am not certain whether this question came within the consideration and review of the parties negotiating, because at the time of the agreement, broadcasting over electric light or power lines by means of carrier current was not in sight. I cannot help feeling, however, that under the present contract, the position of the Telephone Company in this respect is stronger than that of the Radio Group.

"Recommendation

"My suggestion is that such ambiguities as exist, should be cleared up as follows:

"First, by acknowledging that the Telephone Company has exclusive rights in broadcasting by carrier current under its patents and ours over its own lines

and

"Secondly, that the Telephone Company grant to the Radio Corporation an exclusive license under its patents and agree that we may have an exclusive right under our own patents to cover broadcasting by carrier current over *other* lines than those owned or controlled by the Telephone Company."

Sec. 39. RCA and South American Trade.

In the Sarnoff letter to General Harbord we find a section devoted to the South American consortium that requires a bit of explanation. In the summer of 1921 there was fought out in Paris a momentous international contest for the control of wireless communications in South America. England, France, Germany, and the United States were the nations represented at the conferences—not as nations, however, but as national wireless communication systems.[3] The Sarnoff letter discloses that one of RCA's allied corporations, now operating separately, owned the controlling sales organization in the South American countries.

"F. Foreign Field
"8. Issue

"Under the existing contract, neither the Radio Group nor the Telephone Group acquire rights under each other's patents in foreign countries. While it is true that they may manufacture apparatus in the United States under each other's patents, even though such apparatus is intended for export, the situation is that the seller or user of such apparatus in foreign territory is under the risk of infringing foreign patents owned by the other party. This situation is responsible for the present difficulties and threatened suits by each party in South American territory.

"Recommendation

"In my view, it is highly desirable to have the Western Electric Company form part of the consortium in South America insofar as the sale of apparatus is concerned. I will go further and state my belief that the consortium, as at present set up, can hardly expect to be a profitable merchandising venture so long as it has competition from the Western Electric Company and is engaged in a patent war with that company in South America. . . .

"The question of how large the participation of the Western Electric Company in the consortium should be, is a matter for the companies comprising the consortium to determine, but my view is that the

[3] Archer, *History of Radio to 1926*, pp. 227-239.

Western Electric Company is justified in expecting as large a share as, say the French or British have been given in the South American Sales Situation.

"G. Concessions

"My view is that regardless of the merits of the situation under each heading, the manufacturing business in radio broadcasting has assumed such large proportions, as distinguished from its size at the time the contract was drawn, that the Telephone Group will probably not be satisfied to settle the whole question by agreeing to the definitions suggested and making the concessions desired, unless the Western Electric Company is given a portion of the radio manufacturing business. How large this proportion should be, is a matter for trading and, of course, subject to the consent of the Westinghouse and General Electric Companies which, together, obtain at present all of the manufacturing business in patented devices placed by the Radio Corporation. The General Electric and Westinghouse Companies should state how much they are willing to give up in order to settle the existing controversy and obtain harmonious relations with the Telephone Company."

Sec. 40. Concessions, Arbitration or Court Trial.

Having surveyed the field with a thoroughness that revealed his mastery of the controversy, Mr. Sarnoff offered three alternative courses of action. First and most desirable, if it could be successfully accomplished:

"Endeavor to negotiate and trade with the Telephone Company along the lines indicated in this memorandum."

His second suggestion concerns arbitration of the dispute. It is of interest, therefore, to discover what the cross-licensing agreement of July 1, 1920, provided on this score:

"Article XIII—Arbitration

"In case of any differences under this agreement (except in respect of interferences or priority of rights to inventions or patents) shall arise which the parties are unable to adjust between themselves, either party may, by notice in writing served on the other, designate one arbitrator and call upon the other to designate a second arbitrator within thirty days after the receipt of such notice; and the party receiving such notice agrees so to designate an arbitrator. The two arbitrators so designated shall promptly select a third arbitrator. The matter in dispute shall be submitted to the three arbitrators so selected, and the parties agree that the concurring decision of any two of the above-mentioned three arbitrators shall be final and binding upon them. Each party shall pay its own expenses, including the fees of its arbitrator, and the fees and expenses of the third arbitrator shall be paid one-half by each party."

It is probable that Mr. Sarnoff at this time had little confidence in the success of negotiations for an amicable settlement of the points in dispute. The uncompromising attitude of the officials and legal staff of the Telephone Company had already been commented on by him in other reports to his associates.

"Should negotiations fail," he writes, "arbitrate the dispute. I believe that despite the present ambiguities of the contract, our position is sufficiently clear and meritorious to justify resting our case on the decision of competent and impartial arbitrators."

The third alternative was of course the least desirable of all, since an appeal to the courts could not fail to evoke unfavorable publicity for all concerned. A dispute in the ranks of Big Business is always made much of by newspaper reporters; but here is Mr. Sarnoff's proposal:

"Should negotiations fail and arbitration be declined, file suit against the Telephone Company for violation of the present contract and, pending court decision, carry on as at present."

Sec. 41. General Harbord Attempts Mediation.

It is apparent that Mr. Sarnoff had recently put the matter of leasing telephone wires from RCA's rival to the acid test and had become convinced that the Telephone Company had no intention of making concessions. The following interesting correspondence is to be found in the files of the General Electric Company:

(A letter from Mr. Sarnoff to A. H. Griswold of the American Telephone Company, dated January 25th, 1923.)

Dear Mr. Griswold:

As you are no doubt aware, we are at present constructing two radio broadcasting stations, one in the Aeolian Building, in West 42nd Street, New York City, and one in Washington, D. C. It becomes necessary for us at this time to consider the question of installing equipment in these stations to take care of such material as may be transferred to them via telephone lines, such as concerts or public addresses delivered at other points within reasonable distances of the stations.

We would contemplate, more specifically, the permanent leasing of a certain number of lines to certain definite theaters or auditoriums, and install our own transfer and pick-up equipment at the terminals of these lines. In addition, we would desire temporary lines at specific times, for use over short periods of time.

May I ask that you kindly inform me whether or not we may count on securing from you either the permanent or temporary facilities, or both, mentioned above? I would be grateful for an early answer on these points in order that our plans may proceed along definite lines.

Very truly yours,

(Signed) DAVID SARNOFF

This request was apparently followed by personal conferences. Prior to the writing of the Sarnoff recommendation above quoted, Mr. Thayer addressed a letter to Mr. Young, from which it appears that on February 5th representatives of Dr. Goldsmith's department of RCA had telephoned for permission to inspect the WEAF system of remote control at the Capitol Theater. Mr. Harkness, the manager of the station, had denied permission, but had promised to refer the matter to the Telephone Company for a final decision. This matter and Mr. Sarnoff's request of January 25th were referred to in the following letter:

My dear Mr. Young:

I enclose a couple of memoranda.

As I understand it, both of these matters are involved in the question as to connection between a broadcasting studio and a more or less distant point or a broadcasting station and a more or less remote studio, which was one of the matters still under discussion between us.

I do not want our people to seem unresponsive and perhaps you can explain the situation to Mr. Sarnoff and he can defer his requests until you and we have come to some conclusion.

Yours very truly,

(Signed) H. B. THAYER,
President

Although the concluding paragraph of this letter might have been considered as proof that no compromise could be hoped for, General Harbord, the new president of RCA, resolved to make a personal attempt to effect a compromise. On February 14, 1923, he wrote a long letter on the subject to Owen D. Young, in which he modestly declared:

"I have not the temerity to suggest that I can succeed where so many others have failed in this matter, but I have studied the papers and am attempting to summarize the matter herewith. If the conclusions to which I come are approved by you, I suggest we arrange for a meeting with Mr. Thayer and possibly Mr. Gifford, and attempt to reach an agreement."

In prefacing his survey of the situation General Harbord made the following pertinent observations:

"There have been numerous conferences between the subordinate officials of the interested organizations which have had little practical effect except to develop further differences.

"The difficulty appears to me to be that the discussion in such cases has generally taken the form of the legal construction of the contract in the light of developments and events which were unforeseen when the contract was drawn, and to which the parties thereto could not have intended it to apply. It seems to me that attempts to harmonize our differences through that method promise nothing but indefinite discussion. The parties who drew the contract are still alive, and I believe that our differences should be approached in the light of the intent of the contract as far as it can be ascertained from the signatories and by common sense agreement as to what would have been their action had subsequent developments been foreseen.

*   *   *   *

"The present state of affairs is that the Telephone Company is each day getting more aggressive and is consolidating its position in violation of our rights as I see them to such an extent that every day of delay will make it more difficult for them to accept any compromise which we suggest. The need for expedition is therefore apparent.

"With reference to the general intent of the contract, the position of Mr. Thayer is revealed in his comment in his letter of July 10, 1922, on an opinion expressed by Mr. Neave in his letter of June 30th, in which Mr. Thayer states: 'As the contract now stands I have understood it has neither expressed nor implied any obligation on one party to get out of the field of another, provided getting into that field did not involve infringement of patent rights of the other.'

"If this understanding of Mr. Thayer is a correct one, there could have been no purpose in the contract in which each party cedes to the other exclusive rights in certain fields under its own patents.

"My idea of the general purpose of the contract was that it attempted to remove uncertainties, to stimulate new inventions under patents, thereby protecting the reserved fields to each contracting party toward the end that each might be unhampered in best developing such fields in the interest of public service and its stockholders.

"The logical attitude of Mr. Thayer under his opinion quoted above would be that the intention was to allow each group to enter the other party's field by destroying or circumventing its patents or commercial position, by failing to produce new inventions in patents thereby avoiding the necessity of turning over to the other parties exclusive licenses in such fields under one's own patents.

*   *   *   *

"In view of the fact that the broadcasting situation has developed since the contracts were drawn, I doubt if we shall ever be able to reach a harmonious agreement with the Telephone Company unless the Western Electric Company is given a portion of the radio manufacturing business. This, of course, involves the consent of the Westinghouse and General Electric Companies, who divide our manufacturing in the proportions of 60% and 40%. Some such proportion as —General Electric 48%; Westinghouse 32%; and Western Electric 20% might be agreed upon. Naturally, the Western Electric in such case would have to drop out of the field as an independent merchandiser of such radio apparatus as it manufactures.

"If the above outline meets your views, I recommend we attempt to negotiate with Mr. Thayer along these lines. If such negotiations fail, then I believe we should proceed without further delay to arbitrate our points of difference as provided in the contract.

"I believe that in spite of the present ambiguities of the contract, our position is sufficiently clear and has enough merit to justify us risking our case in connection with competent and impartial arbitrators."

CHAPTER
SIX

Attempts at Compromise

Section 42. Superheterodyne Radio Sets.

THE WINTER AND SPRING OF 1923 saw momentous developments in radio broadcasting, with Station WEAF further blazing the trail of commercial advertising. During this period an extensive commercial clientele was built up by the station. Not only that, but dance orchestras, concerts and musical programs were put on the air as sponsored offerings. Radio time was purchased and the program paid for by the advertiser. WEAF was apparently well on the road to financial independence. It is not to be supposed that WEAF's great rival, WJZ, accepted this development with meekness. On the contrary, it seized upon one of the very weapons of competition to turn its blade upon the Telephone Company's minion.

It will be remembered that the Telephone Company had stoutly maintained that it alone had the right to broadcast for hire. It had, in fact, warned the staff of WJZ that should they charge for broadcasting time it would be considered a violation of the rights of the Telephone Company. The energetic Charles B. Popenoe, manager of WJZ, countered by offering to business houses *free time* on the air provided they stand the expense of orchestra or talent adequate to stage a radio program of high quality. This may have seemed, to the staff of WEAF, to have been unfair competition of the rankest sort, for how could they hope to persuade business men to pay stiff fees for broadcasting time as well as stand the expense of programs when they could go to WJZ and get broadcasting time without expense? The wonder is that WEAF could continue its policy of charging fees for broadcasting time, but the fact is that the custom continued to flourish. Possibly that there were not enough free hours available for applicants had some bearing in the matter; but it is also true that WEAF broadcasts were much clearer in tone than those of WJZ—a circumstance that aided the former to maintain its ground as a commercial station.

Several developments in the winter of 1923 deserve special mention as affecting the relations between the Radio Group and the Telephone Company. Every technical advance by one seems to have led to an effort of the other group to equal or excel the offering in question. The General Electric Company, as early as October 15, 1922, had been testing an improved type of wireless transmitter—a vacuum tube with a tungsten filament. The output of this tube was so high that a reasonable number of them in multiple would give as much power as the Alexanderson Alternator. *Radio Broadcast* for January, 1923, hailed this discovery in the following words:

"An announcement of the Radio Corporation just given out states that an experimental tube transmitter has been in successful operation for sixteen hours continuously, sending out sufficient power to transmit perfectly as far as Germany. Instead of the 200-k.w. alternator ordinarily used, six pliotrons, rated at 20 k.w. each, were used to generate the high-frequency power required to excite the antenna. A 15,000-volt supply of continuous current power is required for the plate circuits of these tubes and here also the electron evaporation idea of Richardson is utilized. Two-electrode tubes, plate and filament only, are used as rectifiers, to change the high voltage alternating-current supply available at the station into suitable continuous-current power."

In February, 1923, Major Edwin H. Armstrong, who had been working for several months to develop his superheterodyne radio receiving set, reported to the high command of RCA. The story has been told by the author in the *History of Radio to 1926.*

"For several months Major Edwin H. Armstrong had been working on a radio set of highly original design. He had combined his own ideas with those of another inventor, Harry Houck, and had produced what was later to be known as the Radiola Super-Heterodyne, a set that was destined to revolutionize the radio industry. This was the age of battery sets, and the Armstrong invention was equipped with batteries. It was, nevertheless, so uncanny in its selectivity and sensitiveness that it was possible to operate it without the use of an antenna. It appears that Armstrong first exhibited the device to the astute general manager of RCA, David Sarnoff. Mr. Sarnoff had just concluded arrangements that involved ordering several million dollars' worth of an improved type of radio that had been devised by RCA engineers. He was so impressed by the Armstrong invention that he at once halted these negotiations, much to the disgust of Westinghouse and General Electric, who were all set for quantity production. It was necessary, however, to convince the board of directors of RCA. An interesting incident arose when Major Armstrong took his new radio set to Owen D. Young's apartment for a demonstration, Mr. Young being chairman of the board of directors of RCA. When Major Armstrong came out of the elevator he carried the radio in his arms— the radio in full operation with an opera program in progress. This was so astounding an achievement in radio technique that there was no hesitation about adopting the Armstrong device. Months must elapse, however, before the machine could be offered to the public. It was not until the following summer that RCA announced the new Super-Heterodyne radio set. Not until 1924 was it possible to offer the device to the public in a nationwide market. To the foresight of Elmer E. Bucher, in suggesting the idea and to the genius of Major Armstrong, was due one of the great achievements in the early years of RCA's career." [1]

[1] Archer, *History of Radio to 1926,* pp. 297-298.

Sec. 43. Contest Over the Superheterodyne Patent.

One of the liveliest behind-the-scenes contests in the history of radio broadcasting came to a head over patent rights in the superheterodyne. It appears that the original patent had been issued to Edwin H. Armstrong on June 8, 1920.[2] This patent contained nine claims representing differing degrees of breadth of patent. It will be remembered by those who have read the first volume in this series that from the date of the formation of RCA until July, 1921, a contest was on with the Westinghouse Company. As a strategic move, on May 12, 1920, the International Radio Telegraph Company (Westinghouse affiliate) had acquired license rights under the Armstrong patent. On October 5, 1920, the Westinghouse Company had purchased rights in the patent.[3]

Now, it happened that Ernst F. W. Alexanderson, of the research staff of the General Electric Company, had invented a device that contained some of the scientific principles of the superheterodyne. Stimulated, perhaps, by the rivalry that existed at the time, the legal staff of the General Electric Company promptly contested the Armstrong patent (Interference No. 45,783). The United States Patent Office gave notice of this "Interference" on March 30, 1921. This contest was no doubt one of the master strokes of the Radio Group that brought Westinghouse into the fold on July 1, 1921. Thereafter it did not matter to the corporations how the contest between the claimants might be decided, since each held cross-licensing rights in one another's patents. It did matter, of course, that a valid patent issue to the original inventor. Neither did it matter financially to Ernst F. W. Alexanderson, since he was working under an agreement by which all of his inventions automatically became the property of the General Electric Company. To Major Armstrong, even though he had been paid a large sum for the invention, the loss of any of his patent claims could prove bitterly disappointing. He was destined to lose two of them to Alexanderson on February 23, 1924; but at the time of which we write, the spring of 1923, Armstrong was the reputed inventor of the superheterodyne in all nine of the original claims.

Now comes a development of great significance in the contest between the Radio Group and the Telephone Company. Engineers had never been able to devise anything that could match the superheterodyne as a receiver of wireless impulses. It was known that a man named Levy, who had been with Major Armstrong in France, claimed to have been the real inventor of the superheterodyne principle. The

---

[2] U. S. Patent No. 1, 342, 885.
[3] Archer, *History of Radio to 1926*, p. 197.

Telephone Company had purchased Levy's alleged rights and, in the interval, while Armstrong's radio set was being made ready for wholesale manufacture the Telephone Company produced a number of experimental superheterodyne sets and distributed them among their officials. So marvelous were they that, had they appeared on the market, the simple RCA set would have been outclassed at once. This was due to the fact that Elmer E. Bucher had insisted that a popular-priced model should not have more than two tuning controls. The Telephone Company experimental set utilized the superheterodyne idea to obtain very much more sensitivity by using several tuning controls. To be sure the instrument was as broad as a piano keyboard—heavy and expensive—yet the RCA engineers were obliged to acknowledge its great superiority in power output over their own product.

Knowledge of the existence of this device literally gave Elmer E. Bucher and others responsible for RCA sales the jitters. It is probably true that it was a bit of strategy—most effective strategy as it proved—that knowledge of this latest weapon of competition should be smuggled to potent RCA chieftains.

Sec. 44. RCA Sues Patent Infringers and Gets "Investigated."

It was perhaps inevitable that RCA should sooner or later be obliged to appeal to the courts for protection against alleged infringers of patent rights in radio devices. A test case was brought against the A. H. Grebe Company, a prominent radio manufacturer, alleging infringement of five patents owned by RCA. Since the defendant was only one of many similar violators of RCA's patent rights throughout the nation, the suit aroused widespread outcry against the Radio Corporation. To the unthinking multitude the "little fellow," trying to get along, even though he might be disregarding the patent rights of a great corporation, was the underdog who must be protected against the wicked trust. Coincident with this test suit there developed a campaign of vilification of RCA that must have amazed and distressed the new president of the company. After several months of public castigation, the corporation, whose weakness seems always to have been reluctance to meet adverse propaganda by adequate presentation of its own side of the case, was at length driven to reply.

General James G. Harbord was the spokesman for his company. In explaining why RCA was entitled to the same protection of the laws accorded to other owners of patents he made the following observations as a part of a special article in *Radio Broadcast* for May, 1923.

"It has made great outlay for research and development work in perfecting its own inventions, and to advance the radio art it has also been considered wise to acquire the inventions of others. In no other way could the various improvements and best features of the numerous inventions—no one of them adequate in itself—which are regarded as requisite to satisfactory radio service, have been assembled and made available for the public in any one line of apparatus. . . . Thus far, the public, and a few manufacturers and dealers—some legitimate, but many of them infringers—have profited from the development and production of radio apparatus. The stockholders of this corporation whose money and faith in the patent laws have contributed to the technical achievements largely responsible for progress made have not yet drawn a dollar of profit. . . .

"An infringer of patents has the advantage that he has no patent investment, no research to finance, no responsibility to the art. He can make a thing and sell it. If he makes a dollar profit it belongs to him until the courts take it away from him, which can only happen after a long litigation. The great concern which has made all this development possible, which has spent millions in clearing the road for American radio has to carn something on what it spent in acquiring that pathway. Enforcement of its patent rights with the Federal courts will help it to earn that something. If its rights are not as broad as it believes them to be the courts will say so. In its efforts to test its rights and find out just what they really are and to enforce them the Radio Corporation should have the sympathy of everyone who really wishes the good of the radio art."

There was much more to the letter—a strong defense indeed, yet to the unthinking public no amount of logic could halt the hue and cry against a corporation charged with being a trust. "Trust-busting" is a popular American custom. Members of Congress bestirred themselves to investigate the trust. This brought more headlines in the newspapers as the Federal Trade Commission went into action. It seems that the Radio Corporation, even though not required to do so by law, had filed with the national government copies of all cross-licensing agreements. Thus the Federal Trade Commission had ready at hand the chief facts upon which to base a finding. Federal investigators were soon to appear at the New York offices of the corporation. They were to inspect books and records. They were to question and cross-question right and left—these inquisitors from the Federal Government. RCA's predicament has thus been described by the author in the first volume of this series:

"In vain Owen D. Young and his associates asserted the rectitude of their intentions in forming the great corporation. An international task undertaken at the urgent request of the Federal Government, they averred, should not subject them to attack from the legislative branch of the same government. The inquisitors retorted that the Federal Government had never contemplated the setting up of a monopoly and accused the founders of RCA of taking advantage of the request from the Navy Department to accomplish purposes of their own. RCA responded by producing evidence that they could not have accomplished the allotted task except by a pooling of patents, just as the Government had done in the World War, except that cross licensing was their substitute for the war powers of the Government. Thus was begun the long and expensive contest between the Government and RCA that was destined to make headlines for years thereafter." [4]

Sec. 45. Rival Radio Stations in Bitter Contest.

Publications and congressional investigations, however much they may have injured the Radio Corporation, could not halt its ordinary activities. The feud between the two groups of broadcasting stations went on with increasing tension. What one broadcasting unit attempted the other must "go them one better." When, therefore, RCA and Westinghouse announced a plan to move Station WJZ to the Aeolian Building in the heart of New York City, the owners of WEAF bestirred themselves to give their own station sumptuous quarters in a better location than 24 Walker Street. The story of the activities of the rivals in making ready their new weapons of competition has been told at length by the author in the previous volume. A mere summary will suffice for the present tracing of behind-the-scenes developments.

Station WEAF still carried on the more or less fictional existence of its intended companion station WBAY. RCA's new plans involved a genuine sister station for WJZ. The latter station was to operate on a 455-meter channel. It would broadcast music and entertainment in the lighter vein. The new station, WJY, was to use a 405-meter channel, and would specialize in operas, classical music, lectures and other "highbrow" broadcasting. The situation was not without humorous aspects. On the very day set for the dedication of the new stations at the Aeolian Building, Station WEAF dedicated its new quarters at 195 Broadway.

From this vantage point of time it is safe to say that in the "dedication duello" of May 15, 1923, the RCA stations had the advantage over their rival. Their dedication was in the grand manner, with speeches by famous men. General Harbord and Owen D. Young sounded off in characteristic manner—Mr. Young's speech being a notable tribute to RCA radio broadcasting, as will be seen in the following excerpt:

[4] Archer, *History of Radio to 1926*, p. 299.

"Broadcasting has appealed to the imagination as no other scientific development of the time. Its ultimate effect upon the educational, social, political, and religious life of our country and of the world is quite beyond our ability to prophesy.

"Already it is bringing to the farmer market, weather, and crop reports as well as time signals, which cannot help but be of economic value. In remote communities, where the country parson is no longer in attendance at Sunday morning services, it is filling a great need in spiritual life. Its educational possibilities are being investigated by our foremost national and state educators. It is taking entertainment from the large centers to individual homes. To the blind and the sick it has unfolded a new and richer life. For the purpose of communication it has destroyed time and space." [5]

The change in Station WJZ was rendered the more significant by the fact that it was now taken over entirely by RCA, Westinghouse having formerly operated the station. Unified control of WJZ and WJY, coupled with the fact that the Radio Corporation was now building a station in Washington, D. C.—Station WRC—gave RCA a strong position in its contest with the Telephone Company. Bearing in mind the behind-the-scenes wrangling over pick-up wires we can appreciate the significance of RCA's open defiance of the Telephone Company's mandate in the matter of equipping its New York City stations with permanent pick-up wires.

By arrangement with Western Union a permanent set of cables leading to the station on 42nd Street came up Sixth Avenue from 14th Street and continued as far as the Yankee Stadium. Permanent lines were run from this cable to such well-known centers as the Waldorf-Astoria Hotel, Hotel Astor, Town Hall and the leading theaters. Stations WJZ and WJY were thus in a position to compete effectively with Station WEAF. They continued, moreover, to offer to substantial business houses free time on the air, provided each program so offered should be of the highest order.

Station WEAF found means, however, to counter from an unexpected quarter—the angle of radio announcing. WJZ had already found Milton J. Cross a decided asset. To date, however, he had been valued more as an entertainer than as a star announcer. Coincident with the opening of the new studios at 195 Broadway, Station WEAF had the good fortune to hire as an announcer a visitor who chanced to call to see what radio was all about. The stranger was Graham McNamee, a singer by profession—a juror by accident, with a bit of leisure between trials. McNamee first appeared on the American Telephone Company payroll May 21, 1923. In another connection the author has commented on this event in the following manner:

[5] *Radio Broadcast*, July, 1923, p. 255.

"No greater asset could have been acquired by Station WEAF at this time than the dynamic and volatile McNamee. He was a singer, an entertainer, but above all he had a clarity of voice that captivated radio audiences. In this respect he was a match for Milton Cross of WJZ. Cross was ideally qualified to broadcast the so-called 'highbrow' program but McNamee became at once the announcer-extraordinary of 'low-brow' broadcasts. A prize fight, a ball game and later the great football games found in Graham McNamee an interpreter who could project over the microphone the very spirit of the arena. Even the cadence of his voice as he watched and described what he saw communicated to the radio audience the emotions of the moment. Vast audiences were to hang upon his colorful words; to share his enthusiasms. His own genuine excitement when a knockdown was witnessed, when a baseball was clouted into the bleachers for a home run, or when a touchdown was scored, was carried over the air in a manner so compelling that listeners sometimes forgot their surroundings and cheered.

"Thus Station WEAF introduced a new and vital factor in radio broadcasting—established the McNamee cult, so to speak. In the fifteen years since that date many announcers have aped Graham McNamee—many have come and gone, but like Milton J. Cross, Graham McNamee is still one of the great figures of the radio world." [6]

Sec. 46. Long Distance Short-Wave Broadcasting.

It has previously been noted that David Sarnoff had advocated long distance short-wave broadcasting as early as February 16, 1920. He had urged it upon the president of RCA as a major problem that should be undertaken by the corporation. "This may not materialize for some time to come," he wrote, "for it requires a good deal of development, but if we do not tackle it in due time, other radio people may do so." It is true that Mr. Sarnoff was at the time referring to short-wave wireless telegraphy, radio broadcasting of the human voice not yet having been in vogue. The soundness of the prophecy was borne out by developments in the winter of 1923. RCA had not followed Mr. Sarnoff's suggestion, but an industrial ally of the Radio Corporation—the Westinghouse Company had stepped definitely into the field. The moving spirit in the short-wave research by the latter corporation had been radio broadcasting's great pioneer—the father of Station KDKA—Dr. Frank Conrad. It is true that Senatore Marconi was at the same time conducting experiments in the same field, but this in no wise belittles the independent efforts of Dr. Conrad. In the June, 1923, issue of *Radio Broadcast,* appeared an article on the short-wave experiments at East Pittsburgh, from which the following quotation is made:

[6] Archer, *History of Radio to 1926,* p. 306.

"The Westinghouse Company has been carrying on experiments with this method of broadcasting for the past year and has in that time been able to gather a great deal of useful data from these experiments. Frank Conrad, assistant chief engineer of the company, and well known in the radio world because of his station, 8XK, is believed to be the man who first experimented with broadcasting on the very short wave lengths. Before Mr. Conrad got into the work, radio engineers had proved by mathematics that transmission on short waves was impracticable, but he had an idea that their calculations might not be correct, and decided to investigate for himself the possibilities of broadcasting effectively on wave lengths of 100 meters or lower. First he built a set to transmit on 100 meters and found by tests with an amateur operator in Boston that the 100-meter wave length was more selective and more efficient than even 360 meters. Mr. Conrad next arranged to receive programs from the studio circuit over his telephone line. He then connected this telephone line to his 100-meter transmitting set and sent out KDKA's programs simultaneously with the broadcasting on 360 meters.

"In Boston and other places it was reported that this transmission was stronger than the signals received directly from KDKA on 360 meters! This was true enough though his station was much less powerful than the one at East Pittsburgh."

One significant development was to flow from a continuation of these short-wave experiments. It was discovered that without the aid of pick-up wires programs could be broadcast long distances, and rebroadcast by relaying stations. This was a distinct threat at the time to the Telephone Company's closely guarded efforts to develop long distance wire connections between stations as a means of network broadcasting. Had KDKA's short-wave experiments proved entirely successful the Telephone Company's project would have died "a-borning." As it was, however, the early demonstration of rival wire and wireless connections of distant stations came at about the same time.

The story of these competitive efforts is too long to be more than hinted at in this recital of backstage conflict. For a more extended treatment of these developments the reader is referred to *History of Radio to 1926*.[7] In June, 1923, Station WEAF selected the meeting of the National Electric Light Association to stage a spectacular test of network broadcasting. Station WEAF was hooked up by wire lines with WGY in Schenectady, N. Y.; KDKA in Pittsburgh, Pa., and KYW in Chicago, Ill. A special program, originating in one of the sessions, presumably at a banquet of the National Electric Light Association, went out from Station WEAF on the evening of June

---

[7] Archer, *History of Radio to 1926*, pp. 306-308, 310-311, 313-315, 329-330, 351-365.

7, 1923. The success of the attempt was pronounced. It excited great interest in radio circles.

Out of this experiment came network broadcasting—a great and enduring triumph for Station WEAF. Wire lines were demonstrated to be capable of "piping" radio programs, unmarred by static or fading, hundreds of miles from a key station to other stations in the network. Short-wave relaying of programs was thus outdone by land wires, at least at its existing stage of development. Short-wave broadcasting, however, had come to stay. It was destined to play a great part in the future development of radio. Like television, that enigma of modern science, short-wave broadcasting is far removed from the broadcast band of ordinary radio. It might not be inaccurate to say that the short-wave broadcasting band occupies a middle ground between ordinary broadcasting and television, which so closely approaches the ultra short waves of the light spectrum as to encounter the same limitations of projection. It may barely be explained that instead of operating within the atmospheric space between the earth and the so-called Heaviside layer, television impulses travel in the same manner as waves of light and must be rebroadcast at the visual horizon. Short-wave broadcasting, however, knows no such limitations.

Sec. 47. *Westinghouse Challenges Telephone Company.*

It was perhaps inevitable that a corporation so deeply interested in radio broadcasting as the Westinghouse Company should sooner or later have come to a head-on collision with the American Telephone Company on matters of broadcasting. It is true that RCA had long been negotiating on matters vital to all broadcasting interests. These efforts, as we know, had been highly disappointing. Quite possibly, Mr. Young and his associates had decided to adopt different tactics as a last expedient. At any rate, their ally, the Westinghouse Company, on the very day when Station WJZ passed from the control of Westinghouse to RCA, launched a frontal attack on the Telephone Company. A letter, written by Guy E. Tripp, chairman of the board of Westinghouse to H. B. Thayer, president of the American Telephone Company, May 15, 1923, reads as follows:

Dear Mr. Thayer:

We feel that in fairness to your company as well as our own, our respective rights in connection with "broadcasting" should be definitely determined in the very near future. As you know, it is our view that your company has no rights under any of our Letters Patent to establish or maintain any so-called "broadcasting stations" nor to make, use, sell or lease any receiving apparatus for "broadcasting stations." If, therefore, you are making use of any inventions covered by our Letters Patent in either of these ways, it must be in infringement of our patent rights. In case you do not concur in our opinion, then we believe that steps should be taken at once to determine the respective rights of the two companies in connection therewith, and we invite your co-operation for this purpose.

We would be glad to confer with you at any early date as to the procedure to be adopted in connection therewith.

Yours very truly,
WESTINGHOUSE ELECTRIC &
MANUFACTURING COMPANY
(Signed) G. E. TRIPP,
Chairman

President Thayer's reply was mailed not only to Mr. Tripp but also to the chairman of the board of RCA, thus demonstrating that he regarded the matter in hand as of common concern, if not of common origin. The letter itself is an example of diplomatic response that leaves the controversy wide open, without making a single concession or promise of concession. The legal experts of the warring corporations were relied upon to handle the interminable dispute. The issue raised by Mr. Tripp's letter is thus deftly shunted aside in a letter from Mr. Thayer:

Dear General Tripp:

I have received your letter of the 15th instant. Coming directly to its subject matter, I was not personally aware of your company's views as you express them. Our views are directly opposed to them. If it is possible to settle any part of this matter between two parties only, you will find us ready to go ahead with it promptly and follow it up to a finish. On our part it would be a matter coming within the jurisdiction of Mr. Guernsey and Mr. Folk. Shall I ask them to take it up with Mr. Terry?

Since the making of the original contract, there has been rapid development in the radio field along lines not within the vision of the parties to the contract when it was made. This has led to differences which for a long time I have felt should be cleared up. To that end, I entered into negotiations with the General Electric Company, which we assumed was representing your company as well. In this matter nothing has been done since our last move which was made by us five months ago after various suggestions by us including one for arbitration.

Yours very truly,
(Signed) H. B. THAYER,
President

Sec. 48. Negotiations between RCA and Telephone Company Resumed.

It is apparent that upon receipt of copies of the correspondence above quoted Mr. Young at once took measures to reopen negotiations that had long been stalemated. The reason for Mr. Young's temporary withdrawal from contentious conferences now becomes apparent. The election of General James G. Harbord had caused Owen D. Young to decide that out of deference to the new president, negotiations should be held in abeyance until General Harbord could acquaint himself with the facts. We have already noted that General Harbord had indicated to Mr. Young, some weeks earlier, his willingness to participate in future negotiations. This will explain some of the references contained in the following exchange of letters:

(H. B. Thayer to Owen D. Young, May 17, 1923.)

Dear Mr. Young:

I received your telephone messages in regard to resuming discussions on the contract.

The time of the year has come when I am expecting to be away more or less and would not be able to give continuous attention to this matter as would undoubtedly be necessary.

You probably have seen a letter from the Westinghouse Company and my reply, which I sent you yesterday.

It does not seem to me possible that any settlement of these mooted questions between two parties can be very effective without the co-operation and consent of the others. On the other hand, we probably would not arrive very promptly at a determination of these questions if the discussion took the aspect of a town meeting. If the General Electric Company can represent the Radio Corporation, the Westinghouse Company and any others to whom you have extended the license and whose interest you consider are involved, this company can undertake to represent the Western Electric Company and it would rather seem to me that that was a matter that perhaps ought to be cleared up first. So much time has elapsed since my memorandum of last December, that I think we would have to start afresh.

These two things taken together indicate to me that a settlement would probably involve rather protracted negotiations and as the time of the year has come, as I said above, when I am expecting to be away more or less, I would like the burden borne by Messrs. Gifford, Guernsey and Folk.

Mr. Gifford and Mr. Guernsey are both away for the balance of this week. I will try and get into communication with them and find out when they will be free. They will also be away all of the week after next.

Yours very truly,

(Signed) H. B. THAYER,
President

(Owen D. Young to H. B. Thayer, May 17, 1923.)

Dear Mr. Thayer:

Replying to your letter of the 17th, I suggest that General Harbord and Mr. Sarnoff and Mr. Davis sit down with Mr. Gifford, Mr. Guernsey, and Mr. Folk to discuss the situation. I think I told you that after General Harbord had committed himself to come to the Radio Corporation, I did not feel like going forward with these negotiations further until he had had an opportunity to make himself familiar with the situation. He has studied the situation very hard and discussed it, I think, very fully with representatives both of the General Electric Company and the Westinghouse Company. He was obliged to go to the Pacific coast, which took out one month, and therefore, he has only been available for conference during the last three weeks. During that period, I have been so completely tied up that it was impossible for me to sit in.

I will be glad to attend the first conference on Thursday, make the introductions of General Harbord, and then aid in every way I can. I do not know that it is possible to create a situation finally where any one person can speak with authority for both the Westinghouse and General Electric Companies. My impression, however, is that both companies will acquiesce in any arrangement which General Harbord regards as satisfactory for the Radio Corporation. Both companies have a very great regard for General Harbord and I cannot really imagine their not standing by any commitment which he might make.

If this program is agreeable to you, perhaps you will have your secretary fix the time and place, and if you will notify my office, they will in turn notify General Harbord, Mr. Sarnoff, and Mr. Davis.

Yours very truly,

(Signed) OWEN D. YOUNG

Sec. 49. The Deadlock Continues.

The story of travail and tribulation in the development of the radio industry is probably without parallel in industrial annals. There was surely no place in the high command of either of the contending corporate groups for men of timid or irresolute executive methods. They were engaged in a struggle, in which only titans could have survived. Competitors on all sides were reaping golden harvests from the manufacture of apparatus involving patents that had cost the Radio Group staggering sums, yet the true owners were as yet powerless to protect their legal rights against a multitude of infringers. The Radio Corporation was now beset with the dread menace of an anti-trust investigation by the national government. No one could say what would be the verdict of the Federal Trade Commission. Near at hand, however, was the baffling and momentous controversy with the Telephone Company.

General Harbord was already in the thick of the fray, so to speak, but even he soon realized that the problems involved were so difficult of solution and so far reaching in their implications that mere argument and persuasion were of little value. The more the parties expounded their respective viewpoints the farther apart they seemed to drift. Face-to-face conferences thus operated in the same fashion as had the letter-writing campaign.

The controversy, as already indicated, became more acute when the news came to the Radio Group that the Telephone Company was secretly developing a superheterodyne radio set that threatened to dwarf RCA's new Radiola Super-Heterodyne now about to be put upon sale in the national market. This fact of an effective weapon of competition no doubt had its effect upon the RCA-Telephone negotiators, giving the Telephone officials more confidence in their own cause, hence more independence in negotiation. At this stage of the interminable discussions appears the formidable figure of Albert G. Davis, the General Electric Company's ace patent attorney and a member of the board of directors of RCA.

Mr. Davis had been the man to whom, in 1919, the General Electric Company had entrusted the momentous responsibility of representing it in negotiations with the British Marconi Company for the purchase of the latter's rights in the American Marconi Company. Mr. Davis had handled these negotiations with great ability. Aided by the diplomacy of Edward J. Nally, later to be the president of RCA, he had brought back to America vital concessions from the British Company rendering possible the formation of RCA. In every great emergency since that time Mr. Davis had been called upon to "pinch hit" for the Radio Group. A crisis had now been reached that surely required the talents of Albert G. Davis.

Possibly, Davis had been absent from New York up to this time on some other mission. At any rate, in June, 1923, he was given the story of negotiations to date, as will appear from the following letter:

(Mr. Davis to Mr. Young, June 15, 1923.)

My dear Mr. Young:

I spent a very long evening yesterday with Mr. Sarnoff, Mr. C. A. Terry and Dr. Goldsmith on the telephone situation. As a result of this talk and of other talks which he has had, Mr. Sarnoff proposes to submit to General Harbord at 10 o'clock Monday morning a "final" proposal on behalf of the Radio Corporation, which proposal is to be subject to the approval of the manufacturing companies.

Mr. Sarnoff is impressed with the desirability of settling the controversy and his proposal will involve some very substantial concessions to the Telephone Company. From the consideration which I

OWEN D. YOUNG
Commander-in-chief of the Radio Group. International figure in World
War reconstruction.

was able to give last night, at the end of a long day, to the matter, it seems to me on the whole that if the arrangement which Mr. Sarnoff proposes could be put through it would be wise to do so, speaking from the standpoint of the General Electric Company as well as from the standpoint of the Radio Corporation. The matter is, however, so important and has reached such a critical stage that it may be desirable that you should talk this matter over with Mr. Sarnoff between now and Monday morning, if possible.

Very truly yours,

(Signed) ALBERT G. DAVIS

Sec. 50. RCA Proposals Rejected by Telephone Company.

In the light of subsequent developments it is interesting to note the exact nature of the concessions that were drafted by David Sarnoff after the conference referred to in Mr. Davis' letter above quoted. Fortunately, in the files of the General Electric Company we discover a draft of the document. To be sure it does not concede any of the Telephone Company's major contentions, yet it does offer a genuine compromise from the claims hitherto advanced by the Radio Group. The language of the offer is as follows:

New York, June 18, 1923

"MEMORANDUM

"Tentative Proposal from Radio Corporation of America to American Tel. & Tel. Company

"Subject to Consent of

General Electric Company and Westinghouse Electric &

Manufacturing Company

"1. Broadcast Transmission

"Recognize the exclusive rights of the Telephone Group to make, use and sell, broadcast transmitting apparatus; subject to existing rights of the Radio Group to make and use such apparatus for its own broadcast transmission, or re-transmission, of news, music and entertainment, and subject further to the right of the Radio Group to accept contributions and financial support for its broadcast transmitting, or re-transmitting, stations from manufacturers, distributors, dealers, owners of receiving sets and others.

"2. Broadcast Reception

"Recognize the exclusive rights of the Radio Group to make, use, lease and sell, radio broadcast receiving devices, subject to the grant of the following rights to the Telephone Group:

"(a) A non-exclusive right to the Telephone Group to make, use and sell, head-set and loud speaking type telephone receivers.

"(b) A non-exclusive right to the Telephone Group to make, use and sell vacuum tube amplifiers and vacuum tubes for such amplifiers only and power supply devices for such amplifiers and tubes, upon payment to the Radio Group of a royalty of 50% of the selling price of such devices; provided, however, that such royalties shall not be less than a predetermined minimum, on each such device.

"(c) An exclusive right to the Telephone Group to make, use and lease, but not to sell, broadcast receiving devices for multi-party uses where such service is given for pay to a business establishment.

"(d) A non-exclusive right to the Telephone Group to make, use and lease, but not to sell, radio broadcast receivers as a part of a public address system (subject to a suitable definition of a public address system).

"3. Automotive Devices

"A non-exclusive right to the Telephone Group to make, use, lease and sell radio telephone devices for use in two-way radio telephone communication with automotive devices.

"4. Marine Field

"A non-exclusive right to the Telephone Group to make, use and lease, but not to sell, radio telephone transmitting and receiving devices for use on ships, harbor craft, river boats and other navigating vessels where the Radio Corporation has rights to grant such licenses, provided the tolls charged for such service shall be divided between the Radio and Telephone Groups on an equitable basis to be determined upon.

"5. Wire Line Facilities

"The Telephone Group shall furnish wire line facilities to broadcasting stations of the Radio Group upon reasonable terms of payment therefor.

"6. Two-Way Public Service Radio Telephone Communication

"Recognize the exclusive right of the Telephone Group to make, use, lease and sell radio telephone apparatus for use as a part of a public service two-way telephone communication system where both radio transmitting and radio receiving devices are employed at each end."

Mr. Davis tells an interesting story of a conference with President Thayer of the Telephone Company at about this time. Mr. Folk, general patent attorney for the company, sat in as Mr. Thayer's adviser.

Davis had been authorized to attempt to trade with the Telephone people—to swap rights.

He began somewhat confidently offering to surrender this and that "right" of the Radio Group in exchange for certain specified rights claimed by the Telephone Company. At every mention of a Radio "right" Mr. Folk would at once object: "Why, that doesn't belong to the Radio Group—that is ours already." This process continued until Mr. Thayer declared that he was quite willing to negotiate a better contract but, before entering into negotiations, must know who owned the rights concerning which he was to negotiate.

It is evident that Telephone Company officials had by this time developed a state of mind in which major concessions or virtual surrender by the Radio Group would have been the only means of averting a genuine legal contest. Believing in the justice of their own claims to the immense business in radio receiving sets and other apparatus incident to the business, the Telephone Company officials were unwilling to accept a small part when by contest they might conceivably win a large share of that business. They were probably well aware that RCA sales of radio apparatus were then more than double the volume of sales reported during the corresponding period of the previous year. All indications were that the radio boom would continue for years to come, with increasing volume of sales. The prize was well worth the gamble.

Failure of the effort in mid-June had the effect of transferring the responsibility to David Sarnoff. Owen D. Young departed for Europe on June 27, 1923, no doubt on matters of international importance, since he was soon to be drafted for the Reparations Commission. General Harbord accompanied him to attend a conference in London. The following significant letter was written by an assistant of Owen D. Young:

New York, June 27, 1923

Mr. M. P. Rice,
    Schenectady, N. Y.

Dear Mr. Rice:

Mr. Young left this morning for Europe, and was, naturally, not in the office, and therefore unable to read your letter of June 26th which has just been received.

The Telephone situation is known very intimately by Mr. Young already and a few nights ago I sat in a conference in which the entire matter was discussed by General Harbord, Mr. Sarnoff and Mr. Young.

If I may suggest, I think your letter as well as the other letters might be of interest to Mr. Sarnoff as he is the one who is going to take care of this situation during the absence of both General Harbord and Mr. Young. Of course, I have not sent your letters to him but only make this as a suggestion which you may or may not wish to carry out.

I am sending a copy of this letter to Mr. Swope so that when he reads a copy of your letter addressed to Mr. Young he will see the suggestion I have made. It may be possible that you will want to ascertain what his reaction is regarding my suggestion.

Very truly yours,

(Signed) STUART M. CROCKER

CHAPTER
SEVEN

Arbitration Agreed Upon

Section 51. Defining the Issues in Summer of 1923.

DAVID SARNOFF, thus left in charge of negotiations, apparently at once laid siege to the enemy and accomplished genuine progress toward defining the issues. The hitherto nebulous controversy began to assume tangible form. One after another the issues were agreed upon. This does not mean that agreements were reached. On the contrary, points of disagreement were reduced to writing. A month after Mr. Young departed for Europe, Albert G. Davis wrote a letter to be forwarded to him, copies also to be sent to E. W. Rice, Jr., and Gerard Swope, who were on a committee of the RCA board of directors having the radio controversy in charge. The Davis letter is brief—the only record of negotiations that seems to be available for that period. It reads as follows:

New York, July 23, 1923

Owen D. Young, Esquire,
   New York Office.

My dear Mr. Young:

   Mr. Sarnoff has done some very excellent work in his negotiations with the Telephone Company. The matter has come down to two or three things which, as I see it, you may be able to adjust with Mr. Thayer but which cannot be adjusted in any other way. I hope, therefore, that you will be able to take this matter up actively soon after your return.

Very truly yours,

(Signed) ALBERT G. DAVIS

It is apparent that Mr. Sarnoff continued to have the advice and co-operation of Albert G. Davis during the hectic summer weeks preceding his own vacation. It is equally apparent that the combined efforts of the pair could not effect a compromise with the Telephone Company. The most that they could do was to further clarify the issues. Mr. Young's return from Europe in September, 1923, was the occasion for a report from Albert G. Davis under date of September 13th. The author has been unable to discover any copy of this letter, but he has discovered a report by General Harbord to Mr. Young that portrays in vivid language the exact state of affairs and state of mind of the parties on September 17, 1923. Few historians have had the opportunity to present to the world so intensely human a document as this frank letter from the president of the Radio Corporation of America. A virtual industrial empire was at stake. An error of judgment in the high command of RCA might spell ruin for the corporation. Is it any wonder that the gallant soldier frankly avows in this moving document his fears of the outcome?

"I think before we finally decide to embark on arbitration we should consider that an adverse decision by the arbitrator in the matter of broadcast receiving sets . . . would be a very serious blow to us."

In this very letter General Harbord pleads for the surrender of transoceanic rights of RCA as the price of peace. But let us consider the actual language of this historic communication.

(General Harbord to Mr. Young, September 21, 1923.)

Dear Mr. Young:

Mr. Sarnoff and I met with Messrs. Gifford, Guernsey and Folk of the Telephone Company on the 17th inst.

They brought the negotiations up to date by referring to Mr. Sarnoff's memorandum of June 18th, copy of which I enclose you, which elicited the statement from Mr. Gifford that after mature consideration on the part of himself and his associates they had reached the opinion that the Radio proposal did not give the Telephone Company in substance any greater rights than it already has under existing contracts, while asking them to make certain concessions to us which, if granted, would leave them with less than they now have. Further, that the real difficulty in the situation arises out of the sincere belief on the part of each that it has certain rights which the other party, with equal sincerity, disputes. He said, that it seems to the Telephone representatives that it is not possible to arrive at any real solution of our problems without having a disinterested party determine what each party has, or has not, under the present contract, and, accordingly, he suggests that our present differences be submitted to arbitration. . . . As a step toward getting the matter in concrete form for presentation, it was decided that the Telephone representatives and Mr. Sarnoff and myself would endeavor, with the help of our attorneys, to prepare the necessary data which would enable the matter to be submitted to the arbitrator selected in the clearest manner, with the idea that a decision might be obtained with the least possible delay.

It was agreed that our preparation for the present would take the form of each side stating the things which it feels it has the right to do, without regard to its desire to do them or not, and which the other negotiators dispute. We would then attempt to agree on a single statement of such cases, after which I planned to take the matter up with those whose consent would be necessary as a preliminary to further action.

*　　*　　*　　*

I think before we finally decide to embark on arbitration we should consider that an adverse decision by the arbitrator, in the matter of broadcast receiving sets, resulting in our having a non-exclusive license to manufacture them, would be a very serious blow to us. In the negotiations which Mr. Sarnoff and I suggested to you at your home that evening in June, we would be pretty badly crippled if we had an adverse decision against us by an arbitrator, while an honest admission that there were points in dispute not yet settled would be much less serious. On the other hand, the Telephone Company is very aggressive and it is not unlikely that we shall be forced either into arbitration or litigation, whether we will it or not. Litigation, with the inevitable appeals, could not be expected to result in decisions short of from three to five years. Arbitration is a matter that could be over in three months.

* * * *

The desire of the Telephone Company for what they call more liberty in transoceanic telephony is very noticeable. Mr. Thayer apparently did not think as well of our efforts in England to help them as did Mr. Gifford.

I know how important you consider it for us to retain all our rights in transoceanic telephony, but I am not far-sighted enough to see any commercial future for it, and with a contract binding the Telephone Company to stay out of the telegraph business and to give us a share of the tolls, if any, that resulted from transoceanic telephony, I would be willing to trade them the liberty they wish in that field in return for a settlement in our favor of all disputed matters on broadcasting, and I think that an agreement could be reached along these lines.

This liberty to the Telephone Company in transoceanic telephony would mean that they would spend the vast sums which are going to be necessary to carry transoceanic telephony to such commercial future as it may have, and that the benefits of this money spent in research along that line, would be available to us and equally useful in the further development of the transoceanic telegraphy. I need not point out to you that the co-operation in the matter of research between the two companies, which was contemplated by the contract, has never been realized and that an amicable settlement of these differences would probably bring the two organizations together in a way which nothing else can accomplish.

Sincerely yours,

(Signed) J. G. HARBORD

Sec. 52. *Radio Corporation Votes to Arbitrate the Dispute.*

It is apparent that even before making the written report referred to in the preceding section General Harbord had conferred orally with Mr. Young, acquainting him with the general nature of the conference. This is evidenced by the language of a brief and pithy note from Owen D. Young to Mr. Davis, setting in motion the train of events that resulted in the arbitration. All hesitation had now vanished. Young and Harbord had agreed to contest the Telephone Company's claims in formal arbitration hearings:

New York, September 17, 1923

Mr. A. G. Davis,
     Schenectady, New York.

Dear Mr. Davis:

Regarding the matter referred to in your letter of the 13th, General Harbord thinks that it will be necessary for us to have an arbitration in the telephone case before we can make any substantial progress in negotiations. Will you not be thinking over some person whom we might suggest as arbitrator who would be acceptable to both?

Yours very truly,

(Signed) OWEN D. YOUNG

In General Harbord's report, as quoted in the preceding section, it has no doubt been observed that he referred to a telephone conversation with Albert G. Davis on the very day that he was writing the report. Since Mr. Davis was considered an astute lawyer and a very able tactician, it is of dramatic interest to learn what his hopes and fears actually were at this great crisis of affairs. The memorandum was as follows:

"September 21, 1923

"MEMORANDUM OF TELEPHONE CONVERSATION
"WITH MR. A. G. DAVIS

"Mr. A. G. Davis called me by telephone and said he had had a note from Mr. Young to the effect that I had told him we should probably have to arbitrate with the Telephone Company.

"Mr. Davis is very strongly of the opinion that there are certain things which the Telephone Company will endeavor to include in such arbitration which Mr. Thayer, Mr. Folk, and others know plainly are ours under the contract—particularly the matter of the manufacture of broadcast receiving sets except in direct use with their own transmitting stations. . . .

"He says that he believes that if Mr. Young could go to Mr. Thayer and say to him plainly—'Mr. Thayer: You and I know that such and such things were the intent of this contract,' he would get him to make the admission which would bind his company. As it is now, the failure of our negotiations to include Mr. Thayer and Mr. Young has resulted in the matter being handled by Mr. Gifford with Mr. Thayer having no opportunity to hear our side of the case.

"Mr. Davis is anxious to help, and as a choice between litigation and arbitration is not certain which would be to our advantage. He says that under arbitration, the party usually gets the most who claims the most, and generally, he seems doubtful of our success in arbitration, and points out that an adverse decision on the broadcast receiving apparatus would possibly put us out of business if the Telephone Company chose to go into that branch of business.

*   *   *   *

"He reiterated several times he is very strongly of the opinion that Mr. Young should see Mr. Thayer and endeavor to commit Mr. Thayer to an agreement of their understanding of certain parts of the contract, before seriously considering arbitration."

It is significant that Mr. Davis himself should have written to Owen D. Young on the very day of his telephone conversation with General Harbord, reiterating his sentiments. This same letter throws light upon an important development in the disagreement that existed between the two corporate groups. The alert lawyer realized all too well that for the Telephone Company to bring into the proposed arbitration unnecessary issues could handicap the proceedings. He took the attitude that any language of the contract, so clear that reasonable men could not differ upon it, ought to be kept out of the issues to be framed. Inasmuch as it seemed to be the Telephone Company's strategy to inject as much of this as possible into the issues to be framed, something ought to be done about it. Mr. Young's growing prestige in world affairs marked him as the only man in the RCA group who might be able to persuade President Thayer to alter this policy. All this and more will appear in the following letter:

New York, September 21, 1923

Owen D. Young, Esquire,
New York Office.

My dear Mr. Young:

I have your letter of September 17th, with reference to the Radio Corporation-Telephone Company matter. I will try to think of someone who might be suggested as an arbitrator.

I have fully explained to General Harbord the views which I entertain on the subject. The General will talk with you. My points are:

First, Mr. Thayer is not accessible to General Harbord. Mr. Folk goes to Mr. Thayer, spends a few minutes with him, presumably without giving him our story as completely or as sympathetically as we could. Mr. Thayer says what he would do and that is the end of it. There is only one way to get by that situation and that is for you to talk with Mr. Thayer.

Second, if you decide not to do this, I want to remind you of the position which I have taken almost from the beginning of the controversy. There is certain language in the contracts which Mr. Folk and I (and I am sure you and Mr. Thayer also) know was intended to mean certain things, and which Mr. Gifford contends means something very different. It seems to me incredible that the Telephone Company can want to put those particular points in arbitration—that is, that it can want to arbitrate some points as to which it knows we are right, in order to make those points a make-weight before the arbitrator to affect points which are really and honestly controversial.

If I were in your position I should not allow this to be done until I put this question up to Mr. Thayer personally and got him to say yes or no to the proposition that the Telephone Company will put itself in such a position. Some of these points, as General Harbord agrees, are vital to the prosperity of the Radio Corporation.

Very truly yours,

(Signed) ALBERT G. DAVIS

In spite of the utmost efforts of able men no private compromise was possible. The efforts of Sarnoff, Davis, Young, and others had accomplished this much, however: the contentions of the rival groups had become sufficiently clarified that arbitration issues might more easily be drawn. By October all hope of peaceful solution had been abandoned. The first meeting of the board of directors of RCA, after the representatives of the Radio Corporation and the American Telephone & Telegraph Company had reached a tentative agreement, was held on October 19, 1923. The following extract from the minutes of the meeting gives us the first definite commitment of the corporation to arbitrate the dispute.

"EXTRACT FROM MINUTES OF THE MEETING OF THE
BOARD OF DIRECTORS
"RADIO CORPORATION OF AMERICA
"OCTOBER 19th, 1923

"The President reported to the board that representatives of the American Telephone & Telegraph Company and Western Electric Company and representatives of the Radio Corporation of America had agreed, subject to the approval of the United Fruit Company, the General Electric Company and the Westinghouse Electric & Manufacturing Company and also subject to the approval of this board, to arbitrate the questions which had arisen regarding the construction of the so-called 'Telephone Agreement' of July 1st, 1920. After discussion, the board approved in principle the submission of the contract to arbitration and the selection of Roland W. Boyden of Boston, Mass., as arbitrator."

Sec. 53. Radio Group Selects Chief Counsel.

The vote above recorded was merely one of the preliminary stages leading to the desired arbitration. It became needful to submit the matter not only to the three corporations named in the vote but also to each of the allies of RCA for official action. This matter was turned over to William Brown, vice-president and general counsel of the Radio Corporation, whereupon negotiations to this end were undertaken. Correspondence in considerable volume exists between the legal departments of the various corporations seeking to clarify the issues to be adjudicated.

A first draft of the arbitration agreement was submitted by Nathaniel T. Guernsey, vice-president and general counsel of the Telephone Company, on October 25, 1923. In correspondence concerning this draft we learn that RCA and its allies had not yet agreed upon a lawyer to represent them in the arbitration proceedings. It was apparent that Charles Neave, Esq., who had made the unsuccessful attempt at mediation during the previous year was favored for the task. The following letter from the files of RCA is of considerable historical significance:

(William Brown, Esq., to General J. G. Harbord, October 30, 1923.)

Dear General Harbord:

Pursuant to your instructions, I have conferred with the Westinghouse and General Electric Companies and have attempted to see Governor Griggs with reference to consideration of the proposed arbitration agreement recently submitted by Mr. Guernsey.

Owing to the illness of Governor Griggs and his consequent absence from his office, I have been unable to consult him.

For the Westinghouse Company, I have seen Mr. Terry who is of the opinion that the contract as submitted will be acceptable to the Westinghouse Company with the possible exception of Clause 9. As to this Clause, both Mr. Terry and I feel that as now drafted it is likely to prove of little use in that it obligates either party to give aid to the other in patent litigation only when the former will not prejudice its rights in doing so. Such an arrangement would provide an easy means of either party ignoring the call of the other on the theory that its interests might be so prejudiced. Mr. Terry and I are in accord in the opinion that the paragraph should be revised to plainly bind the owner of the patent to join as party plaintiff in a suit brought by the licensee if requested, and the court rulings require that such party be joined on account of its interest in the patent.

For the General Electric Company I have talked with Judge Appleton who tells me that at the request of Mr. Young, he has forwarded the contract to Mr. Jackson at Schenectady with the request that he try to telephone his views to me prior to your meeting with Mr. Young today. I am expecting to hear from him momentarily; but so far he has not called.

* * * *

Mr. Terry states that while from all accounts he and his associates in the Westinghouse Company believe that Mr. Boyden will make a satisfactory arbitrator, they would like some further opportunity to make inquiry. I have told him it is my understanding that representatives of his company have agreed upon Mr. Boyden with Mr. Young and that Mr. Boyden has been asked to serve and has agreed to do so. He further understands that it is probably too late to consider the appointing of anyone else as arbitrator.

* * * *

Mr. Adams and I are making a careful study of all of the data that have been considered in your numerous conferences with view to completing a statement of the points contended for by the Radio Corporation. We have not yet completed our work in this respect but will endeavor to have a report for you within the next week.

Respectfully,

(Signed) WILLIAM BROWN

P. S.

Since the foregoing was written, Mr. Jackson of the General Electric has called me on the telephone and reports that while he considers the agreement as to form, probably acceptable, he believes it is a serious mistake to definitely bind ourselves to arbitrate until the issues are settled. In other words, he thinks we had better thrash out the points that are to be arbitrated and have them in shape before we definitely obligate ourselves to the arbitration. He feels that the scope of the arbitrator is exceedingly wide and that under the arrangements as contemplated, the telephone company might insist upon injecting numerous points which do not properly arise under the contract, all of which might be avoided should the points be determined first and the agreement to arbitrate be executed afterwards.

Mr. Jackson's suggestion might have been worthy of consideration except that the situation has already gone too far for it, as the obligation to arbitrate has been definitely assumed, only the details remaining to be worked out.

W. B.

An interesting aftermath of this letter has to do with the selection of chief counsel to represent the Radio Group. It was shortly decided that the lawyer who would carry the banner for the Radio Group should be sixty-eight-year-old Frederick P. Fish, of Boston.

It may seem a bit fantastic—there were many fantastic angles to this controversy—but Frederick P. Fish, for the six-year period 1901-1907, had been president of the American Telephone & Telegraph Company. He was now to exert the utmost of his legal ability to defeat that great corporation in the prospective arbitration hearings. It is apparent, however, that Ira J. Adams, Esq., head of the patent department of RCA from 1920 to 1929, was to be the wheelhorse in the gathering of evidence and material to be presented at the arbitration hearings.

By good fortune, there exists in the records a letter from William Brown, Esq., of RCA, dated November 1, 1923, that tells the story of how Mr. Fish happened to be chosen and by whom. The letter is addressed to Charles A. Terry, vice-president of the Westinghouse Company. A portion of the text reads as follows:

"It has also been agreed by General Harbord and Mr. Young that it is desirable to have the interests of the Radio Corporation group in the proposed arbitration handled by Mr. Fish of Messrs. Fish, Richardson and Neave."

The letter gives evidence of an energetic beginning of the preliminaries to the arbitration, since it states:

"Mr. Fish will be in New York tomorrow, and General Harbord requests that I endeavor to bring about a meeting between him and the representatives of the Westinghouse and General Electric Companies and the Radio Corporation. I am unable to say at what hour it would be convenient for Mr. Fish to see us, and can therefore not suggest a definite time for the appointment, but would appreciate it if you would have somebody of your organization in readiness to join in such meeting. I shall endeavor to get in touch with Mr. Fish immediately upon his arrival at his office in New York tomorrow morning, to make an appointment, and shall telephone your office as soon as this has been done."

Sec. 54. Arbitration Issues Forecast.

For six weeks following the submission of the original draft of the arbitration agreement, the lawyers who represented the various corporations struggled to perfect its details. In view of the momentous issues involved, with millions of dollars of revenue at stake, it was needful to so frame the claims of each that no rights be inadvertently overlooked. One of the most interesting papers that the author has discovered in searching the files of that period is dated November 1, 1923. It is from the pen of Ira J. Adams, to whom reference was made in the preceding section. The paper was entitled "Memorandum of Points to Be Considered in Arbitration with Telephone Company." Mr. Adams takes up in detail various controverted points in the agreement of July 1, 1920. His discussion of Article V, Section 4, subdivision (d) 2 is of especial interest. The language of the clause was as follows:

" (d) The Telephone Company grants to the General Company . . . (2) Non-exclusive licenses to establish and maintain transmitting stations for transmitting or broadcasting news, music and entertainment from a transmitting station to outlying points, and licenses to make, use, sell and lease wireless telephone receiving apparatus for the reception of such news, music and entertainment so broadcasted. For the protection of the General Company under the license which it receives in this paragraph, it is agreed that the Telephone Company has no license under this agreement to make, lease or sell wireless telephone receiving apparatus except as a part of or for direct use in connection with transmitting apparatus made by it; and for the protection of the Telephone Company under the licenses hereinbelow granted to it, it is agreed that the General Company has no license to equip wireless telephone receiving apparatus sold under this paragraph with transmitting apparatus, or to sell, lease or otherwise dispose of transmitting apparatus for use in connection with receiving apparatus sold under this paragraph."

Having set forth the language under discussion, let us see how Mr. Adams interpreted its various provisions:

Article V—Section (4) (d) (2)

"Q. 1. Has the General Electric Company a license under the Telephone Company patents to sell or lease broadcast transmitters?

"I think it is our interpretation that it does not have this license.

"Q. 2. Has the General Electric Company a license under its own patents to sell broadcast transmitters?

"As a strict matter of wording of the contract, it might have this right. It is not believed, however, that this was the intention.

"Q. 3. Has the Telephone Company a license under G.E. patents to sell broadcast transmitters?

"As a strict matter of language it did not receive this license.

"Q. 4. Has the Telephone Company a license under its own patents to sell broadcast transmitters?

"As a strict matter of language it has, that is, as a matter of language the Telephone Company did not grant this to the G.E. and therefore retained it.

"Q. 5. Did the Telephone Company receive any license whatever under this paragraph (2) of section (d)?

"It is my opinion that it did not receive any and I do not believe that the intention was that it should.

"Q. 6. Has the General Electric Company an exclusive license insofar as the Telephone Company is concerned, to sell sets for receiving broadcasted news, music and entertainment irrespective of the party that is operating the broadcast transmitter?

"It is our belief that it did receive this exclusive license.

"Q. 7. Can the latter part of paragraph (2) be interpreted to give the Telephone Company a license to sell sets for receiving the ma-

GEORGE K. THROCKMORTON
President, RCA Manufacturing
Company.

GUY E. TRIPP
Chairman of the Board, Westinghouse
from 1912 until death in 1927.

MANTON DAVIS
Distinguished lawyer now chief counsel
of RCA. Active in the contest.

ALBERT G. DAVIS
Eminent lawyer. His death in April,
1939, closed a brilliant career.

terial broadcasted from the Telephone Company stations, for example, WEAF?

"It is believed that it did not receive this right as the latter part of the paragraph refers to the sale or use of receiving sets co-operating with transmitting sets used in two-way public service wireless telephony.

"Q. 8. If the license under this paragraph to the General Electric Company is exclusive, does the Telephone Company have the right to sell amplifiers, head sets and loud speakers to be used in connection with our own broadcast receivers?

"To make this matter clear it is the Telephone Company's contention, as I understand it, that as soon as the broadcasted matter is brought into the antenna and through the detector tube it is no longer wireless telephony but wire telephony and it is their privilege to sell amplifiers to amplify the audible tones. To explain further, our receiving set, for instance, may have a detector tube which converts the inaudible radio frequency into a weak audible tone. In the same set we place amplifying tubes, transformers, etc., to increase this weak audible tone to a point where it is of satisfactory loudness. The Telephone Company seem to say that they can cut this receiver into two parts; let us have the detector tube and they take all the rest of it because after the broadcasted material gets through the detector tube the tone is audible and from then on is wire telephony because it is transmitted over wires even though they are only an inch or two in length. It is our understanding that this position is untenable. We believe the Telephone Company has no license to sell an amplifier unit for broadcast reception even though they do have the right to sell this as a public speaking unit, for instance, in connection with their wire telephone service.

"Q. 9. Has the General Electric Company a license to install a common receiving set, for instance, in an apartment with switchboard connections whereby head telephone sets or loud speaker telephones in the various rooms and apartments can be plugged into the common receiving set?

"This type of work is applicable to apartments, hotels, prisons, hospitals, etc.

"It is the position of the Telephone Company that this is their right and not that of the General Electric Company. It is our position that the General Electric Company does have this license though we have never been arbitrary about the matter.

"Q. 10. Has the General Electric a license to pick up its entertainment at a point remote from a broadcasting station, transmit over wire lines to the transmitter and then broadcasted in the usual way?

"The Telephone Company maintain that the General Electric Company does not have this license but that the performers must be taken to the broadcasting station and there give the performance that is to be radiated or broadcasted. It is our belief that the Gen-

eral Electric Company does have this right even though the performers are located three thousand miles away from the broadcasting stations and the connecting link is transcontinental telephone
lines.

"Q. 11. Has the General Electric Company a license to pick up its
entertainment at a remote point and relay it by radio to the broadcasting station where it is broadcasted in the usual way?

"It is our position that the G.E. has this right. The position of
the Telephone Company on this point is not known.

"Q. 12. Has the General Electric Company a license to lease broadcast receiving sets and collect monthly tolls from that part of the
public using the sets?

"It is our position that the G.E. has this right and I believe that
the Telephone Company takes a contrary position.

"Q. 13. Has the General Electric Company a license to use or sell
broadcast receiving sets to be used in a hall, stadium or other place
where the public can assemble to hear the loud speaker either for
direct or indirect profit through the operation, or free of charge?

"It is our belief that the General Electric Company has this
right. I think the Telephone Company will deny this.

"Q. 14. Has the General Electric Company a license to broadcast
a program for the benefit of one or more persons at a definite locality
and for no other purpose; that is, can the General Electric Company
broadcast an entertainment intended specifically to be received by an
alumni association holding a reunion or at a banquet?

"I understand that the Telephone Company denies this right.
It is our position that the General Electric Company has the right."

The foregoing discussion is illustrative of the very thorough manner in which the various phases of the controversy were explored in
advance of the drafting of the fateful issues upon which the future of
great corporations must be decided.

Sec. 55. Federal Trade Commission Report.

In the midst of preparations for arbitration the Federal Trade
Commission rendered its long-expected report. It was dated December, 1923—a document of 347 pages. The summary included in the
first volume of this series is pertinent in this connection.

"This report contained the results of the investigation made by
the Commission in response to a resolution passed by the fourth
session of the Sixty-seventh Congress. No trust-busting crusade could
have been more fully supplied with ammunition than was available
to the National Congress when this monumental report came from
the Government Printing Office. It was indeed a scholarly document
—an invaluable compilation of historical material. Not only did it
contain a detailed exposition of historical background of the for-

mation of the Radio Corporation of America, ninety-four pages in extent, but in a lengthy appendix it offered documentary evidence of the original agreements and the later cross-licensing agreements between the General Electric Company and the other industrial giants who acted as godfathers for RCA."

Enemies of RCA were naturally jubilant over this report of the Federal Trade Commission. To have the latter's most intimate agreements and trade secrets published to the world was indeed a matter of rejoicing both to politicians and rival manufacturers. Even *Radio Broadcast* indulged in verbal broadsides at the alleged iniquitous trust, from which we quote:

"This report is so thorough in its gathering of important facts not generally known in the radio field that it should have the widest publicity. Many items in the daily press, having to do with patent suits, trade agreements, shortage of tubes, etc., can be better understood in the light of this official report of present conditions in the industry.

* * * *

"Here are some authoritative figures which show the tremendous growth of the radio industry. In 1921 the Radio Corporation furnished on order 112,500 tubes; in 1922, 1,583,021; and in 1923, at the rate given in the report the sale of tubes will reach 4,000,000. This means that the radio public has invested about $24,000,000 in tubes alone, in a single year. We do not question these figures. But—isn't it time that more of the 'development cost' of the tube was charged off and the price adjusted more in accordance with the actual manufacturing cost?" [1]

The annual report of the board of directors of RCA for 1923 contained the following reference to the Federal investigation:

"Though not pertinent to the report of operations for 1923, it will not have escaped your notice that the corporation has recently been made the object of a complaint by the Federal Trade Commission. The position of the corporation, with regard to this, has been that it welcomes the opportunity to make a complete review of its history, organization and policies to that body. As a matter of fact we have, during 1923, already opened our records, correspondence, files, minutes of the meetings of our board of directors, together with all our contracts and agreements to the representatives of the Federal Trade Commission. The Commission has reported the result of that survey to Congress in a report which is in main respects highly complimentary to the Radio Corporation. Your directors are confident that when the investigation is fully completed and finally considered, the

[1] *Radio Broadcast*, March, 1924, pp. 371-373.

position of the Radio Corporation will be found to be entirely sound and proper." [2]

At the time this report was written no one in authority at RCA could have foreseen that the complaint referred to, begun on January 25, 1924, was to absorb so much of the time and energy of the officials of RCA, General Electric, Westinghouse, and the other great corporations suspected of monopolistic practices. They might, perhaps, have been gratified could they have known in advance that on December 19, 1928, the Federal prosecutors were to admit the failure of their effort and dismiss the complaint. Foreknowledge of events, however, is not given to man. The outcome of the prosecution is now well known to readers of this volume, and is referred to in this connection merely to show how the confidence of the directors, as expressed in the 1923 annual report, was justified by the outcome of the investigation instituted in that year.

Sec. 56. Vital Preparations Halted by Gout.

As an illustration of the thoroughness with which the contending factions prepared for the drafting of the arbitration agreement, we find in the files of RCA a letter from Dr. Alfred N. Goldsmith, director of the research department, dated November 5, 1923. It is addressed to David Sarnoff. Twenty-four separate items for discussion were listed by Dr. Goldsmith.

One of the items is of especial interest:

"15. Recognition by the Telephone Company that it is required to furnish on demand available wire line connections for the broadcasting stations of the Radio Corporation and its associated companies to sources of program material even in cities where the Telephone Company already has a broadcasting station."

Dr. Goldsmith, the writer of the memoranda, had already had a head-on collision with Telephone Company officials over this vexed question of pick-up lines. He realized very keenly the necessity of final and authoritative decision thereon. Another point advanced by him had to do with television, that will-o'-the-wisp that had so long baffled radio engineers. This was contained in paragraph 19 of his letter. There was an uncertainty whether the transmission of an image could properly be classed as wireless telegraphy and, because of this, both the Telephone Company and Radio Group were claiming jurisdiction over television.

A letter, written on November 15, 1923, by William Brown, Esq., reveals the status of RCA's progress in preparing for arbitration. It

[2] Archer, *History of Radio to 1926*, pp. 325-327.

was addressed to A. H. Jackson, vice-president of the General Electric Company.

"In accordance with a request of Mr. Fish at a conference held here a few days ago, Mr. Adams of our patent department and Mr. Sarnoff are preparing a memorandum of points to be submitted by the Radio Corporation to the Telephone Company as its recital of the matters for arbitration by Mr. Boyden in the proposed Telephone Company-Radio Corporation arbitration of differences between the two companies.

"Mr. Fish was exceedingly anxious that we should not have to rush into this undertaking without the benefit of the counsel and assistance of Mr. A. G. Davis. It was, therefore, arranged that we should have a reasonable period of time for Mr. Fish to acquaint himself with the details of the matter before the execution of the proposed arbitration agreement.

*   *   *   *

"The form of the proposed arbitration agreement was carefully considered by Mr. Young. He felt that, generally speaking, it was satisfactory, but he did not favor the idea of the Radio Corporation being tied down to a short and definite time within which to present its draft of the points to be arbitrated."

The human element intervened to give the parties a bit of additional time to prepare their cases. On December 10th, Frederick P. Fish, in Boston, wrote to William Brown, chief counsel of RCA:

"I have had a combination of troubles which has prevented me from doing much work on the Radio-Telephone matter. A case in the Supreme Court, coupled with a severe cold, a sprained ankle and the gout have been more than I could carry.

"I have now started on the matter and want very much two or three hours' conference with you, Mr. Sarnoff and Mr. Adams.

"I go to New York tomorrow (Tuesday) night. I should be very glad if you could see me Wednesday morning as early as possible at Mr. Neave's office."

Evidently the meeting was held, since we find in the records a telegram from William Brown setting the meeting for 10 o'clock on Wednesday morning. It is apparent that on the day of the scheduled meeting a draft of the arbitration agreement, virtually in its final form, was circulated among the officers of the corporations concerned. Some changes were apparently suggested by Mr. Fish at the meeting in question.

A controversy now developed between Frederick P. Fish and Nathaniel T. Guernsey of the Telephone Company that virtually deadlocked negotiations. The eighth clause in the proposed agreement provided as follows:

"Each party hereto releases the others and the vendees and users of apparatus or systems made by the others from all claims growing out of infringements of patents prior to the date of the determination by the referee, by reason of the manufacture, use and sale of such apparatus and systems by such others, and its resale or use by such vendees and users."

Mr. Fish held out for an amendment to the clause "which will make it clear that if there are to be such releases as the clause contemplates, they are not to form the basis for an argument that there may be a continuance of any acts or conditions which the arbitrator finds improper." In the controversy thus raised Albert G. Davis of the General Electric Company and John W. Griggs of RCA [3] concurred with Mr. Fish. They even went so far as to advocate eliminating the clause altogether.

Mr. Guernsey insisted, however, that RCA had already agreed in principle to the clause, although he could not point to any definite commitment in writing, claiming an oral agreement at a certain conference held by him with General Harbord and David Sarnoff.

At this point in negotiations Frederick P. Fish, who was of advanced age, took to his bed with gout. Proceedings were thus virtually halted until after the Christmas holidays. To be sure there was a good bit of letter writing by William Brown and others, yet gout proved an effective check to all other endeavors.

Sec. 57. A Deadlock Broken.

Clause 8 of the arbitration agreement formed the basis of a joint conference on December 26, 1923, at which Nathaniel T. Guernsey represented the Telephone Company, while David Sarnoff and William Brown were spokesmen for the Radio Group. Mr. Sarnoff opened the discussion by giving his version of the meeting at which it had been claimed that he and General Harbord had agreed "in principle" to the mutual releases of liability. He pointed out that both he and General Harbord were unable to agree that they had made any such commitment. He presented to Mr. Guernsey a written statement from General Harbord to this effect. In the face of these disclaimers Mr. Guernsey admitted that perhaps he had stated the case too strongly, and readily agreed that the parties could not be bound by oral statements of their officials, this being the province of their respective boards of directors.

[3] See Report of William Brown to General Harbord, December 15, 1923.

"Mr. Sarnoff said that with the above point settled, he wanted to make sure concerning the purpose of the clause, namely, whether it is intended to waive monetary damages only between the parties to the date of the finding of the arbitrator, or whether it would also waive the right of either party to complain against the other—continuing, beyond the arbitrator's award, operations found by the arbitrator to be a violation by such party of its rights under the contract. Mr. Guernsey stated that in his opinion the clause related only to a release of monetary damages. He called attention to his having used the same language as in Article XII of the contract of July 1, 1920, between the Telephone Company and the General Electric Company respecting releases between the parties to the date of the contract and argued that a continuation of that arrangement to the date of the arbitrator's findings appeared to him only a fair and reasonable arrangement." [4]

Mr. Sarnoff then offered the suggestion that broke the deadlock between the parties. It is thus reported in the memorandum last quoted:

"Upon inquiry by Mr. Sarnoff, Mr. Guernsey stated that he had no objection to adding to the clause a provision that thereunder neither party should be entitled to continue after the arbitrator's award any practice or operation with respect to which the arbitrator should decide it was operating in violation of the terms of the contracts."

Since this waiver of damages was still subject to official approval or disapproval, Mr. Brown suggested that in case of disapproval the arbitration might be extended to include an award of damages by the arbitrator. To this suggestion Mr. Guernsey was strenuously opposed, declaring that it would be a mistake to turn the arbitration into an accounting proceeding. Here the matter was left to await action on the following day.

One other controversial point was taken up at this conference:

"Mr. Guernsey brought up the matter of Mr. Sarnoff's recent criticism of the Telephone Company *in re* the latter's lack of co-operation in patent suits. Mr. Sarnoff presented a letter from RCA patent counsel which went with detail into specific cases wherein the Telephone Company had failed to join with the Radio Corporation as plaintiff in various suits, as a result of which at least temporary setbacks were occasioned, necessitating certain appeals. Mr. Guernsey conceded that the statements were perhaps correct, but maintained that it would have been a fairer presentation of the matter had RCA patent counsel gone on to say that it was largely by agreement between patent counsel for the two companies that the Telephone Company had been

[4] Memorandum No. 9—December 26, 1923—RCA files.

joined as a defendant rather than as a party plaintiff in some suits, and that in other cases, instead of joining as plaintiff, had by special assignment sought to confer rights upon the Radio Corporation to sue for infringements of patents involved, which assignments have unfortunately since been held by the courts to be insufficient to serve the purpose intended thereby, appeals from which decisions are now pending. Mr. Sarnoff further stated that while the foregoing facts had been presented by RCA patent counsel, the writers were frank to admit that the Telephone Company is now co-operating satisfactorily in such patent litigation by joining the suits as party plaintiff."

On the following morning Frederick P. Fish, now being in New York City, addressed a memorandum to Mr. Guernsey putting into legal phraseology the Sarnoff suggestion of an addition to clause 8. Mr. Fish was evidently not enthusiastic over the phrase, stating that it seemed to him almost unnecessary. "It should be clear," he wrote, "that the release does not amount to a waiver for the future." However, since the attorney for the Telephone Company was adamant in his refusal to delete clause 8, the harmless amendment, as before indicated, was a face-saving gesture that enabled the parties to conclude their long series of negotiations.

Sec. 58. The Arbitration Agreement Signed.

The final draft of the arbitration agreement was prepared on December 27, 1923. On the next day it was formally executed by the duly authorized representatives of the various corporations. The text is of sufficient importance to deserve reproduction in full. It reads as follows:

WHEREAS, under date of July 1, 1920, the GENERAL ELECTRIC COMPANY, a corporation organized under the laws of the State of New York (hereinafter referred to as the General Company), and the AMERICAN TELEPHONE AND TELEGRAPH COMPANY, a like corporation (hereinafter referred to as the Telephone Company), entered into an agreement whereby each company granted to the other certain licenses and rights under patents, which agreement contemplated that under certain conditions each party thereto might grant sublicenses to others; and

WHEREAS, with the consent of the General Company certain rights under said agreement have been extended to the WESTERN ELECTRIC COMPANY, INCORPORATED, also a New York corporation (hereinafter referred to as the Western Company), and with the consent of the Telephone Company certain rights under the said agreement have been extended to the RADIO CORPORATION OF AMERICA, a Delaware corporation (hereinafter referred to as the Radio Corporation), and to the WESTINGHOUSE ELECTRIC AND MANUFACTURING COMPANY, a Pennsylvania corporation (hereinafter referred to as the Westinghouse Company), and to the UNITED FRUIT COMPANY, a New Jersey corporation (hereinafter referred to as the Fruit Company), and to the TROPICAL RADIO TELEGRAPH COMPANY, a Delaware corporation (hereinafter referred to as the Tropical Company), and to the WIRELESS SPECIALTY APPARATUS COMPANY, a New York corporation (hereinafter referred to as the Specialty Apparatus Company); and

WHEREAS, in connection with said extensions, the parties to whom rights were so extended, granted certain rights to others of the parties; and

WHEREAS, honest and substantial differences of opinion have arisen between the parties as to their rights under the said agreement of July 1, 1920, and under the various agreements made in connection with the aforesaid consent to its extension; and

WHEREAS, each of the parties hereto desires to avoid controversy with the others and to have said differences solved by an authoritative construction of the said agreements, which shall be binding upon all of said parties;

NOW, THEREFORE, in consideration of the premises, and of one dollar ($1.00) in hand paid by each of the parties hereto to each of the other parties hereto, the receipt whereof is hereby acknowledged, it is agreed by and between the said AMERICAN TELEPHONE AND TELEGRAPH COMPANY and WESTERN ELECTRIC COMPANY, INCORPORATED (which are hereinafter for convenience collectively referred to as the Telephone Group), and the said GENERAL ELECTRIC COMPANY, RADIO CORPORATION OF AMERICA, WESTINGHOUSE ELECTRIC AND MANUFACTURING COMPANY, UNITED FRUIT COMPANY, TROPICAL RADIO TELEGRAPH COMPANY and WIRELESS SPECIALTY APPARATUS COMPANY (which are hereinafter for convenience collectively referred to as the Radio Corporation Group), as follows:

FIRST: That the contracts and letters out of which said controverted questions arise are the following:

(a) License agreement dated July 1, 1920, between the General Company and the Telephone Company;

(b) Extension agreement dated July 1, 1920, between the General Company, Radio Corporation, Telephone Company and Western Company;

(c) Letter dated July 1, 1920, from the General Company to the Telephone Company, with the assent of the latter;

(d) Letter dated March 9, 1921, from the Telephone Company and Western Company to the General Company, assenting to extension to the Fruit Company and others;

(e) Letter dated June 30, 1921, from the Telephone Company and the Western Company to the General Company and the Radio Corporation assenting to the extension to the Westinghouse Company;

(f) Agreement dated June 30, 1921, between the Telephone Company, Western Company and Westinghouse Company.

Copies of said contracts shall be filed with the referee at the beginning of the hearing, and when so filed shall become a part of the record of the proceeding before him.

SECOND: That MR. ROLAND W. BOYDEN be and he is hereby constituted a referee, with authority and jurisdiction to hear and determine the questions now in controversy between the said parties as to the proper construction of the said agreements and as to their respective rights thereunder.

THIRD: That the hearing before the referee shall be held at such time and place as the referee may fix. Each party may be represented by counsel and may present such evidence as it is advised is material and competent; and in the proceeding the referee shall be governed by the rules that would apply to a suit in equity between the parties involving the same subject matter.

FOURTH: That in order to define the questions which are to be heard and determined by the referee, the Telephone Group and the Radio Corporation Group shall each prepare a concise statement of its claims, both under the licenses granted and to be granted by said agreements and under its own patents (assuming the validity of all the patents), as to all points as to which it believes controversies have arisen or may arise between the parties.

On the 17th day of January, 1924, at 12 o'clock noon, representatives of the two groups shall meet at the office of N. T. Guernsey, Vice-President and General Counsel of the American Telephone and Telegraph Company, 195 Broadway, New York City, and exchange said statements. Within 10 days after the exchange of claims as aforesaid the Radio Corporation shall advise the Telephone Company in writing what claims of the Telephone Group the Radio Corporation Group concedes, and what of such claims it denies, and the Telephone Company shall give to the Radio Corporation like notice in writing as to the claims asserted by the Radio Corporation Group.

Copies of the claims of the respective parties, and of the notices above referred to shall be furnished to the referee, and the controverted questions disclosed by them shall be the questions to be submitted to and decided by him.

FIFTH: That the report of said referee shall be made in writing, and a copy thereof shall be furnished to each of the parties hereto; and thereupon his determination shall constitute an adjudication binding upon each party hereto as finally and conclusively as an adjudication of a court having jurisdiction of the subject matter and of all of the parties; provided, however, that the adjudication established by the determination of the referee shall only extend to, and include the questions actually presented to and determined by him, and shall not estop either of the parties as to any question not so presented and determined.

Each party hereto agrees that it will accept and conform to such determination, and after such determination has been made will not take any proceedings intended either to modify it or set it aside; provided, however, that such determination shall not affect the rights of either party under paragraph 5 of Article VI of said Contract of July 1, 1920.

SIXTH: That all proceedings before the referee shall be reported stenographically by a reporter to be designated by the referee; each party to have such number of transcripts as it may desire, at its own expense.

SEVENTH: That each group shall pay one-half of the fee of the referee and of his disbursements, and shall pay all of its expenses.

EIGHTH: Each party hereto releases the others and the vendees and users of apparatus or systems made by the others from all claims growing out of infringements of patents prior to the date of the determination by the referee, by reason of the manufacture, use and/or sale of such apparatus and systems by such others, and its resale or use by such vendees and users, *reserving the full right to enforce its rights under patents against any such infringement occurring after the determination of the referee.*

In Witness Whereof, each of the parties hereto has caused this instrument and seven replicas thereof (each of which is an original) to be executed in its behalf by its President or other duly authorized officer, and to be attested by its secretary with its corporate seal, on this 28th day of December, 1923.

AMERICAN TELEPHONE AND TELEGRAPH COMPANY,
By (Signed):   H. B. THAYER, President
[seal]
Attest:
   (Signed)   A. A. MARSTERS, Secretary

WESTERN ELECTRIC COMPANY, Incorporated,
By (Signed):   C. G. DuBOIS, President
[SEAL]
Attest:
   (Signed)   GUY C. PRATT, Secretary

GENERAL ELECTRIC COMPANY,
By (Signed):   GERARD SWOPE, President
[SEAL]
Attest:
   (Signed)   M. F. WESTOVER, Secretary

RADIO CORPORATION OF AMERICA,
By (Signed):   J. G. HARBORD, President
[SEAL]
Attest:
   (Signed)   L. MacCONNACH, Secretary

WESTINGHOUSE ELECTRIC AND
MANUFACTURING COMPANY,
By (Signed):   E. M. HERR, President

[SEAL]

Attest:

     (Signed)   WARREN H. JONES, Assistant Secretary

UNITED FRUIT COMPANY,
By (Signed):   A. W. PRESTON, President

[SEAL]

Attest:

     (Signed)   ARTHUR E. NICHOLSON, Assistant Secretary

TROPICAL RADIO TELEGRAPH COMPANY,
By (Signed):   A. W. PRESTON, President

[SEAL]

Attest:

     (Signed)   ARTHUR E. NICHOLSON, Secretary

WIRELESS SPECIALTY APPARATUS COMPANY,
By (Signed):   EDWARD C. PORTER, Treasurer

[seal]

Attest:

     (Signed)   JOHN L. WARREN, Secretary

CHAPTER
EIGHT

The Arbitration of 1924

Section 59. RCA, Telephone Company et al. Accused of Conspiracy.
IT WILL BE OBSERVED that by the terms of Article 4 of the arbitration agreement the representatives of the two groups were to meet in the offices of Nathaniel T. Guernsey, vice-president and general counsel of the American Telephone Company, on January 17, 1924, to exchange formal statements of their respective contentions. The interval was productive of a great mass of correspondence relating to the interchange of official copies of the agreement. Official notices of ratification by the various corporations were likewise exchanged. The vote of conformation in the records of RCA will sufficiently indicate the nature of votes passed by the various corporations.

EXTRACT FROM MINUTES OF THE MEETING OF THE
BOARD OF DIRECTORS
RADIO CORPORATION OF AMERICA
JANUARY 4TH, 1924

"The President reported that in conformity with the resolution passed by this Board on October 19th, 1923, he had executed in behalf of the Radio Corporation of America, an agreement dated December 28th, 1923, between the American Telephone & Telegraph Company and the Western Electric Company, of the one part and the General Electric Company, the Radio Corporation of America, the Westinghouse Electric & Manufacturing Company, the United Fruit Company, the Tropical Radio Telegraph Company and the Wireless Specialty Apparatus Company of the other part, providing for the arbitration of the points in controversy growing out of the agreement of July 1st, 1920, between the American Telephone & Telegraph Company and the General Electric Company. After discussion, on motion, duly made and seconded, the action of the President in executing the said agreement was ratified, approved and confirmed."

On January 17th the representatives of the Telephone Group filed a statement—a twelve-page brief—and on the same day the Radio Group filed their own fourteen-page statement of claims. This does not signify that the parties were ready to proceed with arbitration. On the contrary, further formalities were necessary. On January 25th the Telephone Company filed a letter addressed to the Radio Corporation making a formal denial of the claims contained in the Radio Corporation brief. On the same date the Radio Group filed a formal answer to the Telephone Company brief, discussing each of the twelve subdivisions of the same. Thus formalities were completed. Weeks were to elapse before hearings in the controversy could begin.

While these events were transpiring in New York certain ominous activities were taking place in Washington, D. C. The Federal Trade

Commission had apparently been making ready for a real trust-busting effort against the alleged monopoly disclosed by the report filed by it with the national congress on December 1, 1923. On January 25, 1924, a formal complaint (Docket No. 1115) was filed for trial before the Federal Trade Commission. It contained thirty-one counts, and named the following defendants:

(1) General Electric Company
(2) American Telephone & Telegraph Company
(3) Western Electric Company
(4) Westinghouse Electric & Manufacturing Company
(5) The International Radio Telegraph Company
(6) United Fruit Company
(7) Wireless Specialty Apparatus Company
(8) Radio Corporation of America

The complaint was concurred in by all members of the Commission except Commissioner Van Fleet. Thus the two groups of corporations that, after long controversy, had arranged for arbitration of their differences, on the very day that final answers were filed in their arbitration suit, found themselves pilloried in the public press as malefactors who were to be tried together for an unlawful conspiracy against the American public.

"The Federal Trade Commission charges," the accusation began, "that the various persons, corporate and individual, mentioned in the caption hereof and more particularly hereinafter described and hereinafter referred to as respondents, have been and are using unfair methods of competition in commerce in violation of the provisions of Section 5 of said Act, and states its charge in that respect as follows: etc."

Investigations by congressional committees or commissions have long been an important feature of the American system of government. In no other way, perhaps, can the people of the nation safeguard themselves against insidious forces working in interstate areas, whether in the business field, or in underground subversive activities and the like, except through the inquisitional powers of the Congress. To be sure there is always danger of abuse of the power, yet that seems to be one of the risks that we run in maintaining a free government. A congressional investigation is necessarily a "fishing expedition" that may or may not be productive of results other than publicity for the committee—and for the accused.

The Radio investigation begun in 1924 is perhaps an extreme illustration of a relatively unproductive inquisitorial effort. More than four thousand pages of printed testimony were to be accumulated in the four years and nine months during which the investigation was officially in progress. The eight accused corporations were to spend vast sums for legal services and for expenses of the hearings. Their responsible officials were to be obliged to devote much time and thought that might have been productively employed to the defense of the accused corporations.

The intangible losses from the public suspicion that hampered corporate activities during the years of the inquiry are beyond calculation. Verily, the power to investigate is the power to hamper, if not to destroy accused corporations. The strangest feature of this inquiry was to be the long lapses in the investigation. For example, the corporations were accused in the public press on January 25, 1924, yet not until October 20, 1925, were they to be placed on trial. Thus twenty months intervened between the original anti-trust suit and the formal beginning of the taking of testimony. This process was to continue by "fits and starts" until February 24, 1928. Then, after a lapse of nearly ten months, on December 19, 1928, the Commission was to dismiss the complaint as casually as though it were a mere daily routine.[1] These facts will appear in the progress of our story yet, in justice to the reader and to the corporations concerned, it seems only fair to point out that the above investigation, begun in January, 1924, was fated to be of little consequence in radio annals. To be sure, it may have had, and it probably did have, wholesome effect upon a very

---

[1] The text of the dismissal was as follows:

UNITED STATES OF AMERICA
BEFORE FEDERAL TRADE COMMISSION

At a regular session of the Federal Trade Commission, held at its office in the City of Washington, D. C., on the 19th day of December, A.D., 1928.
COMMISSIONERS:
    Abram F. Meyers, Chairman,
    Edgar A. McCulloch,
    Garland S. Ferguson, Jr.,
    C. W. Hunt,
    William E. Humphrey.

| In the Matter of | DOCKET 1115 |
| GENERAL ELECTRIC COMPANY, ET AL. | ORDER OF DISMISSAL. |

This matter coming on to be heard on the motions of the respondents to dismiss the complaint herein as amended, and the Commission having heard oral argument in support of said motions and oral argument in opposition to said motions, and the Commission having considered briefs filed in support of and in opposition to said motions and the Commission being fully advised in the premises,

IT IS HEREBY ORDERED that the said motions be and the same are hereby granted, and that the said complaint as amended be and the same is hereby dismissed.

By the Commission

(Signed) OTIS B. JOHNSON
Secretary

much entangled industry. It at least brought home to the corporations involved the lesson that interlocking directorates and close commercial alliances should be avoided.

Sec. 60. Litigation over Infringements—Rivalry for Pre-eminence.

The winter of 1924 was notable in radio annals. Not only had the art by this time become an established feature of our national life, but the contest for dominance of the industry had now developed impressive proportions. The American Telephone Company, like the industrial giant that it was, had at last roused itself to do battle for its rights not only with the Radio Corporation group but also with others. For more than two years it had been issuing periodic protests against unlicensed broadcasting by radio stations. The Telephone Company claimed the right that all owners of patents are supposed to possess under the laws of the United States—to say who should be permitted to use the patented inventions. Not that it was threatening to close radio stations, but simply that it was insisting that stations not already licensed by it to use broadcasting devices manufactured under its patents should at once take out licenses, or cease to infringe patent rights.

A test case was inevitable. Such a case was brought against Station WHN of Ridgewood, N. Y., for unlicensed radio broadcasting. The author has treated this litigation in a previous work.[2] For the purpose of the present narrative the story will bear repeating:

"Threat-muttering had ceased to be a virtue when alleged outlaw stations could set up sponsored programs everywhere. The defiance of Station WHN had been particularly exasperating to the guardians of the rights of the stockholders of A. T. & T. They decided to take legal action. This suit was no sooner brought than cries of 'monopoly control' began to be heard on all sides. So great became the clamor that Secretary of Commerce Herbert Hoover was at length drawn into the controversy. In a public expression of his views Mr. Hoover declared:

" 'I can state emphatically that it would be most unfortunate for the people of this country to whom broadcasting has become an important incident of life if its control should come into the hands of any single corporation, individual or combination. It would be in principle the same as though the entire press of the country were so controlled. The effect would be identical whether this control arose under a patent monopoly or under any form of combination, and from the standpoint of the people's interest the question of whether or not the broadcasting is for profit is immaterial.'

[2] Archer, *History of Radio to 1926*, pp. 333-335.

"Thus the A. T. & T. experienced something of the far-flung hostility that had assailed the Radio Corporation of America. Since the suit against WHN was a feeler to test the vexed question of whether the Telephone Company's patents entitled it to a right to license stations to operate there was cause enough for other stations to join the hue and cry. It mattered not to the public that the American Telephone Company was the legal owner of the patents covering broadcasting station equipment now being used even by the so-called outlaw stations. The fact that the Telephone Company was now granting licenses right and left to stations that applied for the privilege seemed to have no influence with the public mind. Here was an iniquitous trust jumping with hobnailed boots all over the little fellow—hence widespread clamor and ballyhoo.

"Having started suit against WHN, however, the lawyers for the Telephone Company, supported by the directors of the company, pressed the case resolutely. They pointed out to the court that a fundamental issue of patent law was involved. Ever since the United States Government had first established the Patent Office it had been the law that the owner of a patent was entitled to legal protection against those who willfully infringe the aforesaid patent rights. Because A. T. & T. stood ready to license WHN on reasonable terms the lawyers contended that the court should order the offending station to comply with the law or cease broadcasting. Before the trial reached the stage where the judges would be called upon to render an official decision the lawyers for Station WHN, realizing no doubt that their case was hopeless despite the nation-wide clamor that they had stirred up, approached the lawyers of A. T. & T. with a suggestion of compromise.

"Thus the test case was settled out of court. Protesting bitterly that the license agreement prohibited the licensee from using the station for revenue as WEAF was doing, Station WHN acknowledged the validity of the Telephone Company patents and signed the usual license agreement. . . . This vindication was no vindication at all so far as the public was concerned. The net result of the effort had been a distinct loss to the Telephone Company."

In the meantime, the rivalry between Stations WJZ and WEAF found expression in spectacular performances by each. WJZ led off on March 7, 1924, with the most ambitious broadcasting experiment ever attempted up to that time—a trans-Atlantic and transcontinental broadcast.

Appropriately enough, the broadcast was of a banquet program of the Alumni of the Massachusetts Institute of Technology, held in the ballroom of the Waldorf-Astoria in New York City. Not only was the program broadcast in the ordinary way by Station WJZ, but tap-off wires from the amplifier panel in the control room carried the program to special wires that extended from New York City to Schenectady. Here Station WGY of the General Electric Company rebroadcast the program both by long- and short-wave transmission. The short-wave had trans-Atlantic coverage, and also was capable of carrying the program inland to short-wave Station KFKX in Hastings, Nebraska. The latter station in its turn rebroadcast the program to Station KGO in Oakland, California. Thus, listeners in England and on the Pacific coast were able to hear the program at virtually the same instant of time.

Station WEAF now accomplished its first permanent radio network. Stations WEAF, WCAP and WJAR were connected by permanent wires, broadcasting simultaneously the same program. One of the first great triumphs of the network was in broadcasting President Calvin Coolidge's Memorial Day oration, May 30, 1924, from the amphitheater at Arlington Memorial Cemetery.

An interesting contribution to the vigorous contest that was being waged between RCA's New York station and the Telephone Company's WEAF was made at this point by David Sarnoff, vice-president and general manager of RCA. Speaking in Chicago, Mr. Sarnoff declared that broadcasting stations were then in an unhealthy condition owing to lack of financial support. He predicted that unless the smaller stations found means of support enabling them to continue in service, broadcasting of the future would be carried on by a few super-stations, which would be supported by the industry itself from returns on the sales of radio apparatus, a definite percentage of the sale price to be set aside for the purpose. This speech struck a responsive chord in the hearts of those who frowned upon WEAF's policy of selling broadcast time to commercial sponsors. The editor of *Radio Broadcast* probably expressed the reaction of such listeners in the following comment on the Sarnoff utterance:

"Naturally, to the business man, this seems the logical solution. It is probably the simplest solution of the problem and possibly it will be the final one. A reasonable percentage on the sales profits in tubes, batteries, accessories, etc., will maintain a good many stations, even after the sale of new sets begins to fall off, and this falling off, by the way, is still a long way in the future." [3]

It is interesting to note that the results of the WHN suit, and especially its manner of settlement, now began to bear fruit of a different nature than the first crop of criticism. Radio stations over wide areas began to fall in line.

On May 16, 1924, the Telephone Company in a press release declared with evident satisfaction that forty radio stations that had

[3] *Radio Broadcast,* July, 1924, p. 221.

formerly been operating in disregard of the company's patent rights had recently applied for and had received licenses to operate. Although there was still more or less controversy over the allegation that licensees were being obliged to agree not to operate for profit, *Radio Broadcast* was informed by the Telephone Company that it had erred in giving credence to the report. In the August, 1924, number of the magazine the editor makes the following retraction:

"In the article in question it was stated that licensed stations were not allowed to broadcast for profit, one of the outlaw stations so claiming. It appears that this was in error, as the present form of licenses, some of which were sent to us, contain no such agreement."

Another uncertainty was cleared up by the letter from the company —uncertainty as to size of license fees. It had been alleged by critics of the Telephone Company that these fees were excessive, and by company officials that they were so modest as to be negligible.

"The license fees," continues the editorial already quoted, "are from $500 to $3000 depending upon the size of the station. They are paid but once. The fee may be paid in installments if so desired by the licensee. The license form seems reasonable enough . . . certainly no more than adequate to cover the various costly developments which the Telephone Company puts at the disposal of the licensee when he is operating one of their equipments."

Sec. 61. The Eve of Battle.

In the meantime, for weeks on end, the arbitration matter had languished. The case had apparently been ripe for trial before the end of January, 1924. It was, moreover, free from the inevitable delays incident to a crowded court docket. In fact, this special court of arbitration had but one case before it—the mighty issue of the Telephone Group vs. Radio Group. How far reaching that issue really was became evident on March 21, 1924, when the annual report of RCA was made public and the following astounding figures of sales of radio apparatus and radio sets became known:

Gross sales for	1923	$22,465,090.71
Same for	1922	11,286,489.41
" "	1921	1,468,919.95

It was natural that the Telephone Group should have manifested more impatience over the delay than had their adversaries who were, for the present, entrenched in the disputed territory of sales—entrenched, and what is more important, reaping a continuing increase of business. Elmer E. Bucher, general sales manager of RCA, and David Sarnoff, vice-president and general manager of the corporation would have been justified had they discussed the matter in hushed whispers. The report of sales for the first quarter of 1924 indicated that the corporation would roll up more than fifty million dollars in gross sales during the current year.

It is not the author's intention to imply that RCA officials had any share in delaying the beginning of arbitration hearings. As a lawyer, he is well aware that deliberate and painstaking preparation is essential to justice, and that lawyers as a class are prone to develop dilatory habits.

Then, too, a lawyer of advanced years and high standing in his profession is bound to have other important commitments that must be fulfilled before any case, however important, can be reached. Such a lawyer was Frederick P. Fish of Boston. His practice, moreover, was not confined to one locality. He was chief counsel in important suits in various parts of the United States. This would account for much of the delay that was experienced in bringing the arbitration hearings to pass.

Another cause for delay was undoubtedly the absence in Europe of Owen D. Young, chairman of the board of RCA, and an all-powerful figure in the so-called Radio Group. Mr. Young had been appointed a member of the First Committee of Experts by the Reparations Commission in December, 1923, and it had been necessary for him to depart at once for Europe. In April, however, he was back in New York. It is apparent from the letter quoted below that a date for the opening of arbitration hearings had been fixed to follow closely upon Mr. Young's return. The letter contains other interesting information:

New York, April 30, 1924

My dear Mr. Young:

At Mr. Swope's request I told Mr. Folk today over the telephone that you had returned and would be glad to discuss the arbitration matter with Mr. Thayer at any time that could be arranged. I told him that you were today in Washington. Mr. Folk said that Mr. Thayer had expressed the hope that he would not be obliged to get in it himself. I said that I was acting as messenger boy, and Mr. Folk said that he too was acting in the same way. His tone was very friendly.

If you do see Mr. Thayer, I regard it of the utmost importance that you should be posted on the main issues in the arbitration, and the line of the negotiations which I have had with Mr. Folk. I would be very glad, of course, to summarize this matter for you at any time. The arbitration hearings begin Tuesday morning in the Telephone Company's office and are expected to continue Tuesday, Wednesday,

Thursday and Friday, so that during that period I shall be pretty thoroughly occupied, at least in the day time, and may be needed for night conferences. I shall be here until 3:30 Friday afternoon and will probably see you at the board meeting at least. I do not at the moment plan to come down to New York until Monday afternoon, though it may be that Mr. Fish will want me to come down Sunday afternoon.

Very truly yours,

(Signed) ALBERT G. DAVIS

P. S. Since the above was dictated Mr. Folk has called me on the telephone saying that Mr. Thayer would be glad to talk to you either Friday or Monday, or at a later date to be arranged. I told him that you were not expected to return to New York until Friday, on which day I suppose either you will telephone Mr. Thayer, or have someone in your office telephone Mr. Thayer's secretary.

Upon Mr. Young's return from Washington he wrote a letter to Mr. Thayer, dated May 2, 1924, concerning the proposed conference which he had apparently been unable to attend. On May 5, Mr. Thayer wrote a gracious reply in which he congratulated Mr. Young on the work that he had been doing in Europe, concluding with the following paragraph which indicates that another postponement of the hearing had been requested by counsel. Mr. Thayer's impatience with delays is evident:

"By the way, Mr. Guernsey tells me this morning that Mr. Fish has to be away next week and I wonder whether you cannot arrange so that the proceedings of the arbitration can go on without interruption even if he temporarily may have to be absent?"

The language above quoted seems to have caused Mr. Young to express himself a bit freely as to the alleged ungenerous attitude of the Telephone Company. He made no written response to the letter, but instead instructed his secretary to communicate his views by telephone. The latter apparently acted with promptness. The reaction was the following warlike response:

(H. B. Thayer to Owen D. Young, May 7, 1924.)
Dear Mr. Young:

Your secretary has informed me of your comment on the last paragraph of my letter of May 5th.

When you come to read that letter, you will note that I did not refer to the postponement of this week on account of Mrs. Boyden's death, but to the suggestion of a postponement next week on account of Mr. Fish's engagements.

It is now nearly seven months since the parties informally agreed to arbitration. The delay has been prejudicial to our interests and I assume has been to yours. My request is that it be arranged so that if Mr. Fish is unable to go on at any time with the proceedings, someone may be ready to go on in his place.

It is understood in our organization that we are not to ask for any postponement nor to consent to any, except on the proposal of the arbitrator.

Yours very truly,

(Signed) H. B. THAYER,

President

In the files of the General Electric Company is a copy of a reply to the above letter, not from Mr. Young himself, who was by this time out of town, but from Albert G. Davis. Since Mr. Davis had been in touch with all phases of the matter for months he was in position to reply forcefully and to the point. The letter was dated May 8, 1924, and ran as follows:

My dear Mr. Thayer:

Mr. Young is out of town. I understand that he has requested that I should reply to your letter of May 7th to him.

We were quite ready to proceed with the arbitration in New York on May 6th, the date which was fixed some weeks ago by agreement between Mr. Fish and Mr. Guernsey. When the arbitrator notified Mr. Fish that, on account of his wife's condition he could not leave Boston, Mr. Fish wrote to Mr. Guernsey, stating his willingness to go ahead in Boston on May 6th, if Mr. Guernsey thought it desirable.

My understanding is that the postponement of the present week was due entirely to the natural request of the arbitrator, following his wife's death. Whether or not the arbitrator would have been ready to go ahead next week, I do not know, but in any event it was impossible because Mr. Fish had a court engagement of long standing in the South, which made it impossible for him to attend.

We cannot agree with your suggestion that in case Mr. Fish is unable to attend any particular session, someone else should take his place. We do not consider that the rights of the Radio Group would properly be protected under such an agreement.

Mr. Fish has worked very hard over this case, devoted an enormous amount of time to it to the neglect, as I personally know, of other matters of great importance. I understand that he intends to push it as rapidly as possible.

Yours truly,

(Signed) ALBERT G. DAVIS

Sec. 62. Telephone Company Steals a March on RCA.

The death of Mrs. Roland W. Boyden occurred in Boston on May 7, 1924. The arbitration proceedings must necessarily wait until the bereaved husband could have opportunity to recover from the shock of the event. In the meantime, a development had occurred in the strained relations between the two groups that caused considerable perturbation at RCA. Mention has been made of the Telephone Company's experimental superheterodyne radio set. The officials of RCA had long been apprehensive lest the Telephone Company, now so belligerent, should actually go into the business of selling them.

In the latter part of April, 1924, a rumor had come to David Sarnoff that the Western Electric Company had not only gone into the market but had actually installed one of their new radio sets in the White House in Washington, at the very time when an RCA set was about to be installed. Naturally, this caused "fireworks" in the home office of RCA. The Washington branch of the company was called upon for information. The reply from F. P. Guthrie to David Sarnoff is illuminating:

April 30, 1924

To: Mr. David Sarnoff
From: F. P. Guthrie
Subject: New Western Electric Superheterodyne—Type 4-B

Dear Mr. Sarnoff:

This afternoon I went to the Navy Department to see the new Western Electric set which has been submitted as being "much better" than our Superheterodyne.

The set which they have bears the type number 4-B, serial number twenty-six, and seems to be a six tube Superheterodyne set, using Western Electric "peanut" tubes. The output of this set goes to an ordinary Western Electric three tube power amplifier, the output of which in turn passes to one of their new parchment-cone Rochelle-salt loud speakers.

The set is operated by storage batteries, and while it seems to give good results, it is not at all ornamental, and seems to use nine tubes to do the work that six tubes in our set do.

The tone of the new loud speaker seems to resemble very closely the tone of the loud speaker in our Radiola X. I called Commander Langworthy's attention to the fact that it would be quite a simple matter to attach the Western Electric loud speaker to our Superheterodyne, so as to get a comparative test of the sets themselves rather than the loud speakers only.

I will keep closely in touch with this situation and advise you of any further developments.

Yours very truly,

(Signed) F. P. GUTHRIE

Mr. Sarnoff's reaction to the report is typical of the man. Before descending upon the Telephone Company with accusations of bad faith, he desired to be armed with authentic information. This accounts for the following letter:

May 1, 1924

Subject: New Western Electric Superheterodyne

Dear Mr. Guthrie:

I have your letter of the 30th ultimo on the above subject. I will be obliged if you will review the situation for me in a memorandum from the beginning, stating just how we came to install a set in the White House and how the Western Electric Company injected itself.

I am rather inclined to think that their action in this case is one that would not be sanctioned by their executive officers if they knew about it, and I want to lay it before them. But before doing so, I should like your full information based on the facts.

Yours very truly,

(Signed) DAVID SARNOFF

Mr. Guthrie's second letter relates at some length the history of radio sets in the White House, the first having been installed by the Shipping Board during the Harding administration. A question had recently arisen of installing a modern set. Mr. Guthrie had recommended a Radiola Super VIII.

"The set was duly received and carefully calibrated at our service station," he reported. "When it was ready for delivery I called Commander ————— by telephone and advised him; he said he would let me know in a few days what to do with it. When he did not call me I went down to see him in order to find out what was up, and he told me that the matter had been somewhat complicated by the fact that the Western Electric Company had requested permission to submit one of their new sets for comparison, which was described as being 'much better' than our superheterodyne."

Demonstration had apparently convinced the official that the Western Electric radio set was indeed as represented—superior in operation to the Radiola Super VIII. Mr. Guthrie closed his recital by saying: "This is essentially a government sale, and as such, it would not seem to be in violation of the agreement between ourselves and the Western Electric Company."

It is significant that in transmitting this report to General Harbord, Mr. Sarnoff wrote in pencil in the upper margin of the letter:

"Guthrie talks like a reasonable man—DS"

Mr. Sarnoff's letter to General Harbord transmitting the correspondence reveals how fully he appreciated the significance of the event and also of other similar sales. His reference to "upsetting the apple cart" was clearly not overdrawn. RCA engineers realized all too well that the Radiola Super VIII then in production, to be sold at popular prices, could not be expected to equal in performance the "sample sets" being produced by the Western Electric Company presumably without much regard to cost of production. The existence of such sets becoming noised abroad might actually destroy the market for Radiola Super VIII. The letter reads thus:

May 19, 1924

Dear General Harbord:

I attach hereto several letters which indicate that the Western Electric Company has actually gone out aggressively to sell superheterodyne sets in the market, and that the effect of this is being noticed throughout the country. We have had numerous inquiries on this subject and are rather embarrassed about how to answer these inquiries or how to handle this subject. I talked with Mr. Harkness personally over the telephone this morning about the case of the Bankers Life Insurance Company of Des Moines, and told him that you and Mr. Gifford had reached an understanding at the time we decided on arbitration, that pending the decision of the arbitrator, neither side would engage in activities beyond those in which they were engaged at the time arbitration was undertaken.

Mr. Harkness said that he quite understood that, but that he did not regard these cases as violating the understanding between you and Mr. Gifford, because they regarded sales such as those made to the Bankers Life Insurance Company as a sale for specific use by customers desiring to receive from a given station. I asked him what would stop these receivers from functioning in the way that any ordinary broadcasting receiver does, namely, to receive from any broadcasting station within close range, but he merely replied that this was "up to the purchaser."

In view of my contemplated absence this week, I suggest the following course:

1. That you refer these papers to Mr. Adams, who should take them up with Mr. Fish for such bearings as they might have on the arbitration proceedings commencing this week.

2. That you take this matter up with Mr. Gifford and acquaint him with the embarrassment to which the Radio Corporation is being subjected pending the decision of the arbitrator.

The mere fact that the Western Electric Company is now actively putting superheterodyne sets on the market will "upset the apple cart," and require each of us to make some explanations to the trade and the public pending the decision of the arbitrator. If the arbitrator should decide that the Telephone Company has not the right to engage in such activities, then it would seem to me that the Western Electric Company would be more seriously embarrassed with the public than they would have been if they had not engaged in them until and unless the arbitrator decided in their favor.

Respectfully,

(Signed) DAVID SARNOFF

Evidently Mr. Sarnoff had already propounded the question of "understanding" between the corporations to Mr. Adams, since we discover in the files a letter from Ira J. Adams to Mr. Sarnoff, dated May 20th, that apparently disposes of the matter. There is no evidence in the records that indicates any further action on the part of Mr. Sarnoff. Neither do we find in the transcript of the arbitration proceedings any reference to the incident. The letter itself is as follows:

May 20, 1924

To: Mr. D. Sarnoff
From: I. J. Adams
Subject: Western Electric Superheterodynes

Dear Mr. Sarnoff:

I have your letter of May 16th with attached correspondence. I do not recall that the companies ever reached any understanding that they would preserve the status quo pending the arbitration. I think you refer to a letter that General Harbord wrote to Mr. Gifford on April 3, 1924, as per attached copy. I am also attaching Mr. Gifford's reply to this letter.

We have been receiving requests for bids on certain apparatus that we may or may not have licenses to supply. In many of the cases we did not have the apparatus designed and we did not want to enter into the business until the arbitrator had definitely decided whether or not we are licensed in the particular fields involved. After declining to quote on these orders the customer usually came back with a request for information as to who is able to supply the apparatus. During the arbitration we did not like to refer orders to the Telephone Company for fear that it might prejudice the arbitration. Consequently I requested General Harbord to make an arrangement with the Telephone Company whereby either company could refer orders to the other without prejudicing or in any way affecting the arbitration. This is the purpose of the two letters that I am referring to.

I do not know of any agreement between the companies whereby each one agrees to preserve the status quo and I doubt that any such agreement has been made, particularly since no one would be able to know what the status quo is. The letters that you sent me, however, are of particular interest in the arbitration and I am sending them to Mr. Fish.

(Signed) IRA J. ADAMS

The letters exchanged between General Harbord and Mr. Gifford, referred to above, related to ordinary exchange of business courtesies and could not be construed as pledging the Telephone Group to refrain from sales of radio sets.

Sec. 63. Arbitration Hearings at Last.

After seven months of delay the arbitration hearings were at length begun. Nathaniel T. Guernsey was chief counsel for the Telephone Group, with George E. Folk and D. C. Tanner as associate counsel. Frederick P. Fish acted as chief counsel for the Radio Group, with Ira J. Adams and Harrison F. Lyman as associate counsel. The first session of the hearings occurred in the Telephone Company offices at 10 A.M., May 20, 1924.

The case was formally opened for the Telephone Company by Nathaniel T. Guernsey. Inasmuch as the referee was more or less unfamiliar with the radio industry it became Mr. Guernsey's first endeavor to trace the history of wireless developments that could have definite bearing upon radio broadcasting. DeForest, Alexanderson, Arnold and Langmuir were brought into the opening address—the speaker endeavoring to explain the contributions of each to the art. He spent much time in a discussion of the vacuum tube and how it operated. He explained the patent situation that existed when the agreement of July, 1920, was signed. The agreement itself upon which the entire controversy hinged was expounded at great length by the speaker. Mr. Guernsey took up paragraph after paragraph of the disputed portions and explained the Telephone Company's contentions as to the meaning of each.

In discussing the claim of the Radio Group that they were entitled to exclusive rights to manufacture and sell radio receiving apparatus, he boldly asserted that the Telephone Company had an equal right "to make, use and sell receiving apparatus either as a part of it or for direct use in connection with our transmitting apparatus." He stated very clearly the rival claims in connection with it.

"There is a radical, fundamental difference between us," he declared, "and it runs into a good many details and it is a very important thing, because the market for receiving sets is a very large one. You will notice that the license . . . with the General Electric Company is, in the first place, a non-exclusive license as to broadcasting stations, and in the next place a license to make, use and sell wireless telephone receiving apparatus. This is not an exclusive license either. It is for the reception of such news, music and entertainment so broadcast. That is, it is to sell for the reception of their own broadcasting . . . Now, it will be our contention that in the first place it is perfectly obvious that somebody thought we were going to make transmitting apparatus; somebody thought that under this contract we were going to make and sell receiving apparatus, and that where the General Electric Company had received the right, non-exclusive, to make, use and sell wireless telephone receiving apparatus for the reception of 'such news and entertainment so broadcasted,' it was intended to give us the right, taking this in connection with some specific provision of the contract, to make, use and sell receiving apparatus either as a part of it, or for direct use in connection with our transmitting apparatus."

Thus, the contention of the Telephone Company, long debated in private conferences, found utterance by the chief counsel for the company in the formal hearing. Mr. Guernsey, in similar manner, discussed other phases of the controversy, such as rights in automotive devices, leased wires, loud speakers, public address systems and the like.

Frederick P. Fish thereupon made his opening statement for the Radio Group. Like the skillful lawyer that he was, Mr. Fish proceeded to damn with faint praise the opening utterances of his opponent, intimating that the latter had not touched upon the vital points in controversy. In view of the fact that Mr. Guernsey had already covered historical aspects of the radio industry, Mr. Fish was able to discuss the contract at once. He argued learnedly that the intention of the parties, as manifested by the language used and the circumstances under which the contract had been drawn, had been "to divide the development into two fields. On the one hand, the public service communication system and the leased wires of the Telephone Company, and, on the other hand, practically everything else to the General Electric Company, because all the rest, to a very large extent and with some exceptions and modifications was the manufacturing of apparatus and the inter-communication system by radio which the General Electric Company was interested in."

In support of this contention he quoted the introductory language of the contract in which the General Electric Company was described in broad terms as a manufacturer, and the Telephone Company as engaged "in the operation of telephone and telegraph systems." Mr. Fish then took up in analytical manner the meaning of wire telephony and wireless telephony, pointing out that the General Electric Company was granted non-exclusive licenses in wireless, both telegraphic and telephonic "for its own communication or convenience." The portion of the contract relating to the grant by the Telephone Company to the Radio Group of "non-exclusive licenses to establish and maintain transmitting stations for transmitting and broadcasting news, music and entertainment from a transmitting station to outlying points" was conceded by Mr. Fish to limit the Radio Group, so far as the language of the license was concerned. He ridiculed the suggestion by his opponent that the Radio Group was limited by the contract to the supplying of broadcast receivers to be used in connection with its own broadcasts—the Telephone Company allegedly having a similar right.

"You take one of these receiving sets," he argued, "and it is open for the man who has it to listen in everywhere. Any station, whether the Telephone, General Electric, Westinghouse, Government telephone or telegraph station, or other stations, any station that he can tune in to, he can hear. It would be perfectly impossible to limit in the slightest degree the use that the purchaser of a receiving set should make of his receiving set." He contended, therefore, that notwithstanding the non-exclusive license to the General Electric Company the Telephone Company had no reserved right to manufacture and sell receiving sets. He pointed out the special clause of the contract providing that the Telephone Company "has no license" to make and sell such devices meant that it "has no right" to do so.

There was much more to his argument on this phase of the controversy. At the suggestion of Albert G. Davis, Mr. Fish advanced the theory that there was no grant from the General Electric Company to the Telephone Company of General Electric patents for transmitting apparatus. He conceded that the Telephone Company had a right "to put out transmitters under its own patents, but it has no right, clearly has no right, under the General Electric Company's patents. As far as receiving is concerned, it has no right under either. It is out of that field. I mean the one-way receiver without being used in combination with the transmitter."

Having voiced this sweeping contention which, if sustained, would virtually destroy the Telephone Company's case, Mr. Fish took up the question of exclusive rights to sell transmitting and receiving sets to amateurs, asserting that this right was exclusively in the General Electric Company and its licensees, thus raising the question of the meaning of the word amateur. It was later to develop that Mr. Fish claimed that virtually all radio listeners were amateurs, whereas Mr. Guernsey took the position that the term applied only to radio tinkers and investigators of wireless phenomena.

Whether broadcasting could be classed as a "public service" came in for a good deal of discussion. The Telephone Company was known to be claiming jurisdiction over broadcasting because the company was engaged in "public service operations."

"The telephone communication system," Mr. Fish asserted, "is a public service corporation in the strict sense. But how about broadcasting? It lacks every element of a public service communication system, or of a public service system. The public have no rights whatsoever to have anything to do with the broadcasting. Broadcasting transmission, of course, goes out on the air. Anybody can listen to it, but they have no rights. At the present time, nobody can foresee that they ever will. . . . No one can go into a broadcasting station and say that he wants to talk or that he wants to advertise."

The noon recess of the first day of the hearing being reached proceedings were adjourned until after lunch. One of the important matters discussed by Mr. Fish in his afternoon statement had to do with the contention of the Telephone Company that wires leading to a broadcasting transmitter from a distant microphone, or leading from a broadcast receiver to loud speakers not directly connected therewith, was wire telephony and hence within its own jurisdiction. Mr. Fish argued that it was radio broadcasting, irrespective of length of wire; that these wires were a part of the wireless broadcasting transmission whether inches or miles in length.

Sec. 64. Testimony of an Important Witness.

The first witness to be called by the Telephone Company in the arbitration hearings was Arnold W. Nichols, electrical engineer and physicist in charge of radio communication and research for the Western Electric Company. After the usual preliminaries of establishing his right to testify as an expert the witness was called upon to discuss the technical features of an ordinary telephone transmitter and its manner of operation. The variation in the strength of the electrical current caused by the vibrations of the human voice was explained. From this Mr. Guernsey took the witness to a discussion of vacuum tubes. For the benefit of the referee, Mr. Nichols gave an excellent description of what went on within such a tube when in operation. He explained how a vacuum tube could be used as a repeater or amplifier. He told how it could be used to impress upon a fading electric current, on which a telephone message was being sent, a new current that would restore to the message-carrier its former power. This, of course, demonstrated how important vacuum tubes had become in long-distance telephony.

The witness was given a lengthy memorandum containing a statement of the development of radio telephony. He was required to read this statement into the record, making such extemporaneous comment as he might desire from time to time. Hertz, Lodge and Marconi were brought into the general picture by a description of their contributions to the art. The Branley Coherer and the spark-gap devices were described, followed by the alternator devices conceived by Fessenden and Alexanderson. The development of the Fleming valve and the deForest Audion occupied considerable space. It will be remembered by those who have read the first volume of this series that the three-element vacuum tube, or Audion, had been purchased from Inventor deForest by the Telephone Company in 1913. The witness read into

HENRY B. THAYER
President of American Telephone and
Telegraph Company during early years.

WALTER S. GIFFORD
President of A. T. & T. One of chief
actors in Radio-Telephone controversy.

GEORGE E. FOLK
One of the Telephone Company's able
lawyers who figures in this story.

EDGAR S. BLOOM
Vice-President of A. T. & T. Active in
Sarnoff-Bloom negotiations.

the record the following summary of the Telephone Company's later efforts to develop the device:

"This device in the form in which it was left by deForest was not able to handle even the relatively small amounts of power required for a telephone repeater and was very unstable and erratic in its action. The Telephone Company began the systematic development of the device to make it a good telephone repeater, and by 1914 this development had progressed so far that not only were telephone repeaters available for the transcontinental line but the power capacity had been increased to such an extent, by the use of vacuum tubes, that it became possible to communicate by wireless from this country to Paris, Honolulu, and Darien. In this experiment by the Telephone Company, the vacuum tube was used as a high frequency generator, modulator, detector, and amplifier.

"Arnold, representing the Telephone Company, and Langmuir, representing the General Electric Company, discovered how to make the deForest tube available at about the same time. Their applications for patents were in interference in the Patent Office, which finally awarded the priority to Arnold. From this award an appeal was taken, which is now pending in the Court of Appeals of the District of Columbia." [4]

A lengthy and technical description of the manner in which the vacuum tube performed its various functions followed the foregoing introduction to the subject. Its use as an oscillating generator, as well as its availability as a detector of wireless waves, each received attention. The part played by the Western Electric Company, a Telephone Company subsidiary, in manufacturing and marketing the vacuum tube was spread upon the record.

The witness explained in detail the method of transmitting electromagnetic waves, describing the differing types of wave lengths and wave frequencies as well as methods of tuning essential to the reception of such waves in a receiving instrument. The referee was certainly given a large helping of technical information in his first day at the arbitration hearing. Tubes were on exhibit before him. A moving-picture demonstration was made of the operation showing the vacuum tube in action, especially in its function as a high-frequency generator. This film and the explanatory comments occupied the balance of the afternoon.

On the following day, at 10 A.M., May 21, 1924, the hearing was resumed with Mr. Nichols on the witness stand. There was more testimony concerning the vacuum tube. The matter covered in the previous day was reviewed. The referee questioned the witness at some

[4] Both inventors were eventually to lose in this contest, the Supreme Court declaring that the invention was not patentable over the prior art.

length concerning waves, frequencies, selectivity and the like. Mr. Nichols was then called upon to relate the story of the efforts of the research laboratories of the Telephone Company, and the Western Electric Company to develop a type of vacuum tube suitable for radio transmission. He explained that a carbon microphone would burn up if subjected to the current needed to send out genuine broadcasting impulses. Hence, "a device was required that would take the relatively weak voice modulation and impress upon the antenna current variations similar to those voice modulations and do that even when the antenna current was large."

Continuing with his story of the development of the vacuum tube:

"During 1914 the tube was still further developed as a power device so that by the latter end of 1914 we had available much larger tubes, and in 1915 it was decided to attempt radio telephone transmission over a moderate distance, making use of vacuum tubes throughout; that is, using tubes first as oscillating generators, then as modulators, then as amplifiers and then as detectors; that is to say, the tube was to perform all the necessary functions in both transmitting and receiving stations."

Mr. Nichols discussed the experiments made by his company in radio telephony by vacuum tubes, used in the manner described, at Montauk, L. I., and Wilmington, Del., in April, 1915. He stated that the experiment was successful, expressing the belief that this was the first time that vacuum tubes had ever been tried in all phases at once. He described later experiments in the same field, and particularly an experiment with 550 vacuum tubes used to amplify the power up to the intensity required for transmission. Experiments to test the possibility of transoceanic wireless telephony were described, and also the experience in collaboration with the United States Navy in the matter of wireless telephone sets for battleships. It appeared that in May, 1916, Secretary of the Navy Josephus Daniels had participated in an experimental wireless radio talk from the battleship *New Hampshire*.

The witness traced the developments in which his company had co-operated with the United States Navy during the World War, showing that by January, 1918, the Western Electric Company was manufacturing in quantity telephone transmitting and receiving apparatus for the navy. More than 2000 sets for this purpose were manufactured for use on war craft. After the close of the War the Western Electric Company decided to develop a radio telephone system for ship-to-shore intercommunication. Two shore stations for this purpose were built in the spring of 1919, one at Deal Beach, N. J., and the other at Green Harbor, Mass. Thus it became possible to discover the problems to be encountered in this type of communication and, by experiment, to endeavor to solve them. Apparently the technicians encountered great difficulties when using more than one transmitter at the same time. Interference proved a very baffling problem indeed.

The superheterodyne system was then put into operation which helped but did not cure the interference difficulty. Out of the experiments had been built up a system of two-way or duplex-radio telephony. Broadcasting tests were said to have been tried at the Deal Beach Station in May, 1920, in the hope that listening amateurs might pick up the telephonic messages. Phonograph records, and cornet music were broadcast. The experiment of reading selections from current journals was also tried with encouraging results. When Mr. Guernsey offered a bundle of letters alleged to have been received from listening amateurs, Mr. Fish reserved his right to object to their reception.

Letters were read by the witness, after which he was called upon for information as to experiments in July, 1920, between the Catalina Islands and Long Beach, California, a distance of about thirty miles.

The next important experimentation was apparently conducted at RCA's transmitting station at Rocky Point, L. I., in the summer and fall of 1922, the Radio Corporation having permitted Telephone engineers the use of the station. These were the famous trans-Atlantic tests, held December 31, 1922, when the engineers were successful in transmitting the human voice across the ocean from New York City to England. The dramatic story was told of how guests, sixty in all, provided with head sets, were able to receive the speech in London. The witness was then led through a long recital of the technical features of radio broadcasting, involving microphone problems, pickup apparatus, loud speakers, head sets, and the like. He discussed experiments made by the Western Electric Company in developing loud speaking receivers, and especially in adapting them to use in ball parks and halls, sketching these experiments in considerable detail. The advent of the vacuum tube repeater was described.

Mr. Fish finally interposed objections to the extensive reading by the witness, arguing that Mr. Nichols should be confined to what he knew, and should not be permitted to read prepared statements. Mr. Fish called attention to the report of the Federal Trade Commission, claiming that it contained a full general statement of the background and history of radio broadcasting. Mr. Guernsey argued for his method of presentation, Referee Boyden finally pacifying the lawyers.

After a recess, Mr. Nichols resumed the stand and discussed high frequency magnetic waves modulated by the human voice, illustrating for the benefit of the referee from models present in the hearing room. This occupied a considerable time. The condensers used in telephone instruments came in for a thorough discussion, after which the witness was taken for a cross-examination by Mr. Fish. The first questions in cross-examination had to do with radio head sets in relation to the telephone system, and how they compared with head sets used by radio listeners. Mr. Fish questioned the witness on the length of time the Western Electric Company had been selling loud speakers like the one in evidence. Later he pointed out that the patent mark on the exhibit gave three dates in the year 1921. The witness was unable to give the information requested. One very pertinent inquiry was whether the Telephone Company had ever employed loud speakers with wired telephony except on special occasions. The witness parried the question by demanding to know what was meant by special occasions, but was finally obliged to answer that loud speakers were not used in the ordinary subscriber's station.

Mr. Fish then pressed the witness to admit that the loud speaker on exhibit was designed for radio rather than for telephone. Mr. Nichols answered that it was not. Whereupon Mr. Fish tried to get him to admit that the transformer used with them had been designed for radio conditions. Again the witness refused to commit himself. Telephone receiving sets were next discussed, but the witness could not state whether the Western Electric Company or the Telephone Company had ever put these sets on the market. Mr. Fish demanded that the witness get information as to "when first they were sold and under what conditions they were sold." Then followed quite an extensive questioning in connection with exhibits in the hearing room. The witness was again wary, and in some cases declared that others were better qualified to answer than he. Mr. Fish questioned the witness on the value of vacuum tubes used as repeaters in making it possible to telephone long distances over wire of reasonably small size.

Sec. 65. Other Telephone Company Witnesses.

Otto B. Blackwell was called as the second witness in behalf of the Telephone Group. It appeared that Mr. Blackwell was one of the engineers in the research and development department of the American Telephone Company. Mr. Guernsey gave him a written statement to be used as the basis of his testimony. He described the carrier-current system, explaining the method by which several messages could be impressed upon the same wire by using differing frequencies, afterward unscrambling them by a number of selecting circuits corresponding to the frequency output of the sending instruments. This was all very technical and no objection was raised to the method of presentation. The direct examination occupied the balance of the day. The hearing was adjourned to May 22nd.

On the following day, at 10 A.M., the parties met again. Before resuming cross-examination, Mr. Fish again read into the record certain portions of the contract relating to the making and selling of broadcasting apparatus, and brought out the question of the Telephone Company's claim of right to control under its patents the sale of broadcasting equipment. He requested of Mr. Guernsey copies of the contracts by which sales were made. Mr. Guernsey agreed to furnish copies of the contracts. He countered with a request for information from the Radio Corporation group first, as to when it had commenced to manufacture and sell head sets and, second, when the Radio Corporation or any member of it had commenced to sell loud speaker receivers and horns and, third, he desired a statement showing to what extent members of the Radio Group had sold transmitting or broadcasting stations and also to what extent they were selling condensers, head sets, horns, and batteries. There was also a request for figures showing extent of sales of receiving sets and loud speakers. In the cross-examination of Mr. Blackwell, Mr. Fish sought to bring out when carrier currents were first used on power circuits, pressing the witness to admit that such use was relatively recent. The witness was unable to state whether it was before or since signing of the contract in controversy.

The third witness in behalf of the Telephone Group was William E. Harkness, vice-president of the American Telephone Company and manager of the broadcasting station known as WEAF. He was called upon to describe in some detail the physical equipment of the station and its manner of operation. He told of the functions of the different employees of the station, and especially of sales research under the commercial department. He gave information as to permanent telephone connections between Station WCAP in Washington and WEAF in New York, also between the latter station and WJAR in Providence. He stated that their wires were secured from the long lines department of the Telephone Company, and that the radio stations had to pay for the service. The extent of radio coverage by broadcasts from WEAF was discussed. Responses from the radio audience were reported on. Different types of organizations came in for a good deal of attention. The witness was asked to distinguish between the ordinary radio listener and the so-called radio amateur, which he did, stating that there had been considerable controversy between the two classes. The radio amateurs, it seemed, were using their transmitting sets in a way to interfere with radio reception. The Telephone Company introduced into evidence, and caused to be marked as an exhibit, "a list of amateur radio organizations previous to July 1, 1920," this being made up largely from issues of the *Wireless Age* from October, 1918, to September, 1920. At this point a question arose as to whether the *Wireless Age* is "a publication owned by the Radio Corporation of America." Mr. Fish objected that during half the period in question there was no Radio Corporation in existence, hence it could not be responsible for accuracy of the exhibit. After a recess witness was taken for cross-examination by Mr. Fish. His first inquiry was concerned with a questionnaire sent out by the Telephone Company to radio listeners. The witness stated that the questionnaire was sent to 25,000 correspondents, about 55% of whom returned answers. It appeared that the first question related to type and make of radio sets being used by the correspondent. Mr. Fish desired tabulation on this point, but Mr. Harkness replied that they were not yet available. The witness was questioned on what was done when stations applied for wire connections for broadcasting purposes. He gave a general description of the process of supplying wire lines. At the end of Mr. Harkness' testimony, Mr. Guernsey introduced affidavits with reference to transmission of music on one-way fire alarm circuits as early as 1905. This is said to have occurred in Montana.

The fourth witness for the Telephone Group was Claude C. Rose, a lawyer in the patent department of the American Telephone Company. He was questioned concerning the use that was being made of telephone lines for the transmission of music, news, and other forms of entertainment. This led to a discussion of the history of the telephone from its early days under Bell to 1922. Thus developed an historical recital that occupied a great deal of hearing time. The cross-examination by Mr. Fish was halted by adjournment at the end of the day, but was resumed on May 23, 1924, at 10 A.M. This proved to be brief and unimportant.

The fifth witness for the Telephone Company was Albert W. Drake, the general commercial manager of the long lines department of the American Telephone Company. He described in detail services rendered by his department, especially to such important customers as the Associated Press, United Press, and other news services. He also pointed out that the Telephone Company was furnishing one-way service to brokerage customers. Cross-examination of the witness failed to bring out anything of consequence. It was followed by a discussion by counsel of statistics as to the amount being spent by the American public in radio, one estimate being $150,000,000 during the calendar year 1923.

John B. Harlow, the sixth witness for the Telephone Company, was the telephone sales engineer for the Western Electric Company. He testified as to a patented device for indicating at remote points the position of power switches, the same having been patented by the Western Electric Company on February 18, 1919, although systems of the same general character had been sold by his company as early as 1914. It appeared that in 1920 it was found desirable to sell these devices through the General Electric Company. Cross-examination of the witness was conducted by Albert G. Davis, the matter being within the patent field in which Mr. Davis was an expert. Mr. Davis brought out that the remote control switchboard idea was embodied in the Panama Canal regulation of the opening and closing of gates in the various locks of the canal. He then got the witness to admit the similarity of the device to an invention by H. P. Davis, assigned to the Westinghouse Company in 1904, and to various other inventions assigned to the General Electric Company between 1905 and 1910.

After a recess Mr. Guernsey, in behalf of the Telephone Company, introduced a verified statement by the comptroller of the Western Electric Company covering the years 1918 to 1923, showing the total sales of the company to have been as follows:

1918	$145,226,000
1919	135,722,000
1920	206,112,000
1921	189,765,000
1922	210,941,000
1923	255,177,000

In response to a question by Referee Boyden, Mr. Guernsey stated that radio sales were "pretty nearly negligible."

Various radio and telephone appliances were offered as exhibits and explained. A catalogue of RCA, dated September 1, 1921, was introduced as having bearings on RCA's current contention as to amateurs being radio listeners. This was followed by other RCA publications; by copies of the Government Radio Service Bulletin; by copies of Federal laws concerning amateur stations and radio operators. A great deal of time was devoted to reading into the record excerpts from these bulletins, magazines, and clippings. Even annual reports of the directors of RCA were offered as exhibits in the case. Speeches by Herbert Hoover, the Secretary of Commerce, were also offered as a part of the Telephone presentation.

The arbitration resumed on May 26, 1924, at 11 A.M. Mr. Guernsey continued with quotations from Herbert Hoover's comments on the importance of radio broadcasting. He also introduced statements by witnesses who had appeared before the Committee on Merchant Marine Fisheries in March, 1924, a good part of such evidence being spread upon the records.

The seventh witness called in behalf of the Telephone Company was E. B. Craft, chief engineer of the Western Electric Company. He was asked to furnish evidence concerning loud speakers sold by the Western Electric Company. A large part of this testimony was technical, intended to show how loud speakers were used in public address systems.

The witness was asked whether he knew anything about the license agreement between General Electric and the Radio Corporation until after the contract of July 1, 1920. Mr. Folk, of the legal staff, interposed that while they knew there was an agreement, they did not know its terms. Whereupon Mr. Fish interrupted the testimony and called Mr. Folk to the witness stand. Mr. Folk asserted that while his company knew that there was some kind of agreement between the two corporations, they had not seen the terms of the same. Mr. Guernsey and Mr. Fish finally admitted that it made no difference whether the Telephone Company knew of the terms of the contract or not.

Sec. 66. The Radio Group Presents Its Case.

Mr. Fish began the presentation of his case by reading from the hearings already quoted by Mr. Guernsey, particularly testimony by William E. Harkness, the manager of Station WEAF. He introduced the agreement of November 20, 1919, between the General Electric Company and the Radio Corporation of America, and also the agreement between the General Electric Company and the American Telephone Company, of July, 1920, as well as other cross-licensing agreements between the various corporations. These were marked as exhibits in the ordinary manner. The history of the United Fruit Company occupied the time until recess. Mr. Fish later offered similar evidence concerning the Marconi Company, Westinghouse, and General Electric. He also brought in annual reports of the Telephone Company.

The first witness for the Radio Group was Frank Conrad, electrical engineer in the employ of the Westinghouse Company. Mr. Conrad related his experience with the company, and how he eventually became interested in wireless telephony. He spoke of the experimental Station 8XK, tracing its history prior to the War and during the War period. He then read from a prepared statement, giving an excellent history of the circumstances leading to the establishment of Station KDKA. His experiments with short-wave broadcasting were also explained. The reaction of radio audiences in various parts of the world were discussed. The witness was taken back to the beginning of KDKA and was asked to outline the chief landmarks in radio history up to the time of the arbitration hearings. Photographs were identified, newspaper clippings discussed and, upon cross-examination by Mr. Guernsey, the witness went into greater detail in regard to his experimental work for the Westinghouse Company. He was asked to comment on the work of inventors from Fessenden to the latest of those who had contributed to the development of wireless telephony. This testimony occupied the balance of the day.

The hearings were resumed on May 27, 1924, at 10 A.M., with Mr. Conrad still under cross-examination. The discussion was technical in its nature, having to do with microphones, tubes, short wave and the like. They discussed transformers. The witness was also called upon to explain how church services were broadcast over KDKA.

John V. L. Hogan was the second witness introduced on behalf of the Radio Group. He was a consulting engineer, specializing in radio. He gave an interesting story of his experience as laboratory assistant for Lee deForest in 1906 and 1907, his later connection with Reginald A. Fessenden, and his work at Brant Rock. Mr. Hogan was called upon to explain the principles of radio transmission, the methods employed, different phases of the art, etc. His testimony was actually of a technical nature, but was couched in language that the layman might easily understand. He was called upon to discuss various pages in his book, *Outline of Radio,* which was offered in evidence. After a recess, the witness was asked to discuss certain technical problems of loud speakers of various types. Mr. Hogan was asked to give in condensed form the general history of technical and scientific development of radio, as well as its commercial development. This occupied the balance of the day.

On May 28, 1924, at 10 A.M., hearings were resumed with Mr. Hogan still on the stand, and still discussing the history of the art. His definition of radio amateurs had special bearing upon the present inquiry because of the Radio Corporation's contentions. He stated that the American Radio Relay League construed the word "amateur" to mean anyone who holds a license from the Department of Commerce to operate a broadcasting device. Mr. Guernsey objected to this evidence because it was based upon conversations and statements of officials of the League. The witness then read from his book, *Outline of Radio,* the portions relating to amateur activities. Mr. Hogan finally called attention to resolutions adopted by the Hoover Radio Conference of 1922, in which an amateur was defined as "one who operates a radio station, transmitting, receiving or both without pay or commercial gain, merely for personal interest or in connection with an organization of like interests."

The witness gave a long discussion of the carrier-current phase of radio transmission. His testimony was interrupted by a recess after which he explained various types of electrical aids for the deaf, enabling them to hear sounds otherwise inaudible. In cross-examination he was taken again over the matter of audiphones, and then brought back to an historical discussion, particularly of vacuum tubes and the Arnold-Langmuir controversy. The deForest-Armstrong litigation was likewise discussed. The witness was still on the stand at the time of adjournment.

On May 29, 1924, the same line of inquiry was followed. In re-direct examination, the witness testified as to different types of radio receiving sets and the technical features of each. Mr. Guernsey took the witness in hand for another session of cross-examination, discussing tuning of sets by the listener. After a recess, Referee Boyden made a statement for the benefit of counsel, tending to show the impressions that he had gained of the state of radio development, and the uncertainties that he desired to have cleared up. One of these related to aids for the deaf. Whereupon Mr. Fish read into the record extracts from a book by an eminent specialist on diseases of the ear.

This was followed by extensive excerpts from a publication known as *Radio News,* and another called *Wireless Age.* Mr. Fish also introduced a folder of letters having a bearing upon the present controversy; in fact, there was a great deal of correspondence that had passed between the Telephone Company and the Radio Corporation officials. All these became a part of the documentary evidence of the case. Even letters from radio listeners were introduced, the entire day being devoted to this type of evidence. The next session of the arbitration was held on June 3, 1924, at which time there was an exchange of information that had been requested by each side.

The third witness called by the Radio Corporation group was John Frazier, who had charge of the telephone system for the Westinghouse Company. He described in detail the method of operation of the circuits used by the broadcasting stations of Westinghouse, particularly those supplied to KDKA by the Pittsburgh Allegheny Telephone Company. When cross-examined by Mr. Guernsey, he amplified statements given in direct examination and explained particularly the method of broadcasting the services of the First Presbyterian Church of Pittsburgh. This led to a discussion of the system of switches in connection with pick-up lines, the testimony becoming decidedly technical. There was re-examination by Mr. Fish, and re-cross-examination by Mr. Guernsey, all of the same general nature.

The Radio Group's fourth witness was H. A. Sullivan, who was at once turned over to Mr. Guernsey for cross-examination concerning figures as to sales that had been submitted as exhibits by RCA. An item of 127,000 transmitting tubes had aroused the lawyer's interest. He pressed the witness to admit that the tubes in question were really to be used for generating high-frequency current, but Sullivan refused to commit himself to anything more than that the engineers had labeled the tubes as transmitting tubes.

Charles B. Popenoe was the fifth witness for the Radio Group. Mr. Popenoe was the manager of Stations WJZ and WJY in New York City. He testified concerning the necessity of pick-up wires as an adjunct to any radio station that would serve the public. Speeches, grand opera, concerts, sporting events, church services, plays and musical comedies could not be broadcast without this system of pick-up lines. He submitted a list of such events that had been broadcast by his stations between May 15, 1923, and May 1, 1924, showing that 978 major events had been picked up in this manner.

Mr. Popenoe was called upon to explain to the referee the main lines that had been established in New York City. In cross-examination much time was devoted to remote control lines, all of which would seem to have emphasized the points that the Telephone Company was least eager to bring out—the necessity of such lines, and the fact that the stations relied upon the Western Union for service which was desired from the Telephone Company. This testimony concluded the Radio Group's main evidence.

Sec. 67. Rebuttal and Arguments.

The testimony being concluded, the attorneys for the contending parties submitted certain documents in rebuttal. Mr. Guernsey, for the Telephone Group, offered a sheaf of letters that had been exchanged between Mr. Gifford, vice-president of the Telephone Company, and Mr. Tripp of the Westinghouse Company, between Mr. Gifford and Mr. Davis of the General Electric, replies from Mr. Davis; letters exchanged between Mr. Thayer and Mr. Owen D. Young; these were marked as exhibits. The attorneys questioned each other as to the contents or meaning of the various exhibits submitted. The questions and answers were spread upon the record.

Referee Boyden finally stated that it was his belief that the case might be concluded on the following day. Mr. Fish demurred, saying that he was unwilling to argue the case until after he had completed a brief. Mr. Guernsey opposed any postponement of the oral arguments, advancing various reasons for his unwillingness to consent to delay, one of them being that he had arranged soon to go abroad with the Bar Association group on a visit to London. One portion of his argument was as follows:

"We all know that we are able to adjust hearings in cases but it seems to me that we ought not to make so much delay before we get briefs in. We have been postponed for this and that and the other for a good while. It is approximately six months since this contract was signed. It took us about two months before we agreed to make the contract—before we could get it signed, and from that time there has been delay, delay, and it does not seem to me that this ought to go over as much as three weeks."

After somewhat of a debate between the attorneys, Referee Boyden decided to set the case down for argument on June 23, 1924, with the understanding that on the morning following the present session all other details would be concluded.

On June 4, 1924, the group met as agreed. G. E. Folk, general patent attorney of the Telephone Company, was put on the stand by Mr. Guernsey to testify as to negotiations for wire lines by Station KDKA prior to the drawing of the contract of June 30, 1921, between the Radio Corporation, General Electric and Westinghouse. He stated that in advance of the execution and delivery of the consent of the Telephone Company to the contract aforesaid, he may have known that there was a radio station, but he had no recollection of any information regarding so-called pick-up lines. To the best of his knowledge, no one in behalf of the Telephone Company had had knowledge of the situation. Mr. Fish declined to cross-examine the witness.

After submitting some more documentary evidence, the rebuttal was closed. The Radio Group then offered proof in sur-rebuttal. It began with a statement by Mr. Fish in connection with the Arnold-Langmuir interference which was, of course, quite complicated. The attorney reviewed the history of the controversy. The suit brought by Westinghouse against the deForest Company under the Armstrong patents was another matter discussed. The Telephone Company countered with what is known as sur-sur-rebuttal proofs. Mr. Folk was recalled to the witness stand to discuss the issues raised by Mr. Fish with reference to the deForest suit. Mr. Fish cross-examined the witness. Referee Boyden also participated in the questioning. The discussion seemed to be to what extent the Telephone Company was assisting the deForest Company in the interference case. L. F. H. Betts was called as a witness by the Radio Group, and was examined by Mr. Fish and cross-examined by Mr. Guernsey. Little was added to the evidence already submitted, but it was believed that sufficient evidence had been presented by both sides to give the referee a working knowledge of actual conditions of the radio industry. It was understood by all that the task of the referee was largely of a judicial nature—the passing upon a complicated document whose legal construction had long been in doubt. The crucial portion of the arbitration was recognized to be the arguments of counsel.

In the interval between the close of the hearings and the appointed day for arguing the case, an interesting development occurred. Mr. Fish wrote to Albert G. Davis that he was greatly troubled over the matter of television and picture point.

"We cannot make an argument that seems to us even plausible to the effect that this is telegraphy. It seems to us that it is outside the subjects specially contemplated in the contract of July 1, 1920, and therefore open to both parties. I understand that this is the attitude of the Telephone Group. Can you get someone to write an argument in favor of your view that this is telegraphy? It may be that Terry or Schairer could do it.

"Or, is it not better to concede the point?

"We have not yet received the copy of Dr. Harris' statement as to the device for helping the deaf. I assume that this will come to us from your office in New York."

Under date of June 7, 1924, Mr. Davis wrote to Mr. Fish's associate the following letter:

My dear Mr. Lyman:

I will write a section on the television matter when I return from Minneapolis. Certainly we cannot concede the point. Whatever else we argue, we must argue that if systems of this character are used for transmitting commercial telegrams, such operation comes in our exclusive field.

Yours truly,

(Signed) ALBERT G. DAVIS

In accordance with the agreement for the postponement, the parties met again on June 23, 1924, for final arguments in the case. Mr. Fish submitted a brief of 234 pages. The arguments were of great length and very learned in their nature; the two arguments filling about 300 pages of typed transcript of record. These arguments may be summarized as follows:

At the outset of his argument Mr. Guernsey conceded that the claims of his company as to wireless telegraphy were too broad. There was no contention as to transoceanic wireless telephone service. The question of whether broadcasting could be termed a public service received considerable attention, the Telephone Group insisting that it should be so regarded. Mr. Guernsey discussed various phases of radio which, he argued, sustained his contention, even quoting speeches by RCA officials at the dedication of Stations WJZ and WJY to prove the point. Taking up the proposition of the true meaning of the term "amateur," he made out a strong case for distinguishing the true radio amateur from the ordinary radio listener. He ridiculed the contention of the Radio Group that the mere tuning of a radio set could make the listener an amateur. In combating the suggestion of the Radio Group that the Telephone Company had had no interest in the manufacturing field prior to July 1, 1920, he called attention to the fact that the Western Electric Company, the manufacturing branch of the company, had done a great volume of such business for years. The right to make, use and sell transmitting apparatus was declared to be the exclusive right of the Telephone Company, not only because of the alleged public service nature of broadcasting, but also by virtue of grants contained in the contract.

Mr. Guernsey argued earnestly for his contention that his company had a right to make and sell radio receiving apparatus. One typical passage of argument was as follows:

"What was that agreement of the parties? It is a reciprocal agreement. No exclusive licenses for receiving sets is granted. Each party was to have the right to make, use, lease and sell receiving sets for direct use in connection with its own transmitting stations, and each party was to respect this right in the other. In the nature of these things, the rights were not absolutely enforceable. The parties knew that. They knew that receiving apparatus that we sold for any purpose could be used to receive what they might transmit, and we knew that any receiving apparatus that they sold for any purpose could be used to receive what we might transmit. I suppose that they contented themselves with this statement of this reciprocal agreement upon the theory that it was equitable and it was the best that they could do under the circumstances.

"Because broadcasting is a public service, it and the receiving apparatus used in connection with it, come within the general grant to the Telephone Company 'for all wireless telephone apparatus connected to or operated as a part of a public service telephone communication system.'

"Receiving apparatus, moreover, is essential in every leased-wire commercial use that is referred to."

Mr. Guernsey argued briefly on a variety of topics including television, which he contended was wire telegraphy and the exclusive right of the Telephone Company. When he reached the topic of loud speakers he argued at some length to convince the referee that it involved wire telephony. A lawyer named Tanner, who represented the Western Electric Company, was called upon by Mr. Guernsey to argue certain points peculiarly within his own jurisdiction. Mr. Tanner discussed the matter of remote control of power switches, arguing against the contention that the General Electric Company had exclusive rights in this field. He contended also that his company could not be held responsible for the use which a customer might make of a product manufactured by the Western Electric Company.

Mr. Fish then opened his argument for the Radio Group but, the day being far spent, the hearing was adjourned until June 24, 1924. When the proceedings reopened on the following day Mr. Fish pointed out that at the time when the contract was made the Telephone Company had never made or sold radio equipment. On the other hand, the General Electric Company had been in the business for many years. The Telephone Company was engaged in nationwide communications by wire telephony with 15,000,000 subscribers. This was the field that it sought to protect in the contract of July 1, 1920. In discussing public service Mr. Fish declared that the phrase had application to the service long performed by the Telephone Company, but had no possible application to the then unknown service of radio broadcasting, for which the listener pays nothing. He referred to Station WEAF as a private enterprise. The fact that broadcasting is subject to regulation is due to the police power of the State, under which many activities are required to be in order, such as smoke nuisance, ventilation and sanitation.

In discussing the question of broadcast receivers Mr. Fish aptly termed it "one of the boiling points" of the controversy. He made an able and effective argument tending to prove that the right was exclusive in the Radio Group. The transmitting apparatus question was also ably handled. In his argument to convince the referee that the word "amateurs" included broadcast listeners he encountered great difficulty, but he strove valiantly to maintain his point. The loud speaker matter came in for attention. A discussion of leased wires and pick-up wires occupied the remainder of Mr. Fish's able argument.

Thus the formal hearings closed June 24, 1924, and the fate of an industrial empire was left with Roland W. Boyden. It is probable that in the history of big business in America no more momentous decision ever rested upon the wisdom and fairness of a single individual. Even judges in the courts may be appealed from to some higher tribunal, or at least to a tribunal composed of several learned justices but, in this case, by agreement of the parties, Mr. Boyden was to render a decision from which there was to be no appeal.

CHAPTER
NINE

An Inconclusive Victory for RCA

GEORGE F. McCLELLAND
Vice-President and General Manager of NBC during its formative years.
Greatly beloved by his associates, who mourned his untimely death.

Section 68. Radio Developments During a Presidential Election.

THE LONG PERIOD OF SUSPENSE following the close of the arbitration hearings—Mr. Boyden's decision not to be handed down even in a tentative form until November, 1924—was no doubt somewhat trying to the officials of the rival groups. Neither side could feel assurance of victory. It was realized that the issue hinged not upon the evidence submitted, since that was intended merely to give the referee a word picture of the radio industry, but upon a careful analysis and interpretation of the terms of the contract of July 1, 1920. Inasmuch as the chief item in dispute, measured in dollars and cents, related to the right to manufacture and sell radio receiving sets, the delay was undoubtedly more disquieting to the Telephone Company than to the Radio Group.

As for RCA, every month of delay meant additional gross revenue from this source. Even before the hearings had closed the volume of radio sales for the first six months of the year 1924 had exceeded that of the entire year of 1923. July, August, September and October were equally productive. More than four million dollars a month now came pouring into the coffers of RCA—thanks to the skillful management of the sales department. Young in years, tireless in effort and usually working far into the night, Mr. Sarnoff was an industrial chieftain who could literally work miracles. He was fortunate also in the loyalty of the sales department. Elmer E. Bucher, its general manager, taking inspiration from the example of his chief, was continually on the firing line, enlarging the territory of sales and entrenching his company's gains in all parts of the nation. Mr. Bucher, it should be pointed out, was not by training or experience a commercial salesman. Mr. Sarnoff had selected him for this important job because of his ability, enthusiasm and loyalty at a time when no one knew anything about radio sales. It was pioneer work in a brand new industry.

The radio broadcasting sector was far from quiet during the summer of 1924. If RCA had an advantage over the Telephone Company in the matter of sales of radio equipment, the advantage was all the other way in the contest between the rival radio broadcasting stations. Station WEAF had by this time perfected its technique in network broadcasting. The universal interest aroused by the national conventions of the Republican and Democratic parties, held in the summer of 1924, gave great impetus to the growth of radio networks. Even before the Republican Convention, which opened June 10, 1924, the Telephone Company had connected by special wires its two operating stations, WEAF and WCAP, with twelve widely separated cities. The proceedings of the conventions were to be broadcast simultaneously over this extensive network.[1] The success of the experiment led to enlargements of the network, so that by autumn we find the following extensive hookup—twenty-two stations carrying a speech delivered by President Coolidge on October 23, 1924:

Key Stations—WEAF, New York City—WCAP, Washington

WJAR	Providence	WMAF	So. Dartmouth
WEEI	Boston	WGR	Buffalo
WCAE	Pittsburgh	WDBH	Worcester
WGY	Schenectady	WSAI	Cincinnati
WGN	Chicago	WOC	Davenport
KSD	St. Louis	WDAF	Kansas City
WOAW	Omaha	KLZ	Denver
KLX	Oakland	KFOA	Seattle
KFI	Los Angeles	KHJ	Los Angeles
KPO	San Francisco	KGW	Portland, Ore.

In the meantime, RCA had done its utmost to overcome the handicap imposed upon it by the refusal of the Telephone Company to furnish leased lines for network broadcasting. Due to the efforts of its resourceful chief broadcast engineer, Dr. Alfred N. Goldsmith, RCA had accomplished a network of its own—a tiny network to be sure, but a genuine network. The manner in which this was accomplished has already thus been set forth in *History of Radio to 1926:* [2]

"WJZ applied to the Western Union for a special line to Schenectady, N. Y., by which WGY and WJZ were hooked up for the convention broadcasts. This scheme worked so well that it was decided to do the like with Station WRC in Washington. Instead of approaching Western Union for a line to Washington, which would have given away the network project, WJZ applied to the Postal Telegraph Company for a line from Washington to a suburb of Philadelphia (Conshohocken) where a repeater station was established. From this point was a line to WJZ. Neither Postal Telegraph nor Western Union were at first aware that they were participating in a bold defiance of the powerful American Telephone Company's ban on network broadcasting by a competitor. Thus WJZ contrived to have WRC and WGY on a special network."

The presidential election of 1924 became deeply indebted to radio broadcasting. President Calvin Coolidge, the Republican standard bearer, a relatively colorless figure as a platform orator, now emerged

[1] For story of radio in the campaign see Archer, *History of Radio to 1926*, pp. 317-330.

[2] Page 344.

as a powerful radio personality. His voice proved ideally suited to radio broadcasting. While his election would no doubt have been assured even without the miraculous agency that came to his aid, yet there is no doubt that the overwhelming nature of the victory that he won in November, 1924, was due in large measure to his radio-reported speeches.

It is probably true that the national election had important bearing on a development that was inaugurated during the summer of 1924. Complaints of interference between broadcasting stations, due to the custom of assigning to all stations the same wave length, had caused the Bureau of Standards to experiment with the assigning of differing wave lengths to different stations in the same locality. Careful tests were made not only of broadcasting results, but also as to the ability of radio stations to adhere to assigned frequencies. In this contest the Westinghouse engineers scored an outstanding triumph. Station WBZ, in Springfield, Mass., Westinghouse owned and operated, made the highest score of all stations that participated in the tests. With an assigned frequency of 890 kilocycles it had not deviated even a fraction of a per cent during the months of the contest.

The result of the experimentation was reflected in the Third Radio Conference held in Washington, in October, prior to the national election. Like its predecessors this conference was attended by the leaders of the radio industry. The action of Secretary Hoover in assigning differing wave lengths to various stations, as he had been doing for some months, had encountered opposition in certain quarters. The leaders of the industry realized that the failure of the national congress to enact legislation on this point rendered the Hoover assignments of dubious value should contest arise in the courts. For this reason they gathered loyally around Mr. Hoover to manifest their approval of the innovation.

David Sarnoff attended this conference. He took occasion to propose that super-power broadcasting stations be authorized as an experiment in various parts of the country. The idea encountered violent opposition from some of the smaller station owners, despite the fact that by super-power Mr. Sarnoff meant stations of 50 kilowatts. A compromise was finally reached by which the Secretary of Commerce was advised to issue revocable licenses for a limited number of experimental stations of 50-kilowatt capacity.

Sec. 69. "Draft Report" of Arbitration Decision.

The eagerly awaited "Draft Decision" of Referee Boyden was finally announced on November 13, 1924. By draft decision is meant a tentative decision, subject to alteration in minor details by the referee.

Roland W. Boyden's letter, in duplicate to counsel for the rival groups, contained the following paragraph:

"I fix December 6, 1924, as the time limit for the submission to me of such suggestions as you may care to make, which suggestions may include whatever you think worthwhile, whether in form or substance. Upon submission of your suggestions to me, will each of you furnish the other with a copy. Upon receipt of this copy of the other's suggestions, will each of you notify me at once whether you wish to reply. If either does, I will then fix a time limit for replies."

It is apparent from contemporary records that Mr. Boyden had guarded his long deliberations so very carefully that neither side had had any advance conjectures as to the trend of his thoughts. It burst upon them, therefore, with joyful surprise to the one side and utter dismay to the other. The nature of the decision is epitomized in the following radiogram dated November 14, 1924, sent by President Harbord to Owen D. Young, who was then on the high seas:

"DRAFT DECISION BOYDEN JUST RECEIVED (STOP) APPEARS SO FAR AS STUDIED TO GIVE US EXCLUSIVE RIGHT SALE RECEIVING SETS RIGHT TO PICKUP WIRES RIGHT TO INSTALL SYSTEMS IN HOTELS AND APARTMENT HOUSES PROBABLE RIGHTS TO SELL LOUD SPEAKERS AND HEAD SETS IN CONNECTION WITH RECEIVING SETS ALTHOUGH STATED TO BE IN WIRE FIELD AND GIVES RIGHT TO COLLECT TOLLS FOR BROADCASTING (STOP)"

On November 17th a second radiogram was dispatched to Mr. Young by General Harbord. It read as follows:

"FURTHER STUDY BOYDEN DECISION SHOWS TELEPHONE GROUP HAS NO RIGHTS BROADCAST TRANSMISSION UNDER PATENTS RADIO GROUP (STOP)"

One of the clearest of the brief summaries of the vital points in the draft decision made at the time was contained in the following letter from Albert G. Davis to the president of the General Electric Company:

Schenectady, N. Y., Nov. 15, 1924

Gerard Swope, Esq., President,
New York Office.

My dear Mr. Swope:

I have received a copy of Mr. Boyden's draft report in the arbitration proceedings. He gives December 6, 1924, as the time limit for the submission to him of such suggestions as either side cares to make for the revision of the report.

There are so many issues and the whole matter is so complex that it is difficult in a short letter to make a satisfactory summary of the decision. I will try to give you the most important.

The really vital question was with reference to broadcasting. The controversy on this point turned on the construction of paragraph V-4 (d) (2) in connection with (3) and in connection with (e) of the same section.

BROADCASTING RECEPTION

The Telephone Company claimed that the only rights which we had were broadcasting receivers for the reception of news, music and entertainment broadcasted by our own stations, while, on the other hand, the Telephone Company had the full right under its own patents to sell all kinds of wireless telephone receiving apparatus. The arbitrator rejects these contentions. He holds that our rights with reference to broadcasting reception are for the reception of any news, music and entertainment, and that the Telephone Company has no rights under its patents, or under any patents, to make, lease or sell wireless telephone receiving apparatus, except as part of or for direct use in connection with transmitting apparatus made by it. He holds that the expression "as part of or for direct use in connection with" refers to a combination of a receiver and a transmitter corresponding to the receiver and transmitter of an ordinary desk telephone, overruling the Telephone Company's contention that the expression "direct use" meant using the receiver to listen to the transmitter. This is, of course, of the utmost importance.

He also holds that the loud speaker, when used for receiving radio, is in our field.

BROADCASTING TRANSMISSION

I gather from the decision that the arbitrator feels that the Telephone Company has no broadcasting transmission licenses under our patents, though, for some reason, he does not seem to decide this point squarely. There is an intimation that we have acquiesced in WEAF and WCAP.

The principal controversy in connection with broadcasting transmission related to the use of pickups and to the right to broadcast for tolls. All of these points were decided in our favor. We can use as many pickups as we want to and make the wires as long as we want to. For example, we can continue to use the wire between New York and Schenectady and to pick up football games at New Haven and Cambridge, etc.

Similarly, and this has to do more with reception than transmission, he holds, if I understand the decision correctly, that the equipment of an apartment house with a broadcasting receiver wired to loud speakers in the various rooms of the house is in our field.

OTHER MATTERS

He decides rather against us on the meaning of the word amateur. This would be very serious if he had not decided in our favor on the points above mentioned. He gives the term a meaning so limited that it does not include a broadcast listener.

The expression "public service" and similar expressions in the contract are construed to exclude broadcasting and to relate to the kind of public service furnished by the Bell System. The expression "leased wires" is similarly construed. It was by giving a broad construction to these expressions that the Telephone Company made its claim to broadcasting reception where an admittance fee was charged or in apartment houses, clubs, hotels, etc. All of these contentions were overruled.

He decides against us on the audiphone, the device for helping the deaf to hear, holding that is in the field of the Telephone Company.

He decides against us on the matter of broadcasting by carrier current over power lines.

He decides in our favor the point with reference to the use of indicating devices in connection with switchboards.

He decides against us one point in connection with transoceanic telephone. The contract provides in substance that if we do not furnish wireless service, the Telephone Company may build its own stations which, however, we have the right to take over at any time on reimbursing the Telephone Company. It was our idea that our only obligation under this clause was to furnish one station in this country capable of transmitting telephone speech. But the arbitrator holds that we are also responsible for furnishing a station in Europe, though not responsible for furnishing the wire line connection in Europe.

He decides in our favor all of the claims of the Telephone Company with reference to ship to shore, which seemed to me absurd, and also gives us the widest possible rights in connection with radio beacons.

Yours truly,

(Signed) ALBERT G. DAVIS

Sec. 70. An Ominous Issue Raised by Telephone Company.

Since the referee had set a time limit for suggested changes in his draft decision the lawyers for the Telephone Group bestirred themselves to prepare arguments calculated to produce a more favorable disposition of the controversy than appeared in the draft decision. The zeal of the attorneys, however, led them into what appears to the author to have been an error in psychological approach to the subject. The opening paragraph was as follows:

"We believe that the referee's unavoidably incomplete knowledge of the extremely intricate art involved in this arbitration with his effort to co-operate in the attempt of the parties to work out this situation, have misled him into a radical departure from the contract which the parties actually made, and into conclusions which amount to an attempt to make a new contract for them."

The discussion itself was scholarly and well reasoned. The losing side, however, invariably pursues a forlorn hope whenever it undertakes to persuade a referee or judge to alter in any material respects a decision upon which he has lavished weeks and months of time and thought. The attorneys for the Radio Group, while naturally elated at the sweeping nature of the victory, were nevertheless ready with their own suggestions of changes in phrasing calculated to remove ambiguities of language or to strengthen their own case.

Singularly enough, among the various efforts of RCA intellectuals to analyze the issues raised by the Telephone Company in its suggestions for changes in the decision, it remained for a layman, Elmer E. Bucher, general sales manager of RCA, to detect and to isolate the greatest issue of all. This he did in a report to David Sarnoff, on December 16, 1924. The portion of his report discussing the issue of illegality reads as follows:

"Finally, the Telephone Group attacks the referee's decision from a new angle, pointing out in the second brief entitled 'Additional Suggestions' that the contract, as interpreted, becomes an agreement by the parties *for non-use in certain fields of inventions of one or both groups,* declaring that

" 'not only does it make the Telephone Group agree not itself to make, use, lease and sell under its own patents whether it has parted with only a non-exclusive license or even whether it has parted with no license at all, but also it makes the Telephone Group agree not to license others to make, use, lease and sell for these particular purposes—in other words, it forces both the Radio Group and the Telephone Group into an agreement for suppression or non-use of inventions in certain fields.'

"It then points out that such an agreement is *illegal* and comes within the scope of the Sherman Anti-Trust Act, citing pertinent court decisions in cases of a similar nature.

"Applying this decision to the present case, the Telephone brief states that it—

" 'leads to the inevitable conclusion that the change in the protective agreement of (d)-(2) of "license" to "rights" renders such agreement illegal.'

"It then points out that where a contract is susceptible to two constructions, one legal and the other illegal, the former will be adopted. In other words, this attack on the *legality* of the original contract can be construed as the 'last straw' of the Telephone Company in a most extraordinary effort to break down the tentative decision of the referee.

"I understand that the referee is faced here with a point of law, i.e., that courts would insist that the legal interpretation be applied rather than the illegal. On more careful reading of the Telephone Group's argument on 'illegality,' it appears that they are based on wrong assumption, namely, on their own interpretations rather than on the precise decisions of the referee."

David Sarnoff at once took alarm, and wrote a letter to Frederick P. Fish, chief counsel in the dispute. Despite the fact that he is not a lawyer, Mr. Sarnoff managed to inject into his letter not only sound law but a goodly offering of common sense. This letter was dated December 17, 1924, and read as follows:

"As to my own views, I can only say that it seems to me the position taken by you in our brief is a stronger one than that taken by the Telephone Company, at least so far as its psychological effect on a referee's mind is concerned. For the Telephone Company to argue that the whole of a contract is illegal because some portion of it does not provide for rights to either party in some subordinate and relatively unimportant field, is to argue strangely. It may well be, and no doubt is true, that in the efforts of the negotiators to cover comprehensively such large fields as wire and wireless telegraphy, wire and wireless telephony, etc., etc., some minor branch was overlooked and not provided for. The original negotiators could not have been expected to visualize every conceivable application of wire and wireless telegraphy and telephony and specify, in detail, the fields of application in so rapidly developing an art. The best proof of this is that fields of application have developed since the signing of the original contract which were neither in view nor considered important at the time the contract was drawn.

"As to broadcast transmission, the main purpose of the original negotiators was to protect their respective fields of operation and this, according to the referee's decision, has been done. Thus, the Telephone Company is adequately protected in its field of two-way communication not only by wire, but also by wireless telephony. If the Telephone Company has not the right under the patents of the Radio Group to sell broadcast transmitting devices (one-way communication), it is because that field of sales was not visualized at the time the contract was drawn, and even today is a relatively unimportant field so far as *sales or profits* go. The tendency is in the direction of reducing rather than increasing the number of broadcast transmitters. Nor do I imagine that the Telephone Company was thinking, at the time the contract was drawn, of obtaining rights under our patents to *sell* radio transmitting devices capable of carrying the human voice and perhaps ultimately competing with their wire system. This is precisely the door they sought to close, and, under the referee's decision, it has been closed.

"May it not well be argued that since the Telephone Company did not desire competition in its field of telephone communication either by wire or wireless, that they preferred that no one, not even themselves, should have the right to *sell* such devices to others?"

Should the contention of illegality prove valid the Telephone Company might escape from a part or all of the obligations of the contract that had cost so much time, effort and money to interpret. Thus, the Radio Group would be deprived of the advantages that should otherwise accrue from their victory in the arbitration.

Sec. 71. Marking Time at RCA.

In the hectic days that followed the filing of the Telephone Company's requests for changes in the referee's report, the legal lights of the Radio Group wrestled with a variety of problems. Analyses of the report and suggestions for changes were apparently made by the RCA lawyers, and by those of the General Electric Company and Westinghouse. Potent officials of the rival groups were also deep in plans for a fresh effort at conciliation. Now that issues had been decided for and against the contending parties, the situation had materially changed since the day when President Thayer had advised Albert G. Davis to find out who owned the rights before attempting to negotiate. The referee had labeled the articles in dispute. It might now be possible to do something about it.

As early as November 21, 1924,[4] Mr. Davis had written to Frederick P. Fish, indicating that Owen D. Young was preparing the basis for future negotiations with Mr. Thayer. It had been agreed, however,

---

[4] The letter reads as follows:

November 21, 1924

Frederick P. Fish, Esquire,
   84 State Street,
      Boston, Mass.

My dear Mr. Fish:

I had a rather careful talk with Mr. Young about the Telephone situation. He feels that when the decision becomes final he should have a talk with Mr. Thayer to see whether the contract as interpreted by the arbitrator is a satisfactory and workable contract, fair to both parties, or whether it can be improved. Mr. Young does not, however, think that it is desirable that he should have this talk before the draft report is confirmed.

In this connection, Colonel Manton Davis of the Radio Corporation expressed to me today very strongly the feeling that it would be unwise to have any negotiations with the Telephone Company until the decision is made final. His point was that it would have a bad effect on the arbitrator's mind and might tend to unsettle it.

Very truly yours,

(Signed) ALBERT G. DAVIS

that no effort of the kind would be advisable until the referee's report could become final. Mr. Young's approach to the subject of trading had been to call upon the legal experts of RCA, General Electric and Westinghouse for reports on what rights could safely be "swapped" in exchange for rights that had been awarded to the Telephone Company by Referee Boyden.

A memorandum exists in the RCA files, under date of December 12, 1924—an interdepartmental communication from William Brown, general counsel of RCA, to Ira J. Adams, chief patent attorney. The language is of interest:

Dear Mr. Adams:

I have had a telephone call from Mr. Young this afternoon that he is being besieged from many quarters with proposals involving modifications of the Telephone Company license agreement calculated to definitely define various things which we have wanted from the Telephone Company, and providing for various things we might be willing to concede to the Telephone Company in return. He wants to discuss some of these matters with Mr. Thayer, but preparatory to doing so he is anxious to have prepared for him a list in as concise form as possible, stating the specific things we have wanted from the Telephone Company which they have heretofore denied our right to have, or things which the present agreement has not provided for, and opposite these respective things in a second column he desires a recital of the specific things we would be willing to give in return for our respective wants.

He desires such a list to be made in co-operation with the Westinghouse and General Electric Companies, so that our recital will speak for the Radio Group.

From your familiarity with the arbitration proceedings, I assume that you more than anyone else are in a position to undertake the preparation of the desired data, and I shall appreciate it if you will give it the earliest attention you can, as Mr. Young is anxious to have it as soon as possible. I shall be glad to co-operate with you to such extent as I can.

(Signed) W. BROWN

Another type of inquiry was also in progress. It must be remembered that the Radio Corporation was an exceedingly busy corporation, carrying on world-wide wireless communications, nationwide sales of radio equipment, as well as conducting an increasingly important business in radio broadcasting. It became imperative, therefore, for those in charge of any activity affected by the arbitration to know at once what legal rights and legal limitations might be involved in the arbitration report. It is apparent that Dr. Alfred N. Goldsmith, chief radio engineer of RCA, with commendable promptness, had addressed searching inquiries to Ira J. Adams. So great were the issues involved that the Adams replies were forwarded to Frederick P. Fish and Harrison F. Lyman for rechecking. It is a tribute to Mr. Adams that both lawyers agreed with his interpretations—and for three lawyers to see eye to eye on any proposition is unusual, to say the least.

It was not until December 20, 1924, that this triune document reached the desk of David Sarnoff for guidance of the radio department. It was necessarily voluminous, yet is of sufficient importance in the development of this historical narrative to deserve special condensation at this point. The following questions, with greatly abbreviated answers, will acquaint the reader with what was believed at the time to be rights awarded to RCA by the Boyden decision:

1. Have we a right to broadcast individual pictures free or for toll?

   Answer: Yes—wireless transmission of pictures a right guaranteed to RCA.

2. Have we a right to broadcast motion pictures (television) free or for a toll?

   Answer: Television not involved in the arbitration but probably an exclusive right of RCA.

3. Should we not ask the referee to define more clearly what is meant by "news, music and entertainment"?

   Answer: No, the matter is being handled by the lawyers.

3a. Banquets not usually described in the press?

   Answer: Comes under definition of "news, music, etc.," and may be broadcast by RCA.

3b. Descriptions of sporting events?

   Answer: News proper for RCA to broadcast.

3c. Church services?

   Answer: Same as 3a.

3d. Special Chapel services?
3e. Lectures in University classroom?
3f. Lectures in studio?
3g. Poetry?
3h. Theatrical performances?
3i. Debates before audience?
3j. Debates before microphone?

   Answer: All of above may be classed as "news, music and entertainment."

4. Have we a right to monitor our transmission by using a loud speaker?

   Answer: Yes.

5. Have we a right to pick up a program originating in a foreign country and after relaying it to America by any desired means, broadcast it from one or more stations?

Answer: Yes.

6. Have we reciprocal right to send programs to foreign countries for rebroadcasting?

Answer: Yes. RCA has transoceanic rights.

7. Have we a right to broadcast on a selective system (i.e., carrier current)?

Answer: Not passed upon by arbitrator but RCA probably has such right.

8. Have we a right to install broadcast receivers in a railroad train?

Answer: RCA probably has the right.

9. Have we a right to control mechanisms, automotive vehicles and the like by radio?

Answer: Each party (RCA and Telephone Group) probably has such right.

10a. Are we permitted to sell loud speakers without radio sets?

Answer: Probably so.

10b. Electrical phonographs?

10c. Combined radiola phonographs?

Answer: Probably, but doubt as to phonograph alone.

11. Is Telephone Company obliged to furnish us with pick-up wires?

Answer: Probably so, but should not be forced.

Sec. 72. Owen D. Young Assembles "Swapping Points."

The issue of illegality of the contract of July 1, 1920, as interpreted by the referee, apparently continued to be agitated. Learned legal opinions were exchanged between the lawyers of the Radio Group. On the same day that Mr. Bucher made his report to Mr. Sarnoff on this subject, Ira J. Adams wrote a painstaking discussion of the point, as well as others, in a special report to Frederick P. Fish. The report bore the date of December 16, 1924. Three days later, however, Mr. Adams transmitted a supplemental discussion that clarified the situation considerably.

"The Telephone Group makes the point that while the Radio Group has a limited right to broadcast, none of the parties has the right to sell apparatus for broadcast transmission. They seem to think that this is an intolerable situation that could not have been contemplated by the parties. It may be more or less of an intolerable situation that will have to be corrected by subsequent negotiations, but nevertheless this should not affect the interpretation of the contract. The contract clearly shows that the parties did not intend it to cover the entire broadcasting field. The Radio Group wanted, and obtained, the right to operate broadcasting stations, so that the purchasers of their receiving sets would have something to listen to. The contract did not give the Telephone Company any right to sell broadcast receiving sets and the arbitrator has so held. It was entirely normal, therefore, for the contract to stop with a grant to the Radio Corporation of the right to operate broadcasting stations with no further grants. The parties did not foresee the tremendous demand for broadcast transmitting sets and the arbitrator cannot be asked to write something into the contract to make up for this short-sightedness. Mr. Sarnoff seems to have been the only one who foresaw the importance of broadcasting and broadcast reception, but I do not believe that he contemplated a large demand for the sale of broadcast transmitters. It is clear that this was an unforeseen demand and that the parties failed to provide for it. The parties could not have been expected to settle all difficulties under patents and the contract was never written in such a way as to take care of every and all fields of use developed in the future.

"The Telephone Company states that no one now has the right to sell vacuum tubes for replacements in the broadcasting sets already sold. This is something that the arbitrator is not concerned with. The Telephone Group arbitrarily assumed to themselves the right to sell broadcast transmitting sets. There was nothing in the contract that they could clearly say gave them this right. They took a chance and now on finding that they were wrong it does not lie in their mouths to complain.

"The Telephone Group also makes the point that the effect of the decision of the arbitrator is to permit the sets of Radio Group to listen only to its own stations. By this they mean that neither party can sell stations for broadcasting and that, therefore, there are no legally operating stations except those operated by Radio Group. This might happen to be the effect, but it was not necessarily contemplated by the contract. As far as the parties knew when the contract was drawn up third parties might be able to operate broadcasting stations that would not infringe any of the patents involved. If there should happen to be such stations the receiving sets sold by Radio Corporation could listen to them. Furthermore, Radio Corporation was licensed to sell amateur broadcasting stations and the receiving sets could listen to those stations. Also broadcasting stations are operated in Canada, Cuba and other foreign countries."

However certain the RCA lawyers may have felt as to the legality of the contract as interpreted by the referee, they were by no means desirous of testing the matter in the courts, with the long delays that would be inevitable. Owen D. Young, ever the diplomat, was awaiting a favorable moment to renew personal negotiations with Mr. Thayer, the president of the Telephone Company. Dr. Goldsmith, Albert G. Davis and Elmer E. Bucher were already drafting trading points. For days Ira J. Adams had been struggling to prepare a document that might present, in parallel columns, for Mr. Young's information the rights that might be needed by each group. On December 24, 1924, Adams wrote a letter to David Sarnoff, from which the following extract is taken:

"Mr. Brown told me that Mr. Young wanted a list of the things that Radio Corporation might need from the Telephone Company and a similar list that the Telephone Company might need from Radio Corporation. He suggested that I arrange these in opposite columns for convenience and consideration.

"Inasmuch as the Telephone Company will no doubt want certain rights that Radio Corporation may be reluctant to give them, I think this letter should pass through your hands for consideration and comments before it reaches Mr. Young.

"I have listed a number of things that I feel quite sure would not be given to the Telephone Company unless something very substantial is given in return, but nevertheless I have listed these so as to start consideration of the matter."

The parallel columns of rights needed by the embattled groups should be of extreme interest to those who desire adequate understanding of the epic struggle now entering into a new phase of development:

Rights Radio Group May Need	*Rights Telephone Group May Need*
1. License under Telephone Group patents to sell central or land stations for radio communication with ships, airplanes and other automotive devices, including railways (except train dispatching), with and without tolls.	1. License under the patents of Radio Group to sell central or land stations for radio communication with ships, airplanes and other automotive devices, either with or without tolls.
2. License under patents of both groups to sell for radio train dispatching.	2. (Telephone Group now have exclusive licenses.)
3. (Radio Group now have exclusive licenses.)	3. License under patents of both groups to sell railway signaling devices.
4. License under patents of both groups to sell for radio communication for all private business purposes.	4. License under patents of both groups to sell for radio communication for all private business purposes.

5. License under the Telephone Group patents to sell radio broadcast transmitting stations for broadcasting any subject matter whatever.

5. License under patents of Radio Group to sell radio broadcast transmitting stations for broadcasting any subject matter whatever.

6. License under Telephone Group to broadcast through its broadcasting stations any matter whatever instead of only news, music and entertainment.

6. License under patents of Radio Group to establish and maintain radio broadcasting stations.

7. License under patents of both groups to sell sets for the reception of carrier-current broadcasting.

7. (Telephone Group now have exclusive licenses.)

8. License under patents of both groups to sell transmitting apparatus for carrier-current broadcasting.

8. (Telephone Group now have exclusive licenses.)

9. License under patents of both groups to sell public address systems.

9. (Telephone Group now have exclusive licenses.)

10. Licenses under patents of both groups to sell deaf phones.

10. (Telephone Group now have exclusive licenses.)

11. Exclusive license under the patents of both groups for radio television.

11. Exclusive license under patents of both groups for wire television.

12. Acknowledgment of our exclusive (unless we through negotiations share this license with the Telephone Group) license to narrowcast and to sell receiving sets for receiving narrowcasting.

12. License under patents of both groups to sell broadcast receiving sets to the public or perhaps through Radio Corporation.

13. Acknowledgment of the non-exclusive license of the Radio Group, except Westinghouse Company, under the patents of the Telephone Group to sell electric phonographs, i.e., phonographs in which the vibration of the needle is converted into electric currents and these currents amplified or not by vacuum tubes and then fed into a loud speaker, as well as modifications of this idea.

13. (Telephone Group has the non-exclusive license by admission in our arbitration pleadings.)

In discussing paragraph 1 of the above, Mr. Adams pointed out that as the contract then stood RCA could not sell land stations for communicating with receiving sets on ships, airplanes, and other automotive devices unless such devices were small enough to be taken off and on the automotive device and considered portable. He pointed out that there was a difference of opinion as to portability of receiving sets, and that it would clear up the commercial situation immensely without hampering either side financially. The chief benefit would be in serving the public with the resulting good will, and the removal of bothersome restrictions on the sales departments of both companies.

As the matter then stood RCA had the exclusive rights to sell the apparatus on the automotive devices themselves (except railway vehicles). The Telephone Company, however, had no license under RCA patents for selling stationary or central equipment for communicating with ships. They could only establish stations for communicating through their public service system.

Mr. Adams' discussion of paragraph 12 contained the following interesting suggestion:

"The chief disappointment of the Telephone Group in this arbitration is its failure to establish that it has the right to sell broadcast receiving devices. There is no doubt in my mind that this was the cause of the dispute that resulted in the arbitration. It therefore may be deemed advisable to give them some rights with some royalty arrangement or other, so that they can put their receiving sets on the market. I do not myself say that this is advisable and I know it will be a very difficult matter to handle because we feel that this rightfully belongs to us. However, the point is listed for consideration."

Sec. 73. David Sarnoff Suggests a Plan.

It appears that in January, 1925, Referee Boyden's report was still being deliberated upon by its author. The parties were evidently becoming a bit apprehensive as to the possibly injurious effect of the forthcoming decision upon their respective activities. On January 15, 1925, Vice-President Walter S. Gifford of the Telephone Company wrote to General James G. Harbord, chief executive of RCA, proposing a thirty-day adjustment period after the final award should be handed down. The proposed stipulation was in the following form:

"Each party to the arbitration now pending before Mr. Roland W. Boyden shall have thirty days from the effective date of Mr. Boyden's final decision within which to adjust its business to that decision, subject to the right of each party to the proceedings to require that such decision shall become immediately effective in whole or in part, at any time before the thirty days expire. Where such demands are made, the decision shall be effective as to matters covered by such demands without any extension of time thereafter."

On January 17, General Harbord replied to Mr. Gifford, expressing full assent of the Radio Group to the proposal. On January 23, 1925, however, David Sarnoff set in motion a plan that was destined to put the referee's decision "in the refrigerator," so to speak, for a long period of time. Mr. Sarnoff proposed that a three-party strategy meeting be held—Owen D. Young, Albert G. Davis and himself to do the powwowing. Mr. Davis was instructed to arrange the meeting. In a letter written to Owen D. Young on January 23, 1925, Mr. Davis stated the purpose of the meeting thus:

"Mr. Sarnoff is very desirous that the three of us should get together for at least fifteen minutes at an early date to discuss certain matters connected with phonograph and radio."

It is apparent that the meeting above requested was held on February 5, 1925. Evidence of the date of the meeting is gleaned from a document in the files of the General Electric Company, entitled "Mr. Sarnoff's Fundamentals," bearing that date, and undoubtedly the subject matter of the discussion at this historic meeting. Again David Sarnoff called attention to his cherished plan of a national broadcasting company, but this time at a crisis of affairs when the great corporations might find it a way out of a broadcasting impasse in which they had become mutually involved. Because of the events that were to flow from this new suggestion it is well to reproduce in full the Sarnoff proposals of February 5, 1925, as they appear to have been recorded for Owen D. Young. To be sure, these "fundamentals" were to undergo transformation and enlargement, but here they are as they appear in the memorandum:

"February 5, 1925

"MR. SARNOFF'S FUNDAMENTALS

"1. *Two-way telephone communication, wire and wireless*
"This is the natural field of the Telephone Group. We should retire from the field in every way, as far as possible, except with respect to transoceanic telephony, which we should hold in the present situation. This would mean giving the Telephone Group non-exclusive licenses for telephones on ships and other moving vehicles and full control of telephony to railways. It would also involve giving up the Manufacturing Companies' present rights in wired wireless on power lines, but the Manufacturing Companies would retain the right for wired wireless for operating switch mechanisms.

"2. *Broadcasting reception by space radio, including the phonograph and the combinations with the phonograph; also including the broadcasting of moving pictures*

"The Telephone Company should step out of this situation and leave the field exclusively to the Radio Corporation.

"3. *Broadcasting over wires*

"The Telephone Group should do this work and the Radio Group should stay out, provided some plan can be devised to prevent the use in one field of devices sold for another field. This could be accomplished if the Telephone Group would lease the devices to the consumer and maintain the control of these devices, including service and replacements, on the ordinary form of telephone contract which prohibits the attachment of foreign apparatus.

"4. *Broadcasting transmission by space radio and program*

"Put all stations of all parties into a broadcasting company which can be made self-supporting and probably revenue-producing, the Telephone Company to furnish wires as far as needed; operation by board of trustees or by the directors of the new company.

"5. *Some arrangement to prevent the difficulties which now arise from the misuse of tubes and other apparatus sold by the parties in incidental lines*

"This might involve all sales of small tubes and loud speakers by the Radio Corporation."

We have no record of Owen D. Young's reaction to David Sarnoff's proposals, yet the presence in Mr. Young's files of this document—apparently the only copy in existence—indicates the profound impression that it made. In Mr. Sarnoff's files at RCA we discover a more imposing document bearing the date of February 14, 1925. Before leaving the topic of the original proposal it may be well to call attention to the fact that in paragraph 4 Mr. Sarnoff revived his long-advocated project of a nationwide broadcasting company. Not only that, but in his reference to the possibility of making the company self-supporting we find the first intimation of a change of attitude toward radio advertising.

Hitherto, Mr. Sarnoff had been a consistent opponent of advertising in connection with radio programs. He had at first urged support of radio by manufacturers and dealers. When convinced that this was impracticable he had tried to start a movement for the endowment of radio stations. This idea failed to win public support and he was driven by the logic of circumstances to accept the advertising concept as the only feasible plan for the financing of broadcasting activities. In the memorandum of February 14th referred to above, Mr. Sarnoff prefaces his plan by a preamble that is somehow suggestive of Owen D. Young's manner of approach to a subject. An interesting development has likewise occurred in the "Fundamentals." The text is as follows:

February 14, 1925

MEMORANDUM
by
DAVID SARNOFF

FUNDAMENTAL CONSIDERATIONS
PROPOSED NEGOTIATIONS BETWEEN RADIO AND
TELEPHONE GROUP

"This memorandum has been drawn with the following basic thoughts in mind:

"A. The maximum development and use of the inventions, patents, facilities and resources of each group should be made, thus bringing the art of wire and radio communication to the highest state of public usefulness.

"B. The main business of each group should be reasonably protected.

"C. The business of each group should be allowed to expand along its natural lines.

*   *   *   *

"Only fundamentals are dealt with herein. If these are agreed to, in principle, no serious difficulty is anticipated in reaching satisfactory conclusions where subsidiary questions or precise details are involved. These fundamentals will serve as a guide and point to the logical solution of minor questions.

"With the foregoing in mind, the following divisions of field are suggested under the present and future patent rights of both groups.

"PROPOSED FIELDS OF THE TELEPHONE GROUP
"Two-Way Telephone Communication

"1. Exclusive rights in two-way telephone communication on land, for public and private service, by wire, by wired radio and by space radio.

"Also

"Exclusive rights in two-way telephone communication, as above, between fixed points on land, between fixed points and moving vehicles on land or in the air, and between moving vehicles on land or in the air.

"Marine Radio Telephony

"2. Non-exclusive rights in two-way radio telephone communication between ship and shore and between ships.

"Space Radio Broadcast Transmission

"3. Non-exclusive rights to one-way broadcast transmission by space radio, in all its applications, including the right to lease or sell such transmitters and to furnish wire service to others for this purpose, but not including the right to use, lease or sell such one-way transmitters for toll or revenue purpose.

"Wired Radio Broadcast Transmission

"4. Exclusive rights in broadcast transmission, over all wires by wired radio and ordinary wire telephony, in all its applications.

"The Radio Group to give up its present non-exclusive rights to carrier-current communication, excepting actuation of switches, etc., on power lines.

"Wired Radio Broadcast Reception

"5. Exclusive rights covering devices used for one-way reception, over wires, of news, music and entertainment; also, wire photography, wire television, setting of time-clocks and all other applications of one-way broadcast reception over wires.

"Note: As the same devices may be used in the Radio Group's field of Space Radio Reception, the Telephone Group should lease, but not sell, wired radio receiving devices. By leasing such devices to the consumer, maintaining control over them and furnishing service and replacements, on the ordinary form of telephone contract, the Telephone Group would be merely following its traditional policy of prohibiting attachment of foreign apparatus to its lines and instruments.

"Electro-Therapeutic Devices

"6. Non-exclusive rights to each group, as at present.

*   *   *   *

"PROPOSED FIELDS OF THE RADIO GROUP
"Radio Telegraphy and Transoceanic Radio Telephony

"1. Exclusive rights, as at present.

"Marine Radio Telephony

"2. Non-exclusive, instead of present exclusive rights:

"Space Radio Broadcast Transmission

"3. Non-exclusive rights to make, use, lease and sell broadcast transmitting devices and exclusive rights to derive revenue and tolls in this field.

"Space Radio Broadcast Reception

"4. Exclusive rights to make, use, lease and sell all devices for one-way reception, by space radio, of news, music and entertainment, including all devices for broadcast reception through space, as now known, selective broadcasting devices which may be developed, radio television, radio photography, time-clock setting and all other applications of one-way space radio reception. The Radio Group to have the exclusive right to derive revenue and tolls in this field in whatever manner it may be found practicable.

"Electric Phonograph Recording and Reproduction

"5. Exclusive rights to make, use, lease and sell all devices and methods applicable to the above field.

"Electro-Therapeutic Devices

"6. Non-exclusive rights to each group, as at present.

*   *   *   *

"PROPOSED BROADCAST TRANSMISSION COMPANY

"The following plan is suggested for the consideration of all parties:

"Form the 'American Broadcasting Company.' The stockholders to be the American Telephone & Telegraph Company, the Radio Corporation of America, the General Electric and Westinghouse Companies and possibly others. The 'American Broadcasting Company' to be controlled by a board of trustees or directors representing the stockholders.

"The primary function of this company shall be, to maintain centralized studios, hire talent, prepare and furnish suitable programs for space radio and wired broadcast systems.

"Such programs may be furnished not only to the charter members of the 'American Broadcasting Company' but also to Independent Broadcasting Stations.

"The subscribing stations shall pay the 'American Broadcasting Company' for such programs and the charges to be based on the principle that the company is to be made at least self-supporting and, if practicable, also profit-earning.

"The 'American Broadcasting Company' to study the public tastes and requirements in connection with broadcast transmission, to formulate and suggest, if not determine policies affecting broadcast transmission, to include legislative matters and international questions, which are rapidly coming to the front in this art.

"This project would not involve a sacrifice of any rights of the individual parties while at the same time it would provide the benefits of organization, centralization, economy, superior programs, and a substantial move toward the stabilization of the art and industry."

In a later memorandum, apparently written in March, 1925, Mr. Sarnoff enlarged upon the provision as to board of trustees of the proposed "American Broadcasting Company" by providing that they be "chosen from the most prominent people and representing various classes of public interest. The board to number about fifteen and the chairman to be approved by the Secretary of the Department of Commerce."

He also added an entirely new paragraph as follows:

"In order to make this plan commercially practicable, it is suggested that all rights to broadcast transmission for tolls or pay be exclusively vested in this company; the proceeds to be used in the public interest by providing the best possible programs."

Thus it appears from the foregoing that another stage in the evolution of the plan for a national broadcasting company was attained. As previously indicated, David Sarnoff had first conceived the plan in June, 1922. At various times since then he had revived the idea, adding each time a bit of detail even as an artist might return from time to time to an unfinished picture to sketch in some new feature, adding a light here, a shadow there, until the entire artistic conception could stand forth in completeness.

Sec. 74. The Lull Before a Major Encounter.

A tense and complicated situation existed in the RCA-Telephone Company deadlock during the winter of 1925. The harassed referee was still striving to perfect his report. Owen D. Young and his associates were busily engaged in preparations to negotiate a trade with the Telephone Company, still relying for advantage upon the Draft Report as the basis for bargaining. To be sure the Telephone Company, months ago, had raised the issue of illegality of the agreement as it had been interpreted by the referee. Since that time, however, Walter S. Gifford who, in January, 1925, had been elected president of the company, had negotiated with RCA in a manner justifying belief that the Telephone legal staff had abandoned the idea. Notwithstanding these disarming developments, however, there was nevertheless being prepared for RCA and its allies a surprise of staggering proportions. One of Wall Street's greatest corporation lawyers—the recent Democratic contestant for the presidency, John W. Davis himself, was at work on a legal opinion that was to descend upon the Radio Group with all the suddenness of a bombshell.

In the meantime, the lawyers for the embattled groups continued to exchange memoranda. Under date of March 3, 1925, we find a three-page letter from Harrison F. Lyman to Frederick P. Fish, discussing proposed changes in the referee's report. It was of a technical nature. The opening paragraph gives us a glimpse of current developments. It runs thus:

"I do not see that the changes which the referee proposes to make in his draft decision are of any real consequence except as they clear up certain points on which the parties asked to have the language made more definite."

It is interesting to note that, despite the galaxy of lawyers already engaged upon different phases of the controversy, it had been deemed expedient to consult still other lawyers. Joseph P. Cotton, an eminent New York attorney, who had drafted the original contract, was brought into the case at this time. A letter in the files of the General Electric Company gives us the following interesting sidelight upon the state of affairs in early March:

New York, March 5, 1925

Dear Mr. Fish:

I have been over the papers which you left with me the other day. Young has not yet sent for me, but here is my position.

(1) From the point of view of my case it would be advantageous if there could be a prompt adjustment of the whole matter.

(2) If that is not possible I should think your group would find it advisable to consider whether or not they would be willing (whether they get anything for the concession or not) to consent to have the referee's report modified before final filing so that there should not exist any substantial field in which there would not be one of the companies clearly entitled to manufacture and to make and sell under all the patents of all companies. It can not be to the advantage of anybody to have deadlocks existing—particularly in regard to broadcasting. Theoretically, the resulting restraint from such a deadlock may be unimportant—practically, it is sure to be thought important.

(3) If in any further agreement there is to be a division of field which permits one company or another to manufacture and sell certain articles under patents for certain purposes only—e.g., for amateur use, for tolls, for one-way service, etc., I think such divisions of field should be reduced to a minimum and only made where clearly referable to the protection of existing business of some company and should be supportable, so far as may be, on common law principles. I think there is going to be some law made in the next few years on this question, and I do not think the present case is a good place to make it.

I will return your briefs shortly.

Very truly yours,
(Signed) Joseph P. Cotton

On March 2, 1925, Roland W. Boyden addressed a letter to Nathaniel T. Guernsey, counsel for the Telephone Group, and Frederick P. Fish, counsel for the Radio Group, in which he advised the parties to the arbitration that his decision was now in final form. The letter contained the following suggestion:

"In order to avoid possible mistakes, will you send me by March 12, 1925, any criticisms of form with respect either to these changes or any other parts of the decision. . . . Unless you arrange otherwise, I will after March 12th send copies of the final decision to each of you and ask you to furnish me with an acknowledgment by each of the companies you represent."

This letter undoubtedly had immediate repercussions in both camps, and accounts for certain activities that followed closely upon its receipt in New York. Under date of March 6th we find a letter from David Sarnoff to Frederick P. Fish, in which he states:

"I have received with a great deal of satisfaction the report of the final decision of the arbitrator in connection with the Telephone contract."

The balance of the letter consisted of expressions of gratitude of the Radio Group for the able manner in which Mr. Fish had handled the arbitration hearings. There was no intimation of any desire on the part of the Radio Group to postpone the official promulgation of the decision. Indeed, there is evidence of eagerness that this should immediately take place. They realized, however, that new agreements would now be in order. The Telephone Company would perhaps be in a more reasonable frame of mind.

It is evident that Radio officials were expecting immediate con-ferences with the Telephone Company when, on March 7th, Albert G. Davis called at Owen D. Young's office with a message from Mr. Tripp of the Westinghouse Company. Mr. Young was not in at the time, but Miss L. V. Morrison, of his office staff, made the following memorandum of the Davis call:

MEMORANDUM FROM MR. A. G. DAVIS

March 7, 1925

Mr. Young:

General Tripp spoke to Mr. Davis at the Radio Board meeting on Friday and said that while he did not wish to take any part in the negotiations with the Telephone Company, he was going to speak to you and ask you to let him sit in with you in order that there might be no danger that something might be worked out which might be unsatisfactory to the Westinghouse Company. He said that it was very difficult to sit back outside and predetermine what line the negotiations should take. He spoke particularly about broadcasting, and gave Mr. Davis the impression that the Westinghouse Company was afraid of giving up any rights in broadcasting. You will remember that the Westinghouse Company behaved in a very peculiar way about the question of having the right to broadcasting for profit and Harry Davis has some radical ideas about the development of broad-casting. Mr. Davis got the impression that perhaps he was not willing to put the Westinghouse broadcasting into the national broadcasting company. It had been my idea that the individuality of the Westing-house and General Electric and other stations would be retained, and that the National Company would furnish part of the program, the individual station furnishing the local program and both names being announced.

(Signed) L. V. MORRISON

It is apparent that Mr. Sarnoff's plan for a national broadcasting company was by this time regarded by the Radio Group as a trading point of major importance. Westinghouse, with by far the largest number of broadcasting stations in the group, had great interests at stake. Mr. Tripp's concern over the expected trading conferences was due to this circumstance. Whether Westinghouse would come into the proposed amalgamation of broadcasting interests was naturally of great importance to the would-be traders.

CHAPTER
TEN

Empire Swapping

Section 75. John W. Davis Writes an Opinion.

THE SCENE WAS NOW SET for one of the most dramatic occurrences in the four-year conflict between the Radio and Telephone Groups. Owen D. Young and his associates had prepared a masterly campaign of negotiation with the Telephone Company. The basis of these negotiations was obviously the "Draft Report" of the referee. Definite rulings had been made on matters long in controversy. The radio people had won their major contentions. Secure in their gains, the victorious allies were ready to use as trading points some of the rights for which the Telephone Group had striven in vain, in exchange for rights which had been awarded to the Telephone Group. The great prize—exclusive rights in manufacture of receiving sets—was no longer in controversy or subject to negotiation. The Draft Report had settled that. Secure in the belief that this was so, and that both parties accepted the report, Mr. Young was ready for diplomatic moves that might clarify remaining uncertainties.

Thus matters stood on March 17, 1925, when Mr. Young's plan of campaign was blasted at the roots by a bombshell from the Honorable John W. Davis—nothing less than a legal opinion, in the Telephone Company's behalf, that denounced the contract upon which the Draft Report was based as illegal and void. If this contention were sound then the Draft Report would be valueless and the supposed victory of the Radio Group would amount to nothing but wasted effort. To be sure the issue of illegality had been raised by counsel for the Telephone Company during the hearings, yet it had been regarded as a far-fetched contention of lawyers who were fighting a losing battle. Now, however, a lawyer of national repute, a former candidate for the Presidency, had revived the issue, with an additional quirk, and had given the Telephone Company ample justification for repudiating the Draft Report in whole or in part. Here, then, was the devastating feature of the new development—that the Telephone Company would rely upon the Davis opinion and reassert its supposed rights. Whether the Davis interpretation was legally sound was entirely beside the point. It was an opinion that sustained the Telephone Company's contentions and legally justified a refusal to abide by the Draft Report. It was a bombshell delivered at a crucial moment. Because of the historical value of this particular legal opinion, the author will attempt to interpret it for the reader.

"You ask," he writes, in the portion of the opinion that is most pertinent, "first, whether such an agreement is void as a restraint of trade either at common law or under the Sherman Act; second, whether if illegal under the Sherman Act, the A. T. & T. Company, is bound, either in law or in morals, to observe the agreement; third, whether if this clause as interpreted be illegal, it is separable from the rest of the agreement, or whether the whole document is tainted by its illegality. I approach the questions in the order stated."

Before presenting more of the Davis opinion it is perhaps in order to explain that the Sherman Act was a Federal statute that was enacted in 1890, designed to prevent monopolies or conspiracies in restraint of trade in interstate commerce or in commerce with foreign nations. It provides in part as follows: "Every contract, combination in form of trust or otherwise, or conspiracy, in restraint of trade or commerce . . . is hereby declared illegal." The act provided for fine or imprisonment, or both, for violation of the act, as well as for other remedies.

It should also be pointed out that a patent is a monopoly granted by the Federal government for a seventeen-year period to the inventor of any useful device. That is to say, the inventor has the exclusive right to make, use and sell the patented article, but he may sell his rights to another or give leases to manufacturers to exploit the invention on any financial basis that he may be able to arrange. Such exploitation would not be construed as being affected by the Sherman Act. How then could a cross-licensing agreement between the owners of patents in the same field offend the Sherman Act by exchanging with each other these rights guaranteed to them under the patent laws? Let us see by what subtlety of legal reasoning the cross-licensing agreement of July 1, 1920, could be said to violate the Sherman Act. Mr. Davis continued thus:

"No one, I take it, will challenge the general right of a patentee to limit the use which may be made of the patent by those whom he chooses to license. If the patent is of such a character that it may be used for more than one purpose, I think there is no question that he can forbid the licensee to use it in any competitive line of business. For instance, if a manufacturer of woolens should procure a patented device which might be used for general weaving, he could license its use to a linen manufacturer on condition that the latter would not use it to weave woolen goods which would compete with those of the patentee. Such a license could not be treated as restricting competition, because it would be addressed only to goods manufactured by the patented process, and these lie within the field of monopoly created by the patent itself.

"It is equally clear that if the patentee makes sale of the patent or grants to another the exclusive right in its use, he may, in order to protect the value of the thing sold or granted, agree to withdraw himself entirely from the use of the patent. This, in short, is what every sale or exclusive grant of a patent amounts to. Such an agreement, in its essence, is really an agreement against infringement.

"But when the patentee on the one hand, or the licensee on the other, agrees to withdraw entirely from any form of competition, as, for instance, in the illustration I use above, if the linen manufacturer should agree not only to abstain from manufacturing woolen goods by the use of the patent but from all manufacture whatever of woolens, a different question would seem to be presented. Such an agreement goes beyond the mere protection of the patent rights involved and attempts to protect the general profits of the patentee. It is a direct restraint upon trade."

Sec. 76. Telephone Company May Rescind Provision as to Receiving Sets.

Having in this manner stated a premise which, if legally sound, could be used effectively in argument, Mr. Davis goes on to discuss a number of cases involving the Sherman Act in which the United States courts had decided in accordance with his views. This point being established Mr. Davis proceeded to discuss the Boyden Draft Report.

"It is true that in *Bement* v. *National Harrow Company* 186 U. S. 70, the licensee specifically agreed that:

" 'It would not, during the continuance of the license, be directly or indirectly engaged in the manufacture or sale of any other float spring tooth harrows, etc., than those which it was licensed to manufacture and make under the terms of the license, etc.'

"At first blush such a covenant seems to be a close parallel of the one we are now considering, but on page 94 the court proceeds to put its own construction on the covenant, saying:

" 'The plain purpose of the provision was to prevent the defendant from infringing upon the rights of others under other patents, and it had no purpose to stifle competition in the harrow business more than the patent provided for, nor was its purpose to prevent the licensee from attempting to make any improvement in harrows. It was a reasonable prohibition for the defendant, who would thus be excluded from making such harrows as were made by others who were engaged in manufacturing and selling other machines under other patents. It would be unreasonable to so construe the provision as to prevent defendant from using any letters patent legally obtained by it and not infringing patents owned by others. This was neither its purpose nor its meaning.'

"Unless the construction adopted by the referee is itself to be construed in some such fashion, I do not see how the contract can escape the prohibition of the law. According to him, the Telephone Company has in substance bound itself, for the life of the contract, not to invade the field of selling broadcast receiving sets, even though it should hereafter come into possession of new devices whose utilization would vastly benefit the industry and, in consequence, the general public.

"The argument advanced in the reply of the Radio Group, page 10, that the contract and every part of it was justified by 'the inextricable confusion of the patent situation' seems to be quite beside the point. It is true that neither party at this time could make commercial apparatus without using the patents of the other party, and such a situation undoubtedly 'not only warranted but necessitated the granting of cross-licenses.' It may be said also that these cross-licenses might be covered by protective agreements as to the use to be made of the patents covered by the licenses, but there is nothing in all this situation which justified an effort to set up for either party in any field a monopoly which extended beyond that afforded by the patents themselves.

" 'Rights conferred by patents are indeed very definite and extensive, but they do not give any more than other rights an universal license against positive prohibitions. The Sherman law is a limitation of rights, rights which may be pushed to evil consequences and therefore restrained.' *Standard Sanitary Company* v. *United States*.

"Now, if the agreement so construed constitutes an illegal restraint of trade, the Telephone Company is clearly discharged from any obligation to observe it, and can set up its illegality under the Sherman Act as a defense to any suit for its breach. This is axiomatic, and the Supreme Court so held in *Bement* v. *National Harrow Company*. Moreover, the moral obligation to observe a contract once entered into is certainly discharged when the contract, upon subsequent construction, proves to contain an illegality not contemplated by the parties at the time of execution."

Sec. 77. Davis Declares Disputed Clause Illegal.

The final phase of the Davis opinion had to do with a well-known legal principle that, if a contract can be shown to have illegal provisions but be valid in other respects, the courts will endeavor to save the contract by striking out the illegal part, provided the contract is separable. If the contract cannot be separated, that is to say, if the illegal portion is so interrelated to the rest of the contract that it cannot be separated, then the entire contract becomes unenforceable. Let us continue with the Davis discussion:

"Coming then to the third and last question, we are called on to consider what effect, if any, this illegality has upon the contract as a whole. Such an inquiry makes it necessary to determine whether the contract is separable or inseparable, divisible or indivisible, in its character.

*   *   *   *

"Whether a contract is divisible or indivisible, in the absence of any express language on the subject, is, under the modern doctrine, a question primarily of intent, although under the ancient rule the independence of mutual covenants and the divisibility of the contract were always to be assumed unless the contrary was stated. At present the effort of the courts is to put themselves in the position of the parties and endeavor to discover whether one portion of the contract would have been entered into lacking the other. This involved an apprehension of the cardinal object of the contract and the weighing of the relative value of the promises it contains. One cannot speak dogmatically on a subject which lies so largely in the field of individual opinion.

"There is, however, a distinct tendency, where the question is one of a contract in restraint of trade, to hold the contract divisible. In *Oregon Steam Navigation Company* v. *Windsor* 20 Wall. 64-70, the rule is thus stated:

" 'Agreements in restraint of trade, whether under seal or not, are divisible, and accordingly it has been held that when such an agreement contains a stipulation which is capable of being construed divisibly, one part thereof as being in restraint of trade, whilst the other is not, the court will give effect to the latter and will not hold the agreement to be void altogether.'

"See also *United States Consol, S. R. Company* v. *Griffin Skelly Company* (a patent case), 126 Fed. 364-370, and Third *Williston on Contracts*, Sec. 1659, 1779 and 1780.

"Reading the present contract in the light of these considerations, I am of opinion that it is divisible in character, and that the illegality which inheres in clause (d) (2) under the referee's construction does not vitiate the agreement as a whole. The only effect of the illegality is to render that particular portion unenforceable. I reach this conclusion by considering, in the first place, the motive which underlies the contract. It was brought about undoubtedly by a desire to solve, through the exchange of cross-licenses, the existing patent deadlock. I think it fair to assume that the attention of the parties was directed not so much to preserving to themselves a monopoly in any especial field as to make it possible for them to enjoy any and all improvements in the art. That they wished to impose restrictions on the licenses they granted is clear, but once these restrictions had been agreed to, it may fairly be assumed that the signing of the contract did not depend on the insertion of a still broader non-competitive clause."

Having voiced his opinion that the clause in the contract relating to receiving sets was illegal and void Mr. Davis proceeded to lay down a twofold dilemma for the Radio Group. If the clause were to be construed as the referee had interpreted it, then it was illegal and void, neither party being entitled to rights under it. If, on the other hand, it were to be construed according to what Mr. Davis believed a sounder interpretation, the illegal restraint of trade might be thrown out and each party would be entitled to manufacture radio receiving sets. In either case the American Telephone Company would win its long-coveted right to enter into competition in the manufacture of radio sets. Thus it appears that the fate of an industrial empire, as we have previously labeled the radio industry, was to be decided on a very intricate legal technicality. For the rounding out of the story at this point it may be well to examine the conclusion of Mr. Davis' legal opinion:

"The only hesitation which I feel in reaching my conclusion is that we are dealing with the protective clause as the referee has construed it and not with the clause as we believe it to be. If I am right in my answer to your first question, the whole clause, under his construction, goes out for illegality, and we do not retain even the limited protection which, under our construction, the clause was designed to afford. We are brought face to face, therefore, with this question: Would the General Company have entered into this agreement if, in consequence, the Telephone Company would have been enabled to sell independent wireless telephone receiving apparatus; and, on the other hand, would the Telephone Company have entered into it, if, in consequence, the General Company could have sold transmitting apparatus for use in connection with the receiving apparatus? One might easily answer in the negative if it were not for the existing patent deadlock and the various fields covered by the agreements to which this protective clause, however construed, does not extend."

Sec. 78. The Telephone Company in Driver's Seat.

Owen D. Young was the first of the Radio chieftains to receive news of this opinion. It is apparent that he required some little time to recover from the shock before acquainting his associates with the contents of the John W. Davis broadside. In the files at RCA is to be found a copy of the Davis opinion with a memorandum attached thereto that testifies more eloquently than many words to Mr. Young's alarm at the development. The memorandum reads as follows:

March 23, 1925

To David Sarnoff:

To be held as strictly confidential and not released until authorized by me.

(Signed) OWEN D. YOUNG

It will be observed that the Telephone Company had now checkmated the Radio Group. Since December, 1924, Mr. Young had been eager to reopen negotiations in an effort to trade with the Telephone Company on the basis of the Draft Report. The Telephone Company had permitted weeks to pass without facing the Radio Group at the

GERARD SWOPE
President, General Electric Company
from 1922 to date.

MEFFORD F. RUNYON
CBS Vice-President in charge of owned
and operated stations.

OTTO S. SCHAIRER
RCA Vice-President in charge of patent
department.

EDWIN M. HERR
Former President Westinghouse Electric
and Manufacturing Company.

council table. Now that conditions had changed, however, a new spirit was manifest in the Telephone camp. On March 27, 1925, Walter S. Gifford, the new president of the American Telephone Company, Mr. Thayer having retired, at a personal meeting with Mr. Young, handed to the latter a three-page typewritten statement of proposed trading points. The proposal was in two parts:

(A) Proposed rights in the Telephone Group.

Under such rights Mr. Gifford listed the following:

I. *In the field of wireless broadcast transmitting stations for broadcasting news, music, entertainment or any other subject matter of general public interest:*
Non-exclusive licenses to make, use and sell.

II. *Long distance "pick-up" wire lines for transmission to broadcasting stations:*
Exclusive licenses, subject to an agreement to give service to the Radio Group as provided in B III.

III. *Local and long distance wire lines for distribution from wireless broadcasting receiving sets (but not including mere wiring in a building, such as a hotel):*
Exclusive licenses.

IV. *With respect to wireless broadcast receiving sets:*
Non-exclusive licenses to make and sell high-grade receiving apparatus in sufficient amount to warrant an interest in the development of wireless receiving apparatus.

V. *In transoceanic wireless telephony:*
Non-exclusive licenses to make and use. (Where Radio Group facilities are not used, some provision to protect the Radio Group in its exclusive rights in wireless telegraphy.)

VI. *With respect to telephone apparatus and systems for communication by and between and with ships, airships and other automotive devices:*
Non-exclusive licenses to make, use and sell.

VII. *For the incidental and portable uses referred to in (d) (4):*
Non-exclusive licenses.

(B) Proposed rights in Radio Group.

Mr. Gifford listed the following:
I. *For wireless broadcast receiving sets:*
Licenses to be exclusive (except for IV A) during the period of the agreement, and non-exclusive thereafter. This would enable the Radio Group to bring suit under the patents of the Telephone Group in this field.

II. *In the field of wireless broadcast transmitting stations for broadcasting news, music, entertainment and other subject matter of general interest:*
Non-exclusive rights to make, use and sell.

III. The Telephone Group to agree, so far as is practical, and to the extent it does so for other broadcasting stations, including its own stations, to furnish long distance "pick-up" wire lines and local "pick-up" wire lines for the broadcasting stations of the Radio Group.

IV. *In transoceanic wireless telephony:*
Non-exclusive licenses to make and use.

V. *With respect to ground stations for communicating with ships, airships, etc.:*
Non-exclusive licenses to make, use and sell.

It was perceived at once that the Gifford proposals, if adopted, would affect the arbitrator's decision in the following important respects:

The Radio Group would receive (1) a more liberal interpretation of the disputed expression, "news, music and entertainment." (2) Non-exclusive rights to sell broadcast transmitters. (3) Limited use of Telephone Company's wire lines.

On the other hand, the Telephone Group would acquire (a) non-exclusive rights under radio patents to sell broadcast transmitters; (b) exclusive rights to pick-up wires for radio broadcasting; (c) exclusive distribution of wireless signals outside a building in which a receiver might be located; (d) limited non-exclusive rights to sell receiving sets; (e) practically exclusive rights in transoceanic and ship-to-shore telephony; (f) non-exclusive rights to certain incidental uses of wireless telephony.

Several of the above trading points were obviously of extreme importance, but none more so than clause (d) above in the matter of sale of receiving sets. This business had now become truly mammoth in its proportions. The annual report of the board of directors of RCA had just been made public and, lo! the gross sales of the corporation for the calendar year 1924 had crossed the fifty-million-dollar mark. That the reader may understand why these corporate groups were battling so strenuously over manufacturing and sales rights in radio apparatus and radio receiving sets it may be well to reprint the statistics of sales:

1921—$ 1,468,919.95
1922— 11,286,489.41
1923— 22,465,090.71
1924— 50,747,202.24

Sec. 79. RCA Mobilizes Its Leaders for New Effort.

Upon receiving Mr. Gifford's memorandum Owen D. Young realized that hopes of an early adjustment of difficulties were vain. Legal opinions and arbitration award had failed to accomplish the hoped-for peace. The Gifford proposals were unacceptable to the Radio Group. In fact, the suggestion of dividing the business of manufacturing and selling of radio receiving sets into two fields was fraught with possibilities of even greater confusion than had hitherto existed. This much, however, had been accomplished. The parties had explored every hope of compromise only to encounter frustration. They had gone down every blind alley, and now both sides realized that some common ground must be discovered on which they could make peace. Obviously they must "swap rights" or go into the courts where pitiless publicity, in addition to the inescapable notoriety of the Federal Trade proceedings then pending in Washington, would await both corporations.

The long period of preparation for "swapping rights" now came to fruition. Among those who had deliberated longest on the controversy, Albert G. Davis and David Sarnoff were outstanding. To them Owen D. Young now turned for a final summing up of trading points. A meeting was arranged for Wednesday, March 31, 1925, at which the lawyers for the respective parties could be present to give advice and assistance to their clients. In the files of the General Electric Company are to be found two versions of this historic meeting, one written by Albert G. Davis and the other possibly by a member of the Telephone Group. They agree in all essential particulars.

Five persons were present in Mr. Gifford's office at the time of this conference: Frederick P. Fish, attorney for the Radio Group; Nathaniel T. Guernsey, counsel for the Telephone Company; Owen D. Young, Walter S. Gifford and Albert G. Davis. Mr. Fish apparently opened the meeting with a suggestion that started fireworks. He proposed that the portion of the arbitrator's report which John W. Davis had criticized be so amended as to eliminate any question of illegality. Whereupon Mr. Guernsey registered violent protest, declaring that such a change would constitute a material alteration and not a mere change in language. He pointed out that the arbitration decision was by Mr. Boyden's declaration in its final form. The Telephone Company refused to agree to the change and thus blocked this strategic move by Mr. Fish. The utmost that could be accomplished at the meeting was thus summarized in the A. G. Davis version:

"It was agreed that Mr. Fish should say to the arbitrator that the parties requested a further delay of thirty days in the handing down of his decision, it being the understanding that in the meantime you and Mr. Gifford would endeavor to arrive at a modification of the agreement between the parties. It was further agreed that if prior to the handing down of the final decision Mr. Boyden, the arbitrator, should die or become incapacitated the draft decision which he has now delivered to us with the changes which he himself made, that is to say, the decision as it now stands, should be accepted by both parties and treated as final and binding. This may mean that the Radio Group and the Telephone Group are not agreed as to the meaning or legal effect of some particular part of the decision. If so, this would have to be worked out as best we can. In fact, we all realize that in the future there is every possibility that differences of opinion may arise as to the meaning of the arbitrator's decision, as they have arisen with reference to the meaning of the original contract."

Apparently after the conclusion of the above meeting Owen D. Young wrote to Mr. Gifford stating that he was then leaving for Harrisburg to be away on the following day. He was, therefore, sending to Mr. Gifford for his perusal summaries that had been prepared by Albert G. Davis and David Sarnoff. Mr. Young explained that the documents had been prepared for his own guidance and not for general purposes. "I asked both Mr. Davis and Mr. Sarnoff," he writes, "to tell me how they thought the field should be divided and set up in order to avoid the kind of conflicts and misunderstandings which we have had in the past. And also how it should be set up to get the maximum development in all of the fields and thereby the utmost public service. I asked them not to consider the question of whether the exchanges of rights between the Radio Group and the Telephone Group was equal and equitable. This aspect of the matter they were requested to ignore. My thought about it is that, in considering the set up, we ought to make the set up right, and then having gotten the right set up, we should adjust the compensation if the transfer of rights is not equal between the two groups. . . . Will you consider the memoranda submitted and then we will discuss the situation on Thursday, if that will be convenient for you, and see how we can make a real start."

An examination of the Sarnoff memorandum of March 31 discloses that it was the "Fundamentals" previously quoted, with some slight improvements added since February. Mr. Davis presented an eight-page memorandum which differs in some respects from Mr. Sarnoff's suggestions. Fortunately, in the files of the General Electric Company we discover a brief letter that explains the relation between the two versions. It reads as follows:

New York, March 31, 1925

Owen D. Young, Esq.,
New York Office.

My dear Mr. Young:

Mr. Sarnoff's memorandum differs from mine principally in the treatment of two-way telephone communication for ships and transoceanic, both of which in my memorandum are exclusive to the Telephone Company. His suggestion is that the Telephone Company have non-exclusive ship rights, but exclusive rights for land vehicles, and that transoceanic be left as it is.

He also makes the radio telegraph on land for leased wire purposes non-exclusive for the Telephone Company, instead of exclusive as I have suggested.

He also suggests that the transmission and pick-up for carrier-current broadcasting on power lines should be in the hands of the Radio Group if the Broadcasting Company is not formed. My suggestion on this subject is under C, page 2.

He has gone farther than I have into the reasons why certain things should be done. I have gone farther than he has into details, such as wave lengths.

We do not disagree in principle on anything, as far as I can find out.

Very truly yours,

(Signed) ALBERT G. DAVIS

Sec. 80. A Joint Committee Attempts Conciliation.

At the meeting proposed by Mr. Young in the letter to Mr. Gifford quoted in the preceding section it was voted to appoint a committee of five to endeavor to reach an understanding. Edgar S. Bloom and George E. Folk represented the Telephone Group, whereas Albert G. Davis (General Electric), Otto S. Schairer (Westinghouse), and David Sarnoff (RCA), were the negotiators for the Radio Group. The committee held various conferences. One meeting in particular, attended by all members of the committee, convened in Mr. Sarnoff's office on April 6, 1925. The agenda of the conference shows that the Radio Group propounded the following solution of the receiving set controversy:

"Non-exclusive rights to manufacture for the Radio Corporation and for sale by Radio Corporation, radio broadcast receiving devices; such devices to be specified and ordered by the Radio Corporation and to be furnished by the Western Electric Company at cost plus 20%. The quantity, per annum, to be determined, but to be in sufficient amount to warrant an interest on the part of the Telephone Company's engineers in the development of wireless receiving apparatus."

We find no record of the discussions and debates at the meeting of April 6th, but the agenda for the meeting held on April 8th testifies to the fact that the representatives of the Telephone Group had already presented demands for manufacturing rights—demands which if granted might have ruined the Radio Corporation. It was to be expected that the Radio representatives would refuse to concur in the suggestions. A deadlock thus resulted in this, the all-important phase of the negotiations.

Thus the matter stood on April 15th when the committee reported back to Mr. Young and Mr. Gifford. The conference had agreed upon about fourteen minor points but the real controversy still remained unsolved as will be seen in the following extract from the report:

The Telephone Group suggests:

Exclusive rights in radio receiving sets to Radio Group except that:

The Telephone Group shall be licensed to manufacture and sell one-way radio receiving sets, including tubes and accessories, under the patents of both groups, subject to the following provisions:

(a) $10,000,000 of such apparatus in each year (figures based on "list price," that is, price paid by ultimate consumers) free of royalty; any sales beyond the $10,000,000 figure to be subject to a royalty of 20 per cent.

(b) Of the said $10,000,000 not more than $2,000,000 per year shall be apportioned to tubes not forming part of a complete set. Separately sold tubes in excess of the amount of $2,000,000, in any one year shall be subject to a royalty of 20%.

(c) The Telephone Group to sell the above devices either direct to the public or through its own direct agents; the title to the property and the control over its disposition to remain in the Western Electric Com-

The Radio Group suggests:

(a) That the Western Electric Company manufacture —% of the requirements of the Radio Corporation for one-way receiving apparatus, tubes and accessories, at cost plus 20% with engineering relations such as exist between the General Electric Company, Westinghouse and Radio Corporation engineers.

Or as an alternative proposal:

(b) That the Western Electric Company manufacture —% of the requirements of the Radio Corporation for one-way receiving apparatus, tubes and accessories, at cost plus 20%. Such apparatus to carry the Radio Corporation monogram and the Western Electric monogram and the statement that it is manufactured for the Radio Corporation by the Western Electric Company and to be sold by the Radio Corporation through the Western Electric Company's jobbing houses.

Under either of the above propositions, the types of devices and their selling prices to be specified by the Radio Corporation. Engi-

The Telephone Group suggests:

pany until the apparatus is sold to the ultimate consumer.

(d) Whenever any part of a complete set is patented, the sale price of the complete set shall be included in making up the above mentioned total of $10,-000,000.

(e) Reasonable notice to be exchanged between the parties as to new devices to be put on the market.

(f) Head sets sold separately shall not be included in making up the above mentioned total of $10,000,000, but each Group shall have a non-exclusive license to make, use and sell head sets for radio reception.

(g) The license to the Telephone Group shall include radio receiving sets for the use of the Associate and Connecting companies of the Bell System, to be used solely by such companies for the purpose of distributing radio programs over their wires, but such sets shall not be subject to royalty and shall not be included in making up the above mentioned total of $10,-000,000.

(h) Sales for export shall not be included in making up the above mentioned total of $10,-000,000, but each Group shall have a non-exclusive license to make and sell for export, subject to the provision of Article VI, 6, that "No licenses under foreign patents are now granted or are to be implied."

The Radio Group suggests:

neering relations such as exist between the General Electric Company, Westinghouse and Radio Corporation engineers, in this field, to be extended to include the Telephone Group.

It is interesting to note the action taken by the committee on Mr. Sarnoff's proposal of an American Broadcasting Company. The plan emerged in the following joint suggestions:

"15. The following plan is jointly recommended subject to working out of details.

Form the 'American Broadcasting Program Company.' The stockholders to be the American Telephone & Telegraph Company, the Radio Corporation of America, the General Electric and Westinghouse Companies and possibly others. The 'American Broadcasting Program Company' to be controlled by a board of trustees or directors chosen from the prominent people and representing various classes of public interest. The board to number about fifteen and the chairman to be approved by the Secretary of the Department of Commerce.

The primary function of this company shall be to maintain centralized studios, hire talent, prepare and furnish suitable programs for telephonic distribution to the public in any manner available from time to time. Such programs may be furnished not only to the charter members of the 'American Broadcasting Program Company,' but also to others.

The subscribing stations shall pay the 'American Broadcasting Program Company' for such programs and the charges to be based on the principle that the company is to be made self-supporting, but not profit-earning. The company may, however, pay interest on borrowed capital, but shall pay no dividends.

In order to make this plan economically practicable, it is suggested that, subject to prior commitments of the parties, all rights to broadcast transmission for tolls or pay be exclusively vested in this company; the proceeds to be used in the public interest by providing the best possible programs.

"This company would derive its revenue from:

1. Toll broadcasting.
2. Contributions from radio manufacturers (based on a percentage of their sales).
3. Sale of programs.
4. Publication and sale of magazine.
5. Erecting, leasing and operating broadcasting stations.
6. Donations from various sources.

"The 'American Broadcasting Program Company' to study the public tastes and requirements in connection with broadcast programs, to formulate and suggest, if not determine, policies affecting broadcasting, including legislative matters and international questions, which are rapidly coming to the front in this art. Such a company would provide the benefits of organization, centralization, economy, superior programs, and a substantial move toward the stabilization of the art and industry."

Sec. 81. Owen D. Young and Walter S. Gifford Write Letters.

Upon receipt of this report Owen D. Young addressed a formal three-page letter to President Gifford of the American Telephone Company, dated April 15, 1925, in which he recited the history of the controversy and declared that his group was considering "a revision of the contract to meet the original intent." He pointed out that this would mean a release of "the patents held by the American Telephone & Telegraph Company, the Western Electric Company, the Westinghouse Company, the United Fruit Company, the Radio Corporation of America, and the General Electric Company for their most advantageous use in the established business of each of the companies. This I regard not only in the interest of the companies themselves, but essential to their full performance of their public duty."

In speaking of the report that had been made by the joint committee on the day above mentioned, Mr. Young made the following pertinent observations:

"That report indicates in detail the points on which they have agreed, and the points on which they have disagreed. We may assume that the points on which they have agreed carry out the original intention, in the sense that they apply the basic principles which underlay our discussion in 1920 to the situation as it has now developed. Therefore, we need only consider the points on which they have disagreed. The main ones, I understand, are two:

"First—The extension of the license to your people to manufacture under the patents and sell radio broadcast receiving devices.

"Second—The question of the acquisition from your company by the Victor Company of devices made by your company under the patents, which devices, whatever they may be called, are adapted for use, and undoubtedly will be used, in the Radio field."

Mr. Young then went on to discuss that bitterest of all controversies—the business of manufacture and sale of radio receiving sets. It will be remembered that in Mr. Gifford's letter of March 27, 1925, there had been the very disarming suggestion that the Telephone Company desired "non-exclusive licenses to make and sell high-grade receiving apparatus in sufficient amount to warrant an interest in the development of wireless receiving apparatus." Although the arbitration award had denied this right to the Telephone Company when construing the language of the contract of July 1, 1920, yet the threat of setting aside that contract for alleged illegality had so worked upon the minds of the leaders of the Radio Group that they had conceded the point. Their delegates had gone into the conference with instructions to agree to experimental operations by the Telephone Company in this long guarded field. To the dismay of the Radio delegates, however, the representatives of the Telephone Company had insisted upon a stipulation of ten million dollars of business, free of royalty, with a twenty per cent royalty upon sales beyond that figure. In other words, the Telephone Company desired a right that might entitle it to destroy the business in radio sets of the Radio Corporation.

The truth of this supposition is apparent. If the Telephone Company could produce a radio set superior to that of its rival, it might capture the national market, paying no royalty on the first ten million dollars in sales and but twenty per cent for sales above that figure. Is it any wonder, therefore, that even in the diplomatic language of Owen D. Young, in his letter of April 15, 1925, there should have crept a note of bitterness and of defiance? Let us continue with Mr. Young's own words:

"I had assumed that it had been agreed from the beginning that the business of manufacturing and selling broadcast receiving devices under the patents lay in the field licensed to us, and not in yours. I also understood that you desired to invade that field and thereby make an exception to the general principle and the original intent, to the extent that it was necessary to do so in order to give your engineers some experience in radio applications and that this was necessary in order to make the best use of such applications in your own field. To that extent I was sympathetic with your proposal, and I still am. The report of the committee includes proposals made by your representatives which seem to me wholly inconsistent even with the exception which you have asked. It seems to me on the face of it to be a proposal to invade the field licensed to us while protecting your own. The invasion of our field, of course, is the same to us whether done by you directly or indirectly through the Victor Company. This, of course, we cannot assent to."

The reaction of President Gifford to this letter was that of a champion to whom vast interests had been committed. He could not admit the validity of Mr. Young's contentions. Like the skillful debater that he was the letter which he wrote to Mr. Young in reply, under date of April 20, 1925, begins with a bit of effective verbal skirmishing. It is not until midway of the letter that Mr. Gifford joins battle in real earnest by discussing the radio receiving set controversy. So important is this statement of the Telephone Company's case that the letter is reproduced in full.

(Walter S. Gifford to Owen D. Young, April 20, 1925.)

Dear Mr. Young:

I have read with interest your letter of April 15th.

Your statements "we are therefore considering a revision of the contract to meet the original intent," and, referring to the report of the joint committee, "we may assume that the points on which they have agreed carry out the original intention," are not in accord with my understanding of the situation. In many cases, as, for instance, the proposal to give to the Radio Group an exclusive license for the distribution of entertainment over electric light, power and traction wires, and the proposal to give the Telephone Group exclusive rights for automotive devices, and in other cases which will suggest themselves to you, there is a direct departure from what has been the intention of the parties up to this time.

If what you have in mind is the purpose of the parties at the time the contract of 1920 was negotiated, the matter is presented from a different aspect. We were both agreed that licenses under our respective patents were necessary "in order that the radio art might be advanced and the industry established." We felt that this could best be accomplished by making the licenses which were to be granted nonexclusive. Upon this question you differed from us, and urged that this purpose could best be carried out under exclusive licenses. As a result, the contract of July 1, 1920, was a compromise in which each made concessions to the view of the other.

The radio art and industry were practically undeveloped when the contract was made. Largely on this account, the application of the contract to new conditions demonstrated that it was not satisfactory as a working contract, and many differences arose as to its construction. As a consequence, the differences between us as to the construction of the contract were submitted to Mr. Boyden, who was to construe the contract and state the intention of the parties as deduced by him from it.

Our experience under the contract up to the arbitration convinced each of us that as construed by Mr. Boyden it would not be a practical, workable agreement, and so we took up the question whether it could be so revised as to iron out the difficulties which we anticipated under it. The effort of our joint committee, as I understand it, has been along these lines. The plan now proposed by it presents not the original intention but a new plan which is open to discussion and still subject to approval of the principals, both on the points on which the committee agrees, as well as on those on which it disagrees.

A fundamental difficulty in the committee's discussion has been with reference to radio broadcast receiving sets. I feel it necessary that we should make and sell a sufficient number to keep us in full touch with all phases of the art. You express yourself as in sympathy with this idea. Whether or not the Radio Group has an exclusive right in the business of manufacturing and selling broadcast receiving devices, I am sure that this has not been, as you state you assume, agreed to from the beginning.

No suggestion that I know of has been made by the Radio Group to meet this necessity which I have stated. The proposal that we make receiving sets of types to be specified by the Radio Corporation, to be sold solely to it, would not meet our basic purpose, which is to afford our engineers experience in the development of the radio art and science. The sole benefit to us would be of a financial nature, which for the purpose of this discussion, is not a controlling consideration.

Referring to the matter of devices for the Victor Company, these devices are something which, under the contract, we are licensed to make and sell, so that for us to make and sell them cannot properly be characterized as an "invasion" of your field. The fact that they might be illegitimately used in your field is a difficulty which inheres in the plan of licenses of the same devices for use in separate fields, and was anticipated from the outset. I entirely agree with you that this imposed upon each party an obligation to exercise its rights in absolute good faith, and that aside from any question of legal obligation there is a moral obligation which forbids either of us to attempt to do by indirection what it has no right to do directly. This moral obligation we have recognized and shall continue to recognize as binding upon us.

I am leaving for Boston tonight but will be back in New York on Wednesday.

Very truly yours,

(Signed) W. S. Gifford,
President

Sec. 82. Sarnoff-Bloom Negotiations Begin.

As early as March 19, 1925, former Federal Judge Julius M. Mayer, of the firm Mayer, Warfield and Watson, had been consulted by the Radio Group concerning the proper interpretation of the words "amateurs" and "entertainment" as used in the contract between the contending corporations. This fact appears in a letter from Ira J. Adams to Judge Mayer under date of March 19th. The incident itself is unimportant in the development of this narrative but is referred to at this time because Judge Mayer was shortly to be entrusted with important duties in connection with the controversy.

It appears that during the course of negotiations between the members of the conciliation committee, David Sarnoff of the Radio Group and Edgar S. Bloom of the Telephone Company had been especially active in discussing the two unsolved contentions—receiving sets and general broadcasting company. By oral agreement between Owen D. Young and Walter S. Gifford, April 27, 1925, the committee was reduced to two—Sarnoff for the Radio Group and Bloom for the Telephone Company. In explaining this change of plan to the Westinghouse Company on May 8th following Mr. Young wrote thus:

"In order that the Telephone situation might be centralized wholly in Mr. Bloom, I agreed to centralize ours in Mr. Sarnoff. Mr. Gifford and I both thought that two men would be able to deal with that question better than a larger number. The matter was referred to these two men, not with power, but just to study and report."

On the same day that this agreement was reached Mr. Young authorized David Sarnoff to continue with negotiations. The latter at once communicated with Mr. Bloom and a conference was arranged for April 29th. This will explain certain references contained in the following communication:

(Albert G. Davis to Frederick P. Fish, Esq., April 27, 1925.)

My dear Mr. Fish:

Mr. Young asked me to say to you that he had another talk with Mr. Gifford this morning in which, among other things, it was agreed that there should be a further extension of the time for the arbitrator to hand down his final decision. It looks as though an agreement would be reached, but there are many details to be worked out which will take a good deal of time. Mr. Gifford will instruct his people to agree with you on another extension. I suggested one month, but no definite time was fixed. Perhaps it might be wise to make it six weeks, but Mr. Sarnoff and General Harbord are sailing for Europe on May 16th and there is going to be great pressure on everybody to get the thing cleaned up by that time, if possible. It is more probable, however, that the trade will be finished by that time and that it will take a couple of weeks or perhaps even longer to work out the contract.

Very truly yours,

(Signed) ALBERT G. DAVIS

Not often, in examining the dusty files containing sober records of commercial negotiations, does the historian encounter flashes of humor, yet in a letter written by Frederick P. Fish, April 28, 1925, in response to the above request we find the following priceless retort of a long-suffering arbitrator:

"Mr. Boyden consents to an extension of thirty days. Upon my telephoning Mr. Boyden, he said:

" 'I may die any minute but if the parties will take the risk, I will allow the extension.'

"I assume that our agreement holds that if any such misfortune should happen, the report of the arbitrator last submitted should stand as his final and accepted report."

Let us now examine the actual state of the negotiations at the time the above letters were written. A counter-proposal had been suggested under which the Telephone Company would be permitted to manufacture receiving sets to be sold by RCA. This was promptly rejected by the Telephone negotiators. An alternative proposal for manufacture and sale by the Telephone Company bears the imprint of Mr. Sarnoff's vigorous mind. The suggestion was as follows: No royalty on the first million dollars of sales but a rising scale of royalty to the tune of an additional 5% on each successive million.

Thus, when the tenth million should be reached, the Telephone Company would be paying 45% royalty. On the fifteenth million it would be paying 70% royalty and at twenty-one million it would reach 100%. The reaction of the Telephone Company to this ingenious proposal, contained in Mr. Sarnoff's agenda for April 29, 1925,[1] is found in an interesting memorandum taken from the files of the General Electric Company of a conference held on the following day. So great is the historical value of this memorandum that it is reproduced herewith in full:

"MEMORANDUM 'D'
"MEMORANDUM OF MEETING BETWEEN MR. BLOOM OF THE TELEPHONE COMPANY AND MR. SARNOFF OF THE RCA—APRIL 30, 1925.

"1. Mr. Bloom informed Mr. Sarnoff that he had discussed with Mr. Gifford the proposal of the Radio Group that the Telephone Group might be licensed to manufacture a portion of the RCA requirements in radio receiving devices, provided such devices are sold through the RCA on the basis that such devices and their selling prices are to be 'specified by the Radio Group.' Mr. Bloom advised that he and Mr. Gifford are in agreement that this plan cannot be considered by the Telephone Group.

"2. Mr. Bloom then discussed the alternative proposal submitted by the Radio Group on April 29, 1925, under Memorandum 'C,' whereby the Telephone Group might sell direct under the condi-

---

[1] The complete agenda was in the following form:

April 29, 1925

MEMORANDUM C

1. License the Telephone Group to manufacture and sell radio broadcast receiving devices on the following basis:
2. First million dollars in each calendar year (and not cumulative)

....no royalties
Second million dollars........................ 5% royalty
Third million dollars..........................10% royalty
Fourth million dollars.........................15% royalty
Fifth million dollars..........................20% royalty
and so on.

The royalty increasing by 5% with each succeeding million dollars.
3. Royalties based on "list price", i.e., price paid by ultimate consumer.
4. In view of the complexities of the patent situation and of the difficulty in distinguishing between patented and non-patented devices, royalties shall be payable on all devices sold by the Telephone Group in this field whether patented or non-patented.
5. The Telephone Group to sell the above devices either direct to the public or through its own direct agents; the title to the property and the control over its disposition to remain in the Telephone Group until the apparatus is sold to the ultimate consumer.
6. Sales for export shall be included, but at the price at which the sale for export is made, not at the retail price in foreign country. The obligation to sell direct to the public shall not apply to the export field.
7. Sets for use of Associated Bell Companies in their exchanges for re-broadcasting radio programs on the telephone lines, no royalty, as per recommendation. Number Seven of committee's report.
8. Head sets sold separately shall not be subject to royalties, but each Group shall have a non-exclusive license to make, use and sell head sets.
9. The above devices not to be sold for use as combination phonograph-radio sets.

tions therein specified, and advised that the royalties set forth in Item 2 were considered prohibitive and suggested the following counter-proposal:

First five million dollars in each calendar year (and not cumulative) .... no royalties
Sixth million dollars .... 5% royalty
Each succeeding million dollars .... 50% royalty

"As to Item 4, Mr. Bloom advised that the Telephone Group could not consider a provision as broad as that with respect to including all non-patented devices in total subject to royalty. He suggested that this should be modified to provide that whenever any part of a complete device is patented, the selling price of the complete device shall be included in the total subject to royalty, similar to the provision contained in Item 3 'D' of the joint report of April 15, 1925. This means that every patented device, whether sold separately or in combination, is subject to royalty and that machinery might be set up to determine as to what is patented or non-patented, as applied to radio receiving devices.

"3. Mr. Bloom advised that the Telephone Group would not object to a limitation of one and one-half million dollars per annum on the total volume of tube sales where tubes are sold separately and such sales not subject to royalty, but being included in the first five million dollars. On such tubes sold separately in excess of one and one-half million dollars per annum, tubes shall be subject to a royalty of 50%.

"4. With respect to Item 9, Mr. Bloom raised the question as to providing for cases where there is an insistent demand for a Telephone Group radio set to be used in combination with the phonograph. Mr. Sarnoff feels that this will be disposed of through contractual arrangements he hopes to consummate with phonograph companies, which will provide such companies with RCA radio sets.

"5. All other items of Memorandum 'C,' except those above referred to, are satisfactory to the Telephone Group."

Sec. 83. A Tentative Agreement Reached.

The Sarnoff-Bloom conferences continued until May 7, 1925, at which time the two men had apparently accomplished what had long been regarded as impossible—had reached an understanding in the domain of industrial relations. This did not mean that they had settled the controversy but simply that they had explored the possibilities of settlement and were ready to make a joint recommendation to the high commands of the belligerent factions. During three years of intermittent effort the best brains of the radio industry had striven in vain for a common ground and now, in less than two weeks, two nimble-minded negotiators had completed the task—but one of them was the persuasive and dynamic David Sarnoff in the first of a series of similar triumphs. Fortunately for the student of history Mr. Sarnoff's report of the conferences is extant—in the files at the General Electric Company home office. In addition to the report quoted in the preceding section, the memorandum discusses the controversy over phonograph companies. The Telephone Company had already become somewhat involved in business negotiations with the Columbia and Victor phonograph companies. This portion of the report was as follows:

"6. As to sales of devices to phonograph companies, Mr. Bloom stated that his company regarded itself as morally bound to sell such devices to the Victor Talking Machine Company and to the Columbia Phonograph Company. He further advised that the Western Electric Company had written a letter to the Columbia Phonograph Company, asking them to say definitely whether they will or will not purchase such devices. If the answer is that the Columbia Company will purchase, then the Western Electric Company insists on being free to sell. If the answer is in the negative, the Western Electric Company will feel itself morally discharged so far as the Columbia Company is concerned. As to the Victor Company, Mr. Bloom desired to send a similar letter to them and at Mr. Sarnoff's request, this letter was not sent. The position of the Telephone Group with reference to the Victor Company is that if the Radio Corporation can get the Victor Company to discharge the Western Electric Company from the moral obligation which it feels it has, then they will not press this situation further. If, however, the Victor Company does not discharge the Western Electric Company, then the Western Electric Company insists on being free to sell such devices to them."

The conferees had also considered certain details of business arrangements to govern the Telephone Company's entrance into RCA's field of sales, arriving at the following conclusions:

"7. The Telephone Group to sell radio receiving devices either direct to the public or through its own direct agents; the title to the property and the control over its disposition to remain in the Telephone Group until the apparatus is sold to the ultimate consumer.

"8. Sales for export shall be included, but at the price at which the sale for export is made, not at the retail price in foreign country. The obligation to sell direct to the public shall not apply to the export field.

"9. Sets for use of Associated Bell Companies in their exchanges for rebroadcasting radio programs on the telephone lines, no royalty, as per recommendation. Number Seven of committee's report.

"10. Head sets sold separately shall not be subject to royalties, but each group shall have a non-exclusive license to make, use and sell head sets.

"11. The above devices not to be sold for use as combination phonograph-radio sets. (As to this paragraph, Mr. Bloom raised the

MERLIN H. AYLESWORTH
President of NBC during its first decade—an important figure in this recital.

question as to providing for cases where there is an insistent demand for a Telephone Group radio set to be used in combination with the phonograph. Mr. Sarnoff informed Mr. Bloom that this will be disposed of through contractual arrangements he hopes to consummate with phonograph companies, which will provide such companies with RCA radio sets.)"

Mr. Sarnoff's report was discussed at a special strategy meeting of Owen D. Young, General Harbord, Albert G. Davis and Gerard Swope, on May 7, 1925. Fortunately, Albert G. Davis made a written memorandum of the meeting which exists in the following form:

My dear Mr. Sarnoff:

As I understand the views expressed by Mr. Young, General Harbord and Mr. Swope this afternoon, they are as follows:

While we feel that the amount of business which the Telephone Group asks for in the radio reception is excessive, they are disposed to go ahead on the assumption that the rights granted the Telephone Group are regarded as such that no outside consideration is passed between the parties, and with the following modification:

The clause which we suggested to protect devices which require a special status in the radio art is not regarded by them as workable. The Telephone Group is selling a small number of loud speakers for hospital announcement and similar purposes and is also selling a few tubes for use in devices for enabling the deaf to hear, etc. These are, as far as we know, the only tubes which it is selling to the public, as distinguished from tubes which are sold to its associated companies and perhaps to other telephone companies for use on the public service systems, with which we are not concerned and which are excluded from all consideration of this matter so long as they are dealt with in such a way that they cannot come on the retail market.

The suggestion is that these gentlemen will recommend the trade if all sales of tubes, loud speakers and other devices which will be useful in the radio art, which devices are sold over the counter in such a way that they might be used for radio purposes, shall be included in the $5,000,000, and so far as they are tubes in the $1,500,000.

I think that this is along the lines of Mr. Bloom's recognition that it is essential to our interests that he should not go through with the proposed trade with Victor, the only difference being that so far as concerns anything which now exists or anything which we can see as surely coming, the phonograph matter is a large and important one and the other things are small and unimportant. I do not think that this concession on the part of the Telephone Group would reduce the quantity of radio tubes and devices more than $100,000 a year.

I see no reason why we should not except public address systems selling for not less than $———, but of course renewal tubes for those systems should be included as tubes in the $1,500,000.

I do not know whether there is any serious reason to apprehend that any large quantities of tubes requiring sale over the counter will develop in any field in which the Telephone Group is licensed under our patents, but if it does it only means a repetition of the present situation and the creating for us of the very dangers which we are now trying to avoid and which Mr. Bloom fully realizes we are justified in insisting should be avoided.

This is not in any sense going back on anything which the committee decided; subject to Mr. Herr's approval, which has not yet been obtained, we are all in favor of accepting Mr. Bloom's suggestion if he will make this additional concession which is negligible so far as concerns anything which now exists. It would of course be possible to provide, if necessary, that in case any important new use should develop in the Telephone Group's fields outside of radio, the Telephone Group would be perfectly free to supply tubes for that use on a leasing basis if it used proper precautions to keep them out of our field.

Very truly yours,

(Signed) ALBERT G. DAVIS

Sec. 84. A Westinghouse Complication.

The suggestions of change in the proposed agreement made necessary further conferences between David Sarnoff and Edgar S. Bloom, but an unexpected complication arose. Apparently, when Mr. Young communicated with the Westinghouse Company with reference to the Sarnoff-Bloom report, he encountered fireworks. Mr. Herr, one of the high officials of the company, expressed dissatisfaction that Westinghouse had been excluded from the final conferences. He called attention to the fact that his company had previously insisted upon having a representative at these conferences, and that Otto S. Schairer had been selected to safeguard Westinghouse's interests. Mr. Herr apparently inferred that Mr. Young had acted in a high-handed manner in substituting a two-man committee for the committee of five. At any rate, he so thoroughly aroused the ordinarily pacific RCA chieftain that the latter wrote an unusual letter—unusual because it reveals Mr. Young in an obviously indignant mood. The letter reads as follows:

May 8, 1925

Mr. E. M. Herr,
    Westinghouse Electric & Mfg. Company,
      150 Broadway, New York City.

Dear Mr. Herr:

Before I took up negotiations with the Telephone Company, General Tripp spoke to me and said he would like to have a representative of the Westinghouse Company sit in on the negotiations so in that way we would all, at the same time, know how the negotiations were going along, and we might prevent them taking a course which, to any one of us, would seem undesirable. Accordingly, representatives of the Radio Corporation were named Mr. Sarnoff, Mr. A. G. Davis, and Mr. Schairer. The Telephone Company was also represented by Mr. Bloom and one or two associates.

When this report came in which left some matters to be agreed upon, I had a talk with Mr. Gifford, and we finally reached the point where the only major difficulty was the question of how the Telephone Group could be given some manufacturing and thereby give their engineers experience without impairing unnecessarily the position of the Radio Group. In order that the telephone situation might be centralized wholly in Mr. Bloom, I agreed to centralize ours in Mr. Sarnoff. Mr. Gifford and I both thought that two men would be able to deal with that question better than a larger number. The matter was referred to these two men, not with power, but just to study and report. Because I had to leave the city, I asked Mr. A. G. Davis immediately to get in touch with Mr. Schairer and explain to him the situation and see if there was any objection to that method of dealing with it.

I am not concerned in this letter with the question of whether or not you accept the recommendations of Mr. Bloom and Mr. Sarnoff, but I am concerned with the question of whether I have carried on these negotiations in the way which it was intended by General Tripp and myself that they should be carried on. I do not want the slightest misunderstanding about that.

Very truly yours,

(Signed) OWEN D. YOUNG

The rift in the camp of the allies had certain immediate consequences. It called a halt to further negotiations. It delayed David Sarnoff's plans for sailing on his proposed European trip at the time originally specified—May 16th. The Westinghouse chieftains expressed discontent with the proposed terms of compromise. They feared that the Telephone Company might destroy the manufacturing end of the radio business enjoyed by General Electric and Westinghouse. Thus Mr. Sarnoff's outstanding achievement in paving the way for compromise was in danger of becoming labor lost.

Fortunately for the Radio Group, the Westinghouse Company was mollified at the meeting of the board of directors of RCA, held on the following day. A vice-president of Westinghouse was added to the Sarnoff committee—Harry P. Davis, the veteran of radio broadcasting, under whose guidance Stations KDKA, WJZ, WBZ and other Westinghouse stations had been instituted. The following extract from the minutes of the meeting of the board of directors of RCA tells its own story:

"May 15, 1925

"The President and the Vice-President & General Manager reported in regard to certain pending negotiations with the American Telephone & Telegraph Company. After discussion, on motion, duly made, seconded and unanimously carried, it was

"RESOLVED, that a committee (consisting of Mr. H. P. Davis, or an alternate, and Mr. D. Sarnoff) be and hereby is appointed to continue the negotiations with the American Telephone & Telegraph Company and to report back to the board."

Sec. 85. The RCA-Telephone Company Accord.

The committee, thus augmented, immediately resumed negotiations. It now developed that the Westinghouse misunderstanding possessed trading value. The fact that the company was opposed to the allotment of five million dollars of business to the Telephone Company, royalty free, enabled Sarnoff and Davis to wangle a reduction in the quota as will be seen in the following report:

May 20, 1925

Mr. Walter S. Gifford, President,
  American Telephone and Telegraph Company,
    195 Broadway,
      New York City.

Mr. Owen D. Young, Chairman of the Board,
  Radio Corporation of America and
    General Electric Company,
      120 Broadway,
        New York City.

Mr. Guy E. Tripp, Chairman of the Board,
  Westinghouse Elec. & Mfg. Company,
    150 Broadway,
      New York City.

Gentlemen:

Supplementing the Draft Report of April 15, 1925 submitted by the committee appointed by the Telephone and Radio Groups, there is attached hereto Memorandum (G), dated May 20, 1925, setting forth the agreement reached between Mr. E. S. Bloom, representing the Telephone Group and Messrs. H. P. Davis and David Sarnoff, representing the Radio Group, regarding the sale of radio receiving devices.

Memorandum (G), referred to above, is to be substituted for the separate recommendations of the two Groups under Item 3, Page 2 of the Draft Report of April 15, 1925.

On the part of the Telephone Group, the above is subject to the same non-exclusive rights in radio telephony as is stated in the case of radio telegraphy on land under Item 8, Page 4 of the Draft Report of April 15, 1925.

Respectfully,

(Signed) EDGAR S. BLOOM
(Signed) H. P. DAVIS
(Signed) DAVID SARNOFF

May 20, 1925

"MEMORANDUM (G)

"1. License the Telephone Group to manufacture and sell radio broadcast receiving devices on the following basis:

TUBES (THERMIONIC DEVICES) SOLD SEPARATELY

One and one-half million dollars ($1,500,000) in each calendar year (not cumulative), no royalties; but not in excess of 800,000 tubes per annum. Tubes sold in excess subject to 50% royalty.

SETS

Three and one-half million dollars ($3,500,000) in each calendar year (not cumulative), no royalties.
On sets sold in excess of three and one-half million dollars ($3,500,000), 50% royalty.

*   *   *   *

"2. Royalties based on 'list price,' i.e., prices paid by ultimate consumer. The Telephone Group to sell radio receiving devices either direct to the public or through its own direct agents; the title to the property and the control over its distribution to remain in the Telephone Group until the apparatus is sold to the ultimate consumer.

"3. Whenever any part of a complete device is patented, the selling price of the complete device shall be included in the total subject to royalty. This means that every patented device, whether sold separately or in combination, is subject to royalty and that machinery will be set up to determine as to what is patented or non-patented as applied to radio receiving devices.

"4. Telephone Group to grant exclusive licenses to Radio Group covering the field of electric phonograph reproduction as applied to devices used in the home.

"5. Sales for export shall be included, but at the price at which the sale for export is made and not at the retail price charged in a foreign country. The obligation to sell direct to the public shall not apply to the export field.

"6. Sets for use of associated Bell Companies in their exchanges for re-broadcasting radio program over telephone lines, no royalty, as per recommendation Number 7 of Committee's Draft Report of April 15, 1925.

"7. Head sets sold separately shall not be subject to royalties, but each Group shall have a non-exclusive license to make, use and sell such head sets.

"8. The above licensed radio devices not to be sold by Telephone Group for use in combination with phonographs.

"9. Each Group shall give to the other at least four months' notice of its intention to place a new type of radio receiving device on the market. As soon as such device is placed on the market, each Group shall, on request, promptly furnish to the other complete manufacturing information and one sample of such device.

"10. The licenses are to remain exclusive or non-exclusive as provided in the proposed contract for the lives of the respective patents, and the quotas and royalties as specified in Paragraph 2 shall also apply during the lives of the patents.

"11. The Western Electric Company not to announce its proposed program of manufacturing and selling radio receiving devices prior to October 1, 1925.

(Signed) E. S. B.
(Signed) H. P. D.
(Signed) D. S.

It is obvious that the accord thus reached related only to the very troublesome matter of manufacture and sale of radio devices, and did not even mention another major problem—the proposed "American Broadcasting Company" so dear to the heart of David Sarnoff. No doubt the latter had sensed the impossibility of settling so great a matter at this time. A letter written to Owen D. Young on the same day that the committee rendered its report makes interesting reading:

Schenectady, May 20, 1925

Mr. Owen D. Young,
    New York Office.

My dear Mr. Young:

I have heard that Sarnoff and H. P. Davis have traded with Bloom. I do not know what they have done about the broadcasting company. It seems to me of the utmost importance, and Mr. Cotton I think, feels the same way, that the broadcasting company trade should go through simultaneously with the main trade. I hope that it will be possible for you to see Mr. Gifford and get these negotiations started immediately.

Yours very truly,

(Signed) ALBERT G. DAVIS

It will later appear that Mr. Sarnoff and others in high command in the Radio Group had already made up their minds to proceed with the broadcasting project independently of the Telephone Company, and had requested information from the latter as to possible lease of wire lines. Having devoted so much time to the reformation of the industrial contract they dared not inject a new element into negotiations until the hoped-for accord should be "signed, sealed and delivered." Inasmuch as the chief members of the Radio Group owned and operated radio stations, it should be a relatively simple matter to organize a general broadcasting company in which all their broadcasting activities could be consolidated. The new corporation might then be in a position to deal with the Telephone Company in a possible merger of broadcasting interests.

Before leaving for Europe David Sarnoff wrote a letter to Owen D. Young, May 20, 1925, relating to the Telephone accord that presumably charts a course of action that was subsequently followed. It is evident that the ship sailed on the same day that the letter was written.

Dear Mr. Young:
SUBJECT: TELEPHONE CONTRACT
I am writing this note, in advance of my sailing, so that it may serve you as a reminder of the following steps which I assume you will wish to take after Mr. Gifford replies to your letter of date, regarding the extension of time in the matter of the arbitrator's decision.

Assuming that Mr. Gifford replies affirmatively to your letter, above referred to, I suggest that a copy of your letter of date to Mr. Gifford, as well as a copy of his reply, should be sent to Mr. Fish with the request that he arrange with the arbitrator, in accordance with the above letters. This can perhaps best be handled, either direct from your office, or, upon instructions from you, I am sure Mr. A. G. Davis will be glad to handle it.

Presumably, you will wish to acquaint the board of directors of the Radio Corporation, at its next meeting, of the recommendations of the joint committee of the Telephone and Radio Groups. If the board approves the proposed trade with the Telephone Group, then I understand it is your intention to request Judge Mayer to act on behalf of the Radio Corporation, in connection with the drawing up of a contract to cover the agreements reached by the committee. I presume you will wish to instruct Judge Mayer direct in this matter, and in that event, his address is c/o Mayer, Warfield & Watson, 61 Broadway, New York City.

Respectfully yours,
(Signed) DAVID SARNOFF

Before sailing for Europe Mr. Sarnoff also wrote a letter to Judge Julius M. Mayer, dated May 21, 1925, transmitting letters and documents in connection with the Telephone negotiations. A part of this letter ran as follows:

"I have just finished a telephone conversation with Mr. Bloom . . . and informed him of the fact that you had been delegated to handle this matter from now on and to represent in this work the Radio Group. I further informed Mr. Bloom that you are the man to determine from now on as to who in the Radio Corporation organization or in the organization of the General Electric Company or Westinghouse Company, should be called in for consultation (if anyone besides yourself is necessary) and that I would approve whatever course you followed in this matter."

In the records of the Radio Corporation are two items of especial interest to readers who have followed the RCA-Telephone controversy thus far:

"EXTRACT FROM MINUTES OF THE MEETING OF THE BOARD OF DIRECTORS RADIO CORPORATION OF AMERICA MAY 21, 1926

"After discussion, on motion, duly made, seconded and unanimously carried, it was

"RESOLVED, that the President be and he hereby is authorized and empowered to enter into an agreement with the American Telephone and Telegraph Company and such other supplemental agreements, as may be necessary, with the Western Electric Company, the General Electric Company, the Westinghouse Electric and Manufacturing Company and the United Fruit Company, for themselves and for their respective subsidiary or controlled companies, along the general lines of the resolution adopted by the board of directors on June 5, 1925.

*   *   *   *

"EXTRACT FROM THE MINUTES OF THE MEETING OF THE BOARD OF DIRECTORS RADIO CORPORATION OF AMERICA JUNE 5, 1925

"Mr. H. P. Davis reported to the board on behalf of the committee appointed May 15, 1925, to continue the negotiations with the American Telephone & Telegraph Company. After discussion, on motion, duly made, seconded and unanimously carried, it was

"RESOLVED, that the proposed arrangement with the American Telephone & Telegraph Company, as reported, be and hereby is approved in principle; that the matter be referred to Judge Julius M. Mayer to agree upon definitive contracts and that, notwithstanding the large allocation of business to the Telephone Company, without royalty, the proper officers of the company be and they hereby are authorized to waive claims of compensation from the Telephone Company, if in their judgment it is deemed wise to do so."

CHAPTER
ELEVEN

Progress Toward a National Broadcasting Company

Section 86. Significant Developments in Summer of 1925.

THE RESPONSIBILITY FOR DRAFTING A "DEFINITIVE CONTRACT" was thus transferred to the able jurist, Judge Mayer. For some time prior to the action of the RCA board on June 5th, Judge Mayer had been working on the case. This fact appears in a letter written by Albert G. Davis on May 29th, which also brings out other matters of interest:

GENERAL ELECTRIC COMPANY

May 29, 1925

Mr. F. P. Fish,
    84 State St.,
      Boston, Mass.

My dear Mr. Fish:

I have talked with Judge Mayer over the 'phone this morning and have explained to him that you do not care merely to tell Mr. Boyden that we want further delay in this situation, but that you want to tell him frankly what is going on so that he will understand why the delay is being requested. I have also told him that you feel it is time Mr. Boyden's bill was rendered and paid, and would like to suggest to Mr. Boyden that he render his bill.

I understand that Judge Mayer agreed in principle. He will discuss the matter with the others interested, including a representative of the Telephone Company and will try to write you at Boston to-night.

I suggested to Judge Mayer that it might be well to have a conference of counsel Friday morning to decide whatever matters have to be decided before the contract is drawn, as for example—shall we let the arbitrator's decision come down? Judge Mayer doubts his authority to have such a conference with the Telephone Company counsel until the Radio Board has approved the proposed contract.

It is now arranged that there will be a meeting in your office at ten o'clock Friday morning, unless Judge Mayer notifies you otherwise, of counsel interested on our side of the case to discuss this question so that one of us may discuss it with the Telephone counsel after the Radio Board has approved the proposed trade.

Yours very truly,

(Signed) ALBERT G. DAVIS

It is not to be supposed that the selection by the Radio Group of a jurist however able to draft a contract would result in the Telephone Group selecting the same man. Judge Mayer, acting with utmost impartiality, might not be able to interpret adequately the desires of the Telephone Company. It came to pass, therefore, that during the summer of 1925, two separate efforts to draft a "definitive" contract were in progress. Judge Mayer apparently went to Europe early in July, presumably already having prepared a tentative draft of the new contract. Mr. Folk, of the legal staff of the Telephone Company, had certainly submitted his draft of a proposed agreement prior to July 6, 1925. This we learn from a letter written by General James G. Harbord on that date to Albert G. Davis, the letter also mentioning a further postponement of the handing down of the Boyden report. The portion of the letter pertinent to our present inquiry reads as follows:

"Mr. Gifford and I have agreed that we will ask, through Mr. Fish, to have Mr. Boyden not hand down his decision prior to October 13th. This means that the time between now and Judge Mayer's return from Europe, about September 15th, will be spent by our Group in studying Mr. Folk's submitted reformation of the contract between the Telephone Company and ourselves, and that no further negotiations or conferences will take place until Judge Mayer returns from Europe, on September 15th. At that time, it will be Judge Mayer's intention to get our Group together and determine on the objections, if any, to the statement of the contract as Mr. Folk has put it."

It should be noted in this connection that Referee Boyden promptly agreed to the suggestion that he postpone the handing down of his decision until October, 1925.

It appears that the Arnold-Langmuir controversy entered into a new phase in June, 1925. The Court of Appeals of the District of Columbia that had been hearing arguments in an appeal in the Arnold-Langmuir interference now found in favor of Langmuir, which was of course a victory for the Radio Group. The Telephone Company, however, at once gave notice of its intention to file a bill in equity to have the decision reviewed. Albert G. Davis favored a conference to attempt to forestall such action. Frederick P. Fish concurred in the plan. General Harbord and President Gifford soon came to an understanding that the bill would not be filed until October. It was hoped that the entire controversy might reach an amicable solution prior to that date.

While these events were transpiring important developments took place in the field of radio broadcasting. Station WEAF, the Telephone Company's pet project in this line, was as usual in the forefront of broadcasting activities. More than a score of stations throughout the country were now under its banner. This does not mean that the regular broadcasts of the New York station were being fed out daily to so extensive a network, but simply that on great occasions the entire circuit joined hands. Station WJZ, RCA's chief broadcasting station, was still limited to a very modest galaxy of stations, largely because of inability to secure suitable wire lines. To be sure it could lease telegraph lines, yet the comparison in results was so markedly in favor of the special long lines of the American Telephone Company that there was little encouragement to the RCA station in this type of network broadcasting.

A significant letter in the files of RCA discloses the fact that, as early as June, 1925, the officials having in charge the destinies of Station WJZ were thinking of establishing trans-Atlantic exchange of radio programs. This letter is dated June 26, and was written by Dr. Alfred N. Goldsmith to Elmer E. Bucher. Dr. Goldsmith was providing Mr. Bucher with suggestions for a proposed report on the desirability of re-broadcasting European programs. One suggestion by Dr. Goldsmith was that broadcasting was getting into a rut, and that "novelties and revolutionary additions to present-day broadcasting are required as a sort of heart stimulant to the present broadcasting situation." It was believed that programs originating in London, Paris or Berlin would excite public interest and stimulate growth in the radio industry. Dr. Goldsmith estimated that an outlay of $175,000 would cover the cost of wire lines and the equipment needful to launch the project.

On June 29, 1926, Mr. Bucher sent a letter to General Harbord in which he made the following pertinent observations:

"Last year we had the stimulus of the Republican and Democratic Conventions which, without doubt, were primarily responsible for the large sales volume of the latter part of 1924. Since that time there have been no startling or novel changes in broadcasting methods except one evening when WJZ and associated stations fairly successfully re-broadcasted the program of the Hotel Savoy in London. Could this be repeated, say twice per week during the forthcoming radio season, I would say offhand that it would be worth millions of dollars to our sales operations."

On July 20, 1925, General Harbord addressed a letter to Thomas F. Logan, a prominent advertising man, in which he asked advice on several points, one of which was as follows:

"Is there any way that the Radio Corporation can secure financial contributions and support for broadcasting without going into the advertising business?"

On July 21, 1925, Owen D. Young wrote a letter to General Harbord that shows the mental attitude of the leading members of the Radio Group toward Mr. Sarnoff's long-advocated plan of a general broadcasting company. The letter was very brief, and ran as follows:

Dear General Harbord:

General Tripp suggests, and therefore it should be studied most carefully, that the Radio Corporation, the Westinghouse and General Electric all might now turn over their stations to a broadcasting company to operate them. The broadcasting company could then itself determine what its policy would be with reference to broadcasting for toll, and all stations could have a unified policy. General Tripp is not insistent that the toll should begin right away, but he would like to have the company organized so that the unified policy could begin right away.

Yours very truly,

(Signed) OWEN D. YOUNG

On the following day, General Harbord replied to Mr. Young's letter calling attention to the fact that the American Telephone Company had originally been included in such plans, and inquiring whether any written or oral commitments had been made in this regard. On July 24, 1925, Miss Morrison, of Mr. Young's office, reported thus by telephone to General Harbord:

"Mr. Young asked Miss Morrison to say to you that his conversations with Mr. Gifford do not in any way obligate the Radio Corporation to include the Telephone Company in any broadcasting company which might be formed, and that there is no reason that he knows of why we should not go ahead on General Tripp's suggestion, excluding the Telephone Company."

In view of the endless delays that had attended past efforts to agree upon anything with the Telephone Company we may be reasonably certain that General Harbord breathed a sigh of relief upon receiving the above message.

Secretary Hoover, of the Department of Commerce, had by this time allotted to several of the more important broadcasting stations the privilege of testing "super-power." Among these stations were WGY, the General Electric Company station in Schenectady, and RCA's New York outlet, WJZ. It will be remembered that when the Radio Corporation opened Stations WJZ and WJY in Aeolian Hall in New York City, the broadcasting towers of the stations had been erected on the roof of the building itself. In testing super-power, RCA engineers, conforming to public misapprehensions at that time, decided that the transmitter would have to be located outside the metropolitan center. Actually, the amount of energy thrown into space by a 50,000-watt transmitter is negligible as an interference factor, and is small compared to other forms of power.

Fortunately for the broadcasting industry, RCA engineers decided to build their broadcasting towers in Bound Brook, N. J., thirty miles distant from New York City. Radio engineers were no longer laboring under the impression that studios and broadcasting towers need be in the same neighborhood. But the RCA experiment was nevertheless of a trail-blazing nature—the first genuine super-power station to go into operation in the United States. It was to have two transmitting sets—one to operate on 455 meters and the other on 100 meters. The station was to be connected with the New York studios by telephone lines entirely enclosed in cable. It was anticipated that so powerful a station would make it difficult for residents of Bound Brook to tune out WJZ in favor of any other station. RCA engineers, however, were already working on the problem in order that no unnecessary antagonism to their own station be developed in the neighborhood.

Another development that was destined to have a profound effect upon American life was the gradual amalgamation of radio and its older sister, the phonograph. The process thus begun was destined to continue into the moving picture field, eventually giving to the world synchronized sound and motion. This may appear very mysterious and even far-fetched, yet it is to the vacuum tube and other devices, born of radio broadcasting, that we owe our modern talking pictures. It is true, however, that nobody at the inception of the movement even dreamed of the marvelous development that lay beyond the horizon of scientific research. It was one of those mysterious leadings of providence that has so often brought blessings to mankind.

Ever since the first radio set had been introduced into the living room of the American home, to take its place beside the phonograph, certain radio engineers had foreseen that eventually both devices would be housed in a single cabinet. The actual physical union had begun years prior to 1925 yet, in the summer of that year, circumstances conspired to give that union official sanction if not parental blessing. The story has thus been told by the author in the first volume in this series:

"The Victor Talking Machine Company, after vainly struggling against the radio tide for years, decided in the spring of 1925 to conform rather than perish. The company already had some of the very necessary elements of a successful radio program—an impressive galaxy of top-notch vocal artists as well as the Victor Orchestra, equal to the best. It will be remembered that John McCormack and Lucrezia Bori had already appeared with the Victor Orchestra and quartette on a radio program. This, no doubt, marked the beginning of the transition to radio broadcasting as an allied art. It was rumored in July, 1925, that the Victor Company had acquired patent rights to a loud speaker developed and patented in France. This speaker was said to be greatly superior to any type yet devised in the United States. In August the Victor Company definitely announced an alliance with the radio industry but expressly disclaimed intention of manufacturing radio sets. Instead, an arrangement was concluded with the Radio Corporation of America to have superheterodyne sets built to be combined with the well-known Victor phonograph. The loud speaker was indeed of French origin. It was announced also that Victor artists would continue to appear on radio programs." [1]

Later developments in the amalgamation of radio, phonograph and moving pictures will be noted hereafter.

Sec. 87. A Broadcasting Foundation Proposed.

In the meantime, a committee that had been appointed by General Harbord on July 20, 1925, was studying broadcasting problems. Dr. Alfred N. Goldsmith had been made chairman of the committee, his associates being Captain Howard W. Angus, P. Boucheron, Thomas F. Logan, and Charles B. Popenoe. The first meeting of the group occurred on July 24, 1925. Under so vigorous and colorful a chairman as Dr. Goldsmith it was natural that this committee of experts should have wasted no time in answering certain queries propounded to it. The following quotation from the report of the committee, rendered on July 28, 1925, is highly illuminating:

"*Question 1.* Is there any way that the Radio Corporation can secure financial contributions and support for broadcasting without going into the advertising business?

"*Answer 1.* The committee is of the opinion that there is no way in which the Radio Corporation could secure such financial returns outside of the advertising business.

*   *   *   *

"*Question 2.* Is it desirable that the Radio Corporation should go into advertising through its broadcast stations, or is it more desirable that we should be the leader of a group which shall be devoted to the entertainment and interest of the broadcast listener rather than to attempt to support our broadcasting activities by advertising?

"*Answer 2.* It is not desirable that the Radio Corporation shall go into toll advertising in its broadcasting stations.

*   *   *   *

[1] Archer, *History of Radio to 1926*, p. 361. Since writing the above the author has discovered in the files of the Radio Corporation evidence that a definite contract with the Victor Company was concluded on May 16, 1925, although the alliance was not generally known until several months later.

" (a) There is a natural conflict of interest between serving the broadcast listener (the purchaser of radio receivers) and serving the advertiser using broadcasting facilities. The listener desires a program of the highest quality as free as possible from all extraneous or irrelevant material, particularly such as may be psychologically distracting from an artistic performance because of its commercial tinge. . . . The tendency of advertising programs is toward direct advertising . . . the tendency of stations devoted entirely to pleasing the listener and without toll payment for advertising programs is to minimize to the utmost any inartistic or irrelevant text.

"(b) The Radio Corporation of America is the largest radio sales organization in the United States. . . . (it) requires the good will of the broadcast listener and this might be jeopardized by the responsibility for the commercial success of toll advertising programs."

The Goldsmith committee turned its attention also to the state of development of radio broadcasting and noted among observable defects a lack of adequate co-ordination between programs of the various stations; confusion in policies as to the hiring of artists and the securing for radio use of copyrighted material. The committee reached the conclusion that the haphazard distribution of broadcasting stations rendered impossible adequate co-ordination. It suggested a "Broadcasting Foundation of America" to include "groups widely representative of the radio industry and of directly associated industries." It listed the following companies as potential supporters of the Foundation:

The Radio Group

Radio Corporation of America
General Electric Company
Westinghouse Company

Automobile Accessories Group

Atwater Kent
Stewart Warner
Bosch Magneto
Splitdorf

Independent Telephone Company Group

Stromberg Carlson
Kellogg
Federal Telephone & Telegraph Company

Independent Radio Manufacturing Group

Crosley
Freed-Eisemann
DeForest
Zenith

Radio Parts and Accessories Group

Willard Storage Battery Company
Brandes, Inc.
Pacent Electric Company
Dubilier
Bakelite Corporation
National Carbon Company
French and Burgess Battery Companies

The phonograph companies "engaged in the production of combination phonograph-radio instruments such as Victor and Brunswick" were suggested as possible patrons of the Broadcasting Foundation.

The Western Union and Postal Telegraph Companies were listed as interested in furnishing "pick-up and intercommunication services for radio broadcasting." No mention is made of the American Telephone Company either as the owner of broadcasting stations or as a possible source of pick-up lines or wire intercommunication.

It is interesting to note that the Goldsmith committee made various practical suggestions as to possible financial support of the Foundation. These suggestions may be summarized as follows:

1. Participants owning broadcasting stations to lease them to Foundation at nominal rental.

2. Participants to contribute to Foundation a "percentage of sales price of their radio products to the distributor, except that RCA would pay the tax for its group of manufacturers."

3. The Broadcasting Foundation would be free to accept tolls for broadcast advertising. Such advertising to be of the good-will type rather than direct advertising.

4. Foundation "may assemble and distribute programs, either of advertising or non-advertising nature, for tolls paid to Foundation by non-member broadcasting stations."

5. Possible philanthropic donations to general funds.

Thus the suggestions previously made by the various members of the committee were whipped into shape. In transmitting the above report to General Harbord the chairman also forwarded supplemental suggestions from Logan, Angus, and Popenoe, each of which contained afterthoughts or reservations from the original draft made on July 24th. Possibly this fact led Dr. Goldsmith to include the following comment:

"The committee seems to feel that it lacked certain information and background which Mr. Sarnoff could have provided and it hoped that he would have the opportunity to consider the report immediately upon his return."

An examination of the letter of Thomas F. Logan, dated July 27th, reveals certain human-interest angles, as will be seen in the following excerpts:

"I feel fairly safe about the general principles outlined in the report but I hope that Mr. Sarnoff will take a crack at it before General Harbord lets it go out as an RCA plan. . . . Mr. Sarnoff has strong convictions on this subject of broadcasting. General Harbord may put the negotiations into his hands. He will have to expound the plan publicly. I wouldn't want to be a member of a committee that had put another pair of handcuffs on him. There will be enough exercise for his Houdini talents in other directions.

"When you get right down to it, some of this broadcasting plan may be tied up with other negotiations, perhaps even with some of the impressions D. S. brings back from Europe."

Captain Angus, in a letter dated July 28th, raised a question as to the wisdom of forming a Broadcasting Foundation without the cooperation of the Telephone Group. He answered his own question by declaring: "If the Radio Group decides to compete with the Telephone Group in the broadcasting field or if the Telephone Group refuses to co-operate, then I am of opinion that the Broadcasting Foundation of America should not be formed, but that the Radio Group should enter the competitive field unhampered by any associates."

He expressed himself in favor of the pooling of the broadcasting stations of RCA, General Electric and Westinghouse under the management of RCA, on the ground chiefly that by centralized management greater efficiency might be attained.

Charles B. Popenoe, a member of the committee and manager of the department of broadcasting of RCA, wrote a letter on July 29, 1925, in which he argued against Captain Angus' conclusions above noted, expressing belief that the Broadcasting Foundation idea was sound. Like Mr. Logan he expressed a desire that David Sarnoff be consulted before any action should be taken.

Sec. 88. Renewed Efforts for a National Broadcasting Company.

It is apparent that upon David Sarnoff's return from Europe in August, 1925, the broadcasting problem was at once brought to his attention. In the RCA files is to be found a letter to Mr. Sarnoff, dated August 10th, and signed by Thomas F. Logan of the Goldsmith committee. Since Mr. Logan was the head of an advertising corporation, he was in a position to advise Mr. Sarnoff on the feasibility of broadcast advertising. What was more to the point, he transmitted a letter from the Jewett Radio and Phonograph Company of Detroit, Michigan, announcing a new 5000-watt broadcasting station to be known as WJR. The Jewett letter stated that the new station would accept "paid publicity features for other industrial concerns."

Mr. Logan pointed out that his company was receiving similar requests from other sources. He called attention to the chaotic condition then existing in the broadcasting field, and concluded his letter with the following argument for the prompt setting up of a national broadcasting company.

"A single national company," he wrote, "set up in the right way, would probably be assured of a gross revenue from advertising, if the service were properly sold, amounting to a sum between $500,000 and $1,000,000 in the second year. Once stabilized the rates could be raised and the ultimate gross would go up accordingly."

It is obvious that Mr. Logan did not expect that the proposed company could operate on a one-million-dollar earning capacity, but believed that rates adequate to self support might eventually be charged. This advice was in line with Mr. Sarnoff's own belief. Many oral conferences were held and the situation was discussed from all possible angles. Circumstances existed, however, that necessitated delays in the formulation of definite plans for a broadcasting company of national character.

The arbitration report was still being withheld, at the request of the parties. There was one development in this matter that was worthy of note, at least so far as the long-suffering referee was concerned. It had been suggested to him by officials of the Radio Group that, notwithstanding the delay, he should be paid for his services. Lawyers of Mr. Boyden's prominence and ability are customarily compensated not merely for the time and labor devoted to such a task but also for the responsibilities assumed and the magnitude of the issues under arbitration. The bill rendered by Mr. Boyden was apparently not regarded by the Radio Group as excessive. In paying it David Sarnoff wrote the following letter:

September 10, 1925

Roland W. Boyden, Esq.,
   60 State Street,
   Boston, Mass.

Dear Mr. Boyden:

In the absence of General Harbord from the city, I wish to acknowledge receipt of your letter of August 31st addressed jointly to Mr. Guernsey, counsel for the Telephone Group, and Mr. Fish, counsel for the Radio Group, and also your bill of the same date in the amount of $37,935.88, chargeable to the Radio Group.

I take pleasure in sending you herewith a check of the Radio Corporation of America in the amount of $37,935.88 and desire to take this opportunity to express to you, on behalf of the Radio Group, our very sincere appreciation of the conscientious manner in which you have handled so difficult a task.

Very cordially yours,

(Signed) DAVID SARNOFF

Judge Mayer was still abroad and the drafting of the definitive contract between the Radio Group and the Telephone Group must necessarily wait until his return to New York. In the meantime, the suggestions of Mr. Folk embodying the Telephone Company's desires in the matter were being studied by Sarnoff and others of the high command. It is apparent that attention was also being focused on the proposed broadcasting company even though it was not considered expedient to do more than deliberate in secret conclave.

A letter written by David Sarnoff to General Guy E. Tripp, chairman of the board of Westinghouse, on September 2, 1925, seems to have accomplished definite results in reviving the interest of Westinghouse in a general broadcasting corporation. Mr. Sarnoff opened his letter with the following sentiment:

"Because I know your desire to keep the broadcasting expenses of the Westinghouse Company down to the lowest possible minimum . . . I am writing you this note in order to bring to your personal attention the pressing need at this time for inter-connection between our group of broadcasting stations. . . . The fact remains that at this date there does not exist a fully developed and effective substitute for wires to connect local stations. This, together with the possession by the Telephone Company of a national network of wires, has naturally given WEAF and its associated stations a great advantage in the air over the Radio Corporation and its associated companies."

The inference from the above statement was so obvious that Mr. Sarnoff might have been expected to voice his pet project of a national broadcasting company. It was the only logical answer to the Telephone Company's challenge, yet David Sarnoff apparently desired that the suggestion should come from Mr. Tripp. So we find him avoiding the conclusion of thought yet affirming that "a permanent solution to this problem must be found."

The vice-president and general manager of RCA continued as follows:

"In the meantime, however, we are faced with the practical situation which requires immediate attention. Mr. Popenoe, our manager of programs, has been successful in securing permission to broadcast a number of important events during the coming winter season, but only on the understanding that he can provide adequate distribution of the programs."

Mr. Sarnoff enumerated a series of programs projected by the Steinway Company, in which great artists of the opera and concert stage were to appear and asserted that the stations of Westinghouse and the General Electric Company were needed to complete the circuit. He stressed the need of wire connections and the high cost of same. His final observation was to point out the possibility of having celebrated artists of the Victor and Brunswick Phonograph Companies broadcast over WJZ, adding the following significant words:

"But here too, the problem of distribution has been raised and the greater facilities of the Telephone Company pointed to.

"May I not ask that you will be good enough to look into this question personally, and at your convenience I shall be glad to learn of your reaction to this matter?"

Mr. Sarnoff had not long to wait. On the very next day General Tripp replied with military terseness that "consideration should be given to the immediate organization of a broadcasting company which should include for the moment only those stations now operated by the Radio Corporation group." General Tripp declared that this plan would permit a proper allocation of expense of providing broadcasting facilities.

At a meeting of the board of directors of RCA, held on September 4, 1925, the Sarnoff-Tripp letters were read and discussed. Lewis MacConnach, secretary of RCA, thus reported to David Sarnoff, not as yet a member of the board, the developments of the aforesaid meeting:

"Mr. Young thought that Judge Mayer should proceed with the memorandum he has and reduce it to a contract form with the Telephone Company, and that it would be better to get that worked out first.

"Mr. Young suggested that General Tripp and Mr. H. P. Davis work out a suggestion for a program for a broadcasting company, and to send copy of the same to Mr. Swope and General Harbord. He stated that the matter could then be considered, and if the suggested program looks reasonable it can be brought to the board. This procedure was agreed to by General Tripp, Mr. Swope and General Harbord." [2]

Sec. 89. Further Attempts to Redraft Telephone Contract.

On September 8, 1925, General Tripp sent to Owen D. Young a two-page memorandum embodying a plan for the "Immediate Organization of a Broadcasting Service Association." The project was to be launched by General Electric, RCA and Westinghouse. The immediate objects of the proposed association were six in number.

"1. The pooling and proper allocation of all expense of operation and development of existing broadcasting stations belonging to the group.
"2. The prevention of duplication of effort in development work having to do with broadcasting.
"3. The establishment of a united front in dealing with the Telephone Company's broadcasting situation.
"4. Unified control and direction of the general development of broadcasting, etc.
"5. A central control over programs.
"6. The establishment of methods of securing income for service."

There was a further suggestion that the proposed association be governed by a board of trustees, one member from each of the parties; the board to control but not to own the stations. It was suggested that the parties contribute funds in some proportion to be agreed upon. Reference was made to the possible setting up of a budget and the right to call for subscriptions. Other ideas were suggested, yet the plan was decidedly nebulous as to details.

General Harbord's reaction to the suggestions was contained in a letter addressed to Owen D. Young on September 16th. "My reaction to this principle," he wrote, "for it is a principle and not a plan— is favorable. I am particularly glad to have it from the Westinghouse representative, inasmuch as it was suggested to them about two years

---

[2] The board of directors of RCA in 1925 had the following membership:

Owen D. Young, Chairman	James G. Harbord
Gordon Abbott	Edward W. Harden
Arthur E. Braun	Edwin M. Herr
Albert G. Davis	Edward J. Nally
George S. Davis	Edwin W. Rice, Jr.
Harry P. Davis	Gerard Swope
John W. Griggs	Guy E. Tripp
John Hays Hammond, Jr.	

ago and declined. We accept it, therefore, in principle, subject to the working out of the details. Ultimately it ought to mean economy and improved service."

General Harbord, further on in his letter, expressed a disturbing thought in the following language:

"Supported as it will be by contributions from the three companies, I am wondering if the contribution made by the manufacturing companies is to be charged to the cost of radio apparatus and thus, eventually, to be borne by the Radio Corporation for all three of us."

Obviously the idea of a general broadcasting company required a great deal of patient thought if it were ever to ripen into a workable plan of operation. The danger of competition from the broadcasting department of the American Telephone Company was clearly visualized by RCA leaders. Dr. Alfred N. Goldsmith, in a letter to General Harbord on September 21, 1925, made the following pertinent observations:

"It is certain that national broadcasting is going to be an extremely competitive enterprise. The Telephone Company will be a most formidable competitor. . . . The Telephone Company is a highly centralized enterprise with a unified engineering policy and with full control of the activities of its research and development engineers. . . . It is simply impossible to compete with such an organization, liberally supplied with fighting funds, unless one's own organization is at least as well planned."

While these negotiations were in progress Judge Julius Mayer was laboring industriously at the difficult task of formulating a new contract between the Radio Group and the Telephone Company. The lawyer representing the Telephone Company in the matter was George E. Folk. This fact, together with other pertinent information, is to be found in the following letter:

MAYER, WARFIELD & WATSON
11 Pine Street
New York

September 26, 1925.

Re—Telephone Agreement

Mr. David Sarnoff,
233 Broadway,
New York City.

My dear Mr. Sarnoff:

I continued today my conference with Mr. Folk, and we have now completely gone over his draft. There are some features which it

appears Mr. Bloom wishes to negotiate with you—I call it re-nego-
tiate. There are not many of these. I think this fact gives us the
opening you and I were talking about. I intend to stop in to see you
Tuesday morning on my way downtown and hope that I may catch
you free for, at any rate, half an hour. I can bring you down to date
on the essentials more quickly this way than by correspondence.

Sincerely yours,

(Signed) JULIUS M. MAYER

Amendments to the draft referred to on September 26th had apparently been transmitted to Mr. Sarnoff. On October 7th, Judge Mayer
wrote another letter to David Sarnoff that demonstrates the laborious
nature of the effort to arrive at an understanding with the Telephone
Company. Judge Mayer's letter contained suggestions for further
correction of the language. By this time, however, the legal experts
had despaired of completing their labors before the October 13th
deadline, when the Boyden report was to be made public. This
accounts for the following letter from the representative of the Telephone Company:

AMERICAN TELEPHONE AND TELEGRAPH COMPANY

BELL SYSTEM

195 Broadway

New York

October 7, 1925.

Edgar S. Bloom
Vice-President

MR. DAVID SARNOFF, Vice President and General Manager,
Radio Corporation of America,
233 Broadway, New York, N. Y.

Dear Mr. Sarnoff:

On July 7th Mr. Fish wrote General Harbord as follows—

"My dear General Harbord:

"Mr. Boyden assents to the suggestion that the coming down of
his opinion be postponed until October 13.

"I have written Mr. Guernsey to this effect.

"Very truly yours,

" (Signed) F. P. FISH"

While this matter is rapidly getting into final shape, it would seem
to me desirable that we arrange to have Mr. Boyden extend the time
for handing down his decision to December 1st. I believe we will be
able to come to a final conclusion considerably in advance of December 1st and I am only suggesting that date so as to avoid the possi-

bility of again requesting a further extension from Mr. Boyden. If you concur in the above, I will appreciate it if you will have the matter presented to Mr. Boyden.

Very truly yours,

(Signed) Edgar S. Bloom,
Vice-President

On the lower margin of the foregoing letter appears the following penciled memorandum:

> "I agreed with Judge Mayer Oct. 13, '25
> to extend this to Jan. 1, '26.
>   "D. S."

The reason for the additional month of delay indicated by Mr. Sarnoff's memorandum apparently arose on October 8, 1925, when a dispute between counsel occurred over the question of vacuum tubes. It was thereupon agreed to refer the matter to David Sarnoff and Edgar S. Bloom for a compromise agreement. On October 9th the two men conferred at length but, since the matter was of an extremely technical nature, they found it impossible to reach a satisfactory agreement. It was accordingly decided to set up a special committee of experts to wrestle with the problem. In a letter to Judge Mayer on October 9, 1925, Mr. Sarnoff wrote as follows:

"Mr. Bloom has agreed to my suggestion that the question of special bases[3] for tubes be considered by a technical committee consisting of one representative each from the different companies concerned. For the Radio Corporation, I nominate Dr. Goldsmith. Will you please ask the General Electric and Westinghouse Companies to nominate a representative to sit on this committee, and when you have received their reply, please advise Mr. Folk, who, after consultation, with Mr. Bloom, will advise the names of the representatives designated by the Telephone Group."

In the files of RCA is to be found a memorandum, dated October 13, 1925, that epitomizes the status of negotiations on that date:

"Supplementing Judge Mayer's memorandum of October 8th regarding conference in Mr. Bloom's office: Judge Mayer states that he and Mr. Folk are now waiting for Mr. Bloom and Mr. Sarnoff to agree on the questions outlined in the above memorandum of October 8th. The lawyers can make no further progress until these questions are determined and they are instructed accordingly.

"These questions, in the main, seem to be the following:

---

[3] Whether bases should be standardized in the same manner as electric light bulbs, or have bases so different that RCA and A. T. & T. could not be used interchangeably.

SUBJECT	*REMARKS*
1. *Broadcast Transmission* (Wire-lines, pick-ups, etc.)	Mr. Bloom to submit proposition to Mr. Sarnoff for consideration of the Radio Group.
2. *Multi-Party or Single Party One-Way Wireless Telephone Service*	Agreement to be reached as to the extent and limitations of this grant by the Radio Group to the Telephone Group (Judge Mayer and Mr. Folk are endeavoring to draw suitable clause to cover this).
3. *Items on which Royalty Is Payable* (Page 11, Paragraph "6" Folk draft.)	Definition is required.
4. *Wireless Telegraphy* (Extent and limits of grant by the Radio Group to the Telephone Group.)	This may require modification of previous understanding.
5. *Transoceanic Two-way Wireless Telephony*	Shall the rights to the Telephone Group be made exclusive instead of non-exclusive as previously contemplated.
6. *Special Bases for Vacuum Tubes*	A Technical Committee has been appointed to consider and report on this subject.
7. *Amateur Wireless Telephony*	The Telephone Group suggested this be made non-exclusive to both groups instead of exclusive to Radio Group as at present but sales by Telephone Group to be included in the total amount licensed.
8. *Quota*	The Telephone Group desires figures raised from 800,000 tubes to 900,000 tubes and from $1,500,000 to $1,800,000, but retaining the same limit of $5,000,000 as previously agreed upon.
9. *Radio Receiving Apparatus for Redistribution in Buildings*	See Judge Mayer's memorandum of October 8, 1925.
10. *Radio Goniometry*	See Judge Mayer's memorandum of October 8, 1925.

It should perhaps be noted that the author has been unable to discover a copy of Judge Mayer's memorandum of October 8th. It is not, however, essential to the development of this historical narrative.

Sec. 90. Westinghouse Company Grows Impatient at Delay.

It has previously been observed that the Westinghouse Company was becoming increasingly concerned over the mounting deficit in connection with its broadcasting activities. Its responsible officials had long since become convinced that the only financial salvation of broadcasting lay in commercial advertising on the air. The Telephone Company had furnished convincing proof that a radio program could be not only popular with broadcast listeners, but also at the same time financially profitable. Prior to the arbitration hearings none of the Radio Group had dared to contest the Telephone Company's claim of right to exclusive exploitation of broadcast advertising. The Boyden decision, tentatively drafted in November, 1924, had denied the supposed monopoly of the Telephone Company. Thus the Radio allies, particularly the Westinghouse Company, had kindled to the prospect of embarking in broadcast advertising.

Interminable delays in the promulgation of the decision had developed, however, and these delays had had the effect of plunging the broadcasting departments of the allies deeper and deeper into "the red." Westinghouse was of course the greatest loser since it possessed more stations than General Electric and RCA combined. The postponement of October 8, 1925, set a new deadline of December 1st, but even this was to be altered on October 13th to January 1, 1926. Westinghouse had evidently counted upon embarking in radio advertising in October, immediately upon the expected publication of the arbitration award. The postponement referred to had the effect of the proverbial last straw. The Westinghouse Company now resolved to act on its own initiative, regardless of consequences.

On October 15, 1925, while David Sarnoff was in the midst of delicate negotiations with Mr. Bloom of the Telephone Company, he was handed the following communication:

October 15, 1925

Mr. David Sarnoff, Vice-President,
 Radio Corporation of America,
  233 Broadway, New York.

Dear Mr. Sarnoff:

Mr. Terry has handed me a copy of your letter of October 9th to Mr. Bloom stating that you asked Judge Mayer to have the referee in the Telephone arbitration withhold his decision until December 1st.

On July 3, 1924, the Radio Corporation adopted a resolution regarding broadcasting for pay which was to become effective upon the final decision of the referee. In view of the fact that the referee has made his decision affirming such right and even though the formal handing down thereof has been withheld at your request, we regard the decision as having been rendered and, therefore, in effect so far as this resolution is concerned and are proceeding in accordance with its provisions.

Very truly yours,

(Signed) E. M. HERR,

President

Inasmuch as the letter arrived on a Thursday, and required the most earnest consideration as well as an exercise of high diplomacy, Mr. Sarnoff appears to have delayed his answer until the following Monday, October 19th. The letter speaks for itself and, in view of its importance, is reproduced herewith in full:

October 19, 1925

Mr. Edwin M. Herr, President,
  Westinghouse Electric & Mfg. Company,
    150 Broadway,
      New York City.

Dear Mr. Herr:

I take pleasure in acknowledging receipt of your letter of October 15, 1925, with reference to the resolution of July 3, 1924, adopted by the board of the Radio Corporation of America regarding broadcasting for pay. It seems to me that the factors involved in this situation are the following:

1. There is a verbal understanding between Mr. Young and Mr. Gifford to the effect that pending the conclusion of negotiations between the Radio Group and the Telephone Group, each side would proceed in accordance with the practices which it followed prior to the arbitrator's informal decision, and that such activities prior to the conclusion of a new contract, would be licensed by each party.

2. My recollection is that there is a further understanding in the above sense resulting from an exchange of letters between Mr. Fish on behalf of the Radio Group and Mr. Guernsey on behalf of the Telephone Group. I cannot at this moment locate this correspondence, though I believe it exists in our files.

3. A plan for a unification of the broadcasting activities of the Westinghouse and General Electric Companies and the Radio Corporation was recently submitted by General Tripp to Mr. Young. The latter forwarded General Tripp's proposal to the Radio Corporation and the General Electric. General Harbord on behalf of

the Radio Corporation formally advised Mr. Young that we are agreeable to the principles suggested by General Tripp and are ready to proceed with an effort to study and work out the details. The General Electric Company, I understand, is studying General Tripp's plan and expects to advise you of its position shortly.

4. The negotiations during the past week or two between Mr. Bloom of the Telephone Group and myself have reached the stage in the matter of broadcasting transmission which I outlined at the meeting of the Radio Board on Friday. As you know, the board authorized me to proceed to develop the proposals of the Telephone Company in greater detail, and this I am planning to do. The negotiations with the Telephone Company are not as yet concluded.

In the light of the foregoing circumstances, I trust you will agree that it would be highly unfortunate, if, pending the conclusions of negotiations with the Telephone Company and the decision as to General Tripp's plan for a unification of the broadcasting activities of the General Electric and the Westinghouse Companies and the Radio Corporation, any single member of the Radio Group should now engage in a line of action which might force the other members of the Radio Group to do the same, and thereby possibly endanger the very delicate negotiations now going on between the Radio Group and the Telephone Company, and the important plan of unification suggested by General Tripp.

I also believe that the engagement of any members of the Radio Group at this time in any new activities which would be the subject of arbitration and in advance of either the final handing down of the arbitrator's decision or the conclusion of a new agreement with the Telephone Company, would be in violation of the understanding previously arrived at between the Radio and the Telephone Groups. As this latter point involves the question of legal interpretation as well as the spirit of the understanding, may I not suggest that Mr. Terry confer on this point with Judge Mayer.

Sincerely yours,

(Signed) DAVID SARNOFF

It is apparent that the foregoing powerful appeal for non-action on the part of the Westinghouse Company produced the desired result, since we find no further reference to the matter in the files of the period. The incident no doubt stimulated those having the Telephone matter in charge to exert every possible effort to bring the negotiations to a successful conclusion.

Sec. 91. Effect of New Telephone Agreement on Victor Contract.

By the last week in October, 1925, the contract with the Telephone Company was in form for intensive study by the leaders of the Radio Group. To be sure there were certain technical and important matters still to be determined by a joint committee of which Dr. Alfred N. Goldsmith was chairman, as well as other incidental considerations. Judge Mayer himself now discovered a disturbing circumstance while making a survey of RCA relations with other corporations. It has previously been indicated that in May, 1925, a business alliance had been concluded between RCA and the Victor Talking Machine Company. In the contract Judge Mayer noted that the Victor Company had reserved a right to terminate the contract in event, among other things, of the termination of the cross-licensing contract with the Telephone Company.

This disturbing discovery was immediately communicated by telephone to the legal department of RCA. This accounts for the following letter from one of the staff lawyers:

October 29th, 1925

Julius M. Mayer, Esquire,
  11 Pine Street,
    New York City.

My dear Judge:

As per your request over the telephone the other day, I have studied the proposed contract with the Telephone Company with relation to our existing agreement with the Victor Talking Machine Company.

In our contract with the Victor Company of May 16th, 1925, it is provided in Article 13 that the Victor Company may terminate the agreement upon at least one year's written notice to the Radio Corporation in the event of the following contingency:

* * * *

"(3) If the licensing or cross-licensing of patents relating to radio devices or devices for electrically reproducing sound from commercial talking machine records, or the relations as regards patents or patent rights relating to such devices now existing between the Radio Corporation and the American Telephone & Telegraph Company, the Western Electric Company and/or any of said corporations mentioned or referred to in the preceding subdivision numbered (1) of this article should be wholly or substantially terminated, whether by agreement or otherwise."

I hardly believe that the provisions of paragraph 4 (B) of Article 5 of the proposed agreement with the Telephone Company comes within the purview of "wholly or substantially terminated" in Section 3 of Article 13 of the contract with the Victor Company, above set forth. Nevertheless, I respectfully suggest that before we sign the contract with the Telephone Company, we obtain a statement from the Victor Company to the effect that this provision in our proposed agreement with the Telephone Company does not wholly or substantially terminate our relations with the Telephone Company and the Western Electric Company within the meaning of Section 3 of Article 13 of our contract with the Victor Company.

Very respectfully,

(Signed) I. E. LAMBERT

Sec. 92. Mr. Bloom Discusses Wire-Line Charges.

Edgar S. Bloom, a vice-president of the American Telephone Company, had long been prominent in negotiations with David Sarnoff in an effort to bring about a satisfactory redraft of the contract between his company and the Radio Group. For several months the officials of the latter group had been engaged in secret negotiations for the launching of a general broadcasting company which was not to include the Telephone Company. It is evident, however, that David Sarnoff had not confined himself to the negotiations immediately in hand. He had propounded to Mr. Bloom as early as February, 1925, the question of rates for wire lines of the Telephone Company. This was in connection with his "Fundamental Considerations" discussed in a previous chapter. More recently, Mr. Sarnoff had renewed his inquiry. Mr. Bloom had at length accumulated the necessary data and, on November 18, 1925, he forwarded to Mr. Sarnoff a highly confidential memorandum. Because of its brevity and its historical importance it is reproduced herewith:

"MEMORANDUM REGARDING BROADCASTING COMPANY

"Prepared for Mr. Sarnoff, November 18, 1925.

"The present network of the American Telephone & Telegraph Company connects broadcasting stations in 14 of the following 16 cities:

New York	St. Paul-Minneapolis
Philadelphia	St. Louis
Washington	Akron
Providence	Pittsburgh
Worcester	Chicago
Boston	Cincinnati
Buffalo	Davenport
Detroit	Cleveland

requiring a total circuit   leage of 3200. The cost of this wire network, including full se   ce by the long lines department of the American Company is   roximately $410,000 per year. This does not include charges for local loops nor the cost of maintaining the broadcasting organizations or studios.

"The gross revenue of our broadcasting department, from those using the station, is at the rate of approximately $750,000 per year. This gross revenue is secured through the use of about 884 hours of

DR. WALTER J. DAMROSCH
His Music Appreciation Hour has been
a radio feature for more than a decade.

RICHARD C. PATTERSON, JR.
Executive Vice-President of NBC from
October, 1932, to March 27, 1936.

JOHN F. ROYAL
NBC Vice-President in charge of programs. Came to NBC in 1931.

FRANK E. MULLEN
Vice-President in charge of advertising
and publicity, RCA.

the 1092 hours attractive time on a paid basis. If the total attractive time could be sold at present rates a gross revenue of approximately $1,400,000 would be developed.

"A contract between the Broadcasting Company and the American Company would provide for (a) the use of a basic wire network as set forth in the contract for a period of 10 years in accordance with the rates and conditions set forth in Exhibit A attached hereto; (b) the extension of the wire network to other points at the same basic rates as set forth in Exhibit A for a contract term in each case of not less than 3 years."

Mr. Sarnoff's immediate reaction was to organize a special committee to study the Bloom memorandum. Because of Dr. Alfred N. Goldsmith's known capacity for immediate and effective action, he was Mr. Sarnoff's choice to act as chairman of the committee. On November 19th the following illuminating letter of instructions was written by Mr. Sarnoff:

November 19, 1925

Dear Dr. Goldsmith:

I attach hereto a highly confidential memorandum submitted to me by Mr. Bloom with his letter of November 18, 1925. The purpose of my sending this to you now is to ask you to promptly study this memorandum and prepare a statement of its meaning in such a form that I may be able to forward it to Mr. Herr and Mr. Swope. I do not believe that the attached memorandum in itself would mean very much to them, because it does not show the real comparison of existing and prospective situations. I may say that my own reaction to the Bloom memorandum is favorable, although I do not undertake now to express an opinion as to the economics of the figures, because I do not know enough about it yet to have an opinion.

In forwarding Mr. Bloom's memorandum and your summary thereon to Messrs. Herr and Swope, I shall ask them to assign one representative each to serve with you on a committee which should consider this proposition and advise as to what our attitude should be toward this proposition.

As I expect you in my home on Sunday, it would be helpful if you could have your memorandum with you so that we may then discuss it.

I again emphasize the importance of keeping this information confidential, as Mr. Bloom informed me he has not discussed this subject with any of his subordinates as yet and does not want them to know about this matter at this time.

Sincerely yours,

(Signed) DAVID SARNOFF

It does not appear that the suggested committee was formed immediately. On the contrary, a very detailed and painstaking report was filed by Dr. Goldsmith personally, on December 1, 1925, in which, among other things, he recommended the creation of a joint committee of the Radio Group to study the economic problems of the proposed broadcasting company. The Goldsmith report was nineteen pages long, being divided into two main divisions. The first division had to do with the comparative annual cost of wires leased from the American Telephone Company and those furnished by the Telegraph Companies. It is interesting to note that Dr. Goldsmith's summary disclosed that to lease lines from the Telephone Company would result in a substantial saving over the other method.

In the second phase of his report Dr. Goldsmith discussed financial problems that would naturally arise upon the establishment of the proposed broadcasting company. He estimated that a national system comprising sixteen stations in fifteen different cities (New York City to be served by two stations—WJZ and WJY) would cost, for long lines and pick-up wires, a total of $800,000.

Dr. Goldsmith's report formed the agenda of a meeting of the board of directors of RCA on December 4, 1925, at which it was voted to appoint a joint committee of Radio Group experts to study the matter in detail. On the same day General Harbord sent to the presidents of General Electric and Westinghouse letters in duplicate, except for the opening paragraph. The following, from the files of RCA, gives us important data on this phase of the negotiations:

December 4, 1925

Mr. Gerard Swope, President,
General Electric Company,
120 Broadway,
New York, N. Y.

Subject: *NATIONAL BROADCASTING COMPANY*

Dear Mr. Swope:

Referring to the discussion of the above subject which took place at the board meeting today, I will be obliged if you will designate two representatives from your company to serve as members of a joint committee of representatives of the General Electric and Westinghouse Companies and the Radio Corporation of America to consider the data which Mr. Sarnoff handed you personally at the meeting today and to report on the following:

1. The economics of a national broadcasting system as a whole which would take over the existing stations and broadcasting business of the American Telephone & Telegraph Company as well as the stations of the General Electric and Westinghouse Companies and the Radio Corporation of America, and merge them into a national unit.

2. The feasibility of the proposed rates quoted by the Telephone Company for wire service, as compared with the corresponding rates for equally high-grade service using the wires of the Telegraph Companies.

I have appointed Dr. Goldsmith, our chief broadcast engineer, and Mr. Popenoe, our program manager, to serve as the two members for the Radio Corporation of America. My suggestion is that the two persons appointed to represent your company on this joint committee should consist of a technical representative acquainted with the technique of broadcasting and a program man familiar with that phase of the business.

Your representative should be prepared to bring to the joint committee the figures showing the cost of operating your present broadcasting stations and the representatives of the Radio Corporation of America will do likewise. It is necessary to put all these figures together in order to determine on the economics of a national system, which would include some or all of the present broadcasting stations. The Telephone Company, in the data submitted, has already stated the cost of operating its stations.

If agreeable to you, Dr. Goldsmith, who has given this matter detailed consideration and who has prepared an analysis of the memorandum submitted by Mr. Bloom, will serve as chairman of the proposed committee. The Telephone Company is anxious to have the present negotiations, which include this important item of broadcast transmission, concluded not later than January 13th, the date of termination of the present agreement relating to the handing down or withholding of the arbitrator's report.

In forwarding his memorandum to Mr. Sarnoff under date of November 18th, Mr. Bloom, vice-president of the American Telephone & Telegraph Company, stated "For reasons which I explained to you, I would appreciate it if this is kept confidential to your higher officials." May I ask that the subject matter be treated accordingly, as Mr. Bloom's subordinates are not aware of the present negotiations in connection with broadcast transmission.

Sincerely yours,

(Signed) J. G. Harbord

It is a singular fact that no references are to be found in the exchange of letters at this time to an event that must seriously have crippled negotiations between the Radio Group and the Telephone Company. Judge Julius Mayer, who had been relied upon to draft the proposed "definitive contract," and who was in the midst of his labors thereon, died very suddenly, on November 30, 1925. The death is said to have been due to a stroke of apoplexy. This sad occurrence caused a transfer of the task to the firm of Paul D. Cravath, of New York City.

CHAPTER
TWELVE

Radio Group and Telephone Company Make Peace

Section 93. Sub-Committee on Broadcasting Receives Instructions.

WITH A CHAIRMAN OF PRONOUNCED VIEWS many a committee has been swept off its feet and committed to policies favored by the chairman even though committee members may not have arrived at independent conclusions as to the proper course of action. Dr. Alfred N. Goldsmith was and is a man of positive opinions, one, moreover, who possesses persuasive ability and an eloquence in self-expression. In his committee, however, were men of equal independence of mind. They represented great industrial interests temporarily yoked together in a common enterprise. Financial success or financial disaster were to depend upon the wisdom or lack of it exercised by this committee.

Dr. Goldsmith had previously advocated the setting up of a strong broadcasting corporation. He had favored outright ownership of a sufficient number of broadcasting stations to insure nationwide scope to its program structure. This idea did not appeal to certain influential members of the committee. Albert G. Davis, representing the General Electric Company, took a positive stand in opposition, as will appear from a letter written by him to Owen D. Young on December 12, 1925.

"The program which Dr. Goldsmith suggests," he wrote, "is that the broadcasting company should buy all of the stations including WGY and KDKA, and should then run this chain of stations, at the same time doing engineering, development work, etc.

"The program which we suggest is quite different. It runs as follows:

"1. The broadcasting company is to be a program company. It is not to own stations.

"2. It is to have the exclusive right to broadcast for tolls, so far as the parties can give it that right.

"3. The stations are to continue to be owned by the present owners and to be operated in their names.

"4. The broadcasting company is to furnish signals [1] to these stations for a certain number of hours per week, and to collect what revenue it can thereby. The stations are to be bound to take these signals and broadcast them subject only to the natural and necessary provision that no station shall be required to advertise its competitor.

"5. The engineering research and development is to be carried on by the manufacturing companies primarily, which companies will be manufacturing transmitting sets for the Radio Corporation to sell to the public."

The writer went on to discuss the various features of his own plan. He pointed out the probable cost of Dr. Goldsmith's plan of purchas-

---

[1] Meaning programs.

ing and maintaining the radio stations owned by the individual members of the Radio Group. He argued that this was unnecessary, and urged that ownership be unchanged. If Westinghouse would close all but two of its stations, the General Electric Company to continue with three stations and RCA to operate two or three units, there would be, he thought, stations enough for the purpose in hand.

"This proposed arrangement," he continued, "would make it possible for us to deal with outside stations, including those which are taking their signals from the Telephone Company, on a basis very similar to that with which we dealt in case of our own stations, which would be a distinct advantage.

"Further, it would greatly lessen the possibility of having the question of monopoly raised again. It seems to me that we should agree, among ourselves, whether this is our program or arrange what our program shall be before we ask any committee to make the sort of report which Mr. Sarnoff wants."

The Goldsmith committee thus becoming deadlocked it became necessary to create a new joint committee with authority to define the general policies of the Radio Group. David Sarnoff was thereupon appointed to represent RCA; Albert G. Davis, General Electric Company, and Harry P. Davis, the Westinghouse Company. On December 18th, this general committee advised the Goldsmith committee in part as follows:

"The proposed company will be owned by the three companies of the Radio Group in proportion to be agreed upon and each of these companies will furnish capital in proportion to its holdings.

"It will have the exclusive right to broadcast for revenue so far as that right can be given it by the three companies and the Telephone Group.

"It will maintain studios and produce programs and will lease or purchase or otherwise acquire such facilities that may from time to time be necessary for distributing programs to a chain of stations on terms to be arranged between the Broadcasting Service Company and the stations.

"In principle the stations of the three companies are to be members of the chain, but no station of the chain is to lose its identity. The three companies are also to give to the Broadcasting Service Company the exclusive right under their patents and copyrights to transmit signals to other broadcasting stations. It is contemplated that the Telephone Company shall not be in the business of furnishing programs, as distinguished from transmitting by wire, programs of others."

The concluding sentence in the above quotation is very significant. It put the author upon inquiry since it was unthinkable, in view of the sheer fighting ability of the Telephone Company, that so astute a negotiator as David Sarnoff would have permitted a suggestion such as this to creep into a letter of instructions. The challenge would have been too great. Although the negotiations looking to the purchase of Station WEAF were entirely oral, the author has learned from living witnesses that prior to December 18, 1925, David Sarnoff and Edgar S. Bloom had been through a long series of conferences upon it. The representative of the Telephone Company quite naturally attached great importance to the potential value of WEAF. He would not listen to Mr. Sarnoff's initial offer of a price slightly larger than the value of the physical assets of the station.

One of RCA's pioneer officials has declared that his recollection is that the first figure named by Mr. Bloom was two and a half million dollars, and that the parties gradually approached each other. The physical assets of WEAF were agreed upon as $200,000—the battle being over the good will of the station and its potential value to the Telephone Company. It was, of course, the key station to a network of nearly a score of stations. Radio advertising was now producing large revenue—$750,000 in a single year with a possible revenue of $1,400,000 at rates then existing. The wonder is that Mr. Sarnoff was able to whittle down the Bloom estimate of good will to the figure of $800,000 which the parties had now mutually agreed upon. In other words, station assets and good will were set at a total of one million dollars.

A significant feature of the instructions given to the sub-committee was the following:

"The charter of the broadcasting company will be broad enough to enable it to own, lease or operate broadcasting stations, and also to make contracts with local stations upon such terms and conditions as may seem proper to it."

The sub-committee was thereupon recast with the following membership:

For RCA—Dr. Alfred N. Goldsmith and Charles B. Popenoe.
For General Electric—Martin P. Rice and W. R. G. Baker.
For Westinghouse—J. C. McQuiston and Frank Conrad (later substitution—Charles W. Horn).

Sec. 94. The Committee Report Accepted by RCA.

By December 30th the sub-committee was ready to advise that an "American Broadcasting Company" be immediately set up to operate on an "experience and information" basis for six months or so before the plan would become final. An interesting feature of the suggestion was that the proposed American Broadcasting Company was to be operated from the broadcasting headquarters of Station WEAF at 195 Broadway, New York City. The sales department, program department, publicity force, station staff announcers, field operators, concert bureau, orchestras, etc., that WEAF had built up were to continue to function under the more ambitious plan. Obviously, this plan hinged upon the purchase of Station WEAF.

On January 5, 1926, a tentative draft of the proposed report was shown by the chairman to David Sarnoff. In the RCA files is to be found a letter from Dr. Goldsmith containing in the margin penciled memoranda in the handwriting of Mr. Sarnoff that disclose the latter's reactions to the proposals. Such lancet-thrusts as the following are to be deciphered:

"Why duplicate stations? (The list showed two stations in Washington and two in New York.)
"How would losses compare with present costs? Our RCA annual costs, about $400,000 (not including new stations), G. E. and Westinghouse annual costs, I should guess to be about $500,000–$600,000."

The committee had estimated the operating deficit for the first year of the broadcasting company at $410,000; second year, $350,000; third year, $250,000. Mr. Sarnoff's queries caused Dr. Goldsmith to send out hurry calls to the committee to supply information as to actual annual costs of stations involved in the project. By January 7th, the data called for by Mr. Sarnoff had apparently been supplied. The total broadcasting expenses of the three corporations for 1925 were listed as follows:

RCA, $370,000; General Electric, $533,000; Westinghouse, $476,500, making a total for the Radio Group of $1,379,500.

In submitting the final report of his committee, January 8, 1926, Dr. Goldsmith went to some length to explain to David Sarnoff the reasons that had actuated the committee in agreeing to duplicate stations in Washington and New York City. The first reason alleged was political, as will be seen from the following:

"When a powerful and long-established group,[2] contractually associated with the Telephone Company's network, has a station now on the network, it is in my opinion necessary to keep it on the network for an indefinite period of time lest the A.B.C. be accused of attempting to monopolize the good syndicated programs."

[2] Obviously referring to the WEAF network served by Station WCAP in Washington.

The second reason advanced by Dr. Goldsmith was labeled "commercial and program reasons." He pointed out the value of two outlets, alleging that radio listeners would differ as to program preferences. Two types of programs would not only better serve the public but should also be more productive of revenue to the proposed broadcasting company, thus decreasing an inevitable deficit in operation. The richness of program material in New York City was also cited as an additional reason for duplication of stations in that sector, WEAF and WJZ.

The thoroughness with which Mr. Sarnoff prepared himself to report to the meeting of the board of directors scheduled for January 22, 1926, is attested by the array of telegrams sent by him to Westinghouse and General Electric Company officials on January 20 and 21 as a means of checking engineering and development costs.

There is a certain amount of finality, so far as the work of the Goldsmith committee is concerned, to be found in the minutes of the meeting of the board of directors of RCA for January 22, 1926:

"The report of the committee on broadcasting, dated January 22, 1926, was read and after discussion, on motion, duly made, seconded and unanimously carried, it was

"RESOLVED that the report of the committee on broadcasting be received and ordered filed with the secretary and the recommendations contained therein, be and hereby are approved."

An important recommendation of the general committee was as follows:

"Your committee therefore recommends that the executive officers of the Radio Corporation be empowered to proceed with negotiations for a definite contract which should be submitted, through your committee, to this board for its final action."

Among the recommendations by the sub-committee were some that may be summarized as follows:

1. It recommended the establishment by the Radio Group and the Telephone Company of a company to be known as the American Broadcasting Company "with suitable provision for participation in the management thereof by individuals representing the Radio Group, in order to enable such representatives to gain experience and information which will permit them to take over the management of 'American Broadcasting Company' at the end of six months or such other period as may be deemed best.

2. "At the end of the period in question, when the American Telephone & Telegraph Company interests in the American Broadcasting

Company are transferred to the Radio Group, it is recommended that the entire management of the American Broadcasting Company (A.B.C.) be taken over and the existing plant thereof be continued with certain modifications."

There was much more to the report, but the recommendations important to our story are those outlined above. On January 25th Mr. Sarnoff wrote a letter to Paul D. Cravath, Esq., who had taken the place of the late Judge Mayer in drafting the new contract with the Telephone Company. The letter accompanied the committee report above described and ran in part as follows:

"All these papers relate to the proposed broadcasting company, as suggested by Mr. Bloom of the Telephone Company whom I advised today [3] that his project is acceptable to the Radio Group in principle, but conditional upon an ultimate satisfactory contract being mutually agreed upon. For the present, at least, the figures contained in the attached report are confidential so far as the Telephone Group is concerned."

It is significant that on the margin of a copy of the above letter now in the files of RCA there appears, in Mr. Sarnoff's handwriting, the following memorandum:

"At conference in Mr. Bloom's office February 1st, Mr. Bloom undertook to draw and submit contract to us covering this matter.   D. S."

Thus a new phase of the seemingly interminable conferences was reached. The main contract was still in the process of being drafted, and now Edgar S. Bloom was undertaking the drafting of a contract for the consolidation of radio broadcasting. No experienced person in the Radio Group could indulge in optimism over the prospect of a speedy termination of the matter. It was in fact, destined to continue for another six months.

Sec. 95. Telephone Negotiations Again Deadlocked.

The arbitrator's report, now fourteen months in suspended animation, was still a live issue so far as the negotiators were concerned. A serious question in fact had arisen whether to attempt to include all vital matters in a new contract or to incorporate by reference the arbitrator's decision, thus making it a part of the contract. The uncertainties on this point are very fully explained in the following letter, now in the files of the General Electric Company:

[3] The vote of the RCA board was taken on Friday, January 22nd. Monday, the 25th, was apparently the next opportunity for a conference with Mr. Bloom.

January 23, 1926

F. P. Fish, Esq.,
   84 State Street,
      Boston, Mass.

My dear Mr. Fish:

I presume that you know that Mr. Cravath has taken Judge Mayer's place in the negotiations with the Telephone Company. I attended a conference on Thursday with Mr. Cravath and representatives of the Radio Corporation and the Westinghouse Company. We went over the whole situation and made a good deal of progress.

It is my understanding that you and I and Judge Mayer thought that the only way to handle the situation was to let the arbitrator's decision come down and then execute a contract which would recite the old contract and the contract to arbitrate, and the arbitrator's decision, and would then modify the original contract (as left after the arbitrator's decision) in certain specific respects only.

It developed at the conference that Judge Mayer had subsequently changed his mind in this matter and had decided that the papers should be so drawn as to avoid the necessity of referring to the arbitrator's decision. It also developed that Mr. Cravath was of the same opinion.

I protested very earnestly against this course saying, among other things, that there were a number of points in the arbitrator's decision of very little importance as to which there was a difference of opinion, and that if an attempt were made to adjust all of these differences now, it would delay the execution of the contract indefinitely. I also spoke of the great difficulties of drawing a contract which would express all the things which the arbitrator decided; certainly, at the time, Mr. Folk's draft made no mention of anything of the sort.

The matter was not settled, but Mr. Cravath expressed himself rather strongly against leaving it in the situation which would require people to read the arbitrator's decision, the original contract and supplemental contract to find wherein any rights were vested.

It occurs to me that it would be very wise for you to see Mr. Cravath on this matter the next time you are in New York.

                    Yours very truly,
                    (Signed) ALBERT G. DAVIS

To the above letter Mr. Fish made a reply that is eloquent of his feelings at the time. It is, moreover, the "swan song" of the lawyer who had borne the responsibilities of the arbitration contest, and deserves a place in this recital.

FISH, RICHARDSON & NEAVE

Boston, January 25, 1926

My dear Mr. Davis:

I feel very much discouraged as to what you say about the situation in the arbitration matter. Apparently a whole year has been wasted and nothing whatever accomplished.

Of course, if you draw a new contract you will eliminate the arbitrator's decision. All your rights will depend upon the new contract and you can get nothing from the arbitrator's decision except what appears in the new contract. You will inevitably leave out some of the things he has decided. Of course, you may do this intentionally. I should be inclined to think that it would be wiser to refer to the arbitrator's contract and accept it as it stands with certain modifications and new features to be agreed upon.

I have no doubt that Mr. Cravath has given full attention to the subject and, of course, the responsibility is on him unless Mr. Young will take a little interest in the matter.

I do not see that it would be helpful for me to talk with Mr. Cravath as I am precluded from dealing with the matter of the proposed contract.

Very truly yours,

(Signed) F. P. Fish

To the student of industrial history the controversy between the Telephone and Radio groups should prove of interest for many reasons. The interplay of negotiations in which patience, mental stamina, alertness, and the power of personality of the negotiators rarely, if ever, have found more complete expression than in the closing months of this great contest. Even to the veteran lawyer, Frederick P. Fish, the twelvemonth of negotiations had seemed to be wasted effort. To be sure progress had been made, but whenever one barrier in negotiations had been cleared a new barrier very shortly was encountered. If in the mere onlookers this process had produced pessimism what must be thought of the physical and mental drain upon the negotiators of the rival groups—David Sarnoff and Edgar S. Bloom?

The following communication, addressed in duplicate to Owen D. Young and General Tripp, explains an impasse that was reached in early February 1926:

Duplicate sent to Mr. Young

CRAVATH, HENDERSON & DEGERSDORFF

52 William Street

New York, February 8, 1926

Hon. Owen D. Young,
Gen. Guy E. Tripp.

Dear General Tripp:

My partner, Swaine, and I have just had a conference with Mr. Sarnoff regarding the negotiations between the Radio Group and the

Telephone Group. Mr. Bloom, on behalf of the Telephone Group, has written a letter to Mr. Sarnoff, of which I enclose a copy, in which, as you will observe, he takes what purports to be a final position of the Telephone Group on four important questions, two of which (No. 2 and No. 3) all on our side agree are fundamental.

It is clear to Mr. Sarnoff and ourselves that there should be an early conference of the experts of the three companies which constitute the Radio Group. We all feel that we are much more apt to make progress at this conference in reaching a conclusion as to what are, and what are not, essential questions, if you two are present. We therefore very much hope that between you you will fix a day and place which will be convenient to you both. On being notified of your decision, we will then assemble the others.

Unfortunately, Mr. Sarnoff has to spend the next two weeks in Washington on military service, so that it seems important that the conference be held this week. Thursday or Friday seem to be the most available days, if they are satisfactory to you.

Very sincerely yours,

(Signed) PAUL D. CRAVATH

P.S. In order to save time, please send word directly to Mr. Sarnoff as to the date and place of meeting.

The first of the four points of disagreement proved to be a plan for protecting the Radio Group against sales of apparatus capable of use in the Radio field (such as tubes, loud speakers, etc.) to an amount in excess of that likely to be used in the Telephone Group field. The Radio Group had insisted—

"That the Telephone Group make quarterly or semi-annual reports of its sales in the Telephone Group field in order that the Radio Group might have information from which it could determine as to whether or not tubes, for example, were being sold beyond the reasonable requirements of the field in which the Telephone Group might be licensed, with the understanding that the Radio Group would make similar reports of its sales."

To this demand the Telephone Group now returned an emphatic negative, as will be seen in the following excerpt from Mr. Bloom's letter to Mr. Sarnoff, under date of February 8, 1926:

"We cannot see our way clear to make such reports and believe that ultimate protection in matters of this character depends primarily upon the good faith of the parties in carrying out the agreement and the general clause of the contract relating to protection of fields."

The second point of difference arose over the desire of the Radio Group to have exclusive license in "one-way wireless telephone reception," whereas the Telephone Group had insisted upon limiting it to "wireless telephone broadcast reception." Mr. Bloom explained the adverse decision on this point thus:

"The important point involved is the question of multi-party or single-party one-way service by wireless telephony for business, official or commercial purposes other than entertainment as distinguished from broadcasting.

"We cannot accede to the suggestion of the Radio Group as to this item for the reason that we would not care to limit ourselves in any way with respect to a wireless telephone service analogous to our wire service."

The third point of contention related to "carrier-current" broadcasting over electric light and power lines. The Telephone Company thus expressed its attitude:

"We have no objection to making this exclusive to the Radio Group subject to the provisions that in the development of this field there must be no interference with the Telephone Company's system, including the normal development thereof and its own exclusive field of carrier-current broadcasting over other than electric light, power and traction lines, and that the Telephone Group must be the judge of that interference. However, we will hold ourselves open to assist, at the request and expense of the Radio Group, in every reasonable way in enabling you to develop methods or devices to be applied to your system to avoid such interference."

The fourth and last item in the unsolved agenda had to do with electrical phonograph recording and reproduction.

Under this item the Radio Group was to have exclusive license for electric phonograph reproduction in the home, and now desired this to be extended to all fields subject to the provisions that the Telephone Group should have the right for uses in connection with its telephone service and talking movies.

Mr. Bloom explained the Telephone Company attitude thus:

"We are willing to grant the exclusive license for electric phonograph reproduction in the home including the use of phonographs in combination with radio receiving sets or in connection with electric light wires but not in connection with telephone or other wires. For use outside of the home, or not in combination with radio receiving sets, or in connection with electric light or telephone wires, the licenses to be non-exclusive, as at present."

Sec. 96. Telephone Company Organizes a Broadcasting Corporation.

Negotiations continued and definite progress toward a general contract was made. Robert T. Swaine, Esq., a law partner of Paul D. Cravath, now appears as an active participant in the drafting of a substitute agreement. On February 20, 1926, the first printed draft of the proposed redraft of the contract of July, 1920, was submitted to scrutiny of the legal and technical experts of the corporations concerned. It consisted of twenty-six pages, being entitled "License Agreement, General Electric Company and American Telephone & Telegraph Company." It made no provision for the radio broadcasting company. By oral agreement, however, that phase was reserved for a separate contract.

On March 17, 1926, a second draft appeared in which were incorporated two important changes in substance that had been agreed upon by Edgar S. Bloom and David Sarnoff in the process of negotiations. On April 2nd Mr. Swaine wrote to Albert G. Davis, in part, as follows:

"In view of what Mr. Folk said this morning I want you to know that my afternoon session with him has confirmed my view that there is every prospect of our being able to agree upon the form of the contract. . . . Specifically, Mr. Folk has accepted the first half of our draft of March 17, with the exception of matters too trifling to be called to your attention and of the following substantial matters:"

Fourteen "substantial matters" were listed, the most important of which related to Mr. Folk's desire for a non-exclusive license for the Telephone Company in one-way wireless receiving sets.

The arbitrator's decision received a bit of attention in a letter written by Albert G. Davis to David Sarnoff on April 3, 1926.

"From something you said to me the other day," he wrote, "I get the impression that you and Mr. Bloom misunderstood the possibility of taking down the arbitrator's decision.

"The present situation is that either party may have a date fixed, not less than ten days off, at which the parties shall file their objections to the arbitrator's decision. He will then rule on the objections."

Mr. Davis then went on to advance a suggestion identical with an attempt that he had made on March 31, 1925. The reader will recall the opinion of John W. Davis, of March 17, 1925, expressing the view that the contract as interpreted by the arbitrator was illegal. Albert G. Davis had attempted, on the date first mentioned, to have certain words in the report corrected. Counsel for the Telephone Company had at that time blocked the attempt. A. G. Davis now returned to the attack by suggesting to Mr. Sarnoff a way of checkmating the John W. Davis opinion on which the Telephone Company obviously still relied.

"If I were doing it," he wrote, "one of the points which I should raise would be the point on which the John W. Davis opinion hangs, because the whole basis of the John W. Davis opinion could be avoided by change of two or three words in the decision, which change would make the decision mean what in my judgment it was intended to mean, and indeed does mean if properly construed."

On April 22, 1926 Robert T. Swaine was able to report, in part, as follows:

"A revised draft of the Radio Telephone agreement is enclosed. This represents the negotiations with Mr. Folk following the conference of last Monday and a conference between Mr. Sarnoff and Mr. Bloom. I am satisfied that it represents the best trade that can be made; indeed there are one or two points on which Mr. Folk has not finally agreed, such as making the license to the Radio Group for distance actuation and control over power lines exclusive.

"You will note that the difficult subject of radio receiving sets has been solved by the following compromise:

"1. As to multiparty service both groups get non-exclusive licenses and reserved rights however being only for apparatus locked for one wave length.

"2. The Telephone Company gets the facility license which both parties get in all fields.

"3. The Telephone Company gets the license for the $5,000,000 quota of program receiving sets (meaning free from royalty—amounts in excess at 50% royalty).

"4. The Radio Group gets exclusive licenses for program receiving sets, subject to the Telephone Company's quota mentioned above."

The copy of the April 22nd version that passed through David Sarnoff's hands is now in the RCA files. Of great human and historical interest are the marginal notations on this document. On a blank sheet of the back cover, in Mr. Sarnoff's characteristic handwriting, is the following:

Mr. Bucher:
    1. This is the last draft. Please read carefully and note my penciled queries.
    2. Please arrange for study of the draft by Messrs. Adams, Goldsmith and yourself and after a review of it by all three, please have Mr. Adams prepare a memo for Mr. Swaine representing the joint views and queries (if any) of the three (including my penciled nota-

W. A. WINTERBOTTOM
Vice-President and General Manager,
RCA Communications, Inc.

CHARLES J. PANNILL
President, Radiomarine Corporation of
America.

CHARLES B. POPENOE
Under whose capable management Station WJZ originated and developed.

O. B. HANSON
From A. T. & T. to WEAF in 1923, now
a Vice-President of NBC.

tions, if they are regarded as relevant) and let me have the memo by Wednesday P.M. or Thursday A.M., so I can pass it along as the present position of RCA with reference to this draft.

D. S.

The penciled queries, made by one who had spent much time on negotiations, reveal the fact that Mr. Sarnoff had not, because of wearisome negotiations in this field, lost his perspective. On the contrary, like a skillful fencer, he was keenly on guard. For example, he questioned the adequacy of the definition of subsidiaries, and the lawyers later cured the defect by inserting three words, "directly or indirectly," as qualifying the verb "owned." In another place, where it was provided that every license should include "all rights necessary to full enjoyment," Mr. Sarnoff queried: "Is this too broad?" with the result that the words were later changed to "all incidental rights," etc. In yet another portion of the document there was a provision relative to co-ordination of sound and pictures in which the lawyers had used the phrase "projection of motion pictures." Mr. Sarnoff called for the addition of the word "still" with the result that the phrase reappeared simply as "projection of pictures." The above examples illustrate the process of evolution through which the new contract was progressing, since the lawyers and experts were themselves busy with the reconstruction of paragraphs and contractual provisions.

A development of major importance in the long contest between the Radio and Telephone groups occurred on May 11, 1926, when the Telephone Company organized a brand new corporation—the "Broadcasting Company of America!" In view of the negotiations then pending for the purchase by the Radio Group of the broadcasting business of the Telephone Company this action is doubly significant. The Radio Group had for months been deliberating upon the setting up of a general broadcasting company which was to own and operate Station WEAF if and when the same should be transferred by the Telephone Company—but now that resourceful organization had created the corporation and had adopted a name very similar to that intended by the Radio Group. To this corporation, moreover, Station WEAF had gone "lock, stock and barrel."

Conjectures as to reasons and motives governing corporate action are at best unsatisfactory, yet the probabilities are that within the American Telephone organization there were those who were enthusiasts for the continuation and enlargement of the broadcasting activities of that great corporation. There were doubtless others who regarded broadcasting as a bit beyond the proper scope of a public utility such as the Telephone Company. To create a separate corporation for broadcasting would thus meet the views of both parties.

The action should not be interpreted as necessarily contrary to the spirit of the negotiations then pending for the sale of the business. It established a "trading position" that might actually facilitate the project. In the light of subsequent events it is probable that the high command of the Telephone Company had by this time become weary of the controversy and would have been glad indeed to be rid of the entire broadcasting mess. It is certain that the jubilation of the broadcasting group was destined to be of short duration.

Sec. 97. Final Stages of Sarnoff-Bloom Negotiations.

On May 17, 1926, a distressing development caused David Sarnoff, who had slipped away for a few days of rest at Atlantic City, to come hurrying back to New York and the daily grind of negotiations. In a letter from Robert T. Swaine he had received the disconcerting news that President Gifford, of the Telephone Company, had repudiated the Bloom compromise on television and two-way wireless telephony. Mr. Folk, the lawyer for the Telephone Company, had submitted three propositions, one of them relating to co-ordination of sound and pictures, that the Telephone Company would be willing to swap for certain concessions by the Radio Group.

The desperate nature of the crisis thus suddenly arising may be glimpsed in the following extract from the Swaine letter:

"I told Mr. Folk that while of course I had no authority to give the final word and would pass his suggestions on, I felt sure that my so doing was a mere matter of form and that if we were to understand that the Telephone Company demanded the three foregoing concessions there was little prospect of the parties reaching an agreement. He reiterated that these concessions were requested only as the price of the concession requested of the Telephone Company by the Radio Group in respect of wire program receiving apparatus and phonographs and that if our suggestion in that respect were withdrawn, the suggestions now made by him would likewise be withdrawn."

Thus the champions of the embattled groups continued to struggle for advantage. Clipped to the Swaine letter above quoted is an undated memorandum, a part of it in David Sarnoff's handwriting, making cryptic reference to the chief features of the conference with Mr. Bloom that must have followed Sarnoff's return to New York City. The very document is eloquent of battle, yet not very illuminating as to what actually occurred. This important fact emerges, however, that four days later Robert T. Swaine was able to transmit to the chieftains of the General Electric Company, the Westinghouse Company, and the Radio Corporation printed copies of what he optimistically labeled "the final draft of the proposed Radio-Telephone agreement." This draft had already been approved by Owen D. Young, General James G. Harbord, and David Sarnoff.

Certain interesting changes, no doubt reflecting further Sarnoff-Bloom negotiations, appear in this draft. The vexed broadcast receiving set controversy had now been whittled down to $3,000,000, royalty free, per year on receiving sets, with a $2,000,000 royalty free provision on tubes and appliances. All sales above these limits were to be subject to a 50% royalty. Thus it appears that the major controversy, largely through David Sarnoff's tireless efforts as a negotiator, had been reduced from menacing proportions to figures that appealed to the Radio Group as fair and reasonable. Incidentally, it should be noted in this connection that the rights thus accorded to the Telephone Company were never thereafter actually exercised. To Mr. Sarnoff's prowess as a negotiator should therefore be added this significant achievement—the obtaining for RCA, without financial payments, of additional and extensive rights from the American Telephone Company. But we are getting ahead of our story. No one, on May 21, 1926, could have been sure that the contract as drafted would actually be signed, or that a contract relating to the broadcasting phase of the controversy would ever be consummated.

On the following day, May 22, 1926, Robert T. Swaine produced the first draft of a proposed service contract between the Radio Corporation and the Telephone Company. This embodied ideas, long discussed between David Sarnoff and Edgar S. Bloom, relative to wire lines for broadcasting service which, it will be remembered, had been hitherto banned by the Telephone Company. The Swaine draft was naturally the lawyer's version of the understanding that might need to be altered by the parties. This accounts for the fact that in his letter Mr. Swaine stated that it was a rough draft that had "not yet been seen by any of the experts of the Radio Group and therefore represents only my own ideas."

Two days later, May 24, 1926, the long-expected agreement concerning the purchase of the broadcasting enterprise of the Telephone Company made its appearance. It emerged, however, not from the office of Mr. Bloom but from the draftsmen who had prepared the two contracts previously mentioned. This first draft included both Station WEAF and the Washington, D. C. Station WCAP, together with the physical assets of both, and the broadcasting good will that had been built in three years by the Telephone Company. Clause IV of the proposed contract read as follows:

"In consideration of the sale, transfer and assignment to it, or to its subsidiary, herein provided for, the Radio Company agrees to pay the Telephone Company the sum of $1,000,000."

The "subsidiary" company was not mentioned by name in the document, although in Clause II there was an intention expressed by RCA to form such a company, in the meantime to use "the present corporate name of the Broadcasting Company."

The contract contained the usual covenant against broadcasting competition by the Telephone Company but, singularly enough, no liquidated damages were named as a penalty except a refund of the money paid in case the Telephone Company should break its contract and set up a competitive broadcasting system. In other words, the million-dollar purchase price was to be returned to RCA, but without interest thereon. The limitation period, moreover, was fixed at seven years, thus demonstrating the care that was being exercised by the lawyers to avoid any semblance of creating a contract in unlawful restraint of trade.

It was to be expected that a tentative draft of so important a contract would be subject to a cross-fire from both sides. A two-page letter from Albert G. Davis to David Sarnoff, dated May 24, 1926, makes an especially vigorous attack upon it.

"I particularly dislike the rigidity of the thing," Mr. Davis wrote, and proceeded to recount his objections. In fact there seemed to be few provisions that met the approval of the writer of the letter.

By May 26, 1926, the sales agreement had undergone changes enlarging it from a four-page printed document to a six-page contract. WEAF now appears as the only station to be sold. Another significant change was a new provision as to refund in case the Telephone Company should enter into competition in the broadcasting field prior to July 1, 1933. The sum to be refunded was set at $800,000, without interest, "being the consideration for good will included in the total consideration of $1,000,000."

The main contract also was being revised, and new versions were appearing at frequent intervals. Thus the month of May passed in diligent preparation for the expected signing of the contracts on June 1, 1926. It is well known, however, that the contracts were not executed on the expected date. The early days of June saw conferences and revisions of the several contracts under discussion. A fourth draft of the contracts was drawn up on June 9th, but further conferences became necessary.

In the files of RCA is to be found a very significant document, under date of June 14, 1926.

*Memorandum of Points for Discussion Between Mr. Bloom
and Mr. Sarnoff*

Mr. Sarnoff's penciled memo

Main Agreement. The terms upon which the Telephone Company will consent to proposed licenses to be granted by the Radio Group—Page 28.

Left for further discussion June 15. Conference with Mr. Bloom.

(In Mr. Sarnoff's handwriting—Splitdorf case)

Purchase Agreement

1. The re-entrance of Bell subsidiaries into the broadcasting business. } Settled

2. The period over which the Telephone Company is to stay out of broadcasting. } Settled

3. The desire of the Telephone Company to engage in program transmission by wire telegraphy. } Settled

4. Date of transfer of broadcasting business. } Settled

Service Agreement

1. Provision covering character of facilities to be furnished. } Settled

2. Provision to cover infringement of patents alleged to control the connection of broadcasting stations by wire. } Discussion

Out of these conferences came a fifth draft of the contracts. It is interesting to note that in place of the previous provision for the indefinite "thirty days after" date of transfer of the broadcasting business now appeared the following definite language in the purchase agreement:

"Article IV

"Said sale, transfer and assignment shall be effected, and payment therefor made, at the office of the Broadcasting Company, 195 Broadway, New York City, on December 31, 1926, or on such earlier date as the parties may mutually agree upon."

Sec. 98. Contracts Signed at Last.

It was perhaps inevitable that negotiations of such far-reaching importance as those that had been going on between the Radio Group and the Telephone Company should sooner or later come to the knowledge of others. The wonder is that the secret was so long guarded. On June 16, 1926, an inter-departmental communication (dated June 14th) between two RCA officials came to Mr. Sarnoff's desk containing the following human-interest news:

"Although negotiations with the Telephone Company and all conversations related to the subject may have been very carefully guarded, however, there is evidence of a leak somewhere. Whether this has any significance so far as the negotiations are concerned, of course, I cannot say. I am therefore reporting that *The New York Times* has a line on the proposed new broadcasting arrangements and are seeking to officially confirm the fact that there are interesting moves on foot.

"I told the *Times* I knew nothing about any merger between RCA and others."

The final paragraph was not so much of a "fib" as might appear. Even at the stage that negotiations had reached, no one could feel sure that the agreements would actually be signed.

On June 21st the lawyers for the Radio Group drew up seven interrogatories addressed to leaders of the group, containing the following preface:

"In anticipation of being able to complete the various contracts between the Telephone Company and the members of the Radio Group at an early date, and in view of the desire to close with the Telephone Company without waiting to complete the arrangements between the members of the Radio Group themselves, it is desirable that the members of the Radio Group reach a preliminary understanding of the principles to govern the disposition of rights among themselves."

The first interrogatory was relative to what extent patent rights of Telephone Company and RCA in radio devices were to be extended to the Westinghouse Company. The second question was whether RCA was to get exclusive selling rights, and G.E. and Westinghouse exclusive manufacturing rights on the "sixty-forty" basis.

The fifth interrogatory was as follows:

"By whom will the original capital of the new Broadcasting Service Company be contributed and in what proportions?"

In the sixth interrogatory the question was asked whether RCA was to handle sales to the new Broadcasting Service.

Curiously enough, the final negotiations that gave genuine concern to David Sarnoff and Edgar S. Bloom related to the possibility of the Telephone Company re-entering the broadcasting field. On June 25th the question was agitated and, on June 28th, D. C. Swatland, a lawyer who was assisting the preparation of the final drafts of the contracts, wrote a memorandum for Mr. Sarnoff in which he referred to the matter thus:

"The present draft makes the penalty [4] effective if the Telephone Company re-enters the field of broadcasting during the life of the service agreement. Mr. Folk's suggestion is that if the Telephone Company re-enters the field after 1933, the licenses which the Radio Group get are only for use in connection with the transmission of programs from owned stations."

A significant memorandum of a conference between David Sarnoff and Edgar S. Bloom, on June 28, 1926, made by Mr. Swatland, contains the following paragraph:

"As a result of a good deal of discussion and some rather hard trading, Mr. Bloom finally consented to Mr. Sarnoff's request for some period beyond 1933, during which the Radio Group might have evidence of a change of attitude, if any, which might result on the part of the Telephone Company, in the event that the main agreement was terminated and the Telephone Company actually re-entered the broadcasting business subsequent to 1933."

The agreement for extension was apparently for three years, with a proviso that after July, 1933, there would be no refund on the good will previously mentioned. As late as June 30th changes were made that necessitated advancing the operative date of the several contracts to July 1, 1926.

The negotiations had now reached so critical a stage that premature publicity was a danger feared and dreaded by both sides. It seems that on July 1, 1926, David Sarnoff had just finished lunching with Edgar S. Bloom, and that a newspaper reporter had approached the pair in the dining room and had informed them that the story of the negotiations would be in the newspapers next day. Mr. Bloom had denied the truth of the report and had declared that "if anything came out in the papers he would make a statement to the effect that the Telephone Company had no intention of selling their broadcasting company, although we had had some negotiations with them regarding pick up wires, etc." On the following day General Harbord received from Mr. Bloom a prepared statement to be released to the press by the Telephone Company in case of news leak. General Harbord thereupon prepared a statement concurring with Mr. Bloom's report, in readiness to refute, if necessary, any harmful publicity.

[4] Meaning return of the $800,000 paid for "good will."

July 1st having passed it was resolved to sign the papers as soon as possible "as of July 1st." It was not until July 3rd that the lawyers for the Radio Group were able to send out the twelve documents for final inspection.

The great day at length dawned when the seemingly endless controversy between the American Telephone Company and the Radio Group could be settled by the signing of a bewildering array of documents. The first ten of these agreements were as follows:

1. Agreement modifying License Agreement of July 1, 1920 between General Electric and the Telephone Company.

2. Agreement dealing with termination, otherwise than as provided therein, of modified License Agreement between General Electric and the Telephone Company.

3. Agreement terminating the agreement for arbitration dated December 28, 1923, between the Telephone Company, Western Electric and all members of the Radio Group including United Fruit and subsidiaries.

4. Letter dealing with the granting of sub-licenses under modified License Agreement by members of the Radio Group.

5. Letter extending to the Telephone Group 90 days within which to change present method of merchandising to that required by main License Agreement.

6. Agreement modifying Extension Agreement and so-called Termination Agreement of July 1, 1920 between General Electric, Radio Corporation, the Telephone and Western Electric.

7. Letter by Telephone Company assenting to the extension of rights by General Electric and Radio Corporation to Westinghouse.

8. Agreement modifying Telephone-Westinghouse agreement of July 1, 1920.

9. Letter by Telephone Company assenting to extension of rights to corporations controlled by Radio Group.

10. Letter by Telephone Company confirming rights of, and consenting to the extension of rights to, United Fruit Company.

The eleventh document to be signed will no doubt figure in radio annals as the most important contract concerning the broadcasting industry that was ever consummated. By it a momentous struggle for supremacy was definitely closed. It involved in its provisions the purchase of the physical assets and the good will of the most efficient broadcasting organization in the world. It provided, moreover, for establishing a nationwide broadcasting service to arise from the consolidation of the broadcasting facilities of Station WEAF and the group of stations owned or controlled by the Radio Corporation and its allies.

Appropriately enough, the man who had battled so tirelessly and effectively to bring it to pass was given the honor of signing the document as the official representative of RCA. This fact is significant of the courtesy that prevailed in the high command. Owen D. Young, chairman of the board and General James G. Harbord, president of RCA, by virtue of their official positions, might, either of them, have elected to sign so important a contract, yet to David Sarnoff went the honor of affixing the final signature not only to the purchase agreement but also to the twelfth and last document—the service contract.

A very important development in radio broadcasting history occurred at this time—no less than the long-dreaded decision that Secretary Hoover had no legal right to assign wave lengths or to make regulations for the industry. It will be remembered that the national Congress had steadfastly refused to enact a radio control law, and that the only law at all applicable was a measure enacted in 1912 for the regulation of wireless stations and to prevent chaos on the air by unlicensed amateurs. Since radio broadcasting had arisen out of wireless telegraphy, an attempt had been made—unsuccessfully—to extend the 1912 law to regulate the new industry. Secretary Hoover had held repeated annual conferences with leaders in the radio industry and, finally, in 1925 had yielded to the appeals of broadcasters themselves and had assumed authority to regulate the industry.[5] The denial of authority in the Secretary of Commerce was precipitated by the Zenith Radio Corporation, which ignored the rules prescribed by Secretary Hoover and was promptly prosecuted by the government. On April 16, 1926, the U. S. Court for the Northern District of Illinois rendered a decision denying the power of the Department of Commerce.

The facts in the Zenith case were as follows:

Station WJAJ in Chicago was owned by the Zenith Radio Corporation. The station applied to the Federal licensing authority for permission to broadcast and was assigned the same radio frequency as that already possessed by Station KOA, the General Electric station in Denver. Only two hours a week were free on this assignment—the inadequacy of which aroused the ire of the owners. By a study of the situation it was discovered that if assigned a certain different channel there would be a possibility of a reasonable time on the air.

The difficulty was encountered in that the channel desired had already been reserved by mutual agreement between the United States Department of Commerce and Canadian authorities for Canadian broadcasting stations. This was one of six channels allotted to Canada, whereas the United States had eighty-nine channels. The Zenith Radio Corporation endeavored to persuade the Secretary of

[5] For a detailed story of Secretary Hoover's valiant attempts to regulate the industry see Archer, *History of Radio to 1926*, pp. 248-320.

Commerce to permit it to operate on the Canadian channel. Not being able to accomplish this, the station authorities prepared to test the validity of the Hoover assignments of broadcast channels. Thus the dreaded test case had arisen, and the radio industry awaited the issue with fear and trembling. The decision, although expected, threw the broadcasting industry into confusion.

On July 8th the Attorney General of the United States removed the last vestiges of control over radio broadcasting by ruling that the Secretary of Commerce had no power to specify wave lengths or to withhold licenses from would-be broadcasters. It seemed inevitable, however, that the resulting chaos in radio broadcasting would force congressional action at an early date.

Sec. 99. Breaking the News at Station WEAF.

We have previously observed that the contest was twofold in its stratas of controversy. The contest that had ended at the council table on July 7, 1926, was that of the "Olympian gods" who were in control of the destinies of giant corporations. To these men the issues had never become personal. No real animosities had developed. Just as lawyers may wrangle fiercely in the courtroom and remain friends, so these champions of the two groups had been able to maintain friendly personal relations. Thus the dove of peace had been able to flutter gently to the council table as the final signatures were affixed to the contracts last mentioned.

The second phase of rivalry between the two groups, however, had been conducted in the broadcasting arena—whose strata was far below that of the group that had made peace. WEAF, it is true, had commanded the heavens and had touched the far corners of the earth with its magic voice, yet relatively humble folk had fought its battles for supremacy. For years a bitter controversy had existed between WEAF and WJZ, the great metropolitan rivals. The very progress of the radio art prior to July, 1926, had been notably advanced by the very efforts of these rivals to outdo each other.

Human nature dictates that rivalry in any great contest engenders animosities between the contending groups. Partisanship is inevitable. In the process of time the staff at WEAF had developed a deep-seated animosity toward the staff at WJZ, and this hostility had been returned in equal measure by the staff of the latter station. Neither group could believe any good of the other. This attitude of mind quite naturally colored their opinions of the corporate group to which each of the rivals belonged. The staff at WEAF held the Radio Corporation of America in abhorrence. They had long rejoiced at their own affiliation with the American Telephone Company—rejoiced that they had no relations with the alleged iniquitous Radio Corporation.

The very teamwork and fierce rivalry with WJZ had caused Station WEAF to develop into the most powerful and influential radio station in America. Let us consider then the dilemma of this devoted group when rumors began to be circulated among them that their beloved station was being "sold down the river" to the Radio Corporation of America.

However closely guarded the secret may have been, it was inevitable that some inkling of the truth should have penetrated to the offices of WEAF between July 7th, when the contracts were signed, and September 13th, when the Radio Corporation made formal announcement of the purchase of Station WEAF. During the period of uncertainty what must have been the thoughts, the fears, the apprehension for the future of the group of co-laborers who had done so much to advance the banner of Station WEAF! Veterans of that station who are still in radio will say little concerning the summer of 1926. That it was a period of gloom and bitterness no one can deny.

Mark J. Woods, general office manager of station WEAF in 1926, now (1939) vice-president and treasurer of the National Broadcasting Company, tells a very interesting story of how his suspicions were first aroused that something was happening to Station WEAF. It will be remembered that the Broadcasting Company of America was incorporated by the Telephone Company on May 11, 1926, for the express purpose of taking over Station WEAF. A few days later one of the lawyers of the Telephone Company who was working on the Radio-Telephone accord requested Mr. Woods to draw up a schedule of all the physical property of Station WEAF. This request disturbed Mr. Woods because it seemed to go beyond any possible need of the present incorporation of the station. It came, moreover, at a time when the young man was endeavoring to clear up his work in preparation for a three weeks' trip to Florida—in fact, for his honeymoon.

Thus, instead of being able to revisit boyhood scenes with his bride, Mark J. Woods was constrained to forego a wedding trip altogether and to embark on an elaborate inventory of desks and chairs, technical equipment, and the thousand and one items that appear on the purchase contract signed by RCA and the Telephone Company on July 7, 1926. Perhaps it should be added that, except for the weekend trip to Atlantic City following the marriage in early June, the young couple had to wait a full year for the Florida honeymoon.

Mr. Woods continued to entertain suspicions of sale of WEAF, but it was not until July 21st that he learned the truth.

The clearest picture that the author has been able to obtain of Station WEAF during this crucial period comes from the pen of Miss Carolla A. Bryant, now executive secretary of Suffolk University, but at that time a newcomer to the ranks of radio. Miss Bryant joined the staff of WEAF as a speed stenographer in June, 1926, during the final stages of the Sarnoff-Bloom negotiations.

"I had been working at the Bryant Teachers Agency," she writes, "a relatively small organization operated by my brother and cousin. I was greatly impressed by employment at 195 Broadway, the mammoth Telephone Building. Station WEAF occupied one-half of the fourth floor—offices and studios. My work at first was purely stenographic, I being one of about ten stenographers. Mark Woods was then the general office manager. My duties at first were to take dictation from salesmen connected with the staff.

"George McClelland was station manager at the time. H. Clinton Smith, whom we called 'Father' Smith perhaps because of his age, was generally regarded as head salesman. He, by the way, was the man who sold the first commercial contract for WEAF—the Queensboro Corporation account. Daniel S. Tuthill, Herbert Foster, Donald Buckham, George Podeyn and William H. Ensign are other salesmen whom I remember to have been there during that summer at WEAF.

"The first strong impression that I received was the utter friendliness of everybody. It was as if I had joined an especially harmonious family. There was teamwork all the way down the line from station manager to office boy. William E. Harkness, the head of the organization, seemed to be loved by everybody—in fact the staff at WEAF appeared to reflect his personality. It was well organized. There was a quiet dignity about the whole establishment, but no stiff formality—a decidedly homey atmosphere throughout. We knew that the station was being operated by the Broadcasting Company of America, a newly organized subsidiary of the American Telephone Company, and for this reason we felt secure and happy in our work.

"I well remember the shock that came to us one morning in the stenographic department when we were called together and told that there was a notice for each of us to read. The spokesman said that there was nothing to be frightened about. We were not to lose our jobs but WEAF had been sold to the Radio Corporation of America. Of course I had not been there long enough to have the same feeling in the matter that the others in the staff seemed to have when they heard the news. Each of them in turn was to read and initial a notice which had been issued by George McClelland. I was one of the last to sign the notice. It was a simple announcement to the effect that the American Telephone Company had sold Radio Station WEAF to the Radio Corporation of America but that for the time being no changes in working schedules, salaries, policies or station set-up need be expected. I have no clear recollection when this event occurred but since I then felt myself to be an accepted member of the family at WEAF it must have been several weeks after I entered the employ of the station.[6] It was generally understood that while the stenographic and

[6] The records of the American Telephone & Telegraph Company show that the name of Carolla A. Bryant first appeared on the payroll June 25, 1926, which was a Friday, thus indicating that Miss Bryant began work about June 21st.

sales force would not be disturbed yet there were to be changes in the head office."

The date of the announcement to the WEAF staff referred to by Miss Bryant has now definitely been established by the author as having occurred on July 21, 1926—two weeks to a day after the actual signing of the contracts between the Telephone Company and the Radio Group. It is apparent that the leaders of both groups had arrived at an understanding that no immediate announcements would be made concerning the merger of broadcasting facilities. The actual announcement apparently was made in three forms—first, to the staff as described by Miss Bryant; second, by a press release in the evening of that day, July 21st and, third, by an announcement over the WEAF microphones on July 22nd.

That the press release was regarded as a "bolt from the blue" is attested by the headlines on the first page of *The New York Times* for July 22, 1926:

WEAF TO MERGE WITH RADIO STATION WJZ
A. T. & T. will Quit Broadcasting Field

The news story ran, in part, as follows:

Broadcasting Station WEAF is to be sold by the American Telephone and Telegraph Company to the Radio Corporation of America which now operates Station WJZ, it was announced last night, and the A. T. & T. is to retire from the broadcasting business. This announcement practically foreshadows the consolidation of two of the best-known broadcasting stations in the East. A statement issued last night by the A. T. & T. began:

"Arrangements have been completed for the sale of Broadcasting Station WEAF to the Radio Corporation of America. The actual transfer will take place before the end of the year.

"It has always been the purpose of the A. T. & T. Company not only to improve the known means of telephone service but to seek any new means which would further facilitate electric communication. This company therefore undertook to develop radio broadcasting in order to discover how it could be made most useful in our business. . . . WEAF was equipped with the best available apparatus known to the art. It was organized to develop the best possible programs and make a careful analysis and study of the reactions on the part of the public to these programs. It was also designed to determine the place of a commercial station, where broadcasting could be done for hire, in the business and social conditions of the day. . . . The further the experiment was carried the more evident it became that while the technical principle was similar to that of the telephone system, the objective of the broadcasting station was quite different from that of a telephone system. Consequently, it has seemed to us after years of experimentation, that the broadcasting station which we built up might be more suitably operated by other interests.

"If WEAF has helped to point the way to that future it has served a useful purpose. In the hands of the Radio Corporation of America with a concurrent experience in radio broadcasting, the future of Station WEAF should be assured."

The *Times* reporter confirms the author's conjecture that the announcement took RCA officials by surprise, writing as follows:

"Efforts to obtain from Radio Corporation officials information as to the possible future of the station were unavailing last night, all officials who could be reached being in total ignorance of the transaction."

It appeared that reporters had been unable to locate General Harbord on the night of the 21st. The sensation created by the action of the Telephone Company, however, put the RCA chieftain "on the spot." Apparently the General had promptly prepared a news release. At a conference that day Mr. Young read and approved the proposed news item, but then declared: "We might as well get our story over while we have a chance." "He took my statement," said General Harbord, "and dictated another in the rough which I later gave out."

The New York Times for July 23rd carried the story in full—a splendid example of making a virtue of necessity—since it gave the projected broadcasting corporation a fine send off. Mr. Young is noted for the clarity of his statements and the lofty idealism with which he clothes his thoughts. The RCA press release was a masterpiece of publicity, painting a glowing picture of the future status of Station WEAF.

The third form of announcement was, naturally, to WEAF's far-flung radio audience. Although the script, discovered by the author in the RCA files, bears no date it was obviously broadcast on July 22, 1926, when the news first broke in the New York papers:

"The daily press of today is carrying a statement regarding arrangements that have been made for the sale of Broadcasting Station WEAF to the Radio Corporation of America. We want to assure you that WEAF will continue to be operated under its present plan and manned by its present personnel. The same programs will continue to come to you, the voices of the same announcers will continue to introduce these features. The programs will be built and presented by the same people. In short, WEAF remains WEAF with an added interest and endeavor to supply you with those programs which you have received so favorably in the past."

CHAPTER
THIRTEEN

The National Broadcasting Company Arises

Section 100. Important Plans for the New Corporation.

THE INK ON THE CONTRACTS of July 1926 had no sooner dried than the Telephone Company officials took measures to close out their Washington, D. C., station. On July 12, 1926, Edgar S. Bloom addressed a letter to David Sarnoff in which he pointed out the "uneconomic situation" that existed in the Capital City so far as broadcasting was concerned. It seems that RCA's station, WRC, was on a time-sharing basis with WCAP, owned by a subsidiary of the Telephone Company. The arrangement as to broadcasting hours caused one station to be idle while the other was on the air. A portion of Mr. Bloom's letter ran as follows:

"I have not mentioned this matter to you pending the disposal of the matters which have been under negotiation between us regarding the modification of the license contract of July 1, 1920. Now that that matter is disposed of I think it would be desirable to actively consider the elimination of the uneconomic condition that now prevails at Washington.

"Mr. Berry had advised me that he would be glad to consider closing down WCAP provided some satisfactory arrangement can be made with your company to take over WCAP's time, with proper assurances that the Washington radio public would receive features which are now presented over WCAP. From our standpoint here, we would be glad to work out some arrangement with you along this general line which would provide a Washington broadcasting outlet for our network features."

On July 14th Mr. Sarnoff replied to the above letter stating that—

". . . the reasons given in your letter appeal to us as very sound, and we shall be glad to effect the arrangement suggested by you at any time that it is convenient to both parties.

"I have asked my assistant, Mr. Angus, to deal with this matter in my absence. Whenever you are ready to discuss the subject further, Mr. Angus will be pleased to call on you or anyone whom you may designate to work out this matter in detail."

It is apparent that an agreement was promptly effected between the Broadcasting Company of America and RCA for the closing down of WCAP. That the change occurred on August 1st is attested by a letter from one of the BCA officials to Captain Angus, under date of August 23, 1926, in which the following reference is made:

"For the old WCAP pick-ups now connected with WRC, and on which you should take over the charges as of August 1, 1926, there are seven more or less permanent locations."

It should be noted, however, that RCA had not yet exercised its option to purchase the Broadcasting Company of America. The agreement itself had provided that the purchase money could be paid at any time prior to December 31st. Until that important transaction should come to pass Station WEAF and the broadcasting activities of BCA would naturally continue as before. There was a very important reason why RCA postponed the taking of title to Station WEAF. Owen D. Young and his associates had in contemplation the setting up of a great broadcasting company. It was never intended by them that RCA should itself take over the station. The option to purchase was thus in reality being held for the benefit of the future corporation. To lay the foundation for so important an enterprise required a great deal of preliminary work—work that would require the entire summer to complete.

To Owen D. Young, chairman of the board of RCA, came the task of organizing the new corporation. Mr. Young was keenly aware that more important even than the legal features of the preparation would be the problem of selecting a president of the corporation. He well knew that no executive then connected with radio could be chosen without causing jealousies and heart-burnings. It was imperative that the man to be appointed should know something of public utilities and should, moreover, have an established reputation in some industry allied to radio. As early as June, 1926, Mr. Young is known to have suggested to his associates the name of Merlin H. Aylesworth.

Mr. Aylesworth was at this time the managing director of the National Electric Light Association. His rise to that position indicated to Mr. Young the type of "career-man" that seemed to be needed for the job. Mr. Aylesworth had been graduated from the University of Denver Law School, and had practiced law for several years prior to becoming chairman of the Colorado Public Utilities Commission in 1914. After four years of service in that important post he had entered the public utilities field and had very promptly been elected to the position of managing director of the National Electric Light Association.

The manner in which the name "National Broadcasting Company" was selected has been explained to the author by General Harbord. He states that a conference was held at Poland Springs, Maine, in which he, Mr. Young and General Tripp of Westinghouse participated. Among other problems settled at this meeting was the name National Broadcasting Company. General Harbord stated that the meeting probably occurred in July or August, 1926. The exact date of this conference is now definitely established. Owen D. Young's records show that he was at Poland Springs on August 2nd and 3rd.

It is known that from July 30th to August 9th General Harbord was in New England on a vacation. After the Poland Springs conference he apparently went on to Bar Harbor for a few days, returning to New York on August 9, 1926.

Sec. 101. Setting Up the National Broadcasting Company.

The management of the new broadcasting company was the subject of further discussions during July of that year. Early in August, 1926, it was officially determined to invite Merlin H. Aylesworth to become president of the National Broadcasting Company. The proposal to Mr. Aylesworth was made at a conference with Mr. Young and General Harbord on August 13, 1926. Mr. Aylesworth promised to take the matter under advisement, some doubt still existing as to the wisdom of severing his connection with the National Electric Light Association.

On August 19th, however, Merlin H. Aylesworth called at the RCA office and accepted the offer.

A genuine problem in diplomacy must have arisen over the selection of a general manager for the new broadcasting corporation. Charles B. Popenoe, under whose able administration Station WJZ had arisen, was an obvious possibility. His selection, however, would very likely alienate the staff at WEAF, the station for which they were shortly to pay one million dollars. The outstanding man in the WEAF organization, apart from William E. Harkness, a dyed-in-the-wool adherent of the American Telephone Company, was George F. McClelland. There was no apparent hesitation on the part of Mr. Young or General Harbord in this matter—McClelland was the man!

On August 24, 1926, Mr. McClelland was summoned to General Harbord's office. The latter's account of the interview gives us a glimpse of the meeting that reflects great credit upon young McClelland. When General Harbord offered him the position of vice-president and general manager of the National Broadcasting Company, George F. McClelland's response must have surprised and pleased the president of RCA. Quoting from General Harbord:

"He asked what was to be our aim—whether purely a money-making affair, or whether we aim to perform a big public service to which the income was somewhat incidental. I reassured him on this point, telling him we had the ambition to give a splendid public service, not unconscious of the fact, however, that if we did it, it would reflect itself to us in profits by that company and increased sales of radio apparatus by our own. He accepted the position without any understanding as to salary."

On September 9, 1926, the National Broadcasting Company was incorporated in the city of Dover, Delaware. Following the accepted custom in such matters there were but three stockholders and ten shares of stock when the corporate organization was set up. Following the usual procedure these ten shares of stock were immediately subscribed to by RCA. The first meeting of the board of directors was held at 11:45 A.M. on the day of incorporation, at which time by-laws were adopted and temporary officers were elected, these officers, of course, being chosen from the original incorporators who made up the board.

On September 13, 1926, a general statement was issued to the public press, signed by Owen D. Young and General James G. Harbord, formally announcing the formation of the National Broadcasting Company. Despite the fact that the statement was a bit pompous and stilted in tone, it was an admirable expression of the plans and purposes of the National Broadcasting Company.

Sec. 102. Origin of NBC's Great Rival.

So much of legend has grown up concerning the origin of the Columbia Broadcasting System that the author has devoted a good deal of attention to uncovering the real facts. It is of particular interest to note that during the very summer when plans were being laid in the councils of the mighty for the launching of the National Broadcasting Company, an obscure promoter hatched in his teeming brain the idea from which NBC's great rival eventually emerged. It is frequently said that truth is stranger than fiction, and certainly the facts lying in the background of the Columbia Broadcasting System's emergence into the radio field are more romantic than any fables that have been related concerning it.

In *Fortune* for June, 1935, is a reference to an almost legendary figure, George A. Coats, that fails to do the gentleman full justice. Mr. Coats is still living—he is still a promoter and quite willing to demonstrate his present promotion scheme. He is obviously a man of keen intellect, a convincing orator of very positive views, possessing a resourcefulness and persistence that explain how one man, without funds of his own, could accomplish the amazing beginning of a national broadcasting network.

Coats had been in Philadelphia, working as a salesman for the Good Roads Equipment Corporation which he himself had promoted in 1924. He was well acquainted with politicians high and low. He had a wide knowledge of current trends and, in 1926, was keen to undertake something new in the promotion line. Radio broadcasting, however, was out of his field, and had not the event occurred that is about to be related, George A. Coats might never have turned his talents to the broadcasting business at all.

It seems that one of his acquaintances in New York City was L. S. ("Hap") Baker, secretary to Paul B. Klugh, then executive chairman of the National Association of Broadcasters. This organization was then small, and struggling for recognition. It was quite up in arms in the summer of 1926 over the question of using copyrighted material over the air. The American Society of Composers, Authors and Publishers—ASCAP—was then engaged in a militant campaign to force the broadcasters of the nation to pay handsome royalties for radio use of copyrighted material. George A. Coats knew enough about the situation to have developed very positive views concerning the alleged iniquitous ASCAP.

The Fourth Annual Convention of the National Association of Broadcasters was being held in early September, 1926, at the Hotel Astor in Times Square—attended by only twenty-five or thirty delegates. At this psychological moment George A. Coats breezed into town and met his friend "Hap" Baker. Possibly, in a desire to enliven a dull meeting, Baker invited the eloquent promoter to come in and talk for a few minutes to the broadcasters on his pet aversion—ASCAP. Sure enough, Mr. Coats stirred up a lively discussion. His denunciation of ASCAP roused the ire of some of the delegates, especially of Powel Crosley, Jr., of WLW, Cincinnati, who warmly defended the organization and denounced its defamer.

Coats may have entered the room with no idea of doing more than to drop a few pearls of wisdom for the benefit of the broadcasters, but in the heat of his verbal encounter with Powel Crosley was evolved a great purpose. He would demonstrate to all and sundry that broadcasters were "saps" should they meekly accept the dictation of ASCAP. The thing to do, he averred, was to organize a great radio program bureau. The idea was formulated and Coats was soon hot on the trail of someone who could head such a bureau. It so happened that Arthur Judson, the manager of the Philadelphia Symphony Orchestra, and widely acquainted with great artists of the concert hall, was immediately invited to come into the venture.

Mr. Judson had already given considerable thought to the future of his own enterprise, the booking of talent for concerts and the like. He had recognized very clearly the threat that was inherent in the vast broadcasting plans of the Radio Corporation of America. This new development might easily take away from independent booking organizations like his own all important patronage. Mr. Judson was in a mood to join hands with Mr. Coats. A corporation was the logical vehicle of operation. Edward Ervin and his mother, Mrs. Harold E. Yarnell, working for Judson in connection with his management of the Philadelphia Symphony and New York Philharmonic Orchestras, were interested in the venture. The only real cash that came into the treasury when the corporation was organized came from Mrs. Bettie F. Holmes (the former Bettie Fleishman), who subscribed $5000 for stock, well knowing that she was taking grave chances of losing her money. So swiftly did George A. Coats work that, on September 20, 1926, the Judson Radio Program Corporation was organized as a New York corporation. This was step number one in a notable series of efforts of an industrious promoter.

Sec. 103. The National Broadcasting Company Elects Officers.

Since the National Broadcasting Company was formed for a purpose that deeply concerned the nation at large it wisely adopted, at the outset of its career, a plan of publicity calculated to keep the nation informed of its activities. At first glance the joint statement by Messrs. Young and Harbord might seem to be open to criticism for overmuch professing of good intentions, but nevertheless it added to the public interest in the new corporation, not yet out of its swaddling clothes. There were legal formalities in plenty to be complied with before the National Broadcasting Company could have in its treasury funds with which to complete the purchase of Station WEAF and to assume control of the latter's extensive broadcasting activities. The author has been privileged to examine various documents and records that were kept with meticulous care by Lewis MacConnach, who was to be secretary of the National Broadcasting Company from October 15, 1926, to the present writing. With characteristic modesty Mr. MacConnach insisted to the author that he was not the first secretary of NBC. An examination of the records demonstrates that although Charles B. Popenoe was elected secretary and treasurer on October 8, 1926, he nevertheless resigned as secretary before the next meeting, as will appear in the following summary of the organization meetings of the corporation.

On October 1, 1926, the way was clear for the perfunctory stages of the National Broadcasting Company to yield to the real business for which the corporation had been organized. On that day a special meeting of the board of directors was held at 150 Broadway, New York City. In accordance with accepted usages, the board now voted to amend the by-laws of the corporation by increasing the number of directors from three to eleven. This being accomplished the following were elected to the board:

Merlin H. Aylesworth
E. W. Harden
Dwight W. Morrow
Guy E. Tripp
Harry P. Davis
E. M. Herr
Gerard Swope
Owen D. Young.

On the same day, the three organizers of the corporation, having performed the functions intended, resigned as directors.

A special meeting of the board was convened on October 8, 1926. Owen D. Young was appointed temporary chairman and Lewis Mac-Connach was designated as temporary secretary. The three resignations were acted upon and James G. Harbord, David Sarnoff and William Brown were elected to fill the vacancies on the board. An election of officers thereupon occurred, with the following result:

Chairman of the board—Harry P. Davis
President of NBC—Merlin H. Aylesworth
Vice-president and general manager—George F. McClelland
Treasurer—Charles B. Popenoe
Secretary—Charles B. Popenoe

On October 15th, however, Mr. Popenoe resigned as secretary of the corporation and, on the same day, at a special meeting of the board Lewis MacConnach was elected permanent secretary. The excellence of the corporate records of the National Broadcasting Company bears eloquent testimony to the ability and the painstaking character of Secretary MacConnach.

The final organization stage was now accomplished by an amendment of the by-laws authorizing an increase of capital stock to thirty thousand shares, one-half of which were to be immediately issued for cash at $100 a share.

A very significant item of business, in fact the chief purpose for which the corporation had been organized, was transacted at this meeting of October 15th, as will be seen in the following:

"EXTRACT FROM THE MINUTES OF MEETING OF
THE BOARD OF DIRECTORS
"NATIONAL BROADCASTING COMPANY, INC.
"HELD OCTOBER 15, 1926

"The President reported having received, and recommended acceptance of, a proposal from the Radio Corporation of America to transfer and assign to this company the former's right to buy Station WEAF and to acquire wire line facilities necessary to the operation of said station, on the basis of this company assuming certain obligations of the Radio Corporation with respect to the purchase of said station and acquisition of said wire facilities, as provided for in two contracts of the Radio Corporation of America of July 1, 1926, with, first, the American Telephone & Telegraph Company and the Broadcasting Company of America, and second, with the American Telephone & Telegraph Company.

"After full discussion of the matter, on motion, duly made, seconded and unanimously carried, it was

"RESOLVED, that it being deemed to be to the best interests of this company to acquire and operate said station, the President and other proper officers of this company be, and they hereby are, authorized to negotiate and conclude, on terms acceptable to the President, a contract or agreement with the Radio Corporation of America for taking over by this company by proper assignment and transfer certain of the rights of the Radio Corporation under the said two contracts of July 1, 1926, namely, for the purchase at $1,000,000 cash, payable not later than December 31, 1926, of broadcasting Station WEAF, together with its physical property, business, good will, contracts and leases, and on payment of prescribed charges therefor, for the acquisition of certain wire facilities necessary to the operation of said station; and further

"RESOLVED, that upon such rights of the Radio Corporation being duly transferred and assigned to this company, the said officers are hereby authorized to make payments and carry out and perform such of the obligations originally assumed by the Radio Corporation of America under said two contracts of July 1, 1926, with respect to the purchase of said Station WEAF and acquisition of said wire facilities as may be accepted and assumed by the President; provided, however, that the rights so to be acquired by this company in and to said Station WEAF and its property, business, good will, contracts and leases and its rights to said wire facilities, as well as its contemplated operation of said station and its rights, function and activities in the field of broadcasting for tolls in connection therewith, shall be subject to determination by the President of this company in conference with the Presidents of the Radio Corporation of America and the General Electric and Westinghouse Companies."

On the same day, at a meeting of the board of directors of the Radio Corporation of America, action was taken on the above matter as appears in the following extract from the minutes of the meeting:

"OCTOBER 15, 1926

"The President reported that he is advised that the National Broadcasting Company, Inc., is desirous of taking over certain of the interests of the Radio Corporation of America under the two contracts of July 1, 1926, of the Radio Corporation with, first, the American Telephone & Telegraph Company and the Broadcasting Company of America relating to the purchase of Station WEAF and its equipment, and, second, with the American Telephone & Telegraph Company, relating to wire facilities. After full discussion of the matter, on motion, duly made, seconded and unanimously carried, it was

"RESOLVED, that the President and other proper officers of the company be, and they hereby are, authorized and empowered to transfer and assign, on terms acceptable to the President, the rights of the Radio Corporation of America, (1st) to purchase and acquire Station WEAF, including its physical property, business, good will, contracts and leases; and (2nd) to acquire wire line facilities necessary for the operation of said Station WEAF, all as provided for under the following contracts of July 1, 1926:

" (1) Contract of the Radio Corporation of America with American Telephone & Telegraph Company and Broadcasting Company of America for the purchase of said Station WEAF; and

" (2) Contract of the Radio Corporation of America with the American Telephone & Telegraph Company relating to the acquisition of wire line facilities, for use in connection with the operation of said Station WEAF."

Sec. 104. An Advisory Council Is Planned.

It had long been known that Owen D. Young had a very ambitious plan in mind for the public-relations aspect of the National Broadcasting Company. It was no surprise, therefore, when at the first genuine business meeting of the board of directors, October 15, 1926, Mr. Young brought forward his plan for the formation of an advisory council as a means of giving the new corporation the benefit of all shades of thought among leaders in civic life.

As the leader of the Radio Group, Mr. Young apparently resolved to assemble a group of advisers whose wisdom and integrity were already nationally established. The board of directors accepted the recommendation and appointed a committee to deal with the matter, as appears in the following extract from the minutes of October 15th:

"RESOLVED, that the matter of constituting an advisory council and defining its powers, be and hereby is referred to a committee consisting of Messrs. Owen D. Young, Guy E. Tripp, James G. Harbord, Edward W. Harden and the President for consideration and report at the next meeting of the board."

In the meantime, plans were in progress for the taking over of Station WEAF, title to which still remained in the Telephone Company. The Radio Corporation, as we know, held an option to purchase the station. The first step in legal proceedings was therefore for NBC to acquire the option. On October 29, 1926, the Radio Corporation conveyed to the National Broadcasting Company all its rights in relation to Station WEAF and to other assets that had been specified in the covenant of July, 1926. By the terms of the new agreement the National Broadcasting Company was to assume the payment of the purchase price established by the earlier contract. The agreement was executed in RCA's behalf by General Harbord and in behalf of NBC by M. H. Aylesworth.

During this period, at Station WEAF the staff that had fought so valiantly under the banner of the American Telephone Company was making ready to haul down the old flag and to substitute a new banner. William E. Harkness, whom they loved, had announced his intention to return to the long lines department of the Telephone Company. There was really no place for him in the new organization even if he had wished to remain. To President Aylesworth of NBC the coworkers at Station WEAF would in the future look for orders, and so the entire staff made ready to say farewell to their chief.

Not often in industrial annals can such a situation be encountered as this. Under Mr. Harkness' administration the station had grown to an organization employing one hundred and eleven subordinates. Under the circumstances deep emotions, not usually engendered in business relations, were unleashed. The staff contributed funds for a joint gift to Mr. Harkness. A gold watch was selected and, on the last day of independent operations, a surprise party was staged. George F. McClelland, manager of broadcasting under the old regime, was to make the presentation speech. In the midst of it, however, according to the testimony of those who were present at the highly affecting scene, Mr. McClelland, naturally an emotional man, was overcome by the mass emotions of the moment. He was unable to complete his speech and Mr. Harkness likewise was unable to respond—except in the universal language of tears. According to Mark J. Woods every member of the staff unashamedly wept, and so we may truthfully say that the Telephone Company station dissolved in tears to reappear as the National Broadcasting Company's great network outlet—a larger and greater WEAF.

It is recorded that on October 31, 1926, each of the officers who had served WEAF under Mr. Harkness resigned, to accept reappointment under Mr. Aylesworth of NBC. George F. McClelland, as we know, had already been elected vice-president and general manager of the National Broadcasting Company. Mark J. Woods likewise had been chosen assistant treasurer, both elections having occurred on October 15, 1926.

It is significant that one of Mr. Woods' first duties on November 1st was to sign the million-dollar check by which the National Broadcasting Company purchased Station WEAF. The check was drawn

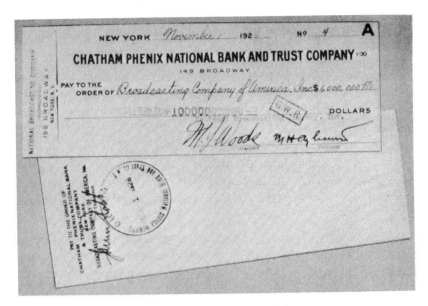

MILLION DOLLAR CHECK
Photostatic copy of both sides of most famous check in radio history

IRA J. ADAMS
RCA lawyer, prominent in negotiations.

MARK J. WOODS
First Treasurer of NBC who signed the million dollar check given for WEAF.

to the order of the Broadcasting Company of America which, in turn, transferred the important slip of paper to the American Telephone Company, and thereafter faded out of the picture as a corporate entity. Station WEAF was now the property of the National Broadcasting Company. All financial transactions beginning with November 1, 1926, were to be in the name of the new company. The canceled check is in the archives of NBC. A photostat of it is included in this volume.

On the morning of November 1, 1926, the staff welcomed the new president of the National Broadcasting Company. Merlin H. Aylesworth had arrived to take over the offices so long occupied by William E. Harkness—to sit at the familiar desk and to issue orders—fortunately, however, relating to the larger affairs of the new corporation. The one consolation—a consolation of major proportions to the staff at WEAF—was that George F. McClelland, of their own official family, had been elected vice-president and general manager of the National Broadcasting Company. They consoled themselves with the thought that McClelland would be their real chief. Not only that but out of the consolidation had come this triumph over their rivals at WJZ—McClelland had become the "boss" of WJZ, triumphing in the councils of the mighty over Charles B. Popenoe, who might have been appointed to the post. As it was, Mr. Popenoe had been elected treasurer of NBC.

By the irony of fate the founder of WJZ, who had been so cordially disliked at WEAF, now came to the offices of the latter as a matter of daily routine. Aylesworth, Popenoe and Captain Angus of RCA were three visible reminders to the WEAF staff that the National Broadcasting Company was a functioning overlord to which they must perforce accord allegiance. For all concerned there were embarrassments and heart-burnings that time and changed environment might eventually alleviate if not entirely cure.

Station WJZ was to remain in its old location in the Aeolian Building—to remain for a full twelve months—while a home for the National Broadcasting Company was being prepared to house both stations under the same roof. The prospect was no doubt heartily dreaded by each staff. It did not require a prophet to foresee major complications when the rank and file of the two rival stations should eventually be obliged to merge. How that merger should be accomplished, and what would happen to heads of departments when the consolidation should become complete, were long to be fruitful topics of speculation. One of the most intriguing was the question of how Phillips Carlin, program manager of Station WEAF, would fare in future competition for advancement with Miss Bertha Brainard, the auburn-haired dynamo who was now assistant program manager of

WJZ. The lady was known to be ambitious and efficient. The age-old prejudice against women in business was likely to encounter the age-old truth that a clever and magnetic woman is a power to be reckoned with even in the councils of the Olympian gods.

G. W. Johnstone, who had served in like capacity for Station WEAF, became publicity manager for NBC. One of the first press releases issued by him in behalf of the new corporation was marked "For Release Monday A.M., November 1st." It was headed: "World Famed Stars in National Broadcasting Company's Opening Program." The first sentence of the release was as follows:

"The most pretentious broadcasting program ever presented, featuring among others, world-famed stars never before heard on the air, will mark the introduction of the National Broadcasting Company to the radio public, Monday evening, November 15th."

In the meantime, the committee headed by Owen D. Young was ready to report on plans for the advisory council. At a meeting of the board of directors of NBC, held on November 5, 1926, the committee submitted a list of names of prospective advisors. This report was accepted and Mr. Young was authorized to send to each person on the list a letter of invitation to join the advisory council. Not only that, the letter itself—already drafted by the far-seeing Owen D. Young— was officially approved.

At the meeting of the NBC board held on October 1st an important item of business was transacted. Now that Station WEAF had been taken over and a definite agreement for wire lines had been included in the treaty of peace of July, 1926, the National Broadcasting Company made ready to extend the sphere of activity of Station WJZ, hitherto unable to obtain long lines from the Telephone Company. Perhaps it should be explained that Mr. Aylesworth and his associates were planning to maintain two great radio networks. WEAF was to be the key station of the network already begun by the Telephone Company, whereas WJZ would be made the central station of another network that would include the stations owned by the corporations known as the Radio Group. Although Station WJZ was still owned by RCA it was to be controlled by the National Broadcasting Company. With this background of facts we may understand the significance of the following:

"EXTRACT FROM MINUTES OF THE MEETING OF THE BOARD OF DIRECTORS
"NATIONAL BROADCASTING COMPANY, INC.
"NOVEMBER 5, 1926

"RESOLVED, that the president be and he hereby is authorized to negotiate and conclude contracts with the American Telephone &

Telegraph Company for necessary wire facilities (under the provisions of that company's contract with the Radio Corporation of America), connecting Stations WJZ, New York, WBZ, Springfield, Mass., KDKA, Pittsburgh, Pa., and KYW, Chicago, Ill., in order to form a new network, and that the president be and he hereby is authorized to negotiate and conclude contracts with the American Telephone & Telegraph Company for necessary wire facilities, (under the provisions of that company's contract with the Radio Corporation of America), to extend the present WEAF network, to Stations WSB, Atlanta, Ga., WHAS, Louisville, Ky., WMC, Memphis, Tenn., and WSM, Nashville, Tenn."

Sec. 105. A Momentous Christening Party, for NBC.

The preliminary announcement of November 1st had been devoid of details concerning the proposed christening party. A second release, under date of November 10, 1926, was more specific. It listed such famous artists as Mary Garden, Will Rogers, Titta Ruffo, Weber and Fields, the New York Symphony Orchestra with Walter Damrosch as conductor, Harold Bauer, the New York Oratorio Society, Edwin Franko Goldman Band, a grand and light opera company under the baton of Cesare Sodero, Vincent Lopez and his Orchestra, George Olsen and the orchestras of Ben Bernie and B. A. Rolfe.

The Grand Ballroom of the Waldorf-Astoria in New York City was the setting for the impressive ceremonies that were to mark the launching of the National Broadcasting Company. Over a thousand guests made up the visible audience. Microphones in the ballroom carried to a vast unseen audience the most ambitious radio program ever attempted up to that time. The exercises opened with a five-minute address by NBC's newly elected president, Merlin H. Aylesworth. Mr. Aylesworth told of the plans and purposes of the new company, and stated that the evening's program was to give the assembled guests and the audience out in radio land a glimpse of the goal that the National Broadcasting Company would seek to obtain in the development of radio broadcasting.

Mary Garden was scheduled to sing on the program, but the audience had the experience of hearing her voice from the loud speakers in the ballroom. Milton Cross in Chicago had put her on the air. Her first selection was *Annie Laurie* followed by *Open Thy Blue Eyes* and *My Little Gray Home in the West.*

The New York Times for November 16, 1926, reported the program at some length. A portion of the account was as follows:

"A gala radio program last night from 8 o'clock to midnight, featuring Mary Garden, soprano of the Chicago Civic Opera Company, and Will Rogers inaugurated the National Broadcasting Company, of which WEAF and WJZ form the nucleus."

In commenting on Miss Garden's songs the *Times* reporter demonstrated that not even the most advanced type of radio engineering in 1926 could surmount every obstacle to perfect rendition from a distance:

"The engineers in the audience were startled when they heard what they termed a 'beat note,' a waxing and waning whistle, mixed in with Miss Garden's voice. They explained that this was caused by the interaction of some other wave with WEAF and showed how congested the ether was now."

No such disturbing incident was recorded with Will Rogers' monologue, which was likewise brought in by way of loud speaker. The comedian spoke from his dressing room in the back stage of Memorial Hall in Independence, Kansas. "Fifteen minutes with a Diplomat" was the title of the Rogers contribution, he being the diplomat, visiting European countries and winding up with a call upon President Coolidge at the White House.

Local celebrities of stage and concert hall brought abundant entertainment, running the gamut from the clowning of Weber and Fields to majestic offerings of New York's great orchestras, under leaders of international fame, previously enumerated.

An interesting aftermath of the affair was a news item in *The New York Times* for November 17th, which stated that NBC's christening party had cost $50,000, one-half of which went to the artists who appeared on the program. "In revealing these figures yesterday to the Associated Press," the report continued, "an official of the company said it was expected to make advertising ultimately pay the entire expense of elaborate programs to come."

Sec. 106. An Energetic Beginning for NBC.

The National Broadcasting Company soon demonstrated that it was a very energetic organization. Mr. Aylesworth's experience as an executive, coupled with the galaxy of industrial leaders in the official family of NBC, gave assurance that the activities of the corporation would be wisely directed. Owen D. Young's campaign to organize an advisory council of Radio had so far progressed that at a meeting of the board of directors on December 3rd [1] he was able to submit a list of seventeen

[1] Present at this meeting were the following:
Harry P. Davis, in the Chair
Merlin H. Aylesworth
James G. Harbord
Edwin M. Herr
David Sarnoff
Gerard Swope
Guy E. Tripp
Owen D. Young
Lewis MacConnach, Secretary.

persons eminent in American life for election to the council. The following extract from the minutes of the meeting will be self-explanatory:

"Mr. Young reported relative to the replies which had been received to letter sent to the proposed members of the advisory council, as authorized by the board of directors on November 5, 1926. After discussion, on motion, duly made, seconded and unanimously carried, it was

"RESOLVED, that an advisory council be and hereby is created, with powers and duties as set forth in letter of November 6, 1926 (a copy of which is attached to the minutes of the meeting of the board of directors held on November 5, 1926), and further

"RESOLVED, that the following members shall constitute the said advisory council (subject to additions and substitutions which may be made from time to time by the board of directors)."

The list of those elected, together with identification of the individuals is as follows:

Edward A. Alderman, president, University of Virginia
Walter J. Damrosch, conductor, New York Symphony Orchestra
John W. Davis, lawyer, New York City
Francis D. Farrell, president, Kansas State Agricultural College
William Green, president, American Federation of Labor
General James G. Harbord, president RCA
Charles E. Hughes, lawyer, New York City
Rev. Charles F. MacFarland, General Secretary Federal Council of
    Churches of Christ in America, New York City
Dwight W. Morrow, banker, New York City
Morgan J. O'Brien, lawyer, New York City
Henry S. Pritchett, president, Carnegie Foundation
Henry M. Robinson, president, First National Bank, Los Angeles, Cal.
Elihu Root, lawyer, New York City
Julius Rosenwald, president, Sears Roebuck & Co.
Mrs. Mary Sherman, president, General Federation of Women's
    Clubs in America
General Guy E. Tripp, chairman of board, Westinghouse Company
Owen D. Young, chairman of board, General Electric Company.

In contemplating this distinguished array of potent sponsors we may perhaps be pardoned if we indulge in the query whether ever before in the history of the world any infant corporation has boasted such a scintillating array of official advisers! Not even a newly born crown prince of one of the great Powers of yesteryear could have begun life with more wisdom at his elbow! Verily, Owen D. Young was fulfilling the pledge made to the American public by RCA on September 13, 1926.

Action was taken at this meeting of December 3rd to authorize President Aylesworth to negotiate and conclude contracts for the establishment, in the near future, of a Pacific coast network of NBC. It was also voted to take over the Westinghouse broadcasting station at Hastings, Nebraska. Obviously this station was strategically located for a contemplated agricultural service to the farmers of the Middle West. It so happened that Frank E. Mullen,[2] a World War veteran and journalist, was then conducting a very successful program of agricultural market reports over Station KDKA. He had maintained this service over the same station since the spring of 1923. This explains the action of the board of directors on December 3, 1927, whereby the president was authorized to employ Mr. Mullen. He was to be placed in charge of the project at Hastings, Nebraska. It should be added that the well-known Farm and Home Hour of the National Broadcasting Company owes its original inspiration to the work of Frank E. Mullen.[3]

The meeting of December 3, 1926, was literally packed with important beginnings. The board of directors of NBC realized that, since radio was a new medium of advertising, it would inevitably encounter sales resistance of a twofold character. The public press was bound to resent the diversion of advertising funds into radio channels and could be counted upon to discourage radio advertising on the part of manufacturers and distributors of national importance. The second type of sales resistance of conservative businessmen and corporation executives was reluctance to embark in new and comparatively unproven ventures. As early as the spring of 1926, when it became apparent that the Sarnoff-Bloom negotiations were likely to succeed, Thomas F. Logan, an adviser in advertising matters, had been asked to suggest some man qualified to undertake the task of breaking down sales resistance to radio advertising.

Mr. Logan had suggested the name of Frank A. Arnold, a former magazine publisher, a trade investigator in foreign lands, then an executive of a prominent New York advertising agency. Mr. Arnold, moreover, for six years had been a lecturer on advertising at the Harvard University School of Business Administration. He was known to be deeply interested in the new medium of radio advertising. It

2 Mr. Mullen attended Iowa State College for one year prior to the War. He served overseas for a year and a half, returning to Iowa State College in September, 1919, graduating with a B.A. degree in Agricultural Journalism in 1922.

3 Mr. Mullen was soon transferred to Chicago to organize an executive branch of NBC in that city. In 1930 he set up the Farm and Home Hour. In December, 1934, he was appointed manager of a newly created department of information for the Radio Corporation of America, the position held by him until April 28, 1939, when he was elected Vice-President in charge of Advertising and Publicity of RCA.

ARTHUR JUDSON
Co-founder of Columbia Broadcasting
System.

PAUL W. KESTEN
CBS Vice-President in charge of promotional activity.

MAJOR J. ANDREW WHITE
Radio's pioneer announcer. One of the
organizers of CBS.

EDWARD KLAUBER
Executive Vice-President, Columbia
Broadcasting System.

was an open secret that Mr. Arnold was slated for a position that might be termed "Ambassador at Large to the American business world" for the National Broadcasting Company when it should begin to function. At the meeting of December 3, 1926, Mr. Arnold was elected "director of development," a sufficiently elastic and euphonious title to commend Mr. Arnold to public audiences or private powwows of industrial leaders. His task would be to devise ways and means of acquainting the public with radio's advertising potentialities.

The next important development in the affairs of the National Broadcasting Company is recorded in the minutes of a meeting of the board on December 17, 1926, at which the following action was taken:

"The president referred to the resignation of Mr. Walter J. Damrosch as director of the New York Symphony Orchestra and stated that, in view of Mr. Damrosch's ability and eminent position in the musical world, it would be desirable to have him associated with the National Broadcasting Company, in order that the company might have the benefit of his advice and counsel. After discussion, on motion, duly made, seconded and unanimously carried, it was

"RESOLVED, that the matter of retaining Mr. Walter J. Damrosch be and hereby is referred to the president, with power."

It is well known that Dr. Damrosch later became musical counsel for the National Broadcasting Company. *Who's Who in America* sets the year as 1928, but the treasury records of NBC demonstrate that Dr. Damrosch came to the company as musical counsel on May 1, 1927.

A press release, dated December 20, 1926, disclosed the fact that NBC had set up a board of consulting engineers composed of Dr. Alfred N. Goldsmith, chief consulting engineer of RCA, as chairman, Dr. Ernst F. W. Alexanderson of the General Electric engineering staff, and Dr. Frank Conrad, employed in a like capacity by the Westinghouse Company.

One of the innovations made by NBC at Station WEAF reversed a custom that had been observed since the station was founded—that of complete silence on Christmas Day. The new administration decreed that the staff must report on December 25th for duty—Santa Claus or no Santa Claus. Not only that, but a twelve-hour gala program was arranged, beginning at noontide. It was indeed a musical Christmas Day. Stars and famous orchestras performed in a continuous program that apparently fulfilled the forecast made on November 16, 1926, that advertisers would thereafter carry the financial burden of a gala program.

The Colgate Orchestra; the Coward Comfort Hour, featuring B. A. Rolfe and his Concert Ensemble; the Eveready Novelty Orchestra; the Greenwich Village Orchestra; even the bewhiskered cough drop brothers, "Trade" and "Mark" Smith, occupied afternoon hours. In the evening Handel's oratorio, "The Messiah," was presented from 7:00 to 7:30 P.M. The Balkite Hour, with Walter Damrosch conducting the New York Symphony Orchestra, was a notable feature. The evening's offerings were concluded by Vincent Lopez and his band.

Sec. 107. An Era of Network Expansion.

The WEAF network had enlarged its scope of activities during December, 1926, and was now beginning to be called the Red Network of the National Broadcasting Company—this being in the days before the term "red network" had acquired a sinister significance in quite another phase of American life. The designation was purely for the purpose of differentiating between two networks that were to originate in New York City—WEAF to be the key station of the Red Network and its old rival WJZ to furnish nationwide programs for the Blue Network. New Year's Day was the appointed date for the inauguration of the second network.

As early as December 12th a press release from the busy office of George W. Johnstone, publicity manager of NBC, had heralded the opening program for the Blue Network. The first of a series of broadcasts to be sponsored by the Victor Talking Machine Company was listed for this purpose on January 1, 1927. The program was to be an hour long—9:00 to 10:00 P.M. and to be given twice a month.

On New Year's Day, President Aylesworth, whose importance in civic affairs entitled him to a measure of pontification, gave out an interview that attracted public attention. A part of his statement was as follows:

"The year 1927, I believe, will do much to bring broadcasting forward as a distinct and self-supporting industry in the radio family. For the first time, perhaps, radio broadcasting in the United States, untied from the apron strings of outside support, will find itself squarely on its own feet. . . . It is true that the picture here is marred for the time being by the lack of police regulation in the air which has resulted in a vast amount of station interference. But the situation is far from hopeless. . . . Our government undoubtedly will agree sooner or later on measures of regulation."

The successful launching of the Blue Network was no doubt a stimulus to the project of extending the National Broadcasting Company's growing domain. The first item of business at a meeting of the board of directors of NBC on January 21, 1927, related to the Pacific coast stations. Mr. Aylesworth had made tentative agreements with the chief radio stations in the region, as appears in the following extract from the minutes of the meeting:

"The president reported relative to the status of negotiations with owners of broadcasting stations in Portland, Oregon, Seattle and Spokane, Washington, and San Francisco and Los Angeles, California, for the establishment of a West Coast network. After discussion, on motion, duly made, seconded and unanimously carried, it was

"RESOLVED, that the power given to the president on December 3, 1926, to conclude contracts for the establishment of a West Coast network, be and hereby is continued."

Although Station WEAF was still operating at its old location it was in contemplation that a new site for its broadcasting towers would shortly become necessary. President Aylesworth, at the meeting of January 21, 1927, submitted an estimate of $400,000 to cover the cost of relocation of the station. The board of directors took the following action:

"RESOLVED, that the recommendation of the president for the expenditure of not exceeding $400,000, for the relocation of Station WEAF, be and hereby is approved."

Since neither corporations nor individuals may spend large sums of money without sooner or later encountering the necessity of replenishing the funds from which they draw, it is only natural that the National Broadcasting Company should by this time have faced the prospect of an empty treasury. The following extract from the minutes of the meeting of January 21st is self-explanatory:

"The president reported that to meet the expense incidental to fitting, equipping and furnishing the new studios and offices at No. 711 Fifth Avenue, New York City, and for remodeling and removing Station WEAF to a new location with purchase of a necessary site and equipment therefor, it will be necessary for the board to consider the issuance and sale of additional shares of the company's capital stock. After full discussion of the matter, on motion, duly made, seconded and unanimously carried, it was

"RESOLVED, that the proper officers of the company be and they hereby are authorized to invite subscriptions for the balance of the company's unissued no par value capital stock (12,500 shares), in amounts of 2500 shares, as and when needed, to be sold at $100 per share cash and that the present stockholders of record of the company be afforded the opportunity to subscribe for the whole of said shares in the proportions of their present respective holdings of the company's stock, the proper officers being further authorized to issue and deliver said shares, when and as subscribed and paid for."

A very significant press release, dated January 24, 1927, heralded the advent of David Lawrence [4] as a news commentator on developments in the nation's capital. Appropriately enough, this voluntary public service of the National Broadcasting Company was to begin on Lincoln's Birthday, February 12, 1927. It was announced as a thirteen-week engagement, and its theme slogan was to be "Eight minutes, please, for your government."

Progress in the plan for a Pacific coast network was so rapid that on February 7, 1927, George F. McClelland left New York for California to organize the network and to arrange for broadcasting headquarters on the coast.

On February 18, 1927, the advisory council of the National Broadcasting Company held its organization meeting. Owen D. Young, the father of the project, was chairman of the meeting, as appears in the following extract from a press release under date of February 19th:

"The advisory council of the National Broadcasting Company consisting of the most distinguished Americans in educational, public and social life held its first meeting at the National Broadcasting Company's offices at 195 Broadway, yesterday afternoon to study the further extension of broadcasting service to millions of American homes.

"Radio broadcasting was discussed by Owen D. Young, acting as temporary chairman, and the progress of the National Broadcasting Company was presented by Merlin Hall Aylesworth, president of the company. . . .

"How best to develop national broadcasting from the cultural and educational standpoint was considered by the advisory council. Among the subjects discussed were: Church Activities, Education, Labor, Political Economy, Music, Drama, Women's Activities and Agriculture. For the development of these subjects assignments were made to the following members of the council:

"*Education*—E. A. Alderman, president of the University of Virginia
"*Church Activities*—Dr. Charles F. MacFarland, Morgan O'Brien and Julius Rosenwald
"*Music*—Walter Damrosch
"*Agriculture*—Francis D. Farrell
"*Labor*—William Green
"*Women's Activities*—Mrs. John D. Sherman."

The greatest engineering feat performed by the National Broadcasting Company during its first winter of operation occurred on Febru-

---

[4] David Lawrence began newspaper work in 1903 with the Buffalo *Express*, a reporter until 1906, when he enrolled as a student at Princeton University. During four years in college he was correspondent for the Associated Press. In 1910 he was sent to Washington as staff correspondent for A.P.

ary 22, 1927. Forty-seven radio stations in all parts of the United States were linked together to carry the Washington's Birthday address made by President Calvin Coolidge. In addition to this impressive array of stations three short-wave stations carried the President's voice to the ends of the earth. Thus the pledge made by Owen D. Young and General Harbord in their official declaration of policies for the new corporation five months before was already being fulfilled.

But what, in the meantime, had occurred in the relations between the two key stations of the National Broadcasting Company—the erstwhile rivals WEAF and WJZ? They could no longer vie with each other for spectacular achievements, since both networks were controlled by the board of directors of NBC. All accounts agree, however, that the old rivalry continued—in no whit abated by the enforced association under the same general management. Had the staff at WEAF at once moved into new surroundings the situation would no doubt have been less acute. Continuing, however, in the Telephone Building, in their old offices and studios, yet daily beholding three officials who symbolized a new era, they cherished in their hearts the memory of former days and former triumphs over their rivals at WJZ. Speculation was still rife as to the probable fate of their departmental chieftains when both stations should move to 711 Fifth Avenue. In lounging rooms and out-of-the-way places stenographers and office workers debated among themselves on this and that possibility, but perhaps the most persistent speculation related to the probable head of the program department of NBC—shall it be Phil Carlin or Bertha Brainard?

CHAPTER
FOURTEEN

Travails of a Rival Radio Network

Section 108. A Rival Broadcasting Network—on Paper.

RETURNING TO THE STORY of the Judson Radio Program Corporation which had been organized September 20, 1926, we encounter great difficulty in establishing the exact activities of the organization during the first three or four months of its corporate life. Arthur Judson was apparently fully occupied by his duties in connection with the Philadelphia and New York Philharmonic Orchestras. George A. Coats, however, fortified by a modest fund in the treasury against expenses and salary, was working with energy to make the venture something more than a shoestring. Arthur Judson himself, whether before or after the incorporation it is not clear, had submitted a plan to David Sarnoff for an ambitious artists' bureau project in which Mr. Judson would naturally be the directing genius. No doubt Mr. Sarnoff was bombarded with similar suggestions at the time. He may possibly have consigned the Judson plan to the wastebasket.

In the interval until January, 1927, Mr. Judson continued to entertain hopes that he might any day be called into conference on the artists' bureau plan. When NBC's second network was inaugurated on January 1st, and no summons had come, Mr. Judson and George A. Coats decided to call upon Mr. Sarnoff. Arthur Judson's version of his interview with David Sarnoff is very interesting, largely because of its dramatic conclusion. The general manager of RCA had explained his own relation to the broadcasting set-up and had parried all suggestions that he assist the Judson organization to gain official connection with NBC. When the interview had developed a bit of warmth Mr. Sarnoff declared that he was washing his hands of the matter.

Judson was by this time a bit excited. On the spur of the moment he declared that they would form a network of their own. Whereupon, according to Mr. Judson, David Sarnoff leaned back in a squeaky swivel chair and explained that wire lines alone would cost a million dollars. He questioned the idea that men without adequate finances behind them could hope to establish a radio network. The upshot of the visit was that both Judson and Coats left Mr. Sarnoff's office vowing to high heaven that they would start a network—come what may.

The ever-resourceful promoter shortly organized a new corporation bearing the title, "United Independent Broadcasters." This important event occurred on January 27, 1927. On March 22nd following, the first issue of stock in the new corporation disclosed Edward Ervin as the holder of two hundred shares in his own right, and two hundred other shares apparently held for George A. Coats and Daisy P. Coats. Arthur Judson had an allotment of two hundred shares. These six hundred shares were apparently issued for services or contracts, hence no cash came into the treasury of the corporation. Four hundred shares were still unissued.

In the meantime, George A. Coats was conducting a vigorous campaign to discover "an angel"—a client with funds—to put the new venture on its feet. One of the first essentials was to organize a radio network—at least on paper. It was apparently never contemplated by the directors of the new corporation that it should operate the network. Mr. Coats believed that he could sell a network to some ambitious client. Still apparently operating through funds in the treasury of the Judson Radio Program Corporation he set forth, in company with Edward Ervin, to make a tour of the country. He was being vouched for by Secretary Baker, of the National Association of Broadcasters. At Philadelphia he signed up Station WCAU, whose owner was Dr. Leon Levy, a friend of Arthur Judson. Since none of the three incorporators knew what the costs of operating a network might be, in fact not even NBC having much data at the time, these envoys were virtual babes in the wood.

Dr. Levy named a price of $500 a week for ten hours of broadcasting time. Coats and Ervin were persuaded that this was the best figure they could hope to obtain. WCAU was thus the first station to join the new network. Encouraged by their success the two hopefuls went their way and shortly signed Station WGHP in Detroit. The $500 weekly guaranty to a radio station in those days when income was a serious problem made a hit wherever the hopeful pair presented their credentials. Eleven other stations were signed: WADC in Akron, Ohio, WOWO in Fort Wayne, Ind., WKRC in Cincinnati, Ohio, KMOX in St. Louis, Mo., KOIL in Omaha, Neb., WNAC in Boston, Mass., WGAS in Pittsburgh, Pa., WFBO in Syracuse, N. Y., WAIU in Columbus, Ohio, WMAQ in Chicago, Ill., and WOR in Newark, New Jersey, as the key station of the proposed network.

Their apparent triumph was soon clouded with doubt. To pay $6000 a week merely for network privileges, other staggering expenses to be met before the United Independent Broadcasters could hope to pay its bills, involved the necessity of charging prospective sponsors an hourly rate that would be almost prohibitive. This fact became a sobering realization as the promoter interviewed a succession of prospects. On several occasions he fancied that success was in sight, only to have the project crash on the rocks of a new danger.

It was realized by all and sundry that this paper network could never be more than paper unless "long lines" could be secured from the American Telephone Company. The promoter and his associates had already been rebuffed by W. E. Harkness, now back in the long lines department. The fact that the corporation had no money and no clients made their situation a bit difficult. Now, however, with actual prospects such as Atwater Kent and various other substantial clients to accompany him to Mr. Harkness' office, Mr. Coats discovered that the Telephone Company was obviously inclined to deny wire lines by naming a price for the same which Coats considered exorbitant. From such an interview the disappointed promoter would retire in defeat. No client, it seemed, would go through with a deal under such circumstances.

Sec. 109. Activities of NBC in Winter of 1927.

The choice of Frank A. Arnold as director of development of the National Broadcasting Company has previously been noted. One of the first important bits of publicity for his company achieved by Mr. Arnold in his new capacity occurred on January 7, 1927, when he spoke before the Business Men of Worcester, Massachusetts. The speech was broadcast and also reported widely by the press. Mr. Arnold discussed current advertising programs over the air and compared the new medium with the older type of advertising—in newspapers and periodicals. He contrasted the relative expense of radio and newspaper advertising—a matter of great moment to businessmen in general.

From this time forward Mr. Arnold was a featured speaker before clubs and organizations in various parts of the country. On February 2nd he was a guest of the Kiwanis Club of New York City, at a great banquet held at the Hotel McAlpin. The Boston Advertising Club featured him on February 15, 1927, and the Merchants Association of New York City listened to radio advertising gospel at the Hotel Astor on March 17th.

Reinforcing this campaign of publicity President Aylesworth, on March 18, 1927, announced that the advertising budget of the National Broadcasting Company for the year 1927 would top the $2,000,-000 mark. Everything that the new corporation set its hand to in those days was grist for the press relations department of NBC. The corporation was expanding its activities but was still unable to move into a home of its own. President Aylesworth continued to occupy the former Harkness office at 195 Broadway. Station WJZ, in the Aeolian Building, carried on as before. An army of workmen and engineers was struggling with the problems of construction at 711 Fifth Avenue.

Oscar B. Hanson, who had been chief engineer for Station WEAF, was placed in charge of the tremendously important task of providing for two major networks operating from the same studios.

"Our experience at 195 Broadway," he testified before the Federal Communications Commission in December, 1938, "had in a limited way exposed many of the factors that would have to be considered in the design of a large multiple studio plant. Much trouble had been experienced with sound leakage between studios. Noises throughout the building and miscellaneous street noises, particularly automobile horns and fire sirens injected themselves into our broadcasts. Little could be done at 195 Broadway to control this problem without complete demolition and reconstruction of our plant."

Plans for the offices at 711 Fifth Avenue called for eight large studios housed closely together in a steel-framed building. Brass bands would be in operation in various studios. Mr. Hanson declared that the problems involved gave his staff "many a nightmare," yet it was imperative that means be devised to control sounds within the building lest the radio audience think "that we were broadcasting from the Tower of Babel."

For the first time in radio history a soundproofing system was resorted to that may be described as "floating" the walls, floors and ceilings by using felt cushions to prevent vibration from being communicated to structural beams or walls. Dead air space, special sound-deadening material, triple glass windows and double soundproof doors rendered each studio a separate unit. Four of the eight studios were two stories in height, the largest being forty feet wide, seventy-five feet long and having a ceiling height of twenty feet. In order to isolate studio units it became necessary to provide each studio with an individual control and monitor room. Each control room was equipped with a triple glass observation window looking into the studio.

"Such hermetically sealed studios," declares Mr. Hanson, "necessitated a special ventilation system, and again for the first time in broadcast history a studio plant was air conditioned. That is to say, the temperature and humidity were held constant in each studio throughout the year, summer and winter, under varying local conditions." The author can testify to the efficiency of the air-conditioning system at 711 Fifth Avenue. Never in three years of his experience before the network microphones was the temperature found to be other than refreshingly cool, whereas in studios elsewhere one's collar might wilt in a fifteen-minute broadcast, especially in summer weather.

A great multitude of problems were encountered in equipping the Fifth Avenue studios. From the experience of NBC engineers the entire broadcasting industry was to benefit. The system of using drape material on the walls was gradually replaced by true acoustical treatment of walls and ceilings.

At a meeting of the board of directors of NBC, held on April 1, 1927, David Sarnoff, on behalf of a committee having in charge the matter of fitting up offices and studios at 711 Fifth Avenue, reported that $515,000 would be necessary for the project. The board approved the amount. It appeared also that the relocation and equipment of Station WEAF at Belmore, L. I., would cost $337,000, which sum was accordingly voted. At this same meeting Dwight W. Morrow's resignation as a director was accepted with regret.

The broadcasting activities of NBC during the first few months of 1927 revealed great progress in the art, but this was accompanied by a mounting deficit. A deficit, however, was an expected development. The directors, particularly Owen D. Young, were inclined to view the matter as a semi-philanthropic activity which the leading corporations of the radio industry were joining hands in supporting. It was regarded, and characterized by Owen D. Young, as "an investment in the youth of America."

Sec. 110. The Paper Network Discovers a Client.

At one time or another in the hectic early months of the corporate life of the United Independent Broadcasters George A. Coats is said to have virtually concluded bargains with Atwater Kent, Paramount Pictures, and Victor Talking Machine Company. Arthur Judson declares that all three of these efforts occurred prior to the great event which we now relate, yet the author has uncovered evidence that would indicate that the Victor Company at least dallied with the idea in the autumn of 1927.

At any rate the Victor Company was already affiliated with RCA in a phonograph-radio manufacturing alliance. As early as April, 1927, rumors were afloat of a possible phonograph-radio merger. The artists who customarily made records for the phonograph companies might very well be utilized in radio broadcasting. The Columbia Phonograph Company was already in a desperate state—which operated in favor of a certain promoter, George A. Coats. For months Coats had labored unprofitably yet, on a fateful day in the spring of 1927, he chanced to meet a potent official of the Columbia Phonograph Company—a man named Louis Sterling.

The promoter had scented gold at last. Louis Sterling was already alarmed over the rumor that the Victor Company was about to merge with radio. This opportunity to acquire a radio network—to steal a march on Victor—to save Columbia—was apparently providential. This was one occasion when W. E. Harkness, of the long lines department, could not discourage a client. The Columbia Phonograph Company and the United Independent Broadcasters talked terms to such good effect that contracts were signed and, best of all, cash was paid over—a staggering sum—$163,000 as a bonus for use of the paper network!

In the midst of negotiations, however, in order that Columbia might advertise itself and make money at the same time it was resolved to create a new corporation—the Columbia Phonograph Broadcasting System. The ten hours a week provided in the network contracts would be split up and resold to commercial sponsors—the announcement, "This is the Columbia Phonograph Broadcasting Company" being relied upon to advertise Columbia phonographs. In the language of the street, it was a "cock-eyed scheme," yet the enthusiasts at the phonograph company paid their money—and took their chances!

The records show that on April 5, 1927, the Columbia Phonograph Broadcasting System, Inc., was born and christened. Its announced purpose, as stated in its charter, was "to maintain, conduct and manage the business of supplying radio broadcasting service and facilities." Apparently but one thousand shares of stock were issued, the stockholders being Columbia Phonograph Company, A. O. Dillenbeck, James A. Hanff, George P. Metzger, and H. M. Newman. This did not mean the end of United Independent Broadcasters. On the contrary, having apparently scored a great coup in selling ten hours of network time to the phonograph company, the United Independent Broadcasters, Inc., was ready for business in a big way—if business could be secured. The phonograph company had a keen interest in the continuation of the Broadcasters because in the contract between the two corporations was a proviso that should the Columbia Group decide to quit the radio broadcasting during the contract period they could cancel the contract upon thirty days' notice. This clause was purely a legal precaution since, in the optimism of the moment, neither party could have dreamed that the cancellation notice would ever be given.

A development of great importance to the radio industry occurred during the spring of 1927. Reference has been made to the breakdown of control over radio broadcasting in the summer of 1926. For years Representative Wallace White, Jr., of Maine (now Senator White), had sponsored bills for control of radio. A new bill providing for a Federal Radio Commission had been agreed upon in July, 1926, but too late in the session to be perfected before the adjournment of Congress. In the winter of 1927, however, the bill was passed. It was signed by President Coolidge on February 23, 1927.

The first Federal Radio Commission consisted of five members— Admiral W. H. G. Bullard, chairman, Orestes H. Caldwell, Eugene O. Sykes, Henry A. Bellows, and Colonel John F. Dillon. The organization meeting occurred March 15, 1927.

By the terms of the Radio Act of 1927 all existing licenses of radio stations were to expire sixty days after approval of the act, which meant that on April 24, 1927, a new era in the industry would begin. "On April 17th," writes Lawrence F. Schmeckebier,[1] "the commission took its initial action affecting specific broadcasting stations by ordering a change in the frequencies of 129 stations which had been operating

[1] The Federal Radio Commission, Service Monograph of the U. S. Government No. 65, p. 24.

on frequencies other than those previously authorized by the Department of Commerce."

That the commission was faced with an appalling task is self evident. The general public had become tremendously interested in the welfare of radio broadcasting. Radio stations were not slow to enlist their audiences in appeals for consideration of one sort or another. The Federal Radio Commission was soon literally buried under an avalanche of letters and affidavits. One station alone is said to have filed 170,000 official affidavits in evidence, all from radio listeners. The author quoted above declares, on page 55 of his monograph: "Probably no quasi-judicial body was ever subject to so much congressional pressure as the Federal Radio Commission. Much of this, moreover, came at a time when the majority of the commission had not been confirmed." [2]

Sec. 111. Columbia Phonograph Broadcasting System Collapses.

In the meantime, the National Broadcasting Company, under the energetic administration of Merlin H. Aylesworth, was extending its network activities. A second vice-president was added to the list of officers at a meeting of the board on May 6, 1927—Howard W. Angus. On May 25th President Aylesworth's recommendation that a Chicago branch of NBC be established was accepted by the board. Expenditure of $263,000 for that purpose was authorized. With construction going on at Belmore, L. I., at 711 Fifth Avenue, in Washington, D. C., in San Francisco, and now in Chicago, the National Broadcasting Company was certainly justifying the optimistic promises of its sponsors. With so prodigious a beginning it surely seemed beyond the point where competition from rivals could ever be of moment. It is doubtful indeed whether any of the high officials of NBC were even aware that the "paper network" idea was still alive.

On July 17, 1927, the announcement was made that NBC had arranged facilities for nationwide distribution of sponsored programs on all three of its networks—"Red," "Blue," and "Pacific." The first program to go out thus widely was sponsored by the Buick Motor Company of Flint, Mich., on Saturday evening, July 23rd. Arthur. Pryor and his band broadcast over the Blue Network from 9:00 to 10:00 P.M. "Roxy" staged a "super-presentation" over the Red Network from 10:00 to 11:00 P.M. The Pacific Network joined in broadcasting other programs and had a Buick program of its own from 9:00 to 10:00 P.M., Pacific time.

[2] Three of the commissioners were confirmed on March 4, 1927, but one of the three, Commissioner Dillon, died October 8, 1927, and Chairman Bullard died November 24, 1927. It was apparently a man-killing responsibility. Since unconfirmed members were not entitled to salaries one of them, Commissioner Bellows, resigned on October 8, 1927.

The three networks were as follows:

Blue		Red		Pacific	
WJZ	New York	WEAF	New York	KPO	San Francisco
WBZ	Springfield	WEEI	Boston	KGO	Oakland
WBZA	Boston	WCSH	Portland, Me.	KFI	Los Angeles
KDKA	Pittsburgh	WTAG	Worcester	KGW	Portland, Ore.
KYW	Chicago	WJAR	Providence	KHQ	Spokane
WJR	Detroit	WTIC	Hartford	KOMO	Seattle
WFAA	Dallas	WGY	Schenectady	KOFOA	Seattle
KVOO	Tulsa	WFI	Philadelphia		
WBT	Charlotte, N. C.	WRC	Washington		
WJAX	Jackson	WCAE	Pittsburgh		
KSD	St. Louis	WTAM	Cleveland		
WDAF	Kansas City	WWJ	Detroit		
WOC	Davenport	WSAI	Cincinnati		
WCCO	Minneapolis, St. Paul	WMAQ	Chicago		
		KFAB	Lincoln		
WHAS	Louisville	KSD	St. Louis		
WSM	Nashville	WDAF	Kansas City		
WMC	Memphis	WOC	Davenport		
WSB	Atlanta	WCCO	Minneapolis, St. Paul		
		WHAS	Louisville		
		WSM	Nashville		
		WMC	Memphis		
		WSB	Atlanta		

On June 29, 1927, the United Independent Broadcasters added to the list of stockholders by issuing 200 shares to H. M. Newman, who was already affiliated with the Columbia Phonograph Broadcasting System. It allotted the remaining 200 shares to J. Andrew White, the colorful figure whose exploits in radio broadcasting have been set forth in the author's previous volume. Major White was widely known in radio circles. He is said to have been made president of the corporation at this time, such being the recollection of George A. Coats. An examination of contracts signed by the corporation in November, 1927, however, discloses the fact that J. Andrew White signed the documents as vice-president. Be that as it may, J. Andrew White was considered the executive head of the organization.

George A. Coats must have done some very effective undercover work in the summer of 1927 in his efforts to oblige the American Telephone Company to furnish wire lines to the Columbia network. In February, 1939, Mr. Coats explained to the author that because of his acquaintance with powerful political personages he succeeded in getting immediate action through the Interstate Commerce Commission. No doubt the Telephone Company acted without waiting for more than the threat of ICC action. Since it would require months to make ready the long lines needful for the new network and, as we shall see, such lines were actually ready for use by mid-September, Mr. Coats must have accomplished his object in early summer of 1927.

At some time prior to June 17th, when the Radio Corporation of America passed resolutions on his demise, General Guy E. Tripp was taken by death. Thus was removed one of the powerful personages who had figured in the great crises of the radio industry. The board of directors of the National Broadcasting Company, of which he had been a member, adopted appropriate resolutions at its meeting on July 15, 1927. At the same meeting Melvin A. Traylor, an eminent banker, was elected to the board to fill the vacancy caused by the resignation of Dwight W. Morrow. Although the original plans for the new home of the National Broadcasting Company at 711 Fifth Avenue had contemplated occupancy by June, 1927, the magnitude of the undertaking rendered this hope vain. June came and went, with the usual chaos incident to building operations preventing any use of the structure by the National Broadcasting Company.

The Columbia Phonograph Broadcasting System that since April, 1927, had been endeavoring to sell broadcasting time out of its ten-hour-a-week network allotment was encountering great difficulties in this respect. Few corporations, it seemed, cared to pay large sums for advertising over the air on programs so obviously proprietary. There was, in fact, a decidedly awkward feature involved. To announce a program as a presentation, let us say, of the XYZ Corporation over the facilities of the Columbia Phonograph Broadcasting System, might not impress radio listeners. Columbia's salesmen, therefore, met with disappointment everywhere they went. Frank A. Arnold's speeches throughout the country, and the impressive campaign for business by NBC caused the latter corporation to become the beneficiary of whatever radio enthusiasm the Columbia System's salesmen might stir up.

As the time drew near for the new network to go on the air—September 5th—Mr. Sterling requested a postponement of operations until September 19th. This arrangement proved satisfactory to the several stations in the network. On September 19, 1927, the Columbia Phonograph Broadcasting System made its debut—no doubt made it very reluctantly in view of the staggering deficits that loomed ahead. It is said that only one client had been secured as the result of a summer of work—expensive effort at that.

The opening program of the new network was an ambitious offering—the Metropolitan Opera Company, with the *King's Henchman* and Deems Taylor. Prophetically enough, a thunder shower of savage nature arose in the midst of the program, contributing static of demoralizing power.

Arthur Judson and his associates must have experienced dismay on their own account, since they were well aware of the cancellation provision in their contract with Columbia Phonograph Broadcasting System. It did not require a prophet to foresee the prompt cancellation of the contract. The phonograph company was in no financial condition to spend the vast sums that would be required to keep the network in operation.

Both the Judson Radio Program Corporation and the United Independent Broadcasters were thus deeply concerned in the success or failure of the network. The program corporation had a five-year contract to furnish programs, and the Broadcasters were obligated to pay $6000 a week to the network stations even though the client should cancel the operating contract. It should perhaps be pointed out that the Columbia people were to pay for time and talent and operating costs during the life of the contract. When, therefore, in October, 1927, the Columbia Phonograph Broadcasting Corporation, having lost $100,000 in the first month, made known its intention of canceling the contract, Arthur Judson, the only substantial member of the venturesome trio, must have experienced the well-known chills down the spine. His ambitious hopes were apparently doomed. No power on earth, it seemed, could avert destruction. Under these circumstances he took his troubles to Dr. Leon Levy, of Station WCAU, in Philadelphia.

By the irony of fate the October, 1927, issue of *Radio Broadcast*[8] carried the following announcement, which must have fallen upon the discomfited trio like laughter of the gods.

"The United Independent Broadcasters, of which Major J. Andrew White, pioneer sports announcer is a leading official, has given out a list of stations which will form its new network. The key station is WOR, which is the third most popular station in New York, exceeded only by WEAF and WJZ in number of listeners. The other stations are WEAM and WNAC in New England, WFBL, WMAK, western New York, WCAU and WJAS, Pennsylvania, WADC, WAIU, WKRC, Ohio, WGHP, Michigan, WMAQ, Chicago, and KMOX, St. Louis. Although, in point of numbers and station standing, the stations comprising the chain are not everywhere in the lead, it would not take long, given good programs, for such a chain to corner a good part of the radio audience.

"Nothing will help the broadcasting situation so much as real competition to the NBC chains, so that both organizations will conduct a nip and tuck battle for program supremacy."

[8] Page 347.

WILLIAM S. PALEY
President of Columbia Broadcasting System, under whose dynamic leadership the company has made radio history.

Sec. 112. NBC Takes Possession at 711 Fifth Avenue.

At some time during the latter part of the summer of 1927, a small luncheon party was held at one of New York's swanky hotels that involved all the elements of drama. It afforded, moreover, the answer to the long speculation as to the merger of the program departments of WEAF and WJZ. The affair was arranged by NBC's newest vice-president, Howard W. Angus. Phillips Carlin, program manager of WEAF, was invited to attend. There were possibly but four in the party. By pre-arrangement, Mr. Carlin was seated with Miss Bertha Brainard of the WJZ program department. The others apparently knew the object of the luncheon, but Phillips Carlin was entirely in the dark until Miss Brainard broke the news to him that she was to be the program manager of the National Broadcasting Company, and that he was to receive appointment as assistant program manager.

In view of the long existing rivalry between the two stations the announcement, however tactfully made, must have been a great blow to Mr. Carlin. In fact, he has admitted to the author that it "knocked him for a goal"; but Miss Brainard declares that Carlin received the announcement so graciously and was such "a good scout" about it that she was not conscious of his keen disappointment in the matter.

In September, 1927, it was announced by the publicity department of NBC that Don E. Gilman of San Francisco had been appointed resident manager of the Pacific Network, succeeding George Podeyn of the New York office, who had been setting up the organization. It was further stated that Mr. Podeyn had been assigned to Chicago to organize an NBC regional department in that city.

On September 22, 1927, occurred the Tunney-Dempsey prize fight at Soldiers' Field, Chicago. The National Broadcasting Company, apparently for the first time, joined all three networks—Red, Blue and Pacific—in reporting the fight. Sixty-one stations were hooked up. Graham McNamee and Phillips Carlin were NBC's ringside announcers.

On October 1, 1927, a very important event in the history of the National Broadcasting Company occurred. Despite the fact that offices were still unfinished, and that workmen and building paraphernalia were everywhere in evidence, Station WJZ took up its residence at 711 Fifth Avenue. It seems that the lease of the station at the Aeolian Building expired on September 30th. Miss Bertha Brainard and other officials of the station bear testimony to the fact that pioneer conditions existed during their first weeks in the new location. "We walked the corridors on 'duck boards' for a week or so," she declares, "and it was at least six weeks before we got rid of the last of the workmen. They were still plastering offices when we moved in. The lime dust was everywhere. We had shampoos every other day until we decided to be just pioneers and wait until the place could be finished before trying to become really civilized again. The noise of hammering was so bad that we had great difficulty with telephones."

A press release under date of October 15th states that only two of NBC's eight projected studios were complete when WJZ moved into the new building. These, however, represented the greatest advance in studio architecture yet achieved by science. Thus WJZ was given the first opportunity to broadcast from the new studios at 711 Fifth Avenue.

On October 5, 1927, the annual World Series baseball games began with NBC's ace sports announcers, Graham McNamee and Phillips Carlin, in action.

At a meeting of the board of the National Broadcasting Company, held on October 7, 1927, John W. Elwood was taken onto the staff of executives, effective November 1st. It will be remembered by those who have read the author's first volume that Mr. Elwood was secretary of the Radio Corporation in its early days, being later transferred to the Pacific coast in connection with RCA's attempt to organize a trans-Pacific communications department. This effort had encountered great difficulties and delays owing to international intrigues and the political chaos that prevailed in China. Mr. Elwood's return to New York was to bring to the program department of NBC one who possessed deep sympathy with the idea that radio should not only entertain its listeners but should consciously endeavor to lead the masses to higher levels of appreciation of music and of things educational. Mr. Elwood believed in emphasizing at all times radio showmanship, since a program, however excellent, fails of its purpose unless sufficiently attractive to hold the interest of listeners.

An announcement of great importance to the radio industry went out to the daily press on October 20th. The General Motors Corporation had signed a contract for a notable series of network broadcasts to go on the air November 7, 1927.

The forty-eighth anniversary of the invention of the incandescent lamp was celebrated as Edison Night, on Friday evening, October 21st, under the sponsorship of the General Electric Company. Forty-one NBC stations were in the network. Thomas A. Edison himself was on the program, being interviewed at his home in West Orange, N. J., by E. W. Rice, Jr., president of General Electric Company. Goldman's band furnished the musical program.

Station WEAF apparently moved from its old home in the Telephone Building, at 195 Broadway, about October 21, 1927. The last press release from 195 Broadway was dated October 20th, and the first press notice from George W. Johnstone's office, at 711 Fifth Avenue, bore the date of October 26th. Certain it is that during the last week in October the old-time rival radio stations were housed under the same roof and facing the same discomforts of turpentine odors and noisy hammerings previously described.

Miss Carolla A. Bryant, whose illuminating description of breaking the news at WEAF has already been noted, brings us another picture—WEAF in its first weeks at 711 Fifth Avenue. Miss Bryant had by this time become secretary to Phillips Carlin, program manager of the station.

"Before we moved from 195 Broadway," she writes, "every desk and cabinet was tagged and numbered. There was a blue print on which the placing of all this furniture was indicated so everybody knew where to look for his or her desk. Some of us had entirely new equipment. Mr. Carlin's office had new desks and chairs. We had no sooner settled in our new quarters than they began to move us around. Offices were not big enough. Radio was growing so fast that they had to tear down partitions and build new ones. I well remember the awful dust and dirt that got onto our new furniture. I even sat at my desk with bags of cement unpleasantly near me—and workmen messing around, building partition walls. Gerard Chatfield was in charge of this business. He changed us around so much that one night the men, to get even with him, got together and moved everything out of Chat's office except his telephone. They stuck up a sign 'Chatfield's Department moved to Second Floor'—a bare floor that didn't belong to us. Chatfield was fit to be tied next morning."

It required more than mutual discomforts, however, to bring discordant elements into harmony. To be sure there was no open mutiny, yet there was a seething undercurrent of hostility that testified to the persistence of human loyalty to prejudices engendered while working in rival organizations. The staff of WEAF, coming to 711 Fifth Avenue after the staff of WJZ had been in possession for three weeks, were at a disadvantage. Obliged to accept assignment to one or another office group of strangers they were deeply resentful at their altered state. The staff workers of WJZ, on the other hand, in strange quarters, oppressed by dust and turpentine fumes, harried by noise, were in no mood to fraternize with the strangers. In fact, their hostility to the WEAF workers was perhaps equal in intensity to that entertained against them.

The higher executives, as might be expected, were able to observe the amenities of life in their interrelations with former rivals. The only resignation from the WEAF contingent at this time was that of William H. Ensign, a salesman who had been on the staff since October 15, 1923. Mr. Ensign resigned to become manager of the radio department of J. Walter Thompson—an advertising agency. Perhaps, also, it may be said that male workers, high and low, found the merger less irksome than did the so-called gentler sex. It is possible that women are by nature more capable "haters" than are men—and more capable of abiding loyalties—at any rate, the WEAF-WJZ feud seems to have been cherished more ardently among them than among their masculine co-workers.

To be sure Miss Bryant stoutly defends her sex, declaring that the masculine workers were more rebellious than the women. The author has learned, however, that in at least one instance a member of the gentler sex bought a screen and placed it between her desk and that of a girl from the rival organization—a "spite fence" that must have caused heart-burnings in that particular office.

Frank A. Arnold, who for several years was a sort of ambassador at large for NBC, one of the first neutrals to join the organization, has informed the author that the feud between the two groups was one of his major problems during the promotion period from 1926 to 1929, since to speak the truth concerning the excellencies of WEAF was to enrage the WJZ veterans and, on the other hand, to voice his admiration of WJZ was to expose him to hostile comment from the other contingent. Since it was his duty to remain impartial, and to praise whatever was worthy at NBC, he became "suspect" by both groups, especially after the appearance of his book, *The Fourth Dimension of Advertising*, in which the history of both stations necessarily appeared.

Sec. 113. A Sportsman Loses Heavily in Rival Network.

Reference has been made to the action of the Columbia Phonograph Company in notifying the United Independent Broadcasters that in thirty days the network contract would be terminated. It will be remembered that Arthur Judson confided his fears of ruin of the network project to Dr. Leon Levy, the owner of WCAU, the first station to join the network. It was fortunate indeed that he took this action, since Dr. Levy had wide acquaintance among capitalists. He promised to look around, presently announcing that a Philadelphia millionaire and sportsman—Jerome H. Louchheim—might be interested in entering the business of radio broadcasting. Judson and his persuasive ally, George A. Coats, lost no time in waiting upon the capitalist. Sure enough, Mr. Louchheim was interested! The possibilities intrigued him, but the possibilities of adequate financing of the network intrigued the hard-pressed shoestring promoter even more. So eloquent and persuasive did George A. Coats become that Mr.

Louchheim agreed to take over the network when it should be relinquished by the Phonograph Company.

This naturally involved the calling in of the Louchheim lawyer, who chanced to be Ralph Colin, the present chief legal adviser of the Columbia Broadcasting System. At a recent conference with the author Arthur Judson related a dramatic story of his experience at the crucial moment of the Louchheim transaction. Lawyer Colin had followed his client's instructions. He had prepared the important papers but now, when the principals had gathered—J. Andrew White, Arthur Judson and George A. Coats on the one side, and the financier on the other—the lawyer felt it his duty to express misgivings in the matter.

This he proceeded to do, with devastating logic. He pictured the network idea as a bottomless pit into which his client was proposing to dump a quarter of a million dollars. Another quarter million, he declared, would soon be necessary. Colin even pictured losses running into millions of dollars. To Mr. Judson these words were so very dismaying that he lost all hope, until he was electrified by Jerome H. Louchheim's reaction. Pen in hand the latter looked up at his lawyer and said very calmly: "What you say may possibly be true, but after all it is my money." He then affixed his signature to the documents.

Legal formalities in plenty were to follow. It was decided to utilize the corporate structure of the United Independent Broadcasters as a means of accomplishing the object in hand. The original shares were now in the hands of the following persons:

Arthur Judson	200 shares
J. Andrew White	200 "
Edward Ervin	200 "
George A. Coats	100 "
Daisy P. Coats	100 "
H. M. Newman	100 "
A. O. Dillenbeck	100 "
Total	1000 shares

The records show that on October 31, 1927, an amendment to the certificate of incorporation was filed, increasing the authorized capitalization from 1000 to 3000 shares.

In order to provide for adequate wire lines a contract was negotiated between the United Independent Broadcasters and the American Telephone Company. The corporation was obliged to deposit $100,000 as a guaranty of faithful fulfillment of its contract. A schedule of charges indicated that the first nine months of operation of the network would cost more than $250,000 for wire lines alone, and for the twelve months from July 15, 1928 onward, the cost would exceed $1,163,000. The contracts were executed in behalf of the United Independent Broadcasters on November 9, 1927, by J. Andrew White, vice-president.

On November 10, 1927, Jerome H. Louchheim, Isaac D. Levy and Leon Levy acquired control of the corporation by the following transactions. They purchased 20 shares of Newman's stock and 1000 shares of the newly authorized stock, so that their respective holdings were as follows:

Jerome H. Louchheim	765 shares
Isaac D. Levy	128 "
Leon Levy	127 "
Total	1020 shares

The cash receipts to the corporation treasury for the above shares of stock amounted to $135,000. Thus fortified with funds, the United Independent Broadcasters were in a position to fulfill the guaranty requirement with the Telephone Company and to bargain with the Columbia people. Either some very clever trading occurred or else the sellers became panicky at their situation since, for $10,000 in cash and thirty-three hours of broadcasting time, the Columbia Phonograph Company turned over to the purchaser not only the network contract but also the stock and the corporation itself. Thus the Columbia Phonograph Broadcasting System came into the hands of the Louchheim interests. On November 19th the name of the corporation was changed to the "Columbia Broadcasting System, Incorporated." The network was continued under that name. Thus two corporations existed for the same purpose.

A serious problem existed in connection with the $500-a-week guarantees to the network stations. In order to mitigate the danger it was arranged by Louchheim that Major White should visit each of the network stations and endeavor to persuade them to sign new contracts at a considerably lower figure. In this task J. Andrew White was completely successful.

Under its new management the network began an active campaign for radio advertising. Results were disappointing to Mr. Louchheim. The National Broadcasting Company naturally attracted the lion's share of network business. Customers who had decided to go on the air at all naturally preferred one of the great networks instead of the Columbia chain that seemed doomed to failure. The financier very shortly regretted that he had not taken the advice of his lawyer, Ralph Colin. By December 31, 1927, the two corporations had lost

$303,262.89, the United Independent Broadcasters having the greater deficit of the two—$220,066.48.

In order to keep the corporation in a solvent condition Mr. Louchheim dipped again into his private funds and put into the treasury an additional $50,000. His friend, Isaac D. Levy, added $14,000 to his investment. Louchheim received 250 shares at this time, and to Levy was issued 70 shares. At the same time the Judson Radio Program Corporation received an allotment of 180 shares in return for services. Thus, at the year's end 2500 of the authorized 3000 shares of stock (of the original United Independent Broadcasters Corporation) had been issued.

More money being needed in the treasury, on January 5, 1928, Harry F. Louchheim bought 75 shares of stock and paid $15,000 for the same. Since this sum was only a drop in the bucket, if we may use the simile—the bottomless pit being more appropriate—on January 13th Jerome H. Louchheim took 375 shares and parted with $75,-000. Arthur Lipper now appears as an adventurer in the gentle art of losing money. For 50 shares he exchanged $10,000 in cash. Thus all of the authorized shares of stock were exhausted. Losses continued at a heartbreaking pace. Mr. Louchheim had already had more than enough of the adventure but, like the true sportsman that he was, he made ready for more financial sacrifices.

On May 21, 1928, a certificate of amendment of the corporation charter was filed increasing the authorized capital stock from 3000 to 5000 shares. On June 14, 1928, Jerome H. Louchheim took 1000 shares of stock and deposited in the treasury $100,000, the shares now being valued at $100 instead of $200 as formerly. On the same date, Harry F. Louchheim bought 50 shares and paid $5000. With this substantial addition to its funds the Columbia Broadcasting System continued its dizzy career of deficit making. By mid-July it needed additional funds. On July 20th Mr. Louchheim reluctantly parted with an additional $10,000 and received another allotment of 100 shares; Isaac D. Levy was induced to venture a like amount.

By this time George A. Coats had become extremely unpopular with Jerome H. Louchheim. It was but human for the latter to trace his woes to the eloquent promoter. As for Coats, his interest in the venture apparently grew more academic as the months passed. While he was no doubt sorry for the Louchheim losses he was nevertheless a bit resentful at being blamed for having performed a superb bit of promotion. After all, no promoter can do more than to lead the investor to the grand opportunity—come what may of the venture. When Mr. Louchheim began to utter threats of closing up the whole unprofitable enterprise—pocketing pride and losses—the threats carried dismay to Arthur Judson and J. Andrew White, who would lose by the collapse of the network. George A. Coats now attempted to discover a purchaser for the Louchheim interests although, according to his own admissions, the irate gentleman made uncomplimentary remarks concerning him even to prospective purchasers. Nothing came of these efforts; and so the corporation continued to cry "more! more!" and Mr. Louchheim wrathfully to respond.

On September 11, 1928, the last chapter in Louchheim losses was written. He then took 400 shares of stock and parted with $40,000. David Bortin bought 275 shares—price $27,500, and Isaac D. Levy took 75 additional shares—price $7500. Of the 5000 outstanding shares the unfortunate Louchheim apparently held 2890 shares and Isaac D. Levy about 1000 shares. The situation was exceedingly desperate, yet a great day was about to dawn for the Columbia Broadcasting System—a mere stripling was to celebrate his twenty-seventh birthday by becoming a radio broadcasting magnate.

Returning now to the National Broadcasting Company we find that as early as November, 1927, it had outgrown its quarters at 711 Fifth Avenue. On November 11th the following action was taken by the board of directors:

"The president reported the necessity for additional space for the company's offices and stated that the eleventh floor of the building at No. 711 Fifth Avenue could probably be obtained for this purpose and requested authority to negotiate for a lease of the said space. After discussion, on motion, duly made, seconded and unanimously carried, it was

"RESOLVED, that the matter of negotiating for a lease of the eleventh floor of the building at No. 711 Fifth Avenue, New York City, on the best terms obtainable, be and hereby is referred to the executive officers of the company, with power."

On January 6, 1928, President Aylesworth was able to report the conclusion of negotiations for the lease of the eleventh floor of the building for the period between November 1, 1927 and April 30, 1946. This action was ratified by the board.

Sec. 114. Enter William S. Paley—Radio Wizard.

William S. Paley, the magician who has built the great Columbia network, deserves extended mention in any history of radio. He was born in Chicago, September 28, 1901, son of Samuel Paley of the Congress Cigar Company. At seventeeen, young William entered the University of Chicago, but a year later accompanied his father to Philadelphia where they were to open a branch factory. The death of young Paley's grandfather called the father to Chicago to take over heavy responsibilities. Eighteen-year-old William was left in

Philadelphia as manager of the new factory. This was his first real business experience, but the youth realized his need of technical training. He matriculated at the Wharton School of Finance of the University of Pennsylvania, winning a degree of Bachelor of Science in 1922. He was thereupon made production and advertising director of the Congress Cigar Company.

Mr. Paley's introduction to radio broadcasting came after Station WCAU was established in Philadelphia. Representatives of the station waited upon the young advertising manager and persuaded him to sign for a radio program one hour long once a week, the cost of each program being $50. So little did William S. Paley realize the limitations of one station that he involved himself in some embarrassment at the time by writing to the Congress Cigar agents in various parts of the country suggesting that they listen to his program and report their reactions. Of course they could hear nothing.

The program was very simple—the La Palina Boy (advertising a brand of cigars) playing a piano and singing songs. A few soloists appeared on the program. When the father, Samuel, and the uncle, Jacob Paley, returned from a business trip in Europe they were disgusted with the young man's supposed lack of judgment. They ordered the program and contract canceled. Then a surprising thing happened. An indignant radio audience began to write letters of protest at the cancellation of the program. Jacob Paley remarked to Samuel, the father, one day, that for all the money they were spending in newspaper advertising they never received comments, yet they were continually being asked why the La Palina Boy was no longer on the air.

Young William was now given a free hand in the matter. By this time the Columbia network had been formed. Mr. Paley arranged for a twenty-six-week program over the network beginning in January, 1928. Although the La Palina Boy had been popular, young Paley was convinced that a young lady would attract more smokers to a program than any boy could do. Thus originated one of the earliest radio dramatic skits—"The La Palina Smoker"—"La Palina," a glamour girl surrounded by "wise-cracking" young men. The program cost, according to a story in *Fortune* for June, 1935, $6500 a, week, but William S. Paley has recently stated to the author that $4000 would be more nearly accurate. Whatever the cost, the program brought results. From 400,000 cigars a day sales mounted to 1,000,000 a day. Small wonder that William S. Paley was soon keen about radio. From Dr. Leon Levy, the owner of Station WCAU, he learned, in the summer of 1928, that Jerome H. Louchheim was anxious to sell the Columbia network.

Although the young man had inherited a large fortune in his own right he wisely decided to enlist his wealthy relatives in the purchase of the network. William S. Paley was too shrewd a business man to have overlooked the opportunity of a bargain in taking over the supposed white elephant. It has been estimated, but never confirmed, that the original Paley family investment was around $300,000, but since the purchase was only a controlling interest—2515 shares—it seems unlikely that they could have paid any such sum—Louchheim himself only valuing the shares at $100. The original purchase was made in the following manner—concluded, by the way, two days before William S. Paley became twenty-seven years old:

The Paley Family Investment on September 26, 1928

William S. Paley purchased from Jerome H. Louchheim, Harry F. Louchheim and Arthur Lipper	2085 shares
Jacob Paley, from Jerome H. Louchheim	150 "
Jacob Paley, from Arthur Lipper	20 "
Lillian Paley, from Arthur Lipper	10 "
Samuel Paley, from Jerome and Harry Louchheim	150 "
Benjamin Paley, from Jerome Louchheim	100 "
Total	2515 shares

Strangely enough, even when making this substantial investment, it was apparent that the Paley family had no idea that it was to become more than a minor issue in family affairs. Young Paley himself was so sure that his future career was in the tobacco business that he merely arranged for a three-months' leave of absence from his duties at the Congress Cigar Company. He fancied that by December 31, 1928, he could whip the business affairs of Columbia into shape and thereafter, more or less by remote control, keep it on an even keel. With the characteristic self-assurance of youth he was positive that in three months he could accomplish his objective.

Paley moved into the executive department of the network immediately. He soon discovered the awkward situation of two corporations, with identical ownership, carrying on in the same offices and under the same management, and decided to dissolve one of them. He discovered also that the problems of the network were tremendously interesting. He became convinced that by a campaign wisely and strenuously conducted Columbia might in due time win a proper share of the nation's radio advertising. Within three weeks from entering upon his duties as a radio executive William S. Paley decided that he had found his life work, and so notified his father and uncle.

At the end of the year 1928 the youthful network had seventeen stations. During the year it had sold $1,647,928 in radio advertising, yet it had a deficit for the year of $380,822.61. This condition Paley resolved to correct. His first move was to increase the capital stock of the operating company (United Independent Broadcasters) from 5000 to 7500 shares. His second important step was to dissolve the original Columbia Corporation. The name, however, he considered of sufficient importance to warrant a bit of name juggling. The title of the operating corporation was changed from United Independent Broadcasters to "Columbia Broadcasting System, Inc.," the transaction being formally completed by a certificate filed under Section 60 of the Corporation Law of the State of New York, January 3, 1929.

Before dismissing the topic of financial returns from network broadcasting it is of interest to note that the National Broadcasting Company, in 1928, received a gross revenue of $9,964,443.05. It made an actual net profit of $427,239.06, which came within $30,000 of canceling the losses sustained during the previous year. To Owen D. Young and his associates, despite their protestations that the broadcasting company was a bit of public service that they expected to subsidize, this development must have been very encouraging.

President Aylesworth had made a splendid record. With two mutually antagonistic groups to begin with he had nevertheless accomplished, in fifteen months, a nation-girdling system of radio broadcasting. Programs of high quality originating in Station WEAF supplied the Red Network, whereas those originating in WJZ went out over the Blue Network. The new Pacific Network seems to have had the right to select programs from either Red or Blue origin. The system was thus becoming truly national in character. None of the high officials at 711 Fifth Avenue at this time took the new Columbia network as a serious rival. They were as yet unacquainted with the young man who had taken over the executive desk at the headquarters of Columbia.

CHAPTER
FIFTEEN

Radio and Talking Pictures

Section 115. The Romantic Origin of Talking Pictures.

IT HAS PREVIOUSLY BEEN POINTED OUT how great inventions that have revolutionized the social life of humanity have almost invariably arisen as the result of the patient groping of many minds through long periods of time. The germ of the idea may have been discovered before any investigator or inventor was able to glimpse its possibilities or to demonstrate its value to the world. The origin of the "talking picture" is a fresh illustration of this truth. Like radio broadcasting itself, the "talking picture" owes its beginning to the investigations of scientists during the World War in studying problems of sound reproduction. Radio broadcasting was the first great offering of science to result from this effort.

To the credit of great electrical manufacturing corporations be it said that, however their factories may have hummed with activity in the mass production of current models of this or that radio appliance, each of them maintained a research department. This department was continually seeking to improve and perfect the known product. This effort had more behind it than mere scientific zeal or altruistic desire to serve humanity. Heaven uses men and not angels to accomplish human progress. Men engaged in industry have investments to protect. They have competitors to contend with. They must not be caught napping, and so the departments of research of mighty manufacturing corporations have this mission to perform—to keep a step ahead of competitors in the race for perfection of products.

We find the General Electric Company and the Western Electric Company, a subsidiary of the American Telephone Company, as leaders in the race that gave to the world the modern marvel of talking pictures. The laboratories of these corporations conducted incessant experimentation in sound reproducing and recording. So closely did the rivals parallel one another's activities that it is difficult to assign to either exclusive credit for any one development. Historical research, beyond the scope of the present volume, would be needful to build up an authoritative recital in this allied field.

One development that impresses the author as especially significant is that relating to the Hoxie Visual Photographic Recorder, invented about June 1, 1917. Between that date and 1920 the General Electric Company built for the United States Navy several sets of these Hoxie recorders as a means of recording on tape by photography incoming radio signals at high speeds—speeds above the normal copying ability of the wireless operator. Here then was the germ of the modern talking picture, but a germ that was to require years of patient research by scientists before it could be brought to perfection. An important forward step—this time in the laboratories of the Western Electric

Company—was made April 6, 1920. Western Electric engineers conceived the idea of a photographic density recorder for the recording of sound on film. The next observable advance seems to have come in December, 1920, when inventor Hoxie, at the General Electric Company, began experimenting with a recorder, using a vibrating mirror and a photoelectric cell—the principle of his Visual Photographic Recorder. Thus he developed a device which he called the Pallophotophone, thereby virtually attaining the goal being sought by both rival organizations—the electrical recording of sound. The first camera recorder involving the Hoxie principle was completed January 15, 1921. This camera succeeded in actually recording sound on film. At the same time a device was perfected that enabled the new type of film to reproduce the sounds thus recorded. On October 6, 1921, the General Electric Company not only made a sound record on film, but re-recorded the same on a wax disk.

How close science had come to developing the modern "talkie" may be judged by the fact that in August, 1922, the Western Electric Company stole a march on its rival by designing a type of equipment that would reproduce sound in conjunction with a motion picture projector—that is to say, it phonographically reproduced sound which operated while the film was being projected. As a spectacular scientific feat this so-called "lecturing movie" was exhibited by Western Electric engineers at Yale University on October 22, 1922. Western Electric thus scored a triumph over its rival, but a triumph somewhat marred by the fact that movie and talkie failed to synchronize. It was not a case of two hearts that beat as one but two hearts that pulsated separately.

Not to be outdone by its rival the General Electric Company research department, on December 6, 1922, developed a sound reproducer for attachment to a Simplex motion picture projector. It was successfully demonstrated at the General Electric laboratories before executives of the company on April 2, 1923.

There appeared to be no market for the device at that time. No one as yet had the hardihood to advocate the union of the newly discovered film sound track with the seemingly perfect silent moving picture film. This newly born infant could not very well step into the sacred precincts of an art that now commanded the rapt attention of millions of theatergoers. Raucous tones from the backstage might well destroy the illusion of life on the screen. The Hoxie idea, however, was readily adaptable to the making of master phonograph records. In the summer of 1923 the General Electric Company arranged with the phonograph industry for exploitation of its patent rights. In 1925 the Brunswick-Balke-Collender Company was to adopt the system for phonograph recording.

Sec. 116. Efforts to Synchronize Sound and Motion.

The research laboratories of the rival manufacturers, however, were not content with their seeming defeat. A race, more or less nip and tuck, continued to feature their activities in this line. Genuinely synchronized sight and sound pictures were eventually achieved by each.

On October 11, 1923, the Western Electric Company completed its first synchronized sound picture and triumphantly demonstrated the same on October 18th. On November 1, 1923, they made a one-act sketch, and on November 19th gave a private exhibition at their laboratory. This was not a sound-on-film demonstration, however, but synchronized phonograph and moving picture film.

The General Electric Company continued in its endeavors to perfect a sound-on-film device. Beginning a fresh effort August 6, 1923, they designed a new form of sound reproducer for attachment to a standard motion picture projector. They were also working on a new type of sound-on-film camera recorder. The two devices were successfully tested November 10, 1923. It is apparent, however, that the heavy expenses of research and the lack of prospect of immediate returns caused the officials of the General Electric Company to soft-pedal this phase of laboratory activities in favor of phonograph research. There was a more or less clamorous market for phonograph recordings. The problems of recording and reproduction of sound-on-disks, moreover, were similar in kind to those encountered in the field of sound-on-film. This explains to a certain extent why the film idea was not followed up more vigorously by the General Electric Company during the period from November, 1923, to April 14, 1926. It appears, however, that during this apparently fallow period technical committees maintained a continuous oversight of laboratory advances in the phonograph recording field that were equally pertinent to films, if and when they should revive the project.

During this very period, moreover, the Western Electric Company was engaged in the same type of research—the perfection of sound-on-disk. It held no patent rights in the film field and seems to have confined its efforts largely to the one medium. In April, 1926, the Western Electric Company formed an alliance with the moving picture industry that was to galvanize the General Electric Company into action. A broker, Walter J. Rich, had been working on the idea of persuading moving picture interests to utilize the new Western Electric sound-on-disk process to furnish musical accompaniment for screen plays. Rich was given exclusive rights to exploit the idea.

Warner Brothers seems to have been the first motion picture company to grasp the full significance of the scheme. As early as 1925, Warner Brothers acquired from Rich exclusive rights to the system, including the right to sub-lease to other producers. The agreement involved a participation in royalties by the Western Electric Company.

An experimental installation of the Western Electric system was made for Warner Brothers at the so-called Warner Theater on Broadway, in New York City, early in 1925. Encouraged by results Warner Brothers organized the Vitaphone Corporation in April, 1926. This corporation was designed to exploit the talking picture rights that had been acquired from the Western Electric Company, as previously noted.

Sec. 117. The "Jazz Singer" Starts a New Industrial Contest.

It so happened that Warner Brothers, seeking a type of stage play that offered possibilities for a talking movie, fixed upon "Don Juan" as a proper vehicle. This was made into a feature picture. Instead of the usual orchestral accompaniment it had a synchronized musical score. Audiences received the innovation with enthusiasm. Bear in mind, however, that the great test of synchronized voice and motion was not involved in this initial offering. Warner Brothers could not hope to induce "movie" theaters in general to install expensive sound reproducing mechanism without some spectacular demonstration of voice and motion.

The "Jazz Singer," a stage success, was selected for filming. Warner Brothers had cast George Jessel, the star of the stage play, to take the stellar role. A dispute arose over Mr. Jessel's natural desire for extra compensation because of the nature of the film in which he was to sing and act. In exasperation Warner Brothers substituted Al Jolson.[1] The "Jazz Singer," offered to the public on August 6, 1926, made a tremendous sensation not merely because of its novelty, but also because of its genuine entertainment value.

The formation of the Vitaphone Corporation in April, 1926, may possibly have aroused the General Electric Company to the necessity of safeguarding its rights in synchronized sound-motion pictures. At any rate, on May 22, 1926, the General Electric laboratories produced a successful experiment in sound-on-film followed by another on May 24th. The success of the "Jazz Singer" in August, 1926, creating as it did a nationwide furor, precipitated a major contest between the two corporations for protection of their respective rights. In this contest RCA also became involved because it owned important circuit and

---

[1] Franklin, *Sound Motion Pictures*, p. 21.

tube patents, without which neither the General Electric Company nor the Western Electric Company could set up a complete system. The General Electric Company, however, had a legal right to use RCA's patents in the field of talking pictures.

The principal patents upon which talking picture rights were based were owned by the Western Electric and General Electric Companies. These rights, seemingly, were in conflict. It will be remembered that the Western Electric Company was a subsidiary of the nation-girdling American Telephone Company, whereas the General Electric Company was the parent of the Radio Corporation of America. The talking picture development, moreover, came at a time when the long contest between the Radio Group and the Telephone Group had just been settled in the revised agreements of July, 1926.

The Western Electric Company was not slow to adopt the technique of General Electric and RCA. As we have discovered, it was the custom of great corporations to create a new subsidiary corporation to have sole charge of any new and important activity of a commercial nature. In December, 1926, therefore, the Western Electric Company organized a corporation to be known as "Electrical Research Products, Inc.," which was to become a power in talking pictures. It was later familiarly known as ERPI.

This new controversy between Western Electric and General Electric involved entirely new angles. RCA had no inter-company license rights in the General Electric talking picture patents but, as previously indicated, its circuit and tube patents made RCA a factor in the controversy. Since Owen D. Young and other officials of General Electric Company occupied a similar relation to RCA it was a natural development that the two corporations should have joined hands in an effort to gain a commanding position in the future industry. Realizing that talking pictures—already dubbed by humorists as "squawkies"—would need a great deal of technical development, the General Electric Company, early in 1927, gave RCA the advantage of the services of Charles W. Stone, the engineer who had been in charge of developing the GE system of talking pictures. The Westinghouse Company also co-operated in the effort of the Radio Group to perfect the new art. The driving energy of David Sarnoff was now an important factor in the contest. His ability to glimpse far horizons was by this time well known.

In February, 1927, an important private demonstration of the General Electric system of talking pictures was held in the Rivoli Theater in New York City. High executives of the motion picture industry were present. While the demonstration indicated future possibilities for the sound-on-film idea yet the experiment failed to convince hard-headed movie magnates that it was ready for public adoption. It did not yet meet their requirements. The fact that each of them had millions of dollars invested in silent films no doubt had something to do with their reluctance to accept the new vehicle of film production. In August, 1927, RCA succeeded in making an agreement with Paramount Pictures by which it was to supply sound effects, derived from sound-on-film, for the famous war picture, "Wings." This demonstration, although true synchronized sound, was not on the same film. Two films, one for the pictures and the other for sound, were operated simultaneously.

In the meantime, the Western Electric's ERPI had apparently decided that sound-on-film possessed distinct possibilities. It so happened that opportunity presented itself to acquire rights in inventions in sound-on-film devices. It appears that Lee deForest, versatile as always, had taken a lively interest in the quest for some means of bringing silent films to life. Engineers now declare that, had deForest been able to produce in technical perfection the delicate instrumentalities needful to the system that he conceived, genuine talking pictures might have resulted from his efforts. In imagination and technical theory deForest had always been a leader. Unfortunately, the products of his laboratories have not generally measured up to his own qualities as an inventor.

A one-time associate of deForest, Theodore W. Case, had sold to William Fox, of Fox Films, a system of sound reproduction which he had labeled "Phonofilm." Fox made available substantial sums for research work in photographing sound-on-film in an effort to develop a variable density sound system. By 1927 Fox was ready to launch the Fox-Case Movietone. The Western Electric Company now seized the opportunity for an alliance with the Fox Movietone, by which each system became entitled to use the combined excellencies of both.

Sec. 118. RCA Moves to Exploit Its Rights in Sound Reproduction.

In 1927 the so-called "Big Five" of the motion picture industry—Metro-Goldwyn-Mayer Corporation; Paramount; United Artists Corporation; First National Pictures, Inc., and Universal Pictures—were approached by Mr. Stone, the manager of RCA's talking picture laboratories, with various propositions for licenses to use the General Electric system. Protracted negotiations ensued, but the picture companies refused to commit themselves.

David Sarnoff in January, 1928, directed Elmer E. Bucher, the sales manager of RCA, to take over the business management of the talking picture department. At the same time, Dr. Alfred N. Goldsmith, a vice-president as well as chief broadcast engineer of RCA, was ordered to take over the engineering department. The negotiations with the "Big Five" were actively pursued, but, despite the best efforts of RCA's representatives, the motion picture companies previously named determined to use the Western Electric system.

This was truly a staggering blow, but Elmer E. Bucher was already a veteran in industrial warfare. He went back to the offices at 411 Fifth Avenue to figure out what might be left in the industry, and also to develop at once effective films to be used as sales arguments. Mr. Bucher recalls with some pride that he and Charles W. Stone shortly prevailed upon the glamorous Gloria Swanson to come to the studios and take a voice test. To their mutual dismay, however, when the sound was reproduced Miss Swanson's voice had undergone a startling change—it sounded for all the world like that of a man. Thus a new problem was presented to the technical staff. Dr. Goldsmith soon decided that the adjustment of the recording apparatus had caused it to filter out the high tones of Miss Swanson's voice and to record only the lower ones. By widening out the acoustical band he solved the problem of true voice reproduction. Thus the feminine quality of Miss Swanson's voice was reproduced in succeeding trials.

A virtual procession of stage, screen, and concert hall stars thereafter came to the studios for voice and picture tests. Thus a rich offering of possible talent became available for the campaign already in mind to capture a substantial sector of the motion picture field.

It is characteristic of American Big Business that its executives are men of vision—otherwise they could never qualify as captains of industry. The Radio Group had its share of such men. As early as 1927, Owen D. Young and his associates had apparently formulated long-range plans for acquiring a foothold in the motion picture industry. The first move in this direction occurred in the fall of 1927, when RCA interests began to purchase blocks of stock in a corporation known as Film Booking Office, which operated studios for the production of motion pictures. Joseph P. Kennedy, our present Ambassador to the Court of St. James, then at the outset of his spectacular career, was the brains of FBO. A circumstance that added strength to the Kennedy organization was the fact of a close alliance with the Keith-Albee-Orpheum chain of motion picture theaters. The strategic value of acquiring stock ownership in FBO should be at once apparent—it paved the way for the Radio Group to exploit its rights in sound-on-film devices. This, then, was an important step in a campaign to compete with the Western Electric Company in the almost limitless field of moving pictures.

Sec. 119. Radio Marine and Photophone Corporations Launched.

The business for which RCA had originally been organized was now only one of several major activities. The RCA symbol, moreover, had become the hallmark for a nationwide business in radio sets and radio appliances—a business that completely dwarfed the communications phase of RCA's corporate existence. Possibly with some reluctance on their part the board of directors of the Radio Corporation of America decided to set up a new corporation dedicated exclusively to communications. On December 31, 1927, the Radio Marine Corporation was organized under the laws of Delaware to take over the marine radio business of RCA. This involved also a taking over of all physical assets of the parent company that were being employed in marine radio business. The entire capital stock, 25,000 shares, of the new company was issued to RCA in exchange for the physical assets previously indicated.

The activities of Radio Marine included public radio telegraphic service between coastal radio stations in the United States and ships of all nations at sea, later to be governed in this service by provisions established by the International Communications Convention at Madrid, Spain, which was held in 1932. A marine news service, broadcast daily on long wave, was intended to furnish the latest world events for publication in shipboard bulletins or news sheets. Another phase of Radio Marine activity was to take over the sale and servicing of marine radio apparatus.

We now approach the entry of RCA into the public entertainment field. To begin with, we have a background of immense development of the radio industry; the triumphant conclusion of the long contest between the Radio Group and the Telephone Group, followed by the launching of the National Broadcasting Company. These factors alone might have been sufficient to influence the minds of the most level-headed captains of industry. But the spirit of the times was that of universal optimism. The nation was then living in the upsurge of one of the greatest industrial booms in the history of America. The administration of Calvin Coolidge had cut down the national debt at an unbelievable rate. War-time taxes had been revised downward.

Although President Coolidge had declared his intention of retiring to private life, his Secretary of Commerce, Herbert Hoover, seemed destined to succeed him. The Hoover reputation was growing into fantastic proportions. Sober statesmen were proclaiming the industrial millennium. Poverty was shortly to be abolished, they averred. Wages were high—everybody was working—everybody was happy—except the group of harpies who coveted the wealth of the nation for this or that type of "world revolution."

Amusement was all the rage in America. Any board of directors of a great corporation that owned patent rights adaptable for use in one of the greatest scientific boons to amusement in the history of the world would certainly have failed in its duty to stockholders had it neglected to grasp so great an opportunity as apparently presented itself to RCA and its allies in the winter of 1928. With the record of success that was theirs these leaders of the interlocking triumvirate —RCA, GE and Westinghouse—would have been more than human had they failed to respond to the national spirit of optimism that then pervaded all classes of society in America. It is easy, therefore, to understand their confidence as they gathered in Owen D. Young's office on March 22, 1928.

Mr. Young outlined to them the situation as it then existed in the amusement field, and the efforts that had been made by the Radio Group to establish a position in the industry. He pointed out that their rival, the Western Electric Company, might speedily capture the entire motion picture industry unless immediate and vigorous action should be instituted by the Radio Group to exploit its own inventions. The spectacular success of the "Jazz Singer" had taken the nation by storm. Mr. Young stressed the fact that the five great moving picture combinations of the nation had already been captured on long-term contracts by their aggressive rival. Western Electric licensees, moreover, had by this time synchronized for sound a large number of motion pictures, even though their phonograph accompaniment scheme would seem to be greatly inferior to the sound-on-film development owned by the Radio Group.

He pointed out the disturbing fact that the Western Electric Company system was already being installed, or under contract, in upwards of two hundred theaters. This, moreover, was merely the beginning, since contracts with the "Big Five," as well as Fox Films, gave Western Electric an assured market from coast to coast.

There could be but one answer to the challenge. The plan, already formulated by the master minds of the Radio Group, was to form a corporation, to be known as RCA Photophone, to take over the activities then in progress under Elmer E. Bucher and Dr. Alfred N. Goldsmith. David Sarnoff was to be president of the new corporation, with Bucher vice-president in charge of sales, and Dr. Goldsmith as vice-president in charge of engineering phases of the development. It was agreed, moreover, that the new corporation should be owned in the following proportions: RCA 60%; General Electric 24%; Westinghouse 16%.

Photophone was organized under the laws of Maryland shortly after the meeting in Mr. Young's office. So rapidly did the lawyers work that on April 4, 1928, the inevitable amended certificate of incorporation was filed, permitting the new company to set up in business. This does not signify that the organization at 411 Fifth Avenue stood still while these important developments were in progress. On the contrary, an informal alliance with Joseph P. Kennedy's energetic organization, FBO, permitted the Bucher-Goldsmith cohorts to synchronize for sound its first feature picture. This does not mean that they made a new picture with sound track and picture combined on the same film. No, indeed. They took FBO's "Chicago After Midnight" and made a sound film to be operated simultaneously with it. This synchronization was completed in March, 1928, to be promptly released to the few theaters then equipped to operate sound and motion projection.

In May and June, 1928, Photophone attempted the ambitious project of making a synchronized sound film for the fourteen-reel feature, "The King of Kings," thereby scoring a notable success. Unfortunately, however, the sound-on-film idea, although superior to the phonograph accompaniment scheme in fundamental principle, had not yet reached the technical perfection of the phonograph. Photophone's contribution to talking pictures was still inclined to be scratchy and troubled with a variety of mechanically created static.

Sec. 120. Radio Corporation Absorbs Keith-Albee and FBO—Forms RKO.

In 1923, the phonograph reigned as king. To those of little vision it may have seemed that the sudden vogue of radio broadcasting would force an early abdication. To those of clearer sight, however, signs of a future coalescence of the radio and phonograph fields were obvious.

For example, the Western Electric technicians at the laboratories of ERPI, as already indicated, were experimenting with voice reproduction. While the objective was perhaps for the improvement of radio yet the Western Electric Company kept a shrewd eye on every available avenue of use for the new invention. During the crisis in 1925 the Victor Talking Machine Company purchased rights in a Western Electric device that quite revolutionized phonograph manufacture. Out of this effort originated the justly famous Orthophonic Victrola—a truly great advance in the art. Its tone had—and still has for those of us who continue to own one—a mellow richness that glorifies ordinary phonograph records.

It has previously been noted that RCA had formed a sort of alliance with the Victor Company on May 16, 1925, by which it had become possible to combine radio sets and phonographs in the same cabinet. This arrangement had further advanced David Sarnoff's ideal of a "Radio Music Box." More than that, it formed an industrial bond that was to lead the Victor Talking Machine Company into a genuine consolidation with RCA.

In another field, however, RCA and its allies were moving with rapidity. The phonograph situation could wait. Talking picture developments could not. Despite the original handicap of a virtual cornering of the market by Western Electric interests RCA Photophone had conducted a masterly campaign to capture the remnants of the motion picture industry. During the summer and fall of 1928 it had concluded license agreements with the following producers:

Standard Cinema Corp.
Tec-Art Studios, Inc.
Van Beuren Corp.
Tiffany Productions, Inc.
Mack Sennett, Inc.
Educational Studios, Inc.
Pathé Exchange, Inc.
FBO Productions, Inc.
RKO

and numerous contracts for theater-producing equipment.

Photophone's first delivery of complete sound-recording equipment was made on September 11, 1928, to the Pathé Studio at Culver City, California, for joint use of Pathé and FBO. By October 15th the installation was complete—Photophone's first commercial "job." The Mack Sennett Studios were next to be equipped. It is interesting to note that the first picture synchronized for sound to be made by Mack Sennett was "The Lions Roar," which was released December 15, 1928. As might be expected at the period, this initial offering of a studio that specialized in slapstick comedy, "The Lions Roar" had its full quota of custard pies, applied in barrage sequences.

The leaders of the Radio Group, greatly as they admired the salesmanship and skill that had enabled RCA Photophone to acquire so much potential business, were nevertheless chagrined at the prodigious strides made by Western Electric and its subsidiary "Electrical Research Products, Inc." These Radio chieftains were not content to play second fiddle to any other corporate group. They realized that existing markets were limited—that if they were to exploit their own sound system it would be over a period of years and through the agency of a great production company.

Fortunately for RCA, circumstances conspired to throw both corporations into the orbit of its influence. Vaudeville, which had been the life of KAO, was no longer enjoying public favor. Deficits meant bank loans, and loans in turn meant that banking interests soon became owners of large blocks of KAO stock. Bankers were thus in a position to exert pressure on KAO. Film Booking Office had no theaters. A combination between the two had been a logical development, but even in combination the two companies lacked a necessary ingredient to success. The latest form of entertainment—talking pictures —was vitally needed, and RCA furnished the solution. RCA Photophone was already in action, making the very pictures that were needed. RCA chieftains were not slow to embrace the opportunity thus providentially arising. A grand merger of interests was in order. By October, 1928, plans had been completed for incorporation of Radio-Keith-Orpheum. On October 25th the corporation was organized under the laws of Maryland as a holding company. Stock was issued in exchange for outstanding shares of Keith-Albee-Orpheum Corporation and FBO as well as for agreements, non-exclusive licenses and working capital.

The details of finance that were involved in this transaction are beyond the scope of this inquiry. It should perhaps be noted that at the time of the consolidation, the gross assets of KAO amounted to over $67,000,000. Its income from theater admissions alone, during the year 1928, exceeded $30,000,000. Beside this corporate giant FBO Productions, with its gross assets of less than $5,000,000, was a veritable pygmy. Its gross income for 1928, however, exceeded $8,000,000. When the transaction was complete the new holding company, RKO, had total assets of $71,397,699.36 so well balanced by liabilities as to leave an initial surplus of $3,339,000.

A great multitude of theaters or theater leases were included in this transaction. RCA Photophone was thus provided with a potential market of considerable magnitude. At the year's end Photophone had equipped thirty motion picture theaters for sound, whereas its great rival, ERPI, had already completed installation of its equipment in seventy-five theaters. Both organizations were feverishly at work in a large number of motion picture houses.

Sec. 121. Paley Reorganizes Columbia Broadcasting System.

It has previously been noted that William S. Paley, on September 26, 1928, became the owner of the network known as the Columbia Broadcasting System. The first three months of his operation of the network had convinced him of the necessity of certain drastic changes. We have noted elsewhere that on January 3, 1929, the name of the original United Independent Broadcasters was officially changed to the Columbia Broadcasting System, and the corporation that had previously borne that title was dissolved. Coincident with this change came increase of capital stock from 5000 to 7500 shares. The additional stock was issued for cash, bringing into the treasury half a million dollars, to be devoted by the energetic president of the company to an ambitious program of expansion.

Paley still wisely retained Major J. Andrew White as a member of his official family. While it is unlikely that he expected to retain White as a permanent executive—the latter's restless disposition already being demonstrated by his previous career—Major White was nevertheless a radio veteran, and Paley needed him during his own apprenticeship in this new field. The Columbia Broadcasting System was deeply concerned over the problem of inducing famous artists to appear on its programs. Major White became invaluable as a contact man for stage and "Great White Way" celebrities.

Another man, one who was destined to continue with Columbia from that day to this, was Arthur Judson, who had long been a booker of talent of high degree. The great opera stars were especially friendly to Arthur Judson because of past relationships. Although the NBC networks had no need for Judson his services were valuable in the extreme to William S. Paley. It is perhaps not too much to say that the immediate success of the youthful network in winning public favor was due in large measure to Arthur Judson's ability to stage programs of outstanding excellence. William S. Paley was too astute an executive to overlook the necessity of showmanship in program building as the first stage in a campaign to attract advertising sponsors. So we find him working diligently with both White and Judson in a campaign to win public acclaim for the Columbia Broadcasting System.

The bewildering intricacies of high finance to all save experts in accounting is well known. The record of the Columbia Broadcasting System, even in the first year of Paley's administration, discloses a bit of financial legerdemain. The Paley family fortune was not relied upon for the entire financing of the network. On June 26, 1929, we find Columbia borrowing $75,000, and again on July 17th another loan of $50,000, both loans coming from the Chemical Bank and Trust Company. On August 7, 1929, a certificate of amendment to the original corporate charter was filed authorizing an increase of stock from 7500 shares to 100,000 shares of no par value. This new issue, moreover, was to consist of 50,000 shares of class A stock and 50,000 shares of class B stock—each class having the right to elect one-half of the directors. Now comes the amazing part of the transaction—the corporate capital, despite the above increase in authorized number of shares, was actually reduced from $1,040,000 to $700,000— a decrease of $340,000. It is significant that this $340,000 in excess of paid-in capital was immediately credited to surplus—thus creating a sort of cushion to ease the impact of a possible deficit for the year, as well as to establish the corporation on a safer financial basis than it had hitherto possessed.

Thanks to the above bookkeeping transaction Columbia Broadcasting System was able to report a profit of $475,203.13 for the year 1929. If we contrast this with NBC's net earnings for the same year, $713,849.33, we encounter the significant fact that Columbia's gross sales for the year were only $5,053,414.19, whereas the gross sales of NBC for the same period totaled $15,552,518.78. This indicated that young Mr. Paley was destined to give the NBC organization a type of competition that might be difficult to meet, since NBC was spending huge sums in the development of radio broadcasting, whereas Columbia, at this time, was concerned chiefly with the commercial phase of the industry.

Some changes in NBC's official family occurred during the year 1929. On January 10, 1929, one of Radio's great pioneers, Charles B. Popenoe, was taken by death. Pneumonia contracted while visiting relatives at Christmas time ended the career of the founder of WJZ, who was serving NBC as treasurer at the time of his death.

On January 18, 1929, the board of directors of NBC voted to employ a general engineer, thus making way for the promotion of Oscar B. Hanson, who had rendered notable engineering service to Radio since the infancy of Station WEAF.

March 15, 1929, was notable in NBC annals since on that date it inaugurated its plan of electing its principal department heads as vice-presidents of the company. In addition to those already in service the board elected the following vice-presidents:

> John W. Elwood
> George Engles
> Niles Trammell
> Don E. Gilman
> A. L. Ashby
> Frank Russell.

Several of the foregoing were located at a distance from New York City. Frank Russell was in Washington, D. C.; Niles Trammell was in Chicago headquarters, and Don Gilman headed the Pacific coast department. Mr. Ashby became also general attorney for NBC.

At this same meeting Mark Woods was elected treasurer and re-elected assistant secretary of the corporation.

CHAPTER
SIXTEEN

Radio Corporation Unified at Last

Section 122. A Move toward Consolidation of Radio Manufacturing.
DAVID SARNOFF'S DESIRE to secure for the Radio Corporation of America
rights which it did not possess under the original cross-licensing agreements has been referred to repeatedly in the development of this narrative. It will be remembered that in 1919 the business of manufacturing electrical equipment for wireless transmission and reception involved the making of such large and complicated devices as the Alexanderson alternator and its accessories. At its origin, it was intended
that RCA would engage primarily in the communications business.
It would obviously have been wasteful to attempt to equip the new
corporation with the expensive facilities then required in the radio
manufacturing business. At the time, therefore, RCA received the right
to use under General Electric and Westinghouse patents, together
with the right to purchase and sell radio apparatus manufactured by
General Electric and Westinghouse. The rise of a new industry, however, and the great radio boom, changed the entire aspect of affairs.

RCA found itself handicapped in competition with rivals owing
to the fact that competitors invariably manufactured the radio sets
and appliances that they offered to the public. Rivals were able to
change models as frequently as their designers could devise improvements in a rapidly developing art. RCA, on the other hand, as we have
frequently observed, was not a manufacturer under its agreements
with General Electric and Westinghouse. Mr. Sarnoff's ambition to
obtain such rights for RCA was a natural development. It was born
of bitter experience in facing competition of rival manufacturers. He
saw very clearly that RCA could never win complete success without
the unification of manufacturing and selling rights that other corporations enjoyed. To be obliged to secure the approval of three sets of
engineers before plans for radio sets could become official was only
one of the annoyances that forced Mr. Sarnoff into his long-continued
crusade for unification of RCA.

As early as 1927, however, forward-looking officials of the Radio
Group began to respond to the logic of circumstances and to incline
a bit toward David Sarnoff's contention that the existing division of
manufacturing and selling, insofar as it related to radio appliances,
was inefficient. Unified control of manufacturing in one organization
was seen to be necessary if the Radio Group were to hold its own in
competition with rivals. The insistent demand for radio sets—for sets
that combined last-minute developments in the art—gave to competitors an immense advantage over the cumbersome G.E.-Westinghouse-
RCA combination.

On October 25, 1927, the so-called Cravath memorandum was
agreed upon in principle by representatives of RCA, G.E., and Westinghouse. This memorandum provided for the establishment of a

new corporation designed to take over the manufacture of radio sets and appliances. A committee was appointed to study the matter, consisting of the following:

> David Sarnoff, of RCA, chairman
> Harry P. Davis, of Westinghouse
> W. R. Burrows and J. W. Lewis, representing the General Electric Company.

This committee, on April 14, 1928, recommended that the corporation be called Radio Manufacturing Corporation, and that it should consolidate the manufacture of sets and appliances as above indicated. In suggesting corporate ownership of the stock in the new corporation General Electric and Westinghouse were to have all of the common stock on the 60-40 basis, with RCA being given the right to purchase in these proportions a total of 20% of this stock. Ultimate ownership would be:

General Electric	48%
Westinghouse	32%
RCA	20%
	100%

It was not at that time possible for Mr. Sarnoff successfully to advance his claim to manufacturing rights for RCA. To unify manufacturing in a single corporation was a move in the right direction. It was a second forward step toward that goal also, when RCA won a right to even a 20% ownership in the corporation. To be sure it was merely a plan as yet—a plan soon to be overshadowed by a new development.

Sec. 123. Victor Talking Machine Company for Sale.

In the spring of 1928, conditions were peculiarly favorable for a merger of RCA and Victor Talking Machine Company. As a result of technical developments, the radio field and the phonograph field seemed destined to coalesce into the home entertainment field. RCA could take care of this enlargement of its normal field in no better way than by an alliance with the world-famous and respected Victor Talking Machine Company. No one saw this opportunity more clearly than Owen D. Young and David Sarnoff. The Victor executives, on the other hand, now realized the necessity of acquiring rights under radio patents.

On April 20, 1928, Paul D. Cravath and Mr. Sarnoff reported to the RCA board concerning the new development, as appears from the following minutes of the meeting:

"Mr. Cravath and Mr. Sarnoff reported to the board in regard to the pending negotiations with the Victor Talking Machine Company and, after a general discussion of the matter, on motion, duly made, seconded and unanimously carried, it was

"RESOLVED, that the board of directors expresses the view that in general it is sympathetic toward an arrangement with the Victor Talking Machine Company along the general lines outlined at the meeting, but desires that the matter be deferred until Mr. Sarnoff's return from Europe."

Whether Mr. Sarnoff and Owen D. Young had at that time arrived at definite conclusions concerning desirability of a merger of RCA and the Victor Talking Machine Company is not apparent. A committee, however, was presently at work assembling data that might be useful in connection with the matter. The Cravath memorandum continued to be agitated; and thus the weeks passed.

One day in July, 1928, shortly after David Sarnoff's return from Europe, President Shumaker, of the Victor Talking Machine Company, made a luncheon engagement with Mr. Sarnoff and Elmer E. Bucher. Shumaker stated bluntly that his company must have license rights to manufacture radios and combination radio and phonograph sets. It is probable that Mr. Shumaker had expected a denial of this request, since at this very meeting he proposed that RCA purchase Victor "lock, stock and barrel." In the inner circles of the Radio Corporation it was well known that Owen D. Young had declared not long before that this was the only solution of the Victor problem that RCA would entertain.

David Sarnoff was too astute a business man to do more than to concede the possibility of a purchase. Cautiously he explored the situation to discover the best terms upon which the merger might be effected. The phonograph official promised to arrange to meet at the council table with a committee of RCA negotiators. Thus began a long series of conferences in which David Sarnoff's talents as a negotiator found ample scope.

The proposed merger offered distinct possibilities. The Victor Talking Machine Company was a world-wide organization. For a generation Victor phonographs and the Victor trade mark—the listening dog —had been known in all nations. Victor records, moreover, were being made by world-famous artists. This galaxy of talent, if brought into official relation with RCA, might supply the needs of its radio broadcasting and sound picture subsidiaries as well as insure to it a continuance of first-quality phonograph records for combination phonograph-radio sets.

An even more intriguing idea to Mr. Sarnoff was the fact that the physical facilities of the Victor Company would provide RCA with factories for the manufacture of first-quality cabinets for radio and phonograph—facilities that could be utilized for manufacture of radio sets, radio tubes, and radio appliances. To David Sarnoff, who had long dreamed of obtaining manufacturing rights and facilities for RCA, this development was little short of providential. The Cravath plan, as we have seen, had contemplated unification of manufacturing facilities of G.E. and Westinghouse—an improvement over present conditions—but it did not go the whole way. RCA imperatively needed complete unification of manufacturing and sales. If by some miracle RCA might achieve this goal the Victor purchase could be turned to great advantage.

It is improbable that Mr. Sarnoff at this time had any well-defined plan for complete unification of RCA in connection with the Victor merger. The most that he could hope for at the moment would be to accomplish unification of manufacturing and thus to eliminate waste of time and effort that now hampered RCA's activities. If he could accomplish this step he believed that it might eventually lead to the desired goal. He had already wangled a 20% ownership plan for RCA in his attempt at unification. Why not strike for even more concessions when the time should come for the setting up of a new Victor Corporation?

Sec. 124. Radio-Victor Merger Approved by RCA.

The executives of the Victor Company had for some time after the advent of radio failed to recognize its possibilities. Instead of taking advantage of the new development they had tried to stem the tide of radio competition. They had finally acknowledged that alliance with radio was imperative. This realization, and the fact that the bankers—J. &. W. Seligman & Company and Speyer & Company—were pressing for action, were favorable to the Sarnoff committee during its weeks of negotiations. There were many details to be explored, however, in so great a transaction. The total assets of the Victor Company were more than $69,000,000. It was out of the question to raise any such sum in cash. Big Business, however, has a convenient substitute for cash—shares of stock. RCA stock must be utilized. Sufficient assets of RCA must go into the merger to afford a reasonable balance for Victor assets.

By December 28, 1928, negotiations had ripened into definite proposals for consolidation which were being submitted to J. & W. Selig-

FRED WEBER
General Manager of the Mutual Network. An NBC veteran.

EDWIN H. ARMSTRONG
Whose new system of modulated frequency may revolutionize broadcasting.

W. B. LEWIS
CBS Vice-President in charge of programs.

ALFRED J. McCOSKER
Chairman of the Board, Mutual Network.

man & Company and Speyer & Company, the bankers for the Victor Talking Machine Company. It is interesting to observe that RCA's representatives were Owen D. Young and David Sarnoff.

At a meeting of the board of directors of RCA, held on January 4, 1929, the merger idea was approved whereupon David Sarnoff, as executive vice-president, advised the Victor Talking Machine Company of this development. He submitted a draft of a plan of consolidation. On the same day the directors of the Victor Company officially approved the merger and E. E. Shumaker, its president, so advised the officials of RCA. The bankers, however, had ideas on the subject. They proposed the establishment of a sinking fund for the retirement of the preferred stock of the Victor Company.

A very interesting and emphatic letter from Owen D. Young to Frederick Strauss, of J. & W. Seligman & Company, under date of January 14, 1929, began in the following language:

"I am entirely opposed in principle to a sinking fund on a preferred stock, and therefore I should say 'no' to the suggestion in your letter of January 11th. Nor do I think the equities of the situation in any sense justify it."

Evidently Mr. Young's letter had the desired effect, since we find in the files of RCA a letter from Mr. Cravath's office, under date of January 17th, addressed to David Sarnoff, which contains the following significant statement:

"Now that the sinking fund question has been settled there is no reason why the Victor Plan should not be signed and sent to Victor stockholders. It is the intention to have the Plan printed today and signed tomorrow."

By the terms of the proposals to be made to the Victor stockholders the offer was to be presented directly to them. RCA would not be obligated to go through with the merger unless seven-eighths of the common stock of the Victor Company should be deposited with the bankers in exchange for RCA common stock on or before March 4, 1929.

Sec. 125. German Reparations Call Young and Sarnoff to Europe.

At this point Messrs. Young and Sarnoff were suddenly called across the Atlantic. The Reparations Commission was then at a standstill in dealing with the Germans. American mediation seemed to be the only hope of world peace, and so Owen D. Young had been summoned to Paris.

Mr. Young was keenly aware of the nature of the task that awaited him in Europe. The German nation was already rebellious at a continuance of the harsh terms of reparations—terms so distasteful to Germans that there was a possibility of war. Mr. Young's task was thus twofold—to endeavor to persuade the Allies to moderate their demands and, on the other hand, to persuade the Germans to accept a possible compromise. This latter effort would involve rough-and-tumble negotiations. It would require firmness, tenacity and strategy in high degree. Although David Sarnoff was not an official of the Reparations Commission, Mr. Young decided that he was the man in his orbit who measured up to the needs of the hour and so, in January, 1929, he requested Sarnoff to accompany him to Paris and to undertake negotiations with the Germans.

At this time no one expected that Young and Sarnoff would need to be absent more than two or three months. It would require at least that time to complete the exchange of common stock. On February 1, 1929, Owen D. Young and David Sarnoff sailed for Paris.

Shortly after Young and Sarnoff had reached Paris, returns began to come in on the amount of Victor stock being deposited for exchange. Radiograms advised them of the state of affairs from day to day. By March 1, 1929, only 55% of the stock had been deposited. On the following day, however, it had risen to five-eighths. On March 4th, more than the requisite seven-eighths was on hand for exchange. March 15, 1929, was set as the date when RCA stock would be issued in exchange, this action having been authorized at a meeting of RCA stockholders on February 27th.

Although Mr. Sarnoff had expected to return by the beginning of April, 1929, the nature of his task proved so difficult that it became necessary to remain in Europe throughout the months of April and May.

Never was Owen D. Young's judgment of men more brilliantly vindicated than it was when David Sarnoff matched wits and endurance with the potent German statesman, Dr. Hjalmar Schacht. The story of those weeks during which Sarnoff converted a hostile and powerful antagonist, and persuaded the German delegates to accept the so-called Young Plan, is a thrilling story in itself. In speaking at a later time of Mr. Sarnoff's services to the reparations cause, Owen D. Young paid the following tribute:

"He was our principal point of contact with Dr. Schacht of the German delegation, and he did an extraordinary piece of work in negotiating for us with the Germans. Dr. Schacht had confidence in Sarnoff and believed in him. They worked well together. One could easily see that each man in the group of American delegates and experts was effective and at one time did a job that saved that conference; each seemed to have a part in the crisis which prevented it from being wrecked, and that can be said of Sarnoff in particular, for there came a time when only one man could save the situation, and that arose toward the end with Sarnoff and the German delegation."

Sec. 126. David Sarnoff Makes a Fateful Decision.

The machinery of unification, having been started, was carried on even without the benefit of the wisdom and experience of Owen D. Young and David Sarnoff. Early in April, 1929, the committee apparently began preparations to retire the Victor preferred stock. In May, 1929, it organized a new manufacturing corporation—Audio Vision Appliance Company—AVA—to take over the physical assets of the Victor Talking Machine Company. It was agreed that General Electric and Westinghouse should own and control the corporation under somewhat the same plan that had been formulated for the Radio Manufacturing Company, provided for under the Cravath unification memorandum—all of which had existed only on paper. It was conceded that RCA should be represented in stock ownership, but no attempt was made to fix the proportion of ownership.

Since much money was needed to finance the retirement of Victor preferred stock and to put Victor factories in condition for operation under the new dispensation the committee hit upon the idea of borrowing the same from General Electric and Westinghouse. These two corporations at once advanced, on the credit of RCA, $32,000,000 for the purpose in hand. Of this amount $22,500,000 was immediately expended to retire the Victor preferred stock. The balance was devoted to improvements and alterations of the Victor factories.

A second corporation, to be known as Radio-Victor Corporation of America, was also organized to take over the Victor sales organization and to combine with it the commercial department of RCA. Owen D. Young and David Sarnoff arrived in New York on June 14, 1929.

There is ample evidence that the summer of 1929 was the most exciting and momentous in the history of the Radio Corporation of America. For years David Sarnoff had been growing in efficiency as a negotiator in industrial disputes. His recent experiences in Europe had obviously "added cubits to his stature." In his relentless drive for RCA's unification of manufacturing and selling rights in a single organization we find him steadily gaining ground. A completely owned RCA subsidiary to handle sales, was no longer the ultimate goal. He had determined that the time was ripe for complete unification of manufacturing and sales under RCA ownership.

A circumstance that favored the idea at this time was that the new manufacturing organization was already bogged down with problems. Parts of seven separate research and engineering units, representing RCA and the six factories of the group, were now assembled in a veritable Noah's Ark of unassimilated talent. Attempts at unification thus far had operated merely to bring the elements of chaos a bit closer together.

Elmer E. Bucher tells the story of a dramatic taxicab ride, during which David Sarnoff made the fateful decision to fight for complete unification. It happened in the late summer of 1929, after a banquet—at one o'clock in the morning. The two men had discussed the situation—Sarnoff growing more agitated as he talked.

"We have reached the point," he said, as though reasoning with himself, "when I think we can have either participation or unification. Which shall it be?"—flinging his derby hat on the floor of the taxicab in sheer weariness of soul.

"Why ask me?" replied Bucher. "Your mind has always been set on complete unification."

"Yes—yes—I know—complete unification—but can we get it?"

"Why not?"

Mr. Sarnoff picked up his hat—dusty and crumpled—and clapped it on his head.

"Well, boy! Unification it is."

Sec. 127. Unification of Manufacture and Sales for RCA.

David Sarnoff's decision to press for complete unification of RCA at length prevailed in the councils of the mighty. This appears in the following entry from the minutes of the meeting of the RCA board on October 4, 1929.

"RESOLVED, that the board approves in principle the unification of the manufacturing, engineering and selling of the apparatus and devices now being manufactured by the General Electric Company and the Westinghouse Electric & Manufacturing Company and sold by the Radio Corporation of America, the working out of the plan being referred to a special committee of the board (consisting of Messrs. Frederick Strauss, chairman, Cornelius N. Bliss and James R. Sheffield, the president and executive vice-president to serve as members of the committee ex-officio)."

It is significant that the above committee was composed entirely of RCA independents, neither General Electric nor Westinghouse being represented.

Mr. Sarnoff was now in a position to exercise his powers of leadership in the process of organization. The committee soon reported a plan for the setting up of a new corporation to be known as RCA

Victor Company, Inc., to take over the radio manufacturing and engineering activities previously exercised by General Electric, Westinghouse and Victor Talking Machine Companies, as well as the sales departments of RCA and Victor. This report was approved by the RCA board on October 18, 1929. This does not mean, however, that the battle was won, except in the RCA board. General Electric and Westinghouse were still to be reckoned with.

Owen D. Young was David Sarnoff's staunch ally in this effort, bringing to the council board the full power of his personality and breadth of vision. During the process, moreover, Mr. Young became convinced that unification on so vast a scale as contemplated would require a new set-up in the official family of the Radio Corporation. He resolved to relinquish his own position as chairman of the board and to urge the promotion of General James G. Harbord, who had now served for seven years as president. This would pave the way for the dynamic Sarnoff to become the chief executive of the vast radio empire resulting from the merger of the Victor and RCA.

On December 26, 1929, the RCA Victor Company, Inc., was organized under the laws of Maryland. Its corporate purposes were defined, generally, as to manufacture and sell radio, sound recording and reproducing apparatus, records, etc., and the taking over of assets of the Victor Talking Machine Company, together with manufacturing and sales rights of RCA, Victor, RCA Victor, RCA Photophone, Audio Vision Appliance Company, and various other corporations. Thus the way was opened for the fulfillment of David Sarnoff's ambitious program.

Mr. Sarnoff was now the man of the hour in the councils of the RCA—acclaimed not only by Owen D. Young and General Harbord but also by Gerard Swope and Andrew W. Robertson, potent chieftains of General Electric and Westinghouse who, on the opposite side of the council table, had carried on with him tedious and difficult negotiations. Thus it came to pass, on January 3, 1930, that a board meeting of RCA witnessed great and dramatic events.

Owen D. Young tendered his resignation as chairman of the board. The resignation was accepted and Mr. Young was immediately elected chairman of a newly created executive committee. General Harbord thereupon resigned as president and was immediately elected chairman of the board. David Sarnoff, the executive vice-president, was at once elected president of the Radio Corporation of America.

Thus, while still lacking some weeks of attaining his thirty-ninth birthday, David Sarnoff became the chief executive of one of the greatest corporations in America—a corporation, moreover, to whose greatness he had materially contributed. He was now in a position to complete the campaign of unification thus far so brilliantly advanced.

Sec. 128. The Aftermath of Victory.

Although the original plans for the RCA Victor Company had called for stock ownership by the three corporations, the new program of complete unification obviously required a different plan. Mr. Sarnoff now proposed that the General Electric and Westinghouse be compensated for the surrender of manufacturing rights, cash advances, equipment, facilities and other assets by RCA stock. Owen D. Young was the first to agree to the plan, and it soon impressed others in authority as a logical and proper solution. By February, 1930, the idea had been approved in principle.

The consent of General Electric and Westinghouse to the relinquishment of manufacturing and engineering rights in radio appliances was the chief victory of the unification movement. The terms of consolidation, however, required weeks of negotiations. It was not until April 4, 1930, that the unification plan could be presented to and accepted by the RCA board. It is noteworthy that all stock issued to the manufacturing corporations under the unification agreement was stock in RCA, rather than in the new corporations. For this stock, moreover, the two corporations surrendered rights of great value, as well as claims for repayment of the $32,000,000 advanced to AVA in May, 1929. They transferred manufacturing licenses in the radio field, which now included phonograph and moving pictures. They surrendered all right to the substantial share of royalties being collected by RCA from licenses previously paid over to General Electric and Westinghouse. They transferred real estate, factories and machinery, together with manufacturing facilities for radio appliances. The entire stock holdings of the two companies in the following RCA subsidiaries came to RCA in this transaction:

50%	of the outstanding common stock of NBC
40%	" " " " " " RCA Photophone
19.6%	" " " " " " General Motors Radio Corp.
50%	" " " " " " RCA Victor
50%	" " " " " " RCA Radiotron
100%	" " " " " " AVA

RCA also became entitled to other considerations from General Electric and Westinghouse, including manufacturing profits from radio apparatus furnished to RCA by the two corporations since January 1, 1930.

In return for the foregoing—undoubtedly one of the greatest transfers of assets in industrial history—the Radio Corporation of America made payment, not in cash or in tangible assets, but in shares of stock of RCA–6,580,375 of common stock resembling a partnership right in that its value depends upon the solvency and business success of the corporation. By virtue of this transaction David Sarnoff achieved his major objective. He put the Radio Corporation of America in position to battle for its industrial life in the midst of the growing chaos of a world depression. Unification was accomplished by the signing of an agreement known as "Agreement M," on April 23, 1930. Agreements "L" and "M," moreover, extended the term of the contracts for ten years—a circumstance that was to become of great value to RCA.

From time to time after the organization of RCA, attacks upon the "Radio Trust" appeared in the press, and such attacks multiplied as the company prospered. Many of them could be traced to competitors infringing RCA's patents. It has previously been noted that the Federal Trade Commission conducted a four-year investigation of RCA and its allies, only to dismiss the suit of its own volition in 1928. In that investigation, special attention was paid to the legality of the cross-licensing arrangements.

From the beginning, however, the executives of RCA, General Electric, Westinghouse and American Telephone Company were secure in their belief that the cross-licensing arrangements were in all respects legal. Their view was that held by eminent counsel who had been consulted with regard thereto.

On May 13, 1930, the Government brought an anti-trust suit, naming RCA, General Electric, Westinghouse and the American Telephone Company as defendants. The Government contended that interstate and foreign commerce in radio communication and apparatus had been restricted. Among other things it was charged that the original Radio agreements of 1919–1921, and the newly signed unification agreement, were contracts in unlawful restraint of competition in the radio business. The RCA legal department, headed by Manton Davis, now had a major controversy on its hands. Unfortunately, this controversy involved more than the energies of the RCA lawyers. High officials of the corporation were obliged to prepare to testify before Federal tribunals, and to be absent from New York for that purpose, with little time for their regular duties. What has been said of the effect of the suit upon the business of RCA would apply also to the other accused corporations. Coming as this prosecution did in the midst of the greatest industrial depression in the history of the world, the suit could not have failed to cause apprehension as to its possible harmful effect upon the newly unified corporation.

Sec. 129. The Depression Hits RKO.

It will be remembered that on October 25, 1928, the Radio-Keith-Orpheum Corporation had been organized to consolidate Film Booking Office and Keith-Albee-Orpheum into a unified production and exhibition company. With the organization of RKO, its future prospects as a coordinated enterprise in the amusement field, combining theaters, motion picture production, booking offices and engineering departments, were accepted generally as very bright. In 1929, RKO net profits disclosed marked improvement over 1928. Further improvement was shown in 1930, although during the latter year the depression began to show real effects in the amusement field. Amusement was naturally one of the last luxuries to experience the full force of national depression, but RKO finally suffered the same box office and public patronage shrinkage that was playing havoc with amusements in general. Growing unemployment, collapse of security values, and widespread failures of banks created an alarming crisis throughout the nation. Movie patrons soon ceased to storm box office windows. Reduced admission charges could not lure them back. Every production company was eventually in desperate straits.

RKO, with the backing of the Radio Corporation, was probably in a stronger position than many others. In the autumn of 1930, when the Pathé Studios were in a receptive mood—RKO already having contractual relations with the organization—it was decided to purchase the studios and thus acquire additional theatrical talent to supplement RKO's own galaxy of radio stars. Well-known and popular artists on Pathé payroll, such as Constance Bennett, Helen Twelvetrees, and Ann Harding, were thus acquired. The Pathé Studios were purchased in December, 1930.

Optimists, who had proclaimed a speedy return of prosperity—prosperity allegedly lurking around the corner—were soon proved to have been tragically mistaken. The depression intensified and presently RKO found itself in need of additional funds for corporate purposes. It then appeared that bankers were afraid to loan money even to corporations so well sponsored as RKO.

In July, 1931, RKO finally succeeded in negotiating a six-million-dollar loan from Commercial Investment Trust, and Chemical Bank and Trust Company. For this loan RKO issued 6% secured notes, to mature in annual installments. Unfortunately, the sums thus raised proved inadequate to meet the full impact of the business recession. No more funds could be raised by bank loans. RKO could look only to its stockholders and, since RCA owned approximately 25% of RKO stock, a major problem was presented to the Radio Corporation. RCA Photophone, moreover, was largely dependent upon the continuing operation of RKO.

In order to safeguard its rights RCA was virtually driven to rescue RKO from going into receivership. Since economists were already declaring that the depression was virtually touching bottom, and that an upward trend might soon be expected, the board of directors of RCA decided to assume the risks of further financing of the losing venture. Thus it came to pass in November, 1931, that RCA agreed to underwrite RKO's needs.

CHAPTER
SEVENTEEN

The Federal Anti-Trust Litigation

Section 130. Radio Broadcasting in 1930 and 1931.

THE GOVERNMENT ANTI-TRUST SUIT, beginning in May, 1930, did not move very rapidly. Much time was required for formal answers. RCA filed its answer on June 30, 1930—an answer covering seventeen printed pages, denying every separate allegation of wrongdoing. RCA Radiotron also made a formal reply. RCA Victor and RCA Photophone did the like, and on the same day. The General Electric Company, the Westinghouse Company, and other defendants likewise unqualifiedly denied unlawful conduct.

The defendants, in their answers, insisted that the patent cross-licensing agreements they had executed among themselves did not restrain trade but, on the contrary, relieved restraints which theretofore had prevented lawful manufacture and sale of efficient radio devices; that the joint use of many adversely owned radio inventions was necessary in making the complicated apparatus required for effective public service; that their agreements, by putting at an end this patent stalemate, did not restrain competition but had exactly the opposite effect.

It appears that the anti-trust suit against the Radio Group was instituted after the Department of Justice had won a decision in the lower court against certain gasoline companies that had been operating under a so-called patent-pooling agreement. This decision, however, had been carried up on appeal. The Supreme Court, on April 13, 1931,[1] reversed the decision. This development had some bearing, no doubt, upon the RCA suit. Efforts were made, as will presently appear, to iron out difficulties without going to trial.

In the meantime, the National Broadcasting Company had solved one of its perennial problems—that relating to copyright privileges in current music, vocal and instrumental. The powerful organization, American Society of Authors, Composers and Publishers, had naturally pressed for the best possible terms—terms that NBC could ill afford to grant. On February 7, 1930, however, the board of directors of NBC authorized the signing of a compact with ASCAP covering Stations WEAF, WJZ, WRC, KOA and KGO, these being stations from which network broadcasts usually originated. Thus, peace in this sector of controversy was assured.

The economic depression bore heavily even on radio broadcasting. Yet it was noticeable that sponsored programs that had won public favor continued on the air despite the hard times. The Rudy Vallee radio show, which had long been a prime favorite with radio listeners, continued under the same sponsors, and continued to make radio history. Mr. Vallee had not at that time originated his famous variety

[1] *Standard Oil Co. of Indiana* v. *U.S.* 283 U.S. 163.

show, with its changing personnel of guest artists yet, from the outset of his remarkable career, the young man had been an outstanding leader in entertainment by radio. At this writing, Mr. Vallee has been on the air for the same sponsors for nine and one-half years—undoubtedly the longest continuous record of "big time" sponsorship in radio annals. In the early years of the depression his superb showmanship on the air was one of the stabilizing influences of the youthful industry.

Another type of commercial program that took the public by storm reached the height of its popularity at this time. The blackface comedians, "Amos 'n' Andy," became the presiding deities of twilight time. Not only did people listen in their homes to the fifteen minutes of atrocious misuse of the English language, but even in public places and on steamships the radio loud speaker was sure to emit the boastful tones of Andy in some moronic scheme. The plaintive bleat of his wiser companion, Amos, who nevertheless followed Andy into every disaster imaginable, was heard in homes innumerable. The Harlemesque illusion was so complete that it became difficult for people in general to realize that they were listening to Charles J. Correll and Freeman F. Gosden, two clever young white men. Not only did "Amos 'n' Andy" enjoy great popularity in 1930, but they have continued to amuse a nation that has sorely need to forget its troubles.

Sustaining programs have always been important contributions to public enjoyment and enlightenment. Grand opera, announced and commented upon by radio's great personality, Milton Cross, did much in depression years to bring consolation to a jittery public. Into homes of wealth or of poverty, by the magic of radio, came grand opera in all its superb qualities—the free-will offering of the National Broadcasting Company.

Another notable service to popular education on music was the "Music Appreciation" program by Dr. Walter Damrosch, broadcast by NBC to millions of school children in classrooms throughout the country. Sustaining programs of outstanding excellence were then, as now, choice offerings in radio's daily bill of fare. The necessity of showmanship even in educational programs was by this time widely recognized by radio lecturers. To be sure, the era of pioneering—of "firsts" in any field—was largely over.

Among notable developments in NBC history we find that on June 5, 1930, the board of directors authorized President Aylesworth to acquire additional land at Belmore, L. I., to enable WEAF to expand its transmitting facilities. The next important development to be recorded in the minutes of the board occurred at a meeting held January 9, 1931, when contracts with RCA Victor and RCA Photophone were concluded, covering electrical transcriptions. Thus it became possible for RCA's subsidiaries to aid one another within the family circle.

September 10, 1931, marked the passing of radio's godfather—Harry Phillips Davis. He it was who had glimpsed in Dr. Frank Conrad's broadcasting experiments in East Pittsburgh, during the summer of 1920, the possibilities of radio as a vehicle of mass communications. Station KDKA was created at his behest, and for eleven years prior to his death radio had been Harry P. Davis' chief interest in life. He had been chairman of the board of NBC since the corporation was formed.

In the same meeting at which resolutions were adopted by the board on the death of Mr. Davis, an important contract was authorized—the lease of space in the high tower of the Empire State Building for an NBC experimental station in television. Changes in NBC's official family occurred at this time. John F. Royal, who had come to the New York offices on February 15th from Station WTAM in Cleveland, Ohio, as program manager, was now promoted to vice-president in charge of programs. Frank Mason was also made vice-president—in charge of press relations. September 25, 1931, was indeed a great day for vice-presidents—three arriving on this date. The third proved to be Roy Witmer, vice-president in charge of sales.

Sec. 131. RCA Faces a New Danger.

Reference has been made to the anti-trust prosecution of the Standard Oil Company of Indiana, in which the Department of Justice suffered a decided reverse. This development evidently cast some doubt even in Government circles upon the soundness of the Government's position in the pending suit against RCA and its former allies.

Under these circumstances attorneys for the Radio Group consulted the Department of Justice in Washington, at which time the suggestion was made that the case be settled out of court on some mutually satisfactory basis.[2] Conferences, in which Warren Olney, Jr., represented the Attorney General, were held in New York in June, 1931. The effort proved unavailing, since the parties could not agree upon a mutually satisfactory method of solving the difficulty. Judge Olney adhered to the view that the contracts complained of offended the anti-trust law. A suggestion was made that the creation of an "open patent pool" might be one way of curing the cross-licensing pact to which the Department of Justice objected. The Government insisted also that the General Electric Company and the Westinghouse Company dispose of their RCA stock. A further suggestion was that licenses should be offered to the General Electric, to Westinghouse, to

---

[2] These facts recited by Warren Olney, Jr., Assistant Attorney General, in a letter to Charles Neave, October 20, 1931.

the American Telephone Company, and to the Western Electric Company, that would enable each of these corporations to compete with RCA in the radio field.

The only favorable result of the conferences, so far as RCA was concerned, came in a public statement from the Department of Justice to the effect that it had found nothing illegal in the organization of RCA by the General Electric Company in 1919. Here the matter rested so far as the anti-trust suit was concerned.

To David Sarnoff, chief executive of the Radio Corporation, these developments were profoundly disquieting. He was in favor of the democratic principle of free competition, yet for RCA's former partners, while still owning RCA stock, to enter competition against it seemed to him to create new circumstances. He believed that these former partners should aid the corporation to a position where it could compete in the national market and to facilitate it in getting on its feet as a radio manufacturer. Unification had cost heavily in time and effort. Fourteen months after unification a new situation had arisen that might well ruin everything. Under the circumstances there appeared grave danger of dismemberment of the Radio Corporation of America. The blame, if blame there be, might rest upon the operation of the anti-trust laws of the United States, but RCA would be the victim.

We have previously observed that in moments of peril—when great issues were at stake—David Sarnoff had always displayed resourcefulness and courage. His talents as a negotiator in industrial disputes were now recognized on both sides of the Atlantic. On this occasion—of gravest imaginable peril—Mr. Sarnoff executed what is probably one of the most brilliant strategic maneuvers of his career.

The danger, as he foresaw it, was that the leaders of the three corporations, in a situation of such perplexity, might act without realizing the full significance of the threatened dismemberment of RCA. Very well, Mr. Sarnoff would see to it that their attention was called to the possibility that acquiescence on their part might be construed unfavorably by the public. The dual relationship as directors of RCA, and of their own corporations, hitherto occupied by high officials of General Electric and Westinghouse, actually placed these officials in, an unenviable position now that separation had become an issue. Mr. Sarnoff well knew that they were men of high integrity; that if he could so marshal his facts as to convince them of the soundness of his views he might count upon them to work mightily for the salvation of RCA.

David Sarnoff prepared his argument with extreme care. In fact, he had been studying the situation for weeks. He had, no doubt, foreseen an emergency for which he must prepare if he were to protect the rights of RCA stockholders. This phase of the story merits greater attention than is possible to give it in the limits of the present volume. In the light of subsequent events we may regard the Sarnoff strategy as having turned the tide of events then threatening to engulf the Radio Corporation.

Sec. 132. David Sarnoff States RCA's Position.

To Andrew W. Robertson, chairman of the board of Westinghouse, and Gerard Swope, president of the General Electric Company, Mr. Sarnoff stated that circumstances required a definite decision on the following alternative policies: (a) Should the parties proceed to a judicial determination of the issues raised by the Government in the case of *U. S. v. RCA, et al.,* or (b) Should they settle the case as far as possible within the principles laid down by the Department of Justice and with due regard for the rights and interests of all it concerns.

He stated that if the defendants should feel certain that legal opinions given by eminent counsel would prevail before the Supreme Court, then the case should be fought through to a judicial determination. If, however, there was doubt on the point, it would be proper to make a settlement that would enable the Department of Justice to dismiss the case without placing the defendants in a position of admitting violation of the law or without entering into such consent as would prejudice the position of the parties in private litigation under the anti-trust laws.

In outlining his views of basic principles, Mr. Sarnoff painted in vivid colors the situation that must be met to assure the survival of the RCA before the electric manufacturing companies determined their position with respect to the Government suit. He stressed the interests of 85,000 independent stockholders of RCA, who were not connected with the electric companies.

Various proposals and counter proposals were discussed among the parties, but time was pressing and a decision of vital importance to all concerned had to be made. In urging that a settlement be reached, Mr. Sarnoff contended that the sooner it could be accomplished, the better for all concerned. An early announcement by the Department of Justice that the Government had dismissed its case would, he urged, do much to relieve the unfavorable position in which the defendants found themselves. It would prevent much additional private litigation then threatening and would enable a new publicity campaign along constructive instead of merely defensive lines. It would discourage new and menacing legislation on the subject of radio promised at the next Congress. It would probably also enable a settlement out of court of pending treble damage suits resulting from Clause 9 litigation. More important still he stressed the fact that a settlement then would enable the principal officers of RCA to attend to constructive business instead of destructive litigation.

Sec. 133. Radio Group Refuses Government Offer.

As a consequence of Mr. Sarnoff's argument the whole subject of settlement of the Government suit came before joint conferences of high officials of the three corporations. Weeks were spent before a definite policy was agreed upon—a policy of resistance to the plan that had been suggested by the Department of Justice. Since this action was likely to precipitate a major conflict, Owen D. Young was chosen to communicate to the Attorney General the views of the defendant corporations. An eight-page letter, bearing the date of October 1, 1931, summarized the situation.

He recounted the efforts that RCA had made to meet the objections raised by the Department of Justice at the recent conferences. The alliance with General Motors was being dissolved. A modification of the agreement with the United Fruit Company was being drafted and would presently be submitted to the Department of Justice for suggestions. In speaking of the "open-patent-pool" idea, Mr. Young called attention to the "grave and difficult problem of reorganization" that would be involved.

"As you are aware," he wrote, "in acquiring exclusive rights under patents of others of the defendants, the Radio Corporation also received tangible properties and many millions in cash. To attempt to make the readjustment at this time, however, when the hope of improved industrial conditions not only remains unrealized but when the country is in an unprecedented economic and industrial crisis, would be to court financial and industrial disaster."

In discussing the Department's announced objective of restoring competition in the relations of the Radio Group, he pointed out the following significant facts:

"Throughout the country large radio plants owned by competing manufacturers stand idle today because of overproduction resulting from ruinous competition. Distributors and dealers are besieged with competitive lines. Radio equipment on the market is in excess of public demand. For the most part, retail prices of radio sets and radio tubes are fixed at the buyer's, not the seller's option. Profitless sales, stimulated by destructive rivalry, now threaten the financial stability of many factors in the industry.

"Thousands of men and women, the large majority of whom might have remained employed if stable conditions existed, are out of work today, and hundreds of thousands of stockholders today find their

MAJOR LENOX R. LOHR
President NBC since January 1, 1936. World War veteran; General Manager
"Century of Progress Exposition," Chicago 1933–1934.

investments depreciated, not by restraint of competition but because of competition so great as to have demoralized prices and to have made profitable operation largely impossible."

One of Mr. Young's most effective points was contained in the following sentiment:

"The Radio Corporation has many large competitors. It has always seemed to me that in view of the relatively small percentage of the total radio business which is done by the Radio Corporation (less than 20% in receiving sets and less than 40% in tubes), and the intense competition in the radio field, there was no reason why the General Electric and Westinghouse Companies should not carry on their radio business jointly through the Radio Corporation. If the Radio Corporation were not in existence and the General Electric and Westinghouse Companies combined had no greater percentage of the total than the Radio Corporation now has, it seems to me clear that those two companies might today without possible objection under the law, combine their radio businesses into one corporation. If that be true, I am unable to see why there should be a continued effort to break up such unification as already exists."

A brisk exchange of letters between the Department of Justice and members of the Radio Group continued for some weeks, yet no satisfactory basis for settlement could be arrived at. In December, 1931, it developed that the Telephone Company was disposed to make peace with the Department of Justice, regarding itself as a minor defendant in the anti-trust suit, having disposed of its RCA stock nearly ten years previous to this date. Believing that the Attorney General's office would agree to discontinue suit against the Telephone Company, provided it should exercise its right to cancel its cross-licensing agreement by giving the agreed three years' notice, such notice was given on December 18, 1931.

Notwithstanding this division in its ranks the Radio Group continued to negotiate for some basis of agreement with the Department of Justice—a tedious and long-continued effort.

Sec. 134. Radio and the Economic Depression.

The collapse of industry following long-sustained boom cannot be other than tragic in its consequences. The general stock market crash in the autumn of 1929 that may at first have seemed a merited rebuke to Wall Street soon appeared to have been a mere prelude to unending and depressing developments. The nation had been obsessed with a spirit of optimism that had led to a virtual mortgaging of the industrial future of millions of American families. Not the least of the evil consequences of the boom had been the tremendous development of installment buying—the rearing of colossal structures of credit that must collapse with the first wave of unemployment.

The calamity that began in the stock markets soon spread to other phases of American life, despite every effort of the Hoover Administration to check its advances. Heavy losses in securities smote at once banks and trust companies; investment trusts in which millions of people had invested savings; great industries with heavy investments. In short, all institutions and persons to whom security values were important had sustained heavy losses financially, but the blow to morale was even more significant and far reaching in its future consequences. Banks became uneasy. Manufacturers curtailed production. The fatal wave of unemployment began. The installment-buying system sagged dangerously.

People now faced growing unemployment and resultant inability to meet their installment payments. On every hand the false prosperity based upon installment sales experienced the double calamity of a sudden halt of installment buying, and an equally sudden necessity of reclaiming goods on which installment payments had ceased. Thus warehouses became congested with unsold new commodities and with reclaimed second-hand goods.

Retail merchants faced ruin. Manufacturers experienced the sudden halt of orders for goods. The natural and inevitable reaction was widespread unemployment. Thus the stock market collapse, by evil progression, had spread disaster to every home in America. These were, indeed, evil days for industry—new or old.

It was RCA's misfortune that this economic depression was to develop major proportions in the months immediately following unification. The tide of disaster to the business world could not be halted by optimistic utterances from Washington, or by economists who endeavored to reassure a jittery world that prosperity would presently return. The radio manufacturing industry was facing the same dilemma that confronted industry in general, although it is probably true that the very nature of radio aided it somewhat in the struggle to exist. A radio set in the home, for instance, might pluck free entertainment out of the air, thus bringing temporary forgetfulness of the evils that loomed on every hand. Notwithstanding this fact, however, the radio industry was hard hit.

RCA was faced with problems of appalling magnitude. The Government anti-trust suit was of small moment in comparison with the economic and industrial problems that confronted them. Its major activities, aside from radio broadcasting, which developed surprising resistance to the buffetings of the depression, required the most searching scrutiny. It was necessary to eliminate every activity that militated against budget balancing which could possibly be discontinued.

No more vivid picture of industrial crisis in the life of a mammoth corporate group could be desired than the reports prepared by Mr. Sarnoff for the perusal of the directors of RCA. Mr. Sarnoff dealt in utmost frankness with various phases of the activities of the corporation and its subsidiaries. The following summary of gross earnings and net profits for three years, taken from RCA annual reports, discloses the cataclysmic nature of the depression:

	Gross Income RCA & Subsidiaries	Net Profits	Net Loss
1929	$182,137,738.65	$15,892,561.91	
1930	137,037,596.36	5,526,293.44	
1931	102,645,419.92	768,903.34	
1932	67,361,142.55		$1,133,585.65

It should be noted that this problem arose during the first year in RCA's history in which it ever sustained a net loss upon operations. There was no spirit of panic manifest in Mr. Sarnoff's summary of the situation. He was not setting up alibis. Neither was he making excuses for his administration of affairs. On the contrary, we find a calm analysis of the situation, particularly in the phases where greatest losses were being sustained.

It has previously been pointed out that Radio-Keith-Orpheum Corporation, organized in October, 1928, had already met financial reverses. At that time Mr. Sarnoff expressed the view that the entertainment industry was one of the last to feel the evil effects of the new economic situation. During the year 1930 the RKO had earned a net profit of $4,173,210, or twice the amount it earned in the preceding boom year of 1929. But when the economic blow finally struck the entertainment industry it did so with a violence that almost threatened extinction of all the major companies. In order to prevent a complete collapse, the RCA found it necessary to come to the financial assistance of RKO, and the profits of 1930 turned into a loss at the end of 1931 and a still greater loss for the then current year.

It might be supposed that such an appalling situation would have dismayed the forty-one-year-old chief executive of so vast an industry, yet David Sarnoff, in July, 1932, displayed the same confidence in his ability to extricate RCA from its perilous dilemma that we have noted in lesser crises of its affairs.

Naturally, he did not overlook the sources of income that had thus far contributed to the well-being of the corporate group. RCA Communications had turned in a net profit in 1930 of $997,000; in

1931, $661,000, and for the first six months of 1932 had shown a favorable balance of $202,000.

The National Broadcasting Company had made the following record of profits:

	Gross Income	Net Profits
1930	$22,162,000	$1,906,000
1931	29,640,000	2,325,000
1932 (1st 6 mos.)	16,655,000	1,196,000

Sec. 135. RCA Retrenchment and Plans for Future.

Mr. Sarnoff's appraisal of the depression is very illuminating. He stated that the extremely low price levels at which radio sets were offered to the American public by struggling and bankrupt competitors, had made it necessary for RCA substantially to meet such prices in order to remain in that branch of its business. Due to the great number of persons entirely or partly unemployed, public purchasing power had been reduced to levels which would have been regarded as unbelievable in 1929.

In speaking of retrenchment he disclosed that heroic efforts had already been made to stem the tide of disaster. He explained that where the control was in RCA's hands, it had been aggressive in cutting costs of doing business, including reductions in salaries and wages. Since 1930 salary payrolls of RCA and its subsidiary companies had been reduced by 50%. The loyalty and devotion of the officers and personnel of the RCA and its subsidiaries during those most difficult years had been truly remarkable and worthy of the highest commendation.

Responsibility in so great a crisis is a burden that few men could bear. That it operated as a challenge to David Sarnoff is manifest in the following statement to his associates on the board of directors of RCA:

"The outstanding fact is that despite the many difficulties, the Radio Corporation of America has survived the overwhelming tide of depression which has engulfed many industries. It has vastly improved its position in many fields and, through co-ordination of policies and activities, it has been able to translate unification at Camden into a well-knit and efficient organization, turning out the best products at the lowest prices in the history of the radio industry. The new developments resulting from activities of our research engineers in the RCA Victor and Communications Companies during the period following unification are of an outstanding character.

"To date we lead the world in the technical development of the new and promising field of television, which must remake the radio industry.

"The same is true regarding our activities in the fields of ultra-short waves, facsimile communication and high-fidelity recording and reproducing of sound.

"Also during this period we have amicably settled and adjusted many pending suits and greatly improved the position of our company in the field of public relations."

He called attention to the fact that RCA debts had been decreased from $24,775,000 to $17,700,000, and that a vast quantity of obsolete inventory had been disposed of, reducing the same from $31,947,000 in January, 1930, to $5,967,000 in June, 1932. A final expression of hope in the future was worded thus:

"Notwithstanding the difficulties of its position the RCA has demonstrated its ability to withstand the shock of a protracted economic and industrial depression. It has met its obligations and has not defaulted on its commitments. It has maintained its position at a time when public purchases were confined to the barest necessities of food and shelter and when such equipment as radio is classed among luxuries.

"The Radio Corporation of America has been a self-contained unit only during the past two years, and while it inherited the commitments of the preceding ten years, it was obliged to consolidate, coordinate, build and rebuild during a period of economic and financial depression which has seriously shaken the world's business and economic structure."

CHAPTER
EIGHTEEN

The Consent Decree

Section 136. Conferences Looking toward Settlement.

ALTHOUGH THE CHIEFTAINS OF THE RADIO GROUP had given earnest thought to a separation of corporate interests for some months, yet the very complexities of the situation had thus far prevented a meeting of the minds of the parties. Now that the summer of 1932 was over, and the great and mighty of the Radio Group had returned to New York, it was inevitable that a fresh attempt at settlement should have been made.

Again we find David Sarnoff as the central figure of negotiations. Upon him rested the chief burden of protecting the Radio Corporation's widespread interests in a particularly difficult and perplexing recasting of corporate contracts. Mr. Swope's activities on behalf of General Electric were similar to those of Mr. Sarnoff acting for RCA. Mr. Robertson served in a similar capacity for Westinghouse. It appears from the records that at no time during the negotiations in the fall of 1932 did either of these gentlemen vote in RCA meetings on matters under discussion. Mr. Young at the time was Chairman of the Board of the General Electric Company, but his position throughout the negotiations was definitely non-partisan. This fact was universally recognized and Mr. Young was frequently called into conference with those directors of RCA who had no affiliations with either General Electric or Westinghouse. As to specific points of negotiation, Mr. Young almost invariably accepted the position taken by Mr. Sarnoff rather than that taken by either Mr. Swope or Mr. Robertson.

Beginning late in September, 1932, the parties sought a mutual basis for agreement that would protect the interests of the stockholders of their respective corporations. In almost daily meetings gathered the chieftains of the Radio Group—Owen D. Young, David Sarnoff, Gerard Swope, Andrew W. Robertson, General James G. Harbord, and many others who have figured in this story—*Big Business and Radio.* Lawyers representing the three great corporations were also feverishly at work, drafting and redrafting suggestions for this and that type of contract. Every point agreed upon was at once incorporated in its appropriate contractual niche, since the entire group of earnest men were working under the compulsion of an imminent trial of the anti-trust suit.

Although the men participating in these conferences denied violation of Federal laws by their corporations, they, nevertheless, viewed with concern the heavy expense of a trial, the delays, and the uncertainty of the issue. Another impelling circumstance should not be overlooked: the industrial and economic depression had not only prostrated the country, but now threatened to defeat the Hoover Administration at the polls.

However the public at large may have accepted the prospect of a change in administration, and a change in fiscal policies of the national government, many industrial leaders in the New York area had grave apprehensions. Gloomy forebodings for the future of American industry thus overshadowed the conferences of these hard-pressed captains of industry. Thus, oppressed by dangers and forebodings, the negotiators struggled for many weeks.

Sec. 137. Negotiations Begin.

Space will not permit a detailed account of the long series of conferences that were held in New York City and Washington during the hectic weeks of the final stages of the radio negotiations. The following review of negotiations indicates the type of problems under consideration and the manner in which they were settled by the contending parties.

Prior to the first formal exchanges across the conference table, Owen D. Young and David Sarnoff found themselves in agreement upon the basic principles of any compact to be reached between RCA and the two Electric Companies. If General Electric and Westinghouse were to separate from RCA, the terms had to be such as fairly to assure the continued existence of RCA as an independent unit. When these principles were communicated to Messrs. Swope and Robertson, it was discovered that they were in general accord. Since general principles are comparatively elastic, when the parties began to discuss the actual terms of an agreement, they found themselves differing in their interpretation. David Sarnoff now found ample scope for the exercise of his ability as a negotiator.

The negotiations began with a series of proposals and counter-proposals. It was apparent from preliminary skirmishes that the parties were dealing with several distinct subjects, each of which presented more difficulties than are usually encountered in an entire series of negotiations. The principal sectors of combat were as follows:

(1) The manner in which the patent licenses could be rearranged so as to meet the contentions of the Government and, at the same time, leave RCA with all patent rights advantageous in the efficient prosecution of its business. In this field, David Sarnoff proposed, among other things, to secure for RCA rights in the transmitter field which it had not previously held.

(2) The patent rights of the various companies in foreign countries formed a separate subject of lengthy discussion.

(3) It was insisted for RCA that the new licenses to the two electric companies be delayed in operation for a period of from two to three years in order to give RCA a period of transition in which to adapt itself to the new order of things.

(4) The manner in which RCA should settle debts which it owed to General Electric and Westinghouse amounting in all to about $18,000,000, was also the subject of protracted negotiations. At the outset, David Sarnoff undertook to gain for RCA a double advantage from the settlement by suggesting that a portion of these debts be cancelled in return for the conveyance by RCA of certain real property situated at 570 Lexington Avenue in New York City. This transaction would be doubly advantageous to RCA since the building in question was not producing income at the time.

(5) As to the broadcasting phase, David Sarnoff proposed that if the General Electric and Westinghouse Companies were to sever their connection with RCA, the rights of its wholly-owned subsidiary, the National Broadcasting Company, should be adequately protected by agreements governing program relations with stations owned by General Electric and Westinghouse.

(6) A number of miscellaneous subjects of negotiation added to the complexity of the situation. Thus a proposal was made that if the Electric Companies were to dispose of their stock in RCA under the terms of any agreement, such disposition should be made in a manner not unduly to depress the market value of such stock.

Before negotiations were well under way, a meeting was held of those directors of RCA who were in no way connected with either the General Electric Company or Westinghouse. At this meeting, the independent directors formally authorized David Sarnoff to negotiate on the Corporation's behalf. Final terms were to be subject to approval of a committee consisting of all the independent members of the RCA Board. Shortly thereafter, Mr. Lansing P. Reed, eminent corporation lawyer, was engaged as independent counsel to advise with Mr. Sarnoff and with the independent members of the Board respecting the pending negotiations.

Although not directly connected with the Government suit, other matters were pressing for the attention of the heavily burdened negotiators. The economic depression had made necessary an adjustment of the commitments of RCA and some of its subsidiaries for space in Radio City. In the fall of 1932, while the parties were seeking to establish a basis upon which RCA could safely face separation from the Electric Companies, the Radio Corporation was also seeking to obtain a reduction in these lease commitments. It was fully recognized that success in the Radio City lease negotiations was closely connected with ultimate outcome of the negotiations for settlement. It was a prerequisite that RCA be established upon such a firm basis that it have a fair prospect of meeting the depression years that loomed ahead. The Radio City landlords were as insistent as anyone that the settlement leave RCA in a strong position.

Sec. 138. Lawyers Meet—and Disagree!

Lawyers are naturally conservative. Their very profession leads them into technicalities of language. In no field of the law is this truth more manifest than in that dealing with patents and patent rights. In a controversy so enmeshed in the cross licensing of patents as this entire radio complication, it was inevitable that the lawyers of the patent departments of the three corporations should be called upon for aid. Early in October, 1932, the first joint conference of the legal champions of the three corporations was held. Otto S. Schairer represented the Radio Corporation. Albert G. Davis was the representative of the General Electric Company. Harold Smith, a member of the legal staff of the Westinghouse Company, represented the latter organization.

No doubt each lawyer had been instructed to do his utmost for the corporation which he represented. So great were the financial interests involved, it is no wonder that these three men approached their task with utmost circumspection. Each was prepared to do battle for his cause but, since the two manufacturing corporations were natural allies, the contest was not exactly triangular. The conference accomplished this much, however, it established the maximum claims of each of the three corporations.

On the same day that the legal champions held their conference, as above noted, a conference of quite a different nature was held in Washington. David Sarnoff and Charles Neave, Esq., conferred with Judge Olney and an assistant named Lipman concerning the wishes of the Department of Justice in respect to a settlement out of court. This conference may be summarized as follows:

The Department of Justice Insists:

1. A consent decree rather than a dismissal is insisted upon.
2. This must be accomplished before the trial date (presently fixed as November 15, 1932).
3. General Electric and Westinghouse to retire from RCA, dispose of RCA stock, neither to resume relations with RCA except that if one company should "tie up" with an RCA competitor the other would be free to resume relations with RCA.
4. A period of transition.
5. No government compulsion on RCA to grant licenses to General Electric and Westinghouse in any field.
6. Department of Justice interested in character of licenses granted, especially in fields in which the three corporations are now doing business.

7. Discussion of international communications.
8. Department approved principle of settlement of RCA's indebtedness.
9. Department agreed with the view (previously suggested by Mr. Young and Mr. Sarnoff) that no settlement be made that would cripple RCA.

Upon the conclusion of the conference it was stipulated that any written agreements in connection with the hoped-for settlement would be submitted to Judge Olney. An interesting aftermath was that, on the following day, October 8th, Judge Olney wrote a letter to Mr. Neave expressing this afterthought:

"I believe that you and Mr. Sarnoff must have perceived yesterday that the Department was quite appreciative of the difficulties of working out a fair and practical scheme for the divorce of the three companies and wishes to throw no unnecessary obstacles in the way of this being done. I have talked the matter over with Mr. O'Brian and he is quite in accord with me in this, we both feel that the only way in which the Radio Corporation may be properly protected, in case of a divorce, is to put it at the outset in such a position, financially and otherwise, that it can stand on its own feet and take care of itself in the face of competition without the existence of agreements or arrangements designed to protect it against competition."

There was a certain humor in this suggestion. The parties themselves had conceded the point at the outset of negotiations, yet the intervening weeks had been filled with a continuous series of conferences, and they were still unable to reach an agreement upon an application of this simply phrased generality.

A second conference among the three lawyers previously mentioned occurred shortly after the middle of October, 1932. Charles Neave, Esq., was present as a sort of umpire. Without entering into details, the lawyers stoutly maintained their previous contentions. When the results of this conference, dealing with patent problems, were reported to David Sarnoff, he at once conferred with Mr. Schairer to make certain that the report was accurate. He then supported the contentions of RCA's representative by informing Mr. Neave that, in his judgment, the General Electric and Westinghouse contentions departed from the principles laid down in the discussions he had previously had with the heads of the Electric companies. Shortly thereafter, Mr. Sarnoff took the same position in communicating with Mr. Swope.

The strain imposed upon all parties by these negotiations was very great, especially upon RCA's negotiator whose shoulders bore the chief burden. Not infrequently, David Sarnoff might receive reports on the same morning from five or six of his subordinates, experts in their respective spheres. Each report must be digested, weighed and fitted into the already complex situation. There might follow a conference, hours long, with Messrs. Swope and Robertson in which Mr. Sarnoff's full energy would be required in arguing, explaining and negotiating on behalf of RCA. These matters had to be explained to the other independent members of the RCA Board for their approval. Then might follow discussions with Lansing P. Reed, Esq., for his advice on each action as it was taken. Then, too, Mr. Sarnoff was accustomed to weigh the day's agenda, and plan for the next conference. Patent rights, finances, real estate, general legal problems—all had to be given consideration as they arose.

Sec. 139. Radio Chieftains Burn Midnight Oil.

An important joint conference was arranged during the latter part of October, 1932. Responsible officials of the three companies now sat down with their lawyers for a three-hour afternoon session. The patent situation was thoroughly canvassed. Debate seems to have raged in three principal fields:

A. Requirements for protection of NBC.
B. Manufacture and sale of transmitting apparatus.
C. Treatment of RCA debts to the electric companies.

Mr. Aylesworth explained the importance of the General Electric and Westinghouse stations to NBC and it was suggested that these stations be leased to NBC for a term of ten years. Considerable discussion resulted over the terms of the proposed contract, but no accord was reached.

Another debate of a strenuous nature raged over whether RCA should grant general licenses to the Electric Companies in the field of transmitters. Various suggestions were made as to the manner in which RCA's debts might be liquidated. No final understanding was reached upon any of these points, the conference remaining in session until after midnight.

At a meeting of the RCA Board of Directors held on October 28, 1932, Mr. Sarnoff was able to report certain major gains. In the matter of cross-licensing of patents, the parties were virtually agreed except on the item of broadcast transmitters. The broadcasting phase had also been practically settled by an agreement of the Electric Companies to permit NBC to take over the programming of their broadcasting stations.

Following adjournment of this meeting, the independent directors held an extended conference. Owen D. Young remained by invitation to discuss pending matters more at length. He now expressed himself in favor of the complete separation of the corporations provided RCA's economic position could be protected. One of the results of this after-meeting was an agreement that the independent directors of RCA should meet on the following Monday, October 31st, for a special discussion of their problems. Lansing P. Reed, counsel for the independent directors, attended this meeting of October 31, 1932. Distinct progress toward the crystallizing of ideas was made.

Shortly thereafter, Mr. Sarnoff directed various technical experts in RCA's official family to begin the drafting of certain agreements that would be required to express the conferees' conclusions. The trial was then only two weeks away and there were still many points to be settled!

Sec. 140. RCA Refuses an Offer of Compromise.

A great outpouring of advice came to Mr. Sarnoff during the first three days of November. Directors and other key men in RCA's official family offered numerous suggestions, each in his own field. The commander-in-chief of the Radio Corporation's forces was thus gathering ammunition for a major encounter in which he hoped to achieve a final victory for his corporate group.

During the same period, a very important strategy meeting of General Electric and Westinghouse leaders was convened. They realized very keenly that David Sarnoff's relentless drive for concessions must be combated with utmost firmness and wisdom. In this grave situation Owen D. Young became a more or less neutral figure—welcome in the councils of both contending groups and giving to each the advantage of his wisdom and breadth of vision. Despite the fact that he was chairman of the board of directors of General Electric Company, he was above partisanship, much in the position of a father of contentious children. Then, too, Mr. Young was virtually the creator of the Radio Corporation as well as the industrial engineer who had put together the "jig-saw puzzle" that the Government was now striving to rearrange.

At this General Electric-Westinghouse powwow Mr. Young's counsel was of extreme value.

Shortly after this meeting there followed an intensive effort to settle the debt question. The Electric companies submitted various proposals for debt cancellations, none of which measured up to Mr. Sarnoff's requirements. Even though this was the only important point remaining to be disposed of, David Sarnoff refused to yield.

During this entire period, the independent members of the RCA Board were kept fully informed by Mr. Sarnoff of developments and Mr. Lansing Reed, the special counsel of these directors, was also kept posted on day-by-day progress.

Sec. 141. Sarnoff Makes Counter-Proposals.

Thus the first week of November, 1932, passed, distinct progress being made, yet important decisions must necessarily await a final conference of the full board. This meeting was set down for November 9th and the usual call was issued. David Sarnoff prepared for the meeting of the RCA board with extreme precaution. Two separate proposals of settlement by Mr. Sarnoff were made on that day.

The first proposal began with a statement of the indebtedness of RCA to the two companies, followed by Mr. Sarnoff's summary of the General Electric Company's recent offer and also that of the Westinghouse Company. He advanced a very interesting suggestion as may be seen in the following:

Mr. Sarnoff's Counter Proposal

General Electric to cancel	$ 4,609,500
General Electric to acquire Lexington Avenue Building	4,755,500
Westinghouse to cancel	3,073,000
Westinghouse to receive RCA debentures	3,073,000
	$15,511,000
To be assumed by Electric Companies as their contribution toward Radio City settlement on 60–40 basis	2,189,000
	$17,700,000

If the above counter-proposal made by Mr. Sarnoff were to be accepted by the electric companies, the disposition of the debts by each of the electric companies would be:

General Electric Company

To cancel	$5,922,900	
Receive Lexington Ave. Bldg.	4,755,500	
RCA Debentures	875,600	
		$11,554,000

Westinghouse Company

To cancel	$3,948,600	
RCA Debentures	2,197,400	
		6,146,000
		$17,700,000

While it is probable that the above proposal had definite effect upon the minds of Messrs. Swope and Robertson, who attended the meeting of the RCA board on November 9th, it is obvious also that they must have rejected the counter-offer, otherwise Mr. Sarnoff would never have presented a second proposition!

The second proposal read as follows:

Proposed Settlement of Debts
Due by RCA to Electrical Companies

Now due to General Electric Company	$11,554,000
Now due to Westinghouse Company	6,146,000
	$17,700,000

To be disposed of as follows:

Method	G. E. Co.	West. Co.	Total
By cancellation	$ 5,266,200	$3,510,800	$ 8,777,000
By transfer Lexington Avenue Building	4,755,500		4,755,500
By issuance RCA Debentures	1,532,300	2,635,200	4,167,500
	$11,554,000	$6,146,000	$17,700,000

It is apparent that some progress was made toward a settlement along these lines, since one of the votes passed at the meeting of the board was as follows:

"After a full discussion of the matter it was the judgment of the board of directors that, provided mutually satisfactory terms can be arranged between the Radio Corporation of America and the General Electric Company and the Westinghouse Electric & Manufacturing Company, that it would be advantageous for this corporation to settle the Government case on the terms suggested by Mr. Neave as counsel of this corporation. This expression of opinion by the board of directors was on the understanding that the General Electric and Westinghouse Companies hold a similar view as to the settlement of the Government case."

Thus another hurdle was surmounted. If the three corporations were actually committing themselves to a settlement, there was hope for Mr. Sarnoff's latest offer.

The minutes of the board of directors contain many other items of business besides the action with reference to the Government case previously quoted, but they had to do with some incidental business transactions.

Sec. 142. An "All Day and All Night" Contest.

On November 10th, Mr. Robertson informed Mr. Sarnoff that a meeting had been held with Mr. Aldrich of the Chase Bank, and others representing the Rockefeller interests, and that the basis of the financial sett ment as between the Radio Corporation and the two electric com: inies was satisfactory to the representatives of the Rockefeller interests, who agreed, so far as their interests were concerned.

Such a message from the chairman of the board of Westinghouse must have been especially heartening to the president of the Radio Corporation as he prepared to take the settlement into its final stage —sanction by the Department of Justice. Mr. Neave had already gone to Washington to report the latest developments to the Attorney General's office.

Judge Olney conferred with RCA's attorneys on November 11, 1932. The RCA staff had indeed performed prodigies. Many of the agreements called for by Mr. Sarnoff at the beginning of November were now actually in printed form!

Some details were still to come, but the bulk of the job was complete. The following documents were handed to Judge Olney and Mr. Lipman:

> Basic Agreement
> Agreement A-1
> Five letters dealing with period of transition
> Memorandum of Foreign Situation
> Stipulation
> Decree.

It was perhaps inevitable that the representatives of the Department of Justice should endeavor to do a bit of editing of the documents. Edit they did through two days of conferences, yet apparently no material changes were made. The distressing fact remained that on Tuesday the trial was scheduled and much remained to be done before the consent decree could be substituted for trial itself. Mr. Sarnoff had called an extraordinary conference to assemble on Sunday, November 13, 1932.

The climax toward which all the dramatic events of the preceding years had been steadily converging occurred on Sunday, November 13, 1932. On that day, at a meeting which lasted through the day and far into the night, principals and counsel reached general agreement upon all but minor details of the final settlement. That meeting was attended by representatives of RCA, General Electric, Westinghouse and NBC. Mr. Sarnoff had thus far been able to accomplish, in successive campaigns, the establishment of RCA as an integrated unit, possessing manufacturing and selling rights. He now contended that under existing economic and industrial conditions this integrated unit must be made economically strong if it were to survive. A situation had arisen after months of weary struggle, in which there was a

MAJOR EDWARD BOWES
A great radio personality who has retained his popularity since July, 1925.

RUDY VALLÉE
One of radio's outstanding leaders. Under same sponsor since October, 1929.

LOWELL THOMAS
Famous author, traveler and news commentator, broadcasting since 1930.

DR. FRANK BLACK
General Musical Director of NBC since December, 1932.

possibility of virtually freeing RCA from its burden of debts. No record exists of the stirring events of that fateful Sabbath day in November, 1932, but at its conclusion David Sarnoff could point to virtually complete agreements as evidence of the victory he had won.

Two details, minor in their relation to the entire settlement, remained for further discussion. These may be summarized as follows:

1. The question of Mr. Young continuing to sit on the Radio Corporation board, and the position taken by the Westinghouse Company with respect thereto.
2. The question of distribution by the electric companies of their RCA stockholders in such a manner as not to adversely affect the interests of RCA.

The first exception requires explanation. In dealing with the Department of Justice a genuine difficulty had developed over Owen D. Young's service on the board of directors of RCA. The Attorney General had insisted upon absolute and final divorce of the corporations, with no interlocking directorates. Unfortunately, Mr. Young, chairman of the board of the General Electric, was to be automatically ousted from RCA. In spite of pleadings of RCA officials that Mr. Young's services were of great value to the corporation, the most that could be accomplished was permission that Mr. Young might remain for five months. This exception caused Westinghouse representatives, at the meeting of Sunday, November 13th, to protest on the ground of unjust discrimination. If General Electric were to have a representative exempted from the ouster clause [1] then Westinghouse deserved similar treatment. This controversy was finally ironed out by including Mr. Robertson of Westinghouse in the five months' exemption clause.

[1] The clause, when amended to include Mr. Robertson, read as follows:

"ARTICLE III (Consent Decree)

"General Electric Company and Westinghouse Electric & Manufacturing Company, respectively, shall cause all of their officers, directors, employees or agents, who are now members of the board of directors, or other boards or committees of Radio Corporation of America, or of any of its subsidiaries, to resign, within ten days from the date hereof, from such boards and committees, and are hereby enjoined and restrained from thereafter permitting any such officer, director, employee or agent to act as a member of any such board or committee; and Radio Corporation of America and its subsidiaries are likewise enjoined and restrained from thereafter permitting any officer, director, employee or agent of General Electric Company or Westinghouse Electric & Manufacturing Company to become or to act as a member of any such board or committee; provided, however, that for a period of not longer than five months from the date hereof, Owen D. Young and Andrew W. Robertson may continue to serve, at the pleasure of the Radio Corporation of America, as members of the boards and committees of Radio Corporation of America and its subsidiaries, and provided, further, that the Advisory Council of National Broadcasting Company, Inc., so long as its functions shall continue to be merely advisory, shall not be deemed to be a board or committee within the meaning of the foregoing provision."

Sec. 143. The Consent Decree at Last.

There was much to be done before the "peace" of November 13th could be translated into a consent decree. The Department of Justice must give its official approval. The trial date must be postponed for a week. These details were speedily arranged, and the final editing of the papers took place. Since the agreements and other documents relative to the settlement were intimately connected with the so-called "consent decree," the operative date of each was made to coincide with the date of the decree itself—November 21, 1932. Of great significance to this story is the so-called "basic agreement" between the Radio Corporation, General Electric, and Westinghouse Companies. It fills seventeen printed pages. Among important facts recited in this agreement we discover the following:

Radio Corporation of America Owes the Following:

To General Electric Company	$11,695,000
Westinghouse Company	6,243,000
Total	$17,938,000

"The Radio Corporation shall issue or cause to be issued to the electric companies debentures to be dated as of November 21, 1932, and to mature November 21, 1942 . . . in the following amounts:

To the General Company	$1,587,000[2]
To the Westinghouse Company	$2,668,000[3]"

We find in the basic agreement the following significant provision:

"ARTICLE IV.

"Indebtedness.

"The General Company shall release as of the date hereof the indebtedness of the Radio Corporation to it amounting to Eleven Million Six Hundred and Ninety-five Thousand Dollars ($11,695,000), being the balance of a deferred account upon which the Radio Corporation has paid interest from January 1, 1930, to November 1, 1932, at the rate of six per cent (6%) per annum; and the Westinghouse Company shall release, and cause its subsidiary, Westinghouse Lamp Company, to release, as of the date hereof, the indebtedness of the Radio Corporation to the Westinghouse Company and its subsidiary, Westinghouse Lamp Company, amounting to Six Million Two Hundred and Forty-three Thousand Dollars ($6,243,000), being the balance of a deferred account upon which the Radio Corporation has

---

[2] Mr. Sarnoff proposed, on November 9th, $1,532,300, on a smaller estimate of indebtedness.

[3] Mr. Sarnoff's offer, $2,632,200, on a smaller estimate of indebtedness.

paid interest from January 1, 1930, to November 1, 1932, at the rate of six per cent (6%) per annum. The General Company and the Westinghouse Company shall each execute and deliver, or cause to be executed and delivered, to the Radio Corporation such receipts, releases or other evidence of such release as may be required by the Radio Corporation. The Radio Corporation shall pay interest on said accounts up to the date hereof."

Sec. 144. Leases and Agreements Accompanying Decree.

The following documents were officially approved by the Department of Justice, on November 21, 1932:

(1) Stipulation (5 pages)
(2) Consent Decree (10 pages)
(3) Basic Agreement (17 pages)
(4) Agreement A-1 (50 pages)
(5) Exhibit B (8 pages)
(6) Exhibit C-1 (2 pages)
(7) Exhibit C-2 (2 pages)
(8) Exhibit C-3 (2 pages)
(9) Exhibit C-4 (2 pages)
(10) Exhibit C-5 (3 pages)
(11) Exhibit D-1 (17 pages)
(12) Exhibit D-2 (13 pages)

It is obvious that nothing beyond a mere summary of the contents of the twelve documents referred to would be appropriate in this volume.

The stipulation recited briefly the contentions of the parties and the fact that the defendants, "without conceding or admitting the truth of the facts or matters alleged by the petitioner, and without any findings of fact," agreed to a so-called consent decree. The stipulation provided for dismissal of the prosecution against the several defendants and incorporated, by reference, various agreements that had been entered into between the defendants looking to the adjustment of equities in reshaping their original agreements to satisfy the Department of Justice.

The stipulation was signed by Attorney General William D. Mitchell and his assistants in behalf of the United States. Attorneys for RCA, NBC, RCA Communications, RCA Photophone, RCA Radiotron, and RCA Victor, signed in due form. The General Electric and International Electric Companies were represented by a second group of lawyers; Westinghouse and Westinghouse Electric International Company by a third group. The Delaware counsel for all three groups was Charles F. Curley.

The Consent Decree

After reciting pertinent facts the consent decree provided that within three months the General Electric and Westinghouse Companies must divest themselves and their subsidiaries of substantially one-half of their RCA common stock "by distributing such shares ratably" to their own holders of common stock, the balance to be disposed of either by distribution as aforesaid, "or otherwise disposed of" within three years. The distribution of shares, moreover, must be without restrictions. Neither General Electric nor Westinghouse was to be permitted to "knowingly sell or transfer to any one interest" more than 150,000 shares of RCA common. Pending disposition of stockholdings, neither General Electric nor Westinghouse should have any direct voting privileges but, at request of RCA directors, might authorize designated proxies to vote their stock at annual or special meetings of the stockholders. The two corporations were forbidden to acquire future RCA stock.

Another significant provision of the consent decree, as previously noted, called for resignation within ten days, from the board of directors of RCA or its subsidiaries, of all "officers, directors, employees or agents" of either General Electric or Westinghouse, except that Owen D. Young and Andrew W. Robertson might continue for a period not longer than five months. RCA and its subsidiaries were enjoined against permitting any person connected as aforesaid with the other corporations to serve on its board of directors.

The defendants were "enjoined and restrained from recognizing as exclusive or asserting to be exclusive any license for the enjoyment of patents or patent rights" in all patents covered by agreements between RCA and General Electric, dated November 20, 1919; between General Electric and Telephone Company, under date of July 1, 1920; RCA and United Fruit Company, dated March 7, 1921; Westinghouse and the International Radio Telegraph Company, signed on June 29, 1921; General Electric, RCA and Westinghouse pact of July 30, 1921; the modified agreement—General Electric and American Telephone "peace terms" of July 1, 1926; General Electric-RCA-Westinghouse compact of June 11, 1929 and the "Unification Agreement" between General Electric, RCA and Westinghouse Companies of January 1, 1930. Thus, every important cross-licensing contract, by which exclusive licenses had been granted, was modified by the consent decree. The parties were forbidden to enter into new combinations, agreements or understandings, "in restraint of interstate or foreign commerce of the United States in violation of the anti-trust laws" of the same.

There were final provisions as to periodic reports to the Government on progress achieved in carrying out the provisions of the consent decree. The decree itself was signed by Justice John P. Nields, of the U. S. District Court of Delaware, on November 21, 1932.

The Basic Agreement, some provisions of which have already been quoted, was a new compact between the Radio Corporation of America, the General Electric Company and the Westinghouse Company. One of its provisions was that the electric companies should divest themselves of stock ownership in RCA, in accordance with provisions of the consent decree. It also provided that certain exclusive licenses be changed to non-exclusive licenses. The indebtedness of RCA was stated as $11,695,000 to General Electric, and $6,243,000 to Westinghouse. It recited, furthermore, that RCA and its subsidiaries, NBC and RKO, had leased certain space in a projected building at Rockefeller Center which, due to changed economic conditions, would be manifestly greater than the needs of the aforesaid corporations. It appeared that the Rockefeller interests were willing to release the tenants from the excess of space contracted for, in consideration of a stated amount of Class A Preferred Stock of RCA, on certain conditions. These conditions were chiefly that RCA be relieved of certain real estate holdings in New York City, and also of a portion of its indebtedness to the electric companies. The details of settlement may be summarized as follows: (a) License agreements were to be modified. (b) General Electric and Westinghouse pledged themselves to divest themselves of RCA stock "to the extent and in the manner prescribed by the terms and provisions" of the consent decree. They agreed, moreover, to give RCA a primary opportunity to purchase any of its stock that they might thereafter offer for sale. (c) RCA was to transfer to General Electric its building at Lexington Avenue and 51st Street. RCA was likewise to issue debentures—$1,587,000 to General Electric, and $2,668,000 to Westinghouse, the same to be interest free during the first year, with two per cent interest for four years, with a proviso that if RCA's financial condition warranted it the interest would be increased to five per cent. After five years the interest was to be five per cent, the issue redeemable within ten years.

In providing for release of RCA indebtedness the General Electric Company agreed to cancel $11,695,000, and Westinghouse $6,243,000.

The General Electric Company agreed, also, to execute an agreement to NBC concerning the lease to it of certain broadcasting stations. Westinghouse consented to a similar stipulation.

Litigation costs were to be pro-rated: 50% to RCA; 30% to General Electric and 20% to Westinghouse.

Supplemental Agreements

The most important of the supplemental agreements was Agreement A-1 which covered virtually all phases of the future relations between the corporations. Exhibits further clarified the provisions of Agreement A-1 by official letters and notices exchanged between the parties modifying arrangements previously existing between them, the most important of these relating to broadcasting licenses between NBC and the electric companies.

When the consent decree was presented to the court in Delaware, on November 21, 1932, all the contracts referred to above were presented with it. In the stipulation filed in court was the following:

"The Petitioner, by its Department of Justice, has examined all of the Agreements attached hereto, and also the above-mentioned Substitute License Agreement (B2) and Agreements Relating Thereto, and finds no objection to them."

Sec. 145. Net Results of Separation.

The reader will no doubt be interested in a brief analysis of the results achieved in the weeks of negotiation leading to the consent decree. To begin with, when the anti-trust suit was filed in May, 1930, and pressure from the Department of Justice for an unscrambling of the corporate relations began, the Radio Corporation was in grave danger of losing all that it had gained in the so-called "unification agreements." It is not too much to say that, had it not been for the almost fanatical devotion to RCA of its president, David Sarnoff, the corporation might then have gone down in ruin—the common fate of many great corporations in those perilous days. David Sarnoff, by his skill as a negotiator—coupled with a bulldog determination—had achieved the salvation of the Radio Corporation.

He had demanded from General Electric and Westinghouse cancellation of debts, real estate adjustments and patent concessions. In all of these points he was successful. Thus the Radio Corporation was enabled to become strong and financially independent—a young industrial giant that could put its shoulder to the wheel of American industry at a time when stabilizing influences were sorely needed.

Let us now summarize the exchanges of values that took place under the separation:

Financial Exchanges

A cash indebtedness to the electric companies, totaling $17,938,-733.71, was liquidated thus:

(a) Outright cancellation	$8,937,881.94
(b) Lexington Ave. Building	4,745,360.62
(c) Debentures to General Electric	1,587,456.22
(d) Debentures to Westinghouse	2,668,034.93
	$17,938,733.71

By this transaction, moreover, RCA was relieved of real estate which at the time was sustaining operating losses.

Patent Rights

RCA Received

1. Return of non-exclusive licenses under its own U.S. patents for all fields, including right to license others (heretofore having had exclusive rights for radio purposes only).

2. Subject to reservation in 1a, non-exclusive rights under G.E. and Westinghouse and A. T. & T. patents for radio purposes, compensation free, with right to license others and retain royalties, also license and sublicense rights in manufacturing transmitters and transmitting tubes.

3. Non-exclusive licenses to use radio tubes and circuits for certain purposes in fields of power, therapeutics and medical purposes, X-ray apparatus, etc., RCA to pay the usual royalty on sales.

4. Non-exclusive licenses to use radio tubes and circuits for purposes other than named in foregoing—RCA pays the usual royalty to owners.

5. Relief from obligation to manufacture radio sets for G.E. and Westinghouse.

RCA Gave

1a. Consent that G.E. and Westinghouse retain non-exclusive rights under their own U.S. patents for radio purposes, including right to license others under their own patents.

2a. Non-exclusive licenses to make and sell to Federal, state and local governments, radio apparatus under RCA patents, paying RCA the usual royalties thereon.

3a. Non-exclusive licenses from RCA to make broadcasting transmitters for existing G.E. and Westinghouse stations.

4a. Subject to licenses reserved to RCA in #1, royalty-free licenses in fields enumerated in #3, with right to grant sub-licenses and retain royalties.

5a. Non-exclusive in fields enumerated in #4 with right to license others and retain royalties.

6a. G.E. and Westinghouse entitled to license rights in certain fields outside of the radio purposes named, if and when the same may be granted to others, and upon the same terms.

All of the above royalty-yielding licenses were subject to a "favored-nation" clause.

It will be observed that RCA retained the important rights acquired under unification in 1930—the right to manufacture and sell radio apparatus under RCA, G.E., Westinghouse and A. T. & T. patents; to grant licenses and to retain 100% of the royalties. G.E. and Westinghouse were obligated to pay royalties to RCA on radio apparatus manufactured and sold by them under RCA, General Electric, Westinghouse and A. T. & T. patents as a group. In addition, RCA received rights in fields in which it had not theretofore been licensed.

Rights in Foreign Field

Prior to November, 1932, RCA had had very limited manufacturing rights for foreign trade. Under the separation RCA acquired broad and valuable rights in all fields previously exclusive to G.E. and Westinghouse.

Protective Provisions

Under the agreement, G.E. and Westinghouse were given competitive rights to manufacture receiving sets and receiving tubes. This right, however, could not be exercised within two and a half years following the consent decree, thus affording a transition period. It is important to note that under this agreement G.E. and Westinghouse, that had, prior to 1930, shared in royalties received from all sources by RCA, were now themselves obliged to pay the usual royalties to RCA. As a matter of fact, they are today paying royalties under this provision to the Radio Corporation. There was also another protective provision in the agreement: General Electric and Westinghouse could not sell "A" or "B" preferred stock of RCA without giving the Radio Corporation an opportunity to buy it—thus protecting it against stock dumping.

Broadcasting Agreements

Under the terms of the settlement RCA's subsidiary, the National Broadcasting Company, was further strengthened by obtaining the right to program the stations owned and operated by General Electric and Westinghouse. Thus, NBC's network programs had greater basic coverage, advantage resulting in the sales of time for sponsored programs.

In a final analysis of the November, 1932, settlement we discover that RCA really gave up but one important right—exclusivity of manufacturing privileges under the patents of the Radio Group. Even here RCA's surrender was slight, since licenses had already been granted to a large group of radio manufacturers who now pay royalty to RCA. General Electric and Westinghouse are now included in this group.

In the industrial crisis of November, 1932—the beginning of the blackest period in the industrial history of America—to shake off nearly eighteen million dollars of debt, to unload a burden of unprofitable real estate, and to combine in one company a complete research, manufacturing and sales broadcasting and communications organization, was an achievement of incalculable benefit to the Radio Corporation.

Sec. 146. RCA's Economic Triumph.

It is possible that the foregoing summary of negotiations has failed to throw into relief the ultimate results of settlement of the Government suit upon RCA's economic position. These results may be summarized as follows:

Prior to 1930, RCA possessed exclusive selling rights under the radio patents of RCA, General Electric, Westinghouse and American Telephone & Telegraph Company. Of its own accord, however, the Radio Corporation shared such rights with others through its policy of granting licenses for the sale of sets, beginning in 1927, and for the sale of tubes, beginning in 1929. During the same period, General Electric and Westinghouse possessed exclusive radio set and tube manufacturing rights and were manufacturing such apparatus for RCA. General Electric and Westinghouse, likewise, had instituted a licensing policy and began to license set manufacturers in 1927 and tube manufacturers in 1929. Thus RCA, General Electric and Westinghouse acted together in granting the aforesaid selling and manufacturing licenses and, prior to 1930, RCA received 60% of the royalties collected thereon.

Upon unification in 1930 RCA issued to General Electric and Westinghouse 6,580,375.1 shares of its common stock and received in return, among other considerations:

(1) A release from $32,000,000 of indebtedness, plus interest due.
(2) Plants, machinery and equipment for the manufacture of radio apparatus, inventories and work in progress. This property had a depreciated book value on the books of General Electric and Westinghouse of over $13,000,000.
(3) Stock of RCA Photophone, NBC and General Motors Radio Corporation. All of the foregoing was carried on the RCA books at a total valuation of approximately $40,000,000.
(4) The right to retain 100% instead of 60% of the royalties to be received from licensees in the radio field under the patents of RCA, General Electric, Westinghouse and American Telephone & Telegraph Company.
(5) Exclusive licenses to manufacture radio devices, except transmitting apparatus, under RCA, General Electric, Westinghouse and American Telephone & Telegraph Company patents. RCA formerly had no manufacturing rights in this field.
(6) Miscellaneous considerations such as the good-will of the General Electric and Westinghouse manufacturing business, highly trained and experienced personnel, and the like.

At the time of unification no specific valuation was placed upon the manufacturing rights received by RCA. It is apparent, however, that the value of these rights did not lie in their exclusive nature. RCA's difficulties prior to unification had not resulted from its lack of *exclusive* manufacturing rights, but rather from its utter lack of manufacturing rights. The true value of these rights lay in the fact that through their acquisition, RCA became a fully integrated unit in the sense that it, through subsidiary companies, could now manufacture and sell radio apparatus, electric phonographs, and talking moving picture apparatus. Another extremely important feature of unification was the fact that RCA became entitled to retain 100% of the patent royalties paid by licensees.

When negotiations leading to separation opened in September, 1932, all business was in the throes of an unparalleled depression. Despite the obvious advantages to RCA in its new position as an integrated company, it found itself burdened with a large debt and with unproductive real estate holdings.

It was under these circumstances that David Sarnoff had made his original proposals to the Electric Companies with respect to settlement. He was greatly handicapped in negotiations at this time because RCA needed many things and was not prepared to pay heavily for them. Using to the utmost the mutual desire of the parties to settle the Government suit and drawing still more upon his experience as a negotiator, Mr. Sarnoff entered upon his task.

As the separation negotiations proceeded, it became apparent that RCA would be able to retain the major gains of unification, such as the following:

(1) The release from $32,000,000 of indebtedness, plus interest due.
(2) Plants, machinery and equipment for the manufacture of radio apparatus, inventories and work in progress which, in 1930, had a depreciated book value on the books of General Electric and Westinghouse of over $13,000,000.
(3) Stock of RCA Photophone, NBC and General Motors Radio Corporation.
(4) The right to retain 100% instead of 60% of the royalties to be received from licensees in the radio field under the patents of RCA, General Electric, Westinghouse and American Telephone & Telegraph Company.
(5) Miscellaneous considerations such as the good-will of the General Electric and Westinghouse manufacturing business, highly trained and experienced personnel, and the like.
(6) Licenses to manufacture radio devices under RCA, General Electric, Westinghouse and American Telephone & Telegraph Company patents.

The sole loss in separation was of exclusive rights. But, as stated above, exclusivity in and of itself had not been of primary importance at unification. In view of the licensing situation, the loss of exclusivity meant only that RCA had two additional manufacturing and selling licensees.

To offset its loss of exclusivity, which RCA had not in fact exercised for many years, RCA received valuable additional considerations at the time of separation which it was believed more than compensated for anything that it may have surrendered. These additional considerations may be summarized as follows:

(1) Licenses to manufacture transmitters and transmitting tubes, with the right to grant licenses to others. *Prior to separation RCA had no rights in this field.*

(2) The return of non-exclusive licenses under its own United States Patents for all fields, including the right to license others. *Prior to separation, RCA had no rights whatsoever under its own patents in the fields of power, therapeutic and medical purposes and negligible rights in any other field, other than the field of radio purposes.*

(3) Valuable additional rights in foreign countries plus the recapture of rights under its own patents in foreign countries.

(4) Through the transfer of 570 Lexington Avenue, relief from an operating loss which was estimated at the time at $200,000 annually. Valuable modifications of lease commitments of RCA and certain of its subsidiaries in Rockefeller Center, were also secured through negotiations closely connected with the separation negotiations.

(5) Release from approximately $18,000,000 of indebtedness through the cancellation of approximately $9,000,000 thereof and the issuance of debentures and the transfer of real estate for the remainder.

(6) The execution of valuable agreements relating to broadcasting stations, representing substantial profits annually for RCA's wholly-owned subsidiary, NBC.

(7) A transition period during which RCA would be able to adjust itself to the competition of two additional licensees.

(8) An agreement whereby General Electric and Westinghouse companies would pay to RCA, royalties at the same rate as paid by any other company licensed under RCA patents to manufacture and sell radio devices. Thus, instead of the General Electric and Westinghouse companies receiving from the RCA part of the royalties paid to them by licensees—as had been the case prior to Unification—General Electric and Westinghouse companies had now agreed themselves to pay such royalties to RCA.

(9) Settlement of the Government suit and avoiding the risks and expense it entailed.

It is not difficult to understand why RCA did not press General Electric and Westinghouse for return of the stock received by them at unification after it became evident that RCA would eventually prevail in the contest. At the time of unification, RCA stock had been selling on the market at about $40 per share. At the time the afore-mentioned settlement was reached, in the latter part of November, 1932, the same stock was selling at $6 per share. The return of the en-tire stock without the considerations listed above would have been far less beneficial to RCA than the settlement actually made. Indeed, when one observes the whole picture, before, during and after separa-tion, one cannot escape the conclusion that RCA was the company that gained the greatest advantages in this stoutly contested and long drawn economic controversy.

CHAPTER
NINETEEN

Radio and the Industrial Depression

Section 147. Columbia Broadcasting System Makes History.

WHEN THE COLUMBIA BROADCASTING SYSTEM had been under William S. Paley's personal direction for a year or so the general public began to realize that it was likely to be a permanent institution—a stabilizing force in the radio broadcasting industry. Despite the youth and the disarming good nature of the president of the corporation it was soon perceived that he was a man of ability, skillful in industrial bargaining and possessing unusual foresight. He seems to have had a natural flair for high finance. An important business transaction, entered into in September, 1929, was later to demonstrate his soundness of judgment and to prove him a match in a contest of wits for no less a veteran than Adolph Zukor, of the great Paramount-Publix Corporation.

Despite the fact that during the latter months of the boom period prosperity had existed generally in the amusement industry, far-seeing executives in the moving picture field were beginning to experience uneasiness over the growth of radio broadcasting. Radio sets in millions of homes might wean many people from going to movies. Mr. Zukor evidently decided that the young man who was making such progress with Columbia was worth cultivating. In the summer of 1929 the Paramount representative approached Mr. Paley with a suggestion of an alliance. Paramount wished to acquire a half interest in Columbia.

An alliance with Paramount might bring prestige to the youthful network—Hollywood talent to Columbia's microphones. The proposal was intriguing—until the financial phase of it was reached. Adolph Zukor offered the medium of exchange that is used by great corporations—shares of stock. For a half interest in Columbia he finally proposed to exchange 58,823 shares of Paramount-Publix stock. This stock was then at its peak—$65 a share—and the offer meant $3,800,000 worth of stock.

It is evident that shrewd negotiations preceded the final stage of bargaining. When the transaction was consummated, in September, 1929, each man held an important concession from the other. Mr. Paley had a guaranty from the movie magnate that on March 1, 1932, Paramount-Publix would repurchase the stock at $85 a share, conditional, however, upon a guaranty that he had been obliged to give to Mr. Zukor. This guaranty was the seemingly impossible proviso that before March 1, 1932, Columbia should earn a net profit of at least $2,000,000. Should Columbia fail to make a profit of such dimensions, then Paramount-Publix would be under no obligation to redeem its stock.

It is now well known that Columbia earned nearly $3,000,000 net before the time set for the repurchase of the Paramount stock. In the meantime, Columbia's stock had greatly appreciated in value, whereas Paramount stock had plummeted from $65 to $9 a share. As might be expected, Paramount did not have the cash to repurchase its stock, which fact no doubt aided a secret plan of Mr. Paley. It put him in an excellent position to bargain with Paramount. He and his friends now held only half of the CBS stock. They desired to get back into their own hands the huge block of shares held by Paramount. The upshot of the affair was that they redeemed the entire lot, incidentally paying Paramount more than the valuation set upon it in September, 1929. Thus, Paramount, already on the toboggan that was to land it in the mire of insolvency, received over $5,000,000 in cash.

Going back to the year 1929 we find President Paley executing another master stroke. Major J. Andrew White had hitherto been in charge of station relations for CBS. He had accomplished noteworthy results. An opportunity presented itself, however, to secure for this highly important position a member of the Federal Radio Commission itself. The commission was more or less overworked. Commissioner Sam Pickard was offered the attractive position of vice-president of CBS, in charge of station relations. In February, 1929, Pickard became a member of Columbia's official family.

An important addition to the Paley staff came to CBS in 1930—Edward Klauber. Mr. Klauber had been the night city editor of *The New York Times*. Radio broadcasting, however, had stronger appeal than the editorial-room routine. Although gifted with the pen—a creative writer—he could see in radio greater scope for his abilities. His newspaper training had given him an understanding of men— and women—which rendered him an especially valuable addition to Columbia, since it had to deal with artists and prominent personalities who are not easily managed. Mr. Klauber could say "no" even to his chief whenever the latter's enthusiasm for a project grew too exuberant. President Paley quickly recognized Mr. Klauber's ability as a business executive. He was presently made executive vice-president.

In this same year, Laurence W. Lohman became vice-president in charge of operations and Hugh K. Boyce, vice-president in charge of sales. Mr. Boyce continued in this capacity until the autumn of 1938.

It is probable that next to Mr. Klauber in importance of contribution to the upbuilding of the Columbia Broadcasting System would stand the second vice-president in the list as printed in the 1939 Annual Report—Paul W. Kesten. Mr. Kesten has had charge of promotional activity, an exceedingly important phase of the development of a nation-girdling broadcasting network. Mefford R. Runyon, former treasurer, is now a vice-president in charge of owned and operated stations. W. B. Lewis is vice-president in charge of programs. Herbert V. Akerberg is now vice-president in charge of station relations, while

VLADIMIR K. ZWORYKIN
Inventor of the Iconoscope and other
epoch-marking television devices.

PHILO T. FARNSWORTH
Inventor of the Farnsworth System of
Television.

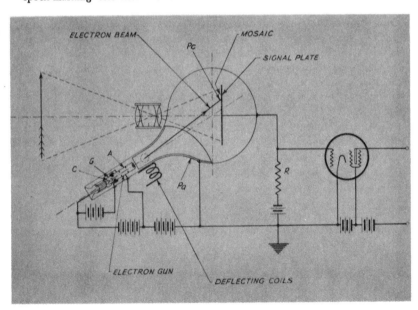

THE ICONOSCOPE
Dr. Zworykin's famous invention. The diagram illustrates the text in
Section 173.

Laurence W. Lohman occupies the responsible post of vice-president in charge of operations. Vice-presidents are apparently very active members of Columbia's official family. Three of them are in charge of important districts—Harry C. Butcher in Washington; H. Leslie Atlass in Chicago, and Donald W. Thornburgh in Los Angeles. Joseph K. White is treasurer and Joseph H. Ream is secretary. Ralph E. Colin, who figured in Columbia's early history, is general counsel, while Joseph H. Ream is general attorney. Frederick A. Willis, whose early activities at Columbia were in connection with the American School of the Air, is now assistant to the president.

Another man who has contributed to the history of radio development is Arthur Judson, one of the founders of Columbia. Prior to 1926, Mr. Judson had long been prominent as a booking agent for artists of grand opera and concert stage. Mr. Paley realized from the beginning of his radio career that musical programs of high quality were essential to the upbuilding of a great network. In order to ensure a supply of dependable talent, an Artists Bureau was established in 1929. A year later, however, it was decided to organize a CBS subsidiary to be called Columbia Concerts Corporation. Arthur Judson became president, a position which he still holds. Under his management the Concerts Corporation has prospered greatly and is now a very strong organization, with an extensive clientele of outstanding artists.

The Columbia Broadcasting System has not neglected the field of public education in music appreciation. Its Sunday Philharmonic concerts, a sustaining program, has won great acclaim by music lovers generally. The artistry of Columbia's offerings, both sponsored and sustaining programs, has long been a conspicuous feature of CBS broadcasting. Columbia's School of the Air is another noteworthy contribution to enlightenment of the general public.

Sec. 148. Radio Corporation Attains Complete Independence.

The consent decree having been officially promulgated, the Radio Corporation took immediate action to carry out its terms. A special meeting of the RCA board of directors was held on November 22, 1932. One of the first items of business was action upon certain changes in directorate called for by the terms of the consent decree. The following resignations from the board were received and accepted—in each case with expressions of regret: Gordon Abbott, Paul D. Cravath, Albert G. Davis, Frank A. Merrick, Edwin W. Rice, Jr., Harold Smith, and Gerard Swope. Except for Owen D. Young of the General Electric Company and Andrew W. Robertson of Westinghouse, the RCA board was now composed entirely of Independents. Thus the way was cleared for the great moment when the Radio Corporation of America should attain complete independence. To quote from the minutes of the meeting:

"The president thereupon informed the board that the matters and things authorized by the board in the meeting of November 14, 1932, had been duly and fully performed; that the stipulation authorized had been signed and the consent decree based thereon had been entered. He thereupon laid before the board a copy of the consent decree entered on November 21, 1932, and of the stipulation on which the decree had been based. He pointed out that to the stipulation laid before the Court there were attached copies of the Basic Agreement, and as Exhibit A thereto the Patent License Agreement," etc., enumerating the various documents. The board thereupon, by formal vote, accepted and approved the settlement of the anti-trust suit.

Before dismissing the topic of separation it should be noted that on the same day, November 22, 1932, the National Broadcasting Company underwent a change in its board of directors. The following action was taken: the resignation of Melvin A. Traylor was received and accepted, with regret. Cornelius N. Bliss was thereupon elected in his stead. Paul D. Cravath was succeeded in like manner by Frederick Strauss. Gerard Swope then resigned and Mark J. Woods was elected in his place, obviously a temporary "holding of the line," since Mr. Woods was to resign three weeks later. Andrew W. Robertson, Edwin M. Herr and Frank A. Merrick quit the NBC board at this same meeting. Mr. Sarnoff, who presided, made a recommendation that no action be taken at the time to elect their successors. It was so voted. Appropriate action was taken on a plan for modification of the Radio City lease and also for the ratification of the settlement under the consent decree. It will be remembered that a new broadcasting setup was provided for in the settlement itself which enabled the National Broadcasting Company to expand its activities.

The economic situation in the United States was by this time in a very grave condition. The election had done much to unsettle public confidence in the future of the nation. The campaign had been very largely waged by radio—millions of people forming their opinions of candidates and issues by listening to the family radio set. The Hoover Administration, which had begun when prosperity was at its peak, had encountered the world depression and the disaster that usually overtakes the administration in power whenever such depressions occur. Mr. Hoover had this cross to bear, and his radio voice had reflected the woes that beset him. He protested that the election of his opponent would bring dire disaster upon the nation. He pictured grass growing in the public streets. Millions of people believed him, yet more millions accepted the promises of his opponent, and so the election had gone to Franklin D. Roosevelt.

The Hoover millions, however, included a large sector of financial and industrial leaders whose apprehensions for the future had no doubt been heightened by the gloomy utterances of campaign orators. The psychology of the hour laid a palsying spell upon the nation. Industry slowed down. Bank failures became epidemic throughout the land. Perilous weeks lay ahead before the old administration could lay down its burdens and the new administration begin its duties.

Thus the Radio Corporation, during the first weeks of its independence, faced appalling financial and industrial problems. At the year's end an audit of its books disclosed that RCA's gross income for 1932 had been $67,361,142, as against $102,645,419 gross income in 1931; $137,037,596 in 1930; and $182,137,738 in 1929. RCA had suffered a net loss for the year 1932 of $1,133,585 despite heroic efforts at retrenchment.

The theatrical world was now in utter chaos. The great Paramount-Publix chain of theaters had long been tottering. On January 26, 1933, it crashed—an event that spread dismay from one end of the nation to the other. Unable to secure financial backing from any source RKO, on the day following the Paramount-Publix collapse, went into receivership. The aggregate investment of RCA in RKO on January 27, 1933, was $16,365,558. Although the Radio Corporation had been unable to stave off receivership for RKO it now, nevertheless, strove to protect its investment by keeping the two Radio City theaters in operation. In order to do so RCA loaned $300,000 to the companies operating the theaters.

Sec. 149. RCA and Its Contest with ERPI.

In considering the whole topic of the Radio Corporation's financial relations with RKO the fact should not be lost sight of that one of the primary purposes of the relation was to provide a market for RCA's sound picture industry and to enable it to compete with the Western Electric Company's ERPI which had entered into contracts with almost the entire industry before RKO was formed.

David Sarnoff, in a statement made to RCA stockholders at their annual meeting, explained the situation:

"One of the main purposes of the investment was to provide at least one major motion picture producing and reproducing organization free to use RCA equipment in the motion picture field. RCA had developed a sound-on-film system of recording and reproducing of motion pictures, but when its apparatus was ready for the market it found that nearly all the large producers and exhibitors of motion pictures were under contract to others, with the result that RCA found itself substantially without a market for its equipment. In RKO such a market was found."

Thus, despite the "frozen investment" and certain actual losses that occurred in connection with the RKO, the Radio Corporation nevertheless attained its objective. Despite receivership of RKO, RCA received substantial amounts in royalties and sales of sound-on-film apparatus. Best of all, the RKO "bridge," however flimsy, enabled RCA to cross to a firmer shore and eventually to win a very strong position in world-wide competition in sound-on-film apparatus.

As previously has been indicated, the indirect beneficial return to the Radio Corporation through RKO channels has been very great. In terms of stimulation of sales in a critical depression period—in advertising value of the relation—and the fact that RCA was enabled through RKO to win a strategic position in the great industry of motion pictures we may perhaps conclude that the whole transaction has been beneficial to the Radio Corporation.

Let us now consider some of the details of RCA's great duel with the American Telephone Company for a "place in the sun" in the motion picture industry. It is well known that both corporations followed the custom of utilizing subsidiaries to develop and operate any highly specialized activity. The Western Electric Company had long been the Telephone Company's electrical manufacturing subsidiary. After the research department of the Western Electric Company had developed a system of sound and motion pictures through the use of phonograph records a new subsidiary was created by it—Electrical Research Products, Inc.—which became known as ERPI. It has previously been noted [1] that the latter organization very promptly "signed up" the five largest motion picture producing firms then in existence. By the terms of the agreement Western Electric recording apparatus was to be installed in all studios and reproducing apparatus in the theaters of their vast chain of movie houses.

We have previously observed that ERPI achieved this master stroke in 1927, leaving RCA's Photophone Company with only ten per cent of the motion picture industry as potential customers. This explains why the captains of RCA's hosts decided to interest themselves in RKO as a means of winning a truly competitive place in the motion picture industry. RKO owned an extensive chain of vaudeville and motion picture theaters. By transforming these theaters into high-fidelity talking picture houses RCA believed that it might eventually make substantial headway in the industry.

It was natural that RCA's activities should for some time have been confined to the motion picture sector represented by RKO. The time came, however, when it was ready to move out into broader fields— that it should encounter ERPI in a competitive way. Then an omi-

1 See Chapter Fifteen, Section 116.

nous potential obstacle became real. The contracts that the latter corporation had concluded with producers and theaters contained such restrictive provisions that unless RCA could find some means of forcing ERPI to release its licensees from such provisions there could be no opportunity for the Radio Corporation to do business with them at all.

ERPI producer licensees, for example, were required: (a) To pay patent royalties to ERPI on all films distributed by them, including films made by RCA licensees; (b) To pay patent royalties on films utilizing any ERPI patents or technical information, even if the producing equipment were furnished by others; (c) To install ERPI equipment in studios and theaters owned by them; (d) To distribute pictures produced by ERPI apparatus only to the theaters equipped and approved by ERPI.

There were other regulations as well. Theater licensees were required to purchase parts from ERPI. These requirements were not considered justifiable because, by cross-license agreements between the Radio Group and the Telephone Group, the RCA apparatus was fully licensed under the patents of the Telephone Group, including ERPI. All in all it was a highly exasperating situation. Negotiations seeking peaceful settlement continued for some time but were unsuccessful. After long and careful investigation of the effect of the ERPI contracts, Mr. Sarnoff and his associates became convinced that legal action would be necessary. Accordingly, a formal complaint was drawn up by RCA counsel alleging unlawful restraint of trade on the part of ERPI. Before filing the complaint, however, the American Telephone Company and ERPI officials were permitted to inspect a copy of the document. The result was that in the latter part of 1935 ERPI officials informally agreed to eliminate the features complained of.

Accordingly, an agreement, dated December 26, 1935, was concluded between RCA on one side and the American Telephone Company and its subsidiaries on the other that gave RCA new and substantial rights. Non-exclusive licenses in a wide variety of fields were received by RCA, as well as the right to grant sub-licenses to others in some fields. The rights received included non-exclusive licenses having to do, for example, with wireless telephony apparatus to be used on shipboard; wireless telephone shore stations for ship-to-shore communication where American Telephone facilities are inadequate or lacking; wireless telephone apparatus for use between stations on land and airplanes or other automotive vehicles; radio and wire broadcasting; submarine signaling; therapeutic and medical apparatus; public address systems; power purposes and household devices; railway signaling; submarine signaling; vacuum tubes and their uses; phonographs; sound recording and sound and picture records themselves.

In some of these fields RCA granted non-exclusive licenses to the Telephone Group.

In addition to the foregoing concessions ERPI wrote letters to its licensees releasing them from the objectionable features of the contracts. Among the more important of these corporations were such well-known producers as Columbia Pictures Corporation, Warner Brothers, Inc., and Twentieth-Century-Fox Film Corporation. ERPI also undertook to give general notice of the abandonment of objectionable features of its license policies.

The above transaction marked the turning point in RCA's campaign to establish itself in a competitive position with ERPI. While the issue, in the last analysis, must necessarily hinge upon the relative merits of the sound recording and reproducing devices manufactured by the rival organizations it is significant that within a year and a half after the settlement of December 26, 1935, President J. E. Otterson of ERPI wrote [2] to Edgar S. Bloom of the Telephone Company the following:

"In the talking motion picture field they [meaning RCA] are competing very actively with us at present, as you know, to develop an affiliation with the large motion picture producers, and competition between us all will doubtless ultimately result in a situation highly favorable to the motion picture interests and opposed to our own."

Recent developments have indeed justified Mr. Otterson's fears of successful competition by RCA. Its sound production system is now used by major producers of the nation's motion pictures.

Sec. 150. Radio Earnings in Depression Years.

Attention has previously been called to the part that radio broadcasting played during the weary years of the depression. The development and marketing of popular-priced radio sets have rendered it possible for virtually every home to provide itself with a set. Thus equipped, even the humblest in the land might tap the same sources of radio entertainment that is possible to the rich and mighty—a manifestation of democracy of profound significance. Radio entertainment, being free to all, has undoubtedly done much to make endurable to the American people the ills of the long-continued depression. Radio sets have thus become not only a stabilizing influence but a necessity as well.

While it is difficult to obtain absolutely accurate statistics on the year by year totals of sales of radio sets since the Radio Corporation achieved its independence, yet the following tabulation [3] is believed to be reasonably accurate:

[2] The letter was dated April 29, 1937.
[3] Prepared by O. H. Caldwell, Editor, *Radio Today.*

INDUSTRY TOTALS INCLUDING RCA
(Wholesale Prices—Retail Practically Double)

Year	SETS Quantities	Sales	TUBES Quantities	Sales	Total Dollar Billing Value
1932	2,446,143	$54,374,700	47,453,380	$18,298,700	$72,673,400
1933	4,157,715	71,165,600	62,761,902	23,147,000	94,312,600
1934	4,478,967	94,859,400	63,247,423	23,315,000	118,174,400
1935	6,030,508	128,399,100	75,961,650	26,564,800	154,963,900
1936	8,320,559	170,853,300	98,304,208	31,942,400	202,795,700
1937	8,083,144	165,390,800	92,055,700	29,870,900	195,261,700
1938	7,107,406	111,914,400	74,690,527	23,093,200	135,007,600

The great popularity of the radio set, even in depression years, not only stabilized the industry but reflected itself in advertising values to radio broadcasting. It is significant that during every year of the depression the National Broadcasting Company and the Columbia Broadcasting System have each rolled up a substantial net profit. The following tabulation is self-explanatory:

Year	NATIONAL BROADCASTING COMPANY Gross Receipts	Net Profits	COLUMBIA BROADCASTING SYSTEM Gross Receipts	Net Profits
1930	$22,161,671	$1,906,370	$ 8,726,884	$ 874,715
1931	29,640,286	2,325,229	14,482,370	2,346,766
1932	29,080,639	1,050,113	15,949,971	1,623,451
1933	24,263,153	507,951	12,402,508	923,794
1934	31,316,793	2,065,301	17,823,387	2,274,119
1935	35,445,571	3,090,807	21,417,182	2,810,078
1936	38,210,749	3,563,668	27,780,300	3,755,522
1937	41,583,339	3,699,386	34,239,896	4,297,566
1938	46,462,086	3,434,301	32,662,993	3,541,741

MUTUAL BROADCASTING SYSTEM

Year	Gross Receipts	Net Revenue
1935	$ 463,857	$ 128,418
1936	1,110,611	546,067
1937	1,650,524	736,656
1938	2,272,662	1,165,132

The story of the Radio Corporation of America, under David Sarnoff's administration since it became a separate entity, is strikingly epitomized by the following from its annual reports:

Year	Gross Revenue	Net Profits	Net Losses
1933	$ 62,333,496.08		$582,093.55
1934	78,756,993.71	$4,249,263.67	
1935	89,228,898.41	5,126,872.55	
1936	101,186,309.90	6,155,936.72	
1937	112,639,497.78	9,024,858.13	
1938	99,968,109.58	7,412,072.42	

Many notable changes have occurred during the period, the obvious tendency being toward simplification and consolidation rather than the earlier trend toward expansion into numerous allied fields, each with a separate subsidiary. The RCA Manufacturing Company, Inc., now combines in itself the activities once performed by RCA Victor, RCA Radiotron and RCA Photophone. The RCA patent department at present includes the research and development activities formerly exercised by the several departments of the subsidiaries above named. The National Broadcasting Company continues to function in its allotted field, with two major networks—the Red Network, with WEAF as the key station, and the Blue Network, served by Station WJZ, as a focal center.

A significant development in the year 1935 was RCA's action in redeeming all its outstanding debentures, amounting to $4,255,000 and a reduction of $1,020,000 in the total of its notes and contracts payable after 1935. Thus the burden of interest payments was substantially reduced. In the same year RCA sold for cash its entire holdings in an English company—Electric and Musical Industries, Limited. Thus $10,255,917 in cash came into its treasury. In the same year it succeeded in selling, as previously indicated, half its RKO holdings, thereby adding to its available cash reserve $5,500,000.

With its heavy debt burdens eliminated and the company restored to profitable operations—the 1934 net profit being $4,249,263, and the net for 1935, $5,126,872—the Sarnoff administration was in a very strong position. It had already accomplished, as before noted, a co-ordination of its various activities. RCA was now in a position to attack its last major problem of reorganization—that of its capital structure.

David Sarnoff was well aware that the industrial depression did not permit the payment of dividends by corporations generally, but he believed that a plan of recapitalization could be worked out that would permit the paying of dividends even to the holders of RCA common, who had never yet in the sixteen years of its history received an RCA dividend. One of Mr. Sarnoff's leading characteristics has been his resourcefulness in emergencies. Dame Fortune, it seems, never knocked but once at his door—or perhaps we might say she never quite reached the door before David Sarnoff was there to accept the proffered opportunity.

The investment market was then depressed, with interest rates lower than when the dividend commitments on RCA's preferred stock had been entered into. Under a plan now proposed by Mr. Sarnoff, the corporation would redeem all its 7% "A" Preferred stock and offer to exchange for each share of "B" Preferred stock one and one-fifth shares of a new $3.50 convertible first preferred stock and one share of Common stock. A special meeting of RCA stockholders was held on April 7, 1936, at which the new plan was approved. From funds in the treasury, and a ten million dollar bank loan, the 7% preferred shares were redeemed. All but two and a half per cent of the outstanding shares of "B Preferred" were exchanged under the plan for the lower-yielding new issue.

The accrued dividends on "B Preferred" were thus reduced from a total of $17,255,182 to $463,391. The annual dividend requirements on preferred stock were thus scaled down from $5,569,100 per annum to $3,235,100, a saving on this score of forty-two per cent. This saving, moreover, would become available for dividends on the common stock.

The subsequent success of the plan is evident from the following: RCA declared its first dividend to common stockholders, in 1937, when there were outstanding 13,853,415 shares of common stock. A dividend of twenty cents a share was paid on this stock, making a grand total to holders of common stock of $2,770,683. The total dividends for the year 1937 were $6,409,226, as compared with $3,222,387 in 1936. The year 1938 witnessed a continuation of dividends to both preferred and common stock, the payments being as follows: to Preferred stockholders, $3,222,743; to Common stockholders, $2,700,724.

Sec. 151. National Broadcasting Company's Era of Change.

It is a significant fact that, within ten years from the beginning of the radio boom, the enterprise had established itself as one of the most stable forces in American life. Radio had changed from amateurish beginnings, with batteries and boxes and gadgets installed in a corner of the kitchen or the "boy's room," to a thing of beauty that visitors might behold in the family living room—had changed from a fad to a necessity. When other industries were closing up shop or going into receiverships radio broadcasting was merely tightening its belt and carrying on. Even in the fateful year 1932, the Columbia

Broadcasting System rolled up an impressive total of net profits—$1,623,451. The National Broadcasting Company, despite its heavy burden of research and its costly expansion program, nevertheless reported net earnings of $1,050,113 for 1932.

The latter corporation was by this time in the throes of internal change. Growing pains are always distressing, and the entire RCA family was experiencing "twinges in the bones." NBC's prospective home at Radio City was in itself a portent of greater changes soon to come within the personnel at 711 Fifth Avenue. The first great change—a major sensation in the family circle—was the resignation of George F. McClelland, the vice-president and general manager of the National Broadcasting Company. This important event was announced, following a meeting of the board of directors, on October 28, 1932.

Needless to say, such an important change in the affairs of a great corporation, especially when the corporation is a subsidiary of a greater organization, does not occur offhand. The cares and burdens of the general manager were great indeed, and Mr. McClelland had carried them for six years. It was perhaps his misfortune to be obliged to compete with William S. Paley of the Columbia Broadcasting System—the brilliant young executive who had come into the field without the commitments and burdens that bogged down the operations of the National Broadcasting Company. It is probably not inaccurate to say that Paley was free to make money, whereas the National Broadcasting Company had been launched by RCA and its allies with an impressive program of research, pioneering, and public service. Columbia, on the other hand, with lighter burdens, could travel a road already cleared. All that NBC had done to educate the business world to the merits of radio advertising, and all the pioneering in other lines that had saddled the older organization with financial burdens, quite naturally benefited Columbia. These facts in no wise should detract from the monumental achievement of William S. Paley in building his network and making it pay impressive dividends.

It was inevitable that the high command of RCA should give thought to a change of administration of the business affairs of the National Broadcasting Company. Curiously enough, a man was selected to succeed Mr. McClelland who had never been identified with the radio industry—the brilliant young Commissioner of Correction of New York City, Richard C. Patterson, Jr. Several weeks before the change was to be effected Mr. Patterson appeared at the 711 Fifth Avenue headquarters as an executive without portfolio to study the general setup. On October 28, 1932, when Mr. McClelland resigned as vice-president and general manager, Patterson was elected to office as executive vice-president of NBC. It should at this time be added that

George F. McClelland was elected at this same meeting to the position of assistant to the president.

It will be remembered that these events occurred at a time when David Sarnoff was in the midst of the final negotiations that preceded the consent decree. No changes of importance at NBC could be expected until other and greater problems had been disposed of. The consent decree was signed on November 21st, and on the following day certain significant events occurred in the board of directors of NBC—resignations from the board of such directors as were affiliated with General Electric or Westinghouse, with the exception of Owen D. Young, as previously noted. By the terms of the consent decree, Mr. Young was permitted to continue on the NBC board for several months.

President Merlin H. Aylesworth continued in office at NBC, yet his time and energies were now divided between NBC and RKO. The new executive vice-president, Richard C. Patterson, Jr., soon began to make changes in personnel at 711 Fifth Avenue. The organization no doubt needed a general overhauling, since it had grown up by a process of accretion around the original amalgamation of staffs of WJZ and WEAF. The Patterson regime, beginning with the dislodgment of the original general manager, was soon to cause uneasiness even to the veterans in the organization at 711 Fifth Avenue.

Richard C. Patterson, Jr., soon began what was gloomily labeled by the persons concerned "a purge"—but under whatever designation it was a thorough process that affected not only those in subordinate positions but others more highly placed. In the case of George F. McClelland we find evidence that the new administration was concerned over its sales organization and disposed to give this popular official an opportunity to reorganize it. On March 22, 1933, a significant development occurred in the board of directors of NBC. On this date Mr. McClelland resigned as assistant to the president and was given the post of vice-president in charge of sales.

In this connection the fact should not be overlooked that the Bank Holiday was then in operation and the nation was in the throes of a great industrial crisis. To place Mr. McClelland at the head of the shock troops of NBC—the sales force—was no doubt a concession to the past and a bid for wavering patronage of commercial sponsors with whom Mr. McClelland was still a power.

Sec. 152. NBC'S Last Months at 711 Fifth Avenue.

It was one of the ironies of fate that befell Owen D. Young when the consent decree of November, 1932, was entered in court. The Department of Justice, in its zeal to eradicate any possible interlocking directorates or the carrying-over of corporate influence, placed every former director or official of the General Electric and Westinghouse Companies on a list of those ineligible to serve NBC—Owen D. Young among them. Now, Mr. Young had been virtually the father of both the Radio Corporation and its subsidiary, the National Broadcasting Company. Each was probably closer to his heart than was the General Electric, since each of them represented the fruition of hopes and plans in which he had been especially interested. Business loyalty and lofty sentiment joined in making Owen D. Young very reluctant to sever his connections with RCA and NBC. A letter exists from Mr. Young to David Sarnoff on this very subject—a long and earnest letter, full of noble sentiments in every way worthy of the man who wrote it. But the consent decree had made the separation necessary, so Mr. Young, in May, 1933, reluctantly, and with deep regret, severed his NBC connections in all respects except membership in the honorary advisory council.

On June 16, 1933, DeWitt Millhauser and Richard C. Patterson, Jr., were elected to the NBC board of directors. Newton D. Baker, U. S. Secretary of War in America's great adventure in European warfare, was likewise elected to the board. Although Merlin H. Aylesworth, in addition to his duties at RKO, continued as president of NBC, the executive vice-president, Richard C. Patterson, Jr., had by this time become its chief executive officer. Reorganization of this and that department resulted in various changes of personnel. However necessary this process may have been it carried dismay to hearts of the pioneers of radio who were still on the NBC payroll.

Although NBC's first years at 711 Fifth Avenue had been characterized by internal friction, caused by merging the old-time rivals, WEAF and WJZ, in the same business organization, yet seven years of association had mellowed these animosities. A spirit of family unity had grown up as well as a genuine affection for the corporate home at 711 Fifth Avenue. The author well remembers the remarkable organization that existed from 1930 to 1933 in the National Broadcasting Building. Elevators opened into a spacious reception room on each floor, presided over by strikingly decorative hostesses. Uniformed page boys were there to escort artists to appropriate studios or to perform this and that necessary service. There was a spirit of friendliness and good cheer not to be encountered elsewhere in great corporations. Even the "Speakers' Studio" at 711 Fifth Avenue was made to resemble a sumptuous drawing room.

The summer of 1933, however, was one of great activity for the NBC family. Home was no longer home but a temporary abiding place. Radio City was now nearing completion, and soon NBC must transfer its operations to the vast structure in which it was thereafter to be housed. Studios and offices had to be planned and equipment built and installed so that the "change over" might be made without interruption in the broadcast schedule.

In the last weeks at the Fifth Avenue home, John W. Elwood, the first secretary of RCA and for several recent years a vice-president of NBC, resigned from the staff on September 15, 1933. This resignation, however, was as nothing in its effect upon the general staff compared with the sensation caused by the resignation of George F. McClelland on October 20, following. McClelland was the last of the prominent "old-timers" of radio—of the office executives who had fought glorious campaigns in the pioneer days of the broadcasting era. Whatever limitations Mr. McClelland may have had as an executive in a highly competitive enterprise, he nevertheless possessed warm human attributes that endeared him to his staff. They had grieved to witness his resignation as general manager of the National Broadcasting Company but now, a few days before the transit to Radio City, his last tie with NBC was severed. He resigned as vice-president in charge of sales.[4]

Sec. 153. Six Years of Progress at Radio City.

The National Broadcasting Company moved from 711 Fifth Avenue to Radio City on November 2 to November 5, 1933. The change from one headquarters to the other was of profound significance to executives and employees. The new offices, the last word in architectural design, were suggestive of the bustle and hustle of radio. There was no homey atmosphere here but, instead, a brisk assembly-line suggestion that could not fail in its psychological effect. Thick carpets on the floors of offices and reception room added to the luxurious appearance of everything but, alas, contributed to the electric

---

[4] The subsequent fate of this popular executive illustrates the hazards of radio. Eleven years in this high-pressure industry had apparently unsettled him for any other calling. Radio was in his blood, so to speak. He could not think of the future except in terms of radio. McClelland at once decided that he would re-enter the radio field on an independent basis. In November, 1933, while NBC was in the act of moving to Radio City, George F. McClelland opened an office at 20 East 40th Street, in New York City, with the intention of setting up a radio network composed of independent stations. To be sure, he had no money and no financial backing save in promises that were destined not to be fulfilled. His plan was to establish a mutual profit-sharing network in which member stations in all parts of the country would be partners. In the eleven months of his effort Mr. McClelland had no office staff save his NBC secretary, Miss Anne Kelley, who had loyally followed him into the new venture. For about six months John A. Holman, of the New York Telephone Company in Albany, who had once been station manager of WEAF, assisted in the task of organization. In June, 1934, Holman, realizing the hopelessness of the undertaking, resigned. McClelland continued until his death on October 12, 1934. A pathetic commentary on the fate of this popular radio veteran is furnished by the success of the idea of a mutual profit-sharing network that he fathered. It has been tried out by the Mutual Broadcasting System—which was being organized at the time of his death. In 1938 it earned a net profit of more than fifty per cent of its gross sales.

atmosphere of the place. To touch a doorknob after hurrying across the aforesaid carpets resulted in a smart electric shock, provided the atmosphere were favorable to the development of static electricity. This condition is true even today—a circumstance that annoyed the author no end during the preparation of this volume, until he learned how to discharge the spark painlessly by touching the door before contacting the doorknob.

At any rate, the new quarters of the National Broadcasting Company, despite the long corridors and the need of a guide at times, soon became familiar ground to the busy staff. The dedication of NBC's new home occurred on November 18, 1933, with a colorful ceremony. David Sarnoff, in London, extended the greetings of the Radio Corporation of America. Owen D. Young, chairman of the board of General Electric, Sir John Reith, managing director of the British Broadcasting Corporation, and General James G. Harbord, chairman of the board of RCA, spoke from the stage of Studio 8 H, on the eighth floor of the RCA building. A dazzling array of artists of stage and screen joined in the celebration—many of them in person and others from distant microphones.

Radio City had received so much publicity during the period of construction that it became at once the Mecca of visitors to New York City. The National Broadcasting Company had long realized that its own activities were of general interest; so, in designing its physical equipment, as much as possible of its technical and operative wonders were made available to public gaze. Much of it was behind plate glass windows fronting corridors along which the awestruck public might be conducted by uniformed guides. The opening of headquarters in Radio City caused throngs of people to seek the privilege of sightseeing tours. Since the Empire State Building had already set the example of charging admission to sightseers, and had derived a tidy revenue for years, the National Broadcasting Company at once resorted to a similar plan. Guided tours, with lecturers to explain the wonders on exhibit, at once became popular. For six years, and at this writing, the conducting of groups of visitors through the broadcasting section and also to the lofty outlook of the high tower of the main building is a thriving business.

David Sarnoff became chairman of the board of NBC in September, 1934, thus bringing into close harmony the policies of the latter corporation and RCA in related matters. The pioneer stage of network building being over, President Aylesworth's talents as an organizer were more and more utilized in connection with RKO, still in receivership and sorely in need of expert guidance.

When the corporation had been organized in November, 1926, the division of responsibility had obviously been necessary. A nationwide task of diplomacy and network building had fully occupied the energies of its able President Merlin H. Aylesworth. As assistant to the president, a general manager of operations, including sale of sponsored time and the thousand and one problems of the two major networks of NBC, was vitally needed. Mr. McClelland had occupied this strategic post for six years. Richard C. Patterson, Jr., his successor, under the title of executive vice-president, had served for three years.

The decision of Mr. Aylesworth, president of NBC, and chairman of the board of RKO, to surrender his burdens at NBC and to confine his energies to the pressing problems of RKO, made it necessary to find a new president for NBC. This occurred in the autumn of 1935. It so happened that at this time Major Lenox R. Lohr had just completed a brilliant task as director of the Chicago World's Fair. The high command of the National Broadcasting Company seized upon the opportunity to engage the services of Major Lohr. At a meeting of the board held on December 27, 1935, the following significant developments occurred: Major Lohr was elected to the board; Mr. Aylesworth resigned as president, and Major Lohr was thereupon elected president in his stead. At this same meeting Mr. Aylesworth was elected vice-chairman of the NBC board.

Even though the new president of NBC had never before been actively engaged in radio he was by profession an engineer. A distinguished record in the World War, followed by seven years of experience as executive secretary of the Society of American Military Engineers, Inc., had preceded his experience as director of the "Century of Progress Exposition" at Chicago. Mr. Patterson continued as executive vice-president for several months while the new president was becoming familiar with the problems of the corporation. On March 27, 1936, Mr. Patterson resigned as executive vice-president.[5]

Mr. Aylesworth continued as vice-chairman of the board and a director of the National Broadcasting Company until September, 1936, thus rounding out ten years of distinguished service to radio broadcasting. Since that time he has been a newspaper executive, but never too busy to join in celebrating new developments in NBC's varied career, as witness the historic inauguration of television service by the corporation at the dedication of the RCA Building at the New York World's Fair on April 20, 1939. NBC's first president was prominent among the dignitaries that graced the occasion.

On November 27, 1936, an event occurred that warmed the hearts of the friends of Edward J. Nally, the Nestor of wireless communications. Although Mr. Nally had reached the age of retirement from

---

[5] Mr. Patterson was appointed Assistant Secretary of Commerce in April, 1938, but it is understood that in July, 1939, he will become chairman of the board of the reorganized RKO, which reorganization was approved in April, 1939.

active business before NBC was organized, yet his continued vigor and his interest in RCA's lively offspring NBC led to his election as a director of the latter corporation. It is a noteworthy fact that the three men who have held the office of president of the Radio Corporation, Edward J. Nally, General James G. Harbord and David Sarnoff, continue to give to both RCA and NBC the benefit of their joint wisdom at the council table. They are in fact warm personal friends and work together in close harmony.

One further change in the official family of NBC should be noted in passing. It will be remembered that Mark J. Woods had been the first treasurer of the corporation. In April, 1934, he was elected assistant executive vice-president and Henry K. Norton had become treasurer, holding the office until September, 1934, when he was succeeded by David Rosenblum. On December 18, 1936, Mr. Rosenblum resigned and Mark Woods was elected vice-president and treasurer, a position that he still holds.

In recognition of the importance of its mission as an educational influence in the life of the nation, the National Broadcasting Company took an important forward step when, on September 1, 1937, it elected Dr. James Rowland Angell, then recently retired from the presidency of Yale University, as its educational counsellor. A well-deserved promotion came to the popular veteran of radio, O. B. Hanson, on November 26, 1937, when he was elected vice-president and chief engineer of NBC.

The advisory council of the National Broadcasting Company continues to function as an important molder of public relations. On January 27, 1939, the following membership was confirmed by the NBC board:

> Owen D. Young (Chairman)
> James R. Angell
> Mrs. August Belmont
> Dr. Henry Sloane Coffin
> Miss Ada Comstock
> Paul D. Cravath
> Walter Damrosch
> John W. Davis
> Francis D. Farrell
> William Green
> General James G. Harbord
> Robert Maynard Hutchins
> Henry S. Pritchett
> David Sarnoff
> Alfred E. Smith

Sec. 154. The Mutual Broadcasting System.

Having surveyed monumental difficulties that beset both NBC and CBS in their first years of operation it is little short of astounding to contemplate the brief but triumphant history of the Mutual Broadcasting System. The plan originated at Station WOR when a prospective commercial sponsor proposed to put on a show that could be broadcast simultaneously over WOR in Newark and WGN in Chicago. He offered to pay each station its standard rate, but insisted that the two stations assume the expense of line charges. The idea was intriguing, and in exploring its possibilities the executives of the two stations quite naturally came face to face with a great idea. Why not organize a small network on a mutual basis? Each station maintained an excellent program department. Each had commercial advertisers who might, with a bit of urging, be induced to patronize such a network. It was evident that through co-operative effort, each station contributing program material and the service of artists, there would be no need of a special network program department. Thus an expensive overhead feature would be eliminated. This was only one of several money-saving ideas that the officials of WOR and WGN worked out in laying the foundation of a mutual network.

George F. McClelland had been working on a similar idea for months, his handicap being that he had no station and no backing. The promoters of this new venture, however, had well-established organizations, background and, best of all, backlog for the launching of the idea. The plan as it ripened at the conference table was for a network whose high officials were to serve without salary from the common venture—each station paying the salary of its own representative in the organization. Wilbert E. Macfarlane of WGN was to be president, and Alfred J. McCosker of WOR would act as chairman of the board.

On September 15, 1934, the Mutual Broadcasting System was formed with the following stations as members: WOR, Newark; WGN,[6] Chicago; WLW, Cincinnati, and WXYZ in Detroit. The first programs of the Mutual Network went on the air from the stations named on October 2, 1934.

It was, of course, inevitable that the work of a genuine network could not be split up between the member stations. The plan was modified to the extent that a general manager was engaged—Fred Weber, an NBC veteran with considerable experience in traffic and program policies of radio networks. Somewhat later, George W.

[6] WGN has since moved to the New York area.

Johnstone, NBC's first publicity director, who had recently joined the staff at WOR, was made director of public relations and special features of WOR and the Mutual Network.

The Mutual Broadcasting System staff is now of modest size, but the overhead expenses are so slight that the network is accomplishing the amazing financial feat of turning in a net profit of more than fifty per cent of its gross receipts—$1,165,132 in 1938 out of a gross revenue of $2,272,662, The present staff at Mutual's headquarters at 1440 Broadway, New York City, in addition to Mr. Weber and Mr. Johnstone above mentioned, are as follows:

Publicity Co-ordinator	Lester Gottlieb
Program Co-ordinator	Adolph Opfinger
Traffic Co-ordinator	Andrew Poole

The term co-ordination is symbolic of the policy of MBS. Co-ordination of program resources, the selection from member stations of program features worthy of network airing, is a responsible task. In some respects this plan has greater potentialities than any single program production plant could have. As already indicated, it is a money-saving scheme that would be hard to equal. In other respects co-ordination is accomplishing noteworthy results for the youthful network.

In 1937 the Colonial Network, the Don Lee Network and the United Broadcasting Company came into the consortium. Independent stations have joined from time to time. The Texas State Network, with twenty-three stations, was one of Mutual's late acquisitions. In May, 1938, it boasted a grand total, in the United States and Hawaii, of one hundred and ten broadcasting stations. The general policy of the Mutual Broadcasting System was explained in the early months of its corporate life as follows:

"The network is to be co-operative, the stations operating the network service, rather than the chain running the stations." This policy, however, in ordinary hands might prove highly demoralizing. The astounding net profit for 1938 conclusively demonstrates that MBS is wisely and ably administered. The officers of this unique network are Wilbert E. Macfarlane of WGN, president; Alfred J. McCosker of WOR, chairman of the board; T. C. Streibert, first vice-president; E. M. Antrim, treasurer and executive secretary; J. A. Cotey, auditor.

CHAPTER
TWENTY

Radio Broadcasting of Today

Section 155. Educational Programs.

THE EDUCATIONAL POTENTIALITIES of radio have been recognized from the beginning of radio broadcasting. Many programs, both sustaining and commercial, have had strong educational characteristics even though not so labeled. Many educational institutions, in early days, however, opened radio stations only to discover that their offerings were not sufficiently appreciated by the public to justify a continuance of the experiment. Some stations have made the mistake of carrying classroom technique to the microphone.

There is much competition on the air. Learned or "highbrow" instruction as such cannot attract and hold a considerable audience. The educational lecturer, if he would be successful before the microphone, must therefore present his message in so attractive a guise that his listeners will keep tuned in because of the human-interest quality of the broadcast. This means that in preparing the material to be presented the radio teacher must bear in mind that entertainment value is of primary importance, since that is the vehicle by which he may convey the message intended. An interesting story, anecdote, or biographical item may each have a rider attached—the message or truth intended to be taught. This is the painless method and, no doubt, the most effective method of teaching by radio.

The earliest form of education by radio seems to have been through the cultural impact upon the masses of truly good music. Grand opera, for instance, that had never before reached the common people except through phonograph records presently became available to radio listeners. To be sure, there was a transition period in which public reaction was tested. Among the pioneers in this field who are still occupying a responsible relation to radio is Franklin Dunham, now educational director of the National Broadcasting Company.

In 1922, Mr. Dunham was in charge of educational activities of Aeolian Hall, in New York City. He at once perceived in radio a new educational possibility. On April 27, 1922, he arranged with Station WJZ, then in Newark, for a recital by Miss Mabel Corlew of the Aeolian Company. This was perhaps one of the first frankly educational attempts in the field of music over the air. It was followed by other Aeolian features, especially after WJZ moved to the Aeolian Building in May, 1923.

By this time Mr. Dunham had become an advisor to the musical department of WJZ. "Literary Vespers" and other attractive musical features of WJZ belong to this period.

After the formation of NBC, Mr. Dunham was chosen as a member of its advisory committee on musical programs. He assisted in arranging details for the launching of Dr. Walter Damrosch's Music Appreciation Hour. Miss Alice Keith seems to have been the chief mover in the project which, by the way, was sponsored during its first year by the Radio Corporation of America. The program was at first known as the RCA Educational Hour, but the title was later changed to its present form.

Turning to frankly educational programs we find that Dr. Levering Tyson, the present director of the National Advisory Council on Radio in Education, was one of the first educators to recognize the significance of the new art in the field of extension courses. Newly assigned to extension work at Columbia University, he was attracted by reports of the KDKA experiments in broadcasting. It was not until after WEAF was well established in New York City that Mr. Tyson had an opportunity to participate in radio work. A series of broadcasts of the poetry of Robert Browning, a WEAF sustaining feature, was the first offering of this nature arranged under the auspices of Columbia University. The first talk in the series, according to the program listings of Station WEAF, occurred on July 17, 1923. They were given by Professor Hoxie N. Fairchild of Columbia University, and were entitled, "Talks on English." [1]

Sec. 156. Schools of the Air.

The Ohio School of the Air, perhaps the earliest ambitious attempt of its kind, was launched by the Ohio State University, January 7, 1929, the Crosley Station WLW co-operating with free broadcasting facilities. In the following year the same University established its famous "Institute for Education by Radio," an annual radio convention of leaders in educational broadcasting. These Institutes have been held every year since 1930.

A second school of the air was established in 1930, largely through the efforts of Miss Alice Keith, who had been chiefly responsible for the Damrosch program. She had endeavored to interest the National Broadcasting Company in the project, but the Advisory Council had frowned upon it. A sponsor, however, was found—the Grigsby-Grunow Company—and it was launched over the Columbia Broadcasting System as the American School of the Air, with Miss Keith as broadcasting director, on February 4, 1930. It appears that Columbia assisted in rounding out the daily programs by contributing somewhat of free time on the air. The sponsor, however, soon withdrew from the project and the Columbia Broadcasting System found itself with the project "on its doorstep."

In the meantime, the National Broadcasting Company ventured a bit into the educational field. At about the time the American School of the Air was launched, Vice-President John W. Elwood of NBC,

[1] Archer, *History of Radio to 1926*, p. 321.

then in charge of educational features, invited the author to give a series of talks on "Early Colonial History" to school children who were then listening to Dr. Damrosch's Music Appreciation Hour—the lectures to open in April after the Damrosch series should end. On April 11, 1930, the author began an eight-week series over the Red Network of NBC—some forty stations participating. The first talk was entitled, "Miles Standish and the Redskins," in a series known as "Founding a Nation."

It should also be added that after the history series had come to an end the author, at Mr. Elwood's invitation, gave a series of coast to coast broadcasts on the spirit and purpose of the laws of the land. Beginning in July, 1930, these talks, entitled "Laws that Safeguard Society," continued in fifteen-minute periods once a week for three years until June, 1933. The author's talks on "Early Colonial History" ran contemporaneously in New England and continued without interruption until September, 1934.[2]

The Music Appreciation Hour and the series referred to above constitute but a minor fraction of the educational offerings of the National Broadcasting Company.

Returning to the Columbia Broadcasting System we find that it adopted the orphaned American School of the Air and promptly gave it substance and active support. Frederick A. Willis, now assistant to the president at Columbia, was its first active director. Upon his promotion, Edward R. Murrow was placed in charge. When Mr. Murrow was selected for his present important post as European representative of Columbia the present director, Sterling Fisher, was appointed. Beginning, as did the Ohio School of the Air, with a fairly close approach to classroom instruction the American School of the Air has developed a technique that combines entertainment with instruction. History, for example, combines narration and dramatization. Director Fisher, in an article contributed to *Radio Guide,* for March 4, 1939, gave the following graphic explanation of the scope of the work now being conducted by the American School of the Air:

"Today the 'American School of the Air,' which represents only one aspect of Columbia's many educational series, is heard in some 100,000 classrooms by an estimated 3,000,000 children every day. These include the cosmopolitan groups found in city schools, children sitting at the rustic desks of country schoolhouses, in 'progressive' private schools, Indian children on reservations, and even orphans and the handicapped in private and public institutions. At least four hundred great city school systems have installed radios in

[2] The author's radio talks were given without compensation—a bit of public service in which NBC joined by furnishing radio facilities. More than ninety radio stations participated during the series.

their classrooms and auditoriums, so that the pupils can listen to radio education during the week. The number is constantly growing. Columbia's station KLZ reports that the 'American School of the Air' programs are now being listened to throughout the entire school system of Denver. In Chicago, the 'American School of the Air' is rapidly becoming a regular part of the school curriculum."

Generally speaking, all radio stations in the United States are devoting a goodly proportion of broadcasting time to educational programs. Radio has become a real force in the educational field. It is not improbable that there will be a progressive development in this direction. Fads and novelties grow stale, but worthwhile programs do not.

The British Broadcasting Corporation, which is a monopoly supported by a tax on radio sets, has maintained a School of the Air for many years. Broadcasts to school children, adult education in the form of lectures and general cultural programs such as music, drama and the like have been features of its radio service. Since the corporation is supported in the manner specified, it is perhaps less responsive to the tastes of the multitude. A program committee decides what type of broadcasts may assist in raising the general level of culture and acts accordingly. Brochures and outlines of courses or of broadcasts are made available to the listener.

In Germany, at least prior to the present regime, there was a tendency to dedicate certain stations to educational broadcasts, thus segregating the purely educational broadcasts from the general type. Some European countries have followed the lead of Germany, whereas others have found the English system to their liking. Experience in all countries seems to confirm the belief that government control of radio broadcasting systems is not conducive to progress in the art. Radio thus controlled may easily become an instrument of propaganda in behalf of dictators or government factions.

Sec. 157. The Variety Show Vogue.

In an art so vital and progressive as radio it is difficult indeed to set one's mental camera for a still picture purporting to display its leading characteristics. A moving picture it truly is. Radio audiences, after all, control the program trends of the industry. Program directors may and frequently do offer new features to the radio public, yet the listener really sits in the driver's seat. Listener response, not necessarily by mail or by telephone, determines the development or discontinuance of any type of program.

Just as in the movies slapstick comedy and early crudities gave place to more subtle types of entertainment, so also has radio moved on from one plane to another, each successive stage an advance in the evolution of the art. Since the range of human interest is relatively limited we may expect that, until television becomes an established factor in entertainment from the heavens, the emotions excited by the sense of hearing will be the limit of radio's possibilities. Music will no doubt always play an important part in radio broadcasting.

Notable results in music appreciation by the common people have already been accomplished by the great networks. Dr. Walter Damrosch's splendid contribution to the musical education of the public, in collaboration with the National Broadcasting Company, is an instance in point. Grand opera and symphony concerts have long been broadcast to radio listeners. The Columbia Broadcasting System's Philharmonic concerts have attained great popularity. Sponsored programs, such as the Atwater Kent broadcasts of early days, the RCA Magic Key, and many other notable programs, have offered music of high quality. Radio has undergone great changes in recent years. Few types of programs that were popular ten years ago continue to enjoy public favor.

A notable exception to this rule, however, is the radio variety show inaugurated by Rudy Vallée in October, 1932. To be sure, RKO had done some experimenting in this field by picking up vaudeville programs from theaters, the first of such experiments having occurred on January 22, 1932. The Vallée variety show, however, was designed for the Fleischmann-sponsored program. Its success marked the beginning of the radio variety show era. For more than six years it has continued, with no evidence of waning popularity. The old adage—"Variety is the spice of life"—seems to apply especially to radio entertainment. Here we find, in combination, orchestral music, popular song hits, comedy, drama, the inevitable "gags," and a visible audience in the studio.

This latter feature grew up from the variety show vogue. Unlike some of the early orchestra leaders who occupied the spotlight alone, Mr. Vallée boldly challenged convention by introducing on his program great stars of stage and screen whose popularity with the public led to increased demand for tickets of admission to his broadcasts— studio admission already being an established custom. Since troupers of the stage need the response of a visible audience to stimulate their efforts, studio applause became a necessary evil in connection with the "variety show."

Perhaps it should be noted that although the present-day radio variety show is built around a star performer or orchestra leader yet the production department of an advertising agency is largely responsible for the show itself. The sponsor pays the bills; the advertising agency builds the show and is represented at rehearsals, even in productions by master showmen like the originator of the idea.

Some notable radio variety shows of the past, like that of Ed Wynn, are no longer on the air. A comparative newcomer to the radio scene is at present the reigning favorite—a ventriloquist's dummy, Charlie McCarthy. Edgar Bergen is the ventriloquist and, probably in the history of stage or screen, he has never been surpassed in this field. The wise-cracking, egotistical, romantic, wooden effigy, by Bergen's magic, has become the most popular personality on the air.

Such well-known figures as Jack Benny, Bing Crosby, Kate Smith, Fred Allen, Eddie Cantor, George Burns and Gracie Allen, Kay Kyser and Rudy Vallée are headliners in the present variety show field. In fact there is a considerable list of important programs of this nature on the air. Crossley ratings for April, 1939, indicate that Charlie McCarthy is "tops," and others named followed in the order given. Radio popularity, however, is ephemeral, and the leaders of today may be reshuffled tomorrow.

The latest development in the variety show—the drift toward Hollywood talent—is no doubt attributable to Rudy Vallée. While broadcasting from New York he had drawn talent from Broadway, but when in the Film City, engaged in the making of films, the persuasive maestro began to introduce film stars to his radio audiences. The innovation proved very popular and nowadays Hollywood actors are in great demand. What effect it will have upon the movie industry does not yet appear, although some moving picture producers are up in arms against it for its alleged tendency to detract from the box-office appeal of screen artists.

Sec. 158. Radio Serials—Radio Comedians.

The variety show radio program may and usually does offer a sample of radio drama. The serial sketch on the air is in fact one of the earliest forms of radio programs. Since radio must rely entirely upon the sense of hearing—until television can add the tremendously important boon of sight—it is relatively circumscribed. Everything must be so handled that by the sense of hearing alone the radio listener can follow the plot and share the human emotions intended to be portrayed.

In the early days of moving pictures, serials were found to be effective lures for movie audiences. Week after week devotees followed the adventures of celluloid heroes and heroines. Whether in connection with the "Perils of Pauline" or any other thriller of early days, the device was effective largely because appeal to the sense of sight stirs emotions and imagination. Radio, however, being limited to sound, has been working on problems of mass appeal much less effectively. Dialogue or out-and-out description must be relied upon to conjure up a mental picture of what is supposed to be happening. Characters also must be visualized by the audience to stir sympathy or hatred as the case may be. Obviously, the serial presentation offered, and still offers, the best available means of accomplishing this result with radio audiences. A single quarter-hour broadcast of "Amos 'n' Andy," to take one simple illustration, could not possibly give the listener the illusion of reality that could come from a series of broadcasts showing the development of some of Andy's crazy schemes to attain opulence or glory in Harlem.

Serials in radio have varied greatly in quality and in type, but the aim has always been to leave the listener in suspense even without the bromidic appeal of the sponsor's announcer to listen to the next broadcast and learn what happens to the hero or heroine. Radio serials have run the gamut from the hilarious "KUKU Hour" staged by Raymond Knight in early days to the more sophisticated dramatic offerings of the present time. Some programs that have no serial qualities whatsoever have nevertheless contrived to attract listeners week after week because of an artificial feud going on between two program leaders. Walter Winchell, "who sees all and tells all" started the vogue years ago by criticizing Ben Bernie's program. The "Old Maestro" replied in kind and the "feud" continued. Jack Benny and Fred Allen, at the present time, are working the same audience-stimulating device.

As before indicated, however, the true serial is one in which action is left unfinished in one broadcast and the listener must watch for the next in the series, usually discovering that a new crisis arises that necessitates further attention. Narrative recitals such as those of fiction or history may also effectively employ the device of suspense to hold the continued interest of a radio audience. Various radio artists, however, have developed great listener appeal without employing the element of suspense.

The radio comedian has always been popular with radio audiences, but unless a particular comedian has a good "gag" writer, or can do the job himself, his popularity speedily withers. A joke that convulsed Julius Caesar may still throw a studio audience into a frenzy of thunderous mirth, but it does not have the same effect upon the listening public. It requires more than studio guffaws into the long-suffering microphone to render a "wise-cracking" or "kidding" program permanently popular. It is no coincidence that the Edgar Bergen–Charley McCarthy program stands at the head of the popular radio programs of today. Originality and genuine humor are precious commodities in a world where a limited number of jokes have been grievously overworked. The Crossley poll demonstrates the relative popularity of comedy programs, but even here we find the variety show and the dramatic skit as essential features. This brings us to the realization that radio programs of today, especially the half-hour or hour commercials, are similar to old-fashioned vaudeville. They combine so many diverse features that it is difficult to classify them as preponderantly one thing or another.

The popular programs of the present day are much alike—orchestra, vocalist, comedian, dramatics, wise-cracking, etc., but only one boasts a Charlie McCarthy. It is safe to say that no radio show can develop a new and successful feature without speedily being imitated by others—hence the similarity above noted. It is beside the point that one program is original and the other an imitation. The imitation may indeed prove more popular than the original. After all, the public is fickle. It loves new faces, new voices, change, innovations—and every trouper of stage or screen is painfully aware of this truth.

Sec. 159. Radio Dramatics.

There are those high in authority in radio who believe that radio dramatists are destined to make important contributions to the literature of the drama. John F. Royal, vice-president in charge of programs of the National Broadcasting Company, has expressed to the author his conviction that radio will revitalize American literature. He declares that more and more demands will be made by radio upon American authors and composers in order to supply high-grade material for use on the air. Drama for the theater of the air, poetry and prose for radio programs, songs and music—all will be needed to meet the demands of a mighty industry.

It is certainly true that we have witnessed distinct evolution in radio dramatics during the past decade. A new technique has developed. The "movies" experienced the same process of trial and error from crude beginnings—melodrama of the garish type and slapstick comedy, in which custard pies were all-important—moving picture production progressed upward to the level of perfection that characterizes the better movie of today. Radio had a greater handicap than mere inexperience. Born blind, so to speak, it had to accomplish its results with only one of the five senses—the sense of hearing. Radio dramatists were quick to respond to the needs of the hour.

It is undoubtedly true that the present-day radio listener is less susceptible to the magic of radio. Radio, like all continuing blessings of society, has become commonplace. Increasing skill of the radio dramatist, however, has more than kept pace with this change. One such radio skit, in the autumn of 1938, for example, purporting to portray an invasion of the New Jersey countryside by fierce warriors from Mars, caused a veritable panic among gullible radio listeners over a wide area. This was testimony to the skill of the radio tragedian,

Orson Welles, and also a lesson to the industry that there is such a thing as packing too much high-power melodrama in a radio skit.

A full decade of development lies behind radio dramatics. Love and hate, action and reaction, adventure and more adventure have been the chief themes of the radio drama as of all others. Always there has been the villain and the hero, the criminal and the organized forces of society striving to protect the public from his depredations, to furnish themes for the new type of dramatic productions.

It is a noteworthy fact that the "Lux Theater of the Air," a sponsored program on a Columbia network, stands in third place in the April, 1939, Crossley survey of the most popular features on the air. "Big Town," a dramatized series in which Edward G. Robinson, famous bad man of the movies, enacts for the radio characterization of officers of the law in relentless pursuit of criminals, is seventh in the list of popular programs. These dramatic skits, by the way, are based upon actual criminal cases, just as the series by Warden Lawes of Sing Sing portray the efforts of society to protect itself against the enemies of law and order. "Gang Busters," by Phillips Lord, is another deservedly popular series of the same general nature. In passing, it should be noted that radio is performing a noteworthy service in debunking the popular false conception of the gangster and criminal as Robin Hoods, built up during the Prohibition era, when such gentry were popular at the back doors of thirsty citizens.

Sec. 160. Audience Participation Programs.

·An interesting development of recent years in radio is that of audience participation in studio programs. This custom may possibly have originated with the versatile Major Edward Bowes, whose Capitol Family musical programs have delighted radio audiences for more than a decade. Not content with that triumphant feature, Major Bowes inaugurated an all-amateur program or opportunity night, that became even more popular than his musical program. Acting as master of ceremonies with inimitable wit and repartee that could match even the "wise guys" that presented themselves, the Major soon developed not only an appealing program but was able to organize his amateurs into groups that went on tour and earned real money— for themselves and for the astute originator of the idea.

This was essentially audience participation. Others took it up and developed wide diversity of programs—spelling bees and contests of one kind or another. Programs in which groups of the fair sex compete with men in answering questions are very popular. Not content with studio audience participation, enterprising announcers stage "Vox Pop" interviews with pedestrians on the street, in theater lobbies and elsewhere. Such interviews are a bit hard on the persons interviewed, and radio men are obliged to make allowances. A recent variation of the theme is called "Information, Please!" in which a small group of experts is subjected to questions sent in by radio listeners. Suitable rewards are paid for acceptable questions, and the experts are kept busy indeed on broadcast evenings.

Sec. 161. Forums and Discussions.

Radio has already played a mighty part in shaping national destiny. Political discussions and political addresses by rival candidates have largely supplanted the old style of campaign oratory by candidates for the presidency of the nation. The number of people who could see and hear the standard bearer of a great political party was always very limited. Through the magic of radio and the great radio networks a present-day candidate can project his personality and his views into homes where millions of voters may be listening. A pleasing and persuasive voice thus becomes an asset of tremendous value to a candidate. In state and local elections radio is also of great importance. The cost of radio time, and the fact that people still attend political rallies and love to applaud their candidates, insisting upon seeing them and hearing them talk, conspire to preserve something of the old-style political campaign.

In intervals between elections the radio forum is growing in popularity. Town meetings of the air—some of them on nationwide networks, such as the weekly broadcast over a nationwide network by NBC, known as "Town Meeting of the Air"—are very popular. Many problems of national and international importance are discussed pro and con by speakers of recognized standing, thus giving the people an opportunity to hear both sides of controversial questions ably presented. Judging by current developments throughout the world we may safely assume that this type of program is to occupy more and more importance in American life.

Sec. 162. Reporting the News.

The first great demonstration of radio broadcasting, as we know, was KDKA's initial offering—report of the Harding election returns, on November 4, 1920. Reporting the news has always been a feature of radio broadcasting. These reports vary in length from news flashes of sufficient importance to interrupt some other program for a few seconds or a minute, to the fifteen-minute survey of the news by some famous news commentator. Of course, there is the quarter-hour news period that is featured by most radio stations several times a day, but even this is usually interlarded with commercial plugs—pills and salves, shoes and other forms of physical salvation. Everybody is interested in the latest news, it seems.

The news commentator program has been a continuous feature since vital Floyd Gibbons startled America with his machine-gun utterances about a decade ago. The author well remembers his first meeting with Floyd Gibbons and his surprise at discovering that the famous correspondent actually talked like other human beings. In radio's early days, however, there was much experimentation in methods of delivery. The Gibbons tempo was much faster than that of Walter Winchell, the chief vocal speedster of the present day.

Lowell Thomas is one of America's leading news commentators. For nearly a decade, five nights a week Mr. Thomas has interpreted the news of the world to the American people. He began as news commentator. His whimsical humor has long delighted radio audiences; but judging by a recent performance in describing the search in the jungle for a husband for a captive lady panda, only to discover, when the quest was successfully ended, that the original captive was no lady, demonstrates that Mr. Thomas has increased in stature as a spinner of yarns.

Hans V. Kaltenborn is a news commentator who has made a distinguished record before the microphone. Broadcasting since 1922, he has been news editor of the Columbia Broadcasting System since 1930.

Frederick William Wile was one of the first network commentators on political topics, beginning over WRC, September 17, 1923. He was with the National Broadcasting Company for several years but, in 1929, became associated with the Columbia Broadcasting System, commenting on national and international affairs.

Boake Carter until recently has been a news commentator on a sponsored program, Philco Radio and Television Corporation, the series beginning in 1932. Incisive and positive views on political questions have featured Mr. Carter's appearances at the microphone.

Edwin C. Hill, whose radio broadcast "The Human Side of the News," now sponsored by Amoco, is a feature of present-day broadcasting, began his career at the microphone in 1932.

Dorothy Thompson (Mrs. Sinclair Lewis) is now a prominent political commentator as well as a newspaper columnist whose writings are widely syndicated.

In addition to the news commentator we have the regular radio news service. Newspaper hostility has at times caused considerable difficulty to radio networks in maintaining a news service. In early days the great news-gathering agencies such as the Associated Press, the United Press and International News Service, were quite indulgent toward radio broadcasting. By 1933, however, the clients of the three organizations above named raised such a clamor, radio cutting into their advertising patronage, that the edict went forth that radio stations and networks would no longer have the privilege of news tips from these sources. Radio audiences clamored for the accustomed news service, and so NBC, Columbia, Mutual, and regional networks such as Shepard's Yankee Network in New England, promptly organized news-gathering facilities. A. A. Schechter became NBC's news editor; Paul White held a similar position with Columbia. The effort proved expensive, but after six months of rivalry the American Newspaper Publishers Association apparently took alarm lest radio broadcasting might establish newspapers of its own. An agreement was reached which resulted in the Press-Radio News Service. This service involved brief news bulletins followed by the admonition, "for further details see your daily newspapers."

Sec. 163. Sound on tape vs. Electrical Transcriptions.

The electrical transcription of radio programs has long been resorted to as a means of supplying high-grade programs to stations unable to carry the feature by the so-called "live talent" method. Commercial advertisers have thus been able to employ well-known orchestras or other means of advertising their product, recording the program and sending the same in disk form to radio stations for use on the air. The electrical transcription is an improved type of phonograph record. It is especially designed for use in broadcasting. Radio networks in early days frowned upon any attempt to substitute "canned" music or drama for live talent, but in recent years even the National Broadcasting Company maintains a highly scientific transcription department.

It was perhaps inevitable that advances in the art of manufacture of sound-on-films for motion picture use should sooner or later be applied to program building for radio broadcasting. The transcription method does not lend itself to editing. Motion picture perfection, however, is attained by the most exacting type of editing. A radio engineer, James Arthur Miller, is reported by *Time* for March 13, 1939, as having made very considerable progress in adapting the motion picture system of cutting and editing of films to the needs of "canned" radio programs. To quote from *Time:*

"Engineer Miller's theory is that most radio shows, concerts, interviews, could and should be staged, directed, polished up and edited beforehand, Hollywood style, and then transmitted from recordings. With radio's prevalent system of disk recording, cutting and editing is almost impossible. But with Millertape, a complete, timed-to-the-second radio show can be pieced together by matching approved takes, just as Hollywood film editors make feature films from the results of many days of takes and retakes. Expert editors and retouchers with Millertape can eliminate single words, can even correct lisps and other lingual mishaps.

"Millertape has been used abroad for four years, mostly for BBC and the J. Walter Thompson Agency in London, which records commercial shows in England, airplanes them to Luxembourg and Radio Normandie for airing. Last week Millertape's first big job in U. S. radio was under way; cutting the hour long Ironized Yeast Good Will Hour into half-hour (2,000 foot) recordings for transmission from 46 local stations in the United States and Canada."

This innovation will no doubt encounter opposition from radio listeners who have a prejudice against using transcriptions or recordings over the air. It may also be viewed with alarm by "big time" radio artists who will see in it a threat to radio shows that now go out over great radio networks. Whether this type of program building will ever win sufficient popularity to challenge the live-talent network show is, of course, a matter for time to decide. It does offer possibilities of perfectly timed programs of very high quality for any broadcasting station to be put on the air at a convenient hour without interfering with commercial programs, which is one of the inconveniences of present-day network broadcasting. If the Charlie McCarthy program, for instance, were thus available to all stations to be put on at any time it might, however, lead to curious results. We might encounter the duplication of programs that has arisen in the case of popular songs in the past, when a radio listener has had the misfortune to encounter it on the dial several times within the hour. The author well remembers the nightmare of "The Dream Walking," when every station seemed to have some moonstruck youth burbling it into the microphone whenever one desired to use his radio set. It required real agility to escape the overworked and not over-intelligent refrain.

Sec. 164. Frequency Modulation.

One of the intriguing developments of radio in the year 1939 is a system of broadcasting that has emerged from the laboratory of Major Edwin H. Armstrong, inventor of the feed-back circuit, super-regenerative and superheterodyne receivers and other epoch marking radio devices. The new system is called frequency modulation, or Apex System, as distinguished from amplitude modulation—the system under which present-day radio broadcasting is accomplished. The distinction means much to radio technicians, but to laymen it is just another bewildering scientific abstraction.

Major Armstrong did not invent frequency modulation, which dates back to experimentation with the Poulsen Arc. Many experimenters prior to 1924 had tried their hand at this type of transmission and had each pronounced it unworkable. Major Armstrong refused to accept the verdict and, where others had failed, he eventually demonstrated that by an original method of his own he could harness the unruly element and put it to the use of man. This required years of patient research and the expenditure of large sums—out of the inventor's private fortune—but by 1935 he had so far perfected the system that he was able to announce his method of frequency modulation before the New York section of the I.R.E.

Amplitude modulation utilizes a fixed frequency operated with variable power. If we could visualize the process we might note that the steadily flowing output of energy involved in the amplitude modulation system broadens under the influence of loud sounds but narrows under the mild impact of soft tones. The microphone acts somewhat like a throttle in regulating the energy output of ordinary radio broadcasting.

In Major Armstrong's system the power output would be constant, but the frequency of the broadcast wave would vary over a wide range from a few cycles for soft tones to nearly the full width of the broadcast channel for loud tones. The broadcast channel, by the way, for frequency modulation would need to be about five times as wide as that for ordinary radio broadcasting. Fortunately, the Armstrong system operates in ultra-high frequencies, outside the range of old-style radio transmission. In this respect it resembles television. In wave lengths from one to ten meters there is said to be room for more than thirteen hundred stations using the Armstrong frequency modulation—thus opening a new frequency spectrum for radio transmission. One of the great virtues of the new system is that it practically eliminates static, whether man-made or the static of atmospheric disturbances such as thunderstorms. It has, moreover, a clarity and power beyond that of amplitude modulation. Of course it will require a radio short-wave receiving set of special design. It is generally understood that one prominent electrical manufacturer is already at work upon transmitters and receivers for the Armstrong system—the General Electric Company.

The system is being tried experimentally in various parts of the country. Major Armstrong has erected a powerful transmitting station at Alpine, N. J.—Station W2XMN. Signals from this station have been picked up at a similar station on Mt. Washington, three hundred miles distant. The latter station is being used for experimentation in frequency modulation. John Shepard, 3rd, who has made such a success in New England of his Yankee and Colonial Networks, is deeply interested. The fact that so practical a radio magnate as Mr. Shepard is spending large sums on the new Armstrong system is significant. Mr. Shepard has stated to the author that a frequency modulation station high in air, as on a mountaintop, should be heard in all parts of New England. He is building such a station in Paxton, Mass. The Shepard station is on a mountaintop where it is expected to have a range of one hundred miles in all directions.

Sec. 165. Federal Communications Commission.

In a previous chapter [3] the early activities of the Federal Radio Commission have been recorded. The original membership of five was composed as follows: Admiral W. H. G. Bullard, chairman; Orestes H. Caldwell; Eugene O. Sykes; Henry A. Bellows and Colonel John F. Dillon. The Commission organized as a working unit on March 15, 1927. The Radio Act of 1927 had provided that the licensing authority of the Commission should be transferred to the Secretary of Commerce at the end of one year, whereupon the Commission should become an advisory and appellate body. So great were the difficulties encountered by the Commission, however, that before the statutory period had expired a House Committee reported the necessity of continuing the license authority in the Commission.

In Schmeckebier's *The Federal Radio Commission,* the resulting congressional action is thus explained:

"In January, 1928, three bills were introduced to meet the situation. The only bill that emerged from the Committee was S 2317, which was reported to the Senate on February 3, and passed by that body on February 6. The bill as reported from the Committee did not provide for a change in term of office of the commissioners, but as amended by the Senate it legislated all the commissioners out of office on February 23, 1929. . . . The House did not agree with the proposal of the Senate to legislate the commissioners out of office, although many members were dissatisfied with the results of the work, particularly in regard to the division of broadcasting facilities between the several zones. It was charged that discrimination had been exercised against the South and West and that preference had been given to high-power stations in the North and East." [4]

The so-called Davis Amendment of the 1928 legislation provided for five broadcasting zones and "a fair and equitable allocation among the different states thereof in proportion to population and area." This act, approved March 28, 1928, extended the licensing authority of the Commission until March 16, 1929. Unfortunately, the members of the Commission could not agree upon their interpretation of the terms of the provisions of the Davis Amendment. In an

[3] Chapter Fourteen, Section 109.
[4] Published by the Brookings Institution in 1932.

effort to reduce the number of broadcasting stations, 164 stations were notified that they must prove that "public interest, convenience or necessity" would be served by renewal of their licenses. This created considerable turmoil, but through voluntary surrender of licenses or denial of renewal requests a total reduction of 109 stations out of a previous total of approximately 700 eventually resulted.

On March 4, 1929, new legislation was enacted which not only affected existing law but the terms of service of the commissioners. On December 18, 1929, new radio legislation was enacted which provided for an engineering division, a necessary adjunct to a commission charged with so important a task as oversight of radio broadcasting. On June 17, 1930, a set of rules and regulations for radio stations was promulgated under this new law. Radio legislation was now of frequent occurrence. The very fact that the functioning of the Federal Radio Commission had controversial angles, that it was obliged to deny applications for licenses as well as to "call onto the carpet" licensees who may have violated radio regulations, no doubt stimulated congressional interest in the activities of the Commission.

The Federal Radio Commission, through seven stormy years, was a political football forever in danger of being kicked off the field. Exactly this fate overtook it in June, 1934, when it was legislated out of existence, to be succeeded by the present Federal Communications Commission. The scope and purpose of the FCC were enumerated by the act entitled "Public, No. 416" approved by the President, June 19, 1934, as follows: To regulate interstate and foreign commerce in communication by wire and radio so as to make available so far as possible to all the people of the United States, a rapid, efficient, nationwide, and worldwide wire and radio communication service with adequate facilities at reasonable charges, for the purpose of the national defense, and for the purpose of securing a more effective execution of this policy by centralizing authority heretofore granted by law to several agencies, and by granting additional authority with respect to interstate and foreign commerce in wire and radio communication.

Thus, two important ·objects were accomplished—first, consolidation of functions heretofore lodged in various governmental agencies and second, a reorganization of the Commission itself. Seven commissioners, with terms ranging from one year to seven years, were now appointed. All future appointments were to be for the full term of seven years. Two members of the former commission were appointed to the new—Eugene O. Sykes for seven years, and Thad H. Brown for six years. Mr. Brown is still on the FCC—Eugene O. Sykes having resigned in March 1939. The membership of the Federal Communications Commission, as constituted on July 1, 1934, was as follows:

Eugene O. Sykes, 7 years (Resigned March 1939)
Thad H. Brown, 6 years (On present Commission)
Paul A. Walker, 5 years (On present Commission)
Norman S. Case, 4 years (On present Commission)
Irvin Stewart, 3 years (Resigned June 30, 1937)
George Henry Payne, 2 years (On present Commission)
Hampson Gary, 1 year (Resigned December 31, 1934)

Anning S. Prall was appointed to succeed Hampson Gary, serving until his death on July 23, 1937. The present chairman, Frank R. Mc-Ninch, and T. A. M. Craven, were appointed in 1937 to fill the two vacancies on the Commission. Mr. McNinch had been chairman of the Federal Power Commission, and by special order of President Roosevelt was given a leave of absence from the Power Commission and authorized to straighten out alleged abuses in the Communications Commission.

The vigorous administration of Chairman McNinch has done much to place the FCC on an efficient basis. Reorganizations of departments and reforms of various kinds have been in order. One of the most significant problems of the FCC is thus stated in the "Fourth Annual Report" for the fiscal year ending June 30, 1938:

"Because of their large number,[5] and the requirement that licenses be renewed every six months the broadcast stations claim a large share of the Commission's attention. . . . Formerly, recommendations made by the examiners were, in part, the basis for a great majority of the Commission's decisions. Under the new practice each hearing is to be conducted by the Commission, by a commissioner, or by one of the more suitably qualified employees, chiefly lawyers. The Commission, instead of the person who presided at the hearing, will file a proposed report of findings of fact and conclusions of law in each case, which report shall be public. Opportunity will be afforded for the filing of exceptions and oral argument before the Commission issues its final report or order. This procedure provides for 'fair play' by apprising the parties of the proposed decisions before they are made final, as the Supreme Court advocated in its decision in the Morgan and other cases."

Regulation of radio broadcasting, however, is only one of the many duties delegated to the FCC. Radio telephony, radio telegraphy, wire telegraphy, wire telephony, television and facsimile are different phases of regulatory duties imposed by federal laws on this very busy commission.

[5] Referring to the 763 broadcasting stations in the United States.

Original Commission

Admiral W. H. G. Bullard (Pa.); Mar. 15, 1927–Nov. 24, 1927 (deceased)

Orestes H. Caldwell (N. Y.); Mar. 15, 1927–Feb. 23, 1929

Eugene O. Sykes (Miss.); Mar. 15, 1927– (Member of FCC)

Henry A. Bellows (Minn.); Mar. 15, 1927–Oct. 31, 1927

Col. John F. Dillon (Cal.); Mar. 15, 1927–Oct. 8, 1927 (Deceased)

Later Appointees

Sam Pickard (Kan.); Nov. 1, 1927–Jan. 31, 1929 (Became vice-president in charge of station)

Henry A. Lafount (Utah); Nov. 14, 1927–July 10, 1934.

Ira E. Robinson (W. Va.); Mar. 29, 1928–Jan. 15, 1932

Gen. C. McK. Saltzman (Iowa); May 2, 1929–July 19, 1932.

William D. L. Starbuck (N. Y.); May 2, 1929–May 23, 1934

Thad H. Brown (Ohio); Jan. 31, 1932– (Member of FCC)

James H. Hanley (Neb.); April 1, 1933–July 10, 1934

Federal Communications Commission

Former Members

Hampson Gary (Texas); July 11, 1934–Dec. 31, 1934

Anning S. Prall (N. Y.); Jan. 17, 1935–July 23, 1937 (Deceased)

Irvin Stewart (Texas); July 11, 1934–June 30, 1937

Eugene O. Sykes (N. Y.); July 11, 1934–Resigned March 1939

Present Members

Frank R. McNinch, Democrat; term 1937–1942–chairman

T. A. M. Craven, Democrat; term 1937–1944

George H. Payne, Republican; term 1934–1943

Thad H. Brown, Republican; term 1934–1940

Paul A. Walker, Democrat; term 1934–1939

Norman S. Case, Republican; term 1934–1945

Frederick I. Thompson, Democrat; (April 5, 1939, replacing commissioner Sykes)

Among other agencies whose activities tend to stabilize the radio industry is the National Association of Broadcasters. It was organized during the years when radio broadcasting stations were facing great problems incident to pioneer beginnings. In 1922 virtually all stations were operating on the same wave length which meant that stations in the same locality must operate on a time-sharing basis. Not only that but station managers were facing the very serious copyright problem. ASCAP, the militant guardian of copyright privileges of composers, authors and publishers, was already clamoring for substantial royalties from radio stations that used popular music on the air. The fact that every radio station was then operating at a heavy loss to its owners rendered a defensive organization imperative. A group of managers of broadcasting stations got together and formed the association.

One of the announced purposes of the organization was to make popular music available to broadcasting stations. The annual conventions of the organization became notable events in which the current ills of radio-land were canvassed. Remedies were proposed and committees were organized for effective collaboration.

The First Annual Convention was held October 11, 1923, at the Commodore Hotel, New York City. The officers elected at that convention were as follows: President, Eugene McDonald, Jr., WJAZ, Chicago, Illinois; Vice President, Frank W. Elliot, WOC, Davenport, Iowa; Vice President, John Shepard, 3rd, WNAC, Boston, Massachusetts; Secretary, J. Elliott Jenkins, WDAP, Chicago, Illinois; Treasurer, Powel Crosley, Jr., WLW, Cincinnati, Ohio.

So important is the work of this organization that in February, 1938, a plan was adopted to make the office of President a paid position, the incumbent to devote his entire time to the task with adequate personnel with headquarters in Washington, D. C. Neville Miller, Esq., former Dean of the Law School of the University of Louisville and later mayor of Louisville, is President of NAB. Edwin M. Spence is Secretary-Treasurer. A board of directors representing seventeen districts from Massachusetts to the Pacific coast is actively functioning. Numerous committees have been formed to co-ordinate widespread activities of the organization.

CHAPTER
TWENTY-ONE

Historical Background of Television

Section 166. Experiments with the Selenium Cell.

ONE OF THE MOST INTRIGUING PROBLEMS of present-day radio is television—that elusive sprite that for a full decade has been "just around the corner," yet has never stepped forth into the broad highway of everyday progress. Television was announced as a possibility prior to the development of radio broadcasting, yet owing to the tremendous technical problems that have confronted television research scientists and engineers it is only now becoming possible to offer to the public assurances that the laboratory stage of the art has ended. In the month in which these words are written, May, 1939, a definite beginning of television broadcasting has been made by the Radio Corporation of America through the National Broadcasting Company in New York City coincident with the opening of the New York World's Fair.

Never in the history of mankind, it is believed, has so intensive and so expensive a campaign of scientific research been waged as in the case of television. As early as 1873 discoveries were made that suggested to men of science that at some far day means would be perfected whereby mankind might attain the power to see things at a distance beyond the range of human vision. They labeled this dream of the future "television"—vision afar off. In 1873, which was before the telephone was invented, the significant fact was discovered that a chemical element known as selenium [1] was sensitive to light. The manner in which this fact was discovered illustrates how the use of one invention may open the way to new scientific advances. Selenium was used in building up high electrical resistances incidental to the operation of the Atlantic cable in its early days. The terminal station at Valentia, on the west coast of Ireland, was the scene of the discovery. An attendant named May noted one afternoon that his instruments were behaving in a very unorthodox manner. It so happened that a ray of sunshine was playing upon the selenium. By repeated experiments he found that whenever the sunlight touched the selenium the needle of the galvanometer moved. It was necessary to protect the device from sunlight. The discovery may not have meant much to the attendant, but to science it was a matter of great importance. Selenium was definitely sensitive to light.

This important fact is said to have been first communicated to the world by Willoughby Smith. It was soon discovered that when used in connection with electrical experiments in complete darkness selenium offered effective resistance to the passage of the electrical current, yet under the influence of light this resistance greatly diminished.

[1] Selenium was discovered by a Swedish chemist, Berzelius, in 1817. It was found in a deposit formed in vitriol chambers. One form of selenium, the gray or crystalline variety, was found to offer very high resistance to the passage of electricity, a curious phenomenon that excited the interest of scientists.

Thus a "light microphone" was discovered. It was a new scientific truth—and scientists began to investigate its possibilities. If electrical currents could be affected by varying rays of light, and means could be devised of instantly translating this electrical variation into terms of light at the other end of the circuit, then a beginning would be made toward the realization of a dazzling mental concept. Thus the "photo-conductive cell" became known among scientists even at a time when the electrical art was concerned chiefly with problems of wire transmission.

In 1877, M. Senlecq produced a device which he labeled a "telectroscope." By electro-magnetic means he hoped to reproduce at a distance the effects of light and shade in the object to be televised. The image was to be projected onto the ground glass of a camera obscura. By tracing the image with a selenium point or pencil it was hoped that variations of light and shade would cause the selenium "microphone" to set up corresponding variations of electric current. It was as yet a mere dream of science, impossible of fulfillment. Among those who investigated the possibilities of the idea was Alexander Graham Bell, the inventor of the telephone. In 1880, several persons, including Bell, took out patents for television apparatus.

By this time the selenium cell was in general use in such experiments. Multiple wires were used, each wire connected with a selenium cell. Thus a mosaic of the intended picture was attempted to be transmitted. G. R. Carey, an American inventor, in 1875 attempted to imitate the human eye by constructing a cylindrical mosaic consisting of a large number of tiny selenium cells appropriately wired.[2] A receiver of chemically prepared paper was stretched between two disks, an incandescent device containing carbon or platinum elements being relied upon to trace the picture on this chemically treated paper. Even if the device had worked television would not have resulted but merely a means of transmitting a still picture by wire, which is now accomplished by facsimile, to be explained hereafter.

Again we have an illustration of the truth that what one generation of scientists may have dreamed over and virtually laid aside, in the process of time, because of new inventions, may be revived by scientists and perfected after the originators of the conception are in their graves. The history of television is one of decades of frustration, of hopes that flamed and died out, to be revived when new discoveries in other fields might offer tantalizing possibilities.

Sec. 167. Futile Attempts at Television.

The selenium cell, as we have seen, had provided the means—a crude means in early days—of "utilizing" light to control electrical energy.

[2] *Scientific American*, Vol. 40, p. 309—1879.

Scientists eventually admitted that their efforts, in the stage that electrical inventions had then attained, gave little hope of accomplishing television by use of the selenium cell. In 1887, however, an announcement was made that set science on a new quest—Hertz's celebrated discovery of electro-magnetic waves, which had been forecast theoretically by Clerk Maxwell many years previously.

In connection with his investigations of electro-magnetic waves Hertz, about 1888, observed a photoelectric effect and reported it to the scientific world. He discovered that spark discharges set up by his apparatus passed more readily when rays of ultra-violet light lay in their path. Various investigators took up the quest: Stoletow, Wilhelm Hallwachs, Julius Elster and Hans Geitel working together, and J. J. Thomson; each made important contributions to knowledge of photoelectric effects. By using a chemically active substance, sodium amalgam being the most responsive substance then known, it was possible to construct a cathode suitable for use in a photoelectric cell, or phototube. The cathode, when activated by short-wave radiation typical of the ultra-violet portion of the spectrum, was capable of emitting streams of electrons. Because these were liberated under the influence of light they were called photoelectrons. This was another scientific abstraction that was later to assume great importance in the art of television.

One of the results of experimentation that has bearing on our present inquiry developed in 1897, when J. J. Thomson, in Cambridge, England, demonstrated the true character of the electron as the smallest particle of the electrical structure of the atom. The function of these electrons in the modern iconoscope—the television camera tube—will later be explained. At the time, however, the discovery was merely another phenomenon, intriguing to scientists but without immediate value. The electrons liberated from the cathode behaved like bullets in leaping to a positive electric terminal, or anode as it is called. Investigators in electrical science found that a partial vacuum assisted in a study of electron characteristics. A suitable glass bulb was devised in which the cathode and the anode or positive terminal could be enclosed—the air evacuated in the ordinary way. Out of this apparently useless device was later to emerge present-day television. Other developments, however, were to intervene. New instrumentalities were to be devised.

Elster and Geitel continued in their efforts to perfect the photoelectric cell. By 1912 they had greatly increased the sensitivity of the device. In the meantime, Dr. Albert Einstein, in 1905, had propounded a theory to account for the fact that the liberated electrons depended both for number released and speed of transit upon various factors. Far be it from the author to attempt to explain any theory enunciated by the expounder of the doctrine of relativity. Suffice it to say that Dr. Einstein materially assisted scientists who were laboring in this field.

Not only did the three-electrode vacuum tube play an important part in developing telephony and radio broadcasting but it also has its place in the history of television. Electrical science thus advanced from stage to stage, originating new devices, combining older inventions and thus developing scientific instrumentalities that would have staggered the credulity of an earlier generation of scientists. Television of today owes its existence to so many types of invention and to so great an array of scientific truths that it is difficult indeed to present an orderly historical picture. Such a recital would require a complete volume in itself. Suffice it for the present to keep in mind the progress being made in several more or less converging avenues of science.

The development of the photoelectric cell and of the three-electrode vacuum tube are but two of the elements that were later to be utilized in the electrical laboratories from which television has emerged. Let us glance briefly at another development in the unfolding drama of scientific approach to the goal of television. This development is known as scanning, which involves the well-known law governing the visual persistence of images.

Sec. 168. Experiments with Mechanical Scanning.

The invention of the scanning disk marked a distinct epoch in television history, since for nearly fifty years it was to prove the chief hope of scientists in their quest for television. To be sure, the scanning disk was not to solve the problem, yet as a will-o'-the-wisp it offered alluring possibilities.

Because the human eye retains, for a tenth of a second, any visual impression, scientists utilized this fact in an effort to develop the illusion of continuous motion by substituting a fresh image before the preceding image could fade out. Ten such substitutions per second would cause a flickering picture, but it was discovered that a minimum of sixteen frames per second [3] would result in reasonably steady vision. Here, then, was the principle of the motion picture that now plays so great a part in public entertainment. Here also was the germ of television. There was this difference, however, between the motion picture and television: the first could be accomplished by mechanical means—a film fed through a projector at a certain speed would produce, on a screen, the desired illusion of life and motion.

Television, on the other hand, involved problems of scie..e that were to baffle physicists for generations. As early as 1884, Paul Nip-

---

[3] The RCA system of television now uses thirty frames per second, a practice that has been recommended to the Federal Communications Commission by the Radio Manufacturers Association.

kow, a German experimenter hit upon the idea of the scanning disk. This device was pierced with a spiral pattern of tiny holes so arranged that if the disk were spun every portion of an image would become visible in succession through one or another of the perforations. The light reflected from the scene, varying according to intensity of light or shade, would pass through the revolving disk and impress itself upon the selenium in the photo-conductive cell which was then being used. The televisor, as it was called, thus became a converter, setting up variations of electrical energy, representative of the lights and shades of the picture, that were capable of being registered and reproduced at the other end of the circuit. With a synchronized scanning disk at the latter point—a neon gas discharge lamp being utilized as an illuminating medium—it became possible to accomplish at least the beginnings of television.

A definite advance toward the goal of television was made by a Swedish inventor, A. Ekstrom, in 1910. Instead of dividing the optical image into numerous elements he suggested the use of a moving spot of light sufficiently intense to reflect to the photoelectric tube every element of the picture as the scanning process went on. This suggestion led to the first genuine demonstrations of television.

Among those investigators who toiled with great persistence at the task of developing systems of television were C. Francis Jenkins, with his prismatic disk, and Dr. Ernst F. W. Alexanderson, with a system of rotating mirrors. The Jenkins idea involved the use of two revolving disks set at right angles. Each disk had a prism section of variable angle near the outer rim, the whole being of optical glass. When rotated a beam of light was made to bend backward and forward, with lateral and perpendicular motions, thus resulting in scanning. The scheme was ingenious, but it did not effectively accomplish the hoped-for results.

Dr. Alexanderson's system of rotating mirrors involved the use of twenty-four mirrors set on a cylindrical drum and revolving at high speed. The image to be televised was focused by means of a lens, a brilliant source of light being used. An ingenious method of blending seven beams of light was provided. Seven photoelectric cells were required. There was much more to the system, but it obviously was not the answer to the problem of television.

The Bell Telephone Laboratories experimented for a time with a scanning system involving the use of a perforated disk. On both sides of the Atlantic the quest for television continued—the ingenuity of man seemingly exhausting itself in a multiplicity of schemes for mechanical scanning. John Logie Baird, in England, was one of those especially active in the quest.

With the persistence of the true scientist, Dr. Alexanderson, after discarding his mirror wheel, returned to the perforated scanning disk. By using high frequency mercury vapor lamps he succeeded in attaining a brilliancy that made possible an actual television picture. This important event occurred on July 5, 1927. The picture, to be sure, was a 48-line reproduction, which was crude, indeed, in comparison with the 441-line pictures in present-day television.

Having made a beginning the inventor pressed his investigation using the Kerr cell. This produced more satisfactory results. In September, 1927, a model of a self-contained television receiver for home use was attempted.

The scanning disk was eighteen inches in diameter, driven by an AC motor, its speed being controlled by a hand-operated key to attain approximate synchronization. Again it was a 48-line picture that must be viewed through a magnifying glass. Four of these models were made and placed in homes in Schenectady for experimental use. It was soon discovered that in utilizing a wave length of approximately 30 meters multiple images were produced, which indicated that reflection from Kennelly-Heaviside layer was responsible for the mischief. By using a vertical antenna instead of the customary horizontal type some progress was made in overcoming the difficulty. Intensive and painstaking experimentation went on in connection with this effort to achieve television by means of the scanning disk.

The scanning disk, as we have previously noted, gave no end of trouble. A succession of able investigators, such as Jenkins, 'Baird, Mihaly, Karolus and Alexanderson, struggled to perfect the mechanical scanning disk; various methods were tried, but each failed to accomplish the desired results. Jenkins gave his first laboratory demonstration of television on June 14, 1923.

At about the same time that Dr. Alexanderson was achieving television in Schenectady, J. L. Baird, in England, accomplished somewhat similar results, giving a public demonstration of his system on January 27, 1926. He, too, used the revolving perforated disk system. Improved illumination enabled each to accomplish what previous inventors had found impossible.

Sec. 169. Invention of the Iconoscope.

Fortunately, however, some investigators were turning attention to the cathode ray for scanning. Boris Rosing, a Russian professor, devised a plan for a television receiver that dispensed entirely with mechanical parts and substituted the cathode ray. In 1911, Campbell Swinton, prior to publication of a description of the Rosing device, suggested in a printed article an apparatus in which the cathode ray could be used both at the transmitting and the receiving ends of the circuit. He suggested, moreover, a mosaic of tiny cubes of light-sensitive substance upon which the image or scene might be focused. The mosaic was to be traversed by the cathode ray, each cube or element of the mosaic in turn being intended to discharge an electrical impulse corresponding to, and caused by, the amount of light or shade of the image focused upon it.

Here at last we find a foreshadowing of modern electronic television. Campbell Swinton's theory was perhaps the closest approach but the hoped for result was to await the discoveries of later investigators.

The story of the quest for acceptable television is of great scientific interest; but so far as the general public is concerned the real story of modern television begins with the application of electronic methods to television. Vladimir K. Zworykin and Philo T. Farnsworth are generally considered the outstanding inventors in this field of investigation on this side of the Atlantic.

Vladimir K. Zworykin made very important contributions to the art. Zworykin was a radio expert for the Signal Corps in the Russian Army during the World War. Like some other loyal subjects of the old regime he came to the United States in 1919. His first real opportunity came in 1920 in the form of a position as a research engineer for the Westinghouse Company. Having developed a keen interest in problems of television, some of his first American inventions were made in the laboratories of Westinghouse. In 1930 he entered the employ of RCA and is now director of the Electronic Research Laboratory of the RCA Manufacturing Company at Camden, N. J. The greatest single contribution to modern television is the Zworykin "Iconoscope"—an electronic device which uses the cathode ray for scanning the light-image of the scene to be transmitted, to convert it into electrical impulses.

Philo T. Farnsworth is another investigator who has made important contributions to electronic television. Farnsworth is said to have begun his career in television research when a freshman in high school (1922), in connection with a course in chemistry. His first attempt was exceedingly ambitious—nothing less than electronic scansion of an image, one of the basic principles of his present system of television. For a fifteen-year-old lad to delve in such mysteries marked him as a future pioneer in the television field. It was not until 1930, however, that the scientific world accepted Farnsworth's theories as practical.

In England, research and development of the Electric & Musical Industries Company, Ltd., under the direction of Mr. I. Shoenberg, made outstanding contributions in the development of the Marconi-EMI television system adopted and now used by the British Broadcasting Company.

Sec. 170. RCA and Electronic Television.

When the Radio Corporation of America began its program for the development of television, it was by no means committed to any one method. Coincident with the early use of mechanical scanning methods, research in the laboratory was under way on a new approach to the subject through the Zworykin iconoscope. To David Sarnoff the device had powerful appeal. His interest in and his support of the new idea was to prove very stimulating to the technical staff of RCA. Thus it came to pass that Dr. Zworykin, of the RCA Manufacturing Company, was enabled to pursue an independent course of inquiry. His was the electronic approach, and because RCA liberally supported him in the quest he was eventually able to give to the world the iconoscope, one of the truly great modern inventions.

In December, 1938, O. B. Hanson, vice-president and chief engineer of NBC, in testimony before the Federal Communications Commission, gave an excellent summary of RCA-NBC television experimentation, from which the following is quoted:

"It was ten years ago—1928—that NBC engineers directed their attention to television studies and at that time worked jointly with RCA engineers on early experiments. Our original equipment consisted of a 48-line mechanical scanning system, a 250-watt transmitter and several mechanical scanning type receivers. It was, of course, obvious that a 48-line picture could hardly be expected to transmit much detail but it served to study the problems involved. Several hundred lines were of course desirable, but no method of obtaining that many scanning lines mechanically was known, and if it had been we had hardly reached that stage of development. Soon we took the next possible step and advanced to 60 lines, and by June, 1930, we had our new system in operation at the NBC Times Square Studio at 42nd Street, New York City.

"This was still a mechanical scanning system, using the flying spot for direct studio pickup at 60 lines per picture and 20 pictures per second. Installed with this equipment was a 500-watt television transmitter operated on a channel 2100 to 2200 kc (140 meters). Over a period of the next twelve months, further improvements were made, such as, improved scanning equipment, better photo cells, etc. The transmitter was increased in power output to 1 kw. In passing it is perhaps of interest to mention that pictures from this station were received quite regularly by amateur experimenters over a wide area and even as far as Kansas. There were letters in our files from more than 200 observers.

"From these early experimental television transmissions, it was obvious that more detail must be transmitted if television was some day to become a great public service. More lines per picture were required and this, in turn, required a greater radio frequency band width.

FACSIMILE RECEIVER
RCA's latest development. Charles J. Young beside it.

RCA TELEVISION RECEIVING SET
Triumph of science in electronic research.

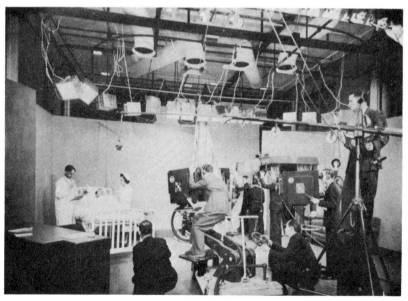

TELEVISION STUDIO
Three television cameras will be noted, also a microphone on a swinging boom to pick up the dialogue.

Space in the short-wave radio spectrum was not available and it was evident that the ultra-short waves offered the only opportunity for expansion. Little else but theory was known about the generation or transmission characteristics of these ultra-short waves or ultra-high frequencies. So NBC and RCA engineers decided to build a new television plant atop the Empire State Building making use of ultra-high frequencies. This plant was completed and put in experimental operation in January, 1932. Improved mechanical scanning of 120 lines was used, both for transmission of motion picture film and direct studio pickup. The frame frequency was 24 pictures per second. In the reproduction of the transmitted pictures, the cathode-ray tubes, using electronic scanning, replaced the cumbersome, noisy mechanical scanning. This was the first step toward an electronic system. The overall result was improved detail and flickerless pictures."

The iconoscope was developed to the point where it was considered ready for tests in a television system about 1933. The technical staff of RCA had turned its attention to the development of a system based upon the use of the iconoscope, having already become satisfied that mechanical scanning was not the answer to the age-long problem of high definition television. Profiting by discoveries in its laboratories and by the possibilities of ultra-short waves the RCA staff was enabled to solve many of the very intricate problems of the electronic approach in record time. It was obvious that television, which required six hundred times the width of the ordinary broadcast channel, necessitated a totally new type of transmitter and antenna. Many intricate and precise controls were needful because in television the timing of functions must be measured in micro-seconds (millionths of a second).

O. B. Hanson has given an admirable description of the activities of the RCA technical staff in developing the RCA system of television. The following quotation is from his testimony before the Federal Communications Commission previously quoted:

"In the meantime, Dr. Zworykin of the RCA Manufacturing Company had invented an electronic device which was to completely revolutionize television technique. . . . Dr. Zworykin named his device the 'Iconoscope,' recognized as the greatest single contribution to television.

"This device completely eliminated the cumbersome mechanical scanning devices previously used for television pickup, and what was most important permitted the immediate increase in the number of scanning lines previously blocked because of mechanical limitations. No longer would the actor be required to perform in a darkened room, where the sole source of light was the flickering beam from the noisy mechanical scanner, projected from an adjacent soundproof room. Actors could now perform in a studio having aspects similar to a well-lighted motion picture studio. The 'Iconoscope' was silent in operation and could be mounted on a tripod and moved about the studio at will, a considerable step forward from the mechanical scanning devices."

In 1933, RCA made its first tests in the field of a system developed to use the iconoscope. These tests were a triumph for electronic television. Pictures of 240 lines—double the capacity of the mechanical scanners previously used—were successfully transmitted on ultra short waves. The kinescope—a cathode ray tube—another electronic device, was used to reproduce the television picture at the receiver. The successful application of these two electronic devices laid the foundation for the RCA electronic system of high definition television. Also, it was during these tests that television pictures were first transmitted by radio relay. Pictures were picked up in New York City, transmitted to an intermediate point at which they were amplified and sent to Camden, N. J. Intensive experiments followed and further progress was made toward the goal of true television.

Previous efforts with mechanical scanning devices had produced either flickering images of very small size or pictures lacking in detail—crude beginnings that offered tantalizing promise rather than present satisfaction.

In view of the disappointing nature of previous attempts on the part of various great corporations to develop a satisfactory system of television, it required considerable courage on the part of David Sarnoff to commit the Radio Corporation of America to the heavy expense of developing the Zworykin system—a radical departure from orthodox attempts at television. After two years of this effort in the secrecy of the laboratories, however, encouraging progress being made, the RCA chief executive resolved upon the bold step of testing the new devices under actual conditions in the field. This would involve heavy expenditures and so in February, 1935, we find a preliminary announcement being made to the stockholders in which it was stated that RCA "was diligently exploring the possibilities of a field demonstration . . . in order that subsequent plans may be founded on experience thus obtained."

At the annual meeting of RCA stockholders, May 7, 1935, Mr. Sarnoff made an extended statement on the television situation, announcing that RCA would at once begin work on a new television transmitting station in New York City. Television receiving sets in limited number would also be necessary and a program service must likewise be set up in order to explore the possibilities and the needs of the new medium of communication. His estimate of the time requisite to prepare for actual field tests was from thirteen to fifteen months.

A summary of the progress that had been accomplished to May, 1935, by RCA television engineers gives interesting historical data:

"Upon a laboratory basis we have produced a 343-line picture, as against the crude 30-line television picture of several years ago. The picture frequency of the earlier system was about 12 per second. This has now been raised to the equivalent of 60 per second. These advances enable the reception, over limited distances, of relatively clear images whose size has been increased without loss of definition."

The concluding paragraph of the Sarnoff statement is very significant in view of what has since transpired:

"While the magnitude and nature of the problem of television call for prudence, they also call for courage and initiative without which a new art cannot be created or a new industry established. Your Corporation has faith in the progress which is being made by its scientists and its engineers, and the management of the Radio Corporation of America is exploring every path that may lead to an increasing business for the radio industry and to a new and useful service to the public."

How accurately Mr. Sarnoff had gauged the time necessary to prepare for field tests is demonstrated by the fact that thirteen months after the announcement above quoted field tests began. This historic beginning was made on June 29, 1936,—the first organized television experimentation in America. By November, 1936, Mr. Sarnoff was able to report, at a special television demonstration to the press, that RCA, in cooperation with NBC, was now successfully transmitting television signals over an area of forty-five miles from its transmitter at the Empire State Building. After discussing the more obvious results of the effort Mr. Sarnoff declares:

"Basic research is a continuing process in our laboratories not only that the problems of television may be solved but also to develop other uses of the ultra-short and micro-waves which possess such vast potentialities in this new domain of the ether."

Sec. 171. Field Experiments by RCA.

In the meantime, the British Broadcasting System was pursuing television experimentation along the lines of an electronic system. This fact appears in a statement issued by Mr. Sarnoff to RCA stockholders in April, 1937.

"Recently," he declares, "the authorities responsible for television in England adopted the Marconi-EMI system of television in preference to the other systems which they tested. The system thus adopted as the English standard is based on RCA inventions."

A further triumph of the RCA system was also reported at this time, April 6, 1937:

"The Columbia Broadcasting System has just announced its plans to enter the field of experimental high-definition television. That company has placed with us, this week, an order for the manufacture of a modern RCA television transmitter to be installed on the Chrysler Building in New York City."

In the same statement Mr. Sarnoff reveals the fact that RCA engineers had reached a new stage of television development—441 lines per frame instead of the 343 lines of the previous year. "This improvement," he reported, "provides greater detail and clarity. It has also made it possible to double the size of the picture from approximately 5½ x 7 inches to 7½ x 10 inches."

The RCA stockholders' meeting of April 5, 1938, was the occasion for an illuminating report on facsimile and television by David Sarnoff. Since the technical problems of facsimile are much less complicated than those of television, facsimile had already reached the stage of commercial utility, as will appear in the following extract from the Sarnoff report:

"The fundamental technical problems of facsimile have been solved, and the immediate question is largely that of determining useful and self-supporting services for the medium."

That this problem was in process of solution was indicated by the following statement in the same report:

"Various broadcasting stations will shortly commence experimental transmission by facsimile of news bulletins and pictorial material to a limited number of receivers in their local areas. The RCA Manufacturing Company is now building facsimile transmitters and several hundred receivers which have been ordered by independent broadcasting stations for this purpose."

In the field of television Mr. Sarnoff was able to report to the stockholders the following:

"Television pictures are larger, sharper, and more brilliant than a year ago, due to marked improvements in both transmitting and receiving apparatus. Developments now under way look toward the acceptance by the industry of definite technical standards, which must be established before any public television service is practicable. Meanwhile, the NBC is continuing its study and experiments with television programs, both inside and outside the studio. The new NBC mobile television unit, the only apparatus of its kind in the United States, is being tested on outside pickups. This is an all-important field for experiment, since on-the-spot pictures of news events are certain to furnish one of the most useful and popular services of television."

Sec. 172. RCA Launches Television Broadcasting.

After years of research in television there still remained a division of thought among leaders in the radio field as to its feasibility. Millions of dollars had been spent upon the development. Many other millions would be necessary to overcome remaining obstacles. Manufacturers had long resisted public impatience in its clamor for "radio vision" because they did not wish to offer television apparatus until acceptable standards of performance could be assured. Recent advances in the art, however, caused David Sarnoff, in the summer of 1938, to take the lead in a movement to launch television in conjunction with the New York World's Fair. A decisive announcement was made at a meeting of the Radio Manufacturers Association on October 20, 1938. The following quotation is from Mr. Sarnoff's address:

"Some years ago I recommended to the RMA board the creation of a special sub-committee for the purpose of keeping itself informed on television progress. This suggestion was adopted and the committee is still functioning. During these years the RCA has made several demonstrations of its television system to its licensees and to others. . . . The results of the experimental field tests of television in the New York area conducted by the RCA and its broadcasting and manufacturing units, have convinced us that television in the home is now technically feasible.

"We are aware, however, that many technical, artistic and financial problems still confront those who would establish an acceptable and regular public service of television programs to the home. These problems must be solved before a national service of network television programs can be made available to the public. Meanwhile, RCA, which has pioneered in the development of television, has made substantial progress, first in its research laboratories, and second, through its field tests and experimental broadcast programs. We believe that the problems confronting this difficult and complicated art can be solved only by operating experience gained from actually serving the public in their homes. Therefore, RCA proposed to take a third step in the solution of these problems by beginning a limited program service to the public from its New York television transmitter on the Empire State Building. This transmitter will serve an area having a radius of approximately fifty miles.

"As publicly announced some time ago, RCA proposes to demonstrate television to the public at the New York World's Fair which is expected to open on April 30, 1939. The National Broadcasting Company contemplates that by the time the Fair opens, it will be on the air with television programs for at least two hours out of each week.

Recent reports in the public press are to the effect that the Columbia Broadcasting System contemplates installing its television transmitter in the Chrysler Building in New York City. These reports further indicated that television programs will be transmitted from this station by the time the World's Fair opens.

"The RCA Manufacturing Company, which built and sold the television transmitter to Columbia, has offered and is prepared to sell television transmitters to broadcasters and others who may desire to enter this new field.

"RCA believes that the development of its television system has now reached a stage where it is practicable to supply television receivers to satisfy the demand of the public in those localities where television transmissions are now or may become available. Therefore, it is planning to manufacture a limited quantity of television receivers which it expects to market by the time the World's Fair opens. We are informed that a number of other radio manufacturers in the United States are also preparing to manufacture and sell television receivers in such areas as may be served with television programs.

"Only a little more than six months remain between now and the time that the World's Fair is expected to open. Those who desire to market television receivers by that time will find it necessary to make their plans now for manufacturing them. RCA is prepared to assist its licensees who may desire to manufacture television receivers, and so far as practicable, will be glad to sell to them such television parts as they may wish to purchase. Our television test equipment is now complete at RCA's license laboratory. We will continue to measure and test television receivers for licensees as we have done for them with sound broadcast receivers. Engineers and executives of our licensees seeking additional information will be welcomed at RCA laboratories, manufacturing plants and broadcasting studios.

"Opportunities to compete in the erection of television transmitters, the establishment of television program services, and the manufacture and sale of television receivers to the public, are available to the radio industry and to others in the United States. We hope that full advantage will be taken of these opportunities to help build a new industry and to establish a greater public service."

The foregoing announcement from the chief executive of the Radio Corporation of America operated as the launching of a new industry. All manufacturers were thus given fair warning that RCA would manufacture television apparatus, but that RCA-licensed competitors could do the same. The race was on. Several manufacturers have already entered into television set production.

At the New York World's Fair grounds on April 20, 1939, a very impressive ceremony occurred. The RCA Exhibit Building was being dedicated and to give historical significance to the occasion the first public demonstration of television occurred. David Sarnoff, under whose leadership the new art had received such impetus, addressed the audience. "The Birth of a New Industry" was the subject of his notable address delivered before the television cameras in the courtyard of the building. The guests within the darkened interior, clustered around a score of television sets, were afforded the unique experience of seeing the backs of the various speakers as they went out into the courtyard, while at the same instant in the television sets they beheld the face and form of the same person emerging into the sunlight.

Mr. Sarnoff's speech was noteworthy. The following excerpts reveal some of its highlights:

"We are now ready to fulfill the promise made to the public last October when after years of research, laboratory experiments and tests in the field, costing millions of dollars, the Radio Corporation of America announced that television program service and commercial receivers would be made available to the public with the opening of the New York World's Fair. . . . There is something tremendously inspiring to all of us in the RCA Family in launching a new service whose purpose is constructive, into a world where destruction is rampant . . . Human aspiration and intelligence are at constant war with the forces of reaction and destruction. When a major victory is won, civilization is able to make a giant stride forward. The coming of radio was one of those victories. After ages in which nature had maintained the barriers of time and distance between men and nations, radio eliminated them, and enabled man to send a whisper around the earth.

"And now we add sight to sound.

"It is with a feeling of humbleness that I come to this moment of announcing the birth in this country of a new art so important in its implications that it is bound to affect all society. It is an art that shines like a torch of hope in a troubled world. It is a creative force which we must learn to utilize for the benefit of all mankind."

It was a matter of deep regret to Mr. Sarnoff as well as to the world in general that Senatore Marconi could not have lived to participate in RCA'S great day at the World's Fair. It is well known that Guglielmo Marconi was the idol and the inspiration of David Sarnoff's youth. In later years a bond of friendship grew up between the two radio pioneers and when in September, 1936, RCA's official family joined in celebrating the thirtieth anniversary of David Sarnoff's entrance into radio Marconi sent an affectionate radiogram to the guest of honor. The great inventor's death in 1937 terminated the relationship but not the pupil's reverence for his master.

In voicing to the author his regret that the father of wireless transmissions could not have lived to join in the television dedication of April 20, 1939, Mr. Sarnoff declared:

"The great work of Marconi, the inventor, is known to all the world, but his spirit and his faith are known best to those who had the privilege of working with him and of knowing him. Marconi never ceased to dream of radio and its endless possibilities. Thirty years after his first great invention in the art, Marconi was still inventing and exploring. Beam transmission and reception, short waves, centimeter and millimeter waves were the objects of his researches right up to the day of his passing. He was a pioneer at the start and a pioneer at the finish."

CHAPTER
TWENTY-TWO

Television and Facsimile

Section 173. The Zworykin Iconoscope.

IN DESCRIBING PRESENT-DAY TELEVISION in simple terms it is necessary
to begin with the familiar principle that we are able to see an object
because of light waves that are reflected from it to the eye. Without
light there can be no visible image. The first step in television is to
capture these light waves in a device that is so constituted that it will
convert them into electric currents which we can feed into a suitable
transmitting antenna. After years of experimentation, Dr. Zworykin
has developed what is known as the "Iconoscope," or in Greek, "image
observer."

The "Iconoscope" is in reality a "television microphone" whereby
light waves are converted into electric currents. Obviously, the "Iconoscope" performs some of the functions of a camera. In fact, it has a
plate or film, a thin sheet of mica covered with individual photoelectric cells so very tiny that a microscope is necessary to distinguish
them. Microscopic cells are essential to a clear picture. The amazing
fact is that scientists have been able to develop such infinitesimal
photoelectric cells and to make each individual cell a separate unit
for the development of an electrostatic charge in proportion to the
amount of light that falls upon it.

With the "Iconoscope," like the camera, a lens is used for focusing on
the sensitive mosaic plate the picture intended to be broadcast. With the
picture thus focused an amazing thing occurs whenever the plate is
exposed to light. This plate, by the way, is not like the film of a camera in respect to exposure. In the camera, when the exposure has been
made, the film must be removed. Its work is done. Not so in the television camera. These microscopic photoelectric cells are enduring—
living, pulsating atoms of magic. Cells upon which no light falls will
remain in equilibrium, but wherever light touches the plate a positive charge of electricity, in proportion to the light, is developed in
the cells affected, due to emission of photoelectrons. In other words,
the action of light causes a cell to lose some of its electrons.

If this were all that happened inside the "Iconoscope" no television
result would be accomplished; but now comes the all-important scanning process. Science has made great strides since mechanical scanning was discarded for the electron beam, a tiny pencil of electrons
that sweeps the surface of the plate in horizontal strokes so inconceivably fast that 441 horizontal "lines" merge in a continuous picture
or frame for transmission—30 frames per second.

The mica plate on which the photoelectric cells are superimposed
is connected with a signal plate and a wire leading from the "Icon-

oscope." Through this wire races the electric current released from each cell as the electron beam traverses it and restores negative electrons. The action of the electron gun is, therefore, somewhat similar to that of a brush that sweeps across the mosaic, releasing the stored charges in successive cells. Thus, a stream of electric impulses races through the wire at the back of the plate capable of controlling the transmitter and thus of being broadcast to a synchronized receiver at a distance. These impulses are naturally very weak, but in the process of transmission they pass through vacuum tubes and amplifiers that build them up to useful proportions. Immediately the electron beam passes over a cell it is ready for further reception of light. Thirty times a second the scanning of the complete picture is repeated—charge and discharge in orderly sequence.

The "Iconoscope," by the way, is a self-contained unit, a bit like a huge, deformed electric light bulb. It has a base like that of a vacuum tube with a long neck in which the gun, or source of the scanning electron beam, is located. The bulb portion is very large and may be spherical or, in its latest form, cylindrical. The plate or mosaic is inside the bulb and is set at an angle in order that the lens may focus the picture upon it free from obstructions. The cathode in the neck of the bulb is covered with certain chemical compounds that give off negative electrons when heated by an electric current. The electron beam passes through a small side tube into the bulb chamber, its rays being directed and deflected by ingenious devices that cause it to scan the picture. As before indicated, it describes 441 lines horizontally across the mosaic 30 times a second.

This scanning process itself would not be as efficiently possible at such speed if purely mechanical means were resorted to. By human ingenuity, however, a way was discovered whereby the electron beam could be directed and made to perform a task beyond the dream of magicians or scientists of any age earlier than the amazing present. By the use of coils, through which could flow currents of special wave form, the deed was done. The deflecting currents in the coils are regulated by oscillating vacuum tubes and so-called deflection circuits. The stream of negative electrons becomes like a jet from a hose tracing an orderly pattern across the mosaic.

It is interesting to note that the British Marconi Company acknowledges with gratitude the monumental contributions to television made by RCA's great director of electronic research. On May 10, 1939, H. A. White, Chairman of the Board of Marconi's Wireless Telegraph Company, Ltd., at the annual meeting made the following statement:

"Before leaving this subject, I should like to express the hope that none of us who are interested in television research will ever forget how much we owe to Vladimir Zworykin, the eminent inventor of the iconoscope."

Sec. 174. The RCA Television Receiving Sets.

A television receiving set is, of course, an exceedingly important part of the system. Television impulses, when captured, must be fed into vacuum tubes to be amplified before they are capable of being reconverted into light images. Under the well-known RCA system a device known as a "Kinescope," a form of cathode-ray tube, is employed for this purpose. The "Kinescope" has a plate that differs somewhat from that in the "Iconoscope." It is really one end of the tube itself which is made nearly flat and coated with fluorescent material. This material is capable of glowing or giving off light whenever the electron beam is played upon it. The glowing spot—about the size of a pin head—traverses the field within the tube in exact synchronism with the "Iconoscope" beam at the transmitter end. The spot varies in intensity in response to the incoming electrical impulses, thus reproducing the lights and shadows of the picture being televised. This unique paint brush, traveling its 441-line circuit 30 [1] times a second, is so inconceivably rapid in its motion that the steady picture appears to the eye in its entirety.

An important fact with reference to the "Kinescope" is that although the process goes on within the tube yet the end of the tube is constructed of clear glass, thus permitting the picture produced within to be seen by the television beholder.

An excellent description of the engineering problems connected with this phase of television is to be found in a lecture given by Arthur VanDyck, engineer in charge, RCA License Laboratory, before the Brooklyn Institute of Arts and Sciences, February, 1937. The following quotation is from the lecture:

"Of course there are many engineering problems associated with this apparatus. The most interesting ones are those associated with what is called 'synchronization,' or the necessity of keeping the flying beam of the 'Kinescope' in perfect step with the flying beam of the 'Iconoscope,' even though they may be miles apart with only a tenuous

---

[1] In order to attain flickerless pictures engineers have resorted to interlaced scanning—alternate lines being scanned each time, so that 60 half-pictures are flashed each second. This accomplishes the purpose much better than if the 441-line field were covered in a single scanning.

radio connection between. Obviously these two must be kept together very accurately, even though they are moving very rapidly over the picture. It would not do at all to have the beam at the transmitter picking up the sparkle of highlight in the eye of the beautiful television lady artist, while the receiver beam was working where her nose was supposed to be.

"The object to be attained may be stated simply. It is merely that the electron beams of the 'Iconoscope' and the 'Kinescope' are to be kept in perfect step with each other. Each is to travel across its plate or screen in horizontal lines. Each is to start at the upper left corner let us say, move across the first or top line at the proper speed, quickly jump back to the left and start on the second line just below the first line, complete that, jump back for the third, and so on until it has covered all 441 lines, finishing at the lower right corner. Then it must jump up to the upper left corner and begin again on the top line. Perhaps we should note here that the method of scanning actually used in modern systems does not move the spot in quite such a simple regular fashion, but has a more complex movement such as doing lines alternately, all the odd-numbered ones first, and then the even-numbered ones. This is known as 'interlaced scanning' and provides several important technical refinements and benefits. It is not necessary to study this more complex method, however, to understand the basic fundamentals of the system, and we may assume that the beam travels over the picture from top to bottom, line after line progressively.

"The beams in each case are made to move by magnetic fields produced by currents in coils mounted on the sides of the 'Iconoscope' and 'Kinescope.' If the right currents are fed into these coils at the right times, the beams will move as desired. The currents can be obtained from vacuum tubes arranged as oscillators, but one beam is at the transmitter and one is at the receiver miles away. We must have these oscillators working absolutely together—because if they deliver their currents out of step by even as little as one one-millionth part of a second, the reproduced image will have no likeness to the original. So they must be tied together somehow. At present this is accomplished by making the generators of currents at the transmitter into masters of the situation. They are arranged to send out short timing signals, called synchronizing signals, and there are two of them, one for keeping the beams together horizontally, and one for keeping them together vertically. These signals are additional to the picture signals, so that a television transmitter sends out three different signals, one describing the picture, and two to keep the beams in step horizontally and vertically. Of course if they were all sent out simultaneously they would interfere with each other. Therefore, the synchronizing signals are sent out very quickly during the short time intervals when the beams are not being used for the picture, but are occupied in jumping back from right to left preparatory to starting a new line of the picture. This means, in effect, that each receiver of all those which may be 'looking-in,' is continuously receiving instructions and assistance, from the transmitter, by means of which it is enabled to keep its 'Kinescope' picture beam exactly in step with the scanning beam at the transmitter."

Sec. 175. The Farnsworth Television System.

This historical survey deals with radio developments in America. It, therefore, concerns itself chiefly in the television field with the work of the two great pioneers in electronic research—Dr. Zworykin, whose inventions have contributed to the RCA television system, and Philo T. Farnsworth, who began his career in electronics when a mere adolescent. It is an amazing fact that before young Farnsworth was old enough to vote he had so far perfected his system of television that he applied for a patent thereon, this important event occurring on January 7, 1927. The patent No. 1773980 was issued August 26, 1930. Mr. Farnsworth's approach to the problem differs in some respects from the Zworykin or RCA system.

Mr. Farnsworth, while utilizing the electron gun in the receiver does not employ a scanning beam in the transmitter image or pickup tube. How then does he transmute the light image into signal currents to be broadcast by an antenna? To scientists the answer is simple, yet to the uninitiated the process is apparently even more complex than the system already described. We have noted that the image to be televised under the RCA system is imposed on a mosaic of photoelectric cells and is scanned by a beam of electrons moving rapidly over its surface. Under the Farnsworth system, however, the optical image is focused sharply upon a photoelectric-sensitive cathode. This photoelectric cathode is formed as a thin translucent film of a photo-sensitive material on the end of the glass tube itself. Varying intensities of light in the optical image set up corresponding photoelectronic emissions which play upon a sort of target forming in their path to the target what may be called an electron image, an electronic duplicate of the optical image.

Instead of scanning this electronic image in the Zworykin manner the image itself, in its entirety, is moved across a tiny aperture in a target member that rises like a pencil or rod in the plane of the electron image. The target aperture is not in the end of the rod but in the side facing the oncoming electron barrage. The scanning is done line by line, as successive portions of the electron image move past the tiny aperture. Beginning at the left-hand corner the image describes two motions, left to right and progressively downward to the last line when it snaps back to begin all over again. This cycle is repeated at a rate sufficient to accomplish the purpose.

How is this ghostly electron image made to behave in any such intelligent manner? By the same means that the electron beam of the "Iconoscope" is made to scan the photoelectric screen—by the use of deflecting coils.

This process sounds a bit more simple than the Farnsworth system only because we have intentionally passed over a very important process by which the electron barrage is made to travel in parallel lines from the optical image to its counterpart, the electron image—which may be six inches or more distant. The difficulty in arraying the electron barrage in parallel lines arises from the fact that the natural tendency of such discharge is to spread out from the point of emergence in a cone-shaped spray. This tendency is controlled by wrapping the tube itself in a focusing coil activated by direct current. This sets up a magnetic field in which the lines of force are parallel to the axis of the tube. This causes the electron beams to travel in parallel lines—a relation which persists even when the paths of the electrons are made to describe the two motions already indicated by the Farnsworth scanning process.

It should be added that Mr. Farnsworth provides appropriate means for amplifying the relatively feeble impulses that flow from the collector anode.

The Farnsworth receiving system uses a vacuum tube known as the oscillight, a form of cathode-ray tube. An electron gun and a fluorescent screen are necessary features of the oscillight. The stream of electrons from the gun is focused in a scanning spot on the fluorescent screen. Deflecting coils are used to direct the stream of electrons in a scanning motion synchronized to reproduce exactly the optical image being televised at the other end of the circuit. Magnetic focusing is employed rather than the electrostatic system used in the Zworykin "Kinescope," although either principle may be used. The result is the same—an illuminated image in the receiving set—the goal of television.

Scientists now hint that the cathode ray may in turn give way to some superior means of producing an illuminated image at a distance. To be sure, they will not formulate in words what that new system may be; yet the very fact that they are seeking an improved method furnishes ground for hope. Surely the history of television in the past

FRANKLIN DUNHAM
Educational Director of NBC since 1931.
With Aeolian Company, 1922 to 1931.

DR. JAMES ROWLAND ANGELL
Educational Counsellor of NBC. Former
President of Yale University.

DEDICATION OF RCA BUILDING AT WORLD'S FAIR
President Sarnoff facing a television camera while distinguished audience
inside building hear and see the speaker in the television receiving sets,
April 20, 1939.

decade indicates that even fantastic prophecies by men of science are worthy of respectful consideration.[2]

[2] It is interesting to note that experimental licenses have been issued to the following organizations:

TELEVISION BROADCAST STATIONS
As of February 1, 1939
(Prepared by the FCC)

Licensee and Location	Call Letters
Columbia Broadcasting System New York, N. Y.	W2XAX
Don Lee Broadcasting System Los Angeles, Calif.	W6XAO
Allen B. DuMont Laboratories, Inc. Passaic, N. J.	W2XVT
Farnsworth Television, Inc., of Pa. Springfield, Pa.	W3XPF
First National Television, Inc. Kansas City, Mo.	W9XAL
General Electric Co. Bridgeport, Conn.	W1XA
General Electric Co. Albany, N. Y.	W2XB
General Electric Co. Schenectady, N. Y.	W2XD
General Electric Co. Schenectady, N. Y.	W2XH
General Television Corp. Boston, Mass.	W1XG
Kansas State College of Agriculture & Applied Science Manhattan, Kansas.	W9XAK
National Broadcasting Co. New York, N. Y.	W2XBS
National Broadcasting Co. (Portable) Camden, N. J., and New York, N. Y.	W2XBT
Philco Radio & Television Corp. Philadelphia, Pa.	W3XE
Philco Radio & Television Corp. Philadelphia, Pa.	W3XP
Purdue University West Lafayette, Ind.	W9XG
Radio Pictures, Inc. Long Island City, N. Y.	W2XDR
RCA Manufacturing Co., Inc. (Portable) Camden, N. J.	W3XAD
RCA Manufacturing Co., Inc. Camden, N. J.	W3XEP
RCA Manufacturing Co., Inc. (Portable-Mobile) Camden, N. J.	W1OXX
University of Iowa Iowa City, Iowa	W9XK
University of Iowa Iowa City, Iowa	W9XUI
Zenith Radio Corp. Chicago, Ill.	W9XZV

Sec. 176. Limitations of Television Broadcasting.

Television broadcasting is much more difficult than ordinary radio broadcasting. This is due to the fact, previously mentioned, that the ultra-short waves necessary to high definition television behave much like rays of light. It is not inappropriate to point out that waves of light are cut off by a solid obstruction. A mountain, a building, or any object cuts off light. The same is true to a certain extent of ultra-short waves. Instead of penetrating a building in the manner of ordinary radio waves the television impulse has considerable difficulty with steel-frame buildings. Another difficulty arises from the fact that buildings, water tanks and other obstructions cause reflections that set up a double or even multiple image in a television receiver.

Television, while practically immune to radio's great bugaboo—atmospheric static, nevertheless suffers acutely from forms of disturbance that have little effect upon radio broadcasting. Automobile ignition, for example, seems to create ultra-short waves that cause static in television receivers. As for a diathermy machine, such as is now popular in electrical treatment of certain physical ailments, the effect of operation is quite devastating to television reception in the vicinity. Other electrical appliances cause trouble, but in all such cases engineers are discovering means of curbing, if not entirely suppressing, such disturbances.

It is generally conceded that the broadcast antenna for television transmitters must be located as high as possible. Since there are no convenient mountain peaks in the vicinity of great eastern cities we will no doubt find television stations, at least during the pioneer period, perched on the top of skyscrapers. NBC's transmitter on the tower of the Empire State Building is an instance in point. The present effective range of this television transmitter is about fifty miles, which corresponds to the distance of the visual horizon from that elevation.

The history of television experimentation, however, should cause the thoughtful observer to experience some hesitation in venturing even to question the ability of science directly or indirectly to overcome the visual-horizon difficulty in television broadcasting. In the case of light waves we have enough data to declare the rule, but television data is as yet meager indeed. RCA investigators, while working on Long Island, have picked up blurred and imperfect signals from the television station in London. Whether this indicates that television broadcast waves, after passing off into space beyond the visual horizon, return to earth in a definite trajectory curve we have no definite proof. We are confident, however, that the curtain is just rising on one of the mightiest dramas of science that the human race has ever witnessed. We are sobered by the fact that as recently as 1933 men of science clung to the feasibility of the mechanical scanning disk and scouted the idea of the cathode ray with which Zworykin and Farnsworth have since attained such brilliant results.

Science has already provided a fairly satisfactory answer to the visual-horizon limitation of television by development of the coaxial cable. The chief difficulty about the coaxial cable is that of expense—it costs at present about four thousand dollars a mile and requires a booster station for television every five miles. By means of the coaxial cable it may be possible to establish network broadcasting.

One of the very serious problems of television production is that of program expense. A television show that would be comparable with a modest movie would be very expensive. Although a picture could be shown very widely, recouping its cost and perhaps earning money, the television show would go out on the air in one broadcast—free to all televiewers within range. It is obvious, therefore, that until the industry can overcome the limitations above named and attract commercial sponsors television producers must bear an inordinately heavy expense for the broadcasting of visual programs.

It is important to remember that it may be possible to supply television programs directly to theaters within transmitter range without resorting to the "canned" or film product. A special frequency dedicated to theater reception and outside the range of home sets might accomplish the result. So also the coaxial cable may be utilized to transmit the program from studio to theaters. Scientists, moreover, are continually discovering new methods as well as improving old ones. We have every reason to believe that existing obstacles will eventually be cleared away.

One of the most serious limitations of television is the wide frequency band of the television signal. The "broadcast band" for ordinary radio broadcasting ranges between 550 and 1560 kilocycles. Since radio technicians have made it possible to operate radio stations on frequencies merely 10 kilocycles apart, it is possible to separate this broadcast band into one hundred and one distinct assignments. It is possible, moreover, because of the territorial extent of the nation, to assign the same channel or frequency to different stations in distant locations without much confusion or overlapping coverage. Thus many stations become possible in long-wave broadcasting.

With television, however, we encounter the disturbing fact that a frequency band of 6000 kilocycles is necessary for a complete television channel. In other words, a single television station would call for six times as much space as the entire broadcast band. Fortunately, television is possible only in ultra-short waves—an entirely different part of the radio frequency spectrum than that used for ordinary radio broadcasting. This permits television to operate without interference to radio broadcasting.

Various obstacles exist to the full utilization of the entire range of television frequencies; one of the chief being that engineers have found it difficult to produce transmitters of high power that are capable of operating on the higher frequencies. The result is that seven television channels are all that are being allotted for experimental purposes at this writing. Since television is of very limited range as compared with ordinary radio transmission we may perhaps multiply television assignments by allotting the same frequency to many different localities.

The British Broadcasting Company has been sending out television programs on a regular schedule since July, 1936. By regular schedule, however, is meant a schedule of brief duration at stated hours, and this cannot compare with all day and all evening radio broadcasting. These programs, moreover, are limited to the London area. It should be remembered that broadcasting in England is a government monopoly supported by a tax on radio receiving sets. Funds are thus available for television experimentation, but it is probable that the amount spent by the British Broadcasting Company is very small in comparison with the total of sums that have been expended by private companies in television research in the United States.

One television experience in London suggests the human interest possibilities of this medium in reporting current events. It occurred at the Armistice Day celebration in 1937—at the Cenotaph in the midst of the pomp and ceremony—when the king himself was in the eye of the television camera. An unexpected and unwelcome actor suddenly leaped into the spotlight and caused consternation by denouncing the celebration as hypocrisy and accusing the British Government of secret preparation for war. All this was action that registered for television as well as for newsreel cameras. Thus the lure of the unexpected and the unpredictable is added to the genuine thrill of beholding events as they occur—a very great advantage over the newsreel, whose showing must necessarily occur hours or days after the event, and its outcomes are well known to the public.

Sec. 177. The Future Television Boom.

It is generally agreed by farseeing observers that television will ultimately affect the radio industry as profoundly as the talking motion picture affected the silent screen. The very fact that sight has more universal appeal than sound renders television especially significant. The apparent certainty of this boom, however, should not mislead the public into a belief that great riches are to be had in television stock.

It is obvious that the future television boom will not come as suddenly and impressively as that of radio broadcasting. In the early days of the radio boom almost any amateur could purchase radio parts and assemble a receiving set that would capture from the ether a minimum of radio program and a maximum of static. Because so great a multitude of people invested small sums for radio parts, early manufacturers—including those who infringed existing patents—reaped a golden harvest. Television, however, cannot be achieved by assembling a collection of inexpensive parts, since a television set that will really work must be carefully assembled from relatively expensive equipment. The most inexpensive television set now being offered would cost several times as much as the popular-priced radio set. Families are comparatively few that can afford such luxury at present. Besides this, television broadcasts on a regular program, at the present writing, are confined to the New York City area, which further limits the sale of television sets. Investors in television stock should bear these facts in mind and await with patience the development of the industry.

There is another phase of television development that should be mentioned. Companies that attempt to broadcast television, such as the National Broadcasting Company and the Columbia Broadcasting System, will be obliged to do so without hope of financial return until the time comes when commercial interests can see in television an attractive field of advertising. This means that until a sufficient number of homes can become equipped with television sets to constitute a potential market television advertising will not arise. Commercial licenses have not yet been granted by the Federal Communications Commission—and such would be necessary before television advertising would be possible. This is what is meant by the chasm that must be bridged before a genuine television boom can develop.

The cost of the development of television, as already indicated, has been exceedingly great, owing to the length of time in which experiments have been going on and the expensive nature of the apparatus and methods involved. The aggregate expenditures in this quest on both sides of the Atlantic will probably never be known. It is estimated by a writer in *Fortune* for April, 1939, that in the United States at least thirteen million dollars have been expended in research in this field alone.

Thus we see that television broadcasting, although the pioneer that must blaze the trail and stimulate business for the manufacturer of television equipment, will be delayed in reaping financial benefit from the new enterprise. That television will make giant strides, now that it has actually emerged from the laboratory, the author has no doubts whatsoever.

Sec. 178. The Coaxial Cable.

The coaxial cable represents a triumph of ingenuity of the electrical engineers. Since the American Telephone & Telegraph Company is concerned with wire lines it has expended large sums in developing this means of communication. The cable can be run under the ground or strung on telegraph poles. The coaxial cable consists of a tube or pipe, usually of copper, within which is contained the second wire of the circuit. Contact between wire and pipe is avoided by the use of washers of insulating material strung upon the wire and so spaced as to accomplish the desired result.

The coaxial cable, in its latest form, is utilizing a gas—nitrogen— within the pipe as an additional insurance against loss of energy. The outer surface of the pipe is covered with some insulating material, except in the case of very large cables which are enclosed in a protective tubing usually of lead. In such installations the cable is insulated from the outer cover and gas is used as a filler. At Station WTAM, in Cleveland, a coaxial cable between station and antenna is used in which the outer tubing is of aluminum with an inner diameter of three inches. These pipes are in twenty-foot units, with couplings that permit a smooth and continuous inner surface.

The chief virtue of the coaxial cable is that it is capable of carrying a great number of messages or electrical impulses. It will handle several hundred telephone conversations simultaneously. It may be likened to a river of energy on which may be launched a variety of crafts, supporting each as though it were the only one in the current. Thus at the same instant of time telegraph messages, telephone talks, radio long-line service, facsimile, television and the like may be accommodated. Obviously, radio and television service require that frequencies appropriate to each must be fed to the coaxial cable and, at the point where it is to be tapped out, instruments capable of picking up the aforesaid frequencies must be used.

It should be pointed out, however, that the coaxial cable, at least in its present stage of development, has distinct limitations. One is that television signals sent by this means cannot enjoy as complete a range as those sent by wireless. Another very serious limitation is the necessity of providing relay or booster stations at intervals of from five to ten miles. It is conceivable that television transmission in the future may utilize both television broadcasting and transmission by coaxial cable, depending upon the nature of the service intended. Television to theaters and other similar private needs might well be satisfied by the coaxial cable. Wireless broadcasting, on the other hand, may serve the myriad purposes to which radio broadcasting is adapted.

Sec. 179. Radio Relays.

One of the important recent achievements of the research laboratories of RCA is the development of radio relays. It is well known that it requires thousands of watts of power in the station of origin in order to broadcast television. These television signals, however, are of relatively short range. We have noted that the coaxial cable, one of the agencies being tried in an attempt to overcome television's visual horizon limitation, requires booster stations, or relays every few miles. The new development of radio relays opens new vistas of television progress since the open air is the theatre of operation and relay stations may be spaced from fifteen to twenty miles apart.

We must not picture the relay as a station operated with power comparable to that of the station of origin. On the contrary the RCA radio relay employs only a few watts of power and is a relatively tiny apparatus installed in a protective housing mounted on poles. It combines the element of a receiver attuned to capture the incoming television signals together with a transmitter to amplify and send them on to the next relay. It may be likened to a valve through which the signals—travelling at the speed of light—pass and in transit receive a bath of electrical power that restores the strength and clarity with which they left the originating studio or pick-up point.

Unbelievable magic is involved in this new radio relay system. The mechanism operates unattended and automatically. Once set up and connected to a local power line it does not require human attention. Instantly responsive to television signals of the frequency to which it is attuned the radio relay is a sleepless and tireless slave of its master. It is possible moreover by using a directive antenna to confine the radiated energy in a beam directed toward the next relay in the chain, this station being attuned to the frequency of the beam.

RCA technicians declare that the radio relay gives promise of an ultimate solution of the problem of a television network. Ralph R. Beal, RCA's Director of Research, has expressed the following view to the author:

"Radio relays offer a promising method," he declares, "of carrying television signals between cities to connect television broadcasting stations into networks, and also for effecting intercity distribution of television programs for theatres or for other uses. Such stations would use wavelengths measured in centimeters. By the use of these wavelengths engineers would be able to apply principles and techniques by which transmission between relay points may be accomplished with a few watts of power as compared with the several thousand watts necessary in the television broadcasting station. Research scientists and engineers in the laboratories of the Radio Corporation of America are making rapid advances in the development of electronic devices, methods and systems which will make these very short wavelengths available and useful. When these devices and methods are perfected and applied, a radio relay system can be provided by which television and other means of communication may be carried within and between cities simultaneously."

The RCA radio relay system is not confined to television. Its principles and methods of operation also apply to code telegraphy, facsimile, teletypewriter communication, and radio telephony. In fact RCA has had in actual operation for more than two years a radio facsimile service between New York and Philadelphia employing the radio relay principles. By using the radio relay system in combination with directional methods of transmission the limited range of ultra short waves may in fact prove to be an asset rather than a liability because the very limitation of range of these extremely short waves will by means of the radio relay system enable the same frequencies to be used simultaneously in many different localities without creating mutual interference.

Science has merely begun to explore the possibilities of the radio relay, but it is already sufficiently apparent that in the device lie dazzling possibilities for the future of the entire radio art. This will become more and more apparent as new channels and new services through air are developed. Thus science marches on to new achievements in a continuously developing art.

Sec. 180. Radio Facsimile.

Efforts to transmit pictures electrically began very shortly after the invention of the electric telegraph. Electrical science was then in its infancy. The opening and closing of circuits with corresponding effect at the other end of the line was about all that scientists then knew of the potentialities of electricity. An investigator named Bain attempted the feat by preparing the picture to be transmitted so that an electrical "pencil," passing over its surface, would encounter portions of conductivity and other portions of insulating material, thus accomplishing a crude picture result. In 1848 another investigator, F. Bakewell, attempted by the same principle to accomplish the task. There was an ingenious attempt also by Bakewell to utilize at the receiving end a special paper impregnated with an electrolytic solution which would change color when an electric current passed through it. Different shades of color were accomplished by using varying currents—provided the transmitting and receiving ends of the circuit could be kept in synchronism. Caselli, another pioneer in the field, used the electrolytic process in the same way.

A fairly successful attempt was made to accomplish picture transmission by electro-mechanical means. A small electromagnet which operated a tiny hammer was at the receiving end, a carbon with white paper beneath to receive the blows. At each signal the hammer operated, the force of the blow in proportion to the strength of the electrical impulse.

About 1867 a photographic method was introduced by G. Little. A moving photographic film was utilized at the receiving end. A light, focused as a small spot on the moving film, was regulated by a shutter operated by an electromagnet. This is the basis of present-day photographic transmission by wire, the photoelectric cell and other modern devices being utilized.

The first attempt at commercial transmission of pictures, manuscripts and printed matter, by the scanning method was apparently made by A. Korn, in 1907. The Korn method involved the use of a translucent replica of the original picture scanned by a pencil of light, using a selenium cell to accomplish variations in optical density in accordance with fluctuations in electrical current. It was not until the development of the photoelectric cell that present-day facsimile transmission became possible. Bell Telephone and Western Union engineers have done much to perfect the system for wire transmission.

It should also be noted that since 1924 RCA engineers have been working on problems of picture transmission by radio, and for many years have been operating a commercial service, both domestic and foreign. The Telefunken Company has been one of the most active European companies engaged in facsimile development and transmission. Transoceanic radio is now used extensively to bring up-to-the-minute pictures of European events and personalities to American newspapers. European periodicals receive pictorial news from America by the same agency. Facsimile has thus become an important adjunct of modern life.

Present-day facsimile may be defined as a system of communication in which an electrically controlled device is operated at a distance to reproduce any graphic material. This graphic material may consist of type, script, line drawings, halftone subjects and the like. Material thus reproduced becomes as permanent a record as the carbon copy of an original—in fact, carbon copy is a very appropriate designation for one sort of facsimile, as will be seen hereafter. By means of the facsimile process it is possible to send by wire or radio the desired message with or without illustrations. The copy is a faithful reproduction of the original, since the scanning process that sweeps over the surface of the original is synchronized with the reproducing instrument at the terminal.

The first extensive tests of facsimile began more than a decade ago. Charles J. Young, of the RCA Manufacturing Company, who has been a pioneer worker in this field, has written various descriptive articles concerning the art, from one of which we quote:

"Some ten years ago, when the first extensive tests were being made of radio facsimile transmission for messages and pictures, the thought developed of using this process for actually printing a newspaper in the home by radio broadcast. It grew from a sudden realization that carbon paper offered a very simple way of making a mark on a piece of paper, and that it might be possible to design a mechanical scanning device which would spread carbon dots on the receiving sheet so as to form a facsimile reproduction. A stylus type of machine was tried first. In a short time, however, the printer bar and helix type of recorder was devised, and it then became apparent that a receiver simple enough for home use was an actual possibility.

"During the years since then many machines have been built and many problems encountered and solved. In the recorder itself the printer unit is the heart of the device and this has been constantly improved, with resulting better definition of copy. Various methods of synchronization have been investigated and some of them applied to actual operation. The structure of the recorder has passed through many stages from purely laboratory apparatus to finished designs for particular applications. Paper and paper-feeding systems have been studied. Some of this work was directed to commercial communication services, operating from shore to ship and from city to city; but the central and motivating idea has always been the one of making practical a facsimile broadcast service.

"As work proceeded toward this objective, much assistance has naturally come from the parallel growth of facsimile or picture transmission equipment for wire-line and radio circuits. In particular, many methods of printing the received image on the paper have appeared and these have been tested and considered for the home broadcast receiver."

Facsimile renders a variety of services, ranging from simple tape facsimile to letter-size "News Flashes" with illustrations. The equipment varies with the size and the type of service to be rendered.

Sec. 181. Methods of Recording Facsimile.

There are four common systems of recording facsimile:
(1) The photographic recorder
(2) The ink recorder
(3) The electrolytic recorder
(4) The carbon paper recorder

Each system depends at the transmitting point upon the same fundamentals: (a) a copy to be transmitted; (b) a scanning apparatus somewhat similar to television; and (c) a transmitting apparatus. In facsimile scanning the "picture" is broken up into picture elements to be transmitted to a distant recorder where they are re-assembled to form a copy of the original. Halftones in newspaper work may have more than four thousand dots per square inch, whereas really fine illustrations on glazed paper may have as many as fifty-seven thousand dots to a square inch. To send a picture by facsimile now requires ten thousand separate signals per square inch.

The scanning method involves the use of a brilliantly illuminated scanning spot that travels from side to side of the "picture" in regular sequence. A photo-cell is arranged to pick up the light reflected from the scanning surface. The impulse or reaction to the light will depend upon the areas of black, gray or white that may be encountered by the scanning beam. Amplifiers are necessary to build up the electrical impulses flowing from the photo-cell before the same may be broadcast.

Photographic recording is far more difficult than plain black and white facsimile. Sensitized paper is used and must be developed before the result can be known.

The ink recorder provides a visible recording method since ink is atomized into a fine mist and sprayed upon the paper. So fine is this ink jet that the spot made by a single impulse would be less than four one-thousandths of an inch in diameter. Such spots, being multiplied, will make up letters or script, pictures or any other desired reproduction. The ink to be used must be of high coloring and completely free from suspended matter. Carbon inks are unsatisfactory, dyes of one kind or another being used in this method of facsimile. The appearance of the ink recording, if well done, is nearly equal to a photographic copy. The ink is sprayed by means of an air-compressor.

Electrolytic recording depends upon chemical action and, unlike the photographic method above described, becomes visible immediately. The principle of operation is that an electric current passing through paper treated with certain chemicals will turn the paper very dark in color. Paper thus saturated and scanned by stylus contact may be darkened by electric current arranged to operate for signals for black. One disadvantage of this system is that the saturated paper must be moist when passing through the point of printing contact. The heat of the high current necessary for this process causes some types of paper to crinkle or wrinkle, thus marring its appearance.

The carbon paper recorder is one of the simplest and most common of facsimile methods.

"Here the scanning is accomplished with a helix and printer bar, as in the continuous electrolytic recorder. Carbon and white paper are fed between the bar and the helix, and after this are separated so that the surface of the white paper is visible only a few seconds after the printing process. The bar is now allowed to drag the paper, but is normally held away from it by an electromagnetic driver unit similar to that on the 'ink gun.' A signal for black depresses the bar, and a black dot is made by the pressure at the intersection of the bar and helix. The carbon paper is drawn through over guides, and wound up on a take-up spindle. The white paper is fed over a knurled feed roll and held against it by a series of rubber idlers, similar to the paper feed of a typewriter.

". . . This method of recording is very simple, uses cheap paper, and prints a very good copy. It is quite reliable, and complete copy, with no processing necessary, is visible only a few seconds after recording. Its disadvantages are also very pronounced. The printer bar is necessarily heavier than a stylus, or ink-deflecting vane, and therefore the speed of recording is limited. Almost any carbon paper that may be used here will be soft enough to smudge a little when rubbed in the fingers, and the finished print may, therefore, be easily smudged, the same as a carbon copy from a typewriter. More mechanical accuracy is required in building this printing bar than in the electrolytic recorder, as the bar and helix must line up parallel to within a few thousandths of an inch. The depressive motion of the bar is quite limited, and, therefore, a little discrepancy in lining up the bar and helix will result in part of the paper not being printed to a full black. Damping of the bar to eliminate 'bouncing' and echo printing is somewhat of a problem, but can be overcome by overpowering the printing mechanism and absorbing the excess power in a damping arrangement on the bar itself.

"One advantage mentioned separately here for emphasis is that this type of recorder may be used to print more than one copy at a time. If the printer bar action is made sufficiently powerful, several rolls of white and carbon paper may be threaded into the machine, and a number of copies of the facsimile made at the same time. As many as eight separate copies of a message have been made in an experimental set-up. The carbon paper may be of the 'hectograph' type, and extra copies of the recording may then be made by the usual duplication process of hectographing." [3]

[3] Artzt, *Facsimile Transmission and Recording*, Vol. I, RCA Institutes Technical Press, October, 1938, pp. 177-178.

CHAPTER
TWENTY-THREE

David Sarnoff Looks Ahead

Section 182. 1939! An Epilogue or Prophecy is in Order!

WE HAVE NOW BROUGHT the History of Radio to the month of April in the year 1939. It is too much to hope that the author has succeeded in covering every important phase of the epic story. The unfolding panorama of man's mightiest adventure in science has been too vast in its scope to be encompassed within the confines of two volumes or indeed of many volumes. At best it is an unfinished story. From crude earth-bound beginnings scientists have attained unto mastery of limitless space in the heavens. Busy laboratories are even now probing new mysteries or solving old problems that have long resisted solution. What the future will bring, no mortal knoweth!

For months past the author has speculated upon what manner of conclusion or epilogue might properly end this volume, *Big Business and Radio*. Obviously we are at the dawn of a new era. Beyond the horizon of today lie shining fields of achievement yet undreamed by man.

Weeks ago the author consulted David Sarnoff, who has played an important role in the development of the radio art and industry, and requested him to forecast what he believed could be expected in the future development of radio. Mr. Sarnoff smiled at the time but made no promises. The author had no genuine hope that the President of the Radio Corporation would accept such a challenge. To be sure Mr. Sarnoff had made prophecies in times past that had marked him as a man of unusual ability to foresee the future. It has already been pointed out that in 1916—four years before radio broadcasting began at KDKA— Mr. Sarnoff wrote out his vision of a "Radio Music Box", not in terms of the clumsy radio sets of early days but he described the very pushbutton electric radio of today. This and many other prophecies by David Sarnoff are matters of record. Not even his warmest admirers to whom the author confided the incident believed that Mr. Sarnoff would hazard his reputation as a prophet by voicing a forecast of the tomorrow of radio.

But lo! on April 11, 1939, David Sarnoff laid aside his business cares and spent the day in Boston. The author seized the opportunity of this visit to interrogate him as to his views on radio, television and communications of the future and Mr. Sarnoff began a comprehensive reply. This unexpected good fortune caused the author to summon the head stenographer of Suffolk University, College of Liberal Arts, in order that the prophecy might be reported in Mr. Sarnoff's exact words. This was accomplished despite the fact that the young lady at times became so enthralled by the mental pictures conjured up by the speaker's words that she quite forgot to write until called "back to earth" by the author.

It is confidently believed that Mr. Sarnoff's prophecy of April 11, 1939, will hereafter be regarded as one of the most significant of his entire career. Accustomed as the author has become through years of intensive study of the cosmic changes wrought by radio the Sarnoff forecast about to be unfolded impressed him while it was being uttered as one of the most breath-taking visions of modern science. Let us then consider David Sarnoff's prediction as stated in his own words.

Sec. 183. Mr. Sarnoff's Vision of Future Developments.

"It seems to me that the author of this book finds himself writing its last chapter at a time when developments in all forms of communications are writing the first chapter of a new volume in the History of Radio.

"It is impossible to forecast with any degree of precision the events which will follow even during the next few years, to say nothing of the developments which will materialize during the coming decade or so. However, the signs of the times indicate that we are moving rapidly towards perfecting and adopting instantaneous methods of communication which should enable transmission of intelligence of unlimited volume, and over any desired distance, at much higher speeds than have heretofore been possible. These new agencies of communication will serve the eye as well as the ear and thus add enormously to the individual's power to interpret and comprehend the intelligence transmitted.

"Because I appreciate the earnestness of the author's efforts and the compliment of his invitation to express my views as to the future of radio, I shall try to do what is asked of me; but with a full realization of the fact that today's forecast will fall short of tomorrow's accomplishments.

"The fields in which I believe we may reasonably expect to see important future developments are, (a) Telephony, (b) Telegraphy, (c) Radio and Television, (d) The Entertainment Field and (e) Application of the Discoveries of Radio Scientists to Other Fields.

(a) Telephony

"The telephone system of communication as it exists today has been based upon the use of a number of conductors which carry electrical impulses. Great ingenuity has been exercised in making it possible to transmit over a minimum number of such conductors, several telephone conversations, telegraph messages, printer telegraph services and facsimile service. Demands of the future will require new methods for such services. The greater future of telephony lies, I believe, in developments which will make it possible to carry all these and many other services over or through a new kind of cable called coaxial cable. This consists of a hollow tube or pipe of relatively small dimensions, with a single conductor along its central axis.

"Much has already been accomplished by scientists to develop such a cable, but the tremendous possibilities which lie in this and kindred fields are now becoming apparent. That scientists will continue to perfect cables of this kind I have no doubt. Think of the amazing prospect of being able to send over a single cable at the same instant of time, telephone messages, telegraph messages, facsimile service, printer telegraph service and most remarkable of all, television service! To be sure, such a cable is expensive—at present very expensive—yet if we can feed into it all of these types of communications and then provide suitable devices for the recapture at a distance of each, then we may forget its cost. Probably more than a hundred such channels are even now possible, and undoubtedly this number will be greatly increased.

"I look forward with confidence to the time when the cost of long distance telephony will be so greatly reduced that a talk between New York and San Francisco will be no more expensive than between New York and Boston. It is even conceivable that the time may come when people will pick up a telephone and speak with a person in any part of the United States for a nickel or a dime.

"I have spoken of this new type of cable as a land-line system. While it is possible that ocean cables also may utilize this same medium, yet in this field the cost may be almost prohibitive. This is due to the fact that in ocean space there are no customers—and only by large customer demand may the cost of such a cable system be warranted.

"In international communications I believe that radio has great advantages over any kind of cables now on the technical horizon, since radio furnishes direct telephone or telegraph communication with any desired nation. A cable terminates at the shore-end and this requires additional land wires or cable circuits to complete the task. Radio is now used exclusively for trans-oceanic telephone communications.

"(b) *Telegraphy*

"Obviously such a development of telephone communications as is predicted above will require the telegraph systems to keep pace or else they will lose out technically, which means finally losing out financially. It would seem that a final chapter is also being written to the Morse Code. While there is always a residue from yesterday that remains useful today and even tomorrow, yet the residue of usefulness of the Morse Code is rapidly diminishing. The world is moving on and speed is its watchword. The ingenuity of man has devised a system of instantaneous communication known as facsimile that so far outmodes the electric telegraph that the latter must eventually take its niche in the corridors of history.

"Let me give you a crude illustration of the difference between the electric telegraph system and this latest miracle—facsimile. Suppose one wishes to transport a crate of freight from New York to San Francisco. What would you think of a process which would do the job in the following manner? It first broke up the freight into small fragments, then enclosed it in the crate, then hauled it to the train, then carried it across the country, at which point the crate would be taken from the train, the fragments reassembled and the product put together for delivery to the addressee in the form it originally left the factory. One would think that a pretty cumbersome method! Well, that is the present method of telegraphy by the Morse Code. A man writes a telegram and the messenger boy calls for it. It is taken to the telegraph office. There the paragraphs are broken down into sentences; the sentences into words; the words into letters; the letters into dots and dashes. In the form of dots and dashes it is transmitted by wire from New York to San Francisco. At that point the receiving operator reverses the process. He puts the dots and dashes into letters; the letters into words; the words into sentences; the sentences into paragraphs and then a messenger boy delivers the message to the addressee.

"However much of sentiment we may have for the Morse Code or the Continental Code—and I confess to that sentiment myself, having been a wireless operator in my youth—we cannot permit sentiment to delay human progress. Obviously the ideal system of communication would be to take the message in its original form, hold it up to something or other, throw a lever, or press a button, and have an exact facsimile of it made instantaneously at the other end of the circuit. To be sure, facsimile has not yet reached this stage of development, but when it comes—and it will come—we will have a new method of telegraph communication.

"Facsimile has already been in use over the Atlantic Ocean by radio for a number of years. The pictures in the newspapers one sees today coming from abroad are carried by radio. Pictures are also carried within the United States over telegraph wires by the telephone and telegraph companies. But the methods employed are still subject to much further improvement. The instantaneous system that I refer to will not only replace the dot and dash system of Morse telegraphy but it will also make the present teletype system which still deals piecemeal with letters, words and sentences, a less important method in the future. Here again we shall see human progress on the march. Every step of that march is necessary yet steps become but 'footprints on the sands of time'.

"Radio will play an important part in this march of human progress. The discoveries of radio scientists and engineers are now beginning to produce methods and systems which will utilize wave-lengths measured in feet and in inches rather than in hundreds, or thousands of feet. These very short waves will be used in radio circuits for interconnecting cities and for short distance communications. This will be accomplished by a system of automatic or unattended relay stations spaced along the route and so arranged that impulses introduced at one point of the radio circuit will be transmitted automatically through each relay point intermediate to its destination. These new wave-lengths will make it possible to use relay stations of small power to carry simultaneously many channels of communication. Such radio relay circuits will open the way for widespread distribution of television, for flashing facsimile messages between cities, and for many other services of communication.

"When finally developed, the new system of facsimile communication should be cheaper than present-day methods. It should be able effectively to compete with voice communication and perhaps offer competition to the mail-bag. It is conceivable that a letter from New York to San Francisco can one day be carried either over coaxial cables, or through the air, at no greater cost than is now involved in sending it by air mail. And it will surely get there more quickly.

"A newspaper in the home, by radio facsimile, has already been hinted at, and this too, will be advanced through the further development of new communication channels in the air.

" (c) *Radio and Television*

"It must be borne in mind that the principal difference between radio and other means of communication is in the medium. The telegraph and the telephone use wires or cables while radio uses the air, but there is much similarity in the terminal equipment used by each. What has been said about the possible new applications to wires and cables equally applies to radio. Here, too, a last chapter is now being written and a new one beginning.

"The reason for this statement is that the new types of services we are discussing take up room in the air, and present-day wave lengths are insufficient to provide the necessary room for the new services. Despite the phrase 'As wide as all outdoors', there is already traffic congestion in the ether. What the scientist must do is not only to learn how to increase traffic upon present lanes but also to carve out new lanes in the ether. This he began to do with what were once called 'short waves' of 100 meters or so. Today, they are already regarded as 'long waves'. The scientist of the air did not stop with 100 meters. He has been exploring the air and has found useful lanes in wave lengths substantially below 100 meters. Thus present-day international services by radio are conducted on wave lengths varying between 14 and 50 meters.

"The new service of television is being commenced on a wavelength of about 6.5 meters. Television requires transmitting channels about 600 times wider than those used in existing sound broadcasting services. For this reason, ultra short waves are used as they provide space for a television service which otherwise could not be accomplished.

"The scientists of the world are now only beginning to probe the mysteries of that vast new region of the radio frequency spectrum called ultra short waves. These are waves from about 10 meters in length to waves of less than 1 centimeter (1/100 meter) in length. That portion of this new spectrum between 10 meters and 1 meter provides 9 times as much room as is now occupied by all existing radio services regardless of the wavelengths they use; between 1 meter and 1 decimeter (1/10 meter), 90 times as much space is provided and between 1 decimeter and 1 centimeter this space is 900 times greater. Thus between wave lengths of 10 meters and 1 centimeter we find nearly 1,000 times more space in the frequency spectrum than is now occupied by all of the radio services in existence today. The scientists of the world are merely at the threshold of new possibilities in radio. They are just beginning to learn how to use effectively the many wavelengths of this vast domain of the spectrum.

"Ultra short waves open entirely new fields for radio communication. They can provide services especially useful to police and fire departments for the protection of life and property. They will extend the uses of radio in aircraft communication and navigation; in the prevention of collisions in the air and sea transport when obstructions are not visible; in guiding aircraft to land safely, and so on.

"In mobile communication, the use of ultra short waves should make it possible for vehicles on land, in the air and on the water, to establish and maintain contacts with anyone, anywhere. Automobiles may be equipped with simple transmitting, as well as receiving gear, enabling the occupants to talk, as well as to listen, while the cars are in motion. It is also possible to extend the uses of radio so that individuals may carry 'pocket radios' and be able to receive messages and programs wherever they may be. Portable radio transmitting devices of small size, using very little power and operating on centimeter or millimeter waves, may enable individuals to establish instant communication with the main wire or radio systems of the country and thus to obtain a 'connection' with any person in any part of the world. All these are in addition to the services of commercial telegraphy, telephony, high speed facsimile, broadcasting and television, already discussed.

"(d) *Entertainment*

"Let us turn for a moment to what has been accomplished in the amusement field. The addition of sight to sound was certainly the beginning of a new chapter of progress. It may reasonably be expected that when television has reached a substantially commercial stage, radio listeners will not be satisfied unless they can also be viewers. Viewers will not be satisfied unless they can also be listeners. This is the case with talking movies at the present time. People once were satisfied to watch a silent actor on the screen, but when the laboratory gave him an electric tongue he no longer was interesting only to look at. The audience also wanted to listen to what the actor had to say. The same may be expected ultimately with sight and sound by radio.

"In discussing the field of entertainment and the effects wrought upon that field through the creation of these new instrumentalities of mass communication, it is interesting to observe that here we find the problem to be 'production', whereas in practically all other fields of industry the problem is 'consumption'. Let a really good picture be made in a studio and distributed to the theatres of the country. People in great numbers come to the theatres to see that picture. The cry is 'Let us have more such pictures'. A company may manufacture the best radio set, or the best electric refrigerator, or the best electric vacuum cleaner, but it still has to sell the idea and induce the public to purchase the article. Creative advertising must blaze the trail. Partial payments must be permitted. Ticklers for the trade must be resorted to. Not so with real art! From the humblest to the richest they are willing to deposit their 25¢ or $1.00 at the cashier's window at any theatre that runs a real picture or gives a real show.

"What has happened in the entertainment field is that the agencies of distribution have outstripped the agencies of production. It may take six months to a year and a million to two millions of dollars to produce a first-class moving picture, yet it can be shown in the leading theatres of the United States in less than one week. If given on a television network, when such becomes available, it can be shown in 30,000,000 homes in the United States within one hour. 'What comes next?' will be the cry. These agencies of distribution through the new wire mediums and through the air can distribute art instantaneously. The whole nation can consume art instantaneously. But art cannot be created or produced instantaneously. There is the bottle neck of the future. To say this, however, is not to infer that the problem is unsolvable. Indeed it is solvable; but new solutions will have to be created.

"Here opportunity beckons to the young and rising generations. It will require all the creative brains the world can supply to feed the growing demand of the masses, as well as the classes, for more and better art. To meet this need it will require the same degree of imagination and invention on the part of the creative writer, artist and performer that is required from the scientist and engineer in the laboratory. To recognize the need for such material may in itself prove to be the first element of invention. And so the theatre of the future may not only show motion pictures as now, but it may be fed from a central point with the greatest variety show that man has thus far produced. Hundreds or thousands of theatres can make that show available simultaneously to audiences.

"Methods may also be found whereby the show given to the theatre by television will be received only in theatres. The television intended for the home may be a different show, transmitted and received with different kinds of apparatus and on different wavelengths. Not only may the method of transmission and reception be different but the type of show may also be different. The person in the home may be part of the audience looking in upon the city in which he lives; upon the nation, and perhaps upon the world. People always wish to gratify their primal instinct to see what is going on—to listen and to behold. To be able to sit in one's home, at ease, and by means of television to see and to hear events of the world at the very moment those events are taking place will gratify a human desire.

"On the other hand there is the gregarious instinct of humanity to consider—the desire to mingle with the crowd. This, too, is a primal instinct. Where the crowd goes, where ladies wear pretty dresses so that others may see them and use perfume to enhance their charms with the opposite sex—there men also will go and the ancient cycle of life will continue. New amusements will take the place of the old but the concert, the stage and the screen will continue to satisfy that gregarious instinct of humanity. In all these things the wonders of science that I have described and a thousand more yet undreamed of will minister to the life of society in which we live and breathe and have our being.

"(e) *Applications of the Discoveries of Radio Scientists to Other Fields*

"As this new chapter in the future development of radio unfolds, it will reveal abundance of contributions to other arts, to sciences and to industries.

"The principles of electron optics, for example, which find application in television, will mark advances of great scientific significance in other fields. When applied in electronic microscopy, they will make it possible to develop magnification from 10 to 20 times greater than can now be obtained by any known method. The electron microscope will then become an instrument that will permit observation and study of the most minute cell structures in a detail heretofore impossible. It will provide new eyes to search and to behold the unseen. Through this medium it promises to add greatly to our store of knowledge of biology.

"Electron microscopy will make important contributions also in many other fields. An increase of 10 to 20 times in magnification when applied to the science of metallurgy will open up new avenues for the study of alloys. It will greatly increase our knowledge in the field of crystallography. It will facilitate obtaining solutions to problems of industry in the production of both organic and inorganic fibrous material and in other fields of industrial chemistry.

"Think also what it will mean in the science of astronomy! Electron optics may go far in reducing the barriers between man and his knowledge of the planets imposed by limitations of even the most highly perfected optical methods of today. Through electron optics and other instrumentalities applied in the art of communication, the planets of the heavens may be brought thousands of light years nearer to the earth for observation and study. Thus may be revealed to mankind in greater measure the secrets of the universe.

"In the field of medicine, the discoveries of radio scientists are rich in promise of instrumentalities for facilitating diagnosis, and for combating and curing diseases.

"When applied to geophysics, these discoveries will aid man in charting underground geological formations. Mines and oil deposits hitherto unknown will yield to this new X-ray of science. Thus man may find and draw from the earth those things which he seeks in the advancement of our social and economic well being.

"The devices originated by radio scientists and engineers should find widespread application in many other industries. Photoelectric cells, vacuum tubes and electronic devices of all kinds will be utilized for operating machinery; for calipering; for color analysis; for control and timing devices; for grading and sorting and for numerous other purposes. Radio frequency current may be used in preserving food by destroying microscopic agencies of food decay. It will free grains from noxious germs and substances. It will make war on insects that prey upon plant life.

"One of the significant developments in the industrial application of radio frequency current is seen in the metal producing and refining industry. The older processes were largely guesswork, dependent upon human judgment and uncertain methods in the control of temperature and harmful contaminations. Now, however, the exact methods of control of these essentials provided by radio frequency currents in the electric furnace make possible the production of new alloys and metals of a new order of purity which will enable new industries to be founded.

"These new devices will contribute also to the perfection of existing products, and will serve as tools for scientists and engineers to extend their explorations and resolve the unknown of today into the known of tomorrow.

"Science recognizes no impassable barriers in its quest for truth. The radio scientist and the technical specialist in the art forever press on to new horizons. They will not limit their researches to the atmosphere in which we live. They will explore the heavens above and the depths of the earth beneath. The limits of human imagination will be the only possible circumscribing frontier of scientific research.

"But we cannot place upon the scientist alone the responsibility of translating the products of the human imagination into tangible products and services that are of every-day usefulness to mankind. The scientist is only the first link in the chain. Statesmen and administrators in government are guiding forces; as are also leaders in such fields as education and labor. And the scientist must be supported by financial resources, by the imagination and courage of management, and by man-power intelligently directed—in a word, by industry.

"The inventor, as we must appreciate, is a great originator of change in our complex civilization. But great inventions must prove themselves—must run the gauntlet, so to speak, before they emerge as real forces in society. There is natural resistance to change until there is definite evidence of a need for the new idea.

"The statesman in government is the guardian of social progress. Research and invention furnish the raw materials of progress, while industry translates these materials into social and economic benefits. As guardian of our social progress, the statesman in government is vested with the power and duty to regulate, but he can also stimulate progress. He can accomplish this by encouraging invention to develop the arts and sciences and by providing for industry freedom of opportunity for effectively translating inventions into social and economic benefits.

"Progress is the life-blood of industry. Nevertheless, those who risk their financial resources must be convinced of the soundness of the invention which promotes change. They must envision the nature and extent of the change and the preparedness of the public to accept the innovation; and be given opportunity for reward reasonably commensurate with the risks involved.

"To emerge as constructive social forces, great inventions require imagination, skill, courage, faith and finance. Science, industry and government, in cooperation, can follow the road that leads to real progress and provides benefits for all society."

INDEX

Abbott, Gordon, 10, 237*n.*, 391
Actors, use of Hollywood talent on air, 416
Adams, Ira J., Telephone-Radio Group controversy, 77, 116, 123, 145, 146, 147, 178, 210, 262; analysis of controverted points in arbitration issue, 117-20; on rights awarded RCA, 177 f.; drafting of "swapping points," 180-82
Advertising, radio, Sarnoff's attitude toward, 31-33, 75 f., 184; WEAF blazes trail with commercial broadcasts, 32, 54, 55, 64, 71, 89, 138; Telephone Company's attitude toward Radio Group participation in, 60; public reaction to, 64; points way to financial salvation for stations, 71; RCA's attitude toward, 230 f.; role in proposed Broadcasting Foundation, 232; revenue produced by, 253; NBC attitude toward, 292, 307; twofold character of sales resistance to, 294; compared with newspaper and periodical variety, 303; effect of depression upon, 353
Aeolian Building station, 83, 94
Aeolian Company, 411
Aeriola radio sets, 14, 15
Agreement A-1 *re* separation of RCA and allies, 379
Agreements "L" and "M" in RCA unification, 349
Agricultural service programs, 294, 298
Aircraft, radio sets for, 28; *see also* Automotive devices
Akerberg, Herbert V., 390
Alderman, Edward A., 293, 298
Aldrich, Mr., 373
Alexanderson, Ernst F. W., 147, 150, 295; Alternator, 5, 25, 89, 339; contest over superheterodyne patent, 91; efforts to perfect television, 435 f.
All American Radio Corporation, 17*n.*
Allen, Fred, 416, 417
Allen, Gracie, 416
Alloys, application of electron microscopy to, 477
Alternator, Alexanderson's, 5, 25, 89, 339

Amateurs, controversy over meaning of, 28, 40 f., 149, 155, 157, 159, 163, 165, 172; wireless telephony for, 241; opportunity night for, 419
American Broadcasting Company proposed, 187, 205 f., 220, 253, 254
American Marconi, *see* Marconi Company, American
American Newspaper Publishers Association, 422
American Radio Relay League, 159
American School of the Air, 391, 412, 413
American Society of Composers, Authors and Publishers, battle over radio use of copyright material, 283, 353, 428
American Telephone and Telegraph Company, sale of WEAF, 3, 253, 265-67, 270; enters cross-licensing agreement, 6, 7, 9, 10 ff., 19, 27, 36 ff., 56, 59 (*see also* cross-licensing pact); share in RCA, 8, 10; why did it join group? 10-13; controversy over receiving apparatus, 10, 13, 28, 45, 78 f., 103, 118, 119, 147 ff., 164, 167, 171, 179, 193 ff., 199, 200, 201, 203-5, 207 f., 209, 211-13, 241, 260, 262; de Forest Audion, 11, 150, 151; controversy over public service communication, 11, 12, 21, 28, 43, 45, 59, 75, 79, 104, 149, 165, 172; rights in field of wire telephony and telegraphy, 11; in broadcasting field, 12, 26, 27 f., 37, 42-44, 53, 60, 62, 76, 103, 118, 155, 179; regards transmission of human voice as form of telephony, 12; controversy over wire lines, 19-22, 40, 56-59, 79, 83 f., 95, 104, 119, 150, 156, 162, 171, 172, 178, 184, 186, 200, 241, 246-49, 265, 302, 308, 315, 316; alarm over radio broadcasting, 20, 40; radio stations, 27, 44 (*see also* WEAF); hostilities with Radio Group begin, 27, 50-68; begins to sell RCA stock, 28; under attack as monopoly, 28, 133-36; controversy over meaning of "amateurs," 28, 40 f., 149, 155, 157, 159, 163, 165, 172; over communication involving automotive devices, 28, 37, 104, 178, 180, 182, 199, 209; over loud

Folk, George E., supports Telephone Company's refusal to lease wires, 58-61; share in Radio Group-Telephone negotiations, 104, 110, 112, 113, 140, 147, 158, 162, 203, 240; draft of proposed agreement, 226, 235, 238, 241, 261, 262, 264, 269
Football game broadcasts, 63, 71
Fortune, 282, 319, 459
Forums and discussions, 420
Foster, Herbert, 274
"Founding a Nation," broadcasts, 413
Fourth Dimension of Advertising, The (Arnold), 314
Fox, William, 328
Fox-Case Movietone, 328
France, contest for control of wireless communications in South America, 81
Frazier, John, testifies for Radio Group in arbitration proceedings, 160
Freed-Eisemann Company, 17n., 27
Frequencies, *see* Wave lengths
Frequency modulation, 423-25

"Gang Busters," 419
Garden, Mary, 291, 292
Gary, Hampson, 427, 428
Geitel, Hans, efforts to perfect photoelectric cell, 433
General Electric Company, control of Alexanderson Alternator, 5, 25, 89, 339; enters cross-licensing agreement, 6, 11 f., 25, 27, 37 ff., 59, 147, 148 (*see also* Cross-licensing pact); relation to RCA, 6, 7 f., 9, 10, 15, 25-27, 33, 82, 86, 339, 356; controversy over receiving apparatus, 10, 13, 28, 45, 78 f., 103, 118, 119, 147 ff., 164, 167, 171, 179, 193 ff., 199, 200, 201, 203-5, 207 f., 209, 211-13, 241, 260, 262; over public service communication, 11, 12, 21, 28, 43, 45, 59, 75, 79, 104, 149, 165, 172; rights in broadcasting field, 12, 26, 27 f., 37, 42-44, 60, 62, 76, 103, 118, 179; experimentation with radio sets, 14-16; wire lines controversy, 19-22, 40, 56-59, 79, 95, 104, 119, 150, 156, 162, 171, 172, 178, 184, 186, 200, 241, 246-49, 265; radio stations, 21, 53, 367, 370, 382; attitude toward acquisition of manufacturing rights by RCA, 26, 339 f., 345, 346 f., 348; carrier-current dispute, 28, 39 f., 61 f., 79-81, 155, 172, 178, 181, 186, 260; controversy over "for amateur purposes," 28, 40 f., 149, 155, 157, 159, 163, 165, 172; over loud speaking devices, 28, 42-44, 76-78, 153, 154, 158, 164, 171, 178, 215; over communication involving automotive devices, 28, 37, 104, 178, 180, 182, 199,

209; over combined telephone-telegraph sets, 28, 41 f., 72; interest in proposed national broadcasting setup, 30, 31, 32, 252; vain attempt at mediation of quarrel with Telephone Company, 36-48; lawyer selected to mediate, 37 f.; row over transoceanic communication, 37, 38, 110, 111, 163, 172, 178, 183, 186, 199, 200, 203, 241; trouble occasioned by exclusive and non-exclusive rights, 38; Neave advises further exchange of licenses, 38 f.; dispute over vacuum tubes, 46, 47, 72, 76, 179, 184, 204, 213, 215 f., 219; Telephone Company's formal complaints, 72; experiments with tungsten filament in vacuum tubes, 89; contest over superheterodyne patent, 91; negotiations with British Marconi Company, 102; controversy over two-way communication, 104, 174, 183, 185, 203, 241, 264; attitude toward Guernsey draft of arbitration agreement, 116; analysis of cross-licensing pact made by I. J. Adams, 117-20; suspected of monopolistic practices, 122; text of arbitration agreement, 126-30; arbitration of 1924, 132 f., 139-65; accused of conspiracy, 134; charge of illegality against original agreement, 172-75, 178, 188, 193-98, 201, 207, 261, 349; broadcasting expenses for 1925, 254; proposed redrafts of July, 1920 contract, 261-63, 265; Edison Night broadcast, 312; efforts to perfect talking pictures, 323, 324, 325 f.; phonograph research, 324 f.; "Jazz Singer" starts new industrial contest, 326-28; share in RCA Photophone, 331; antitrust suit, 349, 353, 355; the consent decree, 364-86; conferences looking toward settlement, 365; negotiations begin, 366-68; RCA's indebtedness to, 367, 370, 371, 372 f., 375, 376, 379, 380, 385; lawyers meet—and disagree! 368-70; chieftains burn midnight oil, 370, 373-75; RCA refuses offer of compromise, 371; Sarnoff makes counter-proposals, 372 f.; leases and agreements accompanying decree, 377-80; net results of separation, 380-82; provisions *re* patent rights, 381; broadcasting agreements, 382; protective provisions, 382; RCA's economic triumph as result of separation, 382-86; *see also* Radio Group
General Motors Corporation, 312, 358
Geophysics, application of electron microscopy to, 477
Germany, contest for control of wireless

educational field, 412; news-gathering facilities, 422

National Electric Light Association, 97

National Harrow Company v. Bement, 195, 196

Neave, Charles, vain attempt at mediation of Radio Group-Telephone row, 27 f., 36-48, 71, 73, 74, 77, 85; advises further exchange of license, 38 f.; recommendations as to carrier-current dispute, 39 f.; defines phrase, "for amateur purposes," 40 f.; recommendations re combined telephone-telegraph sets, 41; re broadcasting devices and loud speakers, 42-44; re broadcasting stations' dispute, 44; re multiple reception of broadcast material, 45; suggested as chief counsel for Radio Group, 115; re settlement of anti-trust suit out of court, 368 f., 373, 374

Network broadcasting, principle of, used in WEAF broadcast of Chicago football game, 63; WEAF experiments in, 71, 97, 138, 167; use of leased wires in, 79

New Hampshire, experimental broadcast from, 152

Newman, H. M., 306, 308, 315, 316

News, music and entertainment, scope of phrase, 177

Newspapers, service compared with that of radio, 30; resent radio advertising, 294; hostility toward radio reporting of the news, 420-22

New York Oratorio Society, 291

New York Symphony Orchestra, 291, 296

New York Times, see Times

New York Tribune, see Tribune

New York World's Fair, television broadcasting launched at, 405, 431, 443-46

Nichols, Arnold W., testifies for Telephone Company, 150-54

Nipkow, Paul, idea of scanning disk, 434

North American Company, experimentation in carrier-current broadcasting, 62

Norton, Henry K., 406

O'Brian, Mr., 369

O'Brien, Morgan J., 293, 298

Ocean cables, 471

Ohio School of the Air, 412

Ohio State University, 412

Olney, Warren, Jr., suggestions re settlement of anti-trust suit against Radio Group, 355, 368 f., 374

Olsen, George, 291

One-way communication, controversy over, 174, 260, 261

"Open-patent-pool" suggested as means to end radio anti-trust suit, 355, 358

Opera broadcasts, 63, 354, 411, 415

Opfinger, Adolph, 408

Opportunity night, 419

Optics, electron, principles of, 476

Oregon Steam Navigation Company v. Windsor, 197

Orthophonic Victrola, 332

Oscillight in television, 454

Otterson, J. E., on RCA competition in motion picture field, 396

Outline of Radio (Hogan), 159

Pacific coast network of NBC, 294, 296, 297, 298, 307, 311, 321; radio stations in, 308

Paley, Benjamin, 320

Paley, Jacob, 319, 320

Paley, Lillian, 320

Paley, Samuel, 318, 319, 320

Paley, William S., enters radio field, 318-21; acquires Louchheim interest in CBS, 320; reorganizes CBS, 334-36, 389-91, 400

Pallophotophone, 324

Panama Canal, regulation of opening and closing of gates, 157

Paper network, see United Independent Broadcasters

Paramount Pictures, 305, 328

Paramount-Publix Corporation, alliance with CBS, 389; financial crash, 390, 393

Paris, contest for control of wireless communications in South America, 81

Patent rights, cross-licensing only feasible way of breaking deadlock of conflicting, 6, 353; infringement of RCA's, 17, 73, 92-94; Telephone Company suit over unlicensed broadcasting, 136 f., 138; nature of, 137, 194

Pathé Studios, 333, 350

Patterson, Richard C., Jr., joins NBC, 400, 401, 402, 405

Payne, George Henry, 427, 428

Peace Conference at Paris, 5

"Perils of Pauline," 416

Philadelphia Storage Battery Company (Philco), 17n., 27

Philco Radio and Television Corporation, 421

Philharmonic concerts, 391

Phonofilm, 328

Phonograph, controversy over combination radio-phonograph sets, 178, 181, 184, 187, 213, 214, 215, 219, 220, 260; coalescence with radio industry, 229,

HISTORY OF BROADCASTING:
Radio To Television
An Arno Press/New York Times Collection

Archer, Gleason L.
Big Business and Radio. 1939.

Archer, Gleason L.
History of Radio to 1926. 1938.

Arnheim, Rudolf.
Radio. 1936.

Blacklisting: Two Key Documents. 1952–1956.

Cantril, Hadley and Gordon W. Allport.
The Psychology of Radio. 1935.

Codel, Martin, editor.
Radio and Its Future. 1930.

Cooper, Isabella M.
Bibliography on Educational Broadcasting. 1942.

Dinsdale, Alfred.
First Principles of Television. 1932.

Dunlap, Orrin E., Jr.
Marconi: The Man and His Wireless. 1938.

Dunlap, Orrin E., Jr.
The Outlook for Television. 1932.

Fahie, J. J.
A History of Wireless Telegraphy. 1901.

Federal Communications Commission.
Annual Reports of the Federal Communications Commission.
1934/1935–1955.

Federal Radio Commission.
Annual Reports of the Federal Radio Commission. 1927–1933.

Frost, S. E., Jr.
Education's Own Stations. 1937.

Grandin, Thomas.
The Political Use of the Radio. 1939.

Harlow, Alvin.
Old Wires and New Waves. 1936.

Hettinger, Herman S.
A Decade of Radio Advertising. 1933.

Huth, Arno.
Radio Today: The Present State of Broadcasting. 1942.

Jome, Hiram L.
Economics of the Radio Industry. 1925.

Lazarsfeld, Paul F.
Radio and the Printed Page. 1940.

Lumley, Frederick H.
Measurement in Radio. 1934.

Maclaurin, W. Rupert.
Invention and Innovation in the Radio Industry. 1949.

Radio: Selected A.A.P.S.S. Surveys. 1929–1941.

Rose, Cornelia B., Jr.
National Policy for Radio Broadcasting. 1940.

Rothafel, Samuel L. and Raymond Francis Yates.
Broadcasting: Its New Day. 1925.

Schubert, Paul.
The Electric Word: The Rise of Radio. 1928.

Studies in the Control of Radio: Nos. 1–6. 1940–1948.

Summers, Harrison B., editor.
Radio Censorship. 1939.

Summers, Harrison B., editor.
**A Thirty-Year History of Programs Carried on
National Radio Networks in the United States, 1926–1956.** 1958.

Waldrop, Frank C. and Joseph Borkin.
Television: A Struggle for Power. 1938.

White, Llewellyn.
The American Radio. 1947.

World Broadcast Advertising: Four Reports. 1930–1932.